Dictionary of Literary Biography

Documentary Series

8 *The Black Aesthetic Movement,* edited by Jeffrey Louis Decker (1991)

9 *American Writers of the Vietnam War: W. D. Ehrhart, Larry Heinemann, Tim O'Brien, Walter McDonald, John M. Del Vecchio,* edited by Ronald Baughman (1991)

10 *The Bloomsbury Group,* edited by Edward L. Bishop (1992)

11 *American Proletarian Culture: The Twenties and The Thirties,* edited by Jon Christian Suggs (1993)

12 *Southern Women Writers: Flannery O'Connor, Katherine Anne Porter, Eudora Welty,* edited by Mary Ann Wimsatt and Karen L. Rood (1994)

13 *The House of Scribner, 1846-1904,* edited by John Delaney (1996)

14 *Four Women Writers for Children, 1868-1918,* edited by Caroline C. Hunt (1996)

15 *American Expatriate Writers: Paris in the Twenties,* edited by Matthew J. Bruccoli and Robert W. Trogdon (1997)

16 *The House of Scribner, 1905-1930,* edited by John Delaney (1997)

17 *The House of Scribner, 1931-1984,* edited by John Delaney (1998)

18 *British Poets of The Great War: Sassoon, Graves, Owen,* edited by Patrick Quinn (1999)

19 *James Dickey,* edited by Judith S. Baughman (1999)

See also DLB 210

Yearbooks

1980 edited by Karen L. Rood, Jean W. Ross, and Richard Ziegfeld (1981)

1981 edited by Karen L. Rood, Jean W. Ross, and Richard Ziegfeld (1982)

1982 edited by Richard Ziegfeld; associate editors: Jean W. Ross and Lynne C. Zeigler (1983)

1983 edited by Mary Bruccoli and Jean W. Ross, associate editor Richard Ziegfeld (1984)

1984 edited by Jean W. Ross (1985)

1985 edited by Jean W. Ross (1986)

1986 edited by J. M. Brook (1987)

1987 edited by J. M. Brook (1988)

1988 edited by J. M. Brook (1989)

1989 edited by J. M. Brook (1990)

1990 edited by James W. Hipp (1991)

1991 edited by James W. Hipp (1992)

1992 edited by James W. Hipp (1993)

1993 edited by James W. Hipp, contributing editor George Garrett (1994)

1994 edited by James W. Hipp, contributing editor George Garrett (1995)

1995 edited by James W. Hipp, contributing editor George Garrett (1996)

1996 edited by Samuel W. Bruce and L. Kay Webster, contributing editor George Garrett (1997)

1997 edited by Matthew J. Bruccoli and George Garrett, with the assistance of L. Kay Webster (1998)

1998 edited by Matthew J. Bruccoli, contributing editor George Garrett, with the assistance of D. W. Thomas (1999)

Concise Series

Concise Dictionary of American Literary Biography, 7 volumes (1988-1999): *The New Consciousness, 1941-1968; Colonization to the American Renaissance, 1640-1865; Realism, Naturalism, and Local Color, 1865-1917; The Twenties, 1917-1929; The Age of Maturity, 1929-1941; Broadening Views, 1968-1988; Supplement: Modern Writers, 1900–1998.*

Concise Dictionary of British Literary Biography, 8 volumes (1991-1992): *Writers of the Middle Ages and Renaissance Before 1660; Writers of the Restoration and Eighteenth Century, 1660-1789; Writers of the Romantic Period, 1789-1832; Victorian Writers, 1832-1890; Late-Victorian and Edwardian Writers, 1890-1914; Modern Writers, 1914-1945; Writers After World War II, 1945-1960; Contemporary Writers, 1960 to Present.*

Concise Dictionary of World Literary Biography, 20 volumes projected (1999-   ): *Ancient Greek and Roman Writers; German Writers.*

Dictionary of Literary Biography® • Volume Two Hundred Fifteen

Twentieth-Century Eastern European Writers
First Series

Twentieth-Century Eastern European Writers
First Series

Edited by
Steven Serafin
Hunter College of The City University of New York

A Bruccoli Clark Layman Book
The Gale Group
Detroit • San Francisco • London • Boston • Woodbridge, Conn.

Associate Editors:

Jan Čulík
University of Glasgow

Bogdan Czaykowski
University of British Columbia

István Dobos
University of Debrecen

Branislav Hochel
Comenius University

Norma L. Rudinsky
Oregon State University

Contents

Contents

Authors by Nationality

Czech Republic

Karel Čapek
Jakub Deml
Viktor Dyk
František Halas
Jaroslav Hašek
Vladimír Holan
Josef Hora
Egon Hostovský

Vítězslav Nezval
Jiří Orten
Karel Poláček
Jaroslav Seifert
Vladislav Vančura
Jiří Wolker

Hungary

Endre Ady
Mihály Babits
Győző Határ
Gyula Illyés
Attila József
Frigyes Karinthy
Lajos Kassák
Gyula Krúdy

György Lukács
Ferenc Molnár
Zsigmond Móricz
László Németh
Miklós Radnóti
Lőrinc Szabó
Magda Szabó
Áron Tamási

Poland

Jerzy Andrzejewski
Wacław Berent
Tadeusz Borowski
Maria Dąbrowska
Witold Gombrowicz
Wacław Iwaniuk
Jarosław Iwaszkiewicz
Maria Kuncewicz

Bolesław Leśmian
Czesław Miłosz
Zofia Nałkowska
Teodor Parnicki
Bruno Schulz
Stanisław Ignacy Witkiewicz

Slovakia

Jozef Cíger Hronský
Jégé
Ivan Krasko
Martin Kukučín

Laco Novomeský
Timrava
Milo Urban

Plan of the Series

... Almost the most prodigious asset of a country, and perhaps its most precious possession, is its native literary product— when that product is fine and noble and enduring.

Mark Twain*

The advisory board, the editors, and the publisher of the *Dictionary of Literary Biography* are joined in endorsing Mark Twain's declaration. The literature of a nation provides an inexhaustible resource of permanent worth. We intend to make literature and its creators better understood and more accessible to students and the reading public, while satisfying the standards of teachers and scholars.

To meet these requirements, *literary biography* has been construed in terms of the author's achievement. The most important thing about a writer is his writing. Accordingly, the entries in *DLB* are career biographies, tracing the development of the author's canon and the evolution of his reputation.

The purpose of *DLB* is not only to provide reliable information in a convenient format but also to place the figures in the larger perspective of literary history and to offer appraisals of their accomplishments by qualified scholars.

The publication plan for *DLB* resulted from two years of preparation. The project was proposed to Bruccoli Clark by Frederick G. Ruffner, president of the Gale Research Company, in November 1975. After specimen entries were prepared and typeset, an advisory board was formed to refine the entry format and develop the series rationale. In meetings held during 1976, the publisher, series editors, and advisory board approved the scheme for a comprehensive biographical dictionary of persons who contributed to North American literature. Editorial work on the first volume began in January 1977, and it was published in 1978. In order to make *DLB* more than a reference tool and to compile volumes that individually have claim to status as literary history, it was decided to organize volumes by

From an unpublished section of Mark Twain's autobiography, copyright by the Mark Twain Company

topic, period, or genre. Each of these freestanding volumes provides a biographical-bibliographical guide and overview for a particular area of literature. We are convinced that this organization–as opposed to a single alphabet method–constitutes a valuable innovation in the presentation of reference material. The volume plan necessarily requires many decisions for the placement and treatment of authors who might properly be included in two or three volumes. In some instances a major figure will be included in separate volumes, but with different entries emphasizing the aspect of his career appropriate to each volume. Ernest Hemingway, for example, is represented in *American Writers in Paris, 1920–1939* by an entry focusing on his expatriate apprenticeship; he is also in *American Novelists, 1910–1945* with an entry surveying his entire career, as well as in *American Short-Story Writers, 1910–1945, Second Series* with an entry concentrating on his short stories. Each volume includes a cumulative index of the subject authors and articles. Comprehensive indexes to the entire series are planned.

Since 1981 the series has been further augmented by the *DLB Yearbooks,* which update published entries and add new entries to keep the *DLB* current with contemporary activity. There have also been *DLB Documentary Series* volumes which provide biographical and critical source materials for figures whose work is judged to have particular interest for students. One of these companion volumes is devoted entirely to Tennessee Williams.

We define literature as the *intellectual commerce of a nation:* not merely as belles lettres but as that ample and complex process by which ideas are generated, shaped, and transmitted. *DLB* entries are not limited to "creative writers" but extend to other figures who in their time and in their way influenced the mind of a people. Thus the series encompasses historians, journalists, publishers, book collectors, and screenwriters. By this means readers of *DLB* may be aided to perceive literature not as cult scripture in the keeping of intellectual high priests but firmly positioned at the center of a nation's life.

DLB includes the major writers appropriate to each volume and those standing in the ranks behind them. Scholarly and critical counsel has been sought in deciding which minor figures to include and how full their entries should be. Wherever possible, useful references are made to figures who do not warrant separate entries.

Each *DLB* volume has an expert volume editor responsible for planning the volume, selecting the figures for inclusion, and assigning the entries. Volume editors are also responsible for preparing, where appropriate, appendices surveying the major periodicals and literary and intellectual movements for their volumes, as well as lists of further readings. Work on the series as a whole is coordinated at the Bruccoli Clark Layman editorial center in Columbia, South Carolina, where the editorial staff is responsible for accuracy and utility of the published volumes.

One feature that distinguishes *DLB* is the illustration policy–its concern with the iconography of literature. Just as an author is influenced by his surroundings, so is the reader's understanding of the author enhanced by a knowledge of his environment. Therefore *DLB* volumes include not only drawings, paintings, and photographs of authors, often depicting them at various stages in their careers, but also illustrations of their families and places where they lived. Title pages are regularly reproduced in facsimile along with dust jackets for modern authors. The dust jackets are a special feature of *DLB* because they often document better than anything else the way in which an author's work was perceived in its own time. Specimens of the writers' manuscripts and letters are included when feasible.

Samuel Johnson rightly decreed that "The chief glory of every people arises from its authors." The purpose of the *Dictionary of Literary Biography* is to compile literary history in the surest way available to us–by accurate and comprehensive treatment of the lives and work of those who contributed to it.

The *DLB* Advisory Board

Introduction

The *Twentieth-Century Eastern European Writers* volumes of the *Dictionary of Literary Biography* introduces the lives and works of the most prominent literary figures of the century from the national literatures of Albania, Czech Republic, Estonia, Hungary, Latvia, Lithuania, Poland, Romania, and Slovakia. The series serves to acknowledge the contribution of those authors who played a significant role in the growth, development, and preservation of their respective literatures. The diversified literary history of Eastern Europe mirrors the depth and complexity of its social and political history, and for many of the national literatures the very survival of literary tradition as well as spoken and written language is often the most significant legacy handed from one generation of authors to the next. *Twentieth-Century Eastern European Writers, First Series*, includes West Slavic authors writing in Czech, Polish, and Slovak as well as Magyar and Transylvanian authors writing in Hungarian who established their literary careers in the first half of the century. In the decades prior to World War II, Eastern Europe was transformed by the realities of modernity, and the literature produced within the context of transition and turbulence serves as a testament both to the nature of art and to the creative integrity of the artist.

Dominated by the literary trends of romanticism and realism throughout much of the second half of the nineteenth century, Eastern European literature gradually embraced the emerging modernist influences, extending from the French symbolists—Charles Baudelaire, Arthur Rimbaud, Paul Verlaine, and Stéphane Mallarmé—to the Belgian author Maurice Maeterlinck and the Russian poets Fyodor Sologub, Konstantin Balmont, and Valery Briusov. The first decades of the twentieth century juxtaposed traditional against new and experimental literary forms, which resulted in an extraordinarily inventive body of creative work and simultaneously generated heated debate among writers and literary scholars as to the purpose and practice of literature. Hav-

ing endured centuries of social upheaval, political turmoil, civil strife, war, and foreign domination, Eastern Europe at the beginning of the twentieth century was on the edge of disjointed uncertainty. Until the end of World War I, Czech and Slovak lands belonged to the empire of Austria-Hungary. Established in 1867, the dual monarchy of Austria-Hungary was dissolved in 1918; as a result, geographical boundaries throughout much of Eastern Europe and the western provinces of Russia were reshaped to reflect new national identities. The former Czech and Slovak lands were united as Czechoslovakia, which also included sizable German, Hungarian, and Ukrainian as well as smaller Jewish and Polish minorities. In addition, the South Slavic peoples of Serbia, Croatia, Slovenia, Macedonia, Bosnia and Herzegovina, and Montenegro were united as Yugoslavia. Prior to World War I, Hungary included sections of present-day Romania, Croatia, Slovakia, and Ukraine; dissolution of the monarchy reduced the country by more than two-thirds of its former size. Likewise, the dissolution of the monarchy enabled Poland to regain its independence after partition in the early nineteenth century by Austria, Prussia, and Russia.

As newly formed nations arose after the war, the process of redefinition and recovery was convoluted by social, political, and ethnic dissension. Disorientation, internal and external conflict, and economic instability left much of Eastern Europe vulnerable to the rise and aftermath of Nazism in Germany. Following the Munich Conference in 1938, Hitler dismembered Czechoslovakia and established an independent state of Slovakia, while Czech lands became occupied by Hungary and Poland. In September 1939 Poland was invaded by Germany and Russia; as a result, the country was once again partitioned, and German occupation led to the extermination of Polish Jewry as well as other ethnic minorities. In addition, close to two million Poles were sent to their deaths in Kazakhstan, Siberia, and the Soviet Far East. Toward the close of the war Soviet forces gained control of the country from Germany, and in 1945 Poland was reorganized as a Soviet state. In that same year Czechoslovakia was reestablished with some territorial concessions to Russia and likewise fell under Soviet domination. Having allied itself with Germany in return for partial restoration of its former boundaries, Hungary at the end of the war became occupied by the Soviets, thus paving the way for communist control throughout Eastern Europe.

The interrelationship between literature and history is perhaps nowhere more evident than in Eastern Europe, and just as individual countries at the turn of the century were transformed by the modern world, so were their national literatures transformed by modernity. At the forefront of the movement was the generation of Czech authors emerging in the 1890s influenced by the major aesthetic critic František Xaver Šalda, the most significant Czech theoretician of the first half of the twentieth century. The Czech modernist manifesto, written primarily by Šalda and published in the journal *Rozhledy* (Overview) in October 1895, advocated rejection of the traditional and conventional literary techniques that had dominated late-nineteenth-century Czech literature in favor of new means of expression, illustrated in the first decades of the twentieth century in the poetry of Josef Svatopluk Machar, Antonín Sova, Petr Bezruč, Otakar Březina, Jiří Karásek ze Lvovic, and Viktor Dyk, and in the fiction of Karel Čapek, Anna Marie Tilschová, and Božena Benešová.

In the aftermath of World War I, with the establishment of the republic of Czechoslovakia in 1918, Czech literature entered a period of transition. The war experience was of thematic importance for several authors in various genres, notably Tilschová and Benešová as well as Jaroslav Hašek, author of the three-volume epic novel *Osudy dobrého vojáka Švejka za světové valky* (1921–1923; expurgated edition translated as *The Good Soldier: Schweik*, 1930). At the same time a proletarian movement in literature emerged that embraced socialist ideology as a means to initiate social and political change; this movement included the poets Josef Hora and Jiří Wolker, and prose writers Ivan Olbracht, Marie Majerová, and Vladislav Vančura. A later proletarian voice emerged in the poetry of Jaroslav Seifert, who in 1984 became the first Czech author to be awarded the Nobel Prize in literature. Seifert was also instrumental in promoting the development of Czech poetism. Formulated primarily by the theoretician Karel Tieje, poetism was a revolutionary program initiated during the interwar period that advocated imaginative and playful experimentation in all forms of popular culture, as illustrated in the work of Vítězslav Nezval and František Halas, both of whom were influenced by Surrealism and avant-garde theories of literature.

During this same period dramatic production was rejuvenated by the work of brothers Josef and Karel Čapek as well as by František Langer and Emil František Burian. Karel Čapek achieved international recognition as a dramatist, notably with the futuristic play *R.U.R. (Rossum's Universal Robots)* (1920), which warned of the impending threat of totalitarianism that soon became a reality in Czech society. Under the leadership of Šalda, Czech literary criticism continued to flourish, notably in the work of Arne Novák and the Marxist critic Bedřich Václavek, and was further enhanced by the emergence of the Prague Linguistic Circle, which promoted the modern structural linguistics theories of such critics as Jan Mukařovský and Roman Jakobson. However, with the German occupation of Czechoslovakia during World War II, literary production was severely censored, and the works of Jewish writers such as Egon Hostovský and Karl Poláček were banned. Several writers were arrested, tortured, or imprisoned; others died of starvation in labor camps or were killed by the German Gestapo. Among the many who perished during the occupation were Poláček, Josef Čapek, Vančura, Václavek, and the editor and critic Julius Fučík.

In Slovak literature the period of romanticism in the mid nineteenth century coincided with the movement of national revival, which produced a generation of writers that formed around Ľudovít Štúr, including Samo Chalúpka, Jozef Miloslav Hurban, Andrej Sládkovič, Ján Kalinčiak, Janko Kráľ, and Ján Botto. Similar in development to Czech literature, Slovak literature at the turn of the century was dominated by the romantic poetry of Svetozár Hurban Vajanský and Hviezdoslav (Pavol Országh). Slovak realism was promoted at the same time in the short stories and most notably in the two-volume novel *Dom v stráni* (The House on a Hill, 1903–1904) by Martin Kukučín, whose focus on the peasantry and village life influenced such writers as Jozef Gregor Tajovský, Timrava (Božena Slančíková), and Jégé (Ladislav Nádaši). In addition to Timrava, other pioneering women writers included Terézia Vansová, the author of *Sirota Podhradských* (The Podhradský Orphan, 1889), the first Slovak novel written by a woman, as well as Elena Maróthy-Šoltésová and Ľudmila Riznerová-Podjavorinská.

Prior to the establishment of the republic of Czechoslovakia, Slovakia was part of the kingdom of Hungary; thus, much of the literature was dominated by nationalistic concerns for the survival of the Slovak language and cultural heritage. Slovak modernism emerged in the early decades of the twentieth century with the generation of writers who were influenced primarily by symbolism and who gathered around the literary journals *Prúdy* and *Hlas* (The Voice); these included Tomáš Garrigue Masaryk, Vladimír Roy, Jozef Gregor Tajovský, Ivan Krasko, Janko Jesenský, František Votruba, and Martin Rázus. The most prolific dramatist of the period was Ferko Urbánek, the author of more than sixty plays. Other dramatists of note were Pavel Sochán, Jozef Hollý, and Vladimír Konštantín Hurban. The leading critics included Jozef Škultéty, Jaroslav Vlček, František Votruba, and Pavel Bujnák.

The postwar years were an unprecedented period of expansion in Slovak literature, as illustrated by prose writers such as Jozef Cíger Hronský, Gejza Vámoš, Janko Kráľ, Ivan Horváth, and Milo Urban; poets such as Valentín Beniak, Ján Smrek (Ján Čietek), Emil Boleslav Lukáč, Andrej Žarnov (František Šubík), and Rudolf Dilong; and the dramatist Ivan Stodola. Beginning in the early 1920s Slovak literature became increasingly influenced by Marxist theories and the encroachment of Socialist Realism. A generation of writers formed around the Marxist periodical *DAV,* most notably the novelist Peter Jilemnický and the poet Ladislav (Laco) Novomeský. In the years prior to World War II, Slovak literature reflected the increasing influence of Surrealism, illustrated in the poetry of Rudolf Fábry and Vladimír Reisel. However, literary activity throughout the country was significantly curtailed during and immediately following the war.

The literary tradition in Poland, dominated in the last decades of the nineteenth century by the realistic novel, represents a diversified history of extraordinary importance within Eastern European literature. Inheriting the realistic vision of such writers as Jósef Ignacy Kraszewski, Bolesław Prus (Aleksander Głowacki), Eliza Orzeszkowa and the imposing figure of Henryk Sienkiewicz (awarded the Nobel Prize in literature in 1905), Polish literature at the turn of the century embraced the emerging modernist techniques in all genres, but most significantly in poetry and drama. The influence of symbolism and impressionism in the last decade of the nineteenth century was early recognized in the work of such traditional writers as Adolf Dygasiński, Antoni Sygietyński, and Gabriela Zapolska, followed by the generations of writers identified with the *Młoda Polska* (Young Poland) tradition, which extended from the last decade of the nineteenth century to the first two decades of the twentieth. The leading writers of the Young Poland period included poets Kazimierz Tetnajer, Jan Kasprowicz, and Leopold Staff; the dramatist Stanisław Wyspiański; and prose writers Wacław Sieroszewski, Stanisław Przybyszewski, Stefan Żeromski, Wacław Berent, and Władystaw Stanisław Reymont, who was awarded the Nobel Prize in literature in 1924.

During World War I, literary activity in Poland was overshadowed by events that virtually decimated the country; however, with the rebirth of an independent Poland in 1918 there was a resurgence of literature. The leading postwar writers gathered around the literary journal *Skamander* and included the poets Julian Tuwim, Kazimierz Wiersyński, Jarosław Iwaszkiewicz, Antoni Słonimski, Stefan Napierski, and Leszek Serafinowicz (Jan Lechoń). The symbolist poetry of Bolesław Leśmian anticipated the futuristic poets Stanisław Młodożeniec, Bruno Jasieński, Anatol Stern, and Aleksander Wat as well as the "functional" poetry of Tadeusz Peiper, Julian Przyboś, Jan Brzękowski, and Marian Czuchnowski.

The interwar period introduced the poetry of Józef Czechowicz, Jerzy Zagórski, and most notably Czesław Miłosz, who in 1980 became the third Polish author to be awarded the Nobel Prize in literature. Simultaneously there emerged dramatists of distinct importance, such as Ludwik Hieronim Morstin, Jerzy Szaniawski, Karol Hubert Rostworowski, and Stanisław Ignacy Witkiewicz, precursor to the Theater of the Absurd, as well as novelists and short-story writers, notably Zofia Nałkowska, Juliusz Kaden-Bandrowski, Maria Dąbrowska, Ferdynand Goetel, Jan Parandowski, Zofia Kossak, Maria Kuncewicz, Józef Wittlin, Leon Kruczkowski, and one of the best-known Polish writers, Witold Gombrowicz, who from the outbreak of World War II lived in exile for the remainder of his life. Of exceptional merit was the experimental fiction of Bruno Schulz, who was executed by the Gestapo during the German occupation of Poland.

During the German occupation of Poland in World War II, literary activity was severely restricted. Many Polish writers were forced into exile, notably Lechoń, Tuwim, Wittlin, and Wierzyński; others were arrested, deported, or sent to concentration camps. Some, such as Schulz, were executed, while still others perished in the Warsaw Uprising and other resistance activities. Writers remaining in Poland were refused permission to publish their works; as a result, many underground periodicals emerged as an alternative means of literary production, but at great risk for the writers and editors, who were often arrested and executed.

Similar to the West Slavic literatures, Hungarian literature at the turn of the century was formulated in response to modernist influences, most importantly the techniques of the French symbolist poets. In the first decade of the century a group of writers formed around the literary journal *Nyugat* (West), founded in 1908 by critics Ignotus (Hugo Veigelsberg) and Ernő Osvát with the intent to give new expression to Hungarian literature. Composed primarily of poets, notably Endre Ady, Mihály Babits, Oszkár Gellért, Gyula Juhász, Simon Kemény, Ernő Szép, Dezső Kosztolányi, Anna Lesznai, Árpád Tóth, and Milán Füst, the first *Nyugat* generation also included prose writers such as Zsigmond Móricz, Margit Kaffka, and Frigyes Karinthy. The revolutionary themes of social protest advocated in the poetry of Ady, Juhász, and Tóth was likewise explored in the fiction of Móricz and Lajos Nagy. In addition to the *Nyugat* generation, other writers of importance included the poet József Kiss, novelist Sándor Bródy, and the dramatists Dezső Szomory and Ferenc Molnár, the Budapest-born author who immigrated to the United States. Although literary modernism was promoted by such influential critics as György Lukács, Zoltán Ambrus, and Aladár Schöpflin, it was bitterly opposed by conservative critics such as Jenő Rákosi, who advocated a more traditional literature.

Following World War I and the dissolution of the Austria-Hungary monarchy, Hungarian literature was transformed by the trend of populism, associated with such writers as Dezső Szabó, József Erdélyi, János Kodolányi, and most notably Gyula Illyés, and as well by the surrealist techniques incorporated in the fiction of Gyula Krúdy and the futuristic and expressionist techniques incorporated in the poetry of Lajos Kassák. Beginning in the early 1920s Hungarian literature also reflected the increasing attention given to social and psychological developments, illustrated by the works of novelist Mihály Földi and playwright Lajos Zilahy, who, like Molnár, immigrated to the United States. However, the interwar period was dominated by the populist poetry of Illyés, Lőrinc Szabó, Miklós Radnóti, and Sándor Weöres. Proletarian writers of the same period included Lajos Nagy, Andor Endre Gelléri, Zsigmond Remenyik, and the revolutionary poet Attila József, whose body of work is the most significant literary achievement in Hungarian literature prior to the encroachment of World War II and Soviet occupation. Similar to other Eastern European countries, Hungary was devastated by World War II, and the impact on cultural life was traumatic. Many writers fled into exile; others who remained in Hungary were arrested, sent to labor camps, or killed. Hungarian writers who perished during the occupation included Radnóti, Gelléri, Károly Pap, György Sárközi, and Antal Szerb.

Twentieth-Century Eastern European Writers, First Series, represents a collaborative effort to bring together in one volume Czech, Slovak, Polish, and Hungarian writers whose creative output reflects the literary as well as the historical development of their respective countries within the modern era up to and during World War II. Since many of the authors included in the series have limited exposure in the West, the series is designed to provide the English-speaking reader with a more comprehensive understanding and appreciation of Eastern Europe and its literary tradition.

Acknowledgments

This book was produced by Bruccoli Clark Layman, Inc. Karen L. Rood is senior editor for the *Dictionary of Literary Biography* series. Tracy Simmons Bitonti and Penelope Hope were the in-house editors. They were assisted by James F. Tidd Jr.

Production manager is Philip B. Dematteis.

Administrative support was provided by Ann M. Cheschi, Tenesha S. Lee, and Joann Whittaker.

Accounting was done by Angi Pleasant.

Copyediting supervisor is Phyllis A. Avant. Senior copyeditor is Thom Harman. The copyediting staff includes Ronald D. Aiken II, Brenda Carol Blanton, Worthy B. Evans, Melissa D. Hinton, William Tobias Mathes, Jennifer Reid, and Michelle L. Whitney.

Editorial assistant is Margo Dowling.

Editorial trainee is Carol A. Fairman.

Indexing specialist is Alex Snead.

Layout and graphics supervisor is Janet E. Hill. Graphics staff includes Zoe R. Cook.

Office manager is Kathy Lawler Merlette.

Photography editors are Charles Mims, Scott Nemzek, Alison Smith, and Paul Talbot. Digital photographic copy work was performed by Joseph M. Bruccoli.

SGML supervisor is Cory McNair. The SGML staff includes Tim Bedford, Linda Drake, Frank Graham, and Alex Snead.

Systems manager is Marie L. Parker.

Kimberly Kelly performed data entry.

Typesetting supervisor is Kathleen M. Flanagan. The typesetting staff includes Karla Corley Brown, Mark J. McEwan, and Patricia Flanagan Salisbury. Freelance typesetter is Delores Plastow.

Walter W. Ross and Steven Gross did library research. They were assisted by the following librarians at the Thomas Cooper Library of the University of South Carolina: Linda Holderfield and the interlibrary-loan staff; reference-department head Virginia Weathers; reference librarians Marilee Birchfield, Stefanie Buck, Stefanie DuBose, Rebecca Feind, Karen Joseph, Donna Lehman, Charlene Loope, Anthony McKissick, Jean Rhyne, and Kwamine Simpson; circulation-department head Caroline Taylor; and acquisitions-searching supervisor David Haggard.

All of the Czech entries in this volume were translated by Elizabeth S. Morrison.

The editor expresses his appreciation for the contribution of the associate editors whose expertise and commitment to their respective national literatures was instrumental in the development of the series. In addition, he wishes to acknowledge the contribution of the invaluable assistance of the librarians and staff of the Hunter College Library, in particular Norman Clarius. Support for this project was provided by a grant from the PSC-CUNY Research Award Program.

Dictionary of Literary Biography® • Volume Two Hundred Fifteen

Twentieth-Century Eastern European Writers
First Series

Dictionary of Literary Biography

Endre Ady
(22 November 1877 – 27 January 1919)

Pál S. Varga
University of Debrecen

BOOKS: *Versek* (Debrecen: Hoffmann-Kronovitz, 1899);

Még egyszer (Nagyvárad: Adolf Sonnenfeld, 1903);

Új versek (Budapest: Pallas, 1906);

Sápadt emberek és történetek (Budapest: Lampel Róbert, 1907);

Vér és arany (Budapest: Franklin-Társulat, 1908 [1907]);

Az Illés szekerén (Budapest: Singer és Wolfner, 1909 [1908]);

Új csapáson (Budapest: Nyugat, 1909);

Szeretném, ha szeretnének: Versek (Budapest: Nyugat, 1910 [1909]);

A forradalmár Petőfi (Budapest: Pallas, 1910);

Így is történhetik (Budapest: Nyugat, 1910);

A minden-titkok verseiből (Budapest: Nyugat, 1910);

A tízmilliós Kleopátra és egyéb történetek (Budapest: Lampel Róbert, 1910);

Vallomások és tanulmányok (Budapest: Nyugat, 1911);

A menekülő élet (Budapest: Nyugat, 1912);

A magunk szerelme: Versek (Budapest: Nyugat, 1913);

Muskétás tanár úr (Békéscsaba: Tevan, 1913);

Ki látott engem?: Versek (Budapest: Nyugat, 1914);

Gyűjtemény Ady Endre verseiből (Budapest: Pallas, 1918);

A halottak élén (Budapest: Pallas, 1918);

Az új Hellász (Budapest: Amicus, 1920);

Margita élni akar (Budapest: Amicus, 1921);

Rövid dalok egyről és másról, edited by Gyula Földessy (Budapest: Amicus, 1923 [1922]);

Az utolsó hajók (Budapest: Athenaeum, 1923),

Levelek Párisból (Budapest: Amicus, 1924);

Párisi noteszkönyve, edited by Lajos Ady (Budapest: Amicus, 1924);

Endre Ady

"Ha hív az acélhegyű ördög . . ." Ady Endre újságírói és publicisztikai írásai 1900–1904 (Oradea- Nagyvárad: Szent László, 1927);

Vallomások és tanulmányok, edited by Földessy (Budapest: Athenaeum, 1944).

Editions and Collections: *Válogatott versei* (Budapest: Pallas, 1921);

Sápadt emberek és töténetek (Budapest: Athenaeum, 1925);

Antológia Ady Endre verseiből, edited by Lőrinc Szabó (Budapest: Athenaeum, 1927);

Összes versei (Budapest: Athenaeum, 1930);

Jóslások Magyarországról. Tanulmányok és jegyzetek a magyar sorskérdésről, edited by Géza Féja (Budapest: Athenaeum, 1936);

Összes versei (Budapest: Athenaeum, 1936);

Összegyűjtött novellái (Budapest: Athenaeum, 1939);

A tegnapi Páris, edited by Aladár Kovách (Budapest: Bolyai Akadémia, 1942);

Összes versei (Budapest: Athenaeum, 1943);

A forradalmi Ady: Szakasits Árpád eloszavával, edited by János Erdody (Budapest: Népszava, 1945);

Összes versei (Budapest: Athenaeum, 1948);

Párisban és Napfényországban, edited by Földessy (Budapest: Athenaeum, 1949);

Összes versei (Budapest: Szépirodalmi, 1950);

Földrengés előtt (Bucharest: Állami Irodalmi és Művészeti Kiadó, 1952);

Válogatott versei (Budapest: Szépirodalmi, 1952);

Összes versei, 2 volumes (Budapest: Szépirodalmi, 1954);

Válogatott cikkei és tanulmányai, edited by Földessy (Budapest: Szépirodalmi, 1954);

Összes prózai művei, 5 volumes (Budapest: Akadémiai Kiadó, 1955–1964);

Összes versei, 2 volumes (Budapest: Szépirodalmi, 1955);

Összes költeményei (Noviszád: Testvériség-Egység, 1956);

Válogatott levelei (Budapest: Szépirodalmi, 1956);

Novellák, 2 volumes (Marosvásárhely [Tirgu Mures]: Állami Irodalmi és Művészeti Kiadó, 1957 [1958]);

Vallomás a patriotizmusról (Bucharest: Állami Irodalmi és Művészeti Kiadó, 1957);

Ifjú szivekben élek: Válogatott cikek és tanulmányok (Budapest: Móra Ferenc, 1958);

A nacionalizmus alkonya, edited by Sándor Koczkás and Erzsébet Vezér (Budapest: Kossuth, 1959);

A fekete lobogó (Budapest: Kossuth, 1960);

Versek, 2 volumes (Bucharest: Irodalmi és Művészeti Kiadó, 1960)—comprises volume 1, *Új versek; Vér és arany; Az Illés szekerén; Szeretném, ha szeretnének; A minden titkok verseiből; A menekülő élet;* volume 2, *A magunk szerelme; Ki látott engem?; A halottak élén; Az utolsó hajók; Versek; Még egyszer;*

Az irodalomról (Budapest: Magvető, 1961);

Összes novellái (Budapest: Szépirodalmi, 1961);

Összes versei (Budapest: Szépirodalmi, 1961);

Összes versei, 2 volumes (Budapest: Szépirodalmi, 1962)—comprises volume 1, *Új versek; Vér és arany; Az Illés szekerén; Szeretném, ha szeretnének; A minden titkok versei; Margita élni akar; A magunk szerelme; Ki látott engem?;* volume 2, *A halottak élén; Az utolsó hajók; Versek; Még egyszer;*

Léda és Csinszka (Budapest: Magyar Helikon, 1966);

Összes versei (Budapest: Magyar Helikon, 1968);

Összes művei, 3 volumes, critical edition (Budapest: Akadémia, 1969, 1988, 1995)—comprises volume 1, *Összes versei 1891–1899* (1969); volume 2, *Összes versei 1900–1906. január 7.* (1988); volume 3, *Összes versei 1906. január 28 1907* (1995);

Összes versei, 2 volumes (Budapest: Szépirodalmi, 1972);

Összes versei, 2 volumes (Budapest: Szépirodalmi, 1975);

Összes novellái (Budapest: Szépirodalmi, 1977);

Összes versei (Budapest: Szépirodalmi, 1977);

Összes versei, 2 volumes (Budapest: Szépirodalmi, 1989);

A kék álom: Novellák (Budapest: Ferenczy, 1994);

Összes versei, 3 volumes (Budapest: Unikornis, 1995);

A Pokol-játek: Történetek (Budapest: Unikornis, 1999).

Editions in English: *Poems,* translated by René Bonnerjea (Budapest: Vajna & Bokor, 1941);

A Selection of Poems from the Writings of Endre Ady, translated by Antal Nyerges (Washington: Published for the American Hungarian Federation by Indiana University Press, 1946);

Poems, translated by Bonnerjea (Forest Hills, N.Y.: Transatlantic, 1947);

Poems of Endre Ady, translated by Anton N. Nyerges, prepared for publishing by Joseph M. Értavy-Baráth (Buffalo, N.Y.: Hungarian Cultural Foundation, 1969);

Ady Endre 1877–1919, edited by Ferenc Kerényi, translated by Nyerges and Bonnerjea (Budapest: Institute for Cultural Relations, 1977);

The Explosive Country: A Selection of Articles and Studies 1898–1916, selected by Erzsébet Vezér, translated by George Ferdinand Cushing (Budapest: Corvina, 1977);

Selected Poems, translated by Eugene Bard (Munich: Hieronymus, 1987);

Neighbours of the Night: Selected Short Stories, edited and translated by Judith Sollosy (Budapest: Corvina, 1994).

Endre Ady's writings have synthesized the tradition of Hungarian poetry with the most important trends of modern European literature (especially symbolism and expressionism). His work has inspired not only poetic trends that have continued and fully realized his innovations but also, indirectly, those writers that have placed themselves in opposition to his ideas. His art has been influential in the whole Central and Eastern European region; many of his poems were published in Czech, Polish, Romanian, and Slovakian translations during his lifetime. His influence, however, can be felt even beyond the region: his poems have been translated into twenty-two languages, and several editions of his works have been published in Croatian, German, Hebrew, Italian, Spanish, Serbian, and English.

Ady's poetic innovations had no immediate antecedents in Hungarian literature; the last flourishing period in Hungarian lyric poetry was produced by the romantic generation from the 1820s through the 1840s. The lyric poetry of the second half of the nineteenth century was dominated by romantic imitators, late-*biedermeier* poets, and the representatives of a poetic school with no contact with the new European literary trends and similar to the German *poetische Realismus*. Despite some significant but isolated neoclassical and neo-romantic (pre-symbolic) experiments, Hungarian poetry in the last two decades of the nineteenth century became provincial and powerless. Ady brought about a radical change also called "poetic revolution."

Endre Ady was born on 22 November 1877 in Érmindszent, a small village in Szilágy county, eastern Hungary (now in Romania; the village has since been renamed after Ady). His father, Lőrinc Ady, was a small landholder; his mother was Mária Pásztor. Ady's ancestry played an important part in his poetic program: the Ady family had a long recorded history from the fourteenth century. The family had soon sunk into poverty, and for centuries their way of life had resembled that of the peasantry rather than that of the nobility. This dichotomy raised Ady's feelings of both responsibility and empathy toward the peasants. He also attached great importance to the fact that among his parental and maternal ancestors there had been several Calvinist ministers and even a few poets. Calvinism, however, did not mean religious fanaticism in the Ady family.

The villages of the region were inhabited by Hungarian noblemen and Romanian, Hungarian, and Slovakian peasants, while the towns were populated by Hungarian, German, and Jewish burgesses. In terms of religion the population included Calvinist Protestants, Lutherans, Roman and Greek Catholics, Israelites, and followers of the Orthodox faith.

The house where Ady was born, in the Hungarian village then known as Érmindszent

The denominational and multiethnic environment was a crucial experience for Ady.

After finishing elementary school in his native village in 1888, Ady attended a Catholic high school in neighboring Nagykároly (now Carei, Romania) for four years. For another four years he continued his studies in the Reformed high school of nearby Zilah (now Zălau, Romania), from which he graduated in 1896. Then he went to Debrecen, a Hungarian-populated city of atavistic spirit, to study law; but he gave it up in 1898 and started to work as a journalist for various newspapers of the opposition.

In 1899 Ady published his first volume of poetry, *Versek* (Poems), in Debrecen. The book did not generate much interest: although later critics pointed out some traces of the emerging poetic revolution, the poems in this volume are hardly different from other contemporary provincial collections of verse. They reflect conventional emotional situations in the familiar form of late sentimental-*bieder-*

meier lyric poetry. In the same year Ady moved to Nagyvárad (now Oradea, Romania), the most flourishing cultural center of the region, where he became acquainted with the contemporary authors of European literature and philosophy—Emile Zola, Anatole France, Fyodor Dostoyevsky, and Friedrich Nietzsche—through fellow journalists and intellectuals. His second volume, *Még egyszer* (Once More), was published in Nagyvárad in 1903 and also went relatively unnoticed. Though it included some of the topics that later became important in his poetry—such as the anticipation of the radical transformation of Hungarian society and a mythical respect for life—as well as elements of his innovative use of poetic imagery, the sentimental style so characteristic of the first volume had not changed. Later editions of his complete works usually relegate *Versek* and *Még egyszer* to an appendix.

Ady's poetic development had been overshadowed initially by his journalistic career: by the age of twenty-seven he had become the most important journalist in the country. He belonged to the classical tradition of nineteenth-century Hungarian liberalism, but on social and ethnic issues he was closer to the social democrats. He took a stand on almost every important issue in politics, culture, literature, and the arts, and his articles attracted great attention; because of an anticlerical article in 1901, for example, he was sentenced to three days in prison.

Talented provincial journalists of the time usually ended up in the capital since Budapest was becoming an important metropolis in literary and journalistic life. Yet, as a result of an acquaintance, Ady's career did not continue there. In 1903 in Nagyvárad he became involved with Adél Brüll, wife of Ödön Diósi, a trader working in Paris at the time. When she left for Paris to join her husband, Ady decided to follow her. In early 1904 he arrived in Paris as a correspondent for a Budapest newspaper and stayed there almost a year. Diósi had a generous attitude toward his wife's relationship with the poet; he recognized Ady's poetic talent. When he learned that Ady had fallen ill with syphilis, Diósi sacrificed a great amount of money for the poet's medical treatment.

The French cultural and political environment and his love for Brüll had a liberating effect on Ady's talent. Brüll encouraged his interest in French literature: at this time he was greatly influenced by the French symbolists Charles-Pierre Baudelaire, Arthur Rimbaud, Paul Verlaine, and Maurice Maeterlinck. During his first stay in Paris he wrote almost half of the poems for his epoch-making volume, *Új versek* (New Poems, 1906).

When Ady returned home, there was a political crisis in Hungary: in order to avoid social conflicts, the illegally appointed government promised to introduce universal suffrage. Many members of the liberal and social democratic opposition held that such endeavors should be supported. For a short while Ady worked for the public relations office of the government, for which the radical opposition later fiercely attacked him. Nevertheless, in 1905 he wrote the poems that—together with the ones he had drafted in Paris—comprised *Új versek* and brought about a turning point in Hungarian poetry.

Új versek appeared in February 1906. The adjective in the title refers not only to simple chronology and a new period in Ady's artistic career but also to his conscious rejection of contemporary poetic trends. His radical program is proclaimed in the invocation and the epilogue in terms of a synthesis of the antinomies of human life. The volume displays a unified compositional concept: four cycles create a poetic world in which the antinomies are synthesized in a system of mutually complementary symbols. The prologue, "Góg és Magóg fia vagyok én" (Son of Gog and Magog), is based on the widespread medieval historiographical tradition of tracing the history of a country back to the biblical Creation story. Ady links his own figure of the lyric self to this mythologized history, and he sets his poems "brought from the West" against the arrival of the Hungarians from the East one thousand years before. He thus professes his program of synthesis between the archaic Eastern or Asian origin of the Hungarians and their modern Western European identity.

The epilogue, "Új vizeken járok" (translated as "I Walk on New Waters," 1969), is built on the archaic motif of water—symbolizing life and death at the same time—and its protagonist is "the hero of Tomorrow," the sailor conquering all unknown waters, or the lyric self turned into a mythical figure. The language of the poem is a synthesis of sacred and blasphemously profane stylistic layers—for example, "Hajtson Szentlélek vagy a korcsma gőze" (Let Me Be Driven By the Holy Spirit or the Fume of the Pub).

The four cycles of the volume are "Léda asszony zsoltárai" (Psalms for Léda; the name "Léda" is an anagram of "Adél" and a mythological allusion as well), "A magyar Ugaron" (The Magyar Fallow), "A daloló Páris" (Singing Paris), and "Szűz ormok vándora" (Roaming over Virgin Peaks). The poems in each cycle are variations on the indicated theme, with the title poem somewhere in the middle of the cycle. The section titles consist of three words, an allusion to the symbolic meaning of the number three in both Christian tradition and Hungarian folklore. The structural composition of this volume, following Baudelaire's editing pattern, became characteristic of all Ady's later books with the exception of his last, posthumous collection, which he had not edited.

In "Léda asszony zsoltárai," which broke with the conventions and taboos of love poetry, the antinomy of the cycle lies in the nature of love, in which egoism and sacrifice, or suffering and pleasure, represent two aspects of the same feeling. Love—"csók-csatatér" (the battlefield of kisses)—is presented as a physical and spiritual relationship between two autonomous persons, each of whom is destined for but unable to bear the other. The majesty of such a relationship is expressed by suggestive symbols, as in "A vár fehér asszonya" (translated as "The White-Lady," 1941; also translated as "The White-Robed Woman," 1969), "Héja-nász az avaron" (translated as "The Hawk Nuptials," 1969), and "Fehér csönd" (White Silence).

The section titled "A magyar Ugaron" is a radical innovation of a centuries-old tradition in Hungarian poetry. The tradition of the national prophet-poet had been generated by a series of crises in the history of the country between the sixteenth and the twentieth centuries. The most significant prior representative of this tradition, Sándor Petőfi, took on the role of the intellectual leader of the people in an effort to realize an optimistic utopia during the 1848 Hungarian Revolution. As this cycle indicates, Ady did not foresee a utopian future; contrary to the obstinate optimism of the opening verse, the poems of the cycle describe the fate of the Hungarians as hopelessly caught between the East and the West. The central premise of the cycle is that the harmonious paganism of the East and the refined Christian culture of the West do not enrich but rather extinguish each other on Hungarian soil, as in "Krisztusok mártírja" (Christ's Martyr) and "Ihar a tölgyek között" (Maple among the Oaks). A resulting, fatally enervating stagnancy and barrenness are illustrated in "A magyar Ugaron," "A Tisza-parton" (translated as "The Tisza Shores," 1941; also translated as "On the Tisza," 1969), and "Lelkek a pányván" (Souls on the Tether).

The cycle called "A daloló Páris" (Singing Paris) has a similar context. As opposed to the "songless," stagnant Hungarian wasteland, Paris is the city of songs and life, as illustrated in "A Gare de L'esten" (translated as "Gare de l'est," 1941). Thus,

even the translations of poems by Baudelaire, Verlaine, and Jehan Rictus in the cycle have symbolic meanings.

The next cycle, "Szűz ormok vándora," is the first full realization of the vital aesthetics that have permeated all of Ady's works and set him against the program of the "literary poets." One of the outstanding products of his art of creating symbols is the poem "Harc a Nagyúrral" (translated as "Lord Swine Head," 1969), in which the central character is Lord Swine Head, the satanic and merciless lord of Life and the miserly owner of his properties. The fight by the lyric subject for possession of the goods of Life against Lord Swine Head takes place in a mythically enlarged time dimension and ends with man's eternal defeat.

The essence of Ady's poetic technique is his creation of symbols. The poem "Lelkek a pányván," for example, starts with a metaphor (the poet's soul is a prancing colt), but the image of the tethered horse becomes independent, and the idea permeating the whole poem can no longer be related to the concrete images. One of the characteristic features of Ady's genius was his ability to suggestively visualize the desires, fears, superstitions, aggressions, and associations of the unconscious. He projected these elements of the unconscious using the imagery of classical, Christian, and Hungarian (pagan) folk mythologies, changing their original meaning. The poem titled "Búgnak a tárnák" (translated as "The Chasms Moan," 1969), which is based on the image of "The sacred mountain of songs: my soul," projects the poetic self. The sacred mountain "is looking at the sun from its snowy peak," where "brisk goblins are dancing alarmed"; but down below, in the "wicked adits" cut in the deep of the mountain by worries and agonies, "monsters are gathering" to blow up the mountain and its dancing goblins.

In the summer of 1906 Ady went back to Paris as a correspondent and remained in France for a year. In the autumn he went on a three-month journey with Brüll, visiting Marseille, Venice, Naples, Monte Carlo, Nice, and Monaco; however, his relationship with her became increasingly tense. He had financial difficulties while back in Hungary; in addition, because of *Új versek*, he was attacked by the conservative press. Seeking relief from his tensions, he often escaped into the nightlife of Paris. To ease his financial burdens he published his first collection of short stories, *Sápadt emberek és történetek* (Pale Men and Pale Stories, 1907). Ady himself did not think highly of his short stories, and scholars have

7

Adél Brüll, Ady's lover and the "Léda" of some of his poems

treated them as a mere supplement to his lyrical poetry.

In December 1907 Ady published a new volume of poetry, *Vér és arany* (Blood and Gold). Its cycles follow those of the previous volume of poetry and also introduce new themes. The subject matter of *Új versek* is continued in the cycles titled "A magyar messiások" (Hungarian Messiahs), "Mi urunk: A Pénz" (Money, Our Lord), "A Léda aranyszobra" (The Golden Sculpture of Léda), and "A Holnap elébe" (About Tomorrow). The first of these cycles brings something new to Ady's poetry. Ady creates a role similar to that of the prophets in the Old Testament and stresses that the fate of the country is ruined and unredeemable: the Hungarian Messiahs "die a thousand deaths, and the cross has no salvation." The inevitability of revolutionary change is indicated by a symbol created from Hungarian folklore motifs: *Fölszállott a páva* (The Peacock Has Taken Flight).

The forces of the unconscious take the shape of increasingly suggestive mythical figures in the cycle titled "Az ős Kaján" (Ancient Demon Guile). The central character of the title poem is a relative of Lord Swine Head. The Ancient Demon Guile, who has arrived from the East in purple robes, is the master of ecstasy, inspiration, love, and death, and

occasionally he revels and fights with the poet. The emphasis in this poem has shifted from that of "Harc a Nagyúrral": now the lyric subject asks for mercy and would like to stop the fighting, but this time there is no escape. While his mighty enemy "runs to new pagan tournaments," moving "from East onwards to West," the poet is laid under the table "with cold body, frozen-gaily." Another monumental symbolic figure is Jó Csönd-herceg (Good Prince Silence) in the poem "Jó Csönd-herceg előtt" (translated as "In Front of the Good Prince Silence," 1946; also translated as "Good Prince Silence," 1969); he embodies the ancient fears inherent in the deepest layer of human character, and he stands behind the poet as a terrifying giant constantly threatening to crush him. In "Özvegy legények tánca" (translated as "Widow of the Bachelor's Dance," 1969) the "widowed lads" dancing as ghosts on Saint George's night represent the poet's inspiring night visions.

In this volume an entire cycle, "A halál rokona" (Kin to Death), is devoted to the theme of death, which has a different meaning in each poem. In the title poem, which can also be regarded as a decadent credo, death appears as an intimate acquaintance. Another poem, "Sírni, sírni, sírni" (To Weep, Weep, Weep), generalizes the extreme state of mind induced in the lyric self by the sight of a funeral procession that makes him suddenly realize he has irreparably ruined his life. Sometimes death appears as a mythical figure—in "Párizsban járt az Ősz" (translated as "Autumn Came to Paris," 1946; also translated as "The Ghost Got into Paris," 1969) the figure of Autumn runs along the streets of Paris as a shadow, smiling and whispering in the poet's ears about his approaching demise. Sometimes death is an instrument: in "A fekete zongora" (translated as "The Black Piano," 1969) the wild music of the black piano in a brothel expresses the ecstatic moments of life. The poem called "Az én koporsó-paripám" (translated as "My Coffin-Steed," 1946) makes fun of death with gruesome humor: "I am galloping on my coffin-steed laughing."

The volume completely divided Hungarian literary life. Conservative critics attacked Ady while, in spite of their differences, representatives of modern literature united to support him. In 1908 Ady returned to Nagyvárad. During his stay the Holnap (Literary Society of Tomorrow) was formed and published anthologies of important new poets in 1908 and 1909. Writers, poets, critics, and aesthetes made friends under the influence of Ady's poetry; as a result, an intellectual circle soon formed around him, naturally leading to the establishment of a journal attracting the major figures of modern Hungarian literature. This publication, *Nyugat* (West), turned out to be the most important journal of Hungarian literature in the twentieth century. Ady was one of its main contributors until the end of his life. After his death the journal, which was published until 1941, continued in more or less the same spirit.

Success had a paradoxical effect on Ady. On the one hand, he found his poetic revolution justified; on the other, he felt that not even his best friends and most enthusiastic critics really understood its essence. As he indicated in the prologue of *Új versek*, he did not want to divide literary life. His fate was that of the reformers: those writers, critics, and readers who represented the ancient traditions of Hungarian literature—the ones he had wanted to realize the need for innovation—refused him, while "uninvited enthusiasts" praised him and founded a "sect" of modernism in his name. This division made him turn against the best friends who supported his revolution, a breach referred to as the *Duk-duk affér* (Duk-Duk Affair). Later he reconciled with his friends and admirers, but the loneliness he felt among them remained with him to the end of his life. His success also changed his relationship with Brüll: earlier she had been the dominant partner, but as Ady's popularity and recognition grew, she became jealous of everyone who took Ady's attention away from her.

His next volume, *Az Illés szekerén* (On the Chariot of Elijah), came out at the end of 1908. It includes seven cycles: "A Sion-hegy alatt" (Under the Zion Hill), "A téli Magyarország" (Hungary in Winter), "Léda ajkai között" (Between Léda's Lips), "Az utca éneke" (The Song of the Street), "Halálvirág: a csók" (Kiss Is a Death-Flower), "Hideg király országában" (In the Country of King Cold), and "A muszáj Herkules" (Hercules Must). Only the first, second, and fourth cycles offer important innovations.

"A Sion-hegy alatt" first presents religious experience as a theme in Ady's poetry. Now the figure of God occurs in his visions, which so far have included only pagan mythological characters. These visions depict many biblical symbols, but the resultant poetic world is far from the canonized religious system of any church. Ady's poems are based on the idea that God's image is inseparable from the individual who believes in him. The white-bearded God one imagines in childhood is dressed in ragged clothes, has no name, and thus becomes fearsome, as in the poem "A Sion-hegy alatt" (translated as "Beneath Mount Sion," 1946). The decadent and

skeptical man of the turn of the century has the image of God as a dream, as in "Álmom: az Isten" (My Dream is God) and "Az éjszakai Isten" (translated as "The Nocturnal," 1969). Sometimes God becomes a symbol expressing man's existential experience in modern society, or man's worries about the future in this world and beyond. God thus becomes one who "wants" the river of Life, which has "neither source nor end," as in "Isten, a vigasztalan" (translated as "God the Disconsolate," 1941; also translated as "The Cheerless," 1969), or a mighty whale with all the world dancing on his slippery back, as in "A nagy Cethalhoz" (translated as "To the Great Whale," 1946).

The cycle "A téli Magyarország" continues the theme of "A magyar Ugaron" and "A magyar Messiások." One new element is that the poet reflects on the inevitable interdependence of the oppressed nations living in the Danubian basin, as in "Magyar jakobinus dala" (Song of the Hungarian Jacobin). This cycle is closely related to "Az utca éneke," in which the central poem is not the title poem but "A Hadak Útja" (Warriors' Way), from an image of the Milky Way taken from Hungarian mythology before the Hungarians' conversion to Christianity. Combining that image with other ancient elements of Hungarian legend as well as biblical motifs, Ady worked out a system of symbols for the social revolution he thought to be imminent. Several Hungarian historical figures are brought into this system by the poems of the cycle; the most important of these poems is "Dózsa György unokája" (György Dózsa's Grandson). György Dózsa was an early-sixteenth-century member of the lower nobility who became head of a peasants' revolt. The rebellion was defeated and followed by bloody retaliation. Ady professes to be the grandson of the peasant leader, meaning that his social commitment has ancient roots: he continues the feeling of responsibility for the country and the people characteristic of the most outstanding members of medieval and modern Hungarian nobility. Ady's ancient noble origin thus gains meaning in his poetry. This poem also clearly indicates that the social revolution Ady advocated was to be carried out by the peasants. Ady's relationship with the working-class movement was ambiguous: while he generally published his revolutionary poems in their newspaper, *Népszava*, he did not consider factory workers to be the dominant force of renewal. Leaders of the working-class movement looked distrustfully at him as the representative of the "genteel class" and a "decadent" and "unintelligible" poet. Resentment and forgiving self-assurance are mingled in one of his poems,

"Küldöm a frigyládát" (translated as "Ark of the Covenant," 1969), published in *Szeretném, ha szeretnének* (Desire To Be Loved, 1909).

When *Az Illés szekerén* appeared, Ady retired from public life to his native village, but at the beginning of 1909 he traveled for nearly six months, spending time in Paris, Nice, and Monte Carlo. As a result of whole nights without sleep, the disturbed relationship with Brüll, and frequent critical attacks, his health and mood began to deteriorate. To cure himself, he spent the summer in a sanatorium in Kolozsvár (now Cluj-Napoca, Romania) and the autumn in Switzerland. He soon recovered and was relieved to see that a special issue of *Nyugat* in June was devoted to his poetry and put an end to the stormy situation caused by the *Duk-duk affér*. In the autumn Ady moved to Budapest to rejoin literary life and was celebrated on his lecture tours throughout the country.

Published at the end of 1909, *Szeretném, ha szeretnének* consists of nine cycles. The cycle titled "Esze Tamás komája" (Tamás Esze's Pal) continues the theme and technique of "Az utca éneke." Presenting a host of symbolic historical figures, Ady outlines his version of an historical and a political tradition. The most important figures are those taken from the so-called Kuruts movement, an important political phenomenon of the eighteenth century: Hungary had been long subjugated to the Austrian monarchy, and around the end of the seventeenth century armed rebellions for independence sprang up all over the country. The soldiers, coming mostly from peasant stock and partly from noble and intellectual circles, were called "Kuruts." By the beginning of the eighteenth century these insurrections had led to a war that ended with the defeat of the Hungarians. The dispersing Kuruts soldiers had produced a special subculture, and Ady used some of its characteristic features in his Kuruts poems. He further developed this technique during World War I when he wrote the poems for *A halottak élén* (Leading the Dead, 1918).

The rest of the cycles continue the themes of the earlier volumes. The cycle "Két szent vitorlás" (Two Saint Boatswains) includes meditations on the poet's failed relationship with Léda. "A vén komornyik" (translated as "The Old Butler," 1941; also translated as "The Ancient Chamberlain," 1946) includes the confessions of the poet as he feels his death approaching and futilely seeks rest either in Paris or in Budapest. "A harcunkat megharcoltuk" (We Have Fought Our Fight) consists of pieces motivated by the poet's anguish over his poetic revolution coming to a standstill. "A Hágár oltára"

(Hágár's Altar) is made up of poems inspired by young women and lyrically documents the lonely poet's desire to be loved. "A Jövendő fehérei" (translated as "Whites of the Future," 1969) includes poems expressing trust in the poor classes of society who have not been demoralized by the political crises of the turn of the century. "Áldott falusi köd" (Blessed Village Fog) reflects the poet's lost but still desired rural identity. "Rendben van, Úristen" (All Right, Our Lord) depicts the paradoxical feelings of the modern man who has become an unbeliever and yet longs for belief. "Egyre hosszabb napok" (Longer and Longer Days) expresses a decadent desire for death and the feeling of no future.

Ady spent the first five months of 1910 in Paris. His relationship with Brüll got worse, although when she fell ill and had to spend the summer in a sanatorium, he still expressed concern. During the second half of the year he stayed in Budapest and in Érmindszent. His next book, *A minden-titkok verseiből* (Of All Mysteries), appeared at Christmastime and brought about a change in his poetic career; this volume marked the beginning of a transitional period that was fulfilled in 1914.

Ady's poetry so far could be characterized by the fact that the subjects of his poems are clearly outlined and carefully controlled, although the intellectually mature Ady saw some naiveté in his earlier poems. The *ars poetica* of the new volume was determined by the recognition that if individual emotions and thoughts are taken out of the spiritual and emotional whole of the personality, they will be distorted. As a result of this realization, the themes of his poems became more blurred; although the cycles remind the reader of the earlier thematic titles, the names of these cycles involve secrets—"Az Isten titkai" (God's Secrets), "A szerelem titkai" (Secrets of Love), "A szomorúság titkai" (Secrets of Sadness), "A magyarság titkai" (Secrets of the Hungarians), "A dicsőség titkai" (Secrets of Glory), and "Az élet-halál titkai" (Secrets of Life and Death). The themes in each cycle are related in complicated ways. In each cycle, however, there is a new and by now unified and comprehensive experience that becomes dominant: the experience of God. The poet is a man of such exceptional qualities that he knows and discloses God's hidden universality.

Ady's poetic technique also changes in this volume. His lyricism has reached its limits, and the suggestive symbols have been replaced gradually by expressive paradoxes or oxymorons—the sadness of resurrection, the joy of joylessness, owl-faith, or straight star.

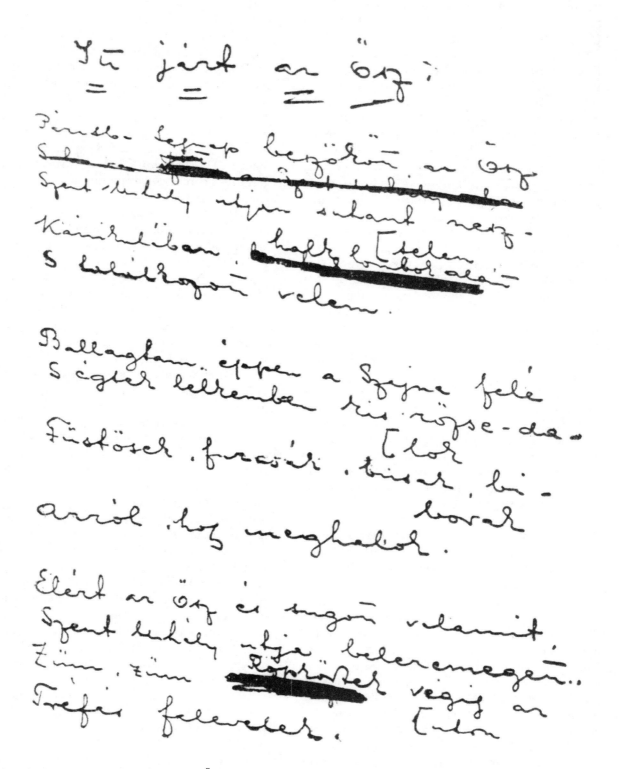

Page from the manuscript for "Párizsban járt az Ősz" (Autumn Came to Paris)–a poem in Ady's collection Vér és arany *(Blood and Gold), published in 1907 (from György Rónay,* Endre Ady, *1967)*

In January 1911 Ady again went to Paris. In March he broke with Brüll (although it was not final yet), and as a result of the accumulating crises in his life, he contemplated suicide. He returned to Budapest for a few weeks and then went back to Paris. He tried to settle his relationship with Brüll, and they traveled to Rome, but in vain: at the end of the journey, she went to Paris, and he returned to Budapest. In that same year he published his *Vallomások és tanulmányok* (Confessions and Essays), which includes some of his most important essays.

In September, Ady returned to his native village and started to work on his new volume of poetry, *A menekülő élet* (This Fugitive Life), which appeared at the beginning of 1912. The volume continues his new poetic credo, but it is highly experimental, with several elements representing a period of transition. The title poem proves that the experience of God in these poems is different from the previous volume. The foreboding of war has diverted the course of Ady's mystic experience. The God of Life is no longer the omnipotent Lord, for there is a terrible Unknown above him whose servant is Death. Nevertheless, the God of Life is still the central motif of the volume, although hidden divinity is no longer revealed in manifestations of individual life. For instance, one of the remarkable poems of the volume, "A Tűz márciusa" (March of Fire), is built on the premise that every nation embodies an individual variety of universal life. This context gives new meaning and function to Hungarian culture belonging to both the West and the East. The changing style of the previous volume is indicated by the titles of the cycles: "A szűz Pilátus" (The Virgin Pilate), "Asszony és temető" (Woman and Cemetery), "Istenhez hanyatló árnyék" (A Shadow Reclining on God), "Harc és halál" (Fight and Death), "Szép magyar sors" (Beautiful Hungarian Fate), and "Szomorú ódák valakihez" (Sad Odes to Somebody).

As a result of a life of debauchery, the poet's health deteriorated again, and his friends collected money for him to go to a sanatorium, where he wrote "Elbocsátó, szép üzenet" (A Message of Gentle Dismissal), the legendary poem expressing his final break with Brüll. He never saw her again. In the sanatorium he also began *Margita élni akar* (Margita Wants to Live), a novel in verse, which was published in serial form in *Nyugat* (it was not published as a separate volume until 1921, two years after the poet's death). It was inspired by autobiographical experiences, and in addition to several current social and political issues, the poems present in a lyric tone the typical patterns of development of the

artists that emerged around the turn of the century. The title character, Margita, is an ideal woman, both a composite of Ady's lovers and a personified symbol of Hungary.

The political events of 1912 had a great impact on Ady: the nationwide social discontent led to street demonstrations and bloody atrocities, and the war in the Balkans against Turkey foreshadowed World War I. These events radically modified Ady's poetic world: in many of his poems Ady attacked the prime minister of the Hungarian government, who turned a deaf ear to the social demands of the masses. The prime minister returned the attack, and Ady's conservative enemies started a press campaign against him.

During the second half of the year Ady traveled between Budapest and Érmindszent. He became addicted to alcohol again, as he had been in 1906–1907, leading to his treatment in early 1913. The money required for a three-month treatment in Maria-Grün, Austria, was provided by Lajos Hatvany, his friend, patron, and an influential figure of *Nyugat* whom Ady had earlier offended. In the meantime Ady's new volume of poems, *A magunk szerelme* (Love of Ourselves, 1913), appeared.

This volume still shows signs of transition: in order to renew the mythical world of his *Új versek* Ady reformulated his earlier subjects in his new expressive poetic style, which was still in the process of formation. He is most successful with his themes of love and social problems. The most important poems outline a mythology centered on the lyric "I," whose will governs the mythical world. One example is "Elbocsátó, szép üzenet"; according to the cruel and humiliating judgment of the legendary haughty man, his lover has ceased to exist since he stopped loving her. This poem is counterpoised by "Valaki útravált belőlünk" (One of Us Has Taken the Road), however: according to this melancholy reckoning, as a result of the break, the man has lost everything valuable in himself. The cruel dismissal is counterpoised in a different way by the poems of the cycle "Ifjú karok kikötőjében" (In the Haven of Young Arms), in which the lyric "I" "creates" the young woman with whom he falls in love again.

Contrary to the often-repeated views of his conservative critics, the lyric "I" used so frequently in Ady's poems is not the reflection of the poet's narcissistic attitude. Both the title of the volume and several poems on personal subjects use the first person in the plural. The grammatical subject in the most significant poems of the cycle "Szent lélek karavánja" (The Caravan of the Holy Spirit) is an actual first-person plural: these lyric pieces have col-

Ady with his mother, Mária (left), and his wife, Berta (right), the "Csinszka" of some of his poems

lective subjects. Those who want a social revolution and advocate a new order merge into one indissoluble mass, as in "Hogy ma vagyunk" (We Exist Today), "Mi kacagunk utoljára" (We Are the Last To Laugh), "Rohanunk a forradalomba" (We are Rushing into Revolution), and "Új tavaszi seregszemle" (New Spring Parade).

Ady spent the rest of 1913, with brief interruptions, in Budapest. His new volume of poetry, *Ki látott engem?* (Who Has Seen Me?), came out in February 1914. It opens with "Megint nagy vizekre" (Off to New Waters Again), a poem reminiscent of the epilogue "Új vizeken járok" of *Új versek*. Ady felt he would soon get over his period of existential crisis and search for new poetic techniques. Yet, the volume is still dominated by experimentation: in contrast to his earlier works, Ady gives a greater role to the traditional cultural patterns than to the elements of his own poetic world of fantasy. His relationship to these elements has also changed: he takes over situations, speech patterns, and typical grammatical and rhetorical figures of speech rather than motifs, images, or symbols from the Bible and medieval and eighteenth-century traditions of Hungarian poetry; his aim is the creation of a new dic-

tion. One of the characteristic poems of this change is "Élet helyett órák" (Hours Instead of Life), which relates the story of a failed love affair by inverting the Song of Songs. Ady's hatred toward the prime minister ruining the country is expressed through the curses of Prophet Hóseás in "A Hóseás átka" (Curses of Hóseás); the tense atmosphere of waiting for the revolution is compared to the frame of mind of those waiting for the Messiah in "Az izgága Jézusok" (Unruly Jesuses); and Ady's political vision is composed in Dante's manner in "Nagy lopások bűne" (The Sin of Big Thefts). In addition, there are poems in which his feelings are expressed in the style and language of Kuruts poetry: "Sípja régi babonáknak" (The Whistle of Old Superstitions), "Szerencsés esztendőt kívánok" (I Wish You a Successful Year), and "Minden rém riogat" (Every Sceptre Scares Us).

After an abortive marriage attempt—the subject of "Élet helyett órák"—and another treatment in a sanatorium, Ady proposed to Berta Boncza. She was a young woman of aristocratic origin and was seventeen years younger than Ady; as a student in Switzerland several years earlier, she had sent him an enthusiastic letter. Her father rejected his proposal, but nonetheless the couple married on 27 March 1915 in Budapest. Ady and his wife moved to the ancient property of the Boncza family in Csucsa (now Ciucea, Romania), near Érmindszent. However, the poet's long-desired quietude was often disturbed by being summoned before the recruiting commission of the Austra-Hungarian army. He was one of those few people who had never believed that World War I served the interests of Hungary and who were certain that Hungary would be defeated, with catastrophic consequences. His feeling of personal threat only strengthened his antiwar attitude. On one occasion the recruiting commission found him fit for military service; he concluded that if drafted, despite his serious illness with syphilis, he would go to war and die on the battlefield as a protest. In the end, his benefactors helped him stay at home, but the threat of going to the front was present until the end of the war, and because of his antiwar attitude he was sharply criticized by papers officially supporting the war. His poems and articles were censored. In 1916 he planned to put out a new volume—with the title "Az új hitető" (The New Persuader)—but because of problems with the printing press of *Nyugat* the book was not published. In March he was briefly treated in a sanatorium in Budapest. In 1917 his father-in-law died, and in the autumn he and his wife moved to her inherited flat in Budapest. At the beginning of 1918 he published *A halottak élén,* which was compiled from his poems of the previous four years, selected with the help of his friend and patron Hatvany. The poems left out were published in a posthumous volume titled *Az utolsó hajók* (The Last Boats, 1923).

A halottak élén is a synthesis of almost all of Ady's earliest themes and poetic techniques, but the frame of the new poetic world becomes the war: the volume creates the mythology of total negativity. The former centralized personality of Ady's poetic world falls apart: first he loses the possibility of uniting with those similar to himself to form a collective subject, as illustrated in "Mégsem, mégsem, mégsem" (After All Not, After All Not, After All Not), because he would find this collective only by "leading the dead." In the next stage the lyric subject is taken out of the center of the mythically described world, as in "Ugrani már: soha" (To Jump: Never), and his role is increasingly narrowed to that of an indifferent eyewitness; in the end he proclaims the death of the mythical lyrical subject in "Az utolsó hajók" (translated as "The Last Boats," 1946). The purpose of history, earlier understood, has been lost, notably in "Tegnapi tegnap siratása" (translated as "Of Yesterday's Yesterday," 1969). The inactive

and unjust God does not bar the way of the Specter of Hell, as illustrated in "Ézaiás könyvének margójára" (translated as "Book of Isaiah," 1969) and "Kicsoda büntet bennünket?" (translated as "Gawd's Punishment," 1969).

The poetic techniques of the poems are also varied. There are symbolic works reminiscent of the first period of his career, notably "Az eltévedt lovas" (translated as "The Lost Rider," 1941; also translated as "The Lost Horseman," 1946). The horseman who has formerly ridden ahead with a clear purpose is now trying to find his way in the jungle of demons; he represents the lost sense of direction of Hungary approaching a collective catastrophe, but he can also be interpreted as the symbol of confused mankind. The poem titled "Az utolsó hajók" is also related to Ady's earlier symbolism: only the boats of "tired fear" and "pert disgust" floating in the sea symbolize the mythical "I," and after these boats are sunk by their boatmen, the sea becomes a dead sea "yawning with salty, cold and bored eyes."

Among the biblical situations, speech patterns, and subjects, the most important function is given to those of the prophets, but Ady inverts that tradition: the prophet, becoming lame, has time left only to curse God, as in "Mai próféta átka" (translated as "The Prophet's Curse," 1969). A New Testament motif, the Holy Communion, is transcribed in a harsh, blasphemous manner in "E nagy tivornya" (This Great Revelry). The expressive language used earlier in the description of the poet's private fights with Lord Swine Head and the Ancient Demon Guile is now used to depict the global man-eating orgy of Frenzy.

Ady drew the viewpoint of the factual and frustrated eyewitness from one of the genres of sixteenth-century Hungarian poetry. The sixteenth and seventeenth centuries were the period of Turkish occupation, an era of bloodshed and inhumanity in Hungarian history; the so-called chronicle poem was the genre of poetic "mass communication" spreading news about events of the war, using primitive poetic means to depict the real nature of war brutalities. Ady uses this tradition as a source in such poems as "Krónikás ének 1918-ból" (A Chronicle Poem from 1918). The feeling of amorality and cynicism after a lost war is represented by Ady's updates of the songs of the Kuruts freedom fighters, who had become vagabonds and criminals after the defeat of the eighteenth-century War of Independence. The meaninglessness of Hungarian participation in World War I is expressed by the presence of a symbolic figure from a Hungarian folktale in "A mesebeli János" (Fabulous János). The techniques of expressionism in Ady's poetry are most successfully realized in the poems renewing such old genres.

The volume also includes some of Ady's love poems to his wife, whom he calls Csinszka. These poems reflect the last trials of escape of the poetic "I" in conflict with himself, as in "Őrizem a szemed" (Guarding Your Eyes).

The most characteristic feature of the poems in this volume is polyphony, meaning not only the simultaneous sounding of several notes but also the interference of different sets of motifs and styles, and even the mingling of different rhythmic systems. A typical example is "Emlékezés egy nyár-éjszakára" (translated as "Recollections of a Summer Night," 1969), which provides an apocalyptic vision by making use of the images of ancient superstitions from Hungarian folklore. Although the speaker identifies with the world revealed in the nightmares, he can still relate the threatening stories as an objective spectator of the events.

With the outbreak of war, however, Ady wrote some poems that reflect the possibility of transgressing the experience of total negativity. Horror and excellence, brutality and humanity appear as aspects of the same unnameable life, as in "A megnőtt élet" (Enlarged Life). This new dynamic experience of life is expressed by a return to the motif of the horseman, as in "Új s új lovat" (A New and New Horse). Ady's last poem, "Üdvözlet a győzőnek" (Greeting to the Victorious), is connected to a concrete historical event: he turns to the victorious powers of World War I, asking them to spare the Hungarian nation, which not only lost the war fighting for foreign interests but also experienced the deepest crisis in its one-thousand-year-long history.

In the summer of 1918 Ady and his wife traveled to Csucsa again on holiday, returning to Budapest in October. In the capital there was a general political crisis: the so-called daisy revolution overthrew the government that had officially admitted that Hungary had lost World War I. Ady sent a telegram of greeting to Count Mihály Károlyi, the new prime minister appointed as a consequence of the radical changes, but the poet could not really be happy about the revolution he had so long expected. He found that this revolution was not the result of a long historical process but that of momentary passions. He maintained that the revolutionary boom would be exploited by unprincipled and immoral people.

Ady's judgment has been proven by history, but in the first stage of the revolution the progressive forces of the bourgeoisie had a decisive role. In January 1919 progressive writers founded a new literary society, the Vörösmarty Academy, and elected Ady their president. The poet's health had been rapidly deteriorating since he returned to Budapest, and therefore he could not deliver his inaugural address, in which he called for the establishment of a new, European Hungary. He died two weeks later, on 27 January.

Without question Ady's creative oeuvre provided a new course for twentieth-century Hungarian poetry. Since his death, opposing political and ideological camps have tried to declare him as their own poet. Those who advocate the principle of indigenous literature have attacked his poetry from the beginning, and this viewpoint is still strong in late-twentieth-century criticism. Ady's self-regulating poetry, however, has defied aesthetic paradigms in every period.

Letters:

Válogatott levelei, edited by György Belia (Budapest: Szépirodalmi, 1956);

Levelei, 3 volumes, edited by Belia (Budapest: Szépirodalmi, 1983);

Levelezése, volume 1, edited by László Vitályos (Budapest: Akademiai Kiado/Argumentum, 1998).

Bibliographies:

Gyula Földessy, "Ady verseinek időrendje," *Ady-múzeum,* 2 volumes (Budapest: Athenaeum, 1924–1925);

Pál Gulyás, *Ady Endre élete és munkái. Bibliográfiai tanulmány* (Budapest: Lantos, 1925);

Albert Tezla, *Hungarian Authors: A Bibliographical Handbook* (Cambridge, Mass.: Belknap Press of Harvard University Press, 1970);

I. L. Halász de Beky, *Endre Ady 1877–1919,* University of Toronto (Toronto: Bibliotheca Hungarica Torontonensis 5, 1977);

László Vitályos and László Orosz, *Ady-bibliográfia 1896–1977* (Budapest: MTA Könyvtára, 1980);

Ferenc Botka and Kálmán Vargha, *A magyar irodalomtörténet bibliográfiája. 1905–1945,* volume 6 (Budapest: Akadémiai, 1982);

Vitályos, *Ady-bibliográfia 1986–87* (Budapest: MTA Könyvtára, 1990).

Biographies:

Lajos Ady, *Ady Endre* (Budapest: Amicus, 1923);

Marcell Benedek, *Ady-breviárium,* volume 1, *Ady élete, emberi arcképe, költői jelentősége, prózai írásai* (Budapest: Dante, 1924);

György Bölöni, *Az igazi Ady* (Paris: Atelier, 1934);

Béla Révész, *Ady és Léda. Ady Endre több mint száz ismeretlen levelével, verskéziratával, 21 fényképpel és egyéb mellékletekkel* (Budapest: Dante, 1934);

Zsófia Dénes, *Élet helyett órák. Egy fejezet Ady életéből* (Budapest: Pantheon, 1939);

Erzsébet Vezér, *Ady Endre alkotásai és vallomásai tükrében* (Budapest: Szépirodalmi, 1968);

Vezér, *Ady Endre. Élete és pályája* (Budapest: Gondolat, 1969);

Imre Robotos, *Az igazi Csinszka* (Budapest: Magvető, 1975);

Sándor Borbély, *Így élt Ady Endre* (Budapest: Móra, 1989).

References:

László Balogh, *Mag hó alatt* (Budapest: Tankönyvkiadó, 1976);

János Barta, "Khiméra asszony serege (Adalékok Ady képzet- és szókincséhez)," in *Magyar Századok (Horvát János Emlékkönyv)* (Budapest: Egyetemi, 1948), pp. 278–298;

Marianna D. Birnbaum, "Innovative Archaism: A Facet in the Poetic Language of Endre Ady," in *The Formation of the Slavonic Literary Languages*, edited by G. Stone and D. Worth (Columbus, Ohio: Slavica, 1985), pp. 243–252;

László Bóka, *Ady Endre élete és művei*, volume 1 of *Bevezetés az Ady-kérdésbe* (Budapest: Akadémiai, 1955);

Dalma H. and S. Brunauer, "Kosztolanyi and Ady," *Journal of Evolutionary Psychology,* 7 (August 1986): 179–190;

Lee Cogdon, "Endre Ady's Summons to National Regeneration in Hungary, 1900–1919," *Slavic Review,* 33 (1974): 302–322;

Zoltán Fábry, *Ady igaza* (Bratislava: Madách, 1977);

Gyula Földessy, *Ady minden titkai. Ady-kommentárok* (Budapest: Athenaeum, 1949);

Földessy, *Ady-tanulmányok* (Budapest: Ethika, 1921);

Földessy, *Újabb Ady-tanulmányok* (Berlin: Ludwig Voggenreiter, 1927);

Lajos Hatvany, *Ady. Cikkek, emlékezések, levelek,* 2 volumes (Budapest: Szépirodalmi, 1959);

János Horváth, *Ady és a legújabb magyar líra* (Budapest: Benkő Gyula, 1910);

Dezső Keresztury, "Endre Ady," *New Hungarian Quarterly,* 35 (1969): 335–344;

István Király, *Ady Endre,* 2 volumes (Budapest: Magveto, 1970);

Király, *Intés az őrzőkhöz. Ady Endre költészete a világháború éveiben 1914–1918,* 2 volumes (Budapest: Szépirodalmi, 1982);

Watson Kirkconnel, *The Poetry of Ady* (Budapest: Society of the Hungarian Quarterly, 1937);

Miklos Kovalovszky, ed., *Emlékezések Adyról,* 5 volumes (Budapest: Akadémiai Kiadó, 1961–1963);

Géza Lengyel, *Ady a műhelyben* (Budapest: Szépirodalmi Könyvkiadó, 1957);

István Loósz, *Ady Endre lírája tükrében* (Szabadka, 1914);

György Lukács, *Ady* (Budapest: Szikra, 1949);

Sándor Makkai, *Magyar fa sorsa. A vádlott Ady költészete* (Cluj-Kolozsvár: Erdélyi Szépmíves Céh, 1927; Budapest: Soli Deo Gloria, 1927);

Péter Pór, "The Symbolist Turn in Endre Ady's Poetry," in *The Symbolist Movement in the Literature of European Languages,* edited by A. Balakian (Budapest: Akadémiai Kiadó, 1982), pp. 361–379;

József Révai, *Ady* (Budapest: Szikra, 1945);

Béla Révész, *Ady Endre életéről, verseiről, jelleméről* (Gyoma: Kner, 1922);

Béla Révész, *Ady tragédiája. A háború, a házasság, a forradalom évei,* 2 volumes (Budapest: Athenaeum, 1924);

Aladár Schöpflin, *Ady Endre* (Budapest: Nyugat, 1934);

Pál Schweitzer, *Ember az embertelenségben. A háborús évek Ady-verseinek szimbolikus motívum-csoportjai* (Budapest: Akadémiai, 1969);

Sándor Sík, "Ady Endre," in his *Gárdonyi, Ady, Prohászka. Lélek és forma a századforduló irodalmában* (Budapest: Pallas, 1928), pp. 133–294;

Péter Szilágyi, *Ady verselése* (Budapest: Akadémiai, 1990);

József Varga, *Ady Endre. Pályakép-vázlat* (Budapest: Magvető, 1966);

Varga, *Ady és műve* (Budapest: Szépirodalmi, 1982);

Varga, *Ady útja az "Új versek" felé* (Budapest: Magyar Tudományos Akadémia Irodalomtörténeti Intézete, 1963);

László Vatai, *Az Isten szönyetege (Ady lírája)* (Washington, D.C.: Occidental, 1963);

Erzsébet Vezér, "Ady—Poet and Special Critic," *New Hungarian Quarterly,* 73 (1979): 101–107;

Béla Zolnai, "Ady és Paul Verlaine álma," in *Nyelv és stílus. Tanulmányok* (Budapest: Gondolat, 1957), pp. 313–342.

Jerzy Andrzejewski

(19 August 1909 – 19 April 1983)

Stanislaw Eile
University of London

BOOKS: *Drogi nieuniknione. Opowiadania* (Warsaw: Prosto z mostu, 1936);

Ład serca. Powieść (Warsaw: Rój, 1938);

Apel (London: Światowy Związek Polaków zza Granicy, 1945);

Noc. Opowiadania (Warsaw: Czytelnik, 1945);

Święto Winkelrida. Widowisko w 3 aktach, by Andrzejewski and Jerzy Zagórski (Kraków: ZZLP, 1946);

Popiół i diament. Powieść (Warsaw: Czytelnik, 1948); translated by David Welsh as *Ashes and Diamonds* (London: Weidenfeld & Nicolson, 1962; Harmondsworth, U.K. & New York: Penguin, 1980);

Aby pokój zwyciężył (Warsaw: Książka i Wiedza, 1950);

O człowieku radzieckim (Warsaw: Książka i Wiedza, 1951);

Ludzie i zdarzenia 1951 (Warsaw: Czytelnik, 1952);

Partia i twórczość pisarza (Warsaw: Czytelnik, 1952);

Ludzie i zdarzenia 1952 (Warsaw: Czytelnik, 1953);

Wojna skuteczna czyli opis bitew i potyczek z Zadufkami (Warsaw: Czytelnik, 1953);

Książka dla Marcina (Warsaw: Państwowy Instytut Wydawniczy, 1954);

Złoty lis (Warsaw: Państwowy Instytut Wydawniczy, 1955);

Ciemności kryją ziemię (Warsaw: Państwowy Instytut Wydawniczy, 1957); translated by Konrad Syrop as *The Inquisitors* (New York: Knopf, 1960; London: Weidenfeld & Nicolson, 1960);

Niby gaj. Opowiadania 1933–1958 (Warsaw: Państwowy Instytut Wydawniczy, 1959);

Bramy raju (Warsaw: Państwowy Instytut Wydawniczy, 1960); translated by James Kirkup as *The Gates of Paradise* (London: Weidenfeld & Nicolson, 1962);

Idzie skacząc po górach (Warsaw: Państwowy Instytut Wydawniczy, 1963); translated by Celina Wieniewska as *He Cometh Leaping upon the Mountains* (London: Weidenfeld & Nicolson, 1965); translation also published as *A Sitter for a Satyr* (New York: Dutton, 1965);

Jerzy Andrzejewski

Apelacja (Paris: Instytut Literacki, 1968); translated by Wieniewska as *The Appeal* (Indianapolis: Bobbs-Merrill, 1971; London: Weidenfeld & Nicolson, 1971);

Prometeusz. Widowisko (Warsaw: Czytelnik, 1973);

Teraz na ciebie zagłada (Warsaw: Czytelnik, 1976);

Już prawie nic (Warsaw: Czytelnik, 1979);

Miazga (Warsaw: NOWA, 1979);

Nowe opowiadania (Warsaw: Czytelnik, 1980);

Nikt (Warsaw: Państwowy Instytut Wydawniczy, 1983);

Intermezzo i inne opowiadania (Warsaw: Czytelnik, 1986);

Gra z cieniem (Warsaw: Czytelnik, 1987);

Z dnia na dzień. Dziennik literacki 1972–1979, 2 volumes (Warsaw: Czytelnik, 1988);

Legendy nowoczesności. Eseje okupacyjne. Listy-eseje Jerzego Andrzejewskiego i Czesława Miłosza, by Andrzejewski and Czesław Miłosz (Kraków: Wydawnictwo Literackie, 1996).

Editions in English: "The Sons," translated by Edward Rothert, in *Contemporary Polish Short Stories*, edited by Andrzej Kijowski (Warsaw: Polonia, 1960), pp. 11–36;

"The Trial," translated by Adam Gillon and Ludwik Krzyżanowski, in *Introduction to Modern Polish Literature: An Anthology of Fiction and Poetry* (New York: Twayne, 1964), pp. 223–235.

MOTION PICTURES: *Miasto nieujarzmione*, screenplay by Andrzejewski and Jerzy Zarzycki, Film Polski, 1950;

Zagubione uczucia, screenplay by Andrzejewski, Zarzycki, Hanna Mortkowicz-Olczakowa, and Julian Dziedzina, Film Polski, 1957;

Popiół i diament, screenplay by Andrzejewski and Andrzej Wajda, Film Polski, 1958;

Niewinni czarodzieje, screenplay by Andrzejewski and Jerzy Skolimowski, Film Polski, 1959;

Bramy raju, screenplay by Andrzejewski and Wajda, Avala Film of Yugoslavia, 1967.

OTHER: Tadeusz Borowski, *Wybór opowiadań*, edited by Andrzejewski (Warsaw: Państwowy Instytut Wydawniczy, 1959);

Ashes and Diamonds, by Andrzejewski and Andrzej Wajda, in *Ashes and Diamonds; Kanal; A Generation: Three Films by Andrzej Wajda*, translated by Bolesław Sulik (London: Lorrimer, 1984), pp. 160–239;

Robinson warszawski, by Andrzejewski and Czesław Miłosz, *Dialog*, 9 (1984): 5–17.

Jerzy Andrzejewski is one of the best-known Polish novelists of the twentieth century. Highly popular in his own country, he has also achieved international recognition: his fiction has been translated into almost all European languages as well as Hebrew, Hindi, Japanese, and Mongolian. Andrzej Wajda's successful 1958 motion-picture production of Andrzejewski's most controversial novel, *Popiół i diament* (1948; translated as *Ashes and Diamonds*, 1962), has reinforced this standing. Always receptive to the moral and political problems of his time, Andrzejewski aimed at conclusions general enough to rouse international interest. His moral authority was undoubtedly enhanced by his political involvement in the dissident movement of the 1970s, which in the long run contributed to the rise of Solidarity and the fall of Communism in Eastern Europe. Andrzejewski was a novelist of many artistic inspirations and fluctuating political affiliations; his literary career reflects the predicament of twentieth-century writers, particularly those in totalitarian states.

Jerzy Andrzejewski was born on 19 August 1909 in Warsaw to Jan and Eugenia Andrzejewski. His father owned a grocery in the center of the city, and Warsaw remained the primary residence of the writer for most of his life. Although few of Andrzejewski's works take place in Warsaw, his attachment to the city, and in particular to its parks and bookstores, is well documented in his reminiscences in *Książka dla Marcina* (The Book for Martin, 1954). Born five years before World War I and reaching maturity during World War II, Andrzejewski watched the growth and then the devastation of his native city.

In 1919 he enrolled in the Jan Zamoyski Gymnasium, one of the best schools in Warsaw; he remembered it as a traditional, politically conservative establishment for children of affluent families. His progress at school was hampered by his devotion to writing poetry, plays, and fiction—an enthusiasm that began when he was thirteen. From 1927 to 1931 Andrzejewski studied Polish language and literature at the University of Warsaw. In 1927 he published his first article in the popular literary journal *Wiadomości Literackie* (Literary News), followed five years later by his first short story, "Wobec czyjegoś życia" (Concerning Somebody's Life), in the Warsaw daily *ABC*. In the late 1930s Andrzejewski published two volumes of fiction, joined the Polish Writers' Union (ZLP), received the Polish Academy of Literature Prize for Young Writers, and became a recognized novelist. He contributed literary and theatrical reviews to *ABC* and *Prosto z mostu* (Straight from the Shoulder), a weekly magazine of the extreme Right; he also served as editor of the literature section of *Prosto z mostu* from 1935 to 1938.

From its beginning, Andrzejewski's fiction was greatly influenced by Joseph Conrad's principle that there is no escape from the prison of the self. In Andrzejewski's first volume of short stories, *Drogi nieuniknione* (Inescapable Ways, 1936), the characters fail to achieve mutual understanding even with the people they are closest to, for innate egoism lies at the core of human existence. Sheltered in their social masks, these characters experience solitude and despondency verging on personal tragedy. Similar anxieties haunt the literary world of *Ład serca* (Mode of the Heart, 1938), Andrzejewski's first novel, which elevated him to the position of a respected moralist. Regarded as an example of Catholic fiction in the manner of the French novelist Georges Bernanos, *Ład serca* places human destiny in the symbolic darkness of a hostile environment: Belorussian forests provide a setting equivalent to Conrad's *Heart of Darkness* (1899). The protagonist, Father Siecheń, stumbles against a "humiliating wall" of misunderstanding that separates him from the parishioners he wants to help. He eventually discovers how much self-love actually underpins actions ostensibly devoted to others. Andrzejewski seems to believe that brotherly love is possible, thanks to God's grace, but ultimately the forces of evil appear more powerful. In Andrzejewski's world of feeble sinners God is far away, while Christian love is finally defeated by despair over the absence of justice and moral order.

During World War II Andrzejewski stayed in Warsaw and participated in clandestine literary activities. He even served as a plenipotentiary for Polish underground authorities with the task of rendering assistance to writers. His traumatic experiences during those years included the ghetto uprising and its burning in 1943 and the almost complete destruction of the city as a result of its anti-German uprising in 1944. From the loft of a suburban house, he watched through old binoculars as Warsaw burned; in *Książka dla Marcina* he recalled: "We knew that the whole city was on fire, one quarter after another. The flames had been on the rampage for six weeks . . . . Less and less frequently we talked about that day when we would be able to go back."

Andrzejewski's war experience is reflected in many of his short stories, which are among the best in modern Polish fiction because of their succinct dramatization of events and occasional but successful irony. The symbolic title of his collection *Noc* (Night, 1945) indicates the pessimistic assessment of human nature well known from *Ład serca*. The forces of evil are now involved on a much larger scale, but from Andrzejewski's perspective the war only intensifies innate human depravity and makes individual loneliness even

Maria Abgarowicz-Czyściecka, whom Andrzejewski married in 1946

more biting. German atrocities come to the foreground in *Apel* (The Roll Call, 1945), a gloomy depiction of Auschwitz, but patriotic stereotypes are undermined as well. In "Wrześniowa oda" (September Ode), published in *Noc*, a party of Polish soldiers keeps on fighting the invading Germans simply because there are no other objectives: "Going home and what then? Frankly, there is only one thing that I could manage to do well. Shooting." The feeling of absurdity dominates several satirical stories about the underground, where pompous nationalist rhetoric does not bear confrontation with reality. Andrzejewski's characters infrequently overcome their selfishness with individual acts of fraternity that are impulsive, irrational, and seemingly inspired by God's grace.

Following the destruction of Warsaw and the end of World War II, Andrzejewski settled in Kraków, which had remained undamaged and gradually became a leading cultural center. He contributed fiction and articles to literary journals and popular magazines, serving also as chairman of the local branch of the ZLP from 1946 to 1947. In 1946 he married Maria Abgarowicz-Czyściecka, with whom he had a son, Marcin. During the postwar years Andrzejewski underwent an ideological transformation, announced in "Propozycje teraźniejszośći" (Present Proposals), a 1945 article for the literary weekly *Odrodzenie* (Renaissance): "The years of madness and hatred have effectively persuaded men of letters that their words, no less than the actions by men of action, must aid [postwar] reconstruction, assisting it without renouncing creativity or diminishing artists' rights, but, on the contrary, by fulfilling the ideal of beauty, which retains moral and thus social values."

Andrzejewski claimed in the same article that "the monstrosity of the last years has instilled in tormented minds the necessity for order and discipline." Despite the fact that he knew about the arrests by the Communist secret police in Kraków of innocent soldiers of the non-Communist Home Army, he soon found values in the ideology of Communism that, according to a later statement, offered him a "magic circle of a well-ordered world." The activist notion of the solidarity of all freedom fighters emerged in the reworked version of his war novella "Wielki Tydzień" (Holy Week), published in *Noc,* but this concept did not contradict the idea of Christian love espoused in *Ład serca.* The writer's full confidence in the Communist Party is reflected in his best-known but politically controversial novel, *Popiół i diament.*

According to the author's diary of May 1947, his work on the novel caused doubts and misgivings: "Whatever I write seems miserable and faint. . . . If I knew how to pray, if I could pray, I would ask for one thing: for a clear mind, for awareness that what I feel is right and true, and accords with my personal convictions." Set in a provincial town in May 1945, this novel portrays a struggle against the Communist takeover. The assassination of the local secretary of the Polish Workers' Party, Szczuka, by a member of the Home Army, Maciek Chełmicki, is shown in the broader context of postwar society and the decline in moral standards of the middle class. *Popiół i diament* fully supports the principle of the infallibility of Party line and maintains that the victory of Communism will be beneficial and is unavoidable. Observing the moral degeneration caused by the war, Andrzejewski concluded that new ideas and civic integrity were to be found principally if not exclusively among activists of the Communist Party. Members of the old intelligentsia and soldiers of the Home Army are described as blind enemies of progress, with a policy of hatred that undermines the foundations of new life and constructive work. The Communists, on the other hand, fighting against great odds for a wonderful future, are elevated to the position of romantic heroes, misunderstood and shunned by an unresponsive and immature society.

Although *Popiół i diament* failed to satisfy the most orthodox among the Marxist ideologues, it eventually became a classic of People's Poland, continually reprinted and prescribed for schools, while its biased portrayal of the postwar struggle for power was denounced only outside the official media. In 1948 Andrzejewski moved to Szczecin and became active in Communist-sponsored organizations, such as the Committee for the Defense of Peace and the Polish-Soviet Friendship Society (TPPR). In 1950 he joined the ruling Polish United Workers' Party (PZPR) and from 1952 to 1956 was a member of the parliament (*Sejm*). Simultaneously, he served as chairman of the Szczecin branch of the Polish Writers' Union and as deputy chairman of its central office in Warsaw. After returning to his native Warsaw, Andrzejewski became editor in chief of the weekly magazine *Przegląd Kulturalny* (Cultural Review), a position he held from 1952 to 1954, and from 1955 to 1956 he was a member of the editorial board of *Twórczość* (Creative Work), the leading literary monthly. His commitment to Communism found a further reflection in political brochures, such as *O człowieku radzieckim* (About the Soviet Man, 1951) and *Partia i twórczość pisarza* (The Party and Writer's Work, 1952). His only attempt at Socialist Realism, however, the satirical novel *Wojna skuteczna* (An Effective War, 1953), ended in failure.

The publication in 1954 of *Złoty lis* (The Golden Fox) in the literary weekly *Nowa Kultura* (New Culture) signaled Andrzejewski's disillusionment with the control exerted over individual experience by collectivist ideas, and the story belongs to the earliest manifestations of the approaching ideological "thaw." *Ciemności kryją ziemię* (Darkness Covers the Earth, 1957; translated as *The Inquisitors,* 1960) exemplifies this trend in its most defiant form. Ostensibly about the Inquisition in medieval Spain, the novel can be read as an allegory relevant to every totalitarian system but certainly inspired by Stalinism. The absolute power, guided by misconceived ideas, allows initially innocent and honest Father

Diego to carry out all the atrocities of the Inquisition, while upholding his status as a man of ideas who is unselfishly committed to a holy cause. Serving the cause, however, eventually becomes an aim in itself, which destroys human sensitivity and subordinates individuals to a barbarous order based on obedience, hatred, and terror.

Bramy raju (1960; translated as *The Gates of Paradise,* 1962) was received as a significant literary event. The novel transforms the story of the thirteenth-century Children's Crusade into a universal parable about ideological euphoria that ultimately turns into illusion and fallacy. Polish readers easily identified the hopes of the adolescent crusaders depicted in the novel with the utopia of Communism. The actual pilgrimage to Jerusalem is presented in *Bramy raju* as a hardly disinterested, worldly affair, motivated by earthly love and carnal desires. Nevertheless, sensual attachment appears as the only authentic value in the pilgrims' experience; their highly motivated but misguided leader, Jacques de Cloyes, deludes others by his erroneous belief in the golden gates to paradise. This unorthodox message is couched in a complex form, which served as protection against the intrusive censorship at the time and made Andrzejewski a leading representative of modernism in Poland. His tale is transmitted by an impersonal narrator but actually consists of five direct confessions by the young crusaders. Still, there is only one high style, in which rhythmic repetitions with variation play a major role. As in detective stories, the mysterious reasons for the crusade are slowly disclosed by its participants, while scattered information builds up the story line and unfolds the message.

More-open contacts with the West allowed Andrzejewski to describe the cultural circles of contemporary Paris in *Idzie skacząc po górach* (1963; published in London under its original title, *He Cometh Leaping upon the Mountains,* 1965, and in New York as *A Sitter for a Satyr,* 1965). He satirically portrays famous artists, especially Pablo Picasso, who appears in the center of the novel as the elderly painter Ortiz. Once again applying his moral criteria concerning human relationships, the author emphasizes the spiritual emptiness of the cultural elite, concealed beneath fine rhetoric and facile conversations. Behind the glamorous facade of modern Paris, people live lonely lives, trapped in themselves and unable to communicate with others. Only Ortiz, a son of Spanish peasants, and White, an arrogant American writer, represent the vigor that is absent in that

environment. Andrzejewski also treats ironically the best-known forms of modernist fiction and fashionable theories such as psychoanalysis. In effect, the narrative eventually changes into a sort of pastiche in which values become relative, in a way symptomatic of Andrzejewski's later fiction.

In the late 1950s Andrzejewski became increasingly alienated from the Communist Party and its policies. In 1957 he left the Party in protest over its refusal to authorize the publication of a new literary journal, *Europa* (Europe), of which he was to be the editor in chief. Yet, these conflicts did not prevent Andrzejewski from being elected chairman of the Warsaw branch of the Polish Writers' Union in 1959. His dissent from the official policy concerning literature became even more open in 1964, when he became one of the signatories of the "Letter of 34." This document in defense of free speech and against the increasing powers of censorship was signed by several prominent writers and academics. Addressed to the Party leadership, it was later denounced by the First Secretary of the Party, Władysław Gomułka. Andrzejewski, however, continued to voice his dissent. In September 1968 he published abroad an open letter to the chairman of the Czechoslovak Writers Union, Edward Goldstücker, in which he protested against Polish participation in the Soviet invasion of Czechoslovakia. As a result the government temporarily suspended the publication of his works, but this censure was counterbalanced by awards in the United States from the Alfred Jurzykowski Foundation in New York (1968) and *Books Abroad* in Oklahoma (1970). He also became a member of the Polish PEN Club in 1969.

Andrzejewski's conflict with the authorities was aggravated by the publication of his short novel *Apelacja* (1968; translated as *The Appeal,* 1971) by the émigré publishing house Instytut Literacki in Paris; it was first published in Poland in the monthly *Twórczość* in 1981. Written as the confession of a "little man" from the lower ranks of the Party apparatus, it gives the impression of an authentic document. Its hero, Konieczny, a former officer of the "people's militia" and a Communist apparatchik, ends up in a mental hospital, persecuted by inner phobias originating in the atmosphere of fear and suspicion that he previously had helped to create. To a large extent a victim of his own making, Konieczny retains a naive, half-religious faith in the Party, which has distorted his personality and language, making him unable to overcome the limits of the official

Zbigniew Cybulski, "the Polish James Dean," as Maciek Chelmicki in the 1958 movie version of Andrzejewski's 1948 novel Popiół i diament, *or* Ashes and Diamonds *(Film Polski)*

newspeak and regain his identity. As a mediocre man of some moral conscience, he demonstrates above all the destructive potential of the totalitarian system.

From the mid 1970s Andrzejewski was at the heart of the democratic opposition in Poland. In January 1976 he signed the "Letter of 101," aimed against changes to the Constitution; these changes included, among other things, a pledge of allegiance to the U.S.S.R. Following the workers' demonstrations in Radom in the same year, he published in Paris an open letter, "To the Persecuted Participants of the Workers' Protest," and was among the founders of the KOR (Committee for the Defense of the Workers), which then formed the focal point of the anti-Communist movement. When clandestine publications became an essential part of cultural life, Andrzejewski served from 1977 to 1981 on the editorial board of *Zapis* (Record), one of the most important literary and political journals. He also delivered weekly lectures at the University of Warsaw.

Andrzejewski's diary, published in the weekly *Literatura* (Literature) from 1972 to 1981, includes his meditations about contemporary life and the arts. In one entry he reflects upon pressures restricting human individuality:

Various mechanisms, social, political and economic, control the human mind. People tend to believe that coercion and captivity are the most dangerous of them. Polish (and not only Polish) history, however, including the years of the last war, seems to prove otherwise. Force becomes particularly destructive only in those cases when people are no longer aware that their thoughts and actions occur under duress. Inner freedom is then dead and resistance immobilized. The mechanism of fashion appears to work in a more perfidious way. Fashion does not coerce, but tempts and cajoles. Fashion is not brutal, not humiliating, but to the contrary: it highlights modernity and progress, it promotes its followers. But by giving so much, it also sanctions inauthenticity.

The last years of Andrzejewski's literary life were marked by growing skepticism, but political dilemmas and commitments often coincided with his response to prevailing literary trends. In the parabolic narrative about biblical Adam and Eve, *Teraz na ciebie zagłada* (Now Annihilation Is Coming upon You, 1976), love is selfish, and dreamers are losers; only Eve appears resilient because of her practical sense of survival. Skepticism combined with the then-fashionable interests in self-conscious fiction characterize Andrzejewski's last novel, *Miazga* (Pulp, 1979). As a critical depiction of the Polish establishment, the work had problems in getting through the censorship. Some fragments had been published in the periodical *Twórczość* in 1966, but the complete text was eventually rejected in 1972. Released by the underground publisher NOWA in 1979 and by a London house (Polonia Book Fund) in 1981, *Miazga* was first published by a state publishing house (Państwowy Instytut Wydawniczy) in 1982. This long period of production affected its final shape and message. Some critics traced its "pulpiness" to the political turmoil and moral anxiety in the aftermath of the student unrest in March 1968, but the author's denial of the viability of the novelistic form represented a much broader attitude, imported from France and popular with the Polish cultural elite. Andrzejewski explained the underlying philosophy behind the novel:

> In the last several years I have not been longing for order. Some old aspirations are certainly still with me . . . , but neither within my own self nor in the world can I spot the slightest vestiges of a structure which would allow me to believe that it is permeated and shaped by an order accessible to comprehension. . . . Literature demonstrates a certain singular tendency to create and duplicate not only authentic existence, but also its patterns. In the literature written in totalitarian states such a model of life must be restricted to unimportant facts, resembling, in a sense, a chronicle of accidents or a book of suggestions and complaints. Apart from this, when an all-embracing form has been eventually fashioned, why not exploit its beneficial shapelessness? This is supposedly pulp.

Miazga is not an anti-novel, despite its links with contemporary French fiction; the author still tells a compelling story and constructs vivid characters. Experiments with form include the equal presentation of events that might have happened and those that "really" took place, paralleled by the corresponding use of conditional and indicative clauses, the incorporation of documents such as the author's diary, a discontinuous plot, and metafictional commentary. The author once again expresses his anxiety about a society ruled by opportunism and expediency, where nobody is without sin, including democratic dissidents and the writer Nagórski, arguably a self-portrait of Andrzejewski.

The novella *Nikt* (Nobody, 1983), about the aging Odysseus, is the final expression of Andrze-

jewski's personal feelings about human loneliness. Both Penelope and Odysseus appear as proud egocentrics, unable to love anybody for fear of losing their freedom. The protagonist even fails to achieve a genuine knowledge of the world, as his own experience eventually seems confusing and largely forgotten, while the very possibility of comprehensive wisdom is questioned. Tormented by the fear of death, Odysseus preserves his heroic image only in legend. Andrzejewski died in Warsaw on 19 April 1983.

Andrzejewski has his admirers and detractors. Artur Sandauer believed that Andrzejewski's works were scarcely original and sometimes approached kitsch. Czesław Miłosz blamed Andrzejewski's postwar mistakes on the superficial character of his posture as a moralist. Well-known writers such as Sławomir Mrożek, Tadeusz Konwicki, and Gustaw Herling-Grudziński condemned *Popiół i diament* as a gross distortion of historical truth. Still, it seems beyond question that Andrzejewski's fiction often presents challenging content and skillful narration, although it is difficult to identify an unquestionable masterwork. A Catholic, a Communist, and a dissident, Jerzy Andrzejewski defies easy classification but inspires interest even in his evident imperfections.

Letters:

Jerzy Andrzejewski, Jarosław Iwaszkiewicz, Listy (Warsaw: Czytelnik, 1991).

Interview:

Jacek Trznadel, *Hańba domowa. Rozmowy z pisarzami* (Paris: Instytut Literacki, 1986), pp. 69–85.

References:

Kazimierz Bartoszyński, "Postmodernizm a 'sprawa polska'—przypadek *Miazgi*," *Teksty Drugie*, 1 (1993): 36–54;

Jan Błoński, "Stygnący popiół," *Teksty*, 2, no. 4 (1973): 73–80;

Endre Boitar, "Kak mozhno stat' realistom sotsializma?" *Canadian American Slavic Studies*, 22, no. 1–4 (1988): 317–327;

Tomasz Burek, "Pisarz, demony i publiczność. Jerzy Andrzejewski," in *Sporne postaci polskiej literatury współczesnej*, edited by Alina Brodzka (Warsaw: IBL, 1994), pp. 169–182;

Jadwiga Czachowska and Alicja Szałagan, eds., *Współcześni polscy pisarze i badacze literatury,* (Warsaw: WSP, 1994), I: 45–50;

Bogdan Czaykowski, "Literatura i polityka w Polsce," *Kultura,* 259 (1969): 98–106; 260 (1969): 89–99;

Jan Detko, *"Popiół i diament" Jerzego Andrzejewskiego* (Warsaw: PZWS, 1964);

Stanislaw Eile, *Modernist Trends in Twentieth-Century Polish Fiction* (London: School of Slavonic & East European Studies, 1996), pp. 166–168, 172–174;

Eile, "The Prison of Self: Moral Dilemmas in Andrzejewski's Fiction," in *New Perspectives in Twentieth-Century Polish Literature,* edited by Eile and Ursula Phillips (Basingstoke & London: Macmillan Press, 1992), pp. 68–86;

Maria Janion, "Krucjata niewiniątek?," *Twórczość,* 43 (April 1987): 96–104;

Andrzej Kijowski, "Traktat o zbawieniu," in his *Arcydzieło nieznane* (Kraków: Wydawnictwo Literackie, 1964), pp. 88–96;

Magnus J. Krynski, "The Metamorphoses of Jerzy Andrzejewski: The Road from Belief to Scepticism," *Polish Review,* 1–2 (1961): 119–124;

Jerzy R. Krzyżanowski, "On the History of *Ashes and Diamonds,*" *Slavic and East European Journal,* 3 (1971): 324–331;

Madeline G. Levine, "The Ambiguity of Moral Outrage in Jerzy Andrzejewski's *Wielki Tydzień,*" *Polish Review,* 32, no. 4 (1987): 385–399;

Alf MacLochlainn, "Romantic Poland's Dead and Gone," *University Review,* 4 (1967): 143–150;

Czesław Miłosz, *Zniewolony umysł* (Paris: Instytut Literacki, 1953), pp. 88–112; English edition, *The Captive Mind,* translated by Jane Zielonko (New York: Knopf, 1953), pp. 82–110;

Zdzisław Najder, "Jerzy Andrzejewski: The Later Novels," *Tri Quarterly,* 9 (1967): 223–228;

Jerzy Poradecki, "Narrator i narracja w *Bramach raju i Idzie skacząc po górach* Jerzego Andrzejewskiego," in *O prozie polskiej XX wieku,* edited by Artur Hutnikiewicz and Helena Zaworska (Wrocław: Zakład Narodowy Imienia Ossolińskich, 1971), pp. 295–310;

Artur Sandauer, *Dla każdego coś przykrego* (Kraków: Wydawnictwo Literackie, 1966), pp. 88–118;

Jürgen Schreiber, *Jerzy Andrzejewskis Roman "Ciemności kryją ziemię" und die Dargestellung der Spanischen Inquisition in Werken der fiktionalen Literatur* (Munich, 1981);

Anna Synoradzka, *Andrzejewski* (Kraków: Wydawnictwo Literackie, 1997);

Teresa Walas, "*O Miazdze* Jerzego Andrzejewskiego, czyli o walce z szatanem," in *Literatura źle obecna* (London: Polonia, 1984), pp. 231–246;

Kazimierz Wyka, *Pogranicze powieści,* second edition (Warsaw: Czytelnik, 1974), pp. 81–94, 405–416;

Helena Zaworska, "Szczerość," *Twórczość,* 38 (September 1982): 113–121.

Mihály Babits

(26 November 1883 – 4 August 1941)

Zoltán Kulcsár-Szabó
Eötvös University, Budapest

BOOKS: *Levelek Iris koszorújából* (Budapest: Nyugat, 1909);

Herceg, hátha megjön a tél is! (Budapest: Nyugat, 1911);

Két kritika (Budapest: Nyugat, 1911);

A gólyakalifa. Regény és néhány novella (Budapest: Athenaeum, 1916); translated by Eva Rácz and revised by Janet Semple as *The Nightmare* (Budapest: Corvina, 1966);

Recitatív (Budapest: Nyugat, 1916);

Irodalmi problémák (Budapest: Nyugat, 1917);

Karácsonyi Madonna (Budapest: Táltos, 1920);

Nyugtalanság völgye (Budapest: Táltos, 1920);

Laodameia (Budapest: Táltos, 1921);

Tímár Virgil fia (Budapest: Athenaeum, 1922);

Gondolat és írás (Budapest: Athenaeum, 1922);

Aranygaras. Mesék (Budapest: Athenaeum, 1923);

Kártyavár. Egy város regénye (Budapest: Athenaeum, 1923);

Sziget és tenger. Versek (Budapest: Athenaeum, 1925);

Halálfiai. Regény (Budapest: Athenaeum, 1927);

Versek, 1902–1927 (Budapest: Athenaeum, 1928);

Élet és irodalom (Budapest: Athenaeum, 1929);

Az istenek halnak, az ember él. Versek (Budapest: Athenaeum, 1929);

Dante. Bevezetés a Divina Commedia olvasásához (Budapest: Magyar Szemle, 1930);

A torony árnyéka. Mesék és novellák (Budapest: Athenaeum, 1931);

Elza pilóta vagy a tökéletes társadalom. Regény (Budapest: Nyugat, 1933);

Versenyt az esztendőkkel! Uj költemények, 1928–1933 (Budapest: Nyugat, 1933);

Az európai irodalom története, 1760–1925, 2 volumes (Budapest: Nyugat, 1934, 1935);

Hatholdas rózsakert (Budapest: Athenaeum, 1937);

Írás és olvasás. Tanulmányok (Budapest: Athenaeum, 1938);

Ezüstkor (Budapest: Athenaeum, 1938);

Jónás könyve (Budapest: Nyugat, 1939);

Keresztül-kasul az életemen (Budapest: Nyugat, 1939);

Mihály Babits

Írók két háború közt (Budapest: Nyugat, 1941);

A második ének (Budapest: Nyugat, 1942);

Hátrahagyott versei, edited by Gyula Illyés (Budapest: Nyugat, 1941).

Editions and Collections: *Összegyűjtött munkái*, 10 volumes (Budapest: Athenaeum, 1937–1939)—comprises volume 1, *Összes versei, 1902–1937*; volume 2, *Írás és olvasás*; volume 3, *Ezüstkor*; volumes 4–5, *Halálfiai*; volume 6, *Tímár Virgil fia; Kártyavár*; volume 7, *A gólyakalifa; Elza* *pilóta;* volume 8, *Összes novellái;* volume 9, *Kisebb műfordításai;* volume 10, *Dante Komédiája;*

Ünnepi beszédei. Születése hatvanadik évfordulójának emlékére (Budapest: Baumgarten Ferenc Irodalmi Alapítvány, 1943);

Összes művei, edited by Sophie Török (Budapest: Franklin-Társulat, 1945);

Jónás könyve (Budapest: Nyugat, 1947);

Hatholdas rózsakert (Újvidék: Testvériség-Egység, 1952);

Az európai irodalom története (Budapest: Európa, 1957);

Művei, 7 volumes (Budapest: Európa, 1957–1964)—comprises volume 1, *A gólyakalifa. Kártyavár;* volume 2, *Drámafordítások;* volumes 3–4, *Halálfiai;* volume 5, *Versfordításai;* volume 6, *Összegyűjtött versei;* volume 7, *Novellák;*

Válogatott versei, edited by Gyula Illyés (Budapest: Móra, 1957);

Válogatott művei, 2 volumes, edited by Tamás Ungvári, György Belia, and Dezső Keresztury (Budapest: Szépirodalmi, 1959);

Jónás könyve (Budapest: Magyar Helikon, 1961);

Művei, 10 volumes (Budapest: Szépirodalmi, 1977–1987).

Edition in English: *21 Poems / 21 Vers,* translated by István Tótfalusi, revised by Robin James Isherwood and Paul Rogerson (Budapest: Maecenas, 1988).

OTHER: *Új anthológia. Fiatal költok 100 legszebb verse,* edited, with an introduction, by Babits (Budapest: Nyugat, 1932).

TRANSLATIONS: Dante, *Pokol* (Budapest: Révai, 1913);

William Shakespeare, *A vihar* (Budapest: Athenaeum, 1916);

Oscar Wilde, *Wilde Oszkár verseiből* (Budapest: Athenaeum, 1916);

Immanuel Kant, *Az örök béke* (Budapest: Új Magyarország, 1918);

Dante, *Purgatórium* (Budapest: Révai, 1920);

Pávatollak. Műfordítások, translated and edited by Babits (Budapest: Táltos, 1920);

Erato. Az erotikus világköltészet remekei, translated and edited by Babits (Wien: Hellas, 1921);

Johann Wolfgang von Goethe, *A napló* (Budapest: Franklin, 1921);

George Meredith, *Az önző,* translated by Babits and Árpád Tóth (Budapest: Genius, 1921);

Théophile Gautier, *Kleopatra egy éjszakája,* (Budapest: Genius, 1922);

Dante, *Dante komédiája. III. A Paradicsom* (Budapest: Révai, 1923);

Charles Baudelaire, *A romlás virágai,* translated by Babits, Tóth, and Lőrinc Szabó (Budapest: Genius, 1923);

Edgar Allan Poe, *Groteszkek és arabeszkek* (Budapest: Franklin, 1928);

Oedipus király és egyéb műfordítások, translated and edited by Babits (Budapest: Athenaeum, 1931)—comprises *Oedipus király, A vihar, Iphigenia Taurisban, Kisebb költmények;*

Amor Sanctus. Szent szeretet könyve. Középkori himnuszok latinul és magyarul, translated and edited by Babits (Budapest: Magyar Szemle, 1933);

Sophocles, *Oedipus király. Oedipus Kolónosban* (Budapest: Franklin-Parthenon, 1942).

Mihály Babits, one of the most imposing figures in Hungarian literature during the first half of the twentieth century, played an instrumental role in the development of Hungarian literary modernism. As a leading contributor and editor of the prestigious literary journal *Nyugat* (West), Babits—together with his contemporaries Endre Ady and Dezső Kosztolányi—established a standard of artistic quality that has influenced generations of Hungarian writers from the postwar era to the present. Although best known as a poet, Babits was accomplished as a novelist, short-story writer, essayist, critic, and literary historian; in addition, his literary translations of both classical and modern poets are considered among the greatest achievements in the history of Hungarian literature.

Mihály Babits was born on 26 November 1883 in Szekszárd, a small Transdanubian town, to Mihály Babits, a judge, and Aurora Kelemen. His parents provided him with a classical, literary education, which certainly influenced his cultural development. "My way was prepared in advance," he wrote in one of the autobiographical essays in *Keresztül-kasul az életemen* (Through and Through My Life, 1939). From 1889 to 1891 Babits attended school in Budapest and then in Pécs, where he finished secondary school in 1901. In that same year he enrolled in the Faculty of Humanities at the University of Budapest, where he studied Hungarian, French, and Latin philology. During this time he also wrote his first poems and composed a handwritten collection of them, which he later titled "Angyalos könyv" (Book of Angels) but never published. As a student he

Babits and Endre Ady, two of the most important figures associated with the prestigious journal Nyugat *(West)*

became interested in Western literatures as well as current European philosophy, most notably the work of Arthur Schopenhauer and Friedrich Nietzsche. In addition, he was strongly influenced by László Négyesy, in whose seminar Babits befriended fellow poets Kosztolányi and Gyula Juhász.

In 1906 Babits earned his degree with a thesis in linguistics, and for the next two years he taught in the state secondary school of Szeged. His poems were first published in 1908 in the anthology *A Holnap* (Tomorrow), one of the most influential publications in the development of modern poetry in Hungary. As a result of this exposure, Babits's poetry began to appear regularly in *Nyugat*. During this time he also began his translation of Dante's *Divina Commedia* (circa 1310–1314), most likely in response to the impressions of his journey to Italy. From 1908 to 1911 Babits worked as a teacher in the Transylvanian city of Fogaras, which he considered a kind of exile; in his poetry he alludes to the bleak landscape of Tomis, the port on the Black Sea where Ovid was exiled.

With the publication of his first collection of poetry, *Levelek Iris koszorújából* (Leaves from Iris's

Wreath, 1909), Babits emerged as a significant and innovative voice in early-twentieth-century Hungarian literature. Despite the harsh critical reaction from the conservative press, which labeled him a "decadent" writer, Babits was praised as a poet of intellectual scope and capacity. Exploring the parameters of poetic form and language, he incorporated a broad spectrum of philosophical and artistic trends with the intent to "modernize" Hungarian poetry. Influenced by literary impressionism and symbolism, Babits envisioned the poetic process as a means to explore the depth and complexity of the human experience, thus creating a lyric poetry of emotional intensity aimed at perception and objectivity. Filled with subtle nuances and striking imagery, poems such as "Sunt lacrimae rerum" (These Are Matters For Tears) and "Hegeso sírja" (Hegeso's Tomb), as noted by critic György Rába, are reminiscent of Charles Baudelaire's "Le Cygne" (written in 1859). Babits investigates the ambiguity of existence; in "Sunt lacrimae rerum" he alludes to "néma lelkek" (dumb souls), "vak árvák" (blind orphans), "süket szemek" (deaf eyes), and "léttelen lények" (beings without being). He also embraces the necessity of acceptance and reconciliation, as illustrated in "A lírikus epilógja" (translated as "The Epilogue of the Lyric Poet," 1988), the final piece in the collection and one of Babits's best-known poems: "A / prison of my own self I must remain, / being subject and object, son and sire, / being, alas, both omega and alpha."

In 1911 Babits was living in Újpest, where he taught secondary school, and in that same year he published his second collection of poetry. During the time he spent in Fogaras, Babits had learned Greek and had developed an interest in both Hellenism and English poetry. He had originally planned to title his second collection "Klasszikus álmok" (Classical Dreams), but instead it was published as *Herceg, hátha megjön a tél is!* (Prince, Maybe the Winter Also Will Arrive!). Often cited as one of his most accomplished works, the volume represents a further extension of Babits's exploration of self and identity, in which he transforms Greek mythology within the context of modern interpretation. Strongly influenced by A. C. Swinburne, most notably by the verse drama *Atalanta in Calydon* (1865) and modernist poems such as "The Triumph of Time" and "The Garden of Proserpine" (1866), Babits blended the humanistic ideals of classical Greece with a broad range of philosophical inquiry inspired by his reading of Nietzsche, Henri Bergson, and Martin Heidegger.

Babits became a teacher at a secondary school in Budapest in 1912, the year he completed *Pokol* (1913), his translation of Dante's *Inferno*. In 1916 he published his first novel, *A gólyakalifa* (The Stork Caliph), a character study exploring the disintegration of personality, in which the tormented protagonist, existing simultaneously in the world of "reality" and in his dreams, orchestrates his own demise in both spheres of identity. Reflecting the influence of pre-Freudian psychology, the novel is reminiscent of Oscar Wilde's *The Picture of Dorian Gray* (1891) as well as Carl Spitteler's *Imago* (1906), taking its title from a tale by Wilhelm Hauff that originates from *The Thousand and One Nights*. As noted by critic Aladár Schöpflin, among others, the novel also incorporates linguistic elements associated with literary expressionism; these elements are further realized in the more fragmented and distorted syntax of the poems collected in *Recitatív*, also published in 1916.

In the years before and during World War I, Babits's poetry became increasingly concerned with social issues, as illustrated by his well-known poem "Május huszonhárom Rákospalotán" (23 May, Rákospalota, 1912), which celebrates a workers' demonstration against the conservative regime. In 1916 his pacifist poems, notably "Húsvét előtt" (Before Easter) and "Játszottam a kezével" (I Played with Her Hands), were vehemently attacked by the "official" conservative press and were responsible for Babits being dismissed from his teaching position. In addition, the publication in 1917 of his antiwar poem "Fortissimo" was cause for the government suppression of an entire issue of *Nyugat*, of which Babits had become an editor in 1916. Undaunted by critical opinion, Babits refused to compromise his moral and aesthetic position and continued writing both poetry and prose, completing in that same year his one-act play *A literátor* (The Literate, performed in 1948 in Budapest) and several papers on literary history, most notably on the work of nineteenth-century Hungarian author János Arany.

In the aftermath of World War I, Babits supported in principle the October Revolution of 1918, and during the communist regime of the "Hungarian Soviet Republic" he was appointed to a professorship at the University of Budapest. However, he soon became disillusioned in his political sympathy, and with the fall of the revolutionary government he was forced to resign his appointment. Nonetheless, in 1918 he completed his translation of Immanuel Kant's *Zum ewigen Frieden* (Perpetual Peace, 1795); and in 1920 he published his translation of Dante's *Purgatorio*. This effort was followed by other collections of translations, notably *Pávatollak* (Peacock Feathers, 1920) and *Erato* (1921), a group of erotic poems, as well as by a 1921 translation, done with Árpád Tóth, of George Meredith's novel *The Egoist* (1879). His collection of short stories *Karácsonyi Madonna* (Christmas Madonna) was published in 1920 as well as a volume of poetry, *Nyugtalanság völgye* (Valley of the Unquiet), which included poems written between 1917 and 1920.

Throughout the 1920s Babits occupied a prestigious position within Hungarian cultural and literary life; but partly as a reaction to the Trianon Peace Treaty of 1920, in which Hungary lost nearly two-thirds of its prewar territory, he became increasingly conservative both politically and aesthetically, and his concept of literature lost much of its experimental and modernistic approach. From 1920 to 1921 Babits shared his apartment with Lőrinc Szabó, the most significant author of the "second generation" of *Nyugat*, which included such writers as Sándor Márai. In effect, the complicated and often contradictory relationship of Babits and Szabó symbolized the evolving disharmony between the traditional lyric poetry identified with *Nyugat* and the emerging poetics of the avant-garde. Ideologically, Babits advocated that the artistic and intellectual community assume a greater degree of social and humanistic responsibility. As a result *Nyugat* became one of the main forums of antiwar sentiment, considered by Babits as a kind of "watchtower" for social consciousness. In contrast, the literary avant-garde extended in a variety of directions, ranging from social protest to social satire.

In 1921 Babits married Ilona Tanner, later a well-known poet and fiction writer who published under the pen name Sophie Török. Shortly afterward Babits's second novel, *Timár Virgil fia* (Virgil Timár's Son, 1922), appeared, followed by *Kártyavár* (House of Cards, 1923). First serialized in *Nyugat* in 1915–1916, *Kártyavár* juxtaposes the internal conflict of a district court judge and the external presence of the modern city (as reflected by the growth of Budapest during that time). As noted by Rába, the true protagonist of the novel is the "collective personality" of the city, linking *Kártyavár* to other "city novels" of the period, notably John Dos Passos's *Manhattan Transfer* (1925) and Alfred Döblin's *Berlin Alexanderplatz* (1929).

Following the appearance in 1923 of his translation with Szabó and Tóth of Baudelaire's *Les Fleurs du mal* (The Flowers of Evil, 1857), which represented a major influence on the development of modern Hungarian poetry, Babits published *Sziget és tenger* (Island and Sea, 1925). Together with *Az istenek halnak, az ember él* (Gods Are Dying, Man Lives On, 1929), this collection solidified the magnitude of Babits's poetic transition, which according to Schöpflin began in 1916 with *Recitatív*. Babits began to withdraw from the lyric exploration of his earlier poetry, preferring instead to protect the values of a self-defined literary canon. Attempting to create a system of direct or symbolic connections between the consciousness of the lyric self and the linguistic mediation of sensual experiences and images, Babits was most concerned with defining the moral and spiritual quality of existence. Babits's ideological position generated heated controversy, and *Az istenek halnak, az ember él* in particular was sharply criticized by many of his contemporaries, most notably by the revolutionary poet Attila József. Written in part as a

response to the critical stance of the avant-garde, Babits's essay "Új klasszicizmus felé" (Toward a New Classicism, 1925) was intended to justify the bases of his aesthetic principles. By the end of the decade, however, Babits altered his own position by embracing a form of "catholicism," interpreted by him in the literary sense of "universality," in which the poetic ideal is absorbed into a broader cultural and political/ideological program.

In the 1930s Babits's position in Hungarian literature was firmly established. In 1929 he was named the editor in chief of *Nyugat*, a position that until 1933 he held jointly with the novelist Zsigmond Móricz. He also became a trustee of the foundation established by the Hungarian-born German aesthetician Franz Baumgarten; this organization was responsible for the Baumgarten Prize, the most important literary award in Hungary. In addition, Babits was named a member of the prestigious Kisfaludy Társaság (Kisfaludy Association), a traditional literary institution established in 1836. His translation of Sophocles' *Oedipus* was published in 1931, followed in 1933 by *Amor Sanctus*, a collection of his translations of medieval Latin hymns, as well as by the novel *Elza pilóta vagy a tökéletes társadalom* (The Pilot Elsa or the Perfect Society), generally considered one of Babits's less successful works. In that same year he published his new collection of poetry, *Versenyt az esztendőkkel!* (Competing with the Years!). Babits's monumental study on European literature, *Az európai irodalom története, 1760–1925* (History of European Literature, 1760–1925), was published in two volumes in 1934–1935, followed by the publication in 1937 of the short novel *Hatholdas rózsakert* (Six-Acre Rosary). This novel continues the story of the protagonist of an earlier novel titled *Halálfiai* (Dead Men, 1927), in which Babits explored the decline of Hungarian society prior to World War I.

That same year Babits was diagnosed as having cancer of the larynx, and in 1938 he underwent a throat operation. In 1939 he published the autobiographical *Keresztül-kasul az életemen*, which is a mosaic-like assembly of short writings in different genres. By the following year he had lost his voice, and from that time on he communicated only in writing.

Published in 1939, the full-length poem titled *Jónás könyve* (The Book of Jonah) is a transformation of the biblical story into an allegory in which modern man, symbolic also of Babits himself, attempts to escape the will of God. The most

Kodácsonnak, aki e vers első olva-
sója volt, kifogyhatatlan nevetéssel
adja a kéziratot – mely ép e napon
készült el – névnapjára 1938-ban
Mihály

26

Jónás könyve

Első rész

Monda az Úr Jónásnak: "Kelj fel és menj
Ninivébe, kiálts a Város ellen!
Nagy ott a baj, megáradt a gonoszság:
szennyes habjai szent lábamat mossák."
Szólt, és fölkele Jónás, hogy szaladna,
de nem hová a Mennybeli akarta,
mivel rühellé a prófétaságot,
félt a várostól, sivatagba vágyott,
ahol magány és békesség övezze,
semhogy a feddett népség megkövezze.
Kerülvén azért Jáfó kikötőbe
hajóra szállott, mely elvinné őtet
Tarsis felé, s megadta a hajóbért,
futván az Urat, mint tolvaj a hóhért!

Az Úr azonban szerzett nagy szelet
és elbocsátá a tenger felett
s kelt a tengernek sok nagy tornya akkor
ingó és hulló kék hullámfalakból,
mintha egy új Ninive kelne-hullna,
kelne s percenkint összedőlne újra.

Page from the manuscript for the 1939 book-length poem in which Babits makes a modern allegory out of the biblical story of Jonah (from
Ágnes Kelevéz, A keletkezo szöveg esztétikája, *1998)*

significant stylistic element of *Jónás könyve* is Babits's use of linguistic archaisms that expressively emphasize the poetic humor. The poem is often interpreted as a meditation on life and artistic choice, suggesting that Babits remained unresolved about the evolution and pattern of his ideological development. The famous beginning of another poem, "Mint forró csontok a máglyán" (Like Hot Bones on the Stake)—"Nem az énekes szüli a dalt: / a dal szüli énekesét" (It is not the singer who creates the song: / the song gives birth to its singer)—encourages such a reading, as does the elegiac poem translated as "Jonah's Prayer" (1988), which was written as a kind of epilogue to *Jónás könyve:* "Words have faithlessly deserted me."

In his last years Babits received considerable recognition for his literary contributions, notably the Italian San Remo Award in 1940 for his translations of Dante; in that same year he was also elected as a member of the Hungarian Academy of Sciences. In 1941 he completed his translation of *Oedipus at Colonus*. Shortly afterward, on 4 August 1941, Babits died in Budapest. His last poems were collected by writer Gyula Illyés and published under the title *Hátrahagyott versei* (Posthumous Works, 1941).

Babits's critical reception has historically placed him as an author of intellectual poetry, one whose public and literary role was based on traditional values. However, there has been renewed interest in Babits's canon as editions of correspondence and other autobiographical documents previously suppressed because of the ideological restrictions during the early Communist era have become available to the public. Babits's poetic work has been the subject of thorough interpretation by Rába; in addition, Babits figures prominently in Csaba Szigeti's studies in the history of lyric prosody (and his critique of the notion of "new classicism") as well as Gábor Tolcsvai Nagy's study that reveals the stylistic plurality of *Levelek Iris koszorújából*. Babits has also been the subject of a feminist reading of his poetry by Annamária Hódosy.

Without question, Babits was one of the most erudite and versatile writers within modern Hungarian literature. Resistant to nationalistic trends of didacticism and propaganda, he matured into an introspective writer who throughout his career showed artistic and moralistic integrity and remained committed to the ideals of enlightened liberalism and humanism.

Letters:

Babits–Juhász–Kosztolányi levelezése, edited by György Belia (Budapest: Magyar Tudományos Akadémia Irodalomtörténeti Intézete, 1959);

Babits–Szilasi levelezes. Dokumentumok, edited by Istvén Gál and Ágnes Kelevéz (Budapest: A Petőfi Irodalmi Múzeum és a Népművélesi Propaganda Iroda közös kiadvanya, 1979);

Babits Mihály és Illyés Gyula levelezése, edited by Mária Iakács (Szekszárd: Tolna megyei könyvtár, 1992);

Kedves Csinszka! Drága Mis!, by Babits and Berta Boncza, edited by Erika Nemeskéni (Budapest: Pesti Szalon, 1994);

A Babits család levelezése, edited by Attila Buda (Budapest: Universitas, 1996).

Interview:

"Itt a halk és komoly beszéd ideje . . ." (Budapest: Pátria, 1993).

Bibliographies:

Albert Tezla, *Hungarian Authors: A Bibliographical Handbook* (Cambridge, Mass.: Belknap Press of Harvard University Press, 1970), pp. 54–63;

Ferenc Botka and Kálmán Vargha, *A magyar irodalomtörténet bibliográfiája 1905–1945* (Budapest: Akadémiai, 1982), I: 127–153;

Anna Cséve, *Babits Mihály kéziratai es levelezése. Katalogus,* 4 volumes (Budapest: Argumentum, 1993).

Biographies:

Zoltán Éder, *Babits a katedrán* (Budapest: Szépirodalmi, 1966);

György Belia, *Babits Mihály tanulóévei* (Budapest: Szépirodalmi, 1983).

References:

Marcell Benedek, *Babits Mihály* (Budapest: Gondolat, 1969);

George Bisztray, "Two Homelands: Mihály Babits and European Consciousness in Modern Hungarian Literature," in *A Journey into History: Essays on Hungarian Literature,* edited by Moses Nagy (New York: Peter Lang, 1990), pp. 145–160;

Gábor Halász, "Egy ízlésforma önarcképe," in his *Válogatott művei* (Budapest: Magvető, 1977), pp. 683–692;

Elemér Hankiss, ed., *Formateremtő elvek a költői műalkotásban* (Budapest: Akadémiai, 1971);

Annamária Hódosy, "Tükör-kép-más-képp," in *Remix,* by Hódosy and Attila Atilla Kiss (Szeged: Ictus, 1996), pp. 180–200;

Gyula Illyés, ed., *Babits emlékkönyv* (Budapest: Nyugat, 1941);

Attila József, "Az istenek halnak, az ember él," in his *Művei* (Budapest: Szépirodalmi, 1977), II: 61–77;

Ágnes Kelevéz, ed., *Mint különös hírmondó* (Budapest: PIM–NPI, 1983);

Dezső Keresztury, "Babits Mihály," in his *Örökség* (Budapest: Magvető, 1970), pp. 368–475;

István Király, "Ady és Babits," in his *Irodalom és társadalom* (Budapest: Szépirodalmi, 1976), pp. 95–112;

Balazs Lengyel, "A Poet's Place," *New Hungarian Quarterly,* 24 (Summer 1983): 64–76;

György Lukács, "Babits Mihály vallomásai," in his *Írástudók felelőssége* (Budapest: Szikra, 1945), pp. 48–75;

G. Béla Németh, "Babits, a másik, a másképpen megújító," *Iris,* 2 (1991): 3–9;

Németh, *Babits, a szabadító* (Budapest: TkK, 1987);

Németh, "Az önmegszólító verstípusról," in his *11+7 vers* (Budapest: TkK, 1984), pp. 5–70;

Lajos Pók, *Babits Mihály* (Budapest: Szépirodalmi, 1967);

György Rába, *Babits Mihály* (Budapest: Gondolat, 1983);

Rába, *Babits Mihály költészete* (Budapest: Szépirodalmi, 1981);

Rába, *A szép hűtlenek* (Budapest: Akadémiai, 1969), pp. 14–213;

Lajos Sípos, *Babits Mihály és a forradalmak kora* (Budapest: Akadémiai, 1976);

Katalin J. Soltész, *Babits Mihály költői nyelve* (Budapest: Akadémiai, 1965);

Dezső Szabó, "Filozopter az irodalomban," in his *A magyar Káosz* (Budapest: Szépirodalmi, 1990), pp. 185–213;

József Szauder, "Babits Mihály költészete," in his *A romantika útján* (Budapest: Szépirodalmi, 1961), pp. 453–760;

Antal Szerb, "Az intellektuális költő," in his *Gondolatok a könyvtárban* (Budapest: Magvető, 1981), pp. 200–221;

Csaba Szigeti, *A hímfarkas bőre* (Pécs: Jelenkor, 1993), pp. 21–36, 125–140;

Attila Tamás, *Költői világképek fejlődése* (Budapest: Akadémiai, 1964);

Gábor Tolcsvai Nagy, "Bizonyosság és kétely határán," *Literatura,* 21 (1994): 73–87.

Wacław Berent

(28 September 1873 – 20 November 1940)

Joachim Baer
University of North Carolina at Greensboro

BOOKS: *Fachowiec. Powieść współczesna* (Warsaw, 1895);
Próchno. Powieść współczesna (Warsaw, 1903);
Źródła i ujścia nietzscheanizmu (Warsaw, 1906);
Idea w ruchu rewolucyjnym (Kraków, 1906);
Ozimina. Powieść (Warsaw: Jakób Mortkowicz, 1911);
Żywe kamienie. Opowieść rybałta, 2 volumes (Poznań: Ostoja, 1918);
Onegdaj (Warsaw, 1933);
Nurt. Opowieści biograficzne, 2 volumes (Warsaw: Gebethner & Wolff, 1934);
Diogenes w kontuszu. Opowieść o narodzinach literatów polskich (Warsaw: Gebethner & Wolff, 1937);
Zmierzch wodzów. Opowieści biograficzne (Warsaw: Gebethner & Wolff, 1939).

Editions and Collections: *Pisma*, 9 volumes (Warsaw: Gebethner & Wolff, 1933–1934)—comprises volume 1, *Fachowiec;* volumes 2–3, *Próchno;* volumes 4–5, *Ozimina;* volumes 6–7, *Żywe kamienie;* volumes 8–9, *Nurt;*

Dzieła wybrane, 6 volumes (Warsaw: Czytelnik, 1956–1958)—comprises volume 1, *Fachowiec;* volume 2, *Próchno;* volume 3, *Ozimina;* volume 4, *Żywe kamienie;* volume 5, *Nurt;* volume 6, *Diogenes w kontuszu;*

Ozimina, edited by Michał Głowiński (Wrocław: Zakład Narodowy im. Ossolińskich, 1974);

Próchno, edited by Jerzy Paszek (Wrocław: Zakład Narodowy im. Ossolińskich, 1979; revised edition, Wrocław, 1998);

Opowieści biograficzne, edited by Włodzimierz Bolecki (Kraków: Wydawnictwo Literackie, 1991)—comprises *Nurt, Diogenes w kontuszu, Zmierzch wodzów;*

Żywe kamienie, edited by Magdalena Popiel (Wrocław: Zakład Narodowy im. Ossolińskich, 1992).

TRANSLATIONS: Friedrich Nietzsche, *Tako rzecze Zaratustra* (Warsaw: Jakób Mortkowicz, 1905);
Christian Dietrich Grabbe, *Żart, satyra, ironia i głębsze znaczenie* (Warsaw, 1911);

Wacław Berent

Knut Hamsun, *Włóczęga* (Warsaw, 1924);
Guy de Maupassant, *Baryłeczka* (Warsaw, 1924);
Romain Rolland, *Żywot Michała Anioła* (Warsaw, 1924);
Lafcadio Hearn, *Opowieści niesamowite i upiorne* (Warsaw, 1924);
Henrik Ibsen, *Wróg ludu* (Warsaw: Instytut Wydawniczy "Biblioteka Polska," 1926);

Charles Kingsley, *Heroje. Czyli klechdy greckie o bohate-rach* (Warsaw, 1926).

Wacław Berent's significance as a prose writer of the *Młoda Polska* (Young Poland) tradition rests on his aesthetic perception of existence as the central value justifying art and life. His difficult, refined style offers a statement of the pursuits of life in which art, mythology, medieval mysticism, and Enlightenment forms of education create values of enduring significance not only for Poland but for all people.

Wacław Berent was born on 28 September 1873 in Warsaw to Paulina Deike and Karol Berent; he was part of an affluent family of merchants who valued education as well as refined living. During his university studies in Zurich and Munich, Berent specialized in the natural sciences and in 1895 published his doctoral thesis in Jena (Germany) on ichthyology. He lived briefly in Kraków but spent most of his life in Warsaw.

Berent's writing career began in the late nineteenth century with the publication of short prose works in periodicals such as *Gazeta Polska* (The Polish Gazette) and *Ateneum,* under the pseudonym Władysław Rawicz; these efforts led to *Fachowiec* (The Specialist, 1895), a major novel in the late Positivist tradition of the period. The nineteen-year-old hero, Kazimierz Zaliwski, follows the call of the time to engage in productive labor in a factory rather than pursue intellectual interests. His ideal is "usefulness" to society as the Positivists of the time understood the term; yet, the value of such alleged usefulness and the idealism behind it are revealed in this first-person narrative as only partially correct. What is lacking is personal satisfaction with the contribution one is making to society. Even though he is a foreman in a factory shop at the end of his "experiment in usefulness," the hero finds the factory environment alien to his nature and his aspirations:

> I live with the others, I push myself into their midst where they don't want me and where they have no use for me, and yet I sense a terrible lack of human association. Sometimes it's hard for me, very hard. I know that I am not the only one in this situation and that there are whole legions of people like me, too limited intellectually to belong with the intelligent ones and too intelligent for the others. These same individuals, however, stay aloof from those who are most like them.

Having thus paid his "dues to the social and literary ideals of the period which were obligatory in the years of his youth," according to scholar Julian Krzyżanowski, Berent moved in a different direction. In the early years of the twentieth century the writings of Friedrich Nietzsche became widely known in Poland as elsewhere in Europe; Berent became a reader and translator of Nietzsche and wrote a study titled *Źródła i ujścia nietzscheanizmu* (Sources and Outlets of Nietzscheanism, 1906). Nietzschean thinking also strongly influenced Berent's novel *Próchno* (Rotten Wood, 1903). This novel about the milieu of the artist in Poland is a statement about the search for values in a confused and rudderless world. A group of highly talented artists—poets, actors, and refined aristocrats—seeks a foothold in a world of defunct beliefs and uncertainties. The novel draws not only on Nietzsche but on Arthur Schopenhauer and Hindu philosophy for intellectual inspiration. Its heroes search for values that transcend this temporary existence, looking instead for what is eternal and enduring. Nietzsche's philosophy is a stepping-stone in a relentless process of transformation in life, attained by means of art and leading to the mystical essence of the "Om."

The metaphoric title of the novel—representing this decaying intellectual world, at the border of two centuries, battling with the despair of existence and in search of an indestructible essence—suggests the transformation of one form of life into something higher. There is a gleam and nobility in this "rotten stuff," as signified in the Russian translation, *Gnilushki* (Rotten Things, 1907). The sense of finding oneself at the threshold of something greater (a Nietzschean concept) was brilliantly assessed by another Russian translator in *Blestjashchaja pyl'* (Gleaming Dust, 1904), and in the German translation, *Edelfäule* (Aristocratic Decay, 1908).

If the suggestion of a transformation from one state of being into something else was Berent's aim in this novel, the means to it was the aesthetic principle: nothing less than beauty. The narration holds to a high level of stylistic elegance and lyricism. The lyrical element is most prominent in the quotations from the Polish romantic poet Juliusz Słowacki; but throughout the novel a kind of music is audible, based on sentence fragments, choice of vocabulary, rich use of alliteration, and use of color. One of the critics of the novel, Jerzy Paszek, has referred to the "dominating aspect of impressionism" in *Próchno.*

This aesthetic vision of life is also prominent in Berent's third novel, *Ozimina* (Winter Wheat, 1911). It is set in a period of social and spiritual instability in which the question of Poland's fate and future, after more than a century of subjugation to foreign

Postcard sent by Berent to Professor Zdzisław Jachimecki, in 1922 (from Władysław Studencki, O Wacławie Berencie, *1968–1969)*

powers, is raised. The place of action is a gathering of various representatives of Polish society in the elegant chambers of Baron Nieman, a conservative representative of the nobility. The novel tries to come to terms with what the future for Poland might be, but it leaves the question unanswered. *Ozimina* is imbued with symbolism and the aesthetic elements of sound and color. Berent suggests Poland's great past, retained in a rich store of memory, through the use of music (specifically the stately rhythms of the polonaise) and visual accents such as the image of the sage jester of three Jagiellonian kings, the Stańczyk, to whom the pensive priest at the gathering is compared.

Use of the aesthetic principle in art precludes providing answers to questions, but it allows for transformation from the level of the temporal to the eternal. This transformation is suggested in the novel through the use of the ancient myth of Demeter and her daughter Persephone, queen of the kingdom of the dead, who returns to the surface of the earth for a third of each year. The myth appears as a vision to one of the characters, a Kraków professor who visits Baron Nieman's salon and offers commentary about Polish history. (The fact that he is a professor at the ancient Kraków University, created by King Kazimir the Great in 1364, lends dignity and weight to his observations.) Poland seems to him in his vision like Demeter looking for her lost child, but the regular and anticipated return of Persephone to the surface of the earth promises a revival of Poland's nationhood in the future.

Berent's art is idealistic, his language stylized. The aestheticism of *Ozimina* has always made it a difficult work for any reader, including highly educated Polish readers. Its language has been described by Paszek as being "najtrudniejszym językowo tekstem" (utterly difficult linguistically). Once again Berent has expressed his theme in a metaphoric title, rich in connotative meaning: Poland at present is "winter wheat," dormant for months, yet with a promise of coming to life and being ready for harvest in the late spring or early summer of the future.

Berent's fourth novel, *Żywe kamienie* (Living Stones, 1918), appeared at the end of the *Młoda Polska* tradition. With his evocation of the spiritual aspirations of medieval Europe, Berent's place in this literary movement attained a rank of indisputable greatness. All of his art is characterized by a visionary quality, by the examination of human life (and the specific situation of Poland in the context of European history) against the background of religious myths and eternal values. The metaphor of "living stones" refers to the human figures decorating the walls of the Gothic cathedrals of medieval Europe. By calling these works of medieval stonemasonry "living," the author hints at the enduring inspirational value of the world of the spirit, passed down from previous centuries.

The pious knight in search of the Holy Grail and the devoted Franciscan friar busy with the illumination of sacred texts were not the only representatives of this spiritual atmosphere; there was also the medieval troubadour wandering among towns and courts in southern France in the twelfth and thirteenth centuries. *Żywe kamienie* is a novel about a band of traveling entertainers and their leader, the goliard. The adventures of this troupe, its leader, and the woman acrobat he loves (both die after a night of revelry in the midst of ruins of antiquity) represent a central feature of the narrative.

Beyond the activities and the multifarious life of medieval Provence, however, Berent once again seeks to assess the significance of art and its enduring triumph. The "essence of art and its relationship to life" was the summation given to Berent's novel by Krzyżanowski. While *Żywe kamienie* is a novel about medieval life, based on profound and detailed research, its thrust is entirely contemporary. Berent meant to convey to his contemporaries the role of art in modern times as a restorative and invaluable element of joy in the face of pervasive melancholy and apathy: "for *our* generation precisely, for the removal of sadness from the face of the earth, for the renewal of human hearts."

With this novel Berent continued not only his artistic theme of aestheticism as a palliative to life but also his tendency toward difficult style. In *Żywe kamienie* the author made an attempt at stylization on medieval artistic models. Paszek calls it a "stylistic pathos, originating from the rhetorical devices of sacred texts." French writer Paul Cazin made a heroic attempt to re-create this novel through a 1931 translation into French.

By the time Poland regained her national independence on 11 November 1918, the *Młoda Polska* tradition, which had been so productive for more than a quarter of a century, had lost its luster and timeliness. Other writers and new artistic problems came forward. Berent for a time joined the editorial board of the journal *Nowy Przegląd Literatury i Sztuki* (New Review of Literature and Art, 1920) and became editor of *Pamiętnik Warszawski* (Warsaw Diary, 1929). For years he was busy as a translator into Polish of works by Nietzsche, Guy de Maupas-

sant, Romain Rolland, Lafcadio Hearn, Henrik Ibsen, and Charles Kingsley. From the late 1920s until 1939 Berent wrote historical biographies on the model of such successful contemporary practitioners as Lytton Strachey and André Maurois. These biographies were assembled in three collections: *Nurt* (Current, 1934), *Diogenes w kontuszu* (A Diogenes in Native Costume, 1937), and *Zmierzch wodzów* (Twilight of the Leaders, 1939).

The impetus for Berent's historical biographies came from the contemporary debate in Polish intellectual circles about appropriate guideposts in Polish history for leaders of the newly independent nation. It was a difficult problem for Poland; Romantic tradition in the nineteenth century had been strong and had preserved certain feelings of national identity. Poland had long been seen as a "martyr nation," nailed to the cross by selfish and powerful neighbors. Even though in 1918 Poland had been restored as an independent country, feelings of martyrdom persisted. To Berent and other representatives of Poland's intellectual elite—including Witold Gombrowicz—this perception of Poland as a martyr was now obsolete.

Berent looked for spiritual guideposts in the period preceding Polish Romanticism, among writers and intellectuals active during the reign of Poland's last king, Stanisław August Poniatowski (reigned 1764–1795), as well as among writers from the period of Polish Classicism and Enlightenment. He also looked to those national leaders who had preserved the spirit of Polish independence not by visions of martyrdom but through thought, learning, and immersion of themselves in the best that Western Civilization in its Enlightenment phase had to offer. Berent's research into the life and times of these representatives of Polish culture, who had lived during a period of crisis in national affairs, led to highly acclaimed biographical sketches of such men as Franciszek Karpiński, Onufry Kopczyński, Henryk Dąbrowski, Franciszek Jezierski, and Julian Niemcewicz. Berent was awarded the National Prize for Literature in 1933 for the sketches included in *Nurt* and was invited to membership in the Polish Academy of Literature in the same year.

Berent was seen as the creative mind who revived the "current" that had kept alive Poland's spirit of self-worth. Although the biographies were much simpler and more direct in style than his previous work, Berent still adhered to a vision of life in which the aesthetic was dominant. The central focus in his heroes' lives was the broadest possible improvement of the spirit through education and creativity. While Berent used historical material for his sketches, he was not as interested in the facts as he was in their spiritual element. He depicted his heroes in their struggle to preserve what was valuable in Polish culture. Twentieth-century poet Czesław Miłosz correctly assessed Berent's aesthetic vision of historical processes and said that Berent had succeeded in restoring hope to himself and others by looking at the men of the Polish Enlightenment. Berent's biographical work was his last project: he died on 20 November 1940 in Warsaw during the German occupation.

A writer with such a pronounced penchant for aestheticism is unlikely to have a broad readership. Paszek in 1990 summed up what Berent stood for: "Wacław Berent was an elitist writer. He did not write easily. He wrote slowly, reflecting well on what he wrote; but, and this is of greatest importance, he wrote with a sharply defined artistic purpose." That purpose was to create beauty.

Letters:

Listy zebrane (Kraków: Wydawnictwo Literackie, 1992);

Pisma rozproszone. Listy, edited by Ryszard Nycz and Włodzimierz Bolecki (Kraków: Wydawnictwo Literackie, 1992).

Biography:

Hanna Muszyńska-Hoffmanowa, *W kręgu Berenta* (Łódź: Wydawnictwo Łódzkie, 1986).

References:

Joachim T. Baer, "Juliusz Słowacki and Wacław Berent in Their Artistic Relationship," in *American Contributions to the Seventh International Congress of Slavists, Warsaw, August 21–27, 1973, II: Literature and Folklore,* edited by Victor Terras (The Hague: Mouton, 1975), pp. 23–37;

Baer, "Symbolism and Stylized Prose in Russia and Poland: V. Brjusov's *Ognennyj angel* and W. Berent's *Żywe kamienie,*" in *American Contributions to the Ninth International Congress of Slavists, Kiev, September, 1983, II: Literature, Poetics, History,* edited by Paul Debreczeny (Columbus, Ohio: Slavica, 1983), pp. 19–38;

Baer, *Wacław Berent: His Life and Work* (Rome: Institutum Historicum Polonicum, 1974);

Baer, "Wacław Berent's *Ozimina:* An Analysis," in *For Wiktor Weintraub: Essays in Polish Literature, Language, and History Presented on the Occasion of His 65th Birthday,* edited by Victor Erlich, Roman Jakobson, Czesław Miłosz, Riccardo Picchio,

and Alexander M. Schenker (The Hague: Mouton, 1975), pp. 43–57;

Włodzimierz Bolecki, *Historia i biografia. Opowieści biograficzne Wacława Berenta* (Wrocław: Zakład Narodowy im. Ossolińskich, 1978);

Bolecki, "Jak czytano 'opowieści biograficzne' Wacława Berenta (1934–1939)," *Pamiętnik Literacki,* 68, no. 4 (1977): 71–112;

Janina Garbaczowska, "Dziedzictwo 'rzeczy listopadowych' po Wyspiańskim w prozie Wacława Berenta," *Ruch Literacki,* 10, no. 4 (1969): 179–187;

Garbaczowska, "Wacław Berent wobec zagadnienia rewolucji," *Ruch Literacki,* 9, no. 6 (1968): 326–338;

Peer Hultberg, *Styl wczesnej prozy fabularnej Wacława Berenta,* translated by Ignacy Sieradzki (Wrocław: Zakład Narodowy im. Ossolińskich, 1969);

Julian Krzyżanowski, *Neo-Romantyzm Polski 1890–1918* (Wrocław: Zakład Narodowy im. Ossolińskich, 1963), p. 268;

Zofia Mołodcówna, *Opowieści biograficzne Wacława Berenta* (Warsaw: Państwowy Instytut Wydawniczy, 1978);

Ryszard Nycz, "Homo irrequietus: Nietzscheanizm w twórczości Wacława Berenta," *Pamiętnik Literacki,* 67, no. 2 (1976): 45–82;

Jerzy Paszek, "Iryzujące aluzje 'Próchna,'" *Pamiętnik Literacki,* 69, no. 4 (1978): 279–296;

Paszek, "Rok 1910 i rok 1911," *Teksty,* 4–5 (1981): 298–303;

Paszek, *Styl powieści Wacława Berenta* (Katowice: Uniwersytet Śląski, 1976);

Paszek, *Wacław Berent–Pisarz Elitarny* (Wrocław: Zakład Narodowy im. Ossolińskich, 1990);

Marian Płachecki, "Powieściowa przestrzeń i poetyka sceny," *Teksty,* 34 (1977): 77–93;

Magdalena Popiel, *Historia i metafora, O "Żywych kamieniach" Wacława Berenta* (Wrocław: Zakład Narodowy im. Ossolińskich, 1989);

Popiel, "Włoskie Berentiana," *Ruch Literacki,* 30 (May–June 1989): 242–249;

Władysław Studencki, *O Wacławie Berencie,* 2 volumes (Opole: Zeszyty Naukowe Wyższej Szkoły Pedagogicznej, 1968–1969);

Janusz Tazbir, "Zapomniana książka wybitnego pisarza," *Przegląd Humanistyczny,* 20, no. 7 (1976): 59–64;

Konstanty Troczyński, *Artysta i dzieło. Studium o "Próchnie" Wacława Berenta* (Poznań, 1938);

Marian Zaczyński, "Repetycje i rewizje: Nad twórczością Wacława Berenta," *Ruch Literacki,* 21, no. 3 (1980): 211–223.

Tadeusz Borowski

(12 November 1922 – 3 July 1951)

John R. Carpenter

BOOKS: *Gdziekolwiek ziemia* (Warsaw: Privately printed, 1942);

Imiona nurtu (Munich: Oficyna Warszawska, 1945);

Poszukiwania. Tracing, by Borowski and Krystyn Olszewski (Munich: Oficyna Warszawska, 1945);

Byliśmy w Oświęcimiu, by Borowski, Olszewski, and Janusz Nel Siedlecki, preface by Anatol Girs (Munich: Oficyna Warszawska na Obczyźnie, 1946);

Pewien żołnierz (Warsaw: Płomienie, 1947);

Pożegnanie z Marią (Warsaw: Wiedza, 1948);

Kamienny świat. Opowiadanie w dwudziestu obrazach (Warsaw: Czytelnik, 1948);

Opowiadania z książek i z gazet (Warsaw: Państwowy Instytut Wydawniczy, 1949);

Mała kronika wielkich spraw, edited by Wiktor Woroszylski (Warsaw: Wydawnictwo Ministerstwa Obrony Narodowej, 1951);

Na przedpolu. Artykuły i reportaże, introduction by Woroszylski (Warsaw: Wydawnictwo Ministerstwa Obrony Narodowej, 1952);

Czerwony maj. Opowiadania, introduction by Kazimierz Koźniewski (Warsaw: Państwowy Instytut Wydawniczy, 1953).

Editions and Collections: *Utwory zebrane,* 5 volumes, edited by Jerzy Andrzejewski, Tadeusz Drewnowski, J. Piórkowski, and Wiktor Woroszylski (Warsaw: Państwowy Instytut Wydawniczy, 1954);

Wybór opowiadań, edited by Andrzejewski (Warsaw: Państwowy Instytut Wydawniczy, 1959);

Pożegnanie z Marią. Wybór opowiadań (Warsaw: Państwowy Instytut Wydawniczy, 1965);

Wybór poezji, edited by Józefa Bartnicka (Warsaw: Czytelnik, 1968);

Opowiadania wybrane, edited by Drewnowski (Warsaw: Państwowy Instytut Wydawniczy, 1971);

Poezje wybrane, edited by Bartnicka (Warsaw: Ludowa Spółdzielnia Wydawnicza, 1971);

Tadeusz Borowski

Poezje, edited by Drewnowski (Warsaw: Państwowy Instytut Wydawniczy, 1972);

Wspomnienia, wiersze, opowiadania, edited by Drewnowski (Warsaw: Państwowy Instytut Wydawniczy, 1974);

Utwory wybrane, edited by Andrzej Werner (Wrocław: Zakład Narodowy im. Ossolińskich, 1991).

Editions in English: "Ladies and Gentlemen, to the Gas Chamber," translated by Jadwiga Zwolska, in *Contemporary Polish Short Stories,* edited by Andrzej Kijowski (Warsaw: Polonia, 1960), pp. 37–66;

This Way for the Gas, Ladies and Gentlemen: And Other Stories, edited and translated by Barbara Ved-

der (London: Cape, 1967; New York: Viking, 1967);
Selected Poems, translated by Tadeusz Pióro, Larry Rafferty, and Meryl Natchez (Walnut Creek, Calif.: Hit & Run Press, 1990).

OTHER: "Chłopiec z Biblią," in *Zeszyty Wrocławskie,* 2 (1947).

There is broad critical agreement that Tadeusz Borowski's stories are among the best that have been written by any writer, in any language, about the German concentration camp at Auschwitz. Borowski explored what Primo Levi called "the grey area" of relative accommodation in the camps. He described this phenomenon directly and with great honesty; it is difficult to overestimate the significance and value of Borowski's writings. Yet, critical assessment is complicated. His writings are varied and often contradictory. The composition of his best writings occurred in a short span of time—approximately four years. The evolution and radical changes in his attitudes often took place rapidly, in months and not years as with most other writers. The difficulties in interpreting Borowski's writings are not only biographical but also textual. Borowski's biographer and editor, Tadeusz Drewnowski, has admitted that the Polish texts of the stories and poems are difficult to establish and that they include many revisions both by the author and by editors. Also, Borowski lost interest in publishing his poetry after 1946; an announced collection of poems, "Rozmowa z przyjacielem" (Conversations with a Friend), was never published. The result was that over the next three decades, new poems were found and published in small groups in periodicals.

Tadeusz Borowski was born on 12 November 1922 into a Polish family living in the Ukrainian town of Zhitomir in the Soviet Union. His father, Stanisław Borowski, an accountant, was a victim of one of the mass arrests in 1926; he was charged with participation in a Polish military organization during World War I. He was sent to a labor camp north of the Arctic Circle in Karelia, where he helped to dig the White Sea Canal. Some of the early biographical accounts of Borowski that were written before 1989 disguised the pretext for his father's arrest because it reflected badly on Soviet authorities. In 1930, during a period of collectivization and hunger, Borowski's mother, Teofila, was sent to a settlement on the Yenisei River in Siberia. The young Borowski was taken in by an aunt. In 1932 Borowski's father was repatriated to Poland as part of an exchange of political prisoners between Poland and the Soviet Union. Later in that year the Red Cross managed to bring the ten-year-old Borowski to Poland, along with his brother. Their mother was repatriated two years later and joined the family in Warsaw.

Warsaw was in an economic crisis at the time. The only employment Stanisław Borowski could find was as a warehouse worker, while Teofila worked as a seamstress at home. Tadeusz was put in a boarding school run by Franciscan monks; when the Germans overran Poland in September 1939, he was not yet seventeen. Secondary school and college education were forbidden to Poles, so Borowski entered the underground University of Warsaw, where he studied Polish language and literature. He also worked part-time as a night watchman in a warehouse on the outskirts of the city. He went to meetings where he and other young people argued heatedly about literature and politics and read illegal publications.

During this time Borowski wrote his earliest poetry. In 1942 he collected his first poems in a mimeographed volume titled *Gdziekolwiek ziemia* (Wherever the Earth). These poems were written in hexameters, unlike most of the poems he wrote in Munich at the end of World War II. In his early poems the war is set at a distance. The poems express grayness and gloom as they present a call to arms as well as a vision of death; they are devoid of any kind of faith. Some critics have called these poems "catastrophist," a label that has been applied to the writings of other Polish poets of the 1930s and early 1940s. One of Borowski's poems, "Widzenie" (Vision), begins with an epigraph from Revelation announcing the coming of the "Days of Wrath." Another poem in this collection, "Pieśń" (translated as "Song," 1990), ends with the phrase, "There will remain after us only scrap-iron / and the hollow, jeering laughter of generations."

In 1940 Borowski met Maria Rundo, the great love of his life. Her name appears in the title of his most famous collection of short stories, *Pożegnanie z Marią* (Farewell to Maria, 1948). Borowski's love poems written to her were not included in his first collection of poems; six of these poems were published in *Arkusz Poetycki* (Poetic Chapbook) in July 1944.

In 1942 Borowski was living with Maria, now his fiancée. One night she did not return; she had fallen into a trap set by the Nazis in a friend's apartment. The following day Borowski searched for her and was arrested in the same apartment. He was first sent to the Pawiak Prison, located at the edge of the Warsaw ghetto, and was imprisoned there for more than two months. At the end of April he was sent in a transport of prisoners to Auschwitz. Maria was sent to Auschwitz in another transport, also in late April. The date is important: after 4 April 1942 "Aryans" were no longer gassed at Auschwitz, except in special cases, and only Jews were gassed en masse. Consequently, Borowski and his fiancée were not subject to the "selections" to which both Jewish and "Aryan" prisoners fell victim. In Auschwitz, Borowski learned that Maria was held in the women's zone nearby; the zones were separated, but he was able to catch an occasional glimpse of her.

In the camp at Auschwitz, Borowski carried telegraph poles and worked as a roofer and a night watchman. He caught pneumonia, and after his recovery he took a class to become a hospital orderly; this experience is described in detail in his story "U nás, w Auschwitzu . . ." (1946; translated as "Auschwitz Our Home (A Letter)," 1967). When Maria became seriously ill, he managed to send her medicine that he obtained through the hospital job. He also gained the position of *Vorarbeiter* (foreman), which gave him special advantages. Probably much of Borowski's life at Auschwitz is described in the stories included in *Pożegnanie z Marią*. The protagonist of most of them is "Tadek," or "*Vorarbeiter Tadeusz*"; the temptation to identify this protagonist with Borowski is great, but the reader must be cautious about doing so. Certain traits of this protagonist are probably exaggerated, while others are understated; he is a deliberate and studied creation. The careful reader can see significant differences in "Tadek" from story to story.

In August 1944 Soviet troops advanced into Germany, and the Germans evacuated surviving Auschwitz inmates to camps further to the west, in Germany proper. Borowski spent the next nine months in the camps of Natzweiler-Dautmergen, near Stuttgart, and Dachau-Allach. Borowski was in Dachau when it was liberated by the American Seventh Army on 1 May 1945. Following his release Borowski spent some time in Munich, visited Paris and Belgium, and also lived at Murnau in Bavaria, the headquarters of those Polish soldiers who had decided not to return to Poland. Biographer Drewnowski quotes one of Borowski's letters (10 March 1946): "I ran from Murnau. I wasn't soldier material—I avoided the meetings, I was no flag-waver, I took to the fields with a stack of books and wandered." Borowski also worked for a Red Cross agency that specialized in reuniting families separated by the war.

Although the year after Borowski's release from Dachau was a time of confusion and uncertainty, it was also the period when he wrote his greatest stories. Most were composed when he was living in the camp for displaced persons at Freimann, on the outskirts of Munich. These stories include "Proszę państwa do gazu" (1946; translated as "Ladies and Gentlemen, to the Gas Chamber," 1960; also translated as "This Way for the Gas, Ladies and Gentlemen," 1967), "Dzień w Harmenzach" (1946; translated as "A Day at Harmenz," 1967), and "Ludzie, którzy szli" (1946; translated as "The People Who Walked On," 1967). They explore the complex interactions among prisoners with brutal honesty, and Borowski avoids depicting the prisoners and their captors in mutually exclusive terms of white or black, virtue or vice, victims or executioners, resisters or collaborators.

Several survivors who have written about Auschwitz, including Sim Kessel and Primo Levi, have stressed that in order to survive, prisoners had to make compromises with the camp administrators and *kapos* (prisoner foremen) and compete with other prisoners. Those who did not make these compromises—for whatever reason—rarely survived. The compromises might be relatively minor and harmless for others, or they could be lethal: most prisoners were victimized by other prisoners. The dynamics of these intricate relationships were complex and unpredictable; lives hung in the balance. Borowski explored the connections with a harsh irony frequently directed against himself or against "Tadek." One of the clearest elucidations of "Dzień w Harmenzach" is the chapter titled "Beta czyli nieszczęśliwy kochanek" (translated as "Beta, the Disappointed Lover") in *Zniewolony umysł* (1953; translated as *The Captive Mind*, 1953), written by Nobel Prize–winning poet Czesław Miłosz. "Beta" was Miłosz's pseudonym for Borowski. Miłosz wrote:

> I have read many books about concentration camps, but not one of them is as terrifying as his stories because he never moralizes, he relates. . . . In his stories Beta clearly defines his social position. He belonged to the caste of clever and healthy prisoners, and he *brags* about his cunning and agility. Life in a concentration camp requires constant alertness; every moment can decide one's life or death.

In the preface to *This Way for the Gas, Ladies and Gentlemen: And Other Stories* (1967) Jan Kott wrote about the impact produced by Borowski's stories when they were first published in Poland between 1945 and 1948:

The stories produced a shock. The public was expecting martyrologies; the Communist party called for works that were ideological, that divided the world into the righteous and the unrighteous, heroes and traitors, Communists and Fascists. Borowski was accused of amorality, decadence, and nihilism. Yet at the same time it was clear to everyone that Polish literature had gained a dazzling new talent. All the publications and all the possibilities the party offered young writers were opened up to Borowski.

This observation sheds some light on Borowski's ambiguous situation in Poland when he returned in 1946. He did not present two-dimensional martyrs and anti-Nazis in his stories about the camps; on the other hand, he had become increasingly hostile to his American liberators. The volume *Byliśmy w Oświęcimiu* (We Were in Auschwitz, 1946), written with Krystyn Olszewski and Janusz Nel Siedlecki, was dedicated to "The American Seventh Army which brought us liberation from the Dachau-Allach concentration camp"; however, Borowski soon started to complain about the American soldiers. In his story "Bitwa pod Grunwaldem" (The Battle of Grünwald, 1946) he wrote contemptuously of the American "Black monkeys in white helmets," and in his letters he bitterly describes "local girls going for walks with Negroes." When he returned to Poland, his descriptions of Americans and the West in general became vitriolic. In broad, somewhat crude strokes he associated the Americans—but also the French, the "liberated" Germans of West Germany, and all Western Europe—with commerce, with reprehensible buying and selling. These were activities, ironically, that he bragged about in his stories in *Pożegnanie z Marią*, although the context was different.

Borowski also wrote many poems in Germany. His poetic output can be divided into three groups: the works included in his 1942 volume *Gdziekolwiek ziemia;* the poems he wrote in the camps and published in Munich in 1945 in his volume *Imiona nurtu* (Names of the Current); and those he wrote after this volume, while he was still residing in postwar Germany. After his return to Poland he ceased writing poetry.

Borowski was repatriated to Poland on the last day of May 1946. In Munich he had learned that Maria was still alive; she had been moved from Birkenau and relocated in Sweden by the Red Cross. Borowski wrote to her. At first she did not want to leave Sweden and go to Communist Poland, but he persuaded her to return in November 1946. He met

Dust jacket for Borowski's second book, a 1945 collection of poetry

her at the border point, and they were married in December of that year.

At the beginning of 1948 Borowski became a member of the Communist Party. Also during this year, *Pożegnanie z Marią* was published as well as more recent stories in the collection *Kamienny świat* (The World of Stone), which appeared in December. The title story of the latter volume presents the narrator as a party activist who makes a resolution to write an "immortal epic" about the true significance of the events, things, and people he has seen. Several critics have noted that the word "epic" in this story was a metaphor for political activism, as opposed to traditional literature—"epic" acts and "epic" commitment. The story was the last serious work of literature that Borowski wrote. Miłosz, in "Beta czyli nieszczęśliwy kochanek," observed that the boundary between literature and propaganda had begun to fade. Borowski plunged into a career as a party propagandist, writing rapidly and abundantly. Some of these works, commissioned by the Sunday newspaper *Rzeczpospolita* (The Republic), were collected in *Opowiadania z książek i z gazet* (Stories from Periodicals and Newspapers, 1949).

In 1949 Borowski spent almost a year in Berlin on a party assignment. His life was becoming increasingly complicated. He returned to Warsaw in March 1950; twice he attempted to commit suicide. Scholar Adolf Rudnicki observed that Borowski had left for Berlin as an enemy of Socialist Realism, but he returned as a strident apostle of that school. The Communist Party had entrusted Borowski with a "secret mission" in Berlin; this situation was described in a thinly veiled short story by Wiktor Woroszylski titled "Człowiek wybiera śmierć" (A Man Chooses Death) in his collection *Okrutna gwiazda* (Cruel Star, 1958). Most references by critics to this episode are unsatisfactory and mix half-truths with untruths, passing in silence over concrete facts or actions that are important to Borowski's biography. The "secret mission" was probably a form of spying, discussed in part by several critics, including Kott in his preface to *This Way for the Gas, Ladies and Gentlemen*, Drewnowski in his biography *Ucieczka z kamiennego świata* (Escape from the World of Stone, 1971), Woroszylski in his introduction to Borowski's five-volume *Utwory zebrane* (Collected Works, 1954), and Rudnicki in "Śmierć w lipcu 1951" (Death in July 1951). None of these versions should be accepted as authority; they are marked by a variety of biases. The reconstruction of the events of this period of Borowski's life is a genuine challenge to the reader, student, and researcher.

Borowski's daughter, Małgorzata, was born in Warsaw on 26 June 1951. On 1 July 1951 Borowski opened the valves of a gas oven in the kitchen of his Warsaw apartment in his third attempt to commit suicide. He died two days later.

Borowski's stories about Auschwitz are on a level with works by Primo Levi and Elie Wiesel. Borowski excelled as an ironist and described the moral contradictions of daily life in the camps with skill and frankness.

Biography:

Tadeusz Drewnowski, *Ucieczka z kamiennego świata. O Tadeuszu Borowskim* (Warsaw: Państwowy Instytut Wydawniczy, 1971).

References:

Addison Bross, "Five Poems [by Borowski]," *Polish Review*, 28, no. 3 (1983): 43–47;

Tadeusz Drewnowski, "Poetycki pamiętnik z podróży," *Miesięcznik Literacki*, 4 (1969): 7, 17–37; 6 (1969): 52–65;

Drewnowski, "Na pół drogi pewnej polityki," *Twórczość*, 27, no. 4 (1971): 30–63;

Drewnowski, "Wyłomy w kamiennym świecie," *Współczesność*, 15 (11–24 November 1970): 6–9;

Andrzej Kijowski, "Tadeusz Borowski," *Życie Literackie*, 24 (1955): 3–4;

Jan Kott, introduction to *This Way for the Gas, Ladies and Gentlemen*, by Borowski, edited and translated by Barbara Vedder (London: Cape, 1967; New York: Viking, 1967);

Frank Kujawinski, "Five Poems [by Borowski]," *Mr. Cogito*, 6, no. 1 (1978);

Tomasz Łubieński, "Anty-Borowski," *Kultura*, 32 (1972): 5;

Czesław Miłosz, "Beta, the Disappointed Lover," in *The Captive Mind*, translated by Jane Zielonko (New York: Random House, 1953), pp. 106–128;

H. Olschowsky, "Reise an die Grenzen einer Moral: Tadeusz Borowskis Auseinandersetzung mit Auschwitz als einem Modell des faschistischen Systems," *Zeitschrift fur Slawistik*, 16 (1971): 615–621;

Adolf Rudnicki, "Śmierć w lipcu 1951," in *Nowa Kultura*, no. 31 (1961);

Christian Skrzyposzek, "Tadeusz Borowski żywy?" *Odra*, 8, no. 5 (1968): 33–39;

Jan Szczawiej, "Drwiący śmiech pokoleń," *Poezja*, 10, nos. 7–8 (1974): 17–22;

Małgorzata Szpakowska, "Kamienny świat pod kamiennym niebem," *Teksty*, 2–4 (1973): 139–145;

Andrzej Tauber-Ziółkowski, "'Pieśni kumejskie' Tadeusza Borowskiego," *Poezja*, 7, no. 7 (1971): 10–19;

Tauber-Ziółkowski, *Sugestie interpretacyjne* (London: Oficyna Poetów i Malarzy, 1972), pp. 53–125;

Andrzej Werner, *Zwyczajna apokalipsa. Tadeusz Borowski i jego wizja świata obozów* (Warsaw: Czytelnik, 1971);

Werner, "Tadeusz Borowski—fenomenologia systemu," *Z Dziejów Form Artystycznych w Literaturze Polskiej*, 24 (1971): 213–252;

Andrzej Wirth, "Odkrycie tragizmu," *Nowa Kultura*, 15 (1962): 3, 6;

Wirth, "A Discovery of Tragedy (The Incomplete Account of Tadeusz Borowski)," *Polish Review*, 12, no. 3 (1967): 43–52;

Wiktor Woroszylski, *O Tadeuszu Borowskim. Jego życiu i twórczości* (Warsaw: Państwowy Instytut Wydawniczy, 1955);

Kazimierz Wyka, "Gdziekolwiek ziemia jest snem," *Odrodzenie*, 23 (1948): 150–159.

Karel Čapek

(9 January 1890 – 25 December 1939)

Jiří Holý
Charles University, Prague

BOOKS: *Zářivé hlubiny a jiné prózy,* by Čapek and
   Josef Čapek (Prague: František Borový, 1916);
Boží muka. Kniha novel (Prague: Jan Otto, 1917);
Pragmatismus čili filosofie praktického života (Prague:
   František Topič, 1918);
Krakonošova zahrada, by Čapek and Josef Čapek
   (Prague: František Borový, 1918);
Loupežník. Komedie o třech dějstvích (Prague: Aventi-
   num, 1920); translated by Rudolf C. Bednar as
   "The Robber": A Comedy in Three Acts (Iowa City,
   1931);
R.U.R. (Rossum's Universal Robots) (Prague: Aventi-
   num, 1920); translated by Paul Selver as *R.U.R.
   (Rossum's Universal Robots): A Fantastic Melo-
   drama* (Garden City, N.Y.: Doubleday, Page,
   1923); translation adapted by Nigel Playfair
   and published as *R.U.R. (Rossum's Universal
   Robots). A Play in Three Acts and an Epilogue,*
   (London: Oxford University Press, 1923);
Kritika slov (Prague: B. M. Klika, 1920);
Trapné povídky (Prague: Aventinum, 1921); translated by Francis P. Marchant, Dora Round, F. P.
   Casey, and O. Vočadlo as *Money and Other Sto-
   ries* (London: Hutchinson, 1929; New York:
   Brentano's, 1930);
*Ze života hmyzu. Komedie o třech aktech s předehrou a epi-
   logem,* by Čapek and Josef Čapek (Prague:
   Aventinum, 1921); translated by Selver and
   adapted by Playfair and Clifford Bax as *"And so
   ad infinitum" (The Life of the Insects.) An Entomo-
   logical Review in Three Acts, a Prologue and an Epi-
   logue* (London & New York: Oxford University
   Press, 1923); translation republished as *The
   Life of the Insects,* in *Chief Patterns of World Drama,
   Aeschylus to Anderson,* edited by William S.
   Clark (Boston: Houghton Mifflin, 1946), pp.
   923–958; also published as *The World We Live In
   (The Insect Comedy),* adapted by Owen Davis
   (New York & Los Angeles: S. French / Lon-
   don: S. French, 1933);

Karel Čapek

Lásky hra osudná, by Čapek and Josef Čapek (Prague:
   Aventinum, 1922);
Továrna na absolutno. Román feuilleton (Brno: Polygra-
   fia, 1922); translated by Thomas Mark as *The
   Absolute at Large* (London: Macmillan, 1927;
   New York: Macmillan, 1927);
Věc Makropulos. Komedie o třech dějstvích s přeměnou
   (Prague: Aventinum, 1922); adapted by Ran-
   dal C. Burrell as *The Makropulos Secret* (Boston:
   J. W. Luce, 1925); also translated by Selver as

The Macropulos Secret: A Comedy (London: R. Holden, 1927);

Italské listy. Feuilletony (Prague: Aventinum, 1923); translated by Marchant as *Letters from Italy* (London: Besant, 1929);

Krakatit. Román (Prague: Aventinum, 1924); translated by Lawrence Hyde as *Krakatit* (London: G. Bles, 1925; New York: Macmillan, 1925); republished as *An Atomic Phantasy. Krakatit: A Novel* (London: Allen & Unwin, 1948; New York: Arts, 1951);

Anglické listy. Pro větší názornost provázené obrázky autorovými (Prague: Aventinum, 1924); translated by Selver as *Letters from England* (London: G. Bles, 1925; Garden City, N.Y.: Doubleday, Page, 1925);

Jak vzniká divadelní hra a průvodce po zákulisí, by Čapek and Josef Čapek (Prague: Aventinum, 1925);

O nejbližších věcech. Feuilletony (Prague: Aventinum, 1925); translated by Round as *Intimate Things* (London: Allen & Unwin, 1935; New York: Putnam, 1936);

Adam Stvořitel. Komedie o sedmi obrazech, by Čapek and Josef Čapek (Prague: Aventinum, 1927); translated by Round as *Adam the Creator* (London: Allen & Unwin, 1929; New York: R. R. Smith, 1930);

Skandální aféra Josefa Holouška (Prague: Aventinum, 1927);

Hovory s T. G. Masarykem I (Prague: Aventinum–Čin, 1928);

Povídky z jedné kapsy (Prague: Aventinum, 1929);

Povídky z druhé kapsy (Prague: Aventinum, 1929);

Zahradníkův rok. Pro poučení všech zahrádkářů napsal Karel Čapek a nakreslil Josef Čapek (Prague: Aventinum, 1929); translated by M. and R. Weatherall as *The Gardener's Year* (London: Allen & Unwin, 1931; New York: Putnam, 1931);

Minda čili o chovu psů (Prague: Orbis, 1930);

Výlet do Španěl. Osvětlený obrázky autorovými (Prague: Aventinum, 1930); translated by Selver as *Letters from Spain* (London: G. Bles, 1931; New York: Putnam, 1932);

Hovory s T. G. Masarykem II (Prague: Aventinum–Čin, 1931);

Marsyas čili Na okraj literatury, 1919–1931 (Prague: Aventinum, 1931); translated by M. and R. Weatherall as *In Praise of Newspapers, and Other Essays on the Margins of Literature* (London: Allen, 1951; New York: Arts, 1951);

Apokryfy (Prague: Adolf Synek, 1932); republished as *Kniha apokryfů,* volume 47 of *Spisy bratří Čapků,* edited by Miroslav Halík (Prague: František Borový, 1945); translated by Round as *Apocryphal Stories* (London: Allen & Unwin / New York: Macmillan, 1949);

Obrázky z Holandska. S kresbami autorovými (Prague: František Borový–Aventinum, 1932); translated by Selver as *Letters from Holland* (London: Faber & Faber, 1933; New York: Putnam, 1933);

O věcech obecných čili Zóon politikon (Prague: František Borový, 1932);

Devatero pohádek a ještě jedna od Josefa Čapka jako přívažek, by Čapek and Josef Čapek (Prague: František Borový–Aventinum, 1932); translated by M. and R. Weatherall as *Fairy Tales, with One Extra as a Makeweight by Joseph Čapek* (London: Allen & Unwin, 1933; New York: Holt, 1933);

Dášeňka čili život štěněte. Pro děti napsal, nakreslil, fotografoval a zakusil Karel Čapek (Prague: František Borový, 1933); translated by M. and R. Weatherall as *Dashenka; or, the Life of a Puppy, Written, Drawn, Photographed and Endured by Karel Čapek* (London: Allen & Unwin, 1933; New York: Holt, 1933);

Hordubal (Prague: František Borový, 1933); translated by M. and R. Weatherall as *Hordubal* (London: Allen & Unwin, 1934);

Povětroň (Prague: František Borový, 1934); translated by M. and R. Weatherall as *Meteor* (London: Allen & Unwin, 1935; New York: Putnam, 1935);

Obyčejný život (Prague: František Borový, 1934); translated by M. and R. Weatherall as *An Ordinary Life* (London: Allen & Unwin, 1936);

Hovory s T. G. Masarykem III (Prague: František Borový–Čin, 1935); translated by Round with *Hovory s T. G. Masarykem I* and *Hovory s T. G. Masarykem II* as *President Masaryk Tells His Story, Recounted by Karel Čapek* (London: Allen & Unwin, 1934; New York: Putnam, 1935);

Mlčení s T. G. Masarykem (Prague: František Borový, 1935);

Tři články o vlastenectví (Prague: František Borový, 1935);

Válka s mloky (Prague: František Borový, 1936); translated by M. and R. Weatherall as *War with the Newts* (London: Allen & Unwin, 1937; New York: Putnam, 1937); translated by Ewald Osers (London & Boston: Unwin, 1985);

Cesta na sever. Pro větší názornost provázena obrázky autorovými a básněmi jeho ženy (Brno: Lidové noviny, 1936); translated by M. and R. Weatherall as *Travels in the North: Exemplified by the Author's Own Drawings* (London: Allen & Unwin, 1939; New York: Macmillan, 1939);

Poster for the National Theatre premiere of Čapek's famous futuristic play, in which he coined the term "robot"

Bílá nemoc. Drama o třech aktech ve 14 obrazech (Prague: František Borový, 1937); translated by Selver and Ralph Neale as *Power and Glory: A Drama in Three Acts* (London: Allen & Unwin, 1938); translated by Michael Heim as *The White Plague, Cross Currents,* 7 (1988): 431–504;

Jak se dělají noviny (Brno: Knihovna Lidových novin, 1937);

První parta (Brno: Lidové noviny, 1937); translated by M. and R. Weatherall as *The First Rescue Party* (London: Allen & Unwin, 1939; New York: Macmillan, 1940);

Matka. Hra o třech dějstvích (Prague: František Borový, 1938); translated by Selver as *The Mother: A Play in Three Acts* (London: Allen & Unwin, 1939);

Jak se co dělá (Prague: František Borový, 1938);

Život a dílo skladatele Foltýna (Brno: Lidové noviny, 1939); translated by M. and R. Weatherall as *The Cheat: A Novel* (London: Allen & Unwin, 1941);

Měl jsem psa a kočku, volume 44 of *Spisy bratří Čapků,* edited by Halík (Prague: František Borový, 1939); translated by M. and R. Weatherall as *I Had a Dog and a Cat* (London: Allen & Unwin, 1940; New York: Macmillan, 1941);

Kalendář. Jak je rok dlouhý, volume 45 of *Spisy bratří Čapků*, edited by Halík (Prague: František Borový, 1940);

O lidech, volume 46 of *Spisy bratří Čapků*, edited by Halík (Prague: František Borový, 1940);

Bajky a podpovídky, volume 49 of *Spisy bratří Čapků*, edited by Halík (Prague: František Borový, 1946);

Vzrušené tance, edited by Halík (Prague: František Borový, 1946);

Ratolest a vavřín, volume 51 of *Spisy bratří Čapků*, edited by Halík (Prague: František Borový, 1947);

Obrázky z domova, edited by Halík (Prague: Československý spisovatel, 1953);

Věci kolem nás. S kresbami a fotografiemi Karla Čapka a s obrázky Josefa Čapka, volume of *Dílo bratří Čapků*, edited by Halík (Prague: Československý spisovatel, 1954);

Sloupkový ambit, volume of *Dílo bratří Čapků*, edited by Halík (Prague: Československý spisovatel, 1957);

Juvenilie, in *Krakonošova Zahrada. Zářivé hlubiny a jiné prózy. Juvenilie*, volume of *Dílo bratří Čapků*, edited by Halík (Prague: Československý spisovatel, 1957);

Poznámky o tvorbě, edited by Halík (Prague: Československý spisovatel, 1959);

Na břehu dnů, edited by Halík (Prague: Československý spisovatel, 1966);

Divadelníkem proti své vůli. Recenze, stati, kresby, fotografie, edited by Halík (Prague: Orbis, 1968);

Čtení o T. G. Masarykovi, edited by Halík (Prague: Melantrich, 1969);

V zajetí slov. Kritika slov a úsloví, edited by Halík (Prague: Svoboda, 1969);

Místo pro Jonathana! Úvahy a glosy k otázkám veřejného života z let 1921–1937, edited by Halík (Prague: Symposium, 1970);

Pudlenka, edited by Halík (Prague: Albatros, 1970);

Drobty pod stolem doby, edited by Halík (Prague: Československý spisovatel, 1975);

O umění a kultuře, 3 volumes, volumes 17–19 of *Spisy Karla Čapka*, edited by Emanuel Macek, Miloš Pohorský, and Zina Trochová (Prague: Československý spisovatel, 1984–1986);

Od člověka k člověku, 3 volumes, volumes 14–16 of *Spisy Karla Čapka*, edited by Milada Chlíbcová, Macek, and Pohorský (Prague: Československý spisovatel, 1988–1991);

Filmová libreta, by Čapek and Josef Čapek, edited by Jiří Pavel Taussig (Prague: Odeon, 1989).

Editions and Collections: *Spisy bratří Čapků*, by Čapek and Josef Čapek, 50 volumes, edited

from 1939 by Miroslav Halík (Prague: Aventinum, 1928–1932; Prague: František Borový, 1932–1947);

Dílo bratří Čapků, by Čapek and Josef Čapek, 20 volumes, edited by Halík (Prague: Československý spisovatel, 1954–1971);

Cesty Evropou. S doprovodem autorových kreseb (Prague: Mladá fronta, 1955);

Výbor z díla Karla Čapka, 5 volumes, edited by Halík (Prague: Československý spisovatel, 1958);

Výbor z díla Karla Čapka, 10 volumes, edited by Halík (Prague: Československý spisovatel, 1972–1975);

Spisy Karla Čapka, 25 volumes, edited by Marta Dandová, Milada Chlíbcová, Emanuel Macek, Miloš Pohorský, Rudolf Skřeček, Zina Trochová, and Jarmila Víšková (Prague: Československý [later Český] spisovatel, 1980–1995);

Univerzitní studie, edited by Miloš Pohorský (Prague: Československý spisovatel, 1987).

Editions in English: *How a Play Is Produced*, by Čapek and Josef Čapek, translated by P. Beaumont Wadsworth (London: G. Bles, 1928);

"The Fathers," selected and translated by Paul Selver, in *An Anthology of Czechoslovak Literature* (London: Kegan Paul, Trench, Trübner, 1929), pp. 285–292;

Tales from Two Pockets, translated by Selver (London: Faber & Faber, 1932; New York: Macmillan, 1943);

Masaryk on Thought and Life: Conversations with Karel Čapek, translated by M. and R. Weatherall (London: Allen & Unwin, 1938);

"On Literature," translated by Dora Round, in *Heart of Europe: An Anthology of Creative Writing in Europe 1920–1940*, edited by Klaus Mann and Hermann Kesten (New York: Fischer, 1943), pp. 496–498;

How They Do It, translated by M. and R. Weatherall (London: Allen & Unwin, 1945);

"Masaryk Tells the Story of His Boyhood," translated by Round, and "T. G. M. Speaks—And Is Silent," translated by Fern Long, in *Hundred Towers: A Czechoslovak Anthology of Creative Writing*, edited by F. C. Weiskopf (New York: Fischer, 1945), pp. 210–227;

Three Novels: Hordubal, An Ordinary Life, Meteor, translated by M. and R. Weatherall (London: Allen & Unwin, 1948; New York: A. A. Wyn, 1948);

R.U.R. and The Insect Play, by Čapek and Josef Čapek, translated by Selver (London: Oxford University Press, 1961);

"Pseudo Lot or Patriotism" and "The Decline of an Era," translated by J. R. Edwards, in *The Linden*

Tree: An Anthology of Czech and Slovak Literature 1890–1960, edited by Mojmír Otruba and Zdeněk Pešat (Prague: Artia, 1962), pp. 197–206;

President Masaryk Tells His Story, translated by M. and R. Weatherall (New York: Arno, 1971);

Toward the Radical Center: A Karel Čapek Reader, with new translations by Norma Comrada and others of *R.U.R.*, *The Makropulos Secret*, *The Mother*, and *The Insect Comedy*, edited by Peter Kussi (Highland Park, N.J.: Catbird Press, 1990);

A Long Cat Tale, by Čapek and Josef Čapek, translated by Milena Jandová (Prague: Albatros, 1996);

A Doggy Tale and Two Tales on Top, by Čapek and Josef Čapek, translated by Norah Hronková (Prague: Albatros, 1997);

The Bird's Tale and Two Tales on Top, by Čapek and Josef Čapek, translated by Lucy Doležalová (Prague: Albatros, 1999);

Fairytales, by Čapek and Josef Čapek, translated by Doležalová (Prague: Albatros, 1999).

PLAY PRODUCTIONS: *Loupežník*, Prague, Národní divadlo, 2 March 1920;

R.U.R. (Rossum's Universal Robots), Prague, Národní divadlo, 25 January 1921;

Lásky hra osudná, by Čapek and Josef Čapek, Prague, Volné jeviště, 1 June 1921;

Ze života hmyzu, by Čapek and Josef Čapek, Prague, Národní divadlo, 8 April 1922;

Věc Makropulos, Prague, Městské divadlo na Král. Vinohradech, 21 November 1922;

Adam Stvořitel, by Čapek and Josef Čapek, Prague, Národní divadlo, 12 April 1927;

Bílá nemoc, Prague, Stavovské divadlo, 29 January 1937;

Matka, Prague, Stavovské divadlo, 12 February 1938.

OTHER: *Nůše pohádek*, 3 volumes, edited by Čapek (Prague: Pražské akciové tiskárny, 1918–1920);

Guillaume Apollinaire, *Pásmo a jiné verše*, translated by Čapek (Prague: František Borový, 1919);

Francouzská poezie nové doby, translated by Čapek (Prague: František Borový, 1920; expanded, 1936);

Molière, *Sganarelle*, translated by Čapek and Otokar Fischer (Prague: B. M. Klika, 1922);

Francouzská poezie a jiné překlady, translated by Čapek, edited by Miroslav Halík (Prague:

Státní nakladatelství krásné literatury, hudby a umění, 1957).

Karel Čapek is regarded as the most important Czech writer before World War II. He worked in many capacities: he was a man of the theater, a translator, a journalist, an essayist, a fiction writer, and an organizer of cultural activities. His views inclined toward tolerant democracy and practical humanism, and he subscribed to the ideology of the first Czechoslovak Republic (1918–1938) and to the views of its first president, Tomáš Garrigue Masaryk.

Karel Čapek was born in Malé Svatoňovice, near Turnov in northeastern Bohemia. His father, Antonín Čapek, was a doctor who came from a family of farmers. His mother, Božena Čapek, collected folklore. The Čapek children were all artistically gifted: Karel's sister, Helena, published several books, and his brother, Josef, was a well-known artist, fiction writer, and dramatist. Karel and Josef wrote several stories and plays together.

As a child Čapek began showing a talent for science and art. From 1901 to 1905 he attended the grammar school at Hradec Králové, where he was an excellent pupil; however, he had to leave, apparently because it was discovered that he was a member of a secret anarchic society. He continued his schooling in Brno and Prague, finishing school in 1909. His first literary works were poems published in the weekly newspaper *Neděle* (Sunday) in Brno as early as 1904, although later he rarely wrote poetry. After 1909 he was publishing essays, short literary articles, and other works with his brother in reviews such as *Horkého týdeník* (Horký's Weekly), *Stopa* (Footprints), *Moravskoslezská revue* (Review for Moravia and Silesia), *Kopřivy* (Nettles), and *Přehled* (Overview). Between 1909 and 1915 he was a student at Charles University in Prague, where he studied philosophy and aesthetics as well as French, German, and English philology. For eight months during 1910–1911 he took time off to visit the Universities of Berlin and Paris, the latter with Josef. While they were in Paris they both became familiar with avant-garde art, particularly cubism and futurism, and after they returned home, they were instrumental in making these forms more widely known. In 1911, with other young artists, they founded the Society of Painters and Artists, which published a magazine titled *Umělecký měsíčník* (Art Monthly). In 1913 they organized the *Almanach na rok 1914* (Almanac for the Year 1914). During this period, between 1908 and 1912, the short pieces that

Čapek with Tomáš Garrigue Masaryk, the first president of Czechoslovakia. Čapek wrote several books about Masaryk's life and ideas.

comprise *Krakonošova zahrada* (Krakonoš's Garden) were published in magazines. (The collection did not appear in book form until 1918.) Other works from the same period were *Zářivé hlubiny a jiné prózy* (Shining Depths and Other Stories, 1916) and the first version of the play *Loupežník* (The Robber), originally a combined effort from 1911. Čapek's definitive text of Loupežník was published in 1920, the same year that the first performance took place at the Národní divadlo (National Theatre) in Prague. These works are entertaining, erotic, and challenging to older literary traditions.

These avant-garde efforts were interrupted by World War I. Admiration for technologically advancing civilization alternated with distrust of the dangerous powers of technology, the unheeding egoism of the capitalist world, and revolutionary, violent ideologies, especially communism and later fascism, that attempted to establish a new world order and a new kind of man. During the war Čapek began to show signs of spondylitis, a serious disease of the spine that was initially diagnosed as terminal and that affected him for many years. Thus, in his work he began to explore man's inner nature and other epistemological and metaphysical questions, as he did in the important collection of stories *Boží muka* (Wayside Crosses, 1917). These stories always start out

with a mystery that cannot be explained rationally—for instance, a solitary footprint in the snow or the disappearance of a young girl. Such mysteries lead the heroes toward a search for the truth, which transcends everyday experience. His philosophy was inspired by Anglo-American pragmatism, which he discussed in *Pragmatismus čili filosofie praktického života* (Pragmatism: A Philosophy of Practical Life, 1918). This philosophy had its roots in tolerance and humanism, which he actively promulgated in his writings and in his positive work ethic.

During the war Čapek helped to edit an anthology of modern French poetry, which was intended to demonstrate cultural and political support for the Allies against hated Austria and Germany. The anthology was not published in its entirety; after the war, however, Čapek's translations of modern French poets from Charles Baudelaire to Guillaume Apollinaire were published independently in 1919 and 1920. These translations had a revolutionary impact—their dynamic evocations of times and places and their linguistic style inspired the postwar generation of Czech avant-garde poets, including Jaroslav Seifert, Vítězslav Nezval, and Konstantin Biebl.

Čapek had finished his studies in 1915 with his doctoral dissertation, "Objektivní metoda v estetice se zřením k výtvarnému umění" (The Objective

Method in Aesthetics with Regard to the Fine Arts). His university teachers expected him to apply for a postdoctoral teaching position and devote himself to an academic career, but he decided otherwise. First he became a tutor in the household of a nobleman, Count Vladimír Lažanský, and in the autumn of 1917 he turned to journalism. He worked first with the paper *Národní listy* (The National Newspaper). After the establishment of Czechoslovakia, *Národní listy* became conservative and nationalistic, attacking President Masaryk; in the spring of 1921 Čapek moved to the liberal democratic paper *Lidové noviny* (The People's Paper), for which he wrote hundreds of articles, literary columns, and essays, mostly on cultural, political, or controversial subjects. The resourceful Čapek was well-suited to the profession of journalism. Under its influence, his fiction moved away from avant-garde exclusivism and became more widely accessible and intelligible: his subjects were more attractive, and he used colloquial language.

In the 1920s Čapek, at the height of his creative powers, began to win world fame as a dramatist. His most renowned work was the fantasy play *R.U.R. (Rossum's Universal Robots)*, published in 1920 and first performed in January 1921 as an amateur production. A few days later it was performed in the National Theatre. In the same year it was performed in Germany, and in 1922 there were productions in Warsaw, Belgrade, and New York; by then it had been translated into thirty languages. Čapek was the first to use the word "robot" (from the Czech word *robota*, meaning labor or drudgery) to mean an artificially constructed being, similar to a man but devoid of any kind of creativity or feeling. In *R.U.R.* the robots, basically modern slaves, increase in numbers throughout the world and gradually take over all human tasks. Meanwhile, however, because they are condemned to inactivity, humans become sterile and lose their natural position in the world. Finally the robots rise in revolt, slaughter the human beings, and seize power. This turn of events seems to seal the fate of humanity, for the robots are not capable of reproduction. In the end, however, human feelings of love and self-sacrifice appear unexpectedly among the robots, and the play ends on a note of hope for the future.

Čapek here examines the themes of rationality and emotionality or intuitiveness in man. He also compares and contrasts certain typical "male" and "female" attitudes and finds both wanting. He warns that man's mind may not be mature enough to deal with his modern technological inventions that have far-reaching repercussions. Čapek expresses horror that such inventions might be misused by market forces and primitive mob behavior, with catastrophic consequences.

Čapek based other works on the concept of similar fantastic catastrophes, notably the novels *Továrna na absolutno* (1922; translated as *The Absolute at Large*, 1927) and *Krakatit* (1924; translated as *Krakatit*, 1925; also translated as *An Atomic Phantasy*, 1948). In *Krakatit* young engineer Prokop invents an explosive capable of destroying the world. Only when his discovery is misused does he realize his responsibility. At the same time, he falls in love with more than one woman, with a similarly explosive force. In this novel Čapek brilliantly foresaw the possibility of a nuclear disaster and symbolized his love affairs with two women: Věra Hrůzová, a professor's daughter, and Olga Scheinpflugová, an actress and writer who became Čapek's wife in 1935. *Krakatit* was made into a motion picture by the Czech director Otakar Vávra in 1947. Two works in a similar vein are the play *Věc Makropulos* (1922; translated as *The Makropulos Secret*, 1925) and *Adam Stvořitel* (1927; translated as *Adam the Creator*, 1929), the latter written in collaboration with his brother. *Věc Makropulos* was first performed in 1922. It deals with the possible immortality of man and inspired Leoš Janáček's world-famous opera of the same title in 1926. *Adam Stvořitel* is about the destruction of the "old" world and the emergence of "new" man.

With these works Čapek became a pioneer of science fiction in literature. The attractive fantasy worlds of his plays did not lead the author into sensationalism; he used them to pose universal human and moral questions. Čapek puts a high value on "everyday normality" and on an approach to life that is unpretentious and constructive. At the same time he satirizes messianic communism, anarchism, and Czech public and political life. Capitalist exploitation and militarism are the main targets of satire in the moral allegory *Ze života hmyzu* (1921; translated as *"And so* ad infinitum*" (The Life of the Insects.)*, 1923; also published as *The Life of the Insects*, 1946, and *The Insect Play*, 1961), written with his brother and first performed in 1922.

In the 1920s Čapek also published several smaller pieces, often on the borderline between literature and journalism. His travel books achieved great popularity. His travels in Italy from March to June 1923 resulted in *Italské listy* (1923; translated as *Letters from Italy*, 1929). He was in Britain from May to July 1924, and as a guest of the London PEN Club he met such writers as John Galsworthy, H. G. Wells, George Bernard Shaw, and G. K. Chesterton. *Anglické listy* (translated as *Letters from England*, 1925) came out later that year. In September 1929 Čapek was in Spain, and *Výlet do Španěl* (translated as *Letters from Spain*, 1931) was published in 1930.

Another theme that interested Čapek—nature and man's place in it—dominates the popular *Zahradníkův rok* (1929; translated as *The Gardener's Year*, 1931) and the posthumously published *Měl jsem psa a kočku* (1939; translated as *I Had a Dog and a Cat*, 1940). Čapek also made a bold foray into the crime and detective story genre in *Povídky z jedné kapsy* (Tales from One Pocket) and *Povídky z druhé kapsy* (Tales from the Other Pocket), originally published in 1929 and translated as *Tales from Two Pockets* in 1932. Most of the stories in the two books were made into Czech motion pictures after World War II. In addition, he wrote fairy tales—*Devatero pohádek a ještě jedna od Josefa Čapka jako přívažek* (1932; translated as *Fairy Tales, with One Extra as a Makeweight by Joseph Čapek*, 1933)—and created Czech apocryphal tales in which, in the style of the Apocrypha, he took a humorous look at famous mythical and historical personages. His collection *Apokryfy* (1932) was posthumously republished as *Kniha apokryfů* (1945; translated as *Apocryphal Stories*, 1949). In all of these works Čapek followed stylistic and semantic principles similar to those in his fantasy works.

When the state of Czechoslovakia was established, Čapek was deeply involved from the beginning in public and cultural life. Between 1921 and 1924 he was producer and repertory adviser for the Vinohrady Theatre in Prague. He was one of the founders and the first president of the Czech PEN Club, representing it at the world forum. In his flat in Prague he organized gatherings of "The Friday Club," a kind of debating society for intellectuals of all political affiliations; even President Masaryk, whom Čapek admired and whose views he promulgated, attended these debates. As a result of his association with President Masaryk, Čapek wrote *Hovory s T. G. Masarykem* (published in three volumes between 1928 and 1935; translated as *President Masaryk Tells His Story*) and its continuation, *Mlčení s T. G. Masarykem* (The Silences of T. G. Masaryk, 1935), exploring Masaryk's life and setting out his philosophical and political ideas.

Čapek's literary work reached its peak with the novels *Hordubal* (1933; translated as *Hordubal*, 1934), *Povětroň* (1934; translated as *Meteor*, 1935), and *Obyčejný život* (1934; translated as *An Ordinary Life*, 1936). *Hordubal* was freely adapted for the screen by the Czech director Martin Frič in 1938 and again made into a motion picture by the Czech director Jaroslav Balík in 1980. The novels form a loose trilogy concerned with epistemological and moral questions. *Hordubal* is the story of a man from the country who returns home to his family after years spent in America; he seeks love and his former way of life, but he is murdered by his wife's lover. *Povětroň* offers three possible interpretations of the identity of an unknown flier who crashes and dies. Once again, reality is shown as ambiguous, with many levels of meaning. The individual, however, conceals within himself this great variety of possibilities. The narrator of the last part of the trilogy, *Obyčejný život*, finds to his surprise that he is able to live his "ordinary life" in several different ways, not only as a conscientious official and bourgeois but also as a beggar and a man indulging in perversion. For a certain time he is also a poet and even a hero. This many-sidedness of human experience is what makes possible an understanding of the world and other people—one founded on equality, brotherhood, and respect for the diversity of opinions among men.

Defense of democracy based on these principles forms the background to all of Čapek's work between the wars, particularly after 1933 when Czechoslovakia was threatened by Adolf Hitler's Germany. This concern is evident in his journalism—in his series of essays on the position and duty of intellectuals, for example—and in his literary works, in which once again he resorted to fantasy subjects. In the novel *Válka s mloky* (1936; translated as *War with the Newts*, 1937) and in the drama *Bílá nemoc* (published, first performed, and filmed in 1937; translated as *Power and Glory*, 1938), he again envisages a catastrophe for civilization and asks who is responsible for it.

Like the robots in *R.U.R.*, in *Válka s mloky* the newts, originally servants and slaves, take over the Earth through the fault of the people and their desire for profits and power; the newts gradually liquidate mankind. Deeply influenced by Čapek's journalistic experiences, *Válka s mloky* is a bitter account of contemporary international politics and business practices ruled by shortsightedness, egotism, and greed. For example, while the newts are waging a war against several human nations, other human nations are selling them supplies and arms.

Bílá nemoc deals with a pandemic of an incurable, infectious disease that strikes down older people. The play is set in a large country led by a fanatical marshal, who is preparing the nation for an aggressive war. His counterpart is Galén, a doctor who has found a cure for the disease but will release it only if the marshal promises peace. The war has already started, however. The marshal, now also struck by the disease, calls Galén to sue for peace, but a fanatical, warlike crowd of the marshal's supporters kills Galén in front of the leader's palace. The disease can be seen as a metaphor for the affliction of totalitarianism and collaboration with brute offical power.

In these works Čapek's criticism is more explicit than in his writings of the 1920s. In the character of the leader of the newts and in the marshal in *Bílá nemoc* readers recognize characteristics of Hitler. Čapek is also more pessimistic than in his earlier writing; both works finish without any hope of a solution.

By the Munich Agreement in the autumn of 1938 France and Britain agreed to German occupation of Czech border territories. Čapek was bitterly disappointed at the capitulation of the democratic world. The first republic of Czechoslovakia, with which he had been in close sympathy ideologically, had collapsed. This fact, and also the unscrupulous attacks of the semifascist Czech press after the Munich Agreement, hastened his death. He died in Prague on 25 December 1938 after a short illness. After the German occupation in 1939 his brother, Josef, was deported to a concentration camp, where he died in April 1945.

During the German occupation and again after the communist takeover of 1948 Karel Čapek was one of the authors who were seldom published and still less respected. The democratic values he defended were at odds with the totalitarian regimes of fascism and communism. Things changed slightly after the publication of Sergei V. Nikolski's Soviet study, in which he interpreted Čapek as a friend of the Soviet Union and a writer who came near to being communist in the 1930s. This perspective made it possible to publish Čapek's books more widely, with the omission of some parts, but to a certain extent it also misrepresented his ideas and work. It was not until after 1989, with the fall of the Communist regime in Czechoslovakia and in Eastern Europe as a whole, that change came and his work could be published without distortion.

Čapek's grave, with a monument designed by his brother, Josef, in the Vyšehrad cemetery, Prague

Letters:

V. Dyk, St. K. Neumann, bratří Čapkové. Korespondence z let 1905–1918, edited by Milan Blahynka, Stanislava Jarošová, and František Všetička (Prague: Nakladatelství Československé akademie věd, 1962);

Listy Olze. Korespondence z let 1920–1938, edited by Miroslav Halík (Prague: Československý spisovatel, 1971);

Listy Anielce, edited by Tomáš Halík (Prague: Supraphon, 1978);

Karel Čapek Věře Hrůzové: Dopisy ze zásuvky, edited by Jiří Opelík (Prague: Melantrich, 1980);

Dopisy z mládí, edited by Opelík, T. Halík, and Jaroslav Slavík (Prague: Společnost bratří Čapků, 1982);

Cesty k přátelství, by Čapek and Fráňa Šrámek, edited by Aleš Fetters (Prague: Československý spisovatel, 1987);

Korespondence, 2 volumes, edited by Marta Dandová, volumes 22–23 of *Spisy Karla Čapka* (Prague: Český spisovatel, 1993).

Bibliographies:

Jiří Opelík, ed., *Miroslav Halík: Karel Čapek. Život a dílo v datech* (Prague: Academia, 1983);

Boris Mědílek, ed., *Bibliografie Karla Čapka* (Prague: Academia, 1990);

Margita Křepinská and Natasha Glazkova, eds., *Karel Čapek. Bibliografie díla a literatury o životě a díle*, 4 volumes (Prague: Slovanská knihovna, 1990).

Biographies:

Helena Koželuhová, *Čapci očima rodiny*, 3 volumes (Hamburg: Sklizeň, 1961–1962); third edition, edited by Jaromír Slomek (Prague: B. Just, 1995);

Helena Čapková, *Moji milí bratři* (Prague: Československý spisovatel, 1962); third expanded edition, edited by Eduard Martin (1986);

Marie Šulcová, *Kruh mého času* (Plzeň: Západočeské nakladatelství, 1975);

Otokar Vočadlo, *Anglické listy Karla Čapka* (Prague: Academia, 1975);

Karel Čapek v vospominaniyach sovremennikov, edited by Oleg Malevich (Moscow, 1983);

Šulcová, *Čapci* (Prague: Melantrich, 1985);

Eckhard Thiele, *Karel Čapek* (Leipzig: Reclam, 1988);

Olga Scheinpflugová, *Byla jsem na světě* (Prague: Mladá fronta, 1988);

Ladislav Vacina, ed., *Jeden i druhý* (Hradec Králové: Kruh, 1988);

Karel Scheinpflug, *Můj švagr Karel Čapek*, edited by Jiří Opelík (Hradec Králové: Kruh, 1991);

Šulcová, *Poločas nadějí* (Prague: Melantrich, 1993);

Šulková, *Brána Věčnosti* (Prague: Melantrich, 1997).

References:

I. A. Bernštejn, *Karel Čapek* (Moscow, 1969);

Bohuslava R. Bradbrook, *Karel Čapek: In Pursuit of Truth, Tolerance, and Trust* (Brighton, U.K.: Sussex Academic Press, 1998);

Josef Branžovský, *Karel Čapek, světový názor a umění* (Prague: Nakladatelství politické literatury, 1963);

František Buriánek, *Čapkovské variace* (Prague: Československý spisovatel, 1984);

Buriánek, *Karel Čapek* (Prague: Československý spisovatel, 1988);

Buriánek, ed., *Krajem bratří Čapků* (Prague, 1983);

Čapek (Brussels: Université libre de Bruxelles, 1995);

Václav Černý, "Dialog F. X. Šalda – K. Č.," in his *Tvorba a osobnost I*, edited by Jan Šulc (Prague: Odeon, 1992), pp. 177–188;

Černý, *Karel Čapek* (Prague: František Borový, 1936);

František Daneš and Světlana Čmejrková, eds., *O Čapkových Hovorech s TGM* (Prague: Academia, 1994);

Sergei Davydov, "Tales from One Pocket. Detective and Justice Stories of Karel Čapek," in *The Structure of the Literary Process*, edited by Peter Steiner, Miroslav Červenka, and Ronald Vroon (Amsterdam: J. Benjamins, 1982), pp. 96–107;

Lájos Dobossy, *Karel Čapek* (Budapest, 1961);

Lubomír Doležel, "Karel Čapek and Vladislav Vančura," in his *Narrative Modes in Czech Literature* (Toronto: University of Toronto Press, 1973), pp. 53–65;

Tomáš Halík, ed., *Karel Čapek ve fotografii* (Prague: Panorama, 1981);

Aleš Haman, "K souřadnicím Čapkova díla," *Literární archív*, 24 (1990): 9–22;

William E. Harkins, "Karel Čapek," in *Anthology of Czech Literature*, edited by Harkins (New York: Columbia University Press, 1953), pp. 177–190;

Harkins, *Karel Čapek* (New York & London: Columbia University Press, 1962);

Jiří Holý, "Čapkova Bílá nemoc," *Literární archív*, 24 (1990): 129–135;

Halina Janaszek-Ivaničkowa, *Karel Čapek czyli Dramat humanisty* (Warsaw, 1962);

Alena Jonáková, "Karel Čapek a avantgarda," *Literární archív*, 24 (1990): 137–157;

Ivan Klíma, *Karel Čapek* (Prague: Československý spisovatel, 1962; second expanded edition, 1965);

Zdeněk Kožmín, *Zvětšeniny ze stylu bratří Čapků* (Brno: Blok, 1989);

Oldřich Králík, *První řada v díle Karla Čapka* (Ostrava: Profil, 1972);

Viktor Kudělka, *Boje o Karla Čapka* (Prague: Academia, 1987);

Lennart Löngren and Karel Šebesta, eds., *Karel Čapek. Bidgrad till ett symposium hüllet i Uppsala 5. April 1990* (Uppsala, Sweden: Uppsala University, 1991);

Michael Makin and Jindřich Toman, eds., *On Karel Čapek: A Michigan Slavic Colloquium* (Ann Arbor: Michigan Slavic Publications, 1992);

Oleg Malevich, *Karel Čapek* (Moscow: Khudozhestvennaia literatura, 1968; second expanded edition, 1989);

Alexander Matuška, *Človek proti skáze* (Bratislava: Slovenský spisovateľ, 1963); published in Czech as *Člověk proti zkáze* (Prague: Československý spisovatel, 1963); published in English as *Karel Čapek: Man against Destruction* (Prague: Artia, 1964);

Jan Mukařovský, "Karel Čapek's Prose as Lyrical Melody and as a Dialogue," in *A Prague School Reader on Esthetics, Literary Structure and Style*, edited by Paul L. Garvin (Washington, D.C.: Georgetown University Press, 1964), pp. 133–149;

Mukařovský, "Vývoj Čapkovy prózy," in his *Kapitoly z české poetiky*, volume 2 (Prague: Svoboda, 1948), pp. 325–356;

Mukařovský, "Významová výstavba a kompoziční osnova epiky Karla Čapka," in his *Kapitoly z české poetiky*, pp. 374–402;

Zdeněk Němeček, "Karel Čapek," in *World Literatures* (Pittsburgh, Pa.: University of Pittsburgh Press, 1956), pp. 53–65;

Sergei V. Nikolski, "Karel Čapek," in *K. Čapek, Izbrannoe* (Moscow: Goslitizdat, 1950), pp. 3–16; published in Czech as *Karel Čapek* (Prague: Československý spisovatel, 1952);

Nikolski, *Karel Čapek–fantast i satirik* (Moscow: Nauka, 1973); published in Czech as *Fantastika a satira v díle Karla Čapka* (Prague: Československý spisovatel, 1978);

Jiří Opelík, "Filmové texty bratří Čapků jako součást jejich díla literárního," in *K. a J. Čapkové, Filmová libreta*, edited by Opelík and Pavel Taussig (Prague: Odeon, 1989), pp. 211–235;

Opelík, "Obyčejný život čili Deukalion," in *Struktura a smysl literárního díla*, edited by Milan Jankovič, Zdeněk Pešat, and Felix Vodička (Prague: Československý spisovatel, 1966), pp. 143–159;

Opelík, ed., *Karel Čapek ve fotografii* (Prague: Středočeské nakladatelství a knihkupectví, 1991);

Ludvik Patera and Dobrava Moldanová, eds., *Karel Čapek 1988* (Prague: Univerzita Karlova, 1989);

František Štícha, ed., *Karel Čapek a český jazyk* (Prague: Karolinum, 1990);

Eva Strohsová, "Román pro služky a Čapkovo směřování k epičnosti," in *Struktura a smysl literárního díla*, pp. 126–142;

Darko Suvin, "Karel Čapek, or the Aliens Among Us," in his *Metamorphoses of Science Fiction: On the Poetics and History of a Literary Genre* (New Haven: Yale University Press, 1979), pp. 270–283;

Alfred Thomas, "Humanism and Relativism in Karel Čapek's *Kniha apokryfů*," in his *The Labyrinth of the Word* (Munich: R. Oldenbourg), pp. 116–131;

Veličko Todorov, *Svetovniat Čech Kniga za Karel Čapek* (Sofia: Universitetsko izdatelstvo, 1990);

Jindřich Toman, "If I Were a Linguist . . . Karel Čapek and/vs. the Prague Linguistic Circle," in *For Henry Kučera. Studies in Slavic Philology and Computational Linguistics* (1992): pp. 365–380;

Ladislav Vacina, ed., *Karel Čapek. Sborník příspěvků z Národní konference k 100. výročí autorova narození* (Hradec Králové: Státní vědecká knihovna, 1990);

Štěpán Vlašín, ed., *Kniha o Čapkovi* (Prague: Československý spisovatel, 1988);

René Wellek, "Karel Čapek," in his *Essays on Czech Literature* (The Hague: Mouton, 1963), pp. 46–61.

Maria Dąbrowska

(6 October 1889 – 19 May 1965)

Bożena Karwowska
University of British Columbia

BOOKS: *Finlandia, wzorowy kraj kooperacji* (Warsaw: Towarzystwo Kooperatystów, 1913);

Kooperatywy na wsi belgijskiej (Warsaw: Towarzystwo Kooperatystów, 1913);

Powstanie 1863: Powitanie wojny i swobody (Warsaw: Uniwersytet Ludowy, 1916);

Dzieci ojczyzny (Warsaw: J. Mortkowicz, 1918);

O wykonaniu reformy rolnej. Objaśnienie ustawy z d. 15 lipca 1920 r. wraz z urzędowym tekstem ustawy i przepisów wykonawczych (Warsaw: Skł. w Księg Rolniczej, 1921);

O zjednoczonej Polsce, jej mieszkańcach i gospodarstwie, second edition (Warsaw: Towarzystwo Wydawnicze w Warszawie, 1921);

Gałąź czereśni i inne nowele (Warsaw: Związek Polskich Stowarzyszeń Spożywców, 1922);

Uśmiech dzieciństwa. Wspomnienia (Warsaw: Towarzystwo Wydawnicze, 1923);

Życie i dzieło Edwarda Abramowskiego (Warsaw: Wydawn. Związku Pol. Stow. Spożywców, 1925);

Ludzie stamtąd. Cykl opowieści (Warsaw: J. Mortkowicz, 1926);

Marcin Kozera (Warsaw: J. Mortkowicz, 1927);

U północnych sąsiadów (Warsaw: Wydawnictwo dzieł literatury europejskiej, 1929);

Noce i dnie, 6 volumes (Warsaw: J. Mortkowicz, 1932–1934)—comprises *Bogumił i Barbara* (1932); *Wieczne zmartwienie* (1932); *Miłość,* 2 volumes (1933); and *Wiatr w oczy,* 2 volumes (1934);

Rozdroże. Studium na temat zagadnień wiejskich (Warsaw: J. Mortkowicz, 1937);

Moja odpowiedź. Refleksje nad polemiką z "Rozdrożem" (Warsaw: J. Mortkowicz, 1938);

Ręce w uścisku. Rzecz o spółdzielczości (Warsaw: J. Mortkowicz, 1938);

Znaki życia. Pięć opowiadań (Warsaw: J. Mortkowicz, 1938);

Geniusz sierocy. Dramat wysnuty z dziejów XVII wieku (Warsaw: J. Mortkowicz, 1939);

Stanisław i Bogumił. Dramat wysnuty z dziejów jedenastego wieku (Warsaw: E. Kuthan, 1948);

Gwiazda zaranna. Opowiadania (Warsaw: Czytelnik, 1955);

Czyste serca (Warsaw: Nasza Księgarnia, 1956);

Myśli o sprawach i ludziach (Warsaw: Czytelnik, 1956);

Szkice z podróży (Warsaw: Czytelnik, 1956);

Szkice o Conradzie (Warsaw: Państwowy Instytut Wydawniczy, 1959);

Przygody człowieka myślącego, edited by Ewa Korzeniewska, introduction by Anna Kowalska (Warsaw: Czytelnik, 1970);

Panna Winczewska (Kraków: Wydawnictwo Literackie, 1980);

A teraz wypijmy–Opowiadania, edited by Tadeusz Drewnowski (Warsaw: Czytelnik, 1981);

Dzienniki, 5 volumes, edited by Tadeusz Drewnowski (Warsaw: Czytelnik, 1988);

Aforyzmy, edited by Aleksander Bogdański (Warsaw: Państwowy Instytut Wydawniczy, 1989).

Editions and Collections: *Zdarzenia. Wybór opowiadań* (Warsaw: Nasza Księgarnia, 1956);

Pisma wybrane, 3 volumes (Warsaw: Czytelnik, 1956);

Dramaty: Geniusz sierocy. Stanisław i Bogumił (Warsaw: Państwowy Instytut Wydawniczy, 1957);

Przyjaźń. Marcin Kozera. Wilczęta z czarnego podwórza (Warsaw: Nasza Księgarnia, 1962);

Pisma rozproszone, 2 volumes, edited by Ewa Korzeniewska (Kraków: Wydawnictwo Literackie, 1964);

Opowiadania, edited by Korzeniewska (Warsaw: Czytelnik, 1967);

Domowe progi, edited by Korzeniewska (Warsaw: Czytelnik, 1969);

Dzienniki powojenne: 1945–1965, 4 volumes, edited by Tadeusz Drewnowski (Warsaw: Czytelnik, 1996).

Editions in English: *A Village Wedding, and Other Stories,* translated by Rachel Kuraho (Warsaw: Polonia, 1957);

"Father Philip," translated by Edmund Ordon, in *Ten Contemporary Polish Stories,* edited by Ordon (Detroit: Wayne State University Press, 1958), pp. 3–36;

"A Change Came o'er the Scenes of My Dream," in *Contemporary Polish Short Stories,* selected by Andrzej Kijowski (Warsaw: Polonia Publishing House, 1960), pp. 143–154;

"The Village Wedding" (excerpt), translated by Kuraho, and "A Happy Creature," translated by Celina Wieniewska, in Maria Kuncewicz, ed., *The Modern Polish Mind: An Anthology* (Boston: Little, Brown, 1962), pp. 150–171, 389–400;

"On a Beautiful Summer Morning," in *Introduction to Modern Polish Literature: An Anthology of Fiction and Poetry,* edited by Adam Gillon and Ludwik Krzyżanowski (New York: Twayne, 1964), pp. 150–169.

OTHER: *Pamiętniki młodzieży wiejskiej, 1918–1939,* compiled by Dąbrowska (Warsaw: Państwowe Zakłady Wydawnictw Szkolnych, 1969).

TRANSLATIONS: Jens Peter Jacobsen, *Niels Lyhne* (Warsaw, 1927);

Samuel Pepys, *Dziennik Samuela Pepysa* (Warsaw: Polski Instytut Wydawniczy, 1952; enlarged edition, 1954);

Anton Chekhov, *Utwory wybrane,* 2 volumes, translated by Dąbrowska, Jarosław Iwaszkiewicz, and Jerzy Wyszomirski (Warsaw, 1953).

Maria Dąbrowska is generally regarded in Poland as one of the most prominent Polish prose writers of the twentieth century. She has not, however, gained a similar recognition outside her native country, although her major novel, *Noce i dnie* (Nights and Days, 1932–1934), and many short stories have appeared in translation in several Eastern and Central European languages. Perhaps the main reason for the lack of wider recognition is the fact that much of her work was directed specifically at Polish readers and dealt with typically Polish issues. Dąbrowska regarded her social class as historically the principal creator of national culture and values. She tried to preserve for this class a significant moral and intellectual place in society by becoming a thoughtful and ethically conscious chronicler of its transformations. Yet, she also was aware that to do full justice to the "truth of this complex world" she had "to take of it an artistic measure," and this attitude gives a universal dimension to her best writings.

As a prose writer Dąbrowska consciously tried to adhere to a form of realism, and her literary works have the character of social documents based on personal experience. She was generally opposed to avant-garde experimentation in literature and attempted to create a prose style free of poeticism—although not lacking in poetic quality—and remarkable chiefly for its transparent "naturalness." In this respect she did not follow the example of her immediate predecessors such as Wacław Berent, whose prose was highly stylized, or Stefan Żeromski, whose work was notable for its often excessive lyricism. One of the important aims of her kind of realism (which some critics have called "modernized realism") was to imbue everyday life and ordinary human relations with epic qualities and to celebrate those characters who perform ordinary tasks with dedication to professional and moral values. The main male character of *Noce i dnie,* modeled to a large extent on the author's father, observes: "I'll say that quiet times, when everyone is doing his job, are also historical. You will see that one day someone will write the story of such quiet and industrious times, and that such history will be real history."

Dąbrowska set herself the task of writing the story of her times by depicting characters and actions that were not larger than life and that illustrated the values and complexity of "toiling for toil's sake" (which she took to be one of the main principles of the social ethic of Polish-descended Joseph Conrad's fiction). But dramatic historical events that demanded more than the heroism of everyday life intervened repeatedly during her literary career.

Dąbrowska was born Maria Szumska on 6 October 1889 in Russów, near the ancient city of Kalisz in west-central Poland. Her parents belonged to the impoverished nobility, and their lives were quite typical of their social class, which was gradually being transformed into a socially conscious intelligentsia. Dąbrowska's father, Józef Szumski, took part in the failed January 1863 uprising against Russian rule and had his land confiscated by the tsarist authorities; he subsequently administered various estates, including Russów, and later bought a house in Kalisz. Dąbrowska's mother completed her education in a private school for girls in Kalisz and worked for a few years as a teacher before marrying Szumski. Maria was the eldest child, with two sisters and two brothers. To Dąbrowska's recollection her childhood was happy, and the children were not aware of the problems their parents faced at that time. Their world was limited to the life of the estate—their home, peasant laborers living in Russów, members of the family living nearby, and the owner of the estate, who visited them from time to time. In Russów, Dąbrowska attempted to write her first "literary prose," based on everyday events in her home. In "Jak zostałam pisarzem" (How I Became a Writer), published in *Pisma rozproszone* (Scattered Works, 1964), she recalled, "When I was not even eight years old the flow of an ordinary day in our home appeared to me suddenly as wonderful and well worth preserving . . . and from six in the morning till late evening . . . I used to write down with a pencil the great story of what was happening at our home from dawn to dusk." Family and rural life in Russów was later incorporated into several of Dąbrowska's literary works, especially *Noce i dnie*.

In 1901 Dąbrowska was sent to Kalisz to begin formal education. She spent the next four years in Helena Semadeni's private boarding school for girls, which she later recalled as a good grounding in patriotism and kindness toward others. After completing grade four she had to move to a Russian school, since education in Polish in Kalisz was limited to junior classes only. In 1905 she participated in a school strike directed against the policy of Russification, especially the use of Russian as an exclusive language of instruction. Unable to return to school after the strike, she spent the next few months at home being tutored and then moved to Warsaw to enroll in a private boarding school run by Paulína Hewelke. There she was taught by several outstanding teachers, among them Ignacy Chrzanowski, who later was professor of Polish literature at the Jagiellonian University in Kraków.

After Dąbrowska completed her education in Warsaw, her parents sent her abroad for further studies—first to Lausanne and then to Brussels. Although the cost of education abroad was quite high, Dąbrowska's mother wished to give her children the best possible learning opportunities. At that time, educational facilities in Poland were quite limited, and Polish families often refrained from sending their children to Russian educational institutions for patriotic reasons. Moreover, higher learning opportunities were even more restricted for women, particularly in the field of natural sciences, which Dąbrowska chose to pursue.

During her stay in Belgium, Dąbrowska became involved in the political activity of Polish immigrant circles. Despite her studies in the natural sciences, she became interested primarily in social problems. In Brussels she met Edward Abramowski, a non-Marxist socialist and a sociologist who was a great proponent of the cooperative movement as a way of making the "enslaved classes" free without the use of the coercive power of the state. Abramowski's ideas had a great impact on Dąbrowska; in 1925 she published a highly positive account of his life and philosophy. His work made her an active and life-long supporter of the cooperative movement and helped her to clarify her approach to literature. Abramowski's views of art were part of his theory of personality and of social development. While he rejected such tendencies as didacticism in literature, he believed that literary work should come from the experiences of the author. Because of Abramowski's ideas, from 1925 Dąbrowska rejected purely fictional plots and attempted to provide "the artistic equivalent" of personally experienced life stories and social phenomena. She followed this program with increasing formal awareness until the end of her life.

In Brussels, Dąbrowska also met her future husband, Marian Dąbrowski, who had to flee the Russian sector of Poland after 1905 because of his involvement in the Polish Socialist Party. In exile Dąbrowski was active in socialist circles and the cooperative movement and was involved, through his brother, Józef, in the attempt to revive Freemasonry in Poland. Though Polish Freemasonry, fol-

Dąbrowska (seated) with her brother Bogumil and sisters, Helena and Jadwiga

lowing old Scottish rules, was limited to men only, Dąbrowska found herself inside a circle of friends deeply involved in the activities of this movement and its attempts to influence Polish life along patriotic and ethical lines. The Dąbrowskis were married in 1911, and in the same year Dąbrowska graduated from the university in Brussels with the degree of *candidat en sciences naturelles* and began studying economic and social sciences in the Université Nouvelle, established by the Belgian socialists.

During this time Dąbrowska began to publish articles and reports in various socialist periodicals in Poland; in 1911 she published some twenty-five articles. As the scholar Zbigniew Folejewski noted, "she gradually developed from an occasional correspondent to Polish periodicals into an accomplished writer, critic, and translator. It was thus she experienced the same literary apprenticeship as her great predecessors in Polish literature, Henryk Sienkiewicz and Bolesław Prus." The journalistic experience helped Dąbrowska to develop her own literary style, a distinctive blend of reality and fiction.

In 1912 Dąbrowska returned to Poland despite the fact that her husband, as a political refugee, could not return with her. She spent most of

the following two years in Warsaw, writing articles on economic, political, and social issues for various newspapers and magazines. She joined her husband briefly in Paris and then in England, where he went on a Cooperative Society fellowship to study the organization of consumer cooperatives. During this time Dąbrowska began to write short stories, and in 1914 the Warsaw weekly *Prawda* (Truth) published "Janek" (Little John), which she regarded as her literary debut.

Dąbrowska spent the World War I years moving from one place to another, writing patriotic pieces for children, working on the editorial board of a pro-independence weekly in Lublin, publishing many articles in a populist journal, taking part in the activities of the *Liga Kobiet* (Women's League), and generally supporting the socialist and populist circles around Józef Piłsudski and his legions. In 1917 Dąbrowska and her husband moved to Warsaw; in 1918 she began working in the Ministry of Agriculture, and a year later she was transferred to the Department of Land Reform, where she worked until 1924. Although in her diary she complained of lack of time to write literary prose, she wrote several short stories based on her early years, some of which were published in 1923 as *Uśmiech dzieciństwa* (The Smile of Childhood), for which she was awarded the Federation of Publishers' Prize in 1925.

Her next strictly literary work, the cycle of short stories *Ludzie stamtąd* (People from Yonder, 1926), although also based on reminiscences from childhood, was artistically and thematically more ambitious. While the stories depict a pattern of rural life that was disappearing because of economic change, the lives of landless peasant laborers (farmhands, night watchmen, shepherds, milkmaids, charwomen) are treated principally as an artistic theme, with a clear focus on the psychology, emotional lives, and value systems of individual characters. The cycle shows a carefully crafted compositional unity and is remarkable for its distinctive style, which blends literary language with the regional dialect spoken by the characters. At the center of the artistic design of the cycle is the search for a convincing articulation of the value and meaning of individual lives that do not amount to much more than working, coping, and experiencing basic human emotions. This goal is achieved not only through psychological insight and vivid delineation of character but also by what the author called "transformation," making the characters occasionally rise above their conceptual limitations. An excellent example of the transformation of dark and complex experience into momentary philosophical clarity occurs in the story titled "Tryumf Dionizego" (The Triumph of Dionysius), in which a milkman finds words that are usually far beyond him in an attempt to console a lonely social outcast called Satan:

> The thing is that when you lose all hope, then for the first time you can see that in reality you have not lost anything, for then the hopes of other people enter your heart. For it is possible to live with what is the property of others. You can lose everything in the world and still have enough left, for your life is in everything . . . in every other human being . . . .
>
> Satan did not listen. And Dionysius went on, silently now, with his thoughts on how joy and sorrow always follow each other. You must experience the one, whether you have any hopes or not, and you cannot escape the other no matter how you try. Your life and your salvation consist of them both.
>
> No use trying to escape from anything. Just live, live with all your power. Even if you don't have anything with which to face catastrophe, meet it with nothing except your courage and your human heart. [quoted in Folejewski]

This interior monologue is brought to an end in a masterly fashion by the intervention of the narrator, who subtly puts this moment of illumination in perspective without undercutting its effect: "Dazzled, he stumbled over a small stone and at once all these thoughts got entangled. He would not be capable of conceiving such thoughts again, not to speak of putting them into words."

Ludzie stamtąd brought Dąbrowska fame and recognition from critics as one of the most interesting and promising writers of her times. The literary success, however, did not bring her happiness; in the same year it was published her husband died, and she experienced a nervous breakdown and serious depression.

Dąbrowska tried to keep herself occupied with various activities, but they distracted her from more serious fiction writing. She continued to write and publish articles on the cooperative movement in various left-wing periodicals, wrote about Conrad and his view of heroism, and translated Danish writer Jens Peter Jacobsen's 1880 novel, *Niels Lyhne*. In 1926 she also took up clerical work, partly for financial reasons and partly to ease her depression, and became more involved in the activities of the Union of Writers and the Polish section of the PEN Club. At the same time, however, she was collecting observations (some of which are recorded in her diary) and reminiscences (including those of her mother, written at Dąbrowska's request) that served as material for her later literary work. Eventually the continuing success of *Ludzie stamtąd* brought Dąbrowska back to literary writing.

In 1927 Dąbrowska made her first attempt at writing a novel. She found the task daunting; she abandoned and resumed the writing several times, trying to move away from the autobiographical form that had become so natural to her. She finally sent the first chapters to the magazine *Kobieta współczesna* (Contemporary Woman) and then felt compelled, despite her dissatisfaction with it, to complete the work, to which she gave the title *Domowe progi* (Home Threshold, 1969). Before the second part of the novel appeared in print, she reworked it thoroughly. By the time the new version appeared, Dąbrowska had already begun work on a third version, which by 1932 became *Bogumił i Barbara*, the first part of *Noce i dnie*. In her novel Dąbrowska depicted the experiences of two generations, using as models her own life as well as the lives of her parents. In fact, all characters in the novel are based on people whom Dąbrowska knew or at least met. The autobiographical and real-life elements, however, are transformed and given artistic shape through a style remarkable for its objectivity, clarity, and conscious "non-literariness" that hides its consummate art and through the use of a complex narrator who, while seldom omniscient, is capable not only of empathy but also of penetrating psychological insight and epic distance. Perhaps the best part of the novel is the study of the relationship of the two major characters, Bogumił and Barbara, whose fairly ordinary married life is imbued with extraordinary interest because of the psychological depth and subtlety of its presentation.

Two further features of *Noce i dnie* contributed to its success: its strong ethical and ideological character and its social dimension. As a follower of Abramowski and a perceptive reader of Conrad, whose moral values she largely regarded as her own, Dąbrowska presented her characters as agents acting within a system of moral values and following or transgressing ethical principles rooted in the experience of generations. The argument of the novel is that the recognition of the simple truths of everyday life and a nonreligious ethical code can help people to find their place in life and be faithful to themselves, to others, and to everyday tasks. At the same time, the main characters are placed in a larger social context against a background of close to 250 minor characters, all of whom face—and are part of—social change within their own class and at large. Because of this broad scope and temporal span *Noce i dnie* is not only a family saga but also a social saga. The entire work appeared in print between 1932 and 1934 and was awarded the 1934 National Literary Prize.

While working on *Noce i dnie* Dąbrowska—according to her diary—wrote several episodes that she did not use in the novel but published as separate short stories. Intense literary work did not, however, keep Dąbrowska away from active involvement in the life of the Polish Union of Writers and the cooperative movement. She took part in inspection tours of establishments organized by the consumers' cooperative *Społem* (Co-ops), traveling extensively and publishing articles on the cooperative movement. In the meantime her personal life had changed; she developed a close relationship with Stanisław Stempowski, a man of deep social commitment and considerable standing in the Freemason circles and among left-wing, populist intellectuals. She could not marry him, however, as he could not bring himself to divorce his wife. Strengthened in her own convictions by his love and friendship, she ventured on several occasions into the political arena, criticizing the persecution of opponents of the governing politico-military circles and deplor-

Marian Dąbrowski, Dąbrowska's husband

ing the spread of anti-Semitism as well as the failure of the landowning class and the political establishment to carry out an extensive land reform.

During this period Dąbrowska also wrote her first dramatic work, *Geniusz sierocy. Dramat wysnuty z dziejów XVII wieku* (The Orphan Genius, 1939), a departure from her usual mode of writing. In this work she went back to historical events and, through the creation of fictional situations, tried to argue for her own vision of history. The idea she wanted to convey focused on the question of talent versus mediocrity and the fact that the latter usually overcomes the former. The drama was scheduled to be performed onstage in Warsaw in 1940; however, the outbreak of World War II intervened.

In September 1939 Dąbrowska and Stempowski left Warsaw for eastern Poland and found themselves under Soviet occupation. Initially they planned to escape abroad but then changed their minds and tried to return illegally to Warsaw. When this course proved impossible, they moved to Brześć and then to Lwów. Dąbrowska had visited Lwów before, so she turned to people she knew there, Stanisława Blumfeldowa and Anna and Jerzy Kowalski, with whom she found refuge. For reasons that still remain unclear the Soviet authorities left Dąbrowska alone despite their largely successful efforts (through intimidation and ideological reeducation) of securing the collaboration of Polish writers and intellectuals in the Sovietization of the occupied territories. Unlike most other Polish writers who found themselves under Soviet rule, Dąbrowska neither participated in the activities of the writers' organization nor published in the communist-controlled press, and she eventually was allowed to return to Warsaw. Dąbrowska's experience of Soviet communism reinforced her attachment to democratic, cooperative forms of socialism, but it may also have made her wary of openly challenging communist methods and doctrine, behind which stood the might of Stalinist Russia.

Dąbrowska spent the period of German occupation mostly in Warsaw. Though she was lecturing in underground educational organizations, she tried to work on a novel and began translating Samuel Pepys's *Diary* (first published in 1825), but the horror of everyday life and the difficulties of making a living brought her to a state of deep depression. After the Warsaw Uprising of August–October 1944, in which she lost a sister and the Poles failed to oust the German army, Dąbrowska found a temporary shelter in Łowicz and in 1945 returned to Warsaw.

Between 1945 and 1955 Dąbrowska was active as a journalist and took part in various activities organized by the official association of writers despite her critical attitude toward the communist regime, Socialist Realism, and ideological censorship. At the same time, she worked on the final version (1954) of her translation of Pepys's *Diary* and translated several of Anton Chekhov's short stories. She also devoted considerable time and care to the writing and rewriting of her own diary, in which she recorded with considerable candor her views of the authorities, of her fellow writers and acquaintances, and of the general situation in Poland as well as many personal observations and details (some quite intimate). She returned to the writing of a novel in which she planned to depict life under the German occupation and the ideological and intellectual predicament of Polish intellectuals faced with the prospect of Soviet Communism. However, she published little of her own work. The first literary work written after the occupation, the short story "W letni poranek" (On a Summer Morning), was published in 1948, and the only longer work by Dąbrowska that appeared during this period was an historical play set in the eleventh century, *Stanisław i Bogumił. Dramat wysnuty z dziejów jedenastego wieku* (Stanislas and Bogumil, 1948).

In 1952 Stempowski died; after his death Dąbrowska prepared for publication his reminiscences and his translation of a volume of Maksim Gorky's writings. In 1954 she moved in with Anna Kowalska, a longtime friend and fellow writer.

With the gradual relaxation of political controls over literature after the death of Jospeh Stalin, Dąbrowska's works began appearing more frequently in various periodicals and in book form. In 1955 a new collection of her short stories, *Gwiazda zaranna* (The Morning Star), was published, and a year later a three-volume selection of her works appeared, followed by a collection of lectures and essays, *Myśli o sprawach i ludziach* (Thoughts on Issues and People, 1956). Interestingly enough, in this late period of her career Dąbrowska began to depict contemporary events and issues in her literary works. Her short story "Na wsi wesele" (translated as "A Village Wedding," 1957) was perceived, in the charged political atmosphere preceding the so-called Polish October period of reform, not only as her intervention in the debate concerning the changes in contemporary peasants' life (such as collectivization) but also as a sign that writers could now try with greater freedom than before to present their own understanding of the socio-economic and political transformations occurring in communist-ruled Poland. Dąbrowska also continued to be active in public life, taking part in various activities of the writers' union and in the peace movement, giving public lectures and readings. After 1955 the first book-length publications devoted to her writing began to appear. She received the State Award for her entire literary oeuvre, and publishers were instructed to pay her top royalties, an advantage reserved for the most highly regarded writers.

Of the short stories published in this period, "Na wsi wesele" is undoubtedly the most substantial and accomplished. In contrast to *Ludzie stamtąd*, in "Na wsi wesele" Dąbrowska is less concerned with individual characters. She constructs her plotless story through encounters, conversations, and thoughts of family members gathered for a wedding in a rural setting at the end of the 1940s, recalling Stanisław Wyspiański's famous play *Wesele* (The Wedding, 1901). She tries to assess the social and political changes in postwar rural life, making it quite clear that Polish peasants are not ready for collectivization. Her main concern, however, is the erosion of the distinctive

Page from the manuscript for the conclusion of Noce i dnie *(Nights and Days, 1932-1934), Dąbrowska's six-volume novel (from*
Zdzisław Libera, Maria Dąbrowska, *1975)*

peasant culture under the pressure of mass culture and the attractions of city life. This concern is reflected especially in the language. Her characters speak three different kinds of Polish: the old peasant dialect, held to slight ridicule in the story; a contemporary peasant language shaped by school and city contacts; and the "newspeak" of the young generation, the children of peasants who moved to live and work in the cities. The story thus unveils the drama of contemporary village culture and the erosion of traditional ways and beliefs by mass culture and new idioms.

The publication of "Na wsi wesele" and Dąbrowska's participation in the public life of communist Poland led some of the more uncompromisingly anticommunist circles of Polish political émigrés to criticize her. She asserted her conviction that only by connecting with the nation could one exert an influence on contemporary developments and have the moral right to judge them. Criticism of Dąbrowska, however, was mostly muted, and she was generally regarded both in Poland and among the Polish émigrés as an indisputable moral authority. This respect for the prudent yet unmistakable moral and ideological independence of the writer became even stronger in the last years of her life, when she increasingly revealed her critical attitude to the communist regime and its policies.

Toward the end of her life Dąbrowska turned to rewriting and correcting the diary she had written for almost her entire life. Though she was still writing and publishing short stories, articles and literary criticism (she continued to be especially interested in Conrad and his writings), as well as trying to complete her novel, work devoted to her diary occupied most of her time. Excerpts from it began to appear in the press. In 1961 she began the serial publication of the novel *Przygody człowieka myślącego* (Adventures of a Thinking Man, 1970) in the weekly *Przegląd Kulturalny* (Cultural Review). The work, however, was received by readers and critics as a disappointing continuation of *Noce i dnie*, with some critics describing its conception and style as anachronistic. As a result of the criticism, the editors of *Przegląd Kulturalny* asked Dąbrowska to shorten the unpublished part of the novel. Dąbrowska, in turn, decided to discontinue its publication in serial form.

Dąbrowska had begun working on the first drafts of *Przygody człowieka myślącego* back in 1938, at which time her goal was to depict the contemporary Polish intelligentsia in a sequel to the presentation in *Noce i dnie*. World War II and the consecutive political changes made the project much more complex. The intelligentsia of the interwar period found itself confronted with two events of unprecedented dimensions: the German occupation, with its horrors; and the Soviet domination of Poland, which began with the Soviet invasion of 17 September 1939 and became consolidated after the defeat of Germany in 1945. It can be argued that the failure of the novel is, at least in some respects, a failure of the entire intellectual formation represented by Dąbrowska, whose political thought sometimes masked a lack of understanding of the situation. In effect the characters and the conception of the novel as a whole prove inadequate in the face of the complexity of historical events, and this fact is primarily responsible for the artistic failure of the book. On the other hand, as several critics have pointed out, some of the individual chapters, when read as separate short stories, have considerable artistic merit as sensitive and acute depictions of life in German-occupied Poland and during the Warsaw Uprising. In fact, Dąbrowska's novel exists in two versions: as *Przygody człowieka myślącego* and as a collection or cycle of short stories titled *A teraz wypijmy–* (And So Let Us Drink Now–, 1981).

During the last two years of her life Dąbrowska was principally devoted to working on her novel and editing and rewriting her diary. Though her health deteriorated dramatically and she had to spend much of her final year in a government health clinic, she tried to continue her public activity. She died in Warsaw on 19 May 1965 without completing her writing projects, although both appeared in print after her death. *Przygody człowieka myślącego* at best gained the critical reputation of a "noble failure." On the other hand, the diary, published as *Dzienniki* in 1988 and as *Dzienniki powojenne: 1945–1965* in 1996, was recognized as one of the most important literary events of the postwar period and as Dąbrowska's second most significant work. Neither of the editions comprises the entirety of the diary. In the first one, many passages are deleted for political reasons, and both omit passages of a sensitive personal nature; in accordance with the author's wishes, the full version cannot be published until fifty years after her death.

Of Dąbrowska's considerable oeuvre, two works seem to possess the staying power of classics, though for different reasons: the collection *Ludzie stamtąd* will be read and admired as her most artistically accomplished work, and *Dzienniki* will stand for a long time as a record of an intense personal drama behind the public image of a courageous and successful life as well as an important document of tragic, complex, yet profoundly interesting times. As for *Noce i dnie,* a work often regarded as her masterpiece, it is probably too long and uneven to retain its position among the best novels of twentieth-century Polish writers, despite the true excellence of some parts of the work.

At a time when several prominent women writers—notably Zofia Nałkowska and Maria Kuncewicz—were producing work that is both feminist and universal, Maria Dąbrowska focused on more-traditional themes in a fashion that places her closer to the major Polish novelists of the nineteenth century rather than those of the twentieth. Her thematic concerns drew their inspiration from left-wing populist and national ideology and a broad humanist ethic, and the woman question does not occur in her writing as a separate major issue. Because she was eminently successful and respected, she had no need to make a special case for herself as a woman writer, nor did she feel that being a woman endowed her with a distinctive perspective on life. Her range of empathy and insight into the human psyche is equally acute in the case of male and female characters of all ages, making her work engaging.

Biography:

Ewa Korzeniowska, *Maria Dąbrowska. Kronika życia* (Warsaw: Czytelnik, 1971).

Bibliography:

Ewa Korzeniewska, *Maria Dąbrowska. Poradnik bibliograficzny* (Warsaw: Biblioteka Narodowa, 1969).

References:

Lesław M. Bartelski, *Dąbrowska* (Warsaw: Agencja Autorska, 1966);

Tadeusz Drewnowski, *Noce i Dnie Marii Dąbrowskiej* (Warsaw: Państwowe Zakłady Wydawnictw Szkolnych, 1965);

Drewnowski, *Rzecz russowska. O pisarstwie Marii Dąbrowskiej* (Kraków: Wydawnictwo Literackie, 1981);

Zbigniew Folejewski, *Maria Dąbrowska* (New York: Twayne, 1967);

Andrzej Kijowski, *Maria Dąbrowska* (Warsaw: Wiedza Powszechna, 1964);

Ewa Korzeniewska, *O Marii Dąbrowskiej i inne szkice* (Wrocław: Ossolineum, 1956);

Korzeniewska, ed., *Pięćdziesiąt lat twórczości Marii Dąbrowskiej. Referaty i materiały sesji naukowej IBL PAN, 1962* (Warsaw: Państwowy Instytut Wydawniczy, 1963);

Zdzisław Libera, *Maria Dąbrowska* (Warsaw: Wydawnictwa Szkolne i Pedagogizne, 1975);

Włodzimierz Maciąg, *Sztuka pisarska Marii Dąbrowskiej* (Kraków: Wydawnictwo Literackie, 1955);

Zofia Szmytrowska-Adamczykowa, *Maria Dąbrowska* (Katowice: Uniwersytet Śląski, 1979).

Jakub Deml

(20 August 1878 – 10 February 1961)

Jaroslav Med
Institute of Czech Literature, Academy of Sciences of the Czech Republic, Prague

BOOKS: *Slovo k Otčenáši Františka Bílka* (Nový Jičín: Nový život, 1904);

Notantur lumina (Stará Říše: Privately printed, 1907); republished as *První světla* (Jinošov: Privately printed, 1917);

Homilie (Stará Říše: Privately printed, 1907);

V Zabajkalí (Šebkovice: Privately printed, 1912);

Rosnička (Šebkovice: Privately printed, 1912);

Hrad smrti (Prague: Privately printed, 1912);

Domů (Prague: Privately printed, 1913);

Moji přátelé (Prague: Privately printed, 1913; enlarged edition, Jinošov, 1917);

Pro budoucí poutníky a poutnice (Prague: Privately printed, 1913);

Tanec smrti (Tasov: Privately printed, 1914);

Miriam (Jinošov: Privately printed, 1916);

Věštec (Jinošov: Privately printed, 1917);

Jsem na Slovensku (Topolčianky: Privately printed, 1920);

Františka Bílka Obětovaný (Tasov: Privately printed, 1922);

Sokolská čítanka (Tasov: Privately printed, 1923);

Česno (Tasov: Privately printed, 1924);

Sestrám (Tasov: Privately printed, 1924);

Tepna (Tasov: Privately printed, 1926);

Hlas mluví k Slovu (Tasov: Privately printed, 1926);

Mohyla (Tasov: Privately printed, 1926);

Z mého okovu (Tasov: Privately printed, 1927);

Do lepších dob (Tasov: Privately printed, 1927);

Dílo Felixe Jeneweina (Prague: Umělecká beseda, 1928);

Můj očistec (Prague: Rudolf Škeřík, 1929);

Mé svědectví o Otokaru Březinovi (Prague: Rudolf Škeřík, 1931);

Katolický sen (Tasov: Privately printed, 1932);

Smrt Pavly Kytlicové (Tasov: Privately printed, 1932);

Pozdrav Tasova (Tasov: Privately printed, 1932);

Sen o Otokaru Březinovi (Tasov: Privately printed, 1932);

Slovo k Hudbě pramenů (Tasov: Privately printed, 1932);

Jak jsme se potkali (Tasov: Privately printed, 1933);

Jakub Deml (courtesy of the National Library of the Czech Republic)

Nové oltáře (Tasov: Privately printed, 1933);

Památný den v Kuksu (Tasov: Privately printed, 1933);

Zapomenuté světlo (Tasov: Privately printed, 1934);

Solitudo (Tasov: Privately printed, 1934);

Štědrý den (Tasov: Privately printed, 1934);

Život, jak já jej vidím (Tasov: Privately printed, 1934);

Princezna (Tasov: Privately printed, 1935);

Cesta k Jihu (Tasov: Privately printed, 1935);

Píseň vojína šílence (Tasov: Privately printed, 1935);

Rodný kraj (Tasov: Privately printed, 1936);

Pohádka (Tasov: Privately printed, 1936);

Jugo (Tasov: Privately printed, 1936);

Matylka (Pardubice: Vlastimil Vokolek, 1937);

Umění (Tasov: Privately printed, 1937);

Vražda (Tasov: Privately printed, 1937);

Verše české, 1907–1938 (Tasov: Privately printed, 1938);

Pupava (Tasov: Privately printed, 1939);

K narození Panny Marie (Olomouc: "Krystal," 1942);

Jméno Ježíš (Olomouc: "Krystal," 1942);

Svatý Josef (Olomouc: "Krystal," 1942);

Ustrnulými nebesy (Tasov: Privately printed, 1946);

Moji přátelé (Tasov: Privately printed, 1947);

Triptych (Prague: Alois Chvála, 1960);

Rodný kraj (Prague: Privately printed, 1967);

Tasov (Prague: Vysehrad, 1971).

Editions and Collections: *Šlépěje*, 26 volumes (Jinošov & Tasov, 1917–1941);

Cestou do Betléma (Brno: Jota a ARCA JIMFA, 1990);

Pout' na Svatou Horu (Brno: Petrov, 1991);

Podzimní sen (Olomouc: Votobia, 1992);

Haluciňák—fragment zápisníku 1948–1960 (Brno: Vetus Via, 1997).

Edition in English: "Dirge," selected and translated by Paul Selver, in *An Anthology of Czechoslovak Literature* (London: Kegan Paul, Trench, Trübner, 1929), p. 264.

TRANSLATIONS: St. Hildegard, *Cesty věz nebo Vidění a zjevení* (Prague: Symposion, 1911);

Slavík svatého Bonaventury (Šebkovice, 1912);

Život svaté Dympny, panny a mučednice (Šebkovice, 1912);

A. K. Emmerichová, *Hora proroků* (Šebkovice, 1912);

Život ctihodné Anny Kateřiny Emmerichové (Šebkovice, 1912);

V. Surius, *Život a některé spisy Ruysbroecka Podivuhodného* (Tasov, 1915);

St. Cyprian, *O divadlech* (Tasov, 1927);

List sv. Vincence Ferrerského Benediktu XIII. o konci světa a příchodu Antikrista (Tasov, 1928);

Audiatur et altera pars (Tasov, 1928);

Rudolf Pannwitz, *Vzpomínka na Otokara Březinu* (Tasov, 1936);

C. Banarsci, *Mléko a krev* (Tasov, 1945);

R. Bellarmino, *O vystupování mysli k Bohu po žebřících věcí stvořených* (Tasov, 1948).

The poet Jakub Deml is one of the most original and controversial figures in Czech literature. It is no exaggeration to call him the most execrated of all Czech poets. His literary output was staggering. Besides poetry, poems in prose, and short stories he also wrote meditations, essays, newspaper columns, pamphlets, critical reviews, religious works, and translations. Poetry and poetic prose, however, formed the most important part of his output.

Deml was born on 20 August 1878 in the little Moravian town of Tasov, where his father was a farmer and village grocer. Deml went to secondary school in the nearby town of Třebíč. While he was still at school, he met the poet Otokar Březina, a leading figure not only in Czech but also in European literary symbolism. Because of his friendship with Březina, Deml decided on a literary career. Even though Březina remained Deml's poetic idol throughout his life, as their correspondence shows, Deml retained his poetic individuality and never identified with symbolism. He left school in 1898 and studied to become a Roman Catholic priest. After his ordination as a priest in 1902 he devoted himself to literature. In 1904 he published his first collection of essays, *Slovo k Otčenáši Františka Bílka* (Some Comments on František Bílek's "Our Father"), followed in 1907 by his first book of poetry, *Notantur lumina*, but he soon came into conflict with his superiors in the church. The young poet-priest could not condone the formalism of many religious pronouncements and the frequent opportunism of the clergy, especially in their relations with the Austro-Hungarian Hapsburgs. Deml was seeking the Absolute. He regarded religious faith as an existential experience of the human heart. Deml's attempts to coordinate religious experience and contemporary life merely served to intensify his conflict with the church authorities.

In 1904 he was removed from his charge and given unpaid leave. In 1912 he was retired and had to move to Prague. He lived like a nomad, going from one temporary abode to another and being thrown on the mercy of friends and acquaintances. This experience profoundly influenced his literary work. Deml's books of poetic prose, *Hrad smrti* (Castle of Death, 1912) and *Tanec smrti* (Dance of Death, 1914), are full of dark anxieties about the life of man, which is constantly negated by death. The concept of man as an outlaw, anxiety-ridden and threatened, wandering aimlessly through life, comes close to expressionism and in many ways anticipates the anguished visions of Franz Kafka.

In Deml's poetry, dreams have an extraordinary significance. Anticipating the surrealists, Deml saw them as the reflection of man's subconscious mind and the source of the poet's imagination. Deml wrote of the relationship between life and dreams: "A dream is often the only credible witness to our innermost being, for when a man is awake he frequently suppresses the truth from himself." Statements of this type led Czech surrealists such

JAKUB DEML

PÍSEŇ VOJÍNA ŠÍLENCE

TASOV MCMXXXV

Title page for Deml's 1935 collection of poems depicting a world in the process of disintegration (courtesy of The Lilly Library, Indiana University, Bloomington, Indiana)

as Vítězslav Nezval to consider Deml their literary forerunner. In Deml's poems in prose, reality and dream often merge into an indivisible whole. Everything is transformed into a torrent of speech. Deml merges thought, the visible world, and language. To prevent himself from using empty forms, he sacrifices style in order to keep the essence of the text. That is the reason his work seems so uncoordinated; commonplace events appear beside deeply spiritual experiences and visions of sheer poetic beauty. Deml never doubted that to be a priest was to be an ascetic, but because of his own tragic experience of life he always agonized over the conflict between asceticism and the enormously powerful temptations of the flesh. In *Moji přátelé* (My Friends, 1913) and *Miriam* (1916) the basic theme is the all-embracing love for the whole of creation through which God speaks to man; consequently, these books make a pleasing light counterpart to the anguished darkness of *Hrad smrti* and *Tanec smrti*. In particular *Moji přátelé*, an evocative poetic address to flowers that is generally regarded as "the prime masterpiece of Czech lyricism," had a fundamental influence on Czech nature poetry.

Deml shows his artistic individuality and originality not only in his poetic works but also, perhaps more than anywhere else, in his total identification of life and the written word. For Deml actual events and language are indivisible. Consequently, when he was writing and publishing poetry and poems in prose, he was at the same time publishing books such as *Rosnička* (A Frog, 1912), *Domů* (Homeward, 1913), and *Pro budoucí poutníky a poutnice* (For Future Pilgrims, 1913). These are collections of Deml's diary entries, in which he often wrote about even the "lowliest" things he encountered. From 1914 the most important part of Deml's work consisted of this type of documentary literature. In that year he began to publish a regular diary, which he called *Šlépěje* (Footprints). It ran continuously until 1941, finishing with the twenty-sixth volume. The loose format of the collections reveals clearly the influence of the French Catholic writer and journalist Léon Bloy. Outstanding poems, prose, and essays take their place beside correspondence, political commentaries, and polemics. Only against the background of this apparent chaos can readers appreciate the unusual wholeness of Deml's writings. Deml the polemicist and ascerbic satirist and Deml the gentle lover of flowers unite in a natural way. It has sometimes been suggested that Deml in fact wrote only one work, a kind of strange "novel of the soul." Deml himself gave credence to this theory when he wrote, "People say I have written quite a number of books. You, dear friend, know better than most that I have been writing only one book."

The creation of an independent Czechoslovakia in 1918 proved to be another watershed in Deml's life. He returned to his native Tasov, where he settled permanently and was received back as a serving priest. For the first time in his life he found, as Gaston Bachelard put it, his own place where he could be happy and where he could leave behind "the loathsome loneliness of one's self" and become part of the wider community of his native parish. No longer alone and having found fellowship that put an end to loneliness, he was moved to create his myth of home as a place where love reigns supreme.

Because love makes no difference between the important and the unimportant, between the great and the small, Deml literally threw himself into the tide of events from which he created his picture of home. In his books from the "Tasov period," *Česno* (The Door to a Beehive, 1924), *Mohyla* (The Gravemound, 1926), *Tepna* (The Artery, 1926), *Hlas mluví k Slovu* (A Voice Speaks to Logos, 1926), and *Z mého okovu* (From my Well Bucket, 1927), the flood of reality is almost overwhelming. Everything that has life, everything mankind is, proceeds from God; existence of everything that is guarantees each individual's existence. In these works Deml is no longer concerned with things but with a boundless, indivisible reality—life. His basic idea is that even seemingly unrelated things have some kind of relationship with everything in creation. Understanding this principle enables readers for the first time to see order and artistic sense in this apparently chaotic writing that might justifiably be termed a "literary collage."

In 1929 Březina, Deml's friend and literary idol, died. Deml tried to come to terms with Březina's literary legacy by writing *Mé svědectví o Otokaru Březinovi* (Otokar Březina As I Knew Him, 1931). His observations about the greatest Czech poet of the day—Březina had been nominated for the Nobel Prize in literature by Karel Čapek—led to bitter condemnation of the book by both Czech writers and the public. To Deml this response seemed like excommunication from the nation, and he felt he was "a failure who had wasted his life." His myth of home was in ruins. Having quarreled with most of his friends and feeling he could no longer stay on in his native town, Deml fled from Tasov. Quite by chance, on a visit to the chateau at Kuks he met a German aristocrat, Count K. Sweerts-Sporck, and his daughter Catherine. In Kuks, Deml tried to assimilate himself into German society and to establish himself clearly as an exile. He even wrote two collections of poems, *Solitudo* (Solitude, 1934) and *Píseň vojína šílence* (Song of the Mad Soldier, 1935), in German. In Kuks, Deml also had a rather ridiculous but tragic affair with the count's daughter. This relationship ended disastrously, and Deml then traveled around aimlessly, visiting Prague, Dubrovnik, Karlovy Vary, and Germany before finally returning to Tasov. There in a moment of inspiration he dashed off his masterpiece in prose, *Zapomenuté světlo* (Forgotten Light, 1934), as a testimony to despair and anguish. The linguist and literary scholar Roman

Jakobson has called this book one of the most tragic in all Czech literature. All Deml's other books from the 1930s, such as *Solitudo*, *Píseň vojína šílence*, *Jugo* (1936), and *Rodný kraj* (Native Land, 1936), are portrayals of a world in the process of disintegration, where the poet can find refuge from suffering only by giving his silent anguish written expression. Poetic grief and loneliness become acrimony as Deml records the world around him in his journal *Šlépěje*. He criticizes President Masaryk and Eduard Beneš. Liberal democracy also comes in for bitter attack, and Deml even indulges in some unpleasant anti-Semitism. Now in the later 1930s Deml was experiencing the greatest crisis of his life, as a priest and as an ordinary human being.

At the beginning of World War II, Tasov emerges again, not as a myth but as a real place, secure and peaceful, where a man can live in harmony with everything and everyone. Past bitterness and hatred seem to be forgotten. The poet accepts his lot tranquilly and devotes himself to his pastoral duties. In this connection Deml wrote many explanatory works on religious subjects—*K narození Panny Marie* (On the Birth of Virgin Mary, 1942), *Jméno Ježíš* (The Name of Jesus, 1942), *Svatý Josef* (Saint Joseph, 1942), and others—but these bore no relationship to his earlier highly original works.

As a result of the political changes in postwar Czechoslovakia, Deml's life took on a completely different character. After the communist coup in 1948 Deml did not share the fate of many of his friends and acquaintances. He was not imprisoned; yet, he felt himself a stranger in his native Tasov. Before the war he had published most of his work privately, but this practice was impossible under communism, and his work was quite unacceptable in the official publishing houses that preferred socialist realism. Deml now wrote little and often immediately destroyed what he did write, fearing the sudden house searches of the communist police. He tried to live like a harmless old village priest who had absolutely no interest in literature or public affairs. However, his poem in prose *Podzimní sen* (Autumn Dream, 1992), which Deml wrote at the age of seventy-three after a visit to an internment camp for monks from disbanded religious orders, bears witness to the continued existence of the great poet behind the self-deprecating facade. This prose poem unquestionably ranks with his best works, such as *Hrad smrti* and *Zapomenuté světlo*, because readers are once again drawn into the strange world of Deml's imagination, where hope and doubt stem from a single source.

It is difficult to place Deml in the mainstream of Czech literature. He himself never accepted any of the avant-garde programs that were influencing literature during his lifetime. Yet, he may be regarded as one of the outstanding exponents of Czech expressionism and a forerunner of surrealism and existentialism. Deml's novelty and originality lay above all in his absolute identification of life and literature. He introduced poetry into a realm it had rarely entered before. It was not lyric poetry as traditionally understood. His new type of poetic imagination had an unacknowledged but definitive influence on modern poetry and prose. Traces of Deml's legacy appear not only in the works of poets such as Vladimír Holan and Ivan Diviš but also in the prose works of Bohumil Hrabal and a host of other Czech authors.

Letters:

Listy Otokara Březiny Jakubu Demlovi (Tasov, 1932);
Listy Jakuba Demla Otokaru Březinovi (Tasov, 1933).

Biographies:

Jan Bartoš, *Znáte Jakuba Demla?* (Velké Meziříčí: Jan Mucha, 1932);
Stanislav Vodička, *Básník Jakub Deml v Tasově* (Velké Meziříčí: Muzeum silnic a dálnic, 1991);
Jiří Olič, *Čtení o Jakubu Demlovi* (Olomouc: Votobia, 1993).

References:

Vladimír Binar, "Neznámé arcidílo Jakuba Demla," afterword in Jakub Deml's *Tasov* (Prague: Vyšehrad, 1971);
Jindřich Chalupecký, "Jakub Deml," in *Expresionisté*, edited by Zina Trochová, Jaroslav Med, and Jan Šulc (Prague: Torst, 1992);
Bedřich Fučík, "Orientační popis některých Demlových krajin," in *Píseň o zemi* (Prague: Melantrich, 1994), pp. 191–244;
Fučík, "Tasov," in *Čtrnáctero zastavení* (Prague: Melantrich, 1992), pp. 89–115;
Jaroslav Med, "Velký z popudlivého plemene básníků," in Deml's *Sen jeden svítí* (Prague: Odeon, 1991);
Alois Plichta, *Tajemství času 1, dokumenty a vzpomínky Demlova advokáta* (Olomouc: Votobia, 1993);
Pozdrav k sedmdesátinám Jakuba Demla (Prague: Vyšehrad, 1948);
Jan Rambousek, *Básník Otokar Březina a Jakub Deml* (Kežmarok: Privately printed, 1931);
František Xaver Šalda, "J. Demla *Hrad smrti* a *Moji přátelé*," *Česká kultura*, 1, no. 16 (1912–1913);
Šalda, "O Jakubu Demlovi," in *Kritické projevy*, volume 10 (Prague: Československý spisovatel, 1957);
Tvar, special Deml issue (September–October 1928);
Albert Vyskočil, "Jakub Deml anebo integrita básníkova zjevu," in *Básníkovo slovo* (Prague: Pourova edice, 1933).

Viktor Dyk

(31 December 1877 – 14 May 1931)

Jaroslav Med
Institute of Czech Literature, Academy of Sciences of the Czech Republic, Prague

BOOKS: *A porta inferi. 1895–1897* (Prague: Grosman a Svoboda, 1897);

Síla života (Prague: Moderní revue, 1898);

Marnosti. Básně (Prague: Moderní revue, 1900);

Stud (Prague: Moderní revue, 1900);

Tragikomedie (Prague: Hugo Kosterka, 1902)—comprises *Pomsta, Zcela vážný rozhovor, Kouzelník, Kouzelník část 2* [fragment], and *Odchod;*

Buřiči. 1901–1902 (Prague: Kruh českých spisovatelů, 1903);

Hučí jez a jiné prózy (Prague: Hejda a Tuček, 1903);

Konec Hackenschmidův. Akta působnosti Čertova kopyta (Prague: Jan Otto, 1904);

Satiry a sarkasmy. 1897–1905 (Prague: Samostatnost, 1905);

Milá sedmi loupežníků (Prague: Kamilla Neumannová, 1906);

Prosinec. Akta působnosti Čertova kopyta (Prague: Jan Otto, 1906);

Episoda. Hra o třech dějstvích (Prague: Nakladatelské družstvo Máje, 1906);

Smuteční hostina. Hra o jednom dějství. Premiéra. Tragikomedie o jednom dějství (Prague: Nakladatelské družstvo Máje, 1906);

Posel (Prague: Nakladatelské družstvo Máje, 1907);

Píseň o vrbě. Prózy (Prague: Jan Otto, 1908);

Pohádky z naší vesnice. 1904–1910 (Prague: Antonín Hajn, 1910);

Giuseppe Moro (Prague: Nová edice, 1911);

Příhody. Ironie a smutky, 1905–1910 (Prague: Antonín Hajn, 1911);

Zmoudření Dona Quijota. Tragedie o pěti aktech (Prague: Spolek českých bibliofilů, 1913);

O Balkánu a o nás (Prague: Antonín Hajn, 1913);

Prohrané kampaně (Prague: František Borový, 1914);

Veliký mág. Drama o pěti dějstvích (Prague: František Borový, 1914);

Lehké a těžké kroky (Prague: Otto Parma, 1915);

Krysař (Prague: František Borový, 1915);

Zápas Jiřího Macků (Prague: František Borový, 1916);

Noci chiméry. Básně, 1900–1916 (Prague: František Topič, 1917);

Anebo. Verše Viktora Dyka (Prague: František Borový, 1918);

Zvěrstva (Prague: Springer, 1919);

Ondřej a drak. Hra o pěti dějstvích (Prague: Aventinum, 1920);

Okno. 1916–1917 (Prague: Ludvík Bradáč, 1921);

Pan poslanec (Prague: Ludvík Bradáč, 1921);

Tichý dům (Prague: E. K. Rosendorf, 1921);

Revoluční trilogie, 1907–1909. Ranní ropucha. Figaro. Přemožení (Prague: E. K. Rosendorf, 1921);

Poslední rok (Prague: Ludvík Bradáč, 1922);

Podél cesty. Básně (Prague: Aventinum, 1922);

Zlý vítr (Prague: Arthur Novák, 1922);

Tajemná dobrodružství Alexeje Iványče Kozulinova (Prague: František Topič, 1923);

Prsty Habakukovy. Humoristický románek z doby Omladiny (Prague: Jan Otto, 1925);

Můj přítel Čehona. Vzpomínky všelijakého člověka (Prague: Šolc a Šimáček, 1925);

Domy. Básně, 1919–1921 (Prague: Kruh českých spisovatelů, 1926);

Vzpomínky a komentáře 1893–1918, 2 volumes (Prague: Ladislav Kuncíř, 1927);

Děd (Mladá Boleslav: Karel Vačlena, 1927);

Inter arma (Prague: Ladislav Kuncíř, 1928);

Zpěvy v bouři. Satiry (Prague: Štěpán Jež, 1928);

Holoubek Kuzma (Prague: Sfinx, Bohumil Janda, 1928);

Soykovy děti (Česká Třebová: František Lukavský, 1929);

Napravený plukovník Švec (Prague: Adolf Neubert, 1929);

Ad usum pana prezidenta republiky (Prague: Adolf Neubert, 1929);

Devátá vlna (Prague: Štěpán Jež, 1930);

Zapomnětlivý. Veselohra o šesti jednáních (Prague: Aventinum, 1931);

Ovzduší mých studentských románů (Prague: Privately printed, 1931);

Děs z prázdna. Román, edited by Arne Novák and J. O. Novotný (Prague: Sfinx, Bohumil Janda, 1932).

Editions and Collections: *O národní stát, 1917–1931*, 7 volumes, edited by J. O. Novotný (Prague: Adolf Neubert, 1932–1938);

Mladost, edited by Zdeňka Dyková (Prague: František Topič, 1933);

Stará galerie, edited by Viktor Kripner (Brno: Atlantis, 1933);

Povídky Emila Šarocha, edited by Arne Novák (Prague: František Topič, 1935);

Spisy Viktora Dyka, 7 volumes, edited by Novák (Prague: František Borový, 1938–1942);

Spisy Viktora Dyka, 3 volumes, edited by Antonín Grund (Prague: František Borový, 1947–1949).

Editions in English: "The Ninth Night, A Play in One Act," translated by Cyril Jeffrey Hrbek, *Poet Lore*, 29, no. 1 (1918): 90–101;

"It Rained the Livelong Day," translated by Paul Selver, in *An Anthology of Czechoslovak Literature*, edited by Selver (London: Kegan Paul, Trench, Trübner, 1929), p. 264;

"An October Day" and "Dreamer's Autumn," translated by Ewald Osers and J. K. Montgomery, in *Modern Czech Poetry*, edited by Osers and Montgomery (London: Allen & Unwin, 1945), pp. 18–19;

"It Rained the Livelong Day" and "The Prison House," translated by Selver, in *A Century of Czech and Slovak Poetry*, edited by Selver (London: New Europe Publishing, 1946), pp. 195–196;

"The Locket," translated by Selver, in *Czech Prose*, edited by William Harkins (Ann Arbor: University of Michigan, 1983), pp. 305–309.

TRANSLATIONS: Alfred Capus, *Slečinka z pošty* (Prague: J. R. Vilímek, 1911);

Gabriele d'Annunzio, *Animal triste* (Prague: Moderní revue, 1912);

Francouzská poezie nové doby v překladech Viktora Dyka, edited by Karel Čechák (Prague: SNKLU, 1957).

Viktor Dyk, one of the most versatile figures in Czech literature, wrote poems, short stories, novels, plays, and essays. He was an exceptionally prolific journalist, writing about politics, current affairs, and cultural matters. His entire canon reflects the complicated, unsettled political and ethnic situation both in the multinational Austro-Hungarian monarchy and in postwar Central and Eastern Europe, as well as the resulting conflicts between Czechs and Germans.

Viktor Dyk was born on 31 December 1877 in Pšovka, a village that is now part of the town of Mělník in central Bohemia. He was the second son of the manager of the Mělník estate of Prince Jiří of Lobkovic. He had an uneventful childhood in a highly cultured patriarchal family with no financial worries. After completing secondary school in Prague he studied in the Faculty of Law at Charles-Ferdinand University in that city, where he engaged in literary pursuits and also became politically active in law societies with radical leanings.

Dyk's first literary efforts—*A porta inferi* (From the Gates of Hell, 1897), *Síla života* (A Life of Power and Vanity, 1898), and *Marnosti* (Vanity,

1900) in poetry, and *Stud* (Shame, 1900) and *Hučí jez a jiné prózy* (The Roaring of the Weir and Other Tales, 1903) in prose—were greatly influenced by the fin de siécle atmosphere cultivated in the decadent literature of Charles-Pierre Baudelaire and Joris-Karl Huysmans. Dyk's conventional, youthful rebellion against authority offered a look at reality through the prism of ennui and death. The theme of almost all his early work was the dark desolation of "the country of the soul." By the turn of the century Dyk was one of the most active poets in the group associated with the journal *Moderní revue* (Modern Review), one of the leading centers of literary symbolism in Central and Eastern Europe.

The Austro-Hungarian government fell in December 1897 after it failed to ratify laws promoting equality of the Czech and German languages. (The Austro-Hungarian monarchy, however, lasted until 1918.) The Germans living in Bohemia and Moravia had foiled every attempt to make Czech and German equal. As a result there was a nationalist revolt in Prague that was put down by the military, an action that was a serious political shock to many members of the younger generations. These events had a fundamental influence on Dyk's lifelong ideological and political attitudes and on the inspiration for his literary work; in a lecture to his students, he said, "A feeling of national solidarity was kindled in me, a feeling that had been firmly suppressed or at least pushed into the background by many other influences." Dyk regarded the impossibility of passing the language-equality laws as a failure of the Austro-Hungarian policy on nationality and also as a "slap in the face not just to official politics but to the entire nation." Dyk incorporated his experiences from the turn of the century in two of his most wide-ranging novels, both subtitled *Akta působnosti Čertova kopyta* (Devious Trickery): *Konec Hackenschmidův* (Hackenschmid's End, 1904) and *Prosinec* (December, 1906). In these novels he combines his personal interpretation of these events with contemporary factual records.

In the anthology of poems *Satiry a sarkasmy* (Satire and Sarcasm, 1905) Dyk included the key poem "Noční elegie" (Elegy of Night), written in 1901. As the poet looks at Prague by night he departs from his decadent skepticism and confesses his love for the oppressed Czech nation. Spleen and resignation alternate with the call to revolt against the present situation. In Dyk's narrative poetry—especially in the balladlike *Milá sedmi loupežníků* (Beloved of Seven Robbers,

Journalist Zdenka Hásková, whom Dyk married in 1928

1906), written in the style of Friedrich Schiller's *Die Räuber* (1781; translated as *The Robbers*, 1792)—the characters are almost anarchic in claiming their right to freedom. Dyk was no less aggressive in *Pohádky z naší vesnice* (Stories from Our Village, 1910), in which he condemns the flaws in the Czech national character and the politics of the Austro-Hungarian government. In his narrative poetry Dyk tended from the beginning toward a concise, austere, epigrammatic style. This tendency was further emphasized by his strict observance of prosody. His poems often culminate in a surprising conclusion.

In 1905 Dyk successfully completed his law studies, but he never worked as a lawyer. Until the end of his life he was an independent writer and a journalist working for many different periodicals. In 1908 Dyk's story collection *Píseň o vrbě* (Song of the Willow) was published. These stories tend

Dyk's grave in the Jewish Cemetery at Olšany, Prague

toward existentialism, exploring the relationship of a man and a woman and analyzing the psychology of love and hate. Nevertheless, at that time Dyk's overriding interest was politics rather than literature. The fight for an independent state became the common factor in his literary and political work as he dedicated himself to the work of the Radical Party for independence. Although this party was not well represented and was totally unimportant in the politics of the Czech lands, it was the only party aiming at political independence and freedom from the Austro-Hungarian monarchy.

All of Dyk's writing was intended to foster the idea of national independence. He fought against the prevailing opportunism of the main political parties and against the small-minded Czech ideal of idyllic rural living. He strongly opposed the idea of universal, cosmopolitan socialism and also condemned the concept of the historical struggle of the Czechs as presented at the time by philosopher and future president Tomáš Garrigue Masaryk. Dyk

wrote a fiercely polemical historical play, *Posel* (The Messenger, 1907), set in the seventeenth century. In *Posel* Dyk uses the religious spirit of Jan Ámos Komenský (the last bishop of the protestant Unity of Brethren and an internationally renowned Czech educational reformer) to symbolize Masaryk's humanity, which Dyk rejects as a weakness; the fighting spirit of Albrecht Wenzel Eusebius von Wallenstein's mercenaries (the armies of Ferdinand II) emerges victorious. The belief that only a radical fight against the Hapsburg dynasty could bring freedom to the Czech nation was the credo of Dyk's literature, politics, and journalism, as evident in his newspaper articles and satirical verses and in his polemics *Prohrané kampaně* (The Lost Campaigns, 1914) and the two-volume *Vzpomínky a komentáře 1893–1918* (Memoirs and Commentaries 1893–1918, 1927).

Dyk's poetic dream about Czech national freedom constantly clashed with the opportunism of Czech politicians and the pettiness of everyday reality. This clash was expressed in Dyk's most often performed play, *Zmoudření Dona Quijota* (Don Quixote Finds Wisdom, 1913), in which the author builds on Miguel de Cervantes's romantic parable about a human being who must follow the noble object of his desires regardless of the circumstances. Don Quixote's tragic heroism and his struggle to achieve an ideal, even if it is only an illusion, reflect Dyk's approach to reality. This play reveals Dyk's belief that people must fight for their aims, even if they are not achievable.

Dyk's most popular prose work, written in neoclassical style, is the short novel *Krysař* (The Ratcatcher, 1915) inspired by the old German fable about the Pied Piper of Hamelin. The novel is in essence a romantic metaphor for the triumph of action over apathy and love of ease. The clash of the protagonist—the Pied Piper, who uses his magic flute to lead people into a chasm—and Jörgen—the simple fisherman who is the only person not to succumb—is again an artistic metaphor for the clash of dream and reality, a major theme of Dyk's work.

Dyk reached the peak of his literary and political career during World War I, which he saw as a rare opportunity in the history of the Czech people to free the nation from the Hapsburg yoke. He subordinated everything he did to this end and became one of the most passionate fighters against the Austro-Hungarian government. In 1916–1917 he was imprisoned for his subversive activities, but imprisonment in no way changed his anti-Hapsburg opinions. After the war he published his prison diary, which he called *Tichý dům* (The Silent House, 1921). All during the war Dyk's emotions fluctuated between two extremes: disgust with Czech government policy, "in which the shadow of Judas shook hands with mocking Wallenrod," and an almost mystic feeling of "brotherhood, in which we were more aware of our dreams than our selves."

The conflict between hope and despair, between the selfish acquiescence of the ordinary Czech citizen and the dream of freedom transcending personal advantage, is the dominant theme that inspired Dyk's most important poetic work, the "War Tetralogy" comprised of collections of his poetry from the years 1914–1918: *Lehké a těžké kroky* (Easy and Difficult Steps, 1915), *Anebo* (Or, 1918), *Okno* (The Window, 1921), and *Poslední rok* (The Last Year, 1922). Although in composing the "War Tetralogy" Dyk had not thought of it as a single work, the poet's own experience of the momentous struggle of the

Czech nation gives the collections a remarkable artistic coherence. In his intimate lyric poetry Dyk had treated his three basic themes of dreams, disillusionment, and reconciliation as a subjective, romantic clash between the ideal and reality. In the poems of the "War Tetralogy" these themes are not treated subjectively but are reflected in the changes in the fate of the nation as perceived by Dyk, the uncompromising nationalist. These collections made Dyk for a time the recognized Czech national bard in the struggle for state and national independence.

As a result of the wartime defeat and dissolution of the Austro-Hungarian Empire, on 28 October 1918 the first independent state for Czechs and Slovaks, the Czechoslovak Republic, came into being. When the new state was established, Dyk was a mature artist and an experienced journalist. For him as a nationalist politician the achievement of independence was the fulfillment of a lifelong dream. Dyk concentrated all his energies on merging the dream with the new political reality. As a member of the senate he represented the ideas of the national conservatives, and as a prolific journalist he constantly urged moral greatness and unity on the nation, warning against all forms of socialist and communist internationalism. His rigid nationalist views became almost a substitute for religious faith. He became increasingly isolated politically and came into conflict with the political beliefs of Masaryk, one of the founders of the state and its first president. Dyk's *Ad usum pana prezidenta republiky* (For the President of the Republic, 1929) is devoted to this quarrel, especially regarding national policy relating to the existence of a large German minority in the Czechoslovak Republic. Dyk was bitterly disappointed at the way politics had developed. As an out-and-out nationalist he remained intensely anti-German. His feelings are reflected in *Podél cesty* (Along the Way, 1922), and *Domy* (Houses, 1926), two tragic, pessimistic anthologies of lyric poetry. He also condemned contemporary Czech politics in his collections of satirical verses *Pan poslanec* (The Ambassador, 1921) and *Zpěvy v bouři* (Songs in a Storm, 1928), and in the short novel *Můj přítel Čehona. Vzpomínky všelijakého člověka* (My Friend Čehona: Everyman's Memoirs, 1925).

His next works also reflect his weariness and disillusionment with the political situation. He gave up dramatic work and concentrated on writing about historical subjects. He looked to the past to find evidence for his ideas about the morality and greatness of the Czech nation. In the novel *Soykovy děti* (Soyka's Children, 1929) he idealized the wartime heroism of an ordinary Czech, and in the novel *Děs z prázdna* (Terror of Emptiness, 1932) he sought justification for his nationalist ideals in the fate of the revolutionaries of 1848. Dyk's exploration of the past naturally also meant finding out about predecessors who directly or indirectly had an influence on his life. Dyk's almost romantic, elegiac work grew out of this connection with the dead. Above all he discovered in death the purifying power of redemption and sacrifice. Dyk's last supreme achievement, his collection of poems *Devátá vlna* (The Ninth Wave, 1930), is about such power. This view of death as a purifier led the poet to a deeper awareness of the most basic questions about human existence.

After a twenty-seven-year-long friendship, Dyk married fellow writer Zdenka Hásková in 1928. At the beginning of May 1931 Dyk and his wife went to Yugoslavia on holiday, first to Dubrovnik and then to the island of Lopud. On 14 May, the day after they arrived on the island, Dyk suffered a fatal heart attack while wading near the shore. He left the legacy of a Czech writer whose nationalist beliefs were unswerving.

Letters:
V. Dyk, St. K. Neumann, bratří Čapkové. Korespondence z let 1905–1918, edited by Stanislava Jarošová, Milan Blahynka, and František Všetička (Prague: Nakladatelství Československé akademie věd, 1962).

Biography:
Jaroslav Med, *Viktor Dyk* (Prague: Melantrich, 1988).

References:
Pavla Buzková, "Drama Viktora Dyka," in her *České drama* (Prague: Melantrich, 1932);

Jan Hajšman, *Viktor Dyk v domácím odboji* (Prague: Legie, 1931);

William E. Harkins, "Viktor Dyk," in *Anthology of Czech Literature*, edited by Harkins (New York: King's Crown Press/Columbia University, 1953), pp. 165–171;

Jan Hartl, *O politickém básníku* (Brno: Moravský legionář, 1931);

Karel Hugo Hilar, *Viktor Dyk. Esej o jeho ironii* (Prague: R. Brož, 1910);

Emanuel Jánský, *Mládí v díle Viktora Dyka* (Prague: E. Hauf, 1937);

Vojtěch Jirát, "Rýmové umění Viktora Dyka," in his *O smyslu formy* (Prague: Václav Petr, 1946);

Zdeněk Myšička, *Viktor Dyk* (Prague: Divadelní ústav, 1971);

Arne Novák, *Viktor Dyk* (Prague: František Borový, 1936);

František Xaver Šalda, "Několik myšlenek na téma básník a politika," *Šaldův zápisník*, 6 (1933–1934): 360–361, 373–375;

Šalda, "Viktor Dyk, básník a politik," *Šaldův zápisník*, 3 (1930–1931): 389–418.

Witold Gombrowicz

(4 August 1904 – 24 July 1969)

Stanisław Barańczak
Harvard University

BOOKS: *Pamiętnik z okresu dojrzewania* (Warsaw: Rój, 1933);

Iwona, księżniczka Burgunda (Warsaw: *Skamander,* 1938; Państwowy Instytut Wydawniczy, 1957); translated by Krystyna Griffith-Jones and Catherine Robins as *Princess Ivona* (London: Calder & Boyars, 1969); also published as *Ivona, Princess of Burgundia* (New York: Grove, 1970);

Ferdydurke (Warsaw: Rój, 1938); translated by Eric Mosbacher as *Ferdydurke* (London: MacGibbon & Kee, 1961; New York: Harcourt, Brace & World, 1961);

Trans-Atlantyk. Ślub (Paris: Institut Littéraire, 1953);

Dziennik, 1953–1956 (Paris: Institut Littéraire, 1957);

Bakakaj (Kraków: Wydawnictwo Literackie, 1957);

Pornografia (Paris: Institut Littéraire, 1960); translated by Alastair Hamilton as *Pornografia,* (London: Calder & Boyars, 1966; New York: Grove, 1966);

Dziennik, 1957–1961 (Paris: Institut Littéraire, 1962);

Kosmos (Paris: Institut Littéraire, 1965); translated by Mosbacher as *Cosmos* (London: Calder & Boyars, 1967; New York: Grove, 1967);

Dziennik, 1961–1966. Operetka (Paris: Institut Littéraire, 1966).

Editions: *Dzieła zebrane,* 11 volumes (Paris: Institut Littéraire, 1969–1977)—comprises volume 1: *Ferdydurke;* volume 2: *Trans-Atlantyk;* volume 3: *Pornografia;* volume 4: *Kosmos;* volume 5: *Teatr;* volumes 6–8: *Dziennik;* volume 9: *Varia;* volume 10: *Wspomnienia polskie;* volume 11: *Wędrówki po Argentynie;*

Dzieła, 10 volumes (Kraków: Wydawnictwo Literackie, 1986–1992)—comprises volume 1: *Bakakaj;* volume 2: *Ferdydurke;* volume 3: *Trans-Atlantyk;* volume 4: *Pornografia;* volume 5: *Kosmos;* volume 6: *Dramaty;* volumes 7–10: *Dziennik;*

Witold Gombrowicz

Iwona, księżniczka Burgunda; Ślub; Operetka; Historia (Kraków: Wydawnictwo Literackie, 1994).

Editions in English: *The Marriage,* translated by Louis Iribarne (New York: Grove, 1969; London: Calder & Boyars, 1970);

Operetta, translated by Iribarne (London: Calder & Boyars, 1971);

A Kind of Testament, edited by Dominique de Roux and translated by Hamilton (London: Calder & Boyars, 1973; Philadelphia: Temple University Press, 1973);

Three Novels: Ferdydurke; Pornografia; Cosmos (New York: Grove, 1978);

Possessed, or the Secret of Myslotch, translated by J. A. Underwood (London & Boston: M. Boyars, 1980);

Diary, 3 volumes, translated by Lillian Vallee (Evanston, Ill.: Northwestern University Press, 1988–1993);

Trans-Atlantic, translated by Carolyn French and Nina Karsov (New Haven: Yale University Press, 1995).

Witold Gombrowicz has been widely recognized as an important figure in twentieth-century Polish literature and is one of the most original and influential of European novelists, playwrights, and essayists of his time. His works, despite the extraordinary degree of technical difficulty involved in the process of their translation, have been translated into all major languages and published or staged worldwide, and his achievement has occasioned a plethora of biographical and critical studies in Polish, French, and English. The first of his four principal novels, *Ferdydurke* (1938; translated as *Ferdydurke*, 1961), is a milestone in the history of Polish fiction; at least three others of his works—the novels *Trans-Atlantyk* (1953; translated as *Trans-Atlantic*, 1995) and *Kosmos* (1965; translated as *Cosmos*, 1967) and the play *Operetka* (1966; translated as *Operetta*, 1971)—deserve the name of masterpiece; his three-volume *Dziennik* (1957, 1962, 1966; translated as *Diary*, 1988–1993) has been hailed by many critics as the single most important Polish book of nonfiction in this century. Yet, the attention—in fact, a veritable cult following—that Gombrowicz's work has attracted in recent decades abounds in bitter ironies. His meteoric rise to international fame, which started only a few years before his death at age sixty-four, contrasted strikingly to his prior reputation, which often had been mired in controversy; his life prior to then, on the whole, had been spent in isolation and neglect. Still, even if success came too late for Gombrowicz to reap all the resulting benefits, he could at least see that his lifelong methodic and relentless struggle for recognition was ultimately not in vain.

Gombrowicz's life falls into three distinct phases separated by two transatlantic journeys; the first of which removed him, as a thirty-five-year-old author of two published books, from his native Poland to Argentina, and the next one, twenty-four years later, brought him back to Europe—though not to Poland, to which he was never to return. He was born on 4 August 1904 to the landed proprietor and industrialist Jan Onufry Gombrowicz and Antonina née Kotkowski, in the country manor of his parents located in the village Małoszyce in central Poland. The youngest of four children (he had two brothers and a sister), Gombrowicz was always the most rebellious, capricious, and undisciplined among them, and his early years spent in the rural provinces, with all their time-honored rituals of country life and traditions of social hierarchy, certainly offered him much to rebel against—although in later years his fundamentally dualistic outlook was perfectly able to include disdain for the conventional social stratification along with programmatic and ostentatious, albeit self-ironic, snobbery—he liked, for instance, to exaggerate *ad absurdum* his family's pretenses to an aristocratic rather than middle-gentry status. In 1911 his family moved to Warsaw, where he was to receive his education. After graduating from high school, he acceded reluctantly to his father's wish and in 1922 began to study law at Warsaw University. He earned his degree in 1927 and left for France, where he spent a year, for most of the time continuing his studies at the Institut des Hautes Etudes Internationales. Upon returning to Poland, he worked for a while as a legal apprentice in Warsaw courts, but he never applied himself seriously to pursuing a career as a lawyer and soon devoted himself entirely to writing.

In 1933 he made his debut by publishing a collection of short stories under the deliberately odd title *Pamiętnik z okresu dojrzewania* (Memoirs Written in Puberty); this collection, with the addition of several stories written later in his life, was reissued in 1957 as *Bakakaj* (Bakakaj). The critical reaction was rather discouraging: most of the reviewers dismissed the book as "immature." Nevertheless, Gombrowicz quickly won recognition in the circles of younger writers. By the mid 1930s he was already enjoying moderate fame as a colorful personality and fascinating interlocutor as well as an insightful literary critic; he even had his "own" table in the exclusive literary café Ziemiańska. It was, however, his first novel, *Ferdydurke*, that became a genuine event in Polish literary life; published in 1938, it was, significantly, attacked immediately by both the extreme right and the extreme left wings of critical opinion and provoked a heated critical debate on avant-garde tendencies in modern Polish fiction. Before World War II, Gombrowicz also published, in the leading literary monthly *Skamander*, his first play, *Iwona, księżniczka Burgunda* (1938; translated as *Princess Ivona*, 1969; also published as *Ivona, Princess of Burgundia*, 1970). The outbreak of war on 1 September 1939 interrupted the serialized publication in a Warsaw tabloid of his pseudonymous parody of

Dust jacket for the first volume of the 1988–1993 English translation of Gombrowicz's Dziennik *(1953–1966)*

a Gothic romance, *Opętani* (Possessed), which was never resumed.

As the last installments of *Opętani* were being printed, however, Gombrowicz was already in, of all places, Buenos Aires. By a strange coincidence, only a few weeks before the German invasion of Poland, he boarded the transatlantic liner *Bolesław Chrobry* as a participant in a trip to Argentina of a small group of young Polish literati, sponsored by the shipping company Gdynia-American Lines. While in Buenos Aires he learned about the outbreak of war and, being unfit for military service anyway, decided not to return. He could not foresee that the capital of Argentina would remain his home for the next quarter of a century.

Gombrowicz's first Argentinian years, while satisfying his need for solitary independence devoid of any ties or obligations, were also extremely difficult in terms of financial insecurity. Initially, the only source of income available to him were articles that he published sporadically in the local press. To

make ends meet, he had to accept whatever job was available: thus, in 1943 and 1944 he worked at the archive of the periodical *Jezuitor Solidaridad,* and in 1947 he took a seemingly better but in fact equally poorly-paid job as a secretary in a Polish bank in Buenos Aires. At the same time, he continued his writing with great determination and made numerous friends in the Argentinian literary circles, mostly among younger writers, some of whom eventually helped him translate his works into Spanish. During the 1940s he was more likely to find some spiritual support among those Argentinian friends than among members of the Polish émigré community, who remained characteristically put off, if not downright antagonized, by what they considered to be irreverent mockery and general "lack of seriousness" in his writing. These charges began to be leveled at him with increasing frequency and aggressiveness after he became more visible as a writer, thanks to his entering in 1951 into steady collaboration with the Paris-based émigré monthly *Kultura.* The consecutive installments of his *Dziennik, 1953–1956* began to appear on the pages of that periodical in 1953, and it was within the book series published by *Kultura* that most of his postwar works came out in book form, beginning with the publication under one cover, also in 1953, of his second novel, *Trans-Atlantyk*, and his second play, *Ślub* (The Marriage). One of the frequent contributors of *Kultura*, the excellent critic Konstanty A. Jeleński, helped Gombrowicz enormously as a promoter of his works in Europe and as their translator into French. Yet, the publication of *Trans-Atlantyk*, a novel that spares nothing in its satirical debunking of the classic stereotypes of the Polish nationalistic tradition, was met with vitriolic attacks from the overwhelmingly conservative émigré critics. Gombrowicz's sense of the absurd "played" much better with his readers in Poland, where the publication in 1957–1958 of four of his books—*Ferdydurke, Iwona, Trans-Atlantyk. Ślub*, and *Bakakaj*–made possible by the brief political "thaw," turned him into a cultural idol of many young critics and readers.

In 1955 Gombrowicz quit his job at Banco Polaco and for a while tried to support himself with grants, royalties for his published and staged works, and the modest income he earned by giving private lectures on philosophy. The year 1958 marked the beginnings of his serious respiratory problems, which became the cause of his death eleven years later. In 1963 he received a grant from the Ford Foundation for a one-year stay in West Berlin, and in April of that year he left Argentina. While in Berlin, he consented to give an interview to a Polish journalist, in which he expressed sincerely his views on many touchy political subjects; published subsequently in Poland along with a scathing commentary by his interviewer, his statements were met with a hostile campaign by the communist media. As a result, no book by Gombrowicz was allowed publication in Poland until his death; in the 1970s the communist authorities were ready to relent and lift the ban, but then the writer's last will (stating that his work could be published in Poland only in its entirety–that is, without censorship cuts) thwarted their designs to publish a bowdlerized edition. Throughout the 1970s and 1980s Gombrowicz's books were read widely in Poland, but thanks only to the clandestine circulation of their émigré editions and underground reprints.

In May 1964 Gombrowicz moved from Germany to France, where during his stay at the Royaumont Abbey as a guest of the *Circle Culturel* of the Royaumont Foundation he met Rita Labrosse, a young Canadian specialist in Romance literature, who became his companion and, in December 1968, his wife. In the fall of 1964 they settled in the small town of Vence in southern France. The last years of Gombrowicz's life were marked by his rapidly growing international fame–in 1967 he received the coveted Formentor Prize and in 1968 was reputed to be one of the top candidates for the Nobel Prize in literature–as well as his deteriorating health. He died 24 July 1969 in Vence after a long struggle with illness.

At first glance whimsical and grotesquely absurd, Gombrowicz's work turns out, on a closer look, to be founded upon an amazingly consistent and complex philosophical system, as original as it is profound. The basic premise of his thought is his obsessive awareness of the human being's solitude and helplessness in confronting the powerful pressure of culture–if "culture" is understood in a Freudian sense, as a collective superego that stifles the authentic impulses of the human self. Accordingly, the chief antinomy that underpins Gombrowicz's philosophical and literary system is the ineffaceable, ubiquitous conflict between the solitary individual and the others, the rest of the human world–in particular, all of society's petrified rituals, customs, stereotypes, and institutionalized relationships, for which Gombrowicz coined an all-encompassing phrase, "the inter-human Church." The individual's natural need is to remain free, independent, spontaneous, and unique, whereas the presence of others crams him or her into the schematic framework of that which is socially and culturally acceptable.

As many critics, notably Jan Błoński and Jerzy Jarzębski, have pointed out, if Gombrowicz had stopped at this point, he would appear to be merely continuing the worn-out line of the argument of Sigmund Freud, if not of Jean-Jacques Rousseau and the whole Romantic tradition. But he is much more original than that. His innately dialectic mind immediately counterbalances the argument with its exact opposite. He is equally aware that, contrary to his need to remain free and unique, the individual also fears isolation and desires the kind of affirmation that can be achieved only through contacts with other people and participation in the "inter-human Church" of their commonly accepted norms of behavior. This contradiction is particularly dramatic in the case of an artist: he wishes to reveal his uniqueness to the audience, but in order to be understood, he must resort to the comprehensible language of approved convention, which, in turn, threatens to destroy his uniqueness. In other words, each public manifestation of the artist's freedom-seeking self is tantamount to his self-imprisonment in a rigid scheme of finished shapes—and thus, it means his death as an artist.

Yet, the situation of the artist, however dramatic, is for Gombrowicz just one version of a more universal paradox of human existence. In his view every individual lives his life in constant suspension between two ideals: maturity and immaturity. These two may variously be called fulfillment and unfulfillment, completeness and freedom, perfection and spontaneity, typicality and uniqueness, or, perhaps most generally, form and chaos. Just as the protagonist of "Tancerz mecenasa Kraykowskiego" (The Dancer of Mr. Kraykowski, Attorney at Law), the opening short story in Gombrowicz's debut collection, sincerely desires to imitate his role model—a certain mature, responsible, smooth, and respected middle-aged lawyer—but at the same time is secretly attracted to anything that is immature, irresponsible, imperfect, and inferior, so virtually all the characters in Gombrowicz's fiction (more often than not, deliberate impersonations of himself and his own neurotic obsessions) are torn between their striving for form on the one hand and for chaos on the other; or the plot consists in a clash between characters symbolizing the striving for form and those symbolizing the leaning toward chaos: a characteristically typical final scene in his works is a duel dissolving into a no-holds-barred general brawl with no clear outcome. As Gombrowicz puts the conflict succinctly in the first volume of *Dziennik:* "The most important, most extreme, and most incurable dispute is that waged in us by two of our most basic strivings: the one that desires form, shape, definition, and the other, which protests against shape, and does not want form."

In both his fictional and his nonfictional writings this basic antinomy takes on the flesh of various specific interhuman relations, from politics to religion to sex. The struggle between form and chaos may reveal itself, for example, in its sociological version, in which aristocracy represents perfect (but also petrified) maturity or form, while peasantry stands for spontaneous (but also inarticulate) immaturity or chaos. It may also be illustrated by the inequality of civilizations: Western civilization is, in that respect, an embodiment of maturity, while the "second-rate" civilizations of countries such as Poland, "the poor relations" of the Western world, represent immaturity. Or the tension between the extremes of form and chaos makes itself felt within the confines of the individual ego, as a self-contradictory, simultaneous yearning for the "perfection" embodied in the complete personality of an adult on the one hand and the "beauty" of a child's or an adolescent's spontaneity on the other.

In fact, all these versions of the basic opposition between form and chaos have a common denominator in the concept of inequality; each opposing pair of notions can be interpreted as a case of superiority confronted with inferiority. According to Gombrowicz the essence of human existence lies in the fact that the individual strives all his life for superiority and form but in reality is by no means unequivocally attracted by these values, since their ultimate attainment would equal spiritual petrification and death. Therefore, the individual secretly desires inferiority, immaturity, and chaos, because only these extremes offer a chance of freedom. Yet, the ultimate attainment of this other goal would mean isolation, the impossibility of any communication or self-affirmation. In the final analysis, the conflict is insoluble. It can only be partly overcome and contained, if not fully resolved, by artistic creativity. Even though the artist can neither escape from nor achieve perfect form, he can at least feel free to "play" with it. He can make both the maturity of artistic convention and his own immaturity "visible" instead of concealing them—and thus, by gaining a salutary distance from both, he can liberate himself to a certain extent from their oppression. It is highly characteristic that Gombrowicz's first book, his collection of short stories, can be read as a series of parodistic vignettes caricaturing the typical literary conventions of clearly recognizable narrative genres and subgenres, such as the mystery novel, the family saga, the novel of adventure, and the Proustian psychological novel set in an aristocratic milieu.

Gombrowicz's way of relating everything to human superiority and inferiority means, in turn, that the focal point of his outlook is neither the individual per se nor society in general but rather what emerges at the point of their mutual clash: what he calls in *Dziennik* the "inter-human Church." His philosophy subscribes neither to individualist nor to collectivist philosophies but to the "third vision" built on the corpses of both: it is a vision, in his own words, of "man in relation to another man, a concrete man, I in relation to you and him . . . Man through man. Man in relation to man. Man created by man."

Essentially a series of philosophical parables meant to provide illustrations of various aspects and

Gombrowicz in 1958 (from Rita Gombrowicz, Gombrowicz w Argentynie, *1987)*

applications of Gombrowicz's system of ideas, his short stories, novels, and plays reveal certain common traits. Their chief shared characteristics have to do with the dialectic nature of the relationship between their first-person narrator (or, in plays, protagonist) and the reality presented. A reality oppresses him, poses problems to solve, and forces him to assume a specific stance or adopt a specific behavior but, simultaneously, the narrator himself attempts to shape reality, to stage and direct events, to manipulate other characters, and to impose some sense upon the world that surrounds him. Accordingly, two basic models of fictional plot coexist in Gombrowicz's works—the model of an investigation (in which reality appears to the narrator/protagonist as a problem to solve) and the model of stage-setting (in which the narrator/protagonist becomes an active manipulator of reality).

The best example of how Gombrowicz juxtaposes and merges these two models is his first and most famous novel, *Ferdydurke,* which perhaps has been surpassed artistically by his later works, yet still remains the most instructive illustration of his philosophy, his vision of the "inter-human Church," his concept of narration, and his use of language. *Ferdydurke* falls into three sharply divided parts, of which the second and third are each preceded by a brief essay and parable. At the outset of the story, the reader meets the narrator (and, at the same time, the chief protagonist of the whole novel), a man in his thirties who, like Gombrowicz himself, has published his first book and has been derided by the critics as an allegedly "immature" and irresponsible author. The narrator is torn between his readiness to embrace any form that would provide him with a modicum of "maturity" and society's acceptance, and his dislike for various specific forms that have so far been imposed on him by others and that he has been unable to accept as representations of his authentic self. What, actually, is his authentic self, and what form could possibly correspond to it? To find an answer, the narrator embarks upon writing another book. Here, however, something absolutely unexpected occurs. A certain Professor Pimko, an old-fashioned high-school teacher, arrives and literally kidnaps the narrator to put him back in school, as if he were still an "immature" teenager.

The subsequent two parts of the novel put the narrator-turned-teenager into three different locales and milieus, each of which represents a different kind of petrified, inauthentic form. After the school sequence, the narrator is placed by Pimko as a subtenant in the house of Mr. and Mrs. Youthful, a middle-aged couple imprisoned, as it were, within their received ideas of what is "modern" and "progressive"; finally, he finds himself in a countryside manor, where the conservative social distinctions between the upper class and the "boors" are still alive. In none of these three places—the school, the "modern" household, nor the traditional manor—can the narrator fully identify with the form that prevails there, nor can he find an authentic form of his own. With grotesque inevitability each of the three plots develops into the narrator's attempts at manipulating the people who surround him, a course of action that is for him the only way of resisting the overwhelming pressure of this or another form that they try to impose on him but which leads each time to a catastrophic conflict resolving itself into a general wild brawl and the narrator's escape.

In his subsequent novels Gombrowicz continued to explore the fundamental problem of form versus chaos, illustrating it with even more intricate fictional plots. *Trans-Atlantyk,* a novel ostensibly based on the author's 1939 Argentinian defection, dissects form in its specific version of patriotic stereotype, while the extreme of chaos, freedom, and youth is identified with rejection of the social norms that such a stereotype creates. There is no other work by Gombrowicz in which language, style, and genre play such a crucial role: a twentieth-century story is told here in the masterfully parodied style of an oral tale spoken by a seventeenth-century Polish nobleman. In *Pornografia* (1960; translated as *Pornografia,* 1966) the relationship between form and chaos or maturity and immaturity takes on the shape of a perverse story of a young couple whose love is "stage-set" and "directed" by a pair of older men—all of this action set against the (imagined rather than experienced) social and political backdrop of German-occupied Poland. Gombrowicz's last novel, *Kosmos,* is his most metaphysical, although, like everything he wrote, it also reveals his extraordinary comic power and his penchant for the grotesque. The central issue discussed in this novel is nothing less than the nature of external reality as reflected in human consciousness: is meaning immanent, or is it merely imposed on reality by the human mind? Gombrowicz asks this question by structuring his novel once again upon the model of investigation and by parodistically referring in its style and construction to the conventions of the mystery story. This peculiar marriage of metaphysics and pulp-fiction poetics pairs *Kosmos,* in a sense, with Gombrowicz's last play, *Operetka,* in which he analogously succeeds in combining the hilarity stemming from his parody of the "divinely idiotic" popular genre with a quite serious discussion of the meaning of modern history. Like the rest of Gombrowicz's body of works, both *Kosmos* and *Operetka* can be read as mad pieces of nonsensical tomfoolery, but they can also be read as profound treatises on the most excruciating puzzles of human existence.

Letters:

J. Majcherek, ed., *Witold Gombrowicz: Listy do Adama Mauersbergera* (Łódź: ŁTPK, 1988);

Andrzej Kowalczyk, ed., *J. Giedroyc, W. Gombrowicz: Listy 1950–1969* (Warsaw: Czytelnik, 1993);

Jerzy Jarzębski, ed., *Gombrowicz: Walka o sławę,* volume 1: *Korespondencja Witolda Gombrowicza z Józefem Wittlinem, Jarosławem Iwaszkiewiczem,* *Arturem Sandauerem* (Kraków: Wydawnictwo Literackie, 1996).

Interview:

Dominique de Roux, *Rozmowy z Gombrowiczem* (Paris: Institut Littéraire, 1969).

Biographies:

Tadeusz Kępiński, *Witold Gombrowicz i świat jego młodości* (Kraków: Wydawnictwo Literackie, 1987);

R. Kalicki, ed., *Tango Gombrowicz* (Kraków: Wydawnictwo Literackie, 1984);

Rita Gombrowicz, *Gombrowicz en Argentynie hswiadectwa i dokumenty, 1939–1963* (London: Puls, 1984);

Joanna Siedlecka, *Jaśnie panicz* (Kraków: Wydawnictwo Literackie, 1987);

Gombrowicz, *Gombrowicz en Europe–temoignages et documents 1963–1969* (Paris: Denoël, 1988);

Tadeusz Kępiński, *Witold Gombrowicz: Studium portretowe* (part 1: Kraków: Wydawnictwo Literackie, 1988; part 2: Warsaw: Alfa, 1994);

Kazimierz Głaz, *Gombrowicz w Vence* (Kraków: Wydawnictwo Literackie, 1989).

References:

Kenneth J. Atchity, "Vision and Perspective in Witold Gombrowicz," *Research Studies,* 37 (1969): 214–216;

Hanjo Berressem, *Lines of desire: Reading Gombrowicz's Fiction with Lacan* (Evanston, Ill.: Northwestern University Press, 1998);

Jan Błoński, *Forma, śmiech i rzeczy ostateczne* (Kraków: Znak, 1994);

François Bondy and Constantin Jeleński, *Witold Gombrowicz* (München: Deutsches Taschenbuch Verlag, 1978);

David Brodsky, "Witold Gombrowicz and the 'Polish October,'" *Slavic Review,* 39 (1980): 459–475;

Manuel Carcassonne, Christophe Guidas, and Malgorzata Smorag, eds., *Gombrowicz, Vingt ans après* (Paris: Bourgois, 1989);

Bogdana Carpenter, "An Aunt or a Book? Narrative Technique in Gombrowicz's *Ferdydurke,*" *Proceedings of the Pacific Northwest Conference on Foreign Languages,* 27, no. 1 (1976): 154–157;

Francesco M. Cataluccio and Jerzy Illg, eds., *Gombrowicz-filozof* (Kraków: Znak, 1991);

Bogdan Czaykowski, "Witold Gombrowicz's *Trans-Atlantyk:* A Novel for New Europe?" *Cross Currents: A Yearbook of Central European Culture,* 12 (1993): 69–77;

Edward J. Czerwinski and Bronislawa Karst, "'Berging' Gombrowicz: A Reappraisal of 'Form-Fastening,'" *Polish Review*, 23, no. 4 (1978): 50–57;

D. de Roux, *Gombrowicz* (Paris: Union Générale d'Edition, 1971);

Andrzej Falkiewicz, *Polski Kosmos* (Kraków: Wydawnictwo Literackie, 1981);

Edward Fiala, "Oficjalność i podoficjalność: O koncepcji człowieka w powieściach Witolda Gombrowicza," *Roczniki Humanistyczne*, 22, no. 1 (1974): 5–150;

R. Georgin, *Gombrowicz* (Lausanne: L'Age d'Homme, 1977);

Michał Głowiński, *Ferdydurke Witolda Gombrowicza* (Warsaw: Wydawnictwo Szkolne i Pedagogiczne, 1991);

George Gömöri, "The Antinomies of Gombrowicz," *Modern Language Review*, 73 (1978): 119–129;

Jerzy Jarzębski, *Gra w Gombrowicza* (Kraków: Wydawnictwo Literackie, 1982);

C. Jeleński and de Roux, eds., *Gombrowicz* (Paris: L'Herne, 1971);

K. A. Jeleński, "Witold Gombrowicz," *TriQuarterly*, 9 (1967): 37–42;

Tadeusz Kepinski, "Witold Gombrowicz and the World of His Youth," *Polish Perspectives*, 21, no. 12 (1978): 45–52;

Diana Kuprel, "Ludic Form and Formal Ludus: The Play of Masks in Witold Gombrowicz's *Operetta*," *Canadian Slavonic Papers*, 36 (1994): 413–428;

Alex Kurczaba, *Gombrowicz and Frisch: Aspects of the Literary Diary* (Bonn: Bouvier, 1980);

Kurczaba, "The Impact of Latin-American Exile on Polish and German Literature: The Case of Witold Gombrowicz and Anna Seghers," *Polish Review*, 23, no. 4 (1978): 58–65;

Zdzisław Łapiński, ed., *Gombrowicz i krytycy* (Kraków: Wydawnictwo Literackie, 1984);

Łapiński, *Ja, Ferdydurke* (Lublin: KUL, 1985);

Patricia Merivale, "The Esthetics of Perversion: Gothic Artifice in Henry James and Witold Gombrowicz," *PMLA: Publication of the Modern Language Association of America*, 93 (1978): 992–1002;

Peter Petro, "The Pyrotechnics of an Infernal Machine: Fictional Reality in Gombrowicz's *Pornografia*," *International Fiction Review*, 6 (1979): 55–61;

Lakis Proguidis, *Un écrivain malgré la critique* (Paris: Gallimard, 1989);

Rochelle H. Ross, "Witold Gombrowicz—An Experimental Novelist," *South Central Bulletin*, 31 (1971): 214–216;

Artur Sandauer, "Witold Gombrowicz: The Man and the Writer," *Polish Perspectives*, 22, no. 1 (1978): 30–48;

E. Sławkowa, *Trans-Atlantyk Witolda Gombrowicza* (Katowice: Uniwersytet Śląski, 1981);

Ewa M. Thompson, "The Reductive Method in Witold Gombrowicz's Novels," in *The Structural Analysis of Narrative Texts*, edited by Andrej Kodjak, Michael J. Connolly, and Krystyna Pomorska (Columbus, Ohio: Slavica, 1980), pp. 196–203;

Thompson, *Witold Gombrowicz* (Boston: Twayne, 1979);

J. Volle, *Gombrowicz, bourreau-martyr* (Paris: Bourgeois, 1972);

Ewa Płonowska Ziarek, ed., *Gombrowicz's Grimaces: Modernism, Gender, Nationality* (Albany: State University of New York Press, 1998).

Papers:

The Beinecke Library at Yale University holds the entirety of Witold Gombrowicz's extant papers: all surviving manuscripts and typescripts of his works, including *Operetka, Kosmos, A Kind of Testament, Dziennik, Wędrówki po Argentynie,* and *Wspomnienia polskie;* manuscripts and typescripts of various shorter texts and manuscript fragments of his longer works; and correspondence with friends, family, and publishers.

František Halas

(3 October 1901 – 27 October 1949)

Richard Svoboda
Institute of Czech Literature, Academy of Sciences of the Czech Republic, Brno

BOOKS: *Sépie* (Prague: Odeon, 1927; revised edition, Prague: František Borový, 1948);

Kohout plaší smrt (Prague: Rudolf Škeřík, 1930; revised edition, Prague: František Borový, 1948);

Tvář (Prague: Družstevní práce, 1931; revised edition, Prague: František Borový, 1946);

Hořec (Prague: E. Jánská, 1933);

Staré ženy (Prague: František Borový, 1935);

Linka Procházková (Prague: Privately printed, 1935); republished as *Malířka Linka Procházková*, (Karel Kryl: Kroměříž, 1948);

Dokořán (Prague: Melantrich, 1936; enlarged edition, Prague: František Borový, 1946);

Torzo naděje (Prague: Melantrich, 1938; enlarged edition, Prague: Melantrich, 1945);

Obrazy (Brno: Skupina výtvarných umělců, 1938);

Naše paní Božena Němcová (Prague: František Borový, 1940; revised edition, Prague: Práce, 1946);

Ladění (Prague: František Borový, 1942; enlarged edition, Prague: František Borový, 1947);

Dělnice (Brno: Rovnost, 1945);

Já se tam vrátím (Prague: Vysočina, 1947);

V řadě (Prague: František Borový, 1948);

Počítadlo (Prague: Orbis, 1948);

František Halas dětem (Prague: Státní nakladatelství dětské knihy, 1954); enlarged as *Před usnutím* (Prague: Albatros, 1972);

Potopa (New York: Edice Svědectví, 1956).

Editions and Collections: *A co?* edited by Ludvík Kundera (Brno: Krajské nakladatelství, 1957);

Básně, edited by Jan Grossman and Vladimír Justl (Prague: Československý spisovatel, 1957);

Potopa–Hlad, edited by Jindřich Chalupecký (Brno: Blok, 1965);

Dílo Františka Halase, 5 volumes, edited by Jiří Brabec, F. X. Halas, and Ludvík Kundera (Prague: Československý spisovatel, 1968–1983);

Tvář rodné země, edited by F. X. Halas (Prague: Československý spisovatel, 1972);

František Halas

Básnické dílo, edited by Bohumil Štorek (Prague: Československý spisovatel, 1978).

Editions in English: "Dead Soldier" and "It Is Time," translated by Ewald Osers, in *Heart of Europe: An Anthology of Creative Writing in Europe 1920–1940*, edited by Klaus Mann and Hermann Kesten (New York: L. B. Fischer, 1943), pp. 526–527;

Our Lady Božena Němcová, translated by Frederick Ost, with a foreword by Pavel Tigrid (Wellington, New Zealand: Handicraft Press, 1944);

"Dead Soldier," "Cemetery," "Sotto Voce," and "It Is
Time," edited and translated by Osers and J. K.
Montgomery, in *Modern Czech Poetry: An
Anthology* (London: Allen & Unwin, 1945),
pp. 62–64;

"Sleep" and "It Is Time," translated by Osers and
Montgomery, in *Hundred Towers: A Czechoslovak Anthology of Creative Writing*, edited by F. C.
Weiskopf (New York: L. B. Fischer, 1945),
pp. 100–101;

Old Women, translated by Karel Offer (London:
Editions Poetry, 1947);

"Death," translated and edited by Albert French,
in *A Book of Czech Verse* (London: Macmillan /
New York: St. Martin's Press, 1958), pp. 94–
95;

"How the Dove Got Her Girdle," translated by
Edith Pargeter, in *A Handful of Linden Leaves:
An Anthology of Czech Poetry*, edited by Jaroslav
Janů (Prague: Artia, 1960), pp. 34–35;

"The Cemetery," "To Prague," "Autumn," and
"Don Quixote at War," translated by Pargeter, in *The Linden Tree: An Anthology of Czech
and Slovak Literature 1890–1960*, edited by
Mojmír Otruba and Zdeněk Pešat (Prague:
Artia, 1962), pp. 180–184;

A Garland of Children's Verse, translated by Barbara
T. Bradford (New York: Lion Press, 1968);

Excerpts from *Sepie, Kohout plaší smrt, Tvář, Hořec*,
and *Staré ženy*, in *The Poets of Prague: Czech Poetry
between the wars*, by Alfred French (London:
Oxford University Press, 1969), pp. 62–63, 81–
82, 85–86, 97–98, 111;

"Selected Poems by František Halas," translated
by Zdenka Brodská and Lyn Coffin, in *Cross
Currents: A Yearbook of Central European Culture*, 11 (1992): 71–78.

OTHER: *Láska a smrt: vybor lidové poezie*, compiled
by Halas and Vladimír Holan (Prague:
Melantrich, 1938; expanded edition, 1946).

František Halas is one of the most important
representatives of Czech lyric poetry of the twentieth century. He was a poet, a translator, an essayist concentrating on literature and art, and a
journalist writing on cultural matters. His name
became identified with the intensive and genuine
search for a poetic form that would encapsulate
the tragic and absurd situation of the individual
in modern, socially stratified society. In times of
difficulty he did not hesitate to speak out in
defense of democratic and humanist principles in
the name of the entire Czech nation.

Halas was born on 3 October 1901 in Brno,
Moravia, to a working-class family of poor textile
workers. His father, František Halas Sr. (1880–
1960), came from a large family of weavers. During Austro-Hungarian rule and also during the
first Czechoslovak republic, as an official representative of the workers, he was prosecuted and
sent to prison. He was also a writer whose fictional
memoirs were published in three volumes: *Kemka*
(1950), *Bez legend* (No Myth, 1958), and *Máje a
prosince* (May and December, 1959). Halas's
mother died of tuberculosis in 1909, and the
eight-year-old František moved with his father to
the nearby parish of Svitavka near Boskovice, an
area where the Halas family had long-standing
connections. It was not only with the early death
of his mother that Halas encountered death in his
childhood; three siblings died soon after they
were born. As a result, one of the recurrent
themes in his work for a long time was variations
on the subject of death.

About that time Halas also began to take a
great interest in literature. He read the works of
Jules Verne and Robert Louis Stevenson, and borrowed Jonathan Swift's *Gulliver's Travels* (1726)
from the workers' library. Memories of his childhood left him with a strong attachment to the
countryside where he grew up. He often went
back there and traveled through the "magic triangle" formed by the parishes of Kunštát, Zboněk,
and Rozseč as the specific sensory images in his
memoirs in prose, *Já se tam vrátím* (I Shall Return,
1947), testify. Halas's only formal education was
gained from the council school that he left in
1916. This information has always come as a
shock to all who were confronted by his exceptional erudition and the scope of his knowledge.
The school was in Husovice, a district of Brno
where he had lived since 1913. From 1916 to 1919
he worked in Píša's Bookshop in Česká Street in
Brno, learning the trade. This position meant
that he met all the Czech literary celebrities in
Brno at the time, and he acquired a literary education.

During World War I his father was in the
Czech Legion in Russia, returning only in 1920,
having traveled by way of Vladivostock, Hong
Kong, and Trieste. Meanwhile, Halas lived hand-
to-mouth with his grandmother. From 1920 to
1921 he was an assistant in Kočí's Bookshop
beside the Old Town Hall in Brno. From 1921 to
1923 he was an active member of the leftist youth
group Modré blůzy (Blue Shirts) and published
in the left-wing press, especially the newspaper

Rovnost (Equality), where he first came to public notice. In December 1922 he was sent to prison for five days for his activities in the communist youth organization Komsomol. In 1922–1923 he worked as an assistant clerk in the Brno Accident Insurance Company. In 1923 and 1924 he published his first poetry and political satire in the communist magazine *Sršatec* (The Firebrand). In 1923 Halas and the left-wing critic Bedřich Václavek founded the Brno group Devětsil. From 1924 to 1925 Halas, Václavek, and Artuš Černík, a well-known journalist writing on cultural affairs, edited the group's first review, *Pásmo* (The Zone). Later, Halas was also on the editorial staff of the magazines *Šlehy* (Witticisms, 1926), *Orbis* (1927–1928), *Rozhledy* (Review, 1935–1938), and *Čteme* (Reading, 1938). After his military service in Brno from 1923 to 1925 Halas set off for six months in Paris from where, as he wrote, he was driven away by hunger. There he met the important Czech artists Jindřich Štyrský and Toyen. He struggled along as best he could, washing dishes and receiving some assistance from the consulate, some from home. At the time he wrote in a letter full of youthful exuberance to Václavek and his wife, "To rut, to roar and go wild! How wonderful it would be to be a sailor!" On the recommendation of the Brno writer, dramatist, and librarian Jiří Mahen he obtained a post in the publishing house Orbis in Prague, where he worked until 1945. From 1926 to 1927 Halas was the permanent arts critic for the social democratic daily newspaper *Právo lidu* (The Rights of the People). While on the editorial staff with Arnošt Vaněček between 1929 and 1935, Halas was largely responsible for publishing a series of editions of new works, including *Mys dobré naděje* (The Cape of Good Hope), and between 1936 and 1942 he helped to launch the series of books *První knížky* (First Titles).

Halas's first book of poems, *Sépie* (Sepia, 1927), has a strong existentialist bias and was already a mature work. The subjects are often life and death, the meaning of human existence, and creativity as a whole. To a certain extent the work is an argument against the poetic idea that all the beauties of the world extol the vision of the world held by some of the communist poets of Halas's generation such as Vítězslav Nezval and Jaroslav Seifert. Halas was already fully integrated into Prague literary life when he became friendly with F. X. Šalda, the most important authority on Czech criticism between the wars. At that time Halas was sharing a flat in Žižkov with the Catholic poet Jan Zahradníček and was often in the company of Vladimír Holan, a poet four years younger than himself. Halas's early poems, strongly influenced by poetism and including the socialist themes of proletarian poetry, were being published regularly in periodicals, but all through this period he was trying to find his own poetic method. In a certain sense he became the opposite of his lifelong friends and former models Jaroslav Seifert and Jiří Wolker.

Halas's method is introspective; he tries to reach and analyze the central elements of emotion and reason and recombine them into a coherent whole. The power of this introspection and the attention Halas gives to every word effectively challenge Nezval's explosive poetry. In spite of this protest, the collection *Sépie* is related to poetism by touches of playful imagination and also by the typographical layout of Karel Teige, a key personality in Czech culture between the wars. Halas's extensive experience of the life of the poorest sections of contemporary society explain his great sympathy, with existentialist overtones, for sufferers from social injustice and his emphasis on ethical and moral values.

The title of the second collection of poems, *Kohout plaší smrt* (The Cock Awakens Death, 1930), illustrates its main theme, the struggle between life and death. This book clearly demonstrates the dominating features in Halas's poetry—playfulness, spontaneity, and acute sensitivity combined with social awareness; but these characteristics simply provide the background for a disenchanted picture of the world. His many images based on oxymorons and paradoxes reflect the inherent tragedy of life. Halas's smoothly flowing chains of free association contrast with his relentless introspective search for values and form that is reflected in discordant staccato expressions. Halas himself commented on this contrast by saying, "I have never professed great technical skill in the poet's craft. Many a time have Hora and Zahradníček tried to thump into my head the secrets of the trochee, iambus, and whatever their fancy names are. To this day I am not familiar with them. Not that I am in any way boasting, that's just how it is. I simply don't understand them. That is why my verse so often sounded harsh and jerky. But what grated on others' ears I heard as heavenly music and went on grinding it out in my own way." His poetry is also exceptional lexically and syntactically. Complex sentences with inverted word order often include a great deal of

Halas (right) with his lifelong friend, the poet Jaroslav Seifert

specialized vocabulary, especially neologisms and archaisms.

Halas's more melodic intimate poetry is chiefly concentrated in the collections *Tvář* (Countenance, 1931) and *Hořec* (Gentian, 1933). Extravagant expressiveness has been replaced in these anthologies by a kind of melancholy, but the basic themes have been retained. Throughout Halas's work, social motifs—such as death, childhood, and love—are constantly repeated. Some suggestions of harmony and happiness can be found in his treatment of love, but even so, love is closely linked with the majesty of death. Halas and another of his contemporaries, the great poet Vladimír Holan, made a collection of Czech lyrical folk poetry called *Láska a smrt* (Love and Death), first published in 1938 and expanded in 1946. The relationship between love and death fascinated both poets and permeated all their work.

In 1931 Halas traveled through France, Italy, and Monaco with Libuše Rejlová, who later became his wife. Before their marriage in 1936

Halas wrote her seven hundred letters. In 1936 he went to join a demonstration in Spain, which at that time was in the throes of civil war. In 1937 a son was born, František Xaver, who later became a translator, historian, diplomat, and editor of his father's work. A second son, Jan, was born in 1945. Jan was the author of personal reminiscences about many Czech literary personalities. Originally intended to be broadcast, these texts were published in 1996 by Český spisovatel in Prague under the title *Dodatky* (Postscript).

The most famous and most controversial of Halas's collections of poetry is certainly the long narrative poem inspired by his grandmother, *Staré ženy* (1935; translated as *Old Women*, 1947), which apostrophizes parts of an aging female body—eyes, hands, hair, womb, and face. As soon as it was published, this imposing dialogue with the human aging process became the subject of controversy. To counter Halas's contentions, Stanislav K. Neumann produced his poetic composition *Staří dělníci* (Old Workers, 1950), and during the orthodox communist, Stalinist campaign in the

1950s *Staré ženy* was used as a pretext for bitter attacks on Halas, who had died a short time before. Ladislav Štoll, a Communist Party ideologue responsible for monitoring literature, led this ideological campaign against Halas's work. Štoll wrote in 1950, "The people simply cannot love Halas's morbid poetry," and in a personal attack he described the poet as "a subjective romantic, a spiritualist full of hypochondriacal anxieties." In obedience to the spirit of the times, František Kautman wrote in 1950, referring directly to the poem *Staré ženy*, "It is a monstrous, formless, deeply pessimistic poem, full of ugliness and panicking about women aging." Nor were those critics slow to stress Halas's "morbidity" and "perversion." His explicit sensuous metaphors and the liturgical form of the poem indicate that Halas's inspiration came from the baroque and catholic traditions in the widest sense. Halas wrote in a letter: "Not having the slightest trace of religious feeling I translate all this into poetry," and *Staré ženy* substantiates this contention:

> old women's hands
> yellower than clay under a coffin
> open and empty
> hands work-roughened and worn
> veils of the Styx
> Gemini of prayer
> damaged sceptres
> nests of varicosity
> the trembling of loneliness
> flowerbeds of veins
> mute intercessors
> drooping pennants
> dismissed aides
> impoverished spendthrifts
> paperweights of dreamlessness.

In 1954 Ludvík Kundera, faithful editor and commentator on Halas's work, came to his defense. Particularly after 1956—when the first, hard-line era of Stalinist communism in Czechoslovakia had passed—many well-known Czech poets and critics, such as Jan Grossman, František Hrubín, Zdeněk Pešat, and Jan Trefulka, repeatedly defended Halas's key position in the development of Czech lyric poetry.

The composition *Dělnice* (The Working Women, 1945), inspired by the author's mother, formed a counterpart to the poem *Staré ženy*. In the collection *Dokořán* (Open Wide, 1936) Halas's vision of the polarity in life becomes sharper, linking together extremes: unshakeable faith and hopeless skepticism, and tragic nothingness and

the glorification of the greatness of man and history. This collection also includes the long poem "Nikde" (Nowhere), an elegiac metaphorical variation on a single word, which resembles a litany. "Nikde" is a vehement testament to the poet's desperate search for elementary certainty in life; in Halas's own words, he touched the depths of his obsession with nothingness and extinction. At the same time Halas's nothingness enters into a kind of dialogue with Edgar Allan Poe's "nevermore" from "The Raven" and with the great Czech Romantic Karel Hynek Mácha's (1810–1836) conception of nothingness.

Halas reacted to the events in Munich in 1938 (when Czechoslovakia was forced by France and Britain to hand over its fortified border regions to Nazi Germany, which in effect made Czechoslovakia defenseless against Hitler) with a passionate, bitingly critical collection, *Torzo naděje* (Fragment of Hope, 1938). In this work he fully identifies with the tragic fate of his betrayed nation. Besides reminiscences of the security of home and childhood, he introduces reminders of the basic values of Czech traditional culture. Reacting against the trauma of topical events, he makes reference to the ancient St. Wenceslas chorale, signifying a thousand years of religion and culture in Bohemia, and to the poet Karel Hynek Mácha, a symbol of revolt and pride. In these poems Halas also celebrates the works of Jan Neruda, the founder of modern Czech civilist poetry. In his composition *Naše paní Božena Němcová* (1940; translated as *Our Lady Božena Němcová*, 1944) he was inspired by the life and work of the eponymous writer. Just as in a similar collection of poems by his contemporary Jaroslav Seifert, Božena Němcová in Halas's long poem stands for suffering and the Czech language, but she is also a symbol of resistance and final victory.

During the crisis of September and October 1938, when the Czechoslovak army was briefly mobilized against Hitler and then withdrawn again, and during the Nazi occupation of Czechoslovakia, Halas was published in the illegal press. With critics Bedřich Václavek and Václav Černý and writer Vladislav Vančura, he founded the National Revolutionary Committee of Writers. He was saved from being arrested by the Gestapo by a doctor from the sanatorium at Tišnov, who gave out the information that Halas was suffering from a fatal disease. Before that, Halas had spent October 1938 in a sanatorium in Vráž, and in 1941 he was in a hospital in Prague and at the spa in Poděbrady.

Halas's only publication during the German occupation was the collection *Ladění* (Tuning, 1942), the poet's return to the playful world of a child's imagination. This collection, which includes many of his occasional poems celebrating personalities in Czech culture, omits the poems "Potopa" (The Deluge) and "Hlad" (Hunger) written during the same time. Only fragments of these two poems have survived. In 1965 they finally were edited and published with commentary.

After the war Halas was a member of the National Assembly. He was head of the Publications Department of the Ministry of Information and also president of the Syndicate of Czech Writers. In October 1945 he undertook to go to France with the ashes of the French poet Robert Desnos, who died in Czechoslovakia. Overwhelmed by official duties and honors thrust upon him by the new regime and disillusioned in the face of the reality of power, Halas longed ever more ardently for the chance to pursue his career as a poet in peace. By 1949, however, he was in the Prague Vinohrady hospital, suffering from chronic heart trouble, and he died on 27 October. Halas was buried in Kunštát in Moravia.

His poems written during the protectorate, full of mobilizing passion and intense moral awareness, became part of the first postwar collection, *V řadě* (In Line, 1948). The book takes stock of the horrors of the Nazi occupation and at the same time bids farewell to dying comrades. The apocalypse of war is described with brutally explicit realism. This collection marked the beginning of another period of intense searching for a new technique of poetic expression, culminating in the book of poems *A co?* (What Now?, 1957), published after the poet's death. In it Halas takes his method of fragmentation to the limit; he mixes the most varied styles of language: rare and newly formed words come up against vulgarisms; he uses fragments of various traditional literary forms; and concrete images clash with abstractions in the innovative poetic world created by Halas. *A co?*, as Zdeněk Pešat wrote, is an evident attempt to "restore the worn-out language of poetry." In this work Halas's skepticism about poetry, his lack of faith in it combined with the desire and the need to write it, reaches its climax. In addition to his own poetry, the translations he made from Slavonic languages, including translations from Aleksandr Pushkin and Juliusz Slowacki, form an integral part of Halas's work,

although many of them were not published until after his death.

František Halas's work is among the most complicated in Czech prewar lyric poetry. As Pešat says, "both the chaos of a world shaken after the first world war by violent social upheavals and the most personal poetic contradictions" are reflected in Halas's work. Indeed, the strength of Halas's innovative poetic vision lies in this tension between the life and experience of the individual and his sensitivity to conflict in history and society.

Letters:

"Z dopisů Františka Halase," *Host do domu*, 1961;

"Z korespondence Františka Halase," *Host do domu*, 1964;

Dvanáct dopisů Františka Halase ženě (Prague: Československý spisovatel, 1965);

J. Hek (Hájek) and Š. Vlašín, *Vzájemná korespondence básníků J. Mahena a F. Halase*, collection NM, series C, volume 11, no. 1, 1966;

Vítězslav Nezval, *Depeše z konce tisíciletí*, edited by Marie Krulichová, Milena Vinařová, and Lubomír Tomek (Prague: Československý spisovatel, 1981), pp. 180–181.

Bibliographies:

Bohumil Marčák, "Soupis příspěvků Františka Halase ve *Slezích*," in *Z časů boje* (Brno: Universitní knihovna, 1962);

Ludvík Kundera, "Bibliografie díla Františka Halase," in *Hlad* (Prague: Československý spisovatel, 1966), pp. 152–154;

Básník úzkosti a naděje František Halas (Úz kosti: Knihovna Jiřího Mahena, 1986);

J. Kubíček, "František Halas. Personální bibliografie o životě a díle," in *František Halas–Spolutvůrce pokrokové kulturní politiky* (Brno: Statni vedecka knihovna, 1987);

Lexikon České literatury, volume 2 (Prague: Academia, 1993), pp. 37–43.

Biographies:

Ludvík Kundera, ed., *Španělský podzim Františka Halase, fakta a dokumenty* (Brno: Museum města, 1959);

Kundera, ed., *Kunštátské akordy. Vzpomínky a vyznání* (Brno: Blok, 1966);

Zdeněk Kalista, in *Tváře ve stínu* (České Budějovice: Růže, 1969), pp. 275–293;

Zdeněk Rotrekl, *Skrytá tvář české literatury* (Toronto: 68 Publishers, 1987), pp. 162–198;

Kundera, *František Halas. Životem umřít* (Prague: Československý spisovatel, 1989), pp. 317–380;

Bedřich Fučík, *Čtrnáctero zastavení* (Prague: Melantrich-Arkýř, 1992).

Zdeněk Pešat, "František Halas," in *Lexikon české literatury,* volume 2 (Prague: Academia, 1993), pp. 37–39.

References:

Milan Blahynka, "Doslov," in *Básnické dílo* (Prague: Československý spisovatel, 1978), pp. 440–453;

Jindřich Chalupecký, "Edice Potopy a Hladu Františka Halase," *Literární archív* (Prague: Památník národního písemnictví, 1966), pp. 123–178;

Bohumil Doležal, "František Halas—mýtus a skutečnost," *Tvář* (1969): 27–31;

Alfred French, *The Poets of Prague: Czech Poetry between the Wars* (London: Oxford University Press, 1969);

František Halas. Spolutvůrce pokrokové kulturní politiky: sborník z konference (Brno: Muzejní a vlastivědná společnost v Brně, 1987);

Jan Grossman, "Halas esejista," *Host do domu,* 11 (1964): 2–6;

Grossman, "Předmluva," in František Halas, *Básně* (Prague: Československý spisovatel, 1957), pp. 7–52;

F. X. Halas, "Halasův esej O poezii," *Česká literatura,* 1 (1967): 47–77;

Aleš Haman, "Nezval a Halas (Pokus o existenciální poetiku)," *Česká literatura,* 4 (1967): 312–341;

William E. Harkins, "František Halas," in *Anthology of Czech Literature* (New York: Columbia University Press, 1953), pp. 203–206;

V. Kolár, "Torzo naděje," in his *Rozumět literatuře* (Prague: SPN, 1986), pp. 335–341;

Zdeněk Kožmín, "Halasův prostor," in his *Studie a kritiky* (Prague: Torst, 1995), pp. 161–166;

Ludvík Kundera, "Básník dokořán," in *Sbohem múzy,* by Halas (Prague: Mladá fronta, 1963), pp. 201–232;

Vladimír Macura, "Neologismus ve struktuře Halasova díla," *Česká literatura,* 3 (1969): 201–227;

Jaroslav Med, "Halas-Trakl-Reynek," *Česká literatura,* 3 (1969): 228–240;

Zdeněk Pešat, *Jak číst poezii* (Prague: Československý spisovatel, 1969), pp. 131–141;

Pešat, "Poezie Františka Halase," in his *Dialogy s poezií* (Prague, 1985), pp. 63–100;

Sylvie Richterová, "Kontury ticha: Oxymóron v moderní české poezii," in her *Slova a ticho* (Prague: Československý spisovatel, 1991), pp. 79–93;

V. Smetáček (Miloslav Červenka), "Růst Halasova Ladění ve světle rukopisů," in his *Literární archív* (Prague: Památník národního písemnictví, 1972), pp. 181–230;

Bedřich Václavek, *Tvorbou k realitě* (Prague: Svoboda, 1937), pp. 25–38;

J. Waczków, *František Halas* (Warsaw: Czytelnik, 1980);

Pavol Winczer, "Litanická forma a Halasovy *Staré ženy,*" *Romboid* (1969): 29–34.

Jaroslav Hašek

(30 April 1883 – 3 January 1923)

Luboš Merhaut
Institute of Czech Literature, Academy of Sciences of the Czech Republic, Prague

BOOKS: *Májové výkřiky a jiné verše,* by Hašek and Ladislav Hájek Domažlický (Prague: Josef Sölch, 1903);

Dobrý voják Švejk a jiné podivné historky (Prague: Hejda & Tuček, 1912);

Trampoty pana Tenkráta (Prague: J. R. Vilímek, 1912);

Kalamajka (Prague: Antonin Svěcený, 1913);

Průvodčí cizinců a jiné satiry z cest i z domova (Prague: Hejda & Tuček, 1913);

Můj obchod se psy a jiné humoresky (Prague: J. R. Vilímek, 1915);

Dobrý voják Švejk v zajetí (Kyjev: Slovanské vydavatelství, 1917);

Dva tucty povídek, edited by K. H. Vik (Prague: Jan Otto, 1920);

Pepíček Nový a jiné povídky (Prague: Tribuna, 1921);

Tři muži se žralokem a jiné poučné historky (Prague: Arnošt Sauer & Jaroslav Hašek, 1921);

Osudy dobrého vojáka Švejka za světové války, volume 1 (Prague: Arnošt Sauer & Václav Čermák, 1921); volume 2 (Prague: A. Sauer & J. Hašek, 1922); volume 3 (Prague: J. Hašek, 1923); expurgated edition, translated by Paul Selver as *The Good Soldier: Schweik* (London: Heinemann, 1930; Garden City, N.Y.: Douldeday, Doran, 1930); complete edition, translated by Cecil Parrott as *The Good Soldier Švejk and His Fortunes in the World War* (London: Heinemann, 1973; New York: Crowell, 1974);

Mírová konference a jiné humoresky (Prague: J. Hašek, 1922);

Švejkův silvestr, by Hašek and Josef Kolář (Prague: A. Fencl, 1922);

Malá zoologická zahrada. Povídky o zvířátkách známých i nově objevených (Prague: Práce, 1950?);

Panoptikum měšťáků, byrokratů a jiných zkamenělin, edited by Zdena Ančík (Prague: ROH, 1950);

Politické a sociální dějiny strany mírného pokroku v mezích zákona, edited by Ančík, Milan Jankovič, and Radko Pytlík (Prague: Československý spisovatel, 1963; revised, edited by Pytlík, 1982);

Jaroslav Hašek

Velitelem města Bugulmy: Z tajemství mého pobytu v Rusku, volume 15 of *Spisy Jaroslava Haška,* edited by Ančík, Jankovič, Pytlík, and Břetislav Štorek (Prague: Československý spisovatel, 1966);

Zábavný a poučný koutek Jaroslava Haška, volume 12 of *Spisy Jaroslava Haška,* edited by Ančík, Jankovič, and Pytlík (Prague: Československý spisovatel, 1973);

Větrný mlynář a jeho dcera: Kabaretní scény a hry bohém-ské družiny Jaroslava Haška, edited by Pytlík and Miroslav Laiske (Prague: Československý spisovatel, 1976).

Editions and Collections: *Sebrané spisy Jaroslava Haška,* 16 volumes, edited by Antonín Dolenský (Prague: Adolf Synek, 1924–1929);

Osudy dobrého vojáka Švejka za světové války, edited by Zdena Ančík and František Daneš (Prague: Naše vojsko, 1954);

Spisy Jaroslava Haška, 16 volumes, edited by Ančík, Daneš, Milada Chlíbcová, Milan Jankovič, Radko Pytlík, and Břetislav Štorek (Prague: Státní nakladatelství krásné literatury, hudby a umění a Československý spisovatel, 1955–1973)—comprises volume 1, *Črty, povídky a humoresky z cest;* volume 2, *Loupežný vrah před soudem;* volume 3, *Dědictví po panu Šafránkovi;* volume 4, *Zrádce národa v Chotěboři;* volume 5, *Fialový hrom;* volume 6, *Utrpení pana Tenkráta;* volume 7, *O dětech a zvířátkách;* volume 8, *Galerie karikatur;* volume 9, *Politické a sociální dějiny strany mírného pokroku v mezích zákona;* volume 10, *Dobrý voják Švejk před válkou a jiné podivné historky;* volume 11, *Májové výkřiky Básně a prózy;* volume 12, *Zábavný a poučný koutek Jaroslava Haška;* volumes 13–14, *Dobrý voják Švejk v zajetí;* volume 15, *Velitelem města Bugulmy: Z tajemství mého pobytu v Rusku;* volume 16, *Moje zpověď;*

Abeceda humoru, 2 volumes, edited by Ančík, Jankovič, and Pytlík (Prague: Československý spisovatel, 1960);

Dekameron humoru a satiry, edited by Ančík, Chlíbcová, Jankovič, and Pytlík (Prague: Československý spisovatel, 1968);

Praha ve dne i v noci aneb Týden mezi Dacany, edited by Jankovič and Pytlík (Prague: Československý spisovatel, 1973);

Výbor z díla Jaroslava Haška, 5 volumes, edited by Pytlík and Jankovič (Prague: Československý spisovatel, 1977–1982)—comprises volume 1, *Politické a sociální dějiny mírného pokroku v mezích zákona;* volume 2, *Procházka přes hranice. Idylky z cest a jiné humoresky* (První dekameron); volume 3, *Lidožroutská historie. Parodie, morytáty a banality* (Druhý dekameron); volume 4, *Reelní podnik. Grotesky a mystifikace* (Třetí dekameron); volume 5, *Osudy dobrého vojáka Švejka za světové války;*

Povídky, 2 volumes (Prague: Československý spisovatel, 1988).

Editions in English: "My Dog Shop," translated by Fern Long, in *Hundred Towers: A Czechoslovak Anthology of Creative Writing,* edited by F. C.

Weiskopf (New York: Fischer, 1945), pp. 56–70;

The Tourist Guide: Twenty-Six Stories, translated by Ivo Havlů (Prague: Artia, 1961);

"Prisoner Sheyba's Rebellion," translated by Havlů, in *The Linden Tree: An Anthology of Czech and Slovak Literature 1890–1960,* edited by Mojmír Otruba and Zdeněk Pešat (Prague: Artia, 1962), pp. 142–153;

The Red Commissar: Including Further Adventures of the Good Soldier Švejk and Other Stories, translated by Parrott (New York: Dial, 1981);

Little Stories by a Great Master, translated by Doris Kožíšková (Prague: Orbis, 1984);

The Bachura Scandal and Other Stories and Sketches, translated by Alan Menhennet (London: Angel, 1991);

"18 Short Sketches by Jaroslav Hašek," translated, with an introduction, by Stáňa Doležalová Williams and Joanna Radwanska, *Slavic and East European Arts,* 7 (Spring 1991): 11–69;

Thus Spake the Good Soldier Švejk: The Best Sayings from Hašek's Švejk, edited by Radko Pytlík, with translations by Cecil Parrott (Prague: Emporius, 1997).

Prague writer and humorist Jaroslav Hašek became internationally known for the novel *Osudy dobrého vojáka Švejka za světové války* (1921–1923; translated and expurgated as *The Good Soldier: Schweik,* 1930; also translated as *The Good Soldier Švejk and His Fortunes in the World War,* 1973). He was also the author of approximately 1,500 stories, sketches, and newspaper columns; in addition, he wrote plays for cabarets. Hašek took his subjects directly from his own life and experiences. His work was closely linked to his unconventional lifestyle, which became the subject of many stories and legends that Hašek himself helped to create. In his best works the spontaneity of his storytelling and overall ironic detachment indicate his belief in unpretentiousness and tolerance. His original practical jokes became a timeless metaphor for a world full of absurdities and misunderstandings.

Jaroslav Matěj František Hašek was born on 30 April 1883 in Prague. Both his father, Josef Hašek, a mathematics teacher and bank official, and his mother, Kateřina (née Jarešová), came from south Bohemian families of farming stock. They lived in Prague under precarious circumstances, moving often because of Josef's alcoholism and financial troubles. Jaroslav attended the secondary school on Žitná Street in Prague, but left in 1898 after academic difficulties. Instead he began to work in a

Hašek and Jarmila Majerová, his first wife, in 1908

the rising generation that stressed individual skepticism and revolt against convention. Reacting against aesthetic decadence and symbolism, they turned their attention directly to their own experiences in their daily lives. They tended to take up anarchic attitudes and to write in a loose, popular, mocking style. Hašek, however, was by nature cynical and anti-literary-establishment, and he soon broke away from contemporary literary movements. For him, writing was a mere job. He wrote mainly for amusement—his own and the public's. Even his first book, *Májové výkřiky a jiné verše* (Cries of May and Other Verse, 1903), jointly written with Ladislav Hájek Domažlický, was a parody, shattering the sentimental delusions of poets and juxtaposing them with the unattractiveness of ordinary life and the contrasts between rich and poor. The activities and the naiveté of writers and artists—including himself—often became the targets of Hašek's mockery. Hašek later only rarely wrote satirical verse, such as *Kalamajka* (1913), which takes its title from the name of an old Czech dance.

In the period prior to World War I, Hašek worked as a publicist and editor, but his primary income came from the hundreds of humorous short stories and anecdotes that were printed in many newspapers and magazines. He used more than a hundred pseudonyms, some of which have probably not been discovered. Thereafter, he published collections of humorous stories: *Dobrý voják Švejk a jiné podivné historky* (The Good Soldier Švejk and Other Strange Stories, 1912), *Trampoty pana Tenkráta* (The Tribulations of Mr. Tenkrát, 1912), *Průvodčí cizinců a jiné satiry z cest i z domova* (1913; translated as *The Tourist Guide: Twenty-Six Stories*, 1961), and *Můj obchod se psy a jiné humoresky* (My Dealings with Dogs and Other Amusing Tales, 1915).

Writing came easily to Hašek. He wrote almost without conscious effort, usually in coffeehouses or pubs from which his manuscripts went straight to the editor or the printer, often without Hašek reading them over. He soon became a popular humorist. Almost every section of society provided him with material, but he found his preferred subjects in town life, in unusual or bizarre details, characters, and situations. The sarcasm in his short pieces often targeted narrow-minded politicians, the church, and the army. He ridiculed bureaucracy and exposed clichés and excessive pettifogging, reducing them to the absurd by the use of a provocative, nonsensical narrative style. He was able to highlight witty, pointed, tragicomic moments of discord and contrasts in lifestyles as well as conflicts between

chemist's shop in Perštýn in central Prague. From 1899 to 1902 he studied at the Commercial Academy on Resslova Street, and after his final examinations he worked in the Slavia Bank. A year later, however, he gave up that job and set off on a journey through Slovakia, Hungary, the Balkans, and Galicia. In the next few years, he visited such places as Bavaria, Switzerland, and Austria and often traveled around Bohemia. He had already begun writing when he was still a student, and his first efforts had been published in newspapers and magazines. These were chiefly amusing accounts of his travels and short literary essays inspired by his roaming through Moravia, Slovakia, and Poland. Gradually, his studies of everyday life and original portraits of simple people became realistic rather than romantically charming, and his extravagant humor was already a signature element.

At the beginning of the century, Czech cultural life was profiting from the modernist influences of the 1890s. Hašek counted himself one of words and deeds or between ideals and harsh reality.

The raciness and irony, almost contempt, in Hašek's narratives were closely related to his own life, which to a certain extent he "created" by playing extravagant, clownish pranks and perpetrating hoaxes with almost dadaistic features. He moved in a peculiar, nocturnal world of licentiousness and fantasy; in pubs he was an entertainer, an alcoholic, and a troublemaker skirmishing with the police. In many of the stories about him it is difficult to separate truth from fiction. The interrelation of his life, literary work, and hoaxes is the determining factor in explaining and interpreting all of Hašek's work.

At first Hašek showed radical and anarchic tendencies. In 1904 he became editor of the north Bohemian anarchic paper *Omladina* (The Younger Generation) and between 1906 and 1907 he was on the editorial staff of the similarly anarchic papers *Chuďas* (Poor Man), *Nová omladina* (New Younger Generation), and *Komuna* (The Commune). In 1907 he was sent to prison for a month for his part in an anarchic rally, and after that he left the movement. In 1910 Hašek married Jarmila Majerová, the daughter of a wealthy stucco decorator and later an author of humorous short stories, novels, and books for young people. However, after his son, Richard, was born two years later, Hašek left his family and again lived his wild life. He also made an apparent attempt to commit suicide in 1911 and spent three weeks in a psychiatric clinic. To earn his living in the years between 1908 and 1913 he had several casual jobs: he edited the magazines *Ženský obzor* (The Female Horizon) and *Svět zvířat* (The World of Animals), worked in the election office of the National Socialist Party, bought and sold dogs, and wrote a gossip column for *České slovo* (The Czech Word).

Through his work as a journalist he perpetrated a remarkable series of frauds and hoaxes. Years later these escapades were collected in a book titled *Zábavný a poučný koutek Jaroslava Haška* (Amusing and Instructive Articles by Jaroslav Hašek, 1973). For the scientific journal *Svět zvířat* Hašek, besides editing humorous tales and anecdotes, added bits to scholarly treatises, caricatured their style, made strange comparisons between the animal and human worlds, indulged in hyperbole, and invented "unknown" animal species. He engaged in correspondence with outraged readers and answered "fan" letters (some of which he wrote himself). Pictorial material was also treated unconventionally; Hašek made innovative use of the technique of collage. These antics made him the pioneer of the so-called journalistic hoax.

Hašek also used his talent for invention on old news items for the paper *České slovo*, changing them into anecdotes. He seized the chance to write for papers of opposing political persuasion—the social democratic *Právo lidu* (The Rights of the People) and the national socialist *České slovo*—giving early warning of the nature of his future political hoaxes. An example is given by Václav Menger in his 1946 biography, *Lidský profil Jaroslava Haška* (A Profile of Jaroslav Hašek):

> Once there was a controversy that filled at least fourteen issues of one of the papers and in the end it was discovered that Hašek had written both sides of the dispute. In the articles he had attacked himself so violently that the editors feared there would be a court case. When the truth came out Hašek could continue to write for both papers only under new pseudonyms.

In the spring of 1911 Hašek perpetrated his most sensational literary and political hoax. He turned his fellow vagabonds from the pub into the Party of Moderate and Peaceful Progress Within the Limits of the Law and took part in a campaign for a by-election to the Imperial Council in Vinohrady, a section of Prague. In his speeches, given in pubs, he parodied political infighting and invented arguments, or made up "happenings" and practical jokes. Although he was not registered as an official candidate, he allegedly earned several dozen votes.

Between the autumn of 1911 and the spring of 1912 Hašek wrote *Politické a sociální dějiny strany mírného pokroku v mezích zákona* (The Political and Social History of the Party of Moderate and Peaceful Progress Within the Limits of the Law), although it was not published until 1963. In this collection, one of his best works, he used various types of writing—including reports, pamphlets, and letters—to record the history of his entourage and his lectures. He included autobiographical details from his travels, journalism, and other experiences, drawing portraits of friends and people from contemporary cultural and social life. He gave exaggerated descriptions of various muddles, misunderstandings, and mistakes. He ridiculed popular rhetoric, and, by caricaturing historical cases, clichés, and paradoxes, he created a lively satire on petty politics, jingoism, hollow pedantry, and compulsive writing. Less flamboyantly, he wrote of the positive aspects and the dangers of the power of words, showing his readers ways to avoid being taken in.

Before World War I, Hašek was a guest actor in Prague cabarets. The Party of Moderate and Peaceful Progress Within the Limits of the Law was

Hašek (right) during his 1911 mock campaign as a candidate for the Party of Moderate and Peaceful Progress Within the Limits of the Law

turned into a cabaret act that was performed on special occasions in wine cellars and restaurants. There were short scenes and one-act plays by Hašek, group plays, and improvisations, in which Josef Mach, Jiří Mahen, and František Langer took part. The book *Větrný mlynář a jeho dcera* (The Miller and His Daughter, 1976), pieced together from surviving manuscripts, records this side of Hašek's life.

In February 1915 Hašek joined the 91st Infantry Regiment in České Budějovice. In May he went with them to Bruck a.d. Leitha, and in June they crossed the Raba River and went by way of Budapest to the Galician front. In September he was taken prisoner during the retreat and sent to a prisoner-of-war camp in Dárnice, near Kiev, and then to Totskoye, near Buzuluk, where he survived a typhoid epidemic. In the spring of 1916 he enlisted in the Czech Foreign Legion, fighting against Austria on the side of the Allies. In the legion Hašek worked as a typist and was secretary to the regimental committee. He also wrote humorous articles and reports for the magazine *Čechoslovan* (The Czecho-Slav), in which he supported the fight for an independent state. In 1917 he was involved in the battle of Zborov, and his valorous conduct was mentioned in dispatches. After the retreat to Ukraine, however, he came into conflict with his superiors when he

criticized the small-mindedness and the overcautious attitude of the Czech National Council in Russia and the leadership of the legion.

After the Bolshevik revolution in Russia, Hašek refused to go with the legion to France, and in the subsequent chaos at the end of 1917 and the beginning of 1918 he became involved in the attempt to establish a revolutionary council of Czech workers and soldiers in Kiev. After that he went to Moscow and joined the Czech Social Democrats (the Bolsheviks). He became a political activist in the Red Army, serving as a press organizer, editor of army magazines in various languages, and publicist. He organized recruitment in Samara. In September he went to Simbirsk; from there he was sent to Bugulma as assistant to the military commander of the town. In 1919 he was in charge of the army printing works in Ufa. After going to Chelyabinsk—and later to Omsk, Krasnoyarsk, and Irkutsk—he worked in the political department for national minorities in the Fifth Army.

During the five years of war and revolution the serious side of Hašek's nature revealed itself. Still impulsive and politically a radical, he gradually began to believe in the idea of social justice for which he might be able to work and live respectably. If the idea of social justice was to be put into practice, it would improve conditions even in Bohemia. But Hašek, always keenly aware of the conflict between dream and reality, eventually seems to have lost this faith.

In 1920 in Krasnoyarsk, Hašek married for the second time—without being divorced from his first wife. He returned with his second wife, Aleksandra (Šura) Lvova, who was employed in a printing works, to Prague by way of Narvik and Stettin. He was expected to work as a political activist in the now-independent Czechoslovakia. The country to which he returned after the war hardly resembled the country he had left, however. His personal circumstances were complicated, and he relapsed into his unconventional lifestyle and started drinking again. He avoided politics and political debate, and his jokes became coarser and more cynical, evidently because of the resignation and spiritual schizophrenia he felt on his return. At the same time he renewed the ironic practical jokes in the spirit of the Party of Moderate and Peaceful Progress Within the Limits of the Law, and he also wrote cabaret acts. For a short time he worked in the cabaret Červená sedma (The Red Seven). Once again he contributed humorous short stories and articles to magazines. These pieces, along with earlier works, were collected as *Dva tucty povídek* (Two Dozen Tales, 1920), *Pepíček Nový a jiné povídky* (Pepíček Nový and Other Stories, 1921), *Tři muži se žralokem a jiné poučné historky* (Three Men and a Shark and Other Illuminating Tales, 1921), and *Mírová konference a jiné humoresky* (Peace Conference and Other Funny Stories, 1922). He recorded his experiences in Russia in the series of stories *Velitelem města Bugulmy* (The Commander of the Town of Bugulma), originally published in magazines in 1921 and in book form in 1966. In these stories, in which his skepticism is obvious, he describes with ironic detachment and satirical exaggeration the absurd quarrels with the professional, dogmatic revolutionary; the conflicts of reason and blind faith in an atmosphere of chaos with continual fighting; and the fortunes of various individuals.

In August 1921 Hašek moved to the village of Lipnice nad Sázavou in southeast Bohemia, where he worked on his novel, *Osudy dobrého vojáka Švejka za světové války*. He had already begun writing it in Prague, where it appeared in installments from 1921 to 1923. When his health deteriorated, he dictated the text of the novel, almost ready for publication, using his encyclopedic memory. However, he did not complete the task. He died on 3 January 1923 as a result of pneumonia and heart failure.

Cover for the first installment of Hašek's celebrated novel about "the good soldier Švejk" (1921-1923)

Hašek had sketched out the character of the good soldier Švejk in two other books. In the collections of short stories *Dobrý voják Švejk a jiné podivné historky* Hašek introduced Švejk as a good-natured idiot who brought antimilitary slapstick comedy into a rigid military situation. Hašek based the comedy on mishaps caused by Švejk's exaggerated willingness to do his duty despite his clumsiness. In *Dobrý voják Švejk v zajetí* (The Good Soldier Švejk in Captivity, 1917) Hašek viewed the eponymous character in a more satirical fashion and with more black humor. But, he was also looking at Švejk in the spirit of the anti-Austrian propaganda as it appeared in the press at the time. Only after wide-ranging postwar revision—influenced by the author's conflicting experiences and his return to his former nonconformist skepticism—was the strange, many-sided, sophisticated folk humorist and storyteller born.

The novel recounts the adventures of ordinary folk from Prague, particularly Josef Švejk, who begins as a crooked dog fancier. In 1914, on the day of the assassination of Archduke Franz Ferdinand and his wife, Sophie, in Sarajevo, Švejk is arrested by the police and imprisoned for treasonous remarks. After proclaiming his absolute loyalty to the Austro-Hungarian monarchy he is examined in a lunatic asylum and freed from police custody. Then he is called up to the army. He suffers from rheumatism but is branded a malingerer. He undergoes "treatment" in a hospital and in prison. He becomes batman to the chaplain, Katz, and later to Lieutenant Lukáš, with whom he goes to České Budějovice to a front-line regiment (after being taken for a Russian spy by the gendarmes). Then they go through Hungary to the Galician front, where, with others in Russian uniform, Švejk is taken prisoner by the military police and condemned to death; but his identity is verified, and he is sent back to his unit.

The book covers an enormous range of events from everyday life as well as war and includes a host of diverse minor characters and incidents. Hašek parodies contemporary texts and official documents. He uses different kinds of language: bureaucratic and military Austro-German; the language of contemporary propaganda, common Czech; and vulgarisms—Hungarian, Polish, and Yiddish expressions. The straightforward unfolding of the plot, however, is swamped by Švejk's many anecdotes and running commentaries, frequently presented in a vast range of contrasting styles and attributing different motives and significance to his actions.

Practically the only way the reader "recognizes" the central, unifying character is through his paradoxical discourses and hyperbole. His other characteristics—origin, physiognomy, psychology, emotions, and intentions—remain vague and confused. What Švejk actually does is revealed predominantly through his language; his idiosyncratic way of speaking changes according to circumstances.

The difficulty of penetrating the fragmented, ambiguous speech and the loose structure of the work means that various contradictory or even misleading interpretations are possible. For example, many critics emphasize Švejk's crafty pragmatism, calling him the embodiment of the Central European mentality and the Czech national character in particular. Even the idealized illustrations by Hašek's friend Josef Lada, which have become a traditional part of the book, can be misleading because Švejk is not really the plump, aging, genial, unattractive fellow Lada depicts. Švejk, however, should not be regarded as having only one side to his character. He is not to be seen merely as a simple-minded coward, a malingerer and saboteur, a stolid egoist, a good-natured or cunning sophist, a folk, or even proletarian, hero.

Likewise, all of Hašek's work, epitomized and dominated by Švejk, has been received in widely different ways. It has been enthusiastically praised and totally rejected. It has been considered negative and optimistic; in fact, it has often touched both extremes. At the same time, critics and interpreters have pointed out affinities with the traditions of Miguel de Cervantes and François Rabelais and with the picaresque novel. They have also sought parallels with the work of Franz Kafka. *Osudy dobrého vojáka Švejka za světové války* has been translated into dozens of languages and has been the subject of many theatrical productions and film adaptations by such figures as Max Brod, Hans Reimann, Erwin Piscator, and Bertolt Brecht.

Osudy dobrého vojáka Švejka za světové války was, above all, written to entertain. However, it transcended the typical antiwar satirical novel. A more profound meaning in the work comes out through the language—fluent and lively, with inventive, intellectual plays on words, revealing its creator's peculiar vision and experience of the world.

Letters:

Lidský profil Jaroslava Haška: Korespondence a dokumenty, edited by Radko Pytlík and Marie Havránková (Prague: Československý spisovatel, 1979).

Bibliographies:

Boris Mědílek, comp., *Bibliografie Jaroslava Haška. Soupis jeho díla a literatury o něm* (Prague: Památník národního písemnictví, 1983);

Augustin Matovčík, *Jaroslav Hašek na Slovensku: Bio-bibliografický prehlad s ukážkami diela* (Martin: Matica slovenská, 1983).

Biographies:

Antonín Bouček, *Padesát historek ze života Jaroslava Haška* (Prague: V. Boučková, 1923); revised as *Kopa historek ze života Jaroslava Haška* (Prague: Zápotočný, 1938);

Zdeněk Matěj Kuděj, *Ve dvou se to lépe táhne* (Prague: Ústřední dělnické knihkupectví a nakl., 1923);

Franta Sauer and Ivan Suk, *In Memoriam Jaroslava Haška* (Prague: Privately printed, 1924);

Ladislav Hájek, *Z mých vzpomínek na Jaroslava Haška* (Prague: Čechie, 1925);

Emil Artur Longen, *Jaroslav Hašek* (Prague: E. Beaufort, 1928);

Kuděj, *Když táhne silná čtyřka* (Prague: Ústřední dělnické knihkupectví a nakl., 1930);

Václav Menger, *Jaroslav Hašek doma* (Prague: Sfinx, B. Janda, 1935); revised as *Lidský profil Jaroslava Haška* (Prague: J. Koliandr, 1946);

Menger, *Jaroslav Hašek v zajetí* (Prague: J. Koliandr, 1948);

Gustav Roger Opočenský, *Čtvrtstoletí s Jaroslavem Haškem* (Vimperk: J. Steinbrener, 1948);

Zdena Ančík, *O životě Jaroslava Haška* (Prague: Československý spisovatel, 1953);

Vladimír Stejskal, *Hašek na Lipnici* (Havlíčkův Brod: Krajské nakl., 1953);

Jaroslav Křížek, *Jaroslav Hašek v revolučním Rusku* (Prague: Naše vojsko, 1957);

Kliment Štěpánek, *Vzpomínky na poslední léta Jaroslava Haška* (Havlíčkův Brod: Krajské nakl., 1960);

N. P. Yelansky, *Jaroslav Gašek v revoljucionnoj Rossii* (Moskva: Socekgiz, 1960);

A. M. Dunayevsky, *Idu za Gašekom* (Moskva: Voyennoe izd., 1963);

František Langer, *Byli a bylo* (Prague: Československý spisovatel, 1963);

Gustav Janouch, *Jaroslav Hašek, der Vater des braven Soldaten Schwejk* (Bern & Munich: A. Francke, 1966);

Radko Pytlík, *Toulavé house* (Prague: Mladá fronta, 1971); revised as *Zpráva o Jaroslavu Haškovi* (Prague: Panorama, 1982);

I. L. Trofimkin, *Jaroslav Gashek* (Leningrad: Prosveshchenie, 1973);

Josef Pospíšil, *Znal jsem Haška* (Hradec Králové: Kruh, 1977);

Cecil Parrott, *The Bad Bohemian: The Life of Jaroslav Hašek, Creator of "The Good Soldier Švejk"* (London: Bodley Head, 1978);

Jan N. Berwid-Buquoy, *Die Abenteur des garnicht so braven Humoristen Jaroslav Hašek: Legenden und Wirklichkeit* (Berlin: BI-HI, 1989).

References:

Hana Arie-Haifman, "Švejk, the homo ludens in *Language and literary theory: in honor of Ladislav Matějka*, edited by Benjamin A. Stolz, I. R. Titunik, and Lubomír Doležel (Ann Arbor: University of Michigan Press, 1984), pp. 307–322;

Václav Bělohradský, "The Retreat into the Uniform and the Disintegration of Order: Švejk as an Integral Part of Central-European Literature," *Scottish Slavonic Review*, 2 (1983): 21–40;

I. A. Bernshtejn, *Pochozhdenia bravogo soldata Shvejka Jaroslava Gasheka* (Moscow: Khudozhestvennaia literatura, 1971);

Přemysl Blažíček, *Haškův Švejk* (Prague: Československý spisovatel, 1991);

Max Brod, "Der gute Soldat Schwejk," in his *Prager Sternenhimmel* (Prague: Orbis, 1923), pp. 212–215;

Jindřich Chalupecký, "Podivný Hašek," in his *Expresionisté* by Zina Trochová, Jaroslav Med, and Jan Šulc (Prague: Torst, 1992), pp. 175–191;

Chalupecký, "The Tragic Comedy of Jaroslav Hašek," *Cross Currents: A Yearbook of Central European Culture*, 2 (1983): 137–153;

František Daneš, "Příspěvek k poznání jazyka a slohu Haškových Osudů dobrého vojáka Švejka," *Naše řeč*, 37 (1954): 124–139;

Bohumil Doležal, "Nedokonalost Haškových 'Osudů,'" in *Podoby*, edited by Adolf Hoffmeister (Prague: Československý spisovatel, 1967), pp. 171–183;

Lubomír Doležel, "Circular Patterns: Hašek and *The Good Soldier Švejk*," in *Poetica Slavica*, edited by J. D. Clayton and G. Schaarschmidt (Ottawa: University of Ottawa Press, 1981), pp. 21–28;

Jaroslav Durych, "Český pomník: Dobrý voják Švejk," in his *Ejhle, člověk!* (Prague: L. Kuncíř, 1928);

Leslie A. Fiedler, "The Antiwar Novel and *The Good Soldier Schweik*," in his *Collected Essays*, volume 2, (New York: Stein & Day, 1971), pp. 224–234;

Emanuel Frynta, *Hašek, the Creator of Schweik* (Prague: Artia, 1965);

Jan Grossman, "Kapitoly o Jaroslavu Haškovi," in his *Analýzy* (Prague: Československý spisovatel, 1991), pp. 22–31;

Mojmir Grygar, ed., *Czech Studies: Literature, Language, Culture* (Amsterdam & Atlanta: Rodopi, 1990);

Andreas Guski, "Mystifikation als Textstrategie: Zum Dadaismus in Hašeks Švejk," *Ars Philologica Slavica*, edited by Vsevolod Setschkareff, Peter Rehder, and Herta Schmid (Munich: 1988), pp. 149–161;

Jiří Hájek, *Jaroslav Hašek* (Prague: Melantrich, 1983);

Milan Hodík, *Encyklopedie pro milovníky Švejka*, edited by Pavel Landa (Prague: Academia, 1998);

Milan Jankovič, *Jaroslav Hašek, literární pozůstalost v Památníku národního písemnictví v Praze* (Prague: Památník národního písemnictví, 1976);

Jankovič, *Nesamozřejmost smyslu* (Prague: Československý spisovatel, 1991);

Jankovič, *Umělecká pravdivost Haškova Švejka* (Prague: ČSAV, 1960);

Jankovič and Radko Pytlík, *Švejk dobývá svět: Výběr z výroků našich i světových kulturních činitelů o Haškovi a Švejkovi* (Hradec Králové: Kruh, 1983);

N. P. Jelanskij, *Ranneje tvorchestvo Jaroslava Gasheka* (Saratov: SGPI, 1960);

Predrag Jirsak, "Talking the World Down According to Hašek," *Cross Currents: A Yearbook of Central European Culture*, 2 (1983):154–158;

Michael Jung and Berndt Kühnel, *Des braven Soldaten Schwejk Leibgerichte und solche, die es geworden wären, wenn er sie kennen gelernt hatte* (Wiesbaden: CSI Communication Services, 1977);

Josef Kalaš, ed., *Jaroslav Hašek ve fotografii* (Prague: Československý spisovatel, 1959);

G. P. Kent, *A Critical and Interpretative Study of Non-Satirical Elements in the Form and Title Hero of the Osudy dobrého vojáka Švejka za světové války by J. Hašek* (Providence, R.I.: Brown University Press, 1978);

Karel Kosík, "Hašek and Kafka: 1883–1922/23," *Cross Currents: A Yearbook of Central European Culture*, 2 (1983): 127–136;

Peter Kosta, "Sprachspiel und Wortspiel in den Abenteuern des braves Soldaten Švejk von J. Hašek," *Slavistische Studien zum X. Internationalen Slavistenkongress in Sofia 1988*, edited by R. Olesch and H. Rothe (Köln-Wien, 1988), pp. 83–96;

Michal Lion, *Der Einfluss von Jaroslav Hašek's "Die Abenteur des braven Soldaten Schwejk" auf die tschechische antimilitaristische Satire der Nachkriegszeit* (Wien, 1977);

Luboš Merhaut, "Haškův svět mystifikace," in his *Cesty stylizace: Stylizace, "okraj" a mystifikace v české literatuře přelomu devatenáctého a dvacátého století* (Prague: ÚČL, 1994), pp. 180–217;

Merhaut, ed., *Světová literárněvědná bohemistika 2: Úvahy a studie o české literatuře* (Prague: ÚČL AV ČR, 1996);

Ivan Olbracht, "Osudy dobrého vojáka Švejka za světové války," in his *O umění a společnosti* (Prague: Československý spisovatel, 1958);

Cecil Parrott, *Jaroslav Hašek: A Study of Švejk and the Short Stories* (Cambridge & New York: Cambridge University Press, 1982);

Willy Prochazka, "Kafka's Association with Jaroslav Hašek and the Czech Anarchists," *Modern Austrian Literature*, 11, nos. 3–4 (1978): 275–287;

Prochazka, *Satire in Jaroslav Hašek's Novel "The Good Soldier Schweik"* (New York: New York University Press, 1966);

Robert B. Pynsent, "The Last Days of Austria: Hašek and Kraus," in *The First World War in Fiction*, edited by Holger Klein (London: Macmillan, 1976), pp. 136–148;

Radko Pytlík, *Kniha o Švejkovi* (Prague: Československý spisovatel, 1983);

Pytlík, David Short, and others, *Jaroslav Hašek and the Good Soldier Schweik* (Prague: Panorama, 1983);

Sylvie Richterová, "Jasnozřivý génius a jeho slepý prorok: Haškův Dobrý voják Švejk," in her *Slova a ticho* (Mnichov: K. Jadrný, Arkýř, 1986);

Angelo Ripellino, *Praga magica* (Torino: Einaudi, 1973);

Susanna Roth, "Le brave soldat Chvéik et le baron de Münchhausen," *Revue des Etudes Slaves*, 58, no. 1 (1986): 109–117;

Walter Schamschula, ed., *Jaroslav Hašek 1883–1983: Proceedings of the International Hašek-Symposium, Bamberg, June 24–27, 1983* (Frankfurt & New York: Peter Lang, 1983);

G. G. Shubin, *Jaroslav Hašek* (Moscow: Znanie, 1982);

Ladislav Soldán, *Jaroslav Hašek* (Prague: Horizont, 1982);

Milada Součková, *A Literary Satellite: Czechoslovak-Russian Literary Relations* (Chicago: University of Chicago Press, 1970);

J. P. Stern, "On the Integrity of the Good Soldier Švejk," in *Czechoslovakia Past and Present*, edited by Miloslav Rechcígl Jr. (The Hague: Mouton, 1968), pp. 972–982;

Jindřich Toman, "Futurismus, dadaismus nebo poetismus?," *Proměny*, 18, no. 2 (1981), pp. 26–32;

Kurt Tucholsky, "Herr Schwejk," *Die Weltbühne*, 23 (1926): 892–897;

René Wellek, "Twenty Years of Czech Literature: 1918–1938," in his *Essays on Czech Literature* (The Hague: Mouton, 1963), pp. 32–45.

Győző Határ

(13 November 1914 –   )

Lóránt Kabdebó
University of Miskolc

BOOKS: *Heliáne. Regény* (Budapest: Magyar Téka Irodalmi Intézet, 1947; second edition, Budapest: Magvető, 1991);

Liturgikon (Budapest: Philebos, 1948);

Pépito et Pépita, French translation by Pierre Grosz (Paris: Julliard, 1963); Hungarian version published as *Pepito és Pepita* (London: Aurora, 1983; Budapest: Szépirodalmi, 1986);

Pantarbesz (Munich: Aurora, 1966);

Bábel tornya. ("A Nagy Etemenanki") misztérium (Stockholm: Ungerska institutet vid Stockholms universitet, 1966; Budapest: Trikolor Press, 1996);

Anibel, volume 1, French translation by Jeanne Faure-Cousin and M. L. [Georges] Kassaï (Paris: Denoël, 1970); Hungarian version published as *Anibel. Regénytrilógia,* 3 volumes (London: Aurora, 1984; Budapest: Szépirodalmi, 1988);

Hajszálhíd. Versek versben, rímek, rigmusok, költemények hárem évtized terméséből, Budapest–Párisz–London (Munich: Aurora, 1970);

Sírónevető. Drámák, 2 volumes (Munich: Aurora, 1972)—comprises *Majomház; Az aranypalást; Némberköztársaság; A libegő; Elefántcsorda; Gargilianus; A ravatal; A kötélvilág; A patkánykirály; Hernyóprém; Bunkócska; Hamu a Mamumondó;*

Az őrző könyve ("Egregor"). "Regényes elmélkedések" és "üzenet a jövőből" (Munich: Aurora, 1974; Szombathely: Életünk, 1992);

Golghelóghi. Rémrettentő képekkel, gonosz kalandokkal teljes csudaságos históriája (London: Aurora, 1976; Szombathely: Életünk, 1989);

Archie Dumbarton. Une histoire criminelle. Roman, French translation by Faure-Cousin and Kassaï (Paris: Denoël, 1977); Hungarian version published as *Éjszaka minden megnő (Archie Dumbarton). Absztrakt regény* (London: Aurora, 1984; Budapest: Magvető, 1986);

Intra muros. Tanulmány a véleményről a hitről, a meggyőződésről (London: Aurora, 1978; Budapest: Pannon Press, 1991);

Győző Határ (portrait by László Gyémánt, Museum of the House of Hungarian Literature, Budapest; courtesy of Határ)

Özön közöny. Elmélkedés (London: Aurora, 1980);

Szélhárfa, 3 volumes (London: Aurora, 1982–1983)—comprises volume 1, *A rákóra ideje;* volume 2, *Félreugrók—megtántorodók;* volume 3, *Antisumma;*

Köpönyeg sors. Iulianosz ifjúsága lélekrajzi regény (London: Aurora, 1985);

Eumolposz–avagy a hazudozás zsoltára (London: Aurora, 1986);

Lélekharangjáték (London: Aurora, 1986);

Az ég csarnokai (London: Aurora, 1987);

Angelika kertje. Mesék, nosztalgiák (London: Aurora, 1987);

A szép Palásthyné a más álmában közösül és más történetek (London: Aurora, 1987);

Csodák országa Hátsó-Eurázia, 2 volumes (London: Aurora, 1988)—comprises volume 1, *Huligánia–abagy a vágyak;* volume 2, *Czodák orsága—avagy a szabadságvágy;*

Medvedorombolás (London: Aurora, 1988);

99

A fontos ember. Regény (Szeged: JATE Press, 1989; London: Aurora, 1989);

Rólunk szól a történet, 3 volumes (London: Aurora, 1990)—comprises volume 1, *Légy minaret!;* volume 2, *A költészet kiskátéja;* volume 3, *Az ige igézetében;*

Halálfej (London: Aurora, 1991);

Üvegkoporsó (London: Aurora, 1992);

Filozófiai zárlatok (London: Aurora, 1992);

Mangun (London: Aurora, 1992);

Életút, 3 volumes (Szombathely: Életünk, 1993–1995)—comprises volume 1, *Oly jó követni ember-élet;* volume 2, *Minden hajó hazám;* volume 3, *Partra vetett bálna;*

A fülem mögött (London: Aurora, 1994);

Léptékváltás (Budapest: Belvárosi Könyvkiadó, 1995);

Álomjáró eberiség (London: Aurora, 1996);

Medaillon Madonna. Last Vintage of Poetry (Budapest: Széphalom, 1997);

A fény megistenülése (Budapest: Terebess Collection, 1998);

Keleti Kulisszák (Budapest: Terebess Collection, 1999).

Editions and Collections: *A léleknek rengése. Válogatott versek, 1933–1988*, edited by Janos Parancs (Budapest: Orpheusz, 1990);

Irodalomtörténet, edited by István Lakatos (Békéscsaba: Tevan, 1991).

Edition in English: *The Right to Sanity: A Victor Határ Reader*, edited by Leslie Kúnos (Budapest: Corvina, 1999).

PLAY PRODUCTIONS: *A patkánykirály*, Nyiregy-háza, Krúdy Theatre, 3 January 1987;

Elefántcsorda, Budapest, National Theater, 28 November 1992; English version translated by H. P. R. Pragai, Exeter, Northcott Theater, 1 February 1995.

TRANSLATIONS: *Huszonöt szovjet egyfelvonás* (Budapest: Soviet-Hungarian Fellowship, 1948);

Vosco Pratolini, *Szegény szerelmesek krónikája* (Budapest: Móra, 1955);

Lawrence Sterne, *Tristram Shandy* (New Hungarian Publishers, 1956);

Lion Feuchtwanger, *Rókák a szőlőben* (New Hungarian Publishers, 1956);

Sterne, *Érzelmes utazás* (Budapest: Europa, 1957);

Stefan Heym, *Keresztes vitézek* (Budapest: Ministry of Defense Press, 1957);

Imposztorok tüköre, translated by Határ, J. Benyhe, and E. Szokoly, edited by R. Honti (Budapest: Europa, 1957);

Jack London, *Válogatott elbeszélések*, 2 volumes (New Hungarian Press, 1968);

London, *Messze földön* (Budapest: Europa, 1975);

Görgőszínpad (Budapest: St. Steven Society Press, 1988).

Győző Határ (who publishes in the West as Victor Határ) is acknowledged as one of the leading post–World War II writers in contemporary Hungarian literature. He is prolific as well as diverse, the author of poetry, fiction, plays, essays, and philosophical texts. He is also a highly regarded translator in several languages. Határ's extensive body of work is shaped by two extremes: he lives removed from the continuity of Hungarian literary life, but nonetheless his work is defined primarily in terms of his cultural heritage. His predicament is similar to that of other Eastern European writers such as Mircea Eliade, Witold Gombrowicz, E. M. Cioran, and Vladimir Nabokov, since Határ, like them, has spent a major part of his life in exile. Consequently, the condition of exile informs his worldview; but unlike other writers of his generation, for Határ, exile serves as a means to identify with the literature of his homeland.

There is a tongue-in-cheek understatement in Határ's complaining in *Hajszálhíd* (Gossamer Bridge, 1970) of being cut off from all customary subject matters of Hungarian literature: "I have sinned, brethren, having grievously breached our patriotic code of literary good manners, what's more I have done so more than once. For I have penned some odd books that, apart from having been written in the language of the Land, have nothing to do with my being Hungarian. Indeed, they could have been written in any of the Western tongues." There is more truth in views on him held by his contemporaries, such as those a fellow poet, Sándor Weöres, related to him in a 1956 letter. Referring to one of Határ's early novels, Weöres remarked:

> Once in the company of writers, we were talking about whether there was a Hungarian novel that might have a chance to achieve worldwide success: one that would not fade into mediocrity in German, English, or French translation but shine as a work of intrinsic value. . . . Lastly, to the great surprise of all of us, we ended up with your novel *Heliáne*: it is European without being Western, interestingly Danubian without being parochial: if translated

into a Western language it would not sink out of sight into the backyard of some great predecessor.

Győző Határ was born in Gyoma, a village in Eastern Hungary, on 13 November 1914, at the stage of World War I when the soldiers were expected to be returning home soon. Határ's father, William Hack, serving in the Austro-Hungarian army, was not able to see his newborn son. Later, his father, a paper-industry expert, became a war invalid who required special care for the remainder of his life. The family moved to Budapest, with Határ's mother, schoolteacher Mary Margaret Túri, in charge, and Határ was soon forced to support himself by whatever means possible. The financial troubles that plagued the family taught Határ at an early age the value of education and perseverence. As a result, he pursued a variety of interests as a means to establish himself in a professional career. He studied architecture and then worked as an architect while simultaneously emerging as a writer. In addition, his knowledge of languages (Greek, Latin, English, French, Russian, German, Italian, Spanish, and Portuguese) turned him into a much-sought-after translator. This work enabled Határ to maintain a relatively high standard of living both before and after World War II while maturing as a writer in almost total obscurity and without the company of Hungarian literati.

Határ's manuscripts written before World War II have for the most part been lost or destroyed. He had been actively opposed to the ruling Right in politics and was arrested as an anti-Nazi on 1 May 1943. Manuscripts found in a search of his house were said to include passages deemed derogatory toward Nicholas Horthy, the regent; the confiscated manuscripts were sent to the regent's office in the palace and were most likely destroyed during the siege of Buda in November and December 1944, when the palace was burned to an empty shell. Nonetheless, the political content of his early novels earned Határ a five-year prison sentence. However, after Hungary was occupied by the Germans in March 1944, Határ was involved in a prison mutiny and managed to escape. In 1945 Határ was able to recover the manuscript of one of his novels, *Csodák országa Hátsó-Eurázia* (On the Outback of Eurasia, Land of Miracles), from the bombed police archives. This work, after some revision, was eventually published in London in 1988 in a two-volume Hungarian edition.

Határ's first published book was *Heliáne* (1947), followed in the next year by a slender volume of poetry, *Liturgikon* (A Book of Liturgies);

Dust jacket for a later edition of Határ's 1980 collection of philosophical meditations

these works were labeled "surrealist" by critics, and for many Hungarian readers Határ became identified with the avant-garde. Although Határ no doubt knew of the avant-garde trends and made use of their devices, his own works indicate essentially different ways of creation. Határ based his writing—in both prose and poetry—on the twin foundations of a headstrong, powerful personality and an absolute mastery of the language.

In poetry, while never turning against classical forms of the past, Határ soon began to experiment with prose poems, at first under the influence of French authors from Aloysius Bertrand to Saint-John Perse. Opposed to German left-wing expressionism as well as parochialism, he was decried as a "Westernizer" and branded as a traitor to the genuine spirit of the Huns. By his originality and his imposing output, however, Határ ultimately opened a new chapter in modern Hungarian poetry.

Határ seeks to establish the preserving power of the "refusal to serve" as compared to a subservient existence; but although he was writing at the same time as Arthur Koestler and George Orwell, Határ's intentions were never explicitly political. In *Heliáne*, for example, the author investigates the extent to which individuals are free to act in a world where all individual activities are predestined. Consequently, he invokes the necessary conflict to pitch his characters into peril, one of whom—a sham philosopher and an amateur painter—dominates his "fellow-artists" with his pseudocharismatic stance and mesmerizing verbiage; yet he is no more than a parody of a "genius." Throughout the novel Határ demonstrates his capacity to entertain as well as challenge his readers; thus *Heliáne* is considered a forerunner to the development of postmodern Hungarian fiction.

The setting of the novel is Panpesvalginesia (Flatfootia), a mythical island chain in the South Seas where the world of the superstitious native "yunyuries" is contrasted with the bohemian society of painters, sculptors, dreamers, and loonies in the capital city. Seated on the summit of the island world is the Fate-God-Beast, the principle of chaotic irrationality—a gigantic, gray-haired buffalo. His beastly stupidity is the counterpoint of "divine wisdom": no human mind can penetrate his erratic streaks or transcendental ignorance.

According to "scientific forecasts," Panpesvalginesia is threatened by a cosmic catastrophe in the passing of the Nigragor—a swarm of comets that, incidentally, signifies the end of the world. As a matter of course, many in the island world continue in the pursuit of pleasure and excess, while the writers and artists care only for immortality. Then Barnabás Bikornutusz arrives to encounter by chance the menagerie of characters headed by a father-figure painter king, the twenty-stone Gábriel Gabreliusz, whose unwritten but studiously blabbered works convince all that Gábriel is their charismatic guru and that Gábrielianism is the most universal, purest artistic and philosophical creed.

Everything in the archipelago of Panpesvalginesia exists "at the same time"; everyone is fully aware of all the details of his or her fate in advance, yet all is accepted with stoic equanimity. Thus, the ascetic and poet Ferenc Nein (an unhappy being who was born hanged on his umbilical cord) knows that he is going to be the victim and executor in a double drama of love. Nepomuk Prozeliusz, a much-respected tainter and adulterator of spices, knows that a falling brick will kill him—he even knows the house from the cornice of which it will fall. Lulof, the bar pianist, a rogue musician and the modest supporter of many parasitic friends, dies of

terror—the terror of being terrified when the comets pass. Hebaminte, the retired Overseer of the Seas and amateur inventor, will survive the disaster, but while out walking, will succumb to a chill—the chill of his death. Actually, Hebaminte is the inventor of the "perfect state-machine," which governs the state without any human intervention and turns natives into docile, "overhead-contact" subjects. Hebaminte escapes from home and fakes his death in order to dedicate the rest of his life to his invention. His wife, the statuesque Mrs. Hebaminte, believes that she is now a widow and looks after her tenant, Barnabás, with intensifying affection.

On one of his aimless strolls, Barnabás falls in love with Heliáne, one of the anointed maidservants of the Holy Prostitution. Knowing that according to the dictate of Fate-God-Beast they may never meet or know each other, the girl takes flight. At the annual Witches' Carnival, however, the Fate-God-Beast provides a suspension of the Law of Fate and allows one day of free will. The couple shares an idyllic encounter, and before the carnival is over, Barnabás decides to snatch Heliáne from the grip of Holy Prostitution and take her to Europe, the home of free will. Then the unhappy and abandoned Mrs. Hebaminte encounters her husband, the inventor, at the carnival; with knife raised high, and shrieking rabidly, she announces that she is possessed—she is the Chosen Witch. The crowd parts before her in holy terror. The frustrated witch throws out her lodger, Barnabás, who is now faced with mounting troubles. Barnabás clings desperately to the Gábrielian church; however, a breach soon occurs in the sect, and the unhinged Barnabás is unable to choose between two tyrannic schools of thought.

The catastrophe of Nigragor's passing takes place; yet, somehow, the world fails to perish. Children reinvent agriculture; shopkeepers restart their business; and Holy Prostitution is thriving again. The Gábrielian sect already counts its dead. In a bout of jealousy, Ferenc Nein shoots the innocent Consolata and himself. Nepomuk Prozeliusz is hit on the head by his brick as scheduled. Hebaminte survives the hell of Nigragor unscathed, only to die of the destined cold breeze. Barnabás is put to a ritual test by being fastened to the "Rock of Terror" at low tide and being released only at the last moment, after which he will learn the fate that has been meted out to him. But Barnabás makes a terrible discovery: his idol, Gábriel, has secretly bought Heliáne out of the brothel-nunnery and married her. Barnabás goes on a rampage. Pigs, geese, and goats fall to his knife, while children flee screaming and people empty the streets. Warriors start chasing

Barnabás, who is attacking the Law of Fate; the mob in pursuit is urged on by Heliáne herself. Under a hail of spears, Barnabás jumps from a steep rock into the sea; there, owing to the miraculous and majestic epiphany of Fate-God-Beast incarnate, he manages to survive. Bedridden on the peaceful island of Roc-Y-Joco, he tells his strange story to the local quack's daughters in a state of delirium.

Following the controversial publication of *Heliáne* and *Liturgikon*, and no doubt provoked by his alienation from the Communist system as it emerged after the siege of Budapest, Hátar was expelled from the Writers' Association in 1949 and was forced to support himself as a translator. Allegedly, author and critic György Lukács was prompted to quip: "Hátar must be given plenty of translations to do and should be well rewarded. It would be a double gain for socialist literature—for the man is an excellent translator—and thus he would be left with no leisure to write works of his own." Hátar's novel in progress, *Az őrző könyve ("Egregor")*. "*Regényes elmélkedések" és "üzenet a jövőből*" (The Book of the Guardian, 1974), written in 1949 during the Stalinist cleansing of art and literature, was an obvious target and proved to be unpublishable at the time for political reasons. This futuristic "history-fiction" was Hátar's attempt to ease his traumatic memories of prison and the war; it circulated initially in typescript among friends.

At the end of 1949 Hátar attempted to leave Hungary without a passport. He was caught on the Yugoslav border and sentenced to two and a half years in prison (one year just for *Az őrző könyve*, which the Hungarian KGB deemed "anti-State" and "anti-Stalinist"), after which he was interned. He was confined for part of his sentence in the same prison where a memorial tablet honored the anti-Fascist prison mutiny he had participated in during the war. As a result of a strike in protest against prison food, he was punished by a transfer to the dreaded maximum security prison at Márianosztra. Confined to a solitary cell, Hátar was mistreated and suffered from malnutrition, resulting in daydream visions and hallucinated dialogues; these formed the basis of the first version of *Golghelóghi. Rémrettentő képekkel, gonosz kalandokkal teljes csudaságos históriája* (Golghelóghi), a drama cycle of nine mystery plays that was later considered his masterpiece. Several decades later, in exile, Hátar reworked the whole cycle from the fragments stuck in his memory and published it in a one-thousand-page volume in 1976.

Released from prison in 1953, Hátar resumed working as an architect for a year, then returned to translating. After soviet tanks crushed the Hungarian uprising in 1956, however, Hátar and his fiancée, Priscilla Rose Mary Pragai, made the decision to leave Hungary. For several months they resided in Vienna before leaving to settle in London, where they were married and Hátar joined the BBC Overseas Services. His talent finally came to fruition during his exile in London. The first of Hátar's works to be published in the West was the novel *Pepito és Pepita* (Pepito and Pepita), first published in a French edition in 1963 under the name Victor Hátar. This book was followed by a succession of works that Hátar had written while in Hungary and that were previously unpublishable, including the novels *Bábel tornya. ("A Nagy Etemenanki") misztérium* (The Tower of Babel, or The Great Etemenankï, A Mystery Play, 1966), published in Sweden; *Anibel* (Anibel, 1970) and *Éjszaka minden megnő (Archie Dumbarton). Absztrakt regény* (By Night Everything Looms Larger, 1977), both of which appeared first in French; and *Köpönyeg sors. Iulianosz ifjúsága lélekrajzi regény* (Turncoat Destiny: An Historical Novel about the Youth of Julian the Apostate, 1985), published in London. In addition, two collections of his short stories were published in 1987: *Angelika kertje. Mesék, nosztalgiák* (The Garden of Angelina: Tales, Nostalgies) and *A szép Palásthyné a más álmában közösül és más történetek* (The Beautiful Mrs. Palásthy Copulates in Somebody Else's Dream, and Other Stories), both in Hungarian.

Avoiding the form of the traditional nineteenth-century novel, Hátar developed his own fictional devices while linking his work to eighteenth-century novels such as Voltaire's *Candide* (1759) and Henry Fielding's *Tom Jones* (1749). He is neither patronizing nor didactic; instead, he surveys human existence by putting discordant characters in conflicting situations and analyzing their actions in microscopic detail. His thematic concerns range from the biological and ethical questions arising from the use of a certain scientific "methodology," illustrated in *Heliáne* and later in *Csodák országa Hátsó-Eurázia*, to the issue of man's degradation and growing helplessness—imprisonment, torture, termination of an individual's rights—as well as the bathos of resisting humiliation, illustrated in *Heliáne* and *Köpönyeg sors*.

Written in 1954–1955, Hátar's novel *Anibel* is a spoof on the Stalinist dictatorship set up by the Soviet quisling Matthias Rákosi. It is also the story of an early infatuation that, in the careerist mind of Simon Sömjén, a "non-party" Stalinist activist and artistic director of the National Theater, grows into a lifelong and unrequited passion that fosters

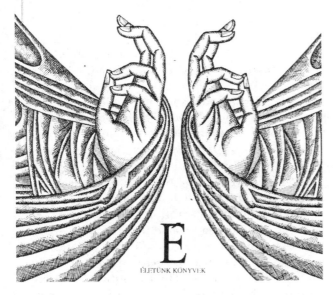

Dust jacket for a later edition of Határ's 1985 novel, in which the situation of the young Julian the Apostate represents that of modern humanity in Communist Hungary

deadly competition between a mother and a daughter. More enriching, however, is the masterful historical novel *Köpönyeg sors*. Written as a kind of bildungsroman, the novel deals with the youthful days of the late-Roman emperor Julian the Apostate. As one of the supernumeraries in the dynasty of the Flavians, Julian lives a guarded existence, always fearful of assassination. He is further threatened by the sorceress-philosopher Sosipatra, who also dreams about the restoration of the Olympians. Határ shows the entrapped "superfluous man" who, by the accident of his birth, is predestined to die and lives only to await his fate.

The idea for the novel derived from Will Durant's *The Age of Faith*, published in 1950 as part of the eleven-volume *Story of Civilization* (1935–1975). Határ revealed in the first volume of his autobiography, *Életút* (Life's Journey, 1993–1995), that a particular passage in the first chapter caught his attention:

Julian wept when he heard how their magnificent shrines were being demolished, how pagan priests were proscribed and their properties distributed among the castrated and the followers [of Christianity]. It may well have happened around this time that he was secretly initiated into the mysteries of Eleusis. It was compatible with the morals of the pagans that someone concealed his apostasy. His tutors, friends and confidants warned him against giving himself away. . . . For ten years he kept up appearances and prayed in public like a Christian, what is more, he even read out from the Holy Bible in the churches of the Christians.

In *Életút* (1993) Határ recalled his reaction to Durant's depiction of Julian:

I felt shocked. I mused for a while on what I had read. I took notes of it and jotted down: "Try to turn it into a short story." In 1984 while looking through my folders I came across this note but felt somehow unsure about it. Still, I decided to try. Soon enough I warmed to the topic and had to realize that it was going to be a "long short story" of about 25–30 pages; in the end the first version actually turned out to be sixty. After giving a rest to it for a month I set to work again to recast it into its final form. It was a crushing disappointment to browse and dip into the text, for it was full of factual-chronological errors. My anxiety deepened to fright when it dawned on me that this was the nucleus of a large novel rather than that of a short story. I flung myself into the nitty-gritty, buying all the sources, those of which until then were not in my library but proved indispensable—Themistius, Libanius, Eunapius, Ammianus Marcellinus, Julian's own books, the lot—for by now it was clear that I could not content myself with second-hand information, hastily picked from historical reference books or English/French translations of quotations. I had to see them in Greek or Latin. . . . I made a huge number of notes and it took me a lot of time to process them, while I found especially difficult to exclude the plentiful/superfluous/unnecessary and not to include those in my delight in having found them. All in all, it took me six months to write the novel. It was a frantic six-month period.

Although *Köpönyeg sors* is set against the background of antiquity, the reader nonetheless confronts the fundamental problems of human fate in the twentieth century. The action is bound within an empire perfectly organized and governed by "ingenious terror"; the subject is how those in power manipulate those victimized by circumstance, and how the victimized are able to survive the manipulation.

Apart from his novels, Határ's output as a poet is also considerable. His collections stand as important events in Hungarian literature in exile: *Hajszálhíd; Lélekharangjáték* (Death Knell Carillon, 1986);

Medvedorombolás (The Purring of a Bear, 1988); *A lélek-knek rengése. Válogatott versek, 1933–1988* (Soul Quake: Selected Poems, 1933–1988, 1990); and *Halálfej* (Death's Head, 1991). His stylistic, rhyming, and rhythmic talents help him portray the irony of human existence. As a poet he shares similarities and differences with his lifelong friend Sándor Weöres. Both are admired as wordsmiths who create worlds of their own through a multitude of contrivances and invented words, thus enriching their medium. Yet, Weöres constructed his poems according to the traditions of myth-creating: through myth the individual merges into a spiritual wholeness, thus both expanding and destroying himself. Határ, on the other hand, moves in the opposite direction: discarding mysticism, he conjures up an independent world in which man plays with language while language plays with man.

Throughout his career Határ produced a steady flow of essays and books on philosophical issues, although much of this work was published decades after it was written. *Pantarbesz* (named for the mythical dragons that carry the Philosopher's stone embedded in their brains), for example, was written in 1949 but remained unpublished until 1966. What many consider his most important work, *Özön közöny. Elmélkedés* (Cosmic Unconcern: Meditations), was finally published in 1980 in London. In this work he attacks the ancient religious and mystical notion that human beings hold a privileged position in the universe—that it was created for them, and that they are able to penetrate into the ultimate nature of reality because the human mind is akin to that reality. The same criticisms apply to modern philosophical concepts, such as the *Geist* (world-spirit) of Georg Wilhelm Friedrich Hegel and the élan vital of Henri Bergson, that are merely elaborations of this idea. He finds the source of these misconceptions in human physiology, especially the dominance of the visual sense. The universe, he contends, is neither friendly nor hostile to humanity; it is simply indifferent.

Another major work composed over the course of his career, the three-volume *Szélhárfa* (Aeolian Harp), was also published in London in 1982 and 1983. Határ originally conceived this work as a commentary on *Özön közöny*, but it soon outgrew this intention. The first volume, titled *A rákóra ideje* (Time Crabwise), surveys the theories of time advanced by such philosophers as Aristotle, St. Augustine, Immanuel Kant, Henri Bergson, and twentieth-century philosopher John McTaggart Ellis McTaggart. Határ then advances his own theory, which holds that time is a product of the human

nervous system. The second volume, *Félreugrók–megtántorodók* (Dodgers and Staggerers), is an historical survey through two millennia of what Adolf von Harnack called the Pauline religion: showing how, much against its will or liking, Judeo-Christianity became a means to preserve and resurrect antiquity—in outlook, morals, taste, mentality, even architecture. Határ concludes that Christianity has outlived its usefulness. The third volume, *Anti-summa* (Anti-SUMMA), is an epitome of the author's own philosophy: guarded and tentative as it is in suspending final judgments, it nonetheless reflects his endeavor to overcome the dead-end sterility of analytic thinking and to outline a new departure in contemporary philosophy.

Határ produced essays on a wide selection of subject matter, from the linguistic implications of the computer revolution to the inherent dangers of Islamic Fundamentalism. Many of these essays were collected in a series of volumes: *Intra muros. Tanulmány a véleményről a hitről, a meggyőződésről* (Intra Muros: An Essay on Opinions, Beliefs, and Convictions), published in 1978; *Rólunk szól a történet*, published in 1990; *Filozófiai zárlatok* (Philosophical Cadences, 1992); *A fülem mögött* (Up My Sleeve, 1994); *Léptékváltás* (Scale Jumping, 1995); and *Álomjáró eberiség* (Sleepwalking Mankind, 1996).

Határ's plays, collected in the two volumes of *Sírónevető* (Laughing–Crying, 1972), plunge the reader into a desolate world identified with the Theater of the Absurd. Yet, they also offer sophisticated post–avant-garde messages in the plots and witty dialogue. Határ's most important contribution to dramatic writing is his play-cycle *Golghelóghi*, a sequence of nine plays meant to be staged on nine consecutive nights.

Taking place at the close of the first Christian millennium, *Golghelóghi* best exemplifies Határ's purposefulness in applying philosophical argument in his creative work. Based on thorough research from the documents and chronicles of the period, the cycle follows the transformation of Golghelóghi from country lad to Lord Protector as he simultaneously suffers the pains of human existence and enjoys the miracle of a life that keeps on renewing and reshaping itself. Within the sequence, the dramatic and tragic become interchangeable with the farcical. The universe becomes a circus in which the master of ceremonies is at best an Oz-like magician. What is not revealed until the end is that watching from above is Satan, seated on his throne, viewing the world with "incommensurable indifference"; huddled at his feet and waiting for his orders is God, who is revealed as a second-rate "craftsgod" who rules the world as a fief from the devil. Satan's last words to God, which close the sequence, attest to his unseen presence throughout the sequence: "By the majestic privilege of an all-upholding pillar, I am retiring to my crowning unconcern and, while you display your miserable radiance, I shall rule over sea and sky—in a princely way."

Although few of Határ's books published in the West found their way to the "Old Country," some copies reached his fellow writers by clandestine channels and were read in confidential circles of friends. People in the universities also circulated transcripts from his books and his fortnightly "Literary Column," which he broadcast regularly, first from the London studios of the BBC and later through Radio Free Europe in Munich. For more than two decades his radio talks became a regular feature and a cause for discussion. His became a household name, and listeners and literary aficionados dubbed him "the Hungarian Alistair Cook." In the 1970s, following the success of Határ's aired translations of English medieval mystery plays at Easter and Christmas, he began to incorporate more of his own work into his literary programs, reading his short stories and prose poems. Many of these transmissions were faithfully recorded all over Hungary (and in the Hungarian-populated parts of Romania and the former Yugoslavia); as a result, the material began to surface in print, which provided a significant impact on the development of the new generation of Hungarian writers.

Beginning in 1986, the Hungarian publishing industry became increasingly receptive to Határ, and editions of his work were published in his homeland for the first time in nearly three decades. With the change of the political situation, Határ emerged as one of the most appreciated authors in contemporary Hungarian literature. In 1989, on his seventy-fifth birthday, he was the first to be honored by the new Republic with the Order of the Gold-Wreathed Star, one of the highest new distinctions in Hungarian letters. This prize was followed in 1991 by the most prestigious award a Hungarian artist can receive, the Kossuth Prize, making Határ the first exiled Hungarian writer to receive the award.

Few of Határ's contemporaries have covered such a wide range of writing as he has. With several volumes of avant-garde poetry and twenty novels to his credit, he became one of the forerunners of the postmodern school; his more than forty plays also present challenges. During two decades with the BBC and later as a contributor to Radio Free Europe, he turned out more than a thousand literary and theatrical reviews. Ultimately, however, the message of all his works turned out to be philosophical, and he will be best remembered as a polymath and philosopher.

Interviews:

Frances Welch, "Rebel with Applause," *London Evening Standard*, 10 January 1990;

Lóránt Kabdebó, interviews in *Életút*, 3 volumes (Szombathely: Életünk, 1993–1995).

References:

Pál Albert, "Hárfás a Kínok Oszlopán," *Irodalmi Újság*, 2 (1964): 15;

Alain Bosquet, "Le Rococo de Victor Határ," *Le Monde*, 7 (1963) : 7;

Ágnes Mária Csiky, "Határ Győző," in her *Volt Egyszer egy Ötödik Síp* (Budapest: Bethlen Gábor Press, 1996), pp. 79–113;

Georges Gömöri, "Conception historique et structure dans les pièces de Witold Gombrowicz et Győző Határ," in *Littérature et Émigration: Dans le pays de l'Europe centrale et orientale*, edited by Maria Delapierre (Paris: Institut de l'études slaves, 1996), pp. 193–202;

Gömöri, "L'Universe de Victor Határ," *La Quinzaine Littéraire*, 4 (1970): 16–31;

Péter Halász, "Határ Győző: *Az őrző könyve, 'Egregor,'*" *Új Látóhatár*, 9 (1975): 20;

Eva Haldimann, "Dichter in D. Emigration," *Neue Züricher Zeitung*, 12 (1977): 17–18;

Haldimann, "Morbide Landkarte," *Neue Züricher Zeitung*, 1 (1989): 30;

Haldimann, "Polyphonie des Exils," *Neue Züricher Zeitung*, 2 (1987): 2;

Lóránt Kabdebó, "A Protean Master: Victor Határ," *New Hungarian Quarterly*, 128 (Winter 1992): 33–42;

Emőke G. Komoróczy, *Felvonásvég a Világszínpadon* (Budapest: Stádium, 1994).

Vladimír Holan

(16 September 1905 – 31 March 1980)

Jiří Holý
Charles University, Prague

BOOKS: *Blouznivý vějíř* (Prague: Svobodná škola umění, 1926);

Triumf smrti (Prague: Ladislav Kuncíř, 1930);

Kolury (Pardubice: Vladim Vokolek, 1932);

Vanutí (Prague: František Borový, 1932);

Torzo (Prague: František Borový, 1933);

Oblouk (Prague: František Borový, 1934);

Kameni, přicházíš . . . (Prague: František Borový, 1937);

Září 1938 (Prague: František Borový, 1938);

Sen (Prague: František Borový, 1939);

Lemuria (Prague: Melantrich, 1940);

První testament (Prague: František Borový, 1940);

Záhřmotí (Prague: Melantrich, 1940);

Chór (Prague: Melantrich, 1941);

Terezka Planetová (Prague: František Borový, 1943);

Cesta mraku (Prague: František Borový, 1945);

Dík Sovětskému svazu (Prague: František Borový, 1945);

Panychida (Prague: František Borový, 1945);

Havraním brkem (Prague: František Borový, 1946);

Rudoarmějci (Prague: Svoboda, 1946; definitive edition, 1947);

Tobě (Prague: Svoboda, 1947);

Prostě (Prague: Československý spisovatel, 1954);

Bajaja (Prague: Československý spisovatel, 1955);

Tři (Prague: Československý spisovatel, 1957);

Zuzana v lázni (Prague: Alois Chvála, 1962);

Bez názvu (Ostrava: Krajské nakladatelství, 1963);

Mozartiana (Prague: Státní nakladatelství krásné literatury, hudby a umění, 1963);

Příběhy (Prague: Československý spisovatel, 1963);

Na postupu (Prague: Československý spisovatel, 1964);

Noc s Hamletem (Prague: Státní nakladatelství krásné literatury, hudby a umění, 1964);

Trialog (Brno: Krajské nakladatelství, 1964);

Bolest (Prague: Československý spisovatel, 1965; expanded edition, 1966);

Na sotnách (Prague: Československý spisovatel, 1967);

Asklépiovi kohouta (Prague: Československý spisovatel, 1970);

Noc s Ofélií, edited by Vladimír Justl (Prague: Restaurace a jídelny v Praze 1, 1973);

Vladimír Holan (photograph by F. Vopata)

Propast propasti, edited by Justl (Prague: Odeon, 1982).

Editions and Collections: *Dvě jezera*, edited by Vladimír Justl (Prague: Spolek českých bibliofilů, 1963);

Noční hlídka srdce, edited by Justl (Prague: Československý spisovatel, 1963);

Sebrané spisy Vladimíra Holana, 11 volumes, edited by Justl (Prague: Odeon, 1965–1988).

Editions in English: "Disaster," in *Modern Czech Poetry*, selected and translated by Ewald Osers and J. K.

Montgomery (London: Allen & Unwin, 1945), p. 60;

"The Accident," in *A Book of Czech Verse*, translated and edited by Alfred French (London: Macmillan, 1958; New York: St. Martin's Press, 1958), pp. 96–97;

"Declaration of Love," "Over the Beloved, Falling Asleep," and "Prologue," translated by Edith Pargeter, in *The Linden Tree: An Anthology of Czech and Slovak Literature 1890–1960*, edited by Mojmír Otruba and Zdeněk Pešat (Prague: Artia, 1962), pp. 250–255;

"The Old Priest," "The Home," "Test II," "Test IV," "Resurrection," "Children," and "Reminiscence," selected, translated, and edited by George Theiner, in *New Writing in Czechoslovakia* (Baltimore & Harmondsworth, U.K.: Penguin, 1969), pp. 115–118;

Selected Poems, translated by Jarmila and Ian Milner, edited by Holan (Baltimore & Harmondsworth, U.K.: Penguin, 1971);

A Night with Hamlet, translated by Jarmila and Ian Milner, edited by Holan (London: Oasis Books, 1980);

"At Mother's after Many Years," "The Cave of Words," and "Memory II," translated by Bronislava Volek and Andrew Durkin, "And Beginning There Is Not," "A Picture Which Is No Abyss," "Over Shelley's Letters," "Snake," and "Somnia et noctium fantasmata," translated by Miroslav Hanák, in *Contemporary East European Poetry*, edited by Emery George (Ann Arbor, Mich.: Ardis, 1983), pp. 205–210;

Mirroring. Selected Poems of Vladimír Holan, translated by C. G. Hanzliczek and Dana Hábová (Middletown, Conn.: Wesleyan University Press, 1985);

"A Night with Hamlet," translated by Clayton Eshleman, in *Conductors of the Pit: Major Works by Rimbaud, Vallejo, Artaud and Holan*, edited by František Galan (New York: Paragon House, 1988).

TRANSLATIONS: Rainer Maria Rilke, *Růže. Okna* (Prague: František Borový, 1937);

Rilke, *Slavení* (Prague: Melantrich, 1937);

Rilke, *Sad* (Prague: František Borový, 1939);

Luis de Góngora y Argote, *Báje o Ákidu i Galatei* (Prague: Melantrich, 1939);

Rilke, *Několik dopisů* (Prague: Melantrich, 1940);

Mikhail Iur'evich Lermontov, *Novic* (Prague: František Borový, 1940);

Iljás ben Júsuf Nizámí, *Sedm princezen*, translated by Holan and Jan Rypka (Prague: Družstevní práce, 1943);

Charles Baudelaire, *Žena* (Prague: Jaroslav Podroužek, 1946);

Charles Vildrac, *Kniha lásky* (Prague: Kruh krásné knihy, 1947; expanded, 1972);

Nikolaj Nikolajevič Aseyev, *Vítězství* (Prague: Svaz československo-sovětského přátelství, 1948);

Georges Chennevière, *Maličko hudby vzdálené* (Prague: František Borový, 1948);

Jean de La Fontaine, *Adónis* (Prague: František Borový, 1948);

Melancholie: básně dynastie Sungské, 960–1279 po Kristu (Prague: František Borový, 1948);

Juliusz Slowacki, *Otec morem nakažených v El-Arish* (Prague: Československý spisovatel, 1953);

Adam Mickiewicz, *Sonety*, in *Spisy Adama Mickiewicze I* (Prague: Státní nakladatelství krásné literatury, hudby a umění, 1953);

Nikolas Lenau, *Albigenští* (Prague: Státní nakladatelství krásné literatury, hudby a umění, 1955);

Paul de Ronsard, *Lásky a jiné verše* (Prague: Státní nakladatelství krásné literatury, hudby a umění, 1956);

de Ronsard, *Básně* (Prague: Státní nakladatelství krásné literatury, hudby a umění, 1957);

Janko Kráľ, *Orel* (Prague: Státní nakladatelství krásné literatury, hudby a umění, 1960);

Cestou, edited by Oldřich Králík (Prague: Státní nakladatelství krásné literatury a umění, 1962);

Avetik Isahakyan, *Abdulalá al Maarii* (Prague: Svět sovětů, 1966);

Tři setkání (Prague: Melantrich, 1972).

OTHER: *Láska a smrt: výbor lidové poezie*, compiled by Holan and František Halas (Prague: Melantrich, 1938).

The great Czech poet Jaroslav Seifert called Vladimír Holan "the black angel." For many years Seifert and Holan were close friends. Their work spanned a long period of time and reached its peak before World War II, remaining at its best both during and after the war. Poetically, however, they were completely different. Seifert saw life as a harmonious whole; his poetry was melodious with a tendency towards melancholy. In Holan's work, on the other hand, the dark, tragic aspects of life are most prominent. His poems are disjointed, full of unexpected changes and sudden interruptions. Holan's language differs sharply from the crystal-clear spoken language that Seifert uses. Holan aims at using the whole range of language. Literary expressions, neologisms, and symbols difficult to understand appear alongside common Czech language and vulgarisms.

Vladimír Holan was born on 16 September 1905 in Prague. Most of his childhood was spent in an area associated with the poet Karel Hynek Mácha (1810–1836), near Bezděz Hill, where his father was a factory manager. "I often went alone to Bezděz. The countryside around Bělá, the pine-woods, the sandy soil, and the gales had a profound effect on me. I loved the bats and the rooks. I once killed an adder by putting it in methylated spirits. I often went to the countryside. I wanted adventure. That is why I collected stamps. To me they symbolized far-away places." From his father, Holan inherited intensity of feeling, a love of solitude, and his melancholy nature. His mother was quite the opposite; she was equable and cheerful. Holan loved her dearly, and the figure of his mother appears frequently in his poems, always connected with childhood, the security of home, and inner purity. While still at secondary school, Holan was enthralled by poetry and began to write and publish verse. After leaving school he went to work as a clerk for the Central Pensions Board, which he hated, finding bureaucracy unbearable. He left for good in 1935, preferring the uncertain life of a freelance writer.

From the beginning of the 1930s Holan and Vilém Závada represented the so-called between generations poets with whom Jan Zahradníček was also closely connected. These poets moved away from poetic enchantment with modern civilization and revolution, and also distanced themselves from avantgarde poetics. They concentrated on existentialist situations and the dark, gloomy side of life. Holan's poetry in particular became the antithesis of the easy-flowing associations in the works of Seifert and Vítězslav Nezval, especially in Nezval's collection *Triumf smrti* (The Triumph of Death, 1930). These poems are full of pauses and sharp edges, and they are intentionally strange and convoluted. They are like fragments of lost associations that are simply hinted at. Readers laboriously uncover them as they read but perhaps cannot fully explain them. The author disregards the normal rules of language. He uses unusual words and equally unusual juxtapositions. It is as if some expressions have a life of their own with no substance in reality. Metaphors, abstract and concrete, follow hard on each other, as illustrated in the poem addressing darkness in Holan's fifth collection, *Kameni, přicházíš...* (You Are Coming, Stone...), published in 1937:

> Once more, oh darkness, axe-like, you penetrate the furniture
>
> shattering into its bruises, as it cracks at night.
>
> Awake, you keep vigil with me in its futility.

Holan with his mother in the late 1930s

> My feelings of gloom
> owe it to the parachute of the spirit
> that it lands near former tenderness
> singing in my speech, singing in my speech
> unearthly of this earth.

To a large extent Holan's collection of prose works, titled *Lemuria* (written between 1934 and 1938, published in 1940), shed light on his vision of the world. There is the mere suggestion of a plot held together by the character Maxima. Besides Maxima's letters and diaries there are quotations from books and essays in which the author explains himself directly. He portrays the world as tragically impenetrable and human life as tragically fragmented: "The keys of the prison doors of our life continually rattle as if someone were trying to keep us shut up behind treble-locked doors." Yet, at times cracks suddenly appear in the enclosing walls. Holan finds traces of poetry, love, and purity. His poetry has a distinctive character based on discord and inner dialogue with two voices alternating; frequent question marks indicate equivocal explanations, and three dots indicate ambiguity.

Surprisingly Holan, the creator of abstract poetic worlds, spoke out clearly when Czechoslovakia was threatened by Adolf Hitler's Germany. Particularly in the poetic cycle *Září 1938* (1938) and *Odpověď Francii* (A Response to France, banned by the censor and not published until 1946) he expressed the nation's determination to defend the homeland and its despair at the capitulation to Nazi Germany in March 1939. In the poem "Noc z Íliady" (An Iliad Night) Holan compares the Czech September mobilization with Homer's epic poem.

After the war Holan continued to write poetry directly connected with social and political problems of the day. Despair at the horrors of war and curses addressed to the German occupying forces along with boundless admiration for the Soviet liberators are two sides of the same coin. One of these remarkable topical collections is *Rudoarmějci* (Soldiers of the Red Army, 1946). It was inspired by Holan's meeting Russian soldiers who had endured service at the front. In *Rudoarmějci* the poet dispenses with complicated poetic devices, intending the work purely as a bare testimony about his unassuming, unsophisticated, naive heroes.

Compared with his first experimental period, the author's style became simpler from the 1940s onward: "I, too, once cast spells with phrases that stopped the reader in his tracks. Today, however, I realize that it can be something absolutely familiar that brings your language down to earth, like a well-worn doorstep, your mother's thimble or a grave." The prevailing mood in Holan's world continued to be tragic. At this point, however, the simple things in daily life had positive value: childhood, the countryside and nature, pure love, the sacrifices people make, and suffering in general. These are the main themes developed in his nontraditional conception of narrative poetry.

After another full-length abstract poem, *První testament* (The First Testament, 1940), there followed *Terezka Planetová* (1943), the poetic story of a young life ruined and a compelling but unexpressed love. In this work Holan also employs unusual metaphors ("the plate of the moon above the house"), elements of lyricism, and complicated reflections, but the meaning of the work is more transparent than before. *Terezka Planetová* foreshadows Holan's poems from the end of the 1940s and the beginning of the 1950s, which were not published until 1963 in the collection *Příběhy* (Tales). In this collection the author's tendency to write poetry resembling prose is more pronounced than before. Gone are regular rhyme and rhythm, replaced by free verse. A life in ruins, an individual condemned to a cruel fate, becomes Holan's main theme. Such, for example, is the life of the heroine in "Óda na radost" (Ode to Joy), the divinely beautiful and pure Lucie, who was "simply full of joy" and "radiated joy to others." The name Lucie is probably an allusion to the Latin "lux"—meaning light, radiance, and also salvation.

However, unlike Friedrich von Schiller's "Ode to Joy," incorporated at the end of Ludwig van Beethoven's *Ninth Symphony*, Holan's poem of the same name does not lead to brotherhood and hope for a happy future. Through no fault of her own, Lucie is the cause of the death of a young man who was overwhelmed by her beauty. Lucie leaves home and works as a seamstress and a cleaner. One day while she is washing the floor she inadvertently knocks over a lighted lamp—the motif of light again—and burns to death in dreadful agony. The horrifying story of Lucie suggests martyrdom but also hints that a malevolent, diabolical fate is at work, as if the author doubted there were any sense in the world and in human existence itself.

Příběhy was written during the most difficult period in the author's life, the cruel era of communist totalitarianism after February 1948, when communists assumed power in Czechoslovakia. Holan was one of the writers who could not publish their work. He earned his living by translating, and his Czech versions of the work by the Spanish master Luis de Góngora y Argote, the Austrian romantic Nikolas Lenau, and the German neoromantic Rainer Maria Rilke are outstanding among his many translations. Moreover, at that time the poet was in deep distress over the incurable illness of his only daughter. He viewed this illness as a curse. For years he almost never went out of his flat. Later he wrote "for fifteen years I talked / to the walls."

However, in his anguished solitude he composed many of the best works in Czech poetry—works that could not be published until the 1960s. Some of these works are the collection of short lyric poems *Bolest* (Pain), written between 1949 and 1955 and published in 1965, and the composition *Noc s Hamletem* (translated as *A Night with Hamlet*, 1980), written between 1949 and 1956 and published in 1964. These works continue the succession of narratives with reflective passages. Again, Holan employs the motifs of walls and precipices referring to the crushing oppression of life, images of life as mere staying alive; but, there are also flashes of a miraculous spark of "Poetry," moments when man catches a glimpse of the hidden meaning of existence. Love is portrayed as animal carnality but also as a promise of tenderness and as an unselfish maternal emotion. In his nocturnal conversation with his alter ego, Hamlet, the poet speculates on whether or not humans are lost creatures. He comes to the conclusion that people must accept the tragic quirks of fate in their lives.

Manuscript for "Mamince" (To Mother), by Holan, reproduced in volume 11 of Sebrané spisy Vladimíra Holana *(1965–1988)*

In the second half of the 1950s Holan wrote practically nothing. The long poem "Toskána" (From Tuscany) is an exception. It was first published in 1963 as part of the collection *Příběhy*. The hero of the poem, who embodies some features of the author, receives a letter from his long-standing lover inviting him to follow her to Venice. There another letter awaits him asking him to follow her to Florence and then to Siena. When he meets her at last, he sees that she is Death.

Holan's last creative period extends from the 1960s into the 1970s. The main features, typical of the author's style, have not changed. However, the former rich accumulation of metaphors has disappeared. More often things are named without circumlocution, and constructions are concise. Paradoxically, feelings of anxiety and futility became stronger in his poetry at the time when he had become a living legend in Czech poetry and a serious candidate for the Nobel Prize in literature, and when he had a huge literary following and a great many admirers. He called one of the poems in his last collection *Sbohem?* (Goodbye?), "Naší dcerce Kateřině" (To Our Daughter Kateřina). This poem was published posthumously in 1982:

Who are you, my little girl and who are we
you who are reading and do not know how to read
you who are writing and do not know how to write
you who are saying things so futile
that it is impossible to live without them?

Holan's daughter Kateřina died in 1977. After her death Holan, whose own health was also bad, lost interest in life and stopped writing poetry. He died on 31 March 1980 in his flat in Prague beside the river Vltava.

Bibliography:

Emanuel Macek, "Soupis původního díla Vladimíra Holana," in *Bagately*, by Holan (Prague: Odeon, 1988), pp. 31–244.

Biographies:

František Hrubín, "Opony," in his *Lásky* (Prague: Československý spisovatel, 1967), pp. 70–73;

Jaroslav Seifert, "Pět kapek Vladimíra Holana," in his *Všecky krásy světa*, edited by Rudolf Havel (Prague: Československý spisovatel, 1985), pp. 316–322;

Vladimír Justl, "Životopis Vladimíra Holana," in *Bagately*, by Holan (Prague: Odeon, 1986), pp. 315–450;

Jan Pilař, "Dům na Kampě," in his *Sluneční hodiny* (Prague: Československý spisovatel, 1989), pp. 373–376;

Bedřich Fučík, "Byla v Holanech věrnost!" in his *Čtrnáctero zastavení*, edited by Vladimír Binar and Mojmír Trávníček (Prague: Melantrich, 1992), pp. 287–300.

References:

Přemysl Blažíček, *Sebeuvědomění poezie. Nad básněmi Vladimíra Holana* (Pardubice: Akcent, 1991);

Jiří Brabec, "Holan," in *Jak číst poezii*, second edition, edited by Jiří Opelík (Prague: Československý spisovatel, 1969), pp. 158–177;

Miroslav Červenka, "Vědomí strasti. Prolegomena k epice Vladimíra Holana," in his *Styl a význam* (Prague: Československý spisovatel, 1991), pp. 107–122;

Jiří Holý, "Poéma–příběh–zpráva," in his *Problémy nové české epiky* (Prague: Ústav pro českou literaturu, 1995), pp. 7–29;

David France Jakubec, "Les trois étapes d'une élaboration poétique," in *Czech Studies*, edited by Mojmír Grygar (Amsterdam: Rodopi, 1990), pp. 127–156;

Vladimír Justl, ed., *Úderem tepny. Sborník ze semináře k interpretaci básnického díla Vladimíra Holana* (Prague: Restaurace a jídelny v Praze 1, 1986);

Zdeněk Kožmín, "Krajnost Holanovy poezie," in his *Studie a kritiky* (Prague: Torst, 1995), pp. 171–180;

Kožmín, "Vladimír Holan: Matka," in his *Interpretace básní* (Prague: Státní pedagogické nakladatelství, 1986), pp. 82–99;

Oldřich Králík, "O metodě básnických překladů Vladimíra Holana," in his *Osvobozená slova*, edited by Jiří Opelík (Prague: Torst, 1995), pp. 424–452;

Rio Preisner, "Zdi," *Studie*, 14, nos. 1–3 (1971): 425–436;

Sylvie Richterová, "Kontury ticha," in her *Slova a ticho*, second edition (Prague: Československý spisovatel, 1991), pp. 79–93;

Richterová, "Polyfonie v díle Vladimíra Holana," in her *Ticho a smích* (Prague: Mladá fronta, 1997), pp. 151–164;

Angelo Maria Ripellino, "Úvod k Vladimíru Holanovi," *Host do domu*, 15, no. 2 (1968);

Alexandr Stich, "Několik marginálních poznámek o jazyku Holanovy poezie," in his *Od Karla Havlíčka k Františku Halasovi* (Prague: Torst, 1996), pp. 242–256.

Josef Hora

(8 July 1891 – 21 June 1945)

Šárka Nevidalová
Ostrava University

BOOKS: *Básně, 1911–1914* (Prague: Zeyerův fond při České akademii císaře Františka Josefa pro vědy, slovesnost a umění, 1915); revised as *První kniha básní* (Prague: František Borový, 1924);

Strom v květu (Prague: František Borový, 1920);

Pracující den (Prague: Holubice, 1920);

Srdce a vřava světa (Prague: František Borový, 1922);

Hliněný Babylon (Prague: Věnceslava Boučková, 1922);

Socialistická naděje (Prague: Komunistické knihkupectví a nakladatelství, 1922);

Kultura a třídní vědomí (Prague: Federace dělnických tělocvičných jednot československých, 1922);

Bouřlivé jaro (Prague: František Borový, 1923);

Z politické svatyně (Prague: Komunistické knihkupectví a nakladatelství, 1924);

Itálie (Prague: František Borový, 1925);

Probuzení (Prague: Dr. Otakar Štorch-Marien, 1925);

Hladový rok (Prague: Čin, 1926);

Struny ve větru, volume 7 of *Dílo Josefa Hory* (Prague: František Borový, 1927);

Mít křídla (Prague: Privately printed, 1928);

Smrt manželů Pivodových (Prague: Pokrok, 1928);

Deset let, volume 9 of *Dílo Josefa Hory* (Prague: František Borový, 1929);

Literatura a politika (Prague: Otto Girgal, 1929);

Tvůj hlas (Prague: František Borový, 1930);

Tonoucí stíny, volume 11 of *Dílo Josefa Hory* (Prague: František Borový, 1933);

Dvě minuty ticha, volume 12 of *Dílo Josefa Hory* (Prague: František Borový, 1934);

Popelec (Prague: František Borový, 1934);

Karel Toman (Prague: František Borový, 1935);

Tiché poselství, volume 13 of *Dílo Josefa Hory* (Prague: František Borový, 1936);

Máchovské variace (Prague: František Borový, 1936);

Domov (Prague: František Borový, 1938);

Dech na skle, 7 volumes (Prague: Knihovna Lidových novin, 1938);

Jan Houslista (Prague: František Borový, 1939);

Zahrada Popelčina, volume 26 of *Dílo Josefa Hory* (Prague: František Borový, 1940);

Zápisky z nemoci (Prague: Melantrich, 1945);

Život a dílo básníka Aneliho, edited by Miloslav Novotný (Prague: František Borový, 1945);

Proud, edited by Novotný (Prague: František Borový, 1946);

Pozdravy, edited by A. M. Píša (Prague: Československý spisovatel, 1949).

Editions and Collections: *Dílo Josefa Hory*, 16 volumes, incomplete (Prague: František Borový, 1927–1940)—comprises volume 1, *Básně* (1927); volume 2, *Strom v květu* (1927); volume 3, *Pracující den;* volume 4, *Srdce a vřava světa* (1929); volume 5, *Bouřlivé jaro* (1927); volume 6, *Itálie* (1933); volume 7, *Struny ve větru* (1927); volume 8, *Hladový rok* (1932); volume 9, *Deset let* (1929); volume 10, *Tvůj hlas* (1940); volume 11, *Tonoucí stíny* (1933); volume 12, *Dvě minuty ticha* (1934); volume 13, *Tiché poselství* (1936); volume 14, *Dech na skle* (1938); volume 15, *Jan houslista* (1939); volume 16, *Zahrada Popelčina* (1940);

Dílo Josefa Hory, 16 volumes, edited by Miloslav Novotný, edited after 1949 by A. M. Píša (Prague: František Borový, 1946–1949; Prague: Československý spisovatel, 1949–1961)—comprises volume 1, *Kořist smyslů* (1948); volume 2, *Kniha srdce a světa* (1948); volume 3, *Kniha času a ticha* (1948); volume 4, *Kniha domova* (1954); volume 5, *Písně hodin večerních* (1950); volume 6, *Zapomenuté básně* (1951); volume 7, *Socialistická naděje a jiné prózy* (1949); volume 8, *Hladový rok* (1949); volume 9, *Dech na skle* (1948); volume 10, *Eugen Oněgin* (1949); volume 11, *Kniha slovanské poezie* (1951); volume 12, *Jesenin a Pasternak* (1947); volume 13, *Kniha satiry a rozmaru* (1953); volume 14, *Z německé poezie* (1954); volume 15, *Poezie a život* (1959); volume 16, *Dny a lidé* (1961).

Editions In English: "Labour," selected and translated by Paul Selver, in *An Anthology of Czechoslovak Literature* (London: Kegan Paul, Trench, Trübner, 1929), p. 293;

"Autumn," translated by Ewald Osers, in *Heart of Europe: An Anthology of Creative Writing in Europe 1920–1940*, edited by Klaus Mann and Hermann Kesten (New York: Fischer, 1943), p. 527;

"The Workwoman Madonna," translated by Oliver Elton, and "Jan the Violinist," translated by Osers and J. K. Montgomery, in *Hundred Towers: A Czechoslovak Anthology of Creative Writing*, edited by F. C. Weiskopf (New York: Fischer, 1945), pp. 53–55;

"Spring," "Autumn," "Sky over Slovakia," "Strings in the Wind," and "Jan the Violinist," selected and translated by Osers and Montgomery in *Modern Czech Poetry* (London: Allen & Unwin, 1945), pp. 36–39;

"The Window," translated and edited by Albert French, in *A Book of Czech Verse* (London & New York: Macmillan, 1958), p. 72;

"Most Beautiful Is the Earth" and "Sonnet," translated by Edith Pargeter, in *A Handful of Linden Leaves*, edited by Jaroslav Janů (Prague: Artia, 1960), pp. 12, 36;

"Song," "Most Beautiful Is the Land," "The Window," "Time, Brother of My Heart," and "A Madonna of the People," translated by Pargeter, in *The Linden Tree: An Anthology of Czech and Slovak Literature 1890–1960*, edited by Mojmír Otruba and Zdeněk Pešat (Prague: Artia, 1962), pp. 88–93;

"Working-class Madonna," from a newspaper article by Hora, criticizing poetism, published in *Rudé právo* on 20 November 1924; excerpts from *Struny ve větru; Dvě minuty ticha;* and *Jan houslista*, in Alfred French's the *Poets of Prague: Czech Poetry between the Wars* (London: Oxford University Press, 1969), pp. 9–14, 49, 56–58, 96, 118.

OTHER: *Komunistický kalendář na rok 1922*, edited by Hora (Prague: Komunistické knihkupectví a nakladatelství, 1921);

Mladá česká poezie, compiled and edited by Hora (Prague: Státní nakladatelství Praha, 1931);

Almanach Kmene 1931–32, edited by Hora (Prague: Kmen, 1932);

Antonín Macek, Výbor z díla, compiled and edited by Hora (Prague: Družstevní práce, 1932);

Průvodce dnešního čtenáře z knih Kmene, compiled and edited by Hora and Libuše Vokrová-Ambrosová (Prague: Kmen, 1934);

Věčný Mácha, edited by Hora and others (Prague: Čin, 1940).

Josef Hora, one of the most important figures in twentieth-century Czech literature, is famous mainly as a poet, but he also won recognition as a prose writer; literary critic; translator from Russian, German, and south Slavic languages; and literary and political publicist. His work created a link with Czech prewar modernism, closely associated with the then-fashionable artistic trends of "vitalism," extolling the exuberance of human life, and "civilism," paying homage to the arrival of a modern, technological civilization. Nevertheless, Hora never wrote purely "vitalist" or "civilist" poetry. His work is strongly influenced by the socialist movements of the 1920s and the 1930s; uncommonly, for this type of poetry, Hora emphasizes the ethics of revolutionary activity in his "proletarian" poems. Hora was never a member of any literary group, nor was he an adherent of any poetic school.

Josef Hora was born on 8 July 1891 in Dobříš near Roudnice. When he was two years old, his father sold the estate that had belonged to his wife's family, and the whole family moved to Prague. In 1896 his parents separated, and Hora, not yet six years old, went with his mother to live with relations in Roudnice, where he attended secondary school from 1902 to 1910 and where he spent a lot of time even during the years 1910 to 1916, when he was studying at the Faculty of Law in Prague. When he was just eighteen, he settled permanently in Prague.

The long years he spent away from the Czech capital undoubtedly influenced Hora's first poetic efforts and his early prose writing. From the age of seventeen he wrote verse that he occasionally published. His work first appeared in June 1908 under the pseudonym Jan Hron in *Vesna* (Spring), a women's fortnightly magazine. Soon afterward, he finished his final secondary-school examinations and, as a result of parental pressure, went to Prague to study. Hora was disappointed in Prague, of which he had high expectations. Studying a subject that offered "good prospects" did not appeal to him, and he almost completely lost faith in his poetic talent. On the other hand, the energetic environment of the big city awakened him out of a certain mental lethargy, and young Hora began working as a journalist. By 1911 he was contributing regularly to *Rudé proudy* (The Red Currents), the regional Podřipsko journal of the Czechoslovak social democrats. For three years he wrote a series, *Dopisy z Prahy* (Letters from Prague), for the

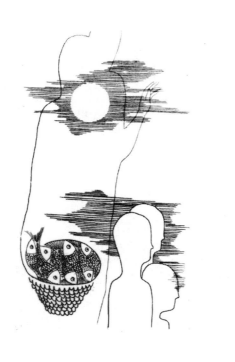

JOSEF HORA

MÍT KŘÍDLA

EDITIO PRINCEPS

V PRAZE 1928

Frontispiece and title page for a collection of Josef Hora's poetry (courtesy of The Lilly Library, Indiana University, Bloomington, Indiana)

paper, giving news about politics and cultural events. At the same time he began writing literary reviews. His success as a journalist restored his self-confidence. The young writer refined his style, began to be less introverted, and soon returned to writing poetry.

Hora published his first book of verse, *Básně 1911–1914* (Poems, 1911–1914), in 1915. The date of publication shows that its verses originate from the period when Czech literature was confronted by different approaches from two generations of writers; the static individualistic poetry of the 1890s was at odds with the trends in poetry of the writers concentrated around the *Almanach na rok 1914* (Almanac for 1914). The new poetry was dynamic and intoxicated with the modern world, its technology, and its civilization. Although Hora did not take part directly in the controversy, he obviously needed to clarify his ideas about his poetry, to lay claim to his place among poets. Hora welcomes the fresh wind in Czech poetry, and in *Básně*, basically his poetic creed, he attempts to find a bal-

ance between a too "primitive" vitalism, which holds up the experience of the senses as the only true value, and the lack of human interest in civilism. This dualism, the conflict between the subjective and the objective, pervades all of Hora's work. At the same time he is constantly searching in his poetry for order, harmony, and meaning in the world and in life. In his first work Hora does not offer solutions to these questions; he merely gives them expression. The mood of this collection is predominantly optimistic.

In the chaos of the war years, *Básně* did not arouse much interest, and Hora did not really begin to be recognized as a poet until 1920, when František Borový published Hora's second collection, *Strom v květu* (A Tree in Blossom). Most of the poems in this book were written during the second half of World War I, so the collection can be viewed as a seamless continuation of the first volume. Hora was depressed by the lack of response to his first volume, by political events, by the war, and by the problem of earning a living. He had no intention of taking up legal work. When he graduated, he went back to Roudnice and worked full time as a publicist and editor for such publications as *Právo lidu* (People's Rights) and *Podřipan* (The Man from Podřipsko). At the beginning of the 1920s, Hora met his future wife, who helped him overcome his personal problems.

The title of the second collection indicates that there is no place in it for Hora's depression. Just as in *Básně*, there is an optimistic feeling about life. Actual experience of war and love give substance to the general plan of the book. In the midst of the hardships of war Hora realizes that even in these painful circumstances it is possible for a feeling of solidarity and unity with the world, later more specifically with the workers, to come into being and grow. Hora develops to the fullest his skill in finding the positive in the negative and in uniting intimate and social themes, the subjective and the objective.

After World War I, Hora moved permanently to Prague. He became involved at the center of cultural and political life and gathered around himself the up-and-coming generation of young poets. At this time Hora's career was moving in two directions: besides working on his own literary work, he spent a great deal of time working as a journalist. By 1919 he was editing the arts column in the social democratic *Právo lidu*. From 1920 to 1929 he did the same job for the communist paper *Rudé právo* (Red Rights), becoming chief editor in 1926. At the same time he published dozens of popular articles in the left-wing and workers' press. He gave lectures, and in 1922 his educational lecture for self-taught workers, *Kultura a třídní vědomí* (Culture and Class Consciousness), was published in book form. Writing literary criticism, and essays and articles on cultural affairs now formed the main part of his work in journalism, a profession that he enjoyed and at which he was successful. Nevertheless, the hundreds of articles that he had published in various newspapers and magazines in the course of twenty-five years, roughly from the end of World War I to the beginning of the 1940s, were no match for his poetry in importance. Just as in his literary work, Hora based his criticism on the principle of duality. According to him a literary work of the highest order is "socially committed," but at the same time it is individual and unrepeatable because it is completely integrated with the personality of its creator.

The most important factor at this happy period of Hora's life was his own writing. In 1922 his satirical novel *Socialistická naděje* (Socialist Hope) was published; in it Hora expressed his opinion of the right-wing policies of the leaders of social democracy. Two years later he published a book of poems and epi-

grams titled *Z politické svatyně* (From the Temple of Politics), but Hora's most important collections are the three works of so-called proletarian lyrical poetry—*Pracující den* (The Working Day, 1920), *Srdce a vřava světa* (The Heart and the Turmoil of the World, 1922), and *Bouřlivé jaro* (Stormy Spring, 1923).

In those years proletarian poetry was a fixed and recognized genre, though of course every one of the proletarian poets—Jiří Wolker, Stanislav K. Neumann, Jaroslav Seifert, Jindřich Hořejší, and others—treated it differently. Just as in his previous collections, Hora combined the intimate and the social, the objective and the subjective. He made liberal use of the symbols of Christianity: revolution, associated with the traditional conception of divine justice, appears justified. Even during the war Hora believed in collective power and social change, and the revolutionary atmosphere after the war confirmed this feeling: only the proletariat can bring about change. Hora now developed his poetic imagery in the completely opposite way from before. From concrete images he moved to abstractions, and specifics became general symbols. This change was surely due to Hora's revolutionary ideas.

The collection *Itálie* (Italy, 1925) revealed even more significant changes in Hora's poetry. All twenty-seven poems in this collection were directly concerned with his journey to Italy in July 1924. Association with this emotional and sensuous southern people brought Hora back into contact with the world of the senses. He began to use details and colors in his poetry. In contrast with his earlier collections, he now moved from abstractions to specifics: symbols became "real things," and sentence construction and poetic terms were simplified. Instead of long subordinate clauses, multiple elements in sentences, and extensive enumerations he used a succession of short metaphorical expressions. Hora's poems became more regular in form, more songlike. The change in Hora's poetic style was in harmony with the rise of poetism in Czech literature. Hora never accepted poetism (a Czech movement, which, according to Karel Teige, approached the world "in such a way that it would become a poem," a lyrical poetry that used the method of free association of ideas) as a poetic program, but certain elements in it did inspire him, especially the emphasis on the sensual and the specific. Of course the proletarian character was not lost in the collection *Itálie*, for Hora was closely associated with contemporary events. A few months after the publication of *Itálie*, the book *Probuzení* (Awakening, 1925), a collection of his older shorter writings, was published. Its theme is the poet's childhood in Roudnice. The novel *Hladový rok*

(The Hungry Year, 1926) has the same background. In it Hora writes about the last year of the war in a provincial town.

In the autumn of 1925 Hora traveled to the Soviet Union, where he spent a month as a delegate to the Society for the Advancement of Relations with the New Russia. After his return the general tone of his poetry changed again. Hora, a poet who regarded the world with optimism, became disillusioned in Russia. In spite of his continued faith in a just, socialist society of the future, he began to see how difficult, if not impossible, it was to attain. He therefore of necessity had to find some new constant as a basis for his poetry, and he found it in the concept of time. The collection *Struny ve větru* (Strings in the Wind, 1927) includes poems written immediately after his journey to the Soviet Union. Consciousness of time is dominant: time is a completely natural, indispensable part of reality; it permeates the whole of nature and every human being. Hora speaks of time both directly and in symbols, in the abstract and in material terms. Time is in no way allegorized; in short, time exists, passes, and is. Such treatment of this phenomenon is fairly unusual in Czech poetry of the day. The "non-material" verses in Hora's poetry most closely resemble the poems of Karel Toman (1877–1946), who like Hora juxtaposes the abstract and the concrete and constructs his poetry on the conflict between them. Hora himself was conscious of this affinity, including poems dedicated to Toman in the collection *Struny ve větru*, and in 1935 Hora wrote of Toman as his literary "mentor."

Hora published the collection *Mít křídla* (Having Wings) in a special private edition in 1928. It included six older poems that dealt with topics relevant to social events and proletarian poetry. Hora's most extensive collection, titled *Deset let* (Ten Years), came out in 1929 and won the state prize. In it Hora takes stock of the ten preceding years. The world that had hardly recovered from the disasters following World War I was heading for further catastrophes, without people having reached the expected happy times. Hora reflects also on his own career as a writer: he is certainly disappointed in the way society has developed, but the existence of the phenomenon of time, which cannot be suspended or changed, fills him with faith in the future. The poet here combines his older and newer creative processes: besides free (unrhymed) verse, which Hora uses to express the most general truths, he also employs highly condensed metaphors. In the spring of 1929 Hora was one of the seven communist writers who protested against the newly introduced, hardline and pro-soviet political program of the new leaders of the Czechoslovak Communist Party and

PROUD

Josef Hora

ZODIAK

Title page for the 1948 edition of Hora's posthumously published 1946 book, one of three memoirs Hora wrote during the five years of illness that ended in his death (courtesy of The Lilly Library, Indiana University, Bloomington, Indiana)

hence were expelled from the party. Yet, Hora still retained his allegiance to socialist doctrine. The best proof of his loyalty is found in the brochure *Literatura a politika* (Literature and Politics, 1929).

By the beginning of the 1930s Hora had became well known in Czech literary circles. The critics praised his books, and Hora won many prizes. He was invited to be on important literary panels and joined editorial boards for literary journals, anthologies, and books. Between 1929 and 1932 he published his own journal, *Plán* (The Plan), a review of literature, art, and science. Until the mid 1930s he was editor of *Literární noviny* (The Literary Gazette), and for two years he edited *Almanach Kmene* (The Kmen Almanac). From 1935 he edited a series of literary monographs, *Postavy a dílo* (Writers and Their Work), which he had devised himself. In the 1930s Hora traveled more. In 1930 he visited Paris; two years later he went to Estonia; and in that same year he wrote an article about his travels, "Chvíle v Estonsku" (A Sojourn in Estonia). The following year he went to Budapest, and in 1938 his last journey took him to Ljubljana, a trip that inspired him to translate Slovenian poetry, published as *Hvězdy nad Triglavem* (Stars Over Triglav, 1940).

In the early 1930s Hora's poetry underwent a fundamental change. The poet—who had always constructed his poetry on some fixed constant, usually the passage of time—began to anchor his poetry within his own inner being, shut off from the outside world. Nevertheless, he did not maintain this position for long. Hora's "quiet" verse changed and became more and more "vociferous," arguing about society and actual social conditions. Some of the poems are tragic in tone. More frequently he writes of loneliness, anguish, helplessness, pain, and death. Time is not hope but proof of vanity and destruction. Hora takes this position in his collections from the 1930s—*Tvůj hlas* (Your Voice, 1930), *Tonoucí stíny* (Drowning Shadows, 1933), *Dvě minuty ticha* (Two Minutes' Silence, 1934), and *Tiché poselství* (The Silent Message, 1936).

The collection *Máchovské variace* (Variations on Mácha, 1936), written for the hundredth anniversary of the publication of *Máj* (May) by the great Czech Romantic poet Karel Hynek Mácha (1810–1836), was Hora's crowning achievement; he had been engaged in a persistent search for the ideal form of poetry since the beginning of the 1930s. In *Tiché poselství* Hora had already sensed the stability and near indestructibility of the traditions of his native land; in *Máchovské variace* Mácha's life and work inspired him. Both poets were keenly aware of time and the passage of time. Mácha's perception of time had, of course, a more tragic basis—he had an overwhelming feeling of futility that was not typical of Hora. The sense of unity that came from identifying with Mácha gave Hora a feeling of strength and liberation. The collection was hailed as the peak of Hora's poetic work. The poet solved the problem of the relationship of life and poetry; he concluded that they cannot be separated: they are complementary.

In the intense and melodious poetry of *Máchovské variace*, Hora draws parallels between the natural world, the romantic Czech countryside, various themes of Mácha's poetry, the abstract concepts of time and space and the basic, unanswerable questions of human existence. Through time and space Hora seeks a reunion of understanding with the poet Karel Hynek Mácha, who lived a hundred years before him but who towers beyond history because of the intensity of his imagination. Hora sympathizes with Mácha, who, as a result of his exceptional insight and poetic talent, stood alone among his contemporaries and whose unsuccessful attempts to unlock the mysteries of human existence remained misunderstood in his time. But these highly intense attempts to tackle perennial, insoluble philosophical problems made Mácha relevant to Man in any age. Art and the attempts of artists to penetrate the wall of mystery surrounding human existence are, in Hora's view, much more real than human existence itself, even though poets do not manage to achieve much more than to catch a glimpse of the magic that lies beyond everyday life.

In the latter part of the 1930s Europe began to awaken to the danger of the spread of fascism. The nation had to adopt a firmer stance; it had to strengthen its position and speak out. Hora, who had previously found a basis for hope in the traditions of the Czech nation in *Tiché poselství*, now published the collection *Domov* (The Homeland, 1938) in which he extolled the great personalities of Czech culture—Mácha, Jaroslav Vrchlický, and František Xaver Šalda. Although the poems are mostly subjective in outlook, their subject matter (such as the nation's approaching tragedy) is highly topical. In the famous "Zpěv rodné zemi" (My Song to My Native Land), the last part of the collection, Hora reacts to a political event—the annexation of Austria by Germany in 1938. This poem, however, included only a muted appeal to patriotism, but during the German occupation Hora began to write the prose poem inspired by the life of Jan Kubelík, *Jan Houslista* (Jan the Violinist, 1939), in which he made a direct appeal for patriotism and resistance. Hora remained faithful, according to Břetislav Štorek, to "the synthesis of writing and life." He had already come to believe in this synthesis when he wrote *Máchovské variace*, in which he presents these elements as a harmonious entity, not parallel to each other but indivisible.

Hora's last work published in his lifetime, *Zahrada Popelčina* (Cinderella's Garden, 1940), is a highly emotional sequel to *Jan Houslista*. The two cycles of poems of *Zahrada Popelčina* are closely linked in both form and content to *Jan Houslista*. Hora develops the synthesizing nature of the work. He reconciles the motif of death with the enduring quality of beauty, created in the first place by man in poetry and art.

Hora's achievements as a translator reached their peak in the 1930s. First, he translated the poems of Sergei Yesenin and Boris Pasternak. Then, in 1937, he translated Aleksandr Pushkin's *Eugeny Onegin* and the poem *Tsygany*, Mikhail Iur'evich Lermontov's *Demon*, and many German authors, including Johann Wolfgang von Goethe, Johann Schiller, and Friedrich Wilhelm Nietzsche. From his student years Hora had devoted a great deal of time to prose writing. However, his prose work is interesting primarily for its descriptions of people engaged in the arts and in society and as commentaries on the life of the author. Hora's most extensive work is the novel *Dech na skle* (Breath on Glass, 1938), dealing with conditions in Soviet Russia. In his psychological novel *Smrt manželů Pivodových* (The Death of Mr. and Mrs. Pivoda, 1928) he departs from his subjective documentary style.

By the beginning of World War II, Hora had become ill with a disease that dragged on for five years. He retired from public life and stopped publishing. The three books that he wrote during this unhappy period—*Proud* (The Flow, 1946), *Život a dílo básníka Aneliho* (The Life and Work of the Poet Aneli, 1945), and *Zápisky z nemoci* (Memoirs from a Sickbed, 1945)—were not published until after his death. The memoirs bear witness to the poet's maturity. They show that he became reconciled to his illness and his fate and that he was able through his art to take a detached view of his own situation and that of the nation. Josef Hora died on 21 June 1945, a few weeks after the liberation of Europe. The day after his death he was given the title of national poet, an honor created for the first time in Czechoslovakian history in his memory.

Letters:

Jarmila Mourková, "Z korespondence Josefa Hory," *Česká literatura* (1961): 351;

Mourková and Jarmila Víšková, "Korespondence Josefa Hory z let 1909–1919," *Literární archív Památníku národního písemnictví* (1987): 19–20.

Bibliographies:

Olga Jirečková and Julie Kuncová, *Dílo Josefa Hory* (Prague: Městská lidová knihovna Prague, 1960);

Saša Mouchová, *Soupis knižního díla* (Prague: Československý spisovatel, 1971).

Biographies:

Dík a pozdrav, edited by F. Halas and Bohumil Novák (Prague: František Borový, 1941);

Václav Černý, *Zpěv duše* (Prague: Václav Petr, 1946);

A. M. Píša, *Josef Hora* (Prague: Vydavatelství Ministerstva financí, 1947);

Jarmila Mourková, *Josef Hora* (Prague: Melantrich, 1981).

References:

Miroslav Červenka, "Itálie," "Jan Houslista," "Máchovské variace," "Pracující den," in *Slovník básnických knih* (Prague: Československý spisovatel, 1990), pp. 74–79, 134–136, 227–229;

Alfred French, *The Poets of Prague: Czech Poetry between the Wars* (London & New York, Oxford University Press, 1969);

William E. Harkins, "Joseph Hora," in *Anthology of Czech Literature* (New York: Columbia University Press, 1953), pp. 195–198;

Zdeněk Kalista, "Josef Hora," in *Tváře ve stínu* (České Budějovice: Růže, 1969), pp. 75–98;

Zdeněk Kožmín, "Čas a prostor v Horově a Nezvalově poezii," in *Studie a kritiky,* edited by Helena Burešová, Pavel Urbanec, and Jiří Rambousek (Prague: Torst, 1995), pp. 456–465;

Jarmila Mourková, "Jan Houslista," in *Rozumět literatuře 1* (Prague: Státní pedagogické nakladatelství, 1989), pp. 342–349;

Miloslav Novotný and A. M. Píša, afterwords in *Dílo Josefa Hory* (Prague: František Borový, Československý spisovatel, 1946–1961);

Josef Palivec, "Hora a Halas," in *Básně, eseje, překlady* (Prague: Torst, 1993), pp. 109–112;

Zdeněk Pešat, "Básník smyslů a času," in *Josef Hora: Prsty bílého hvězdáře,* edited by Pešat (Prague: Československý spisovatel, 1985), pp. 197–243;

Pešat, "Kořist smyslů," in *Dialogy s poezií* (Prague: Československý spisovatel, 1985), pp. 183–193;

Milan Suchomel, "Zpěv revolty a smíření," *Host do domu,* 7 (č.6, 1960): 272–274;

František Xaver Šalda, "O nejmladší poezii české," in *Dílo Františka X. Šaldy 8,* edited by Rudolf Havel (Prague: Československý spisovatel, 1961), pp. 146–158;

Břetislav Štorek, "Josef Hora," in *Dějiny české literatury IV,* edited by Jan Mukařovský (Prague: Victoria Publishing, 1995), pp. 291–309.

Egon Hostovský

(23 April 1908 – 7 May 1973)

Vladimír Papoušek
South Bohemia University, České Budějovice

BOOKS: *Zavřené dveře. Nemocné prósy* (Prague: Václav Horák, 1926);

Stezka podél cesty (Prague: Antoníń Král, 1927);

Ve výhni (Ostrava: Ostravský deník, 1927);

Ghetto v nich (Prague: Pokrok, 1928);

Danajský dar (Prague: František Borový, 1930);

Ztracený stín (Prague: Miloslav Dolínský, 1931);

Případ profesora Körnera (Prague: Melantrich, 1932);

Černá tlupa (Prague: Melantrich, 1933);

Cesty k pokladům (Prague: Melantrich, 1934)—comprises "Pan Lorenz," "Modré světlo," *Ghetto v nich;*

Žhář. Román (Prague: Melantrich, 1935);

Dům bez pána. Román (Prague: Melantrich, 1937);

Kruh spravedlivých. Povídka (Prague: Štěpán Jež, 1938);

Tři starci (Prague: Melantrich, 1938);

Listy z vyhnanství (Chicago: České národní sdružení v Americe, 1941); translated by Ann Krtil as *Letters from Exile* (London: Allen & Unwin, 1942);

Sedmkrát v hlavní úloze. Román (New York: Newyorský deník, 1942); translated by Fern Long as *Seven Times the Leading Man* (London: Eyre & Spottiswoode, 1945; New York: Fischer, 1945);

Úkryt (Texas: Nákladem autorových přátel / New York: Vytiskly New-Yorské listy, 1943);

Cizinec hledá byt. Román (Prague: Melantrich, 1947);

Osamělí buřiči (Brno: Lidové noviny, 1948); translated by Jindra Brumlíková, W. Bechyně, John Lehman, and Willa Muir as *The Lonely Rebels: Three Novelettes* (New York: Arts Inc., 1951)—comprises "Mister Lorenz," "The Revolt in Liossa," "The Mission";

Manipulation of the Zhdanov Line in Czechoslovakia (New York: National Committee for a Free Europe, 1952);

Missing: A Novel, translated by Ewald Osers (New York: Viking, 1952; London: Secker & Warburg, 1952); Czech version published as *Nezvěstný. Román* (Toronto: Nový domov, 1955);

Egon Hostovský (photograph by Vilém Kříž; from the dust jacket for The Plot, *1961)*

Komunistická modla Julius Fučík a jeho generace (New York: National Committee for a Free Europe, 1953); translated as *The Communist Idol Julius Fučík and His Generation* (New York: National Committee for a Free Europe, 1953);

The Midnight Patient, translated by Philip H. Smith Jr. (New York: Appleton-Century-Crofts, 1954; London: Heinemann, 1955); Czech version published as *Půlnoční pacient. Román* (New York: Universum Press, 1959);

The Charity Ball, translated by Smith (London: Heinemann, 1957; Garden City, N.Y.: Doubleday, 1958); Czech version published as *Dobročinný večírek. Román* (New York: Moravian Library, 1958);

The Plot, translated by Alice Backer and Bernard Wolfe (Garden City, N.Y.: Doubleday, 1961; London: Cassell, 1961); Czech version published as *Všeobecné spiknutí* (Prague: Melantrich, 1969);

Tři noci. Román (New York: Společnost pro vědy a umění, 1964); translated by Smith as *Three Nights* (London: Cassell, 1964);

Literární dobrodružství českého spisovatele v cizině, aneb o ctihodném povolání kouzla zbaveném (Toronto: Nový domov, 1966);

Osvoboditel se vrací (Köln: Index, 1972)—comprises *Osvoboditel se vrací* and *Epidemie.*

Edition in English: *The Hideout,* translated by Fern Long (New York: Random House, 1945); republished with *The Black Band,* translated by Jindra Brumlíková and Isabella Athey, as *Hide & Seek: Two Tales of Escape* (London: Eyre & Spottiswoode, 1950).

OTHER: "Biographical Notes by Egon Hostovský," in *Hundred Towers: A Czechoslovak Anthology of Creative Writing,* edited by F. C. Weiskopf (New York: Fischer, 1945), pp. 251–275;

"Participation in Modern Czech Literature," in *The Jews of Czechoslovakia,* edited by Avigdor Dagan, Gertrude Hirschler, and Lewis Weiner (Philadelphia: Society for the History of Czechoslovak Jews, 1968), volume 1, pp. 439–453.

PERIODICAL PUBLICATION: "The Czech Novel Between the Two World Wars," *Slavonic and East European Review,* 21 (1943): 78–96.

Egon Hostovský made an original contribution to twentieth-century European and American literature with works that portray modern man's existentialist feelings of alienation and rootlessness. In his stories Hostovský depicted weak, defenseless individuals (mostly Jews and exiles from Europe) threatened by a hostile world, and he allegorized their fate in terms of the fall of humanity into the dark regions of alienation and the absurdity of stereotyped human relations. Hostovský's works attracted the attention of an international public chiefly during the 1940s and 1950s. At that time, however, Franz Kafka had been rediscovered, and Hostovský's works were often misinterpreted by being linked with his.

Egon Hostovský, the youngest of eight children, was born on 23 April 1908 in Hronov, in East Bohemia. His father, Josef Hostovský, was one of the owners of a textile factory, but this unsuccessful business became the source of family tensions that marked Hostovský's childhood. The author also suffered the loss of his mother, Bedřiška, who died when he was young. During World War I there were material privations, and two of his brothers died of tuberculosis.

From 1919 to 1927 Hostovský attended secondary school in Náchod. By the time he left school he was a budding author: several magazine articles and his first book, the story collection *Zavřené dveře. Nemocné prósy* (A Closed Door, 1926), had already been published. For a short time he was a student in the Arts Faculty at Charles University in Prague under Professor Miloslav Hýsek. In 1929 Hostovský moved to the Arts Faculty in Vienna, where he met Květa Ondráková, the daughter of a businessman from Opočno; she later became his first wife. He abandoned his studies in 1930; returning to Prague, he began to contribute to several periodicals, including *Host* (Guest) and *Kvart* (Quarto), and he worked as a reader for the publishing house Melantrich. He became friends with František Halas, Jaroslav Seifert, and Ivan Olbracht, all well-known Czech authors. In multicultural Prague, Hostovský became more intensely aware of his Jewishness and began to take a greater interest in the fate of the Jews in eastern and central Europe. He supported the so-called theory of assimilation, according to which the Jewish population would gradually merge with the national majority in the country they lived in. He was inspired by the theories of the self-styled Prague philosopher Jindřich Kohn.

The problem that the eastern and central European Jews had to contend with—the alienation and rootlessness they felt as members of minorities within other nations—gave Hostovský a basic theme for his work that he developed to varying degrees in allegories about the relationship of the individual to society as well as about acceptance and rejection, love and repudiation, and personal and metaphysical guilt. During the 1930s Hostovský's distinct literary and intellectual ideas began to take shape. These ideas were most fully developed in his best works from the 1940s and early 1950s—works that were based on an ever more daring analysis of the relationship of the individual to an alienated, hostile world. From novel to novel Hostovský's heroes are increasingly led to the agonizing recognition of their own share of guilt about the state of the world and society.

Hostovský's first stories, printed in the secondary-school student magazine under the pseudonym H. Noge, showed strong literary influences, chiefly of the work of Fyodor Dostoyevsky. The young author loved to portray his heroes as "hurt and

MISSING

A NOVEL

TRANSLATED FROM THE CZECH

BY EWALD OSERS

NEW YORK · 1952

THE VIKING PRESS

Title page for Hostovský's novel about a mysterious journalist, which was first published in an English translation

humiliated" by a hostile world in situations where their lives have been destroyed. He liked to analyze their mental and spiritual states and the rather melodramatic gestures by which they generally attempted to free themselves from the stranglehold of their own destinies. He kept to a similar formula in *Zavřené dveře*, in which the heroes are caught in their own hypersensitive psyches. They are incapable of finding a way of communicating with the outside world, which Hostovský pictured as a chaotic whirlpool of forces threatening the identity of the individual. The title story of *Zavřené dveře* depicts suicides, as well as murders committed by Frank, a physically handicapped teacher who feels humiliated by his disability.

The critics showed little interest in Hostovský's first efforts. Occasionally reviewers criticized the author for expressionist oversimplification and even, like Jiří Žantovský, considered his work an example of "pathological adolescent self-glorification." In spite of the lack of interest on the part of the critics, the obvious literary influences, and the author's manifest immaturity, Hostovský's first works created a basic model for the majority of his later works.

Hostovský's first novel, *Stezka podél cesty* (The Wayside Path, 1927), can also be classed among his juvenilia. It is perhaps a specific response to Dostoyevsky's *Prestuplenie i nakazanie* (1866; translated as *Crime and Punishment*, 1886). *Stezka podél cesty* and Hostovský's next novel, *Ve výhni* (Annihilation, 1927), were published in installments in an Ostrava newspaper in the same year. *Ve výhni* was ignored by literary critics until 1996, although it marks the first appearance of Hostovský's typical concepts of war as a cosmic evil that destroys human relations and of apparent peace that conceals conflict.

Neither readers nor critics showed much interest in Hostovský until 1928, when his novel *Ghetto v nich* (The Ghetto Within) appeared. The main character and narrator, Pavel, is a young Jew who suffers in many ways because of his ethnicity. He is traumatized by his Jewishness, and he feels oppressed above all by his father's resigned attitude to life. Through his love for an Aryan girl, he tries in vain to escape from the restraints imposed on him by family and society. Disappointed and humiliated by the girl, he leaves his father's house, hoping that in this way he will be free; but the title of the novel suggests that the hero will carry his stigmata with him.

The novel was the first of several of Hostovský's works to be reviewed favorably by critics such as Arne Novák, Josef Hora, and František Goetz. It was not only the literary quality of the work and Hostovský's greater experience in narrative writing that were responsible but also the accurate description of the hero's traumas. While in Hostovský's early works the social status of the characters is only vaguely indicated, in *Ghetto v nich* their social levels are quite obvious, which made the novel clearly understandable in the context of the society of the First Republic.

Hostovský began to be hailed by the critics as one of the highest hopes for Czech prose writing, which meant that the author's next works were awaited with keen anticipation. This judgment was supported by a vast amount of publicity in *Literární noviny* (Literary Gazette) announcing the author's new novel *Danajský dar* (A Greek Gift) as early as 1929, though it was not published until the latter part of 1930. In spite of being well received on the whole by the critics, it was not popular with readers. The novel *Ztracený stín* (Lost Shadow) was published the following year. It tells the story of a lowly clerk who blackmails his boss in an attempt to get rid of his feeling of humiliation. It is the first of a series of literary successes at home that continued until the author emigrated for the first time.

Hostovský married Květa Ondráková in 1932; their daughter, Olga, was born in 1936. The 1930s were easily the most fruitful and peaceful years of the author's life. Virtually every year until 1938, the well-known publishing house Melantrich published a novel by Hostovský. He won the respect of the critics and became part of the artistic community in Prague. He was never close to the avant-garde, who at that time dominated the artistic scene, but he was in tune with the emerging writers and poets of the early 1930s, notably Halas, Jan Zahradníček, and Jan Čep. Hostovský and Čep represent the most important preexistentialist prose writing in Czech literature.

By the time he wrote the novel *Případ profesora Körnera* (The Case of Professor Koerner), published in 1932, Hostovský was a mature novelist who could produce a masterly psychological character analysis and at the same time find a subject that would interest the reader. However, in the 1930s there was a whole succession of novelists of this type. The chief difference between Hostovský and other writers is that his works offer something more: in his novels of the early 1930s there are increasing indications that the stories are universal allegories. By suggestion, secret symbols, and cryptic signs, the author gives the impression that the real meaning of the novel is not put into words but is concealed behind the ostensible meaning, indicating that his aim is to lay bare the secret relationship between the individual and the universe.

Případ profesora Körnera tells the story of a Jewish secondary-school teacher who is honest and good-hearted but not good at getting along with his pupils. He tries in vain to find a way of relating not only to them but also to his Aryan wife and the entire predominantly non-Jewish community. All his accommodating gestures are misunderstood as manifestations of weakness. In a single moment his whole life is shattered when he finds out that his wife is having an affair with the family doctor and that he himself is dying of an incurable disease. Yet, even in this tense situation, he again decides to try a gesture of reconciliation. By doing good, he attempts to raise the quality of his hitherto ordinary, unexceptional, and insignificant life. Once again everything he does is interpreted as increasing eccentricity and the reactions of a man facing death. Then he finds out that the doctor's diagnosis was wrong and his life is not in immediate danger.

Elated by this news, he stands in the street and turns to the silent heavens asking for a sign that would vindicate his present way of life. The answer comes in the shape of a rapidly approaching car that strikes him down. Here, for the first time in Hostovský's work, paradox and "cosmic irony" play an important part. His protagonists, vainly seeking deliverance from the inadequacy of their emotional lives, meet these forces ever more frequently.

Other works by Hostovský that depict a man striving to find his place within the mysterious transcendental order of the universe include *Černá tlupa* (The Black Mob, 1933), the stories "Pan Lorenz" (translated as "Mister Lorenz," 1951) and "Modré světlo" (The Blue Light), a revised version of *Ghetto v nich, Cesty k pokladům* (Roads to Treasures, 1934), and *Žhář* (The Arsonist, 1935), for which Hostovský was nominated for the State Prize for Literature in 1936. The following year, *Ztracený stín* was made into a motion picture titled *Vyděrač* (The Extortionist), directed by well-known moviemaker Ladislav Brom.

Also in 1937 another important novel by Hostovský, *Dům bez pána* (House without a Master), was published. The text includes a great variety of Hassidic legends and Talmudic and Cabalistic symbols. The inspiration to use this material came from Hostovský's friendship with Jiří Langer, son of writer František Langer, a renowned translator of Hebrew texts and the enfant terrible of a respected Prague family who believed in the theory of assimilation. After a lengthy stay in a Hassidic community in Belz in Galicia, Jiří Langer became an Orthodox Hassidic Jew. When he returned to Prague, he encouraged Ivan Olbracht and Hostovský to visit Galicia; on this visit he acted as a knowledgeable guide for them. Afterward, both writers used their experiences in the world of Eastern Orthodox Jewry to good effect in their work.

Dům bez pána is the story of Dr. Adler's children, who return to their father's house after his death to seek out his will. The desire to discover the "hidden treasure" and their attempts to put the blame for their failures in life on the actions of their nearest and dearest brings them to the point of hating each other. Their story is combined with that of a hypocritical Hassidic mystic who conceals his limitations behind an assumed air of erudition. The story takes its atmosphere from the all-pervading gloom of the house, with many mysterious phenomena acting as signals to the people looking for the will. Allusions to aspects of Jewish folklore with its many allegories form another important element in the story. In the end it turns out that what the loving father leaves in his will is a message challenging his descendants to be understanding of each other. The mysterious signals are shown to be delusions created by the characters themselves that distort their basic family relationships.

By the second half of the 1930s several foreign translations of Hostovský's work had appeared. *Dům bez pána* was published in Holland in 1939, and a short time earlier a translation of *Žhář* had been published in Belgium. On the tour connected with this publication the author's life reached a critical turning point. Hostovský had gone to Belgium in February 1939, and on 15 March he learned of the Nazi occupation of Czechoslovakia. On the advice of friends who had experienced the Nazi race laws, he decided to ask for asylum in Belgium. At the same time, with the consent of his wife, he applied for a separation in order to protect his family from persecution. Because Belgium was also invaded by the Germans, Hostovský continued his flight through France and Spain to Portugal. In Lisbon, along with many other refugees, he waited for an American visa.

The separation from his family and homeland was painful for Hostovský. The bitter experience of exile became the subject of his most sentimental work, *Listy z vyhnanství* (1941; translated as *Letters from Exile*, 1942). The epistolary novel describes a succession of incidents from the lives of refugees: their secret fears of breaking down and being destroyed, the fleeing crowds, and abandoned children, all intermingled with pictures of family life and the homeland. The work reaches its climax with the narrator's discovery that he personally bears some responsibility for the modern apocalypse and with his emotional declaration of love for his native country and his family. The English translation of the book aroused great interest among Anglo-American readers. *Žhář* also received favorable criticism; for example, in 1942 scholar Carlos Baker reviewed it in *The New York Times Book Review*.

In February 1941 Hostovský set sail from Lisbon for the United States on the ship *Serpa Pinto*. In addition to his writing, he had been working for the Foreign Ministry since 1937, so he was given a job immediately in the Czechoslovak consulate in New York; however, his relations with political and journalist exiles were strained. When *Listy z vyhnanství* was published, some Czech journalists criticized Hostovský as lacking in national feeling and fighting spirit. Hostovský's quarrel with the exiled nationalist intellectuals and supporters of Czech president Edvard Beneš came to a head after the publication of his novel *Sedmkrát v hlavní úloze* (1942; translated as *Seven Times the Leading Man*,

1945). Roman Jakobson began the wave of criticism, in which he was joined by the journalist Stanislav Budín in *New Yorkské listy* (New York Letters) and Jan Muenzer in *Sokolská Besídka* (Sokol Gathering). They censured him for accusing Czech and European intellectuals of tolerating the blight of fascism.

Sedmkrát v hlavní úloze is the story of an energetic, sophisticated writer, Kavalský, who is surrounded by a circle of faithful admirers. Kavalský's flirting with a movement plotting to gain control of the world ends in personal tragedy for him and in the moral collapse of his entire group of followers. Kavalský, self-styled prophet of a new gospel, finally becomes victim of his own fanaticism. The novel was highly regarded by the American intellectual Lewis Mumford, who later became a personal friend of Hostovský. At the same time, Graham Greene became a great admirer of Hostovský and made every effort to promote his work in Britain.

Although some of the exiled Czech intellectuals supported Hostovský in the quarrel over *Sedmkrát v hlavní úloze*, the author was hurt by the personal attacks. Separation from his family, the loss of his public, and the feeling of alienation in a strange land finally led to a nervous breakdown. He recovered through his friendship with Jindra Brumlíková, whom he eventually married. Brumlíková was from a Czech Jewish family; her parents had sent her to be brought up in the United States to save her from the fate of the majority of European Jews.

At the end of the war in Europe, Hostovský tried to contact his family in Czechoslovakia, but most of his relations, including his elderly father and his sisters, had died in concentration camps. Moreover, several of his friends disapproved of his second marriage in America. When he returned to Czechoslovakia in 1947 with Brumlíková and their daughter, intending to settle there permanently, some of these former friends would have nothing to do with him. Brumlíková could not get used to life in Czechoslovakia and went back to America with their daughter that same year. Hostovský, however, was accepted into a circle of younger artists and writers, most of whom had begun their careers just before the war. The group included Zdeněk Urbánek, Bohuslav Březovský, and Josef Hiršal. The younger generation admired Hostovský's talent for convincingly expressing the emotions of existentialist isolation. The first wave of French existentialism had in fact just reached Czechoslovakia, and young authors growing up in the oppressive atmosphere of the protectorate found in it echoes of their own ideas.

Hostovský's novel *Cizinec hledá byt* (A Foreigner Looks for a Flat), published in 1947, is perhaps a perfect example of Czech existentialism. It is the tragic story of an exiled doctor, Marek, who wanders around New York looking in vain for a place where he would have peace to complete his mission of producing a cure for a malignant disease. Followed by a mysterious being who is finally revealed as Death, Marek goes about like a divine messenger unrecognized by humanity; in the end he dies, completely exhausted, without managing to complete his task. *Cizinec hledá byt* and the book of short stories *Osamělí buřiči* (1948; translated as *The Lonely Rebels*, 1951) were the last of Hostovský's books to be published in his homeland for a long time.

After the communist takeover of Czechoslovakia in February 1948 Hostovský went to Norway as a secretary in the Czechoslovak embassy. In February 1950 he resigned his post and emigrated from Norway to the United States. Meanwhile, his second marriage had ended in divorce. Hostovský began to work for the emerging station Radio Free Europe. He regularly wrote commentaries condemning the cultural policies of communist Czechoslovakia. In 1952 an English translation of Hostovský's new novel, *Nezvěstný*, was published as *Missing* by Secker and Warburg in London and Viking in New York. American readers expected the book to be a thriller about the events of the February coup and the mysterious, violent death of the Czechoslovak foreign minister Jan Masaryk; none of the contemporary reviewers failed to point out the fact that Masaryk and Hostovský had been friends. Those expecting a thriller, however, were disappointed. Although the plot is set in the eerie atmosphere of Prague at the time of the coup and Masaryk's death, the book is not a real-life detective story but a characteristic allegory of the modern world destroyed by an ideological cyclone and dominated by the inner workings of industry and politics. In this world a simple human act becomes incomprehensible and even dangerous.

The plot revolves around the secretive central figure of Král, a journalist. His trip to the United States arouses the suspicions of the communist and American secret services. His motives for going to the United States are simple—he is trying to save his sick daughter—but terrible things begin to happen around him. Eventually the people behind the violence and intrigue become its victims themselves. The author imposes on the original spy story more of his examples of cosmic irony. Nobody is capable

of stopping the vortex of forces released, and in the end these forces catch up with and punish guilty and innocent alike; however, the latter are guilty of apathy and lack of awareness. In 1955 the novel was published in Czech by the Toronto publishing house Nový domov.

The same spirit is evident in the next novel, *Půlnoční pacient*, first published in English as *The Midnight Patient* in 1954. This novel is about the relationship of a New York psychiatrist, Malík, and his patient, the spy Alfons. Again a whirlpool of intrigue, mystery, and crime spreads around them. The French director Henri-Georges Clouzot became interested in the subject and made the book into a motion picture titled *Les Espions* (The Spies, 1957). The novel *Dobročinný večírek*, published first in English as *The Charity Ball* in 1957, is an ironic fantasy about the life of European exiles in America. Their strange society gives a ball, during which the extent of their segregation and the isolation of their inner world is gradually revealed. The novel has no central protagonist but is a panorama of wasted human lives. The characters' desires to help or understand others nearly always have the opposite effect, with the result that gradually an incomprehensible chaotic universe unfolds in front of the reader. Because of their unwholesome need for mutual love, these lost exiles destroy each other. In *Dobročinný večírek* Hostovský moves on from the notion of the world as a crystal-clear structure with easily understood laws, as in *Žhář* and *Dům bez pána*, to a much less confident picture of a world of chaos, in which the only realities are the pain and absolute loneliness of human existence. Having sold the film rights for *Dobročinný večírek*, Hostovský was free of financial worries for a time and was able to devote himself to writing.

After his divorce from Brumlíková, Hostovský remarried; his third wife, Regina Weis, was a naturalized American of German extraction. In 1958 their son, Paul, was born. During the 1950s a friendship developed between Hostovský and Mumford, who became a dedicated interpreter of Hostovský's allegories. At the same time, he inspired the author with his theories about where civilization was heading and about the gradual triumph of technology over humanity. Hostovský also became friendly with Waldo Frank, but the latter's uncritical admiration of the Cuban revolutionary Fidel Castro caused a difference of opinion. The critic Orville Prescott of *The New York Times* also wrote sympathetically about Hostovský's work.

In spite of the attention of the critics Hostovský was not completely accepted by American

*Dust jacket for the first Czech edition (1969) of Hostovský's 1961
novel,* The Plot, *about a writer in New York (courtesy of the
National Library of the Czech Republic)*

and British readers. Although his books had generally attractive subjects, Hostovský tended to be a writer for a rather restricted circle of intellectuals. Even they, however, had reservations about the wide-ranging *Všeobecné spiknutí* (1969), published first in English as *The Plot* (1961). The author had worked hard at it after the successful sale of the film rights of his previous book, and he considered it his best work. The story of the writer Bareš, who lives in New York, unfolds on several time levels. As he celebrates his birthday, there are indications that he is disappointed in his surroundings and that he is gradually becoming aware of signs of a widespread plot aimed not only at himself but also at humanity in general. In the eerie atmosphere surrounding him he finds more proof of a conspiracy. Perpetually apprehensive and distrustful of everyone, including himself, he completely loses his mind.

On a different level and forming a contrast to the basic story, there are several flashbacks in which Bareš returns to the idyllic country of childhood, to prewar Prague, and to the year 1948. By going back to these days and finding an analogy between his own childhood and the play of an unidentified New York child, Bareš finally regains his sanity and trust in his relations. Like the novel *Dům bez pána,* this novel includes many incidental stories, allegories, symbols, and visions.

When the novel appeared in English, there were several unfavorable reviews generally criticizing its obscurity and the many cryptic allegorical and symbolic passages. This time neither Greene nor Mumford came to its defense. Hostovský attributed its lack of success to one of the translators, Bernard Wolfe, who tried to impose his own style on the book. The work was not published in Czechoslovakia until the short spell of relaxation of censorship at the end of the 1960s, but then it was favorably received both by readers and critics. Perhaps the reason for such a different reception was that in *Všeobecné spiknutí* Hostovský assumes that the reader has knowledge of Czech life and institutions, various contemporary affairs, and political and cultural associations. True to his style, Hostovský uses symbolic language to describe these things. Many of these associations were outside the experience of foreign readers, including the translator.

Hostovský's Europeanism complicated his relationship with America. Incidentally, American reviewers always stressed this aspect of his work. He loved America as the land that had given him asylum, but at the same time he was afraid of it as it was a place of many strange cultures. He was never able to follow the example of Joseph Conrad and write in English. He tried to partly satisfy his longing for Europe with a two-year stay in Denmark from 1964 to 1966. His family could not adapt to life there, however, so he went back to the United States.

In 1964 the novel *Tři noci* (translated as *Three Nights,* 1964), perhaps one of the best of Hostovský's late works, was published. It is a modern allegory of the loneliness and alienation that tragically constrain the life of man. The principal characters are a husband and wife whose marriage is on the point of breaking up. Věra Wagnerová is an emigrant from Europe who constantly harps about her past; to try to come to terms with that past, she uses drugs and engages in love affairs. Her husband, Pavel Wagner, is a typical middle-class American: healthy, high powered, and optimistic, with no complexes. At the greatest crisis point in their marriage a stranger comes to the door of their flat at midnight on three successive evenings. Both husband and wife are shaken out of their normal outlook on life by the terrible events accompanying this visit. Paradoxically, the arrival of the mysterious stranger marks the beginning of their attempt to come to a new understanding. The third night, however, the visitor tricks Wagner and gets into the closely guarded flat. When Wagner returns, he finds his wife dead: the intruder invading the privacy of the couple was Death. In despair Wagner turns furiously to the silent heavens and decides to commit suicide. However, when a new day dawns, he becomes reconciled to living; the symbolic combination of blue and gold gives him the feeling that some unspecified transcendental hope is at hand. In spite of the author's attempt to end the work on a hopeful note, the tone of the whole novel is rather oppressive. The motif of death, in many guises, permeates the entire work.

Hostovský's final work was the novel *Epidemie* (Epidemic). It was published in 1972 together with the unsuccessful play *Osvoboditel se vrací* (Return of the Liberator). In *Epidemie*, as in *Tři noci*, the prevailing theme is death. For the first time Hostovský also targets the American consumer society, portraying it with a fair amount of black humor. The setting is a typical small American provincial town called Petfield. The hero is a middle-aged man who is convinced that he has lost all his family's respect by losing his job. No longer involved in the daily routine of earning a living, he sees life from a different angle. He discovers a hitherto unknown deadly disease that is spreading through society. When he tries to warn people about it, he is simply ridiculed; so he goes off, despised and forgotten by everyone, to serve the dead in the local cemetery. This grotesque allegory about the collapse of civilization finishes with a gesture of intentional dark irony.

The last two works of black humor indicate that the author had become disheartened by his inability to settle in American society and by the first signs of cancer, which overshadowed the last years of his life. In 1968 Hostovský intended to visit Czechoslovakia but was prevented from doing so by the Soviet occupation. Hostovský's books, which had been banned at home since 1948, appeared again for a short time in the late 1960s but once more ended up being destroyed, including the entire edition of *Půlnoční pacient* that had been prepared for publication by Mladá fronta and was destroyed in late 1969.

From his home in Millburn, New Jersey, Hostovský tried to return to Czechoslovakia at least in spirit through correspondence with the poets František Hrubín, Jaroslav Seifert, and his own daughter Olga. He planned a last visit to Europe in the spring of 1973, although by that time he was seriously ill. "I should so much like to see you and all the rest of you again," he wrote on 14 March in a letter to Olga in Italy. He was unable to satisfy this longing; he died on 7 May 1973 in Montclair, New Jersey.

At first inspired by expressionism and the European psychological novel, Hostovský progressed to writing original allegories in which he examined various types of responsibility. He tried to find the connection between the personal lives of his heroes and the general destruction of human values, and a connection with the triumph of modern technology over the individual. He achieved a distinctive blend of a dynamic plot that is often based on adventure and symbolic language and on allusions that often use the poetry of the psalms and other elements of Hebrew folklore. In the context of world literature Hostovský presents an alternative to the existentialist revolutionariness of Jean-Paul Sartre and the acquiescent Messianism of Fyodor Dostoyevsky and Nikolai Aleksandrovich Berdyayev by characteristically stressing traditional Jewish elements of irony and black humor and by contrasting the eternal, albeit often absurd, intercourse between the individual and the transcendental forces of the universe.

Interviews:

"Nový román Egona Hostovského," in *Zápisník*, edited by Ivan Zvěřina (New York: Universum Press, 1958), pp. 14–15;

A. J. Liehm, "Poslední rozhovor," in *Egon Hostovský*, edited by Rudolf Šturm (Toronto: 68 Publishers, 1974), pp. 160–191.

Bibliographies:

"Knihy Egona Hostovského," in *Padesát let Egona Hostovského*, edited by Jiří Pistorius (New York: Moravian Library, 1958), pp. 76–78;

Jaroslav Kunc, *Česká literární bibliografie 1945–1963. Dodatky k 1.dílu A–M* (Prague: Státní knihovna-Národní knihovna, 1964), pp. 758–761;

"Knihy Egona Hostovského," in *Egon Hostovský*, edited by Rudolf Šturm (Toronto: 68 Publishers, 1974), pp. 197–204;

Egon Hostovský (1908–1973), Medailón a výběrová bibliografie, edited by Petr Barták and Ladislav Vacina (Náchod: Okresní knihovna, 1990);

Ludmila Šeflová, *Knihy českých a slovenských autorů vydané v zahraničí v letech 1948–1978* (Brno: Doplněk, 1993), pp. 85–87.

References:

Jiří Bednář, "Druhý zrak Egona Hostovského" *Plamen,* 10 (July 1968): 63–67;

Jiří Brabec, "Konfliktní přijetí Hostovského románu *Sedmkrát v hlavní úloze,*" *Kritický sborník,* 8, no. 3 (1993): 41–44;

Václav Černý, "O Egonu Hostovském," *Listy pro umění a kritiku,* 1 (1933): 491–499;

Černý, "Fikce přehodnocením skutečnosti u Egona Hostovského," *Listy pro umění a kritiku,* 4 (1936): 81–86;

Paul Engle, "One Man Is Missing as Reds Take Prague," *Chicago Tribune* (18 May 1952): 6;

Pavel Fraenkl, "K problematice sebecitu v díle Egona Hostovského," in *Kalendář česko-židovský 1936–1937* (1937);

Wolf Giusti, *Pagine Boeme* (Roma: Giovanni Volpe, 1970), pp. 214–216;

Olga Hostovská, "Jazyková stránka Hostovského knih z období jeho druhé emigrace," *Literární noviny,* 4, no. 26 (1993): 5;

Kautman, *Návrat Egona Hostovského* (Prague: Klub osvobozeného samizdatu, Protis, 1996);

František Kautman, *Polarita našeho věku v díle Egona Hostovského* (Prague: Evropský kulturní klub, 1993);

Ladislav Matějka, "Tisk o románech Egona Hostovského," in *Rok,* edited by Matějka (New York: Moravian Library, 1957), pp. 128–136;

Vladimír Papoušek, *Egon Hostovský (Člověk v uzavřeném prostoru)* (Prague: H+H, 1996);

Papoušek, "Egon Hostovský a Lewis Mumford," *Česká literatura,* 43 (1995): 510–518;

Papoušek, "Hostovského anglicky psané texty o české literatuře," in *O Karlu Poláčkovi a jiných,* edited by Jaroslav Kolár (Boskovice: Albert, 1995), pp. 215–222;

Vladimír Peška, "Deux Types D'Ecrivains en Exil: Jan Čep et Egon Hostovský," in *Emigration Et Exil Dans Les Cultures Tchèque Et Polonaise,* edited by Hana Jechová and Hélène Władarczyk (Paris: Presses de L'Université de Paris-Sorbonne, 1987), pp. 217–229;

Jiří Pistorius, *Padesát let Egona Hostovského 1958* (New York: Moravian Library, 1958);

Karel Sezima, "Dvojí domov," in his *Mlází* (Prague: Umělecká beseda, 1936), pp. 103–123;

Rudolf Šturm, *Egon Hostovský, Studie a dokumenty o jeho osudu* (Toronto: 68 Publishers, 1974);

Timotheus Vodička, "Ztracená cesta," in *Stavitelé věží* (Tasov: Josef Florian, 1947), 89–103.

Papers:

Egon Hostovský's archive of newspaper clippings is housed in the Manuscript Division, Library of Congress, Washington, D.C. His letters to Lewis Mumford are included in the Lewis Mumford Papers, Special Collections, Van Pelt-Dietrich Library, University of Pennsylvania, Philadelphia.

Jozef Cíger Hronský

(23 February 1896 – 13 July 1960)

Ladislav Čúzy
Comenius University, Bratislava

BOOKS: *U nás* (Martin: Matica slovenská, 1923);
Najmladší Závodský (Kremnica: Mládež, 1924);
Domov (Martin: Matica slovenská, 1925);
Kremnické povesti (Kremnica: Mládež, 1925);
Sedemnásť a sedem múdrostí a iné rozprávky (Kremnica: Mládež:,1925);
Janko Hrášok (Kremnica: Mládež, 1926);
Pod kozúbkom (Kremnica: Mládež, 1926);
Žltý dom v Klokoči (Prague: Mazáč, 1927);
Medové srdce (Bratislava & Prague: Mazáč, 1929);
Proroctvo doktora Stankovského (Bratislava & Prague: Mazáč, 1930);
Smelý Zajko (Martin: Matica slovenská, 1930);
Chlieb (Martin: Matica slovenská, 1931);
Smelý Zajko v Afrike (Martin: Matica slovenská, 1931);
Traja bratia (Martin: Matica slovenská, 1931);
Zakopaný meč (Martin: Matica slovenská, 1931);
Brondove rozprávky (Bratislava: Unás, 1932);
Zábavky strýca Kurkovského (Bratislava: Unás, 1932);
Budkáčik a Dubkáčik (Martin: Matica slovenská, 1932);
Podpolianske rozprávky (Martin: Matica slovenská, 1932);
Sokoliar Tomáš (Martin: Matica slovenská, 1932);
Jozef Mak (Martin: Matica slovenská, 1933); translated by Andrew Cincura (Columbus, Ohio: Slavica, 1985);
Tomčíkovci (Trnava: Spolok sv. Vojtecha, 1933);
Zlatý dážď (Trnava: Spolok sv. Vojtecha, 1933);
Sedem sŕdc (Martin: Živena, 1934);
Zlaté hodinky (Martin: Matica slovenská, 1934);
Strýcovo vrtielko (Martin: Matica slovenská, 1935);
Tri rozprávky (Martin: Matica slovenská, 1936);
Budatínski Frgáčovci (Martin: Matica slovenská, 1939);
Pisár Gráč (Martin: Matica slovenská, 1940);
Tri múdre kozliatka (Martin: Matica slovenská, 1940);
Cesta slovenskou Amerikou (Martin: Matica slovenská, 1940);
Šmákova mucha (Martin: Matica slovenská, 1944);
Na Bukvovom dvore (Martin: Matica slovenská, 1944);

Jozef Cíger Hronský

Predavač talizmanov Liberius Gaius od Porta Collina, in *Nádej víťazná*, edited by Mikuláš Šprinc (Scranton, Pa.: Obrana Press, 1947); translated by John J. Kester as *Seller of Talismans* (Scotch Plains, N.J.: Kester, 1978);
Andreas Búr Majster (Scranton, Pa.: Obrana Press, 1948);
Svet na Trasovisku (Whiting, Ind.: Ján J. Lach, 1960);

Pohár z brúseného skla (Buenos Aires: Zahraničná Matica slovenská, 1964);

Na krížnych cestách (Buenos Aires: Zahraničná Matica slovenská, 1966).

Edition: *Sobrané spisy Jozefa C. Hronského,* 9 volumes (Martin: Matica slovenská, 1938–1944);

Dielo I, II, III (Bratislava: Tatran, 1993).

Editions in English: *Seller of Talismans,* translated by John J. Kester (Scotch Plains: N.J.: Kester, 1978);

Jozef Mak, translated by Andrew Cincura (Columbus, Ohio: Slavica, 1985).

Slovak writers of fiction who began their work in the 1920s tried to supplant classical realism by using various stimuli from other European literatures. Similarly, Jozef Cíger Hronský started out with an orientation toward realism but later changed the direction of his writing and created work with strong elements of expressionism. He managed to convey the modern problems of civilized mankind and their world—especially the damage done to their minds by the phenomenon of war—as well as to reveal instinctive powers of man that both renew his vitality and ensure his capacity to survive.

Jozef Cíger Hronský was born on 23 February 1896 in Zvolen, where his father, Peter Pavol Hronský, worked at a lumberyard and lived with his wife, Jozefína. After completing his elementary education Hronský studied at the Hungarian-language teachers' college in Levice, where he finished in 1914 and received his teaching certification. During 1917 and 1918 he saw action on the Italian front in World War I. On 1 March 1919 he married Anna Valéria Ružináková, the daughter of a print-shop owner. After his return from the war he taught and also began his literary efforts. In addition to literature, he devoted time to painting.

Hronský's literary debut came with the publication in 1923 of the story collection titled *U nás* (Our Way). In *U nás,* as well as in the two following collections, *Domov* (Home, 1925) and *Medové srdce* (Heart of Honey, 1929), he continued in the tradition of classical Slovak realism. Thematically he concentrated on the lives of simple village people, whose main concerns in life are their own individual problems. A frequent motif in these works is the way men and women live together. Hronský's view of the villagers' lives is mostly filled with mild humor and harmony. These early works already display elements of Hronský's later poetics. Realism is made special here through the introduction of the lyricism of nature, which evokes atmosphere in the

story and emphasizes the irrational aspects of human existence. Hronský's clear orientation toward man's inner self practically eliminates the presence of contemporary sociohistorical reality in his first works.

Hronský published his first novel, *Žltý dom v Klokoči* (Yellow House in Klokoč), in 1927. It is a story about a love destroyed by the pursuit of money. The conflict arises when the tyrannical miser Petrovič blocks the love of his daughter Eva and her beloved, Koreň. Despite the tragic outcome, on the whole the novel has a harmonious feeling, as all discord is removed, and life continues upon its designated path. In the following year Hronský began editing the children's magazine *Slniečko* (Sun), which he continued doing until 1935.

His second novel, *Proroctvo doktora Stankovského* (Dr. Stankovsky's Prophecy, 1930), represents a diversion from the village theme but later proved to be an isolated case. In this intellectual novel, which was conceived as a model, Hronský plays out a complex game of love with a particular focus on the rational and emotional principles behind it. The novel is about the love of a woman for three men. The characters represent a clash between reason and emotion. Besides this opposition another one is created, namely the opposition between art and the pragmatism of everyday life. The motif of love is brought to the fore and is represented in an absolute, romanticized way by the female protagonist—a young female painter—(She), by a young writer (He), and by a male painter called Zorin. The world of arts and the intuitive, emotional conception of life by these characters is contradictory to the world of a banker named Eduard. The romanticized atmosphere is emphasized by an irrational prediction about the premature death of the writer (He), which comes true. Relations among characters are complicated. Under the pressure of circumstances the young female painter marries the rich Eduard. Her relationship is based on obligation, not on love. The marriage is not successful, and emotional links with the other two men remain unfulfilled. In this novel Hronský departs from poetics of realism and leans toward his own peculiar variant of expressionism, which he developed almost consciously in his later works, especially his novels.

Hronský's first major artistic success was the novel *Chlieb* (Bread, 1931), a collectivist social novel that takes place after World War I in the village of Bacúch and the small town of Podhrabnice. For the first time the historical dimension comes to the forefront in this work along with the natural and mythical. The novel has noticeable expressionistic tendencies; in it Hronský abandons the traditional, gradual story development. The intertwined accounts of a large number of villagers are developed like a mosaic through the combination of individual sequences. The novel is about the mythical life-affirming power of ordinary people who through their endurance and faith are able to overcome fate's adversities. It is also about man's struggle with existential problems and his constant revival by the power of nature in his attempts to win bread for himself and his family. Of the individually characterized villagers, Metodej Chlebko stands out as an ordinary but intelligent man who has his own original, rational logic. As he typically does with many of his other protagonists, Hronský depicts Chlebko as a character full of contradictions. Chlebko is a loving person who helps his neighbors and yet is also someone who can hate and who lives only according to his own conscience, never surrendering to any higher social authority. In *Chlieb* Hronský indicates that his epic world is divided into both inner and outer worlds: the inner world displays uncertainty, uneasiness, worry, and self-withdrawal; the outer world, while apparently quite firm, is only thus because it counters the transient and because the earth and bread are timeless.

Hronský's preference for the inner world, which neglects emphasizing ties between characters and their sociopolitical context, became the generalized model that predominated Hronský's following novel, *Jozef Mak* (1933; translated, 1985). This novel, according to Albín Bagin, became a contemporary "metaphorical picture of Slovak destiny and misery." The novel's plot centers on the main character, Jozef Mak, starting from the beginning of the twentieth century and continuing until he is about thirty. Mak, a born-out-of-wedlock, disinherited man not unlike a million others, grows up with his mother and brother and has the dreams of a typical village person—he wants to build a house and marry his beloved Maruša. However, he is drafted and war interferes in his destiny. Upon his return home, he can no longer realize his plans. In the house he had begun building he finds his brother, Jano, living with his former love, Maruša. Out of spite, Mak marries the sick and homely Julia only to continue a life filled with misfortune, without the capacity to influence its course of events. Mak does not stand in the way of the destiny that shaped his life but manages, despite his insignificance, through his innate strength, to overcome all obstacles and continue his life.

Hronský and Valéria Ružinákova, whom he married in 1919

In addition to the basic story line Hronský again develops his favorite theme of human interrelationships. This time he sketches the complex position of a man (Jozef Mak) caught between two women: Mak's docile wife, Julia, who embodies the spiritual dimension of love, and his former lover Maruša, a woman who loses her beauty, but not her animal magnetism, and who embodies the biological, instinctual side of love. In the novel Hronský once again employs the expressionistic method of depiction. In the forefront he places individual characters who, above all, live intense and spiritual lives, while the backdrop of nature, upon which the story is set, is largely lyricized. The metaphorical transformation of nature-related motifs has a mythologizing function, which is to convey the philosophical idea that fate is a basic determinant of human existence.

In the 1930s, besides writing novels, Hronský also created several shorter fictional works, mainly short stories. The first in a series of short-story collections from that decade is *Podpolianske rozprávky* (Tales from the Foothills of Polana, 1932). As in earlier works, the stories are dominated by undertones of harmony and occasionally enlivened by subtle humor and irony. Likewise, Hronský again draws the subjects for these stories from village life, a choice that often results in unusual elaborations of anecdotes. The stories are synthesized conceptualizations of realistic plots that subtly penetrate into the psychology of the characters. Only two short stories—"Gajdošov vojna-kôň" (Gajdoš's War-Horse) and "Šimčik a jeho mat" (Šimčik and His Mother)—stand apart from the unified tone of the collection. Both draw upon the motif of war, which shows up not in the foreground but rather as a phenomenon that has a strong impact on the destiny of the characters. In his next collection of short prose, *Tomčíkovci* (The Tomčíks, 1933), Hronský returns to the realm of childhood, which he views as a period of harmony and happiness. The atmosphere of the stories is formed by his selection of motifs, as well as through the heightened poetization of all narrative contexts. He sets the stories in both villages and towns and pays only marginal attention to social conflicts—which therefore do not become disturbing elements.

Shortly afterward, the collection *Sedem sŕdc* (Seven Hearts, 1934) was published. Sharing the subtlety of Hronský's earlier work, this latter collection narrates stories about romantic relationships seen in an unusual manner. The heroine in each of the stories is an exalted woman who experiences love intensely. Each story bears the name of one of the heroines (Tereza, Matilda, Marta, Eleonóra, Paula, Tóna, and Cia), introverts who perceive love in a spiritual, almost transcendental sense. Their love becomes so absolute that they are unable to establish normal contacts with their surroundings, thereby increasing their loneliness. These are mostly tragic stories of women longing for a type of love that can never satisfy their desires.

Hronský left teaching in 1933 and became the secretary of the Matica Slovenská organization. He headed the Matica delegation that visited the United States in order to make contacts with Slovak Americans, a trip lasting from December 1935 to July 1936. He described his experiences on the trip in the book *Cesta slovenskou Amerikou* (A Journey through Slovak America), published in 1940.

Hronský's next novel, *Na krížnych cestách* (At the Crossroads), was published serially in the journal *Slovenské pohľady* in 1939 and in book form in 1966. In this novel he again tried to synthesize the historical and the intimate. The action of the book begins in the nineteenth-century

kingdom of Hungary and continues up to the period just after World War I, immediately after the founding of Czechoslovakia. The intimate atmosphere is populated by three generations whose lives are circumscribed by destiny, love, and national feeling. In 1940 Hronský became the director of Matica Slovenská; his tenure was marked by organizational and artistic efforts of almost heroic proportions.

The poetics of Hronský's work always existed within the worlds of realism and expressionism. In his shorter works he was more likely to veer toward realism, but in his novellas and novels expressionism was almost always present. The culmination of the expressionistic tendencies in Hronský's work is the novel *Pisár Gráč* (Scrivener Gráč, 1940). It is probably his most complicated work and the least susceptible to unequivocal interpretation. The subject of *Pisár Gráč* is quite simple—the protagonist, Pisár Gráč, tries to make sense of his existence after having returned from war and realizing its inhumanity and absurdity. The primary instrument in his search is an attempt to understand the people living around him. Pisár Gráč portrays an intellectual attitude toward life that does not serve as a basis for understanding the world. Hronský fashions the private quest of his protagonist in a complicated way, and Gráč's feelings are transmitted to the reader through first-person narration. Overlapping throughout the narration are various temporal planes, reality and fantasy, and detailed facts and symbols. The novel ends with a catharsis after the characters gradually shed the uncertainties and existential feelings that the war had evoked in them. The overall message of the novel, however, is tragic.

During the Slovak National Uprising in September 1944 Hronský was arrested and imprisoned by the insurgents, though released shortly afterward. In that same year he published a collection of short stories titled *Šmákova mucha* (Šmak's Fly). Their topics vary widely; yet, the author's political orientation toward nationalism can be clearly detected. Also in 1944 the last of his novels published in Slovakia, *Na Bukvovom dvore* (In Bukva's Yard), appeared. Once again the plot is set in a village, and again there are stories about love torn between passion and morality, and between emotion and pragmatism. The protagonists of the novel are firmly linked to the myth of the earth, which nourishes man and at the same time becomes his most important value. Yet, this time, fatalism is overcome to a degree by the activities of the wealthy farmer Michal Bukva, who, through his well-considered actions and enterprises, manages to surmount his emotional barriers.

By the beginning of 1945 Hronský left Martin for Bratislava. He subsequently immigrated to Austria with several other nationally oriented figures from Matica. He then lived in the American zone in Bavaria and later immigrated to Italy, where he lived in Rome until February 1948. As an immigrant he continued to pursue literary endeavors, despite the changed conditions. *Andreas Búr Majster* (Master Andreas Bur), a novel, and *Predavač talizmanov Liberius Gaius od Porta Collina* (Liberius Gaius from Port Collin, translated as *Seller of Talismans*, 1978), a novella, were published in 1948 and 1947, respectively. The latter reconstructs the tale of Liberius Gaius, a peddler of pagan talismans who begins to move closer to the Christian faith because of a statuette of Christ and inexplicable events that happen around him. In 1948 the Italian police arrested Hronský at the misinformed request of Czechoslovak authorities and wanted to extradite him as a war criminal. Hronský managed to avoid this fate, instead immigrating to Argentina, where he spent the rest of his life under difficult conditions.

In his extensive body of work Hronský often focused on atypical protagonists who rise above the environments in which they live. The most recognizable of these heroes is the charcoal burner Master Andreas Búr from the 1948 novel, *Andreas Búr Majster*. His story unfolds at Bojnice Castle, is full of poetry and imagination, and develops on the border between reality and the transcendental. Búr, considered a madman by the villagers, is a character marked by absolute love: love for work, love for his wife Lucia, and love for Amalia, mistress of the castle's owner, Richard. The novel concerns human relationships that are hard to define, the quest to communicate with God, and the power of the individual.

In 1956 Hronský became chairman of the Slovak National Council abroad. His last novel, *Svet na Trasovisku* (The World in a Quagmire/The World of Trasovisku, 1960), was published only after his death and because of his political orientation was unavailable to the Slovak public until the end of the 1980s. Once again, in this novel the basic story line touches on the link between mankind and the nourishing earth, as well as ever-renewing vitality. These ideas are symbolized by the protagonist Martin Hrančok, who returns

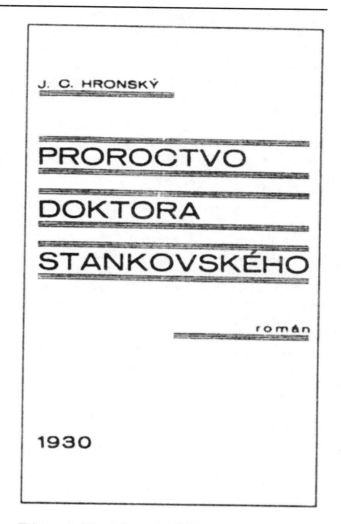

Title page for Hronský's complex 1930 novel that explores the role of art in the world and is also the story of an unfulfilled love affair

home to die but is miraculously healed by the earth. Likewise, the stories of the inhabitants of the small village of Trasovisku are, as before, full of complicated interrelationships. The second theme of the novel has a strong political orientation, while its latter chapters cover the Slovak National Uprising, which Hronský interprets quite differently from the view common in the former Czechoslovakia. Hronský rejects the antifascist orientation of the uprising, instead understanding the rebellion to be an historically illogical and political act that was exported to Slovakia by the Soviet Union and directed against the independence of the Slovak Republic and Slovak statehood. His last published work was a collection of intimate stories with the title *Pohár z brúseného skla* (A Cut-Glass Goblet, 1964).

Hronský also belongs among the most productive and artistically successful writers of children's fiction. He operated on the assumption that it is necessary to evoke in children feelings of justice, faith, and joyful optimism, and his works reflect this orientation. Thanks to Hronský, Ján Kopal says in *Biografické štúdic* (1992), "the genre of imaginative, optimistic works of fantasy was developed as a subset of children's literature." Among his most successful and widely read books today are *Kremnické povesti* (Kremnické Fables, 1925), *Smelý Zajko* (Brave Bunny, 1930), and *Budkáčik a Dubkáčik* (1932).

Jozef Cíger Hronský died on 13 July 1960 in the Argentinean town of Lujan. His books, however, remain part of the treasure of Slovak literature. Many of them have been republished and some translated into other languages. Because of his political orientation, Hronský's name was struck from schoolbooks, and his work was banned from distribution in the 1950s and the first half of the 1960s. However, today a great deal of attention is paid to his work and career. He remains popular with readers, and his works receive increasing attention from contemporary literary critics and scholars.

References:

Libuša Chrašteková, ed., *Jozef Cíger Hronský* (Martin: Osveta, 1995);

Oleg Malevič, "Ešte jedno stretnutie s Jozefom Makom," *Slovenské pohľady*, 87, no. 10 (1971): 53–59;

Alexander Matuška, *J. C. Hronský* (Bratislava: Slovenský spisovateľ, 1970);

Matuška, *Osobnosti* (Bratislava: Slovenský spisovateľ, 1973);

Marta Pataková, *Kompozičná variabilnosť prózy* (Nitre: Pedagogická fakulta, 1990);

Jozek Paučo, *Pamiatke Jozefa Cígra Hronského* (Middletown, Pa.: Filip A. Hrobak, 1960);

Peter Petro, "Jozef Cíger Hronský: A Major Slovak Novelist," *Slovakia*, 30 (1982–1983): 55–56, 142–152;

Ján Poliak, "Vzdelávacia epika," *Slovenské pohľady*, 85, no. 9 (1969): 70–79;

Joseph M. Rydlo, "The World in a Quagmire: The Last Literary Work of Jozef Cíger Hronský," *Slovak Studies*, 15 (1975): 117–142;

Oľga Saboľová, "Poznámky o jazyku a štýle Hronského próz," *Slovenská reč*, 39 (1974): 198–203;

Ján Števček, "Podpolianske rozprávky a Hronského prínos," *Slovenská literatúra*, 15 (1968): 506–510;

Miloš Tomčík, "Matuškov pohľad na J. C. Hronského," *Slovenská literatúra*, 18 (1971): 193–197.

Papers:

Most, perhaps all, of Jozef Cíger Hronský's papers are in the Natica Slovenská (National Library) in Martin, Slovakia. Part of Hronský's papers and manuscripts are in the archives of Matica slovenska in Martin.

Gyula Illyés

(2 November 1902 – 15 April 1983)

András Gerliczki
Nyíregyháza Teacher Training College

BOOKS: *Nehéz föld* (Budapest: Nyugat, 1928);

Sarjúrendek (Budapest: Nyugat, 1931);

Három öreg (Budapest: S Szerző, 1931);

Hősökről beszélek (Cluj-Koloszvár: Korunk, 1933);

Ifjúság (Debrecen: Nagy Károly és Társai, 1934);

Oroszország (Budapest: Nyugat, 1934);

Szálló egek alatt (Budapest: Nyugat, 1935);

Puszták népe (Budapest: Nyugat, 1936); translated by G. F. Cushing as *People of the Puszta* (Budapest: Corvina, 1967);

Petőfi (Budapest: Nyugat, 1936); expanded as *Petőfi Sándor* (Budapest: Szépirodalmi, 1963);

Rend a Romokban (Budapest: Nyugat, 1937);

Magyarok, 2 volumes (Budapest: Nyugat, 1938);

Külön világban (Budapest: Cserépfalvi, 1939);

Ki a magyar? (Budapest: Mefhosz, 1939);

Lélek és kenyér (Budapest: Nyugat, 1939);

Kora tavasz, 2 volumes (Budapest: Révai, 1941);

Csizma az asztalon (Budapest: Nyugat, 1941);

Mint a darvak (Budapest: Nyugat, 1942);

A tű foka (Budapest: Nyugat, 1944);

Egy év (Budapest: Sarló, 1945);

Honfoglalók között (Kolozsvár: Sarló, 1945);

Húnok Párizsban (Budapest: Révai, 1946);

Szembenézve (Budapest: Revai, 1947);

Tizenkét nap Bulgáriában (Budapest: Székesfőváros, 1947);

Lélekbúvár (Budapest: Révai, 1948);

Két férfi (Budapest: Révai, 1950);

Két kéz (Budapest: Athenaeum, l950);

Ozorai példa (Budapest: Szépirodalmi, 1952);

Tűz-viz (Budapest: Művelt Nép, 1952);

Fáklyaláng (Budapest: Szépirodalmi, 1953);

Hetvenhét magyar népmese (Budapest: Ifjúsági, 1953);

Tűvé-tevők (Budapest: Művelt Nép, 1953);

A csodafurulyás juhász (Budapest: Ifjúsági, 1954);

Dózsa György (Budapest: Szépirodalmi, 1956);

Kézfogások (Budapest: Szépirodalmi, 1956);

Új versek (Budapest: Szépirodalmi, 1961);

Ebéd a kastélyban (Budapest: Szépirodalmi, 1962);

Puszták népe (Budapest: Szépirodalmi, 1962);

Másokért egyedül: A kegyenc, A különc (Budapest: Szépirodalmi, 1963);

Dőlt vitorla (Budapest: Szépirodalmi, 1965);

Drámák, 2 volumes (Budapest: Szépirodalmi, 1969);

Kháron ladikján (Budapest: Szépirodalmi, 1969);

Hunok Párizsba (Budapest: Szépirodalmi, 1970);

Hajszálgyökerek (Budapest: Szépirodalmi, 1971);

Tiszták (Budapest: Szépirodalmi, 1971);

Bál a pusztán (Budapest: Szépirodalmi, 1972);

Minden lehelet: új versek (Budapest: Szépirodalmi, 1973);

Anyanyelvünk (Budapest: Magvető, 1975);

Iránytűvel, 2 volumes (Budapest: Szépirodalmi, 1975);

Különös testamentum (Budapest, 1977);

Szellem és erőszak (Budapest: Magvető, 1978);

Beatrice apródjai (Budapest: Szépirodalmi, 1979);

Közügy (Budapest: Szépirodalmi, 1981);

Táviratok (Budapest: Szépirodalmi, 1982);

Sorsválasztók (Budapest: Szépirodalmi, 1982);

A szentlélek karavánja (Budapest: Szépirodalmi, 1987).

Editions and Collections: *Összegyűjtött versei* (Budapest: Nyugat, 1940);

A nép nevében (Pestszentlőrinc: Mátyás, 1942);

Válogatott versek (Budapest: Révai, 1943);

Összes versei, 3 volumes (Budapest: Nyugat and Révai, 1930–1947)—comprises volume 1, *Nehéz föld, Sarjúrendek, Három öreg, Ifjúság, Szálló egek alatt, Hősökről beszélek*, volume 2, *Rend a romokban, Hűtlen a jövő, Külön világban, Új versek;* volume 3, *Szembenézve;*

Válogatott versei (Budapest: Szépirodalmi, 1952);

Három dráma (Budapest: Szépirodalmi, 1957);

Kínai szelence (Budapest: Európa, 1958);

Balaton (Budapest: Corvina, 1962);

Nem volt elég . . . (Budapest: Szépirodalmi, 1962);

Nyitott ajtó (Budapest: Európa, 1963);

Ingyen lakoma, 2 volumes (Budapest: Szépirodalmi, 1964);

Haza a magasban: Összegyüjtött versek 1920–1945 (Budapest: Szépirodalmi, 1972);

Teremteni: Összegyüjtött versek 1946–1968 (Budapest: Szépirodalmi, 1973);

Illyés Gyula összegyüjtött versei (Budapest: Szépirodalmi, 1977);

Szemelt szőlő: válogatott versek, edited by Miklós Béládi (Budapest: Szépirodalmi, 1980);

Konok kikelet: válogatott versek (Budapest: Szépirodalmi, 1981);

Szemben a támadással: Összegyüjtött versek 1969–1981 (Budapest: Szépirodalmi, 1981);

Illyés Gyula művei, 3 volumes, edited by Béládi (Budapest: Szépirodalmi, 1982);

A Semmi közelít: Hátrahagyott versek, edited by Mátyás Domokos (Budapest: Szépirodalmi, 1983);

Csak az igazat: Három színmü, edited by Miklós Borsos (Budapest: Szépirodalmi, 1983);

Menet a ködben, edited by Domokos (Budapest: Szépirodalmi, 1986);

Hetvenhét magyar népmese, edited by Piroska Szántó (Budapest: Móra, 1991);

Illyés Gyula összegyüjtött versei, edited by Domokos (Budapest: Szépirodalmi, 1993);

Illyés Gyula legszebb versei, edited by László Vörös (Budapest: Móra, 1994);

Magyarok: Naplójegyzetek Szekszárd (Babits, 1994).

Editions in English: *Once Upon a Time*, translated by Barna Balogh and Susan Kun, in *Forty Hungarian Folktales* (Budapest: Corvina, 1964);

Selected Poems, edited by Thomas Kabdebo and Paul Tabori (London: Chatto & Windus, 1971);

Petőfi, translated by Cushing (Budapest: Corvina, 1973);

"Spacious Winter," "Sour-Cherry Trees," and "Part of a Novel," translated by Emery George, and "Deep Dusk," translated by Nicholas Kolumban, in *Contemporary East European Poetry*, edited by George (Ann Arbor, Mich.: Ardis, 1983), pp. 239–242;

The Three Wishes, translated by Gerard Gorman (Budapest: Corvina, 1989);

The Tree That Reached the Sky, adapted by Illyés and Benedek Elek, translated by Caroline Bodoczky, Judith Elliott, and Gorman (Budapest: Corvina, 1990);

"The Three Wishes" and "Matthew the Gooseboy," in *Hungarian Folktales* (Budapest: Corvina, 1991).

TRANSLATIONS: *A francia irodalom kincsesháza* (Budapest: Athenaeum, 1942).

The body of works of Gyula Illyés combines popular, national, and universal interests. Most of Illyés's readers and critics share the opinion that his life and works serve as a distinct reflection of the social and political changes in Hungary for much of the twentieth century. Obsessed in his writings with the future of the Hungarian nation, Illyés incorporated throughout his works the plight of the peasantry as a thematic concern. He believed that literature was an essential means to educate people and to bring about constructive change for the betterment of humanity.

Illyés was born on 2 November 1902 in Rácegrespuszta to Janos and Ida (Kallay) Illyés. He spent his early childhood among the agricultural laborers of the *puszta* (prairie). One of his grandfathers was a shepherd, the other a craftsman. His father worked for a nobleman as a mechanic. However, his grandmother on his mother's side arranged for Illyés to learn French from the French governess in the castle and German from the ethnic Germans of the neighboring villages. Until the age of ten he lived on the *puszta;* then he continued his studies in a secondary school in Dombóvár. When his mother got a divorce in 1916, she moved with her son to Budapest and worked as a seamstress to support the two of them. In Budapest, Illyés studied first in a grammar school and then in a commercial school. He graduated from secondary school in 1921. In the same year he enrolled at the University of Budapest, where he majored in French and Hungarian. As a young student he supported the revolution of 1918–1919 and for a brief period participated in the fighting. The police made inquiries about his illegal organizing activities, and as a result he had to leave the country in 1922. After spending some time in Vienna, Berlin, and Luxemburg he eventually settled in Paris. He earned a living by casual labor and learned the bookbinding trade. He studied literature, psychology, and sociology at the Sorbonne. He also became an active participant in the labor movement by giving lectures and organizing cultural programs and made friends with the leading figures of the surrealist movement—Paul Eluard, Tristan Tzara, and Louis Aragon. Some of his poems were published in *Ma* (Today), the avant-garde journal of Lajos Kassák. Illyés's activist and surrealist poems advocated the rights of liberty and rebellion and emphasized his social commitment.

He returned home from Paris in 1926. The five years spent in France made him realize that his memories, relationships, language, and education connected him to Hungary. Although he wrote some French poems, he felt that his artistic duty was to picture the Hungarian reality. It was the poet Milán Füst (1888–1967) who called the attention of the editors of *Nyugat* (The West) to Illyés after he read Illyés's poem titled "Szomorú béres" (Sad Field Hand) in the *Láthatár* (Horizon). From 1927 Illyés's works were published in *Nyugat*, and his first volume of poetry, *Nehéz föld* (Heavy Earth), also appeared in this journal in 1928. Most of the characters in the book are agricultural laborers, poor peasants, prodigal sons returning to the village, or wanderers who feel at home in nature. The volume pictures the homeland and speaks through the voice of the poor, as in "Énekelj, költőő" (Sing, Poet). The texts of the poems illustrate Illyés's identification with the land and its people, notably in "Szomorú béres," "Jel" (Sign), "Tékozló" (The Prodigal Son), and "Szerelem" (Love). *Nehéz föld* presents colorful poetry, in which can be recognized the influences of Horace, Dániel Berzsenyi, Milán Füst, and József Erdélyi.

In 1929 Mihály Babits and Zsigmond Móricz took over the editorship of *Nyugat*. At this time Illyés became close friends with Babits, who as an editor supported young writers and whose apartment became a literary meeting place.

Illyés's second volume, titled *Sarjúrendek* (Aftermath), was published in 1931. The new volume is a farewell to youth as well as a preparation for

Flóra Kozmutza, the inspiration for Attila József's "Flóra" cycle. Illyés married her in 1939.

manhood. Taking the role of a national poet openly expressing public issues, Illyés attempts to enliven the tradition of the descriptive, narrative, and lyric poems of the popular national poetry of the previous century, as in "Dunántúli reggel" (Transdanubian Morning), "A ház végén ülök" (Sitting at the Back of the House), and "Itt az első csillag" (Here Is the First Star). His poems are simple, direct, and objective in style. He pictures the peasant characters with sensitive realism. In his "Elégia" (Elegy) he contrasts the peasant family with the figures of the politician, the soldier, and the poet. The influences of Sándor Petőfi and János Arany can be traced in his poem "A ház végén ülök," which is about his grandmother who helped him to prepare for the role of a poet.

In 1931 Illyés received the Baumgarten Award. That he received this award three more times before 1936 indicates his rising fame. During this time he also became friends with the writer Attila József. The determinant values of Illyés's poetry became the consciously chosen popular character, realistic objectivity, and the revival of epic forms. In his three successive epic poems—*Három öreg* (Three Old Men, 1931), *Hősökről beszélek* (I Am Talking about Heroes, 1933), and *Ifjúság* (Youth, 1934)—Illyés strove to write modern, narrative poetry. He had wanted to write a longer epic poem depicting nationalism, revolution, and history and began writing one on György Dózsa, but he finished only the initial passages, published in 1930 as "Dózsa." In *Három öreg* Illyés writes with gentle affection in a confessional tone about his two grandfathers and the old field hand who taught Illyés how to write. *Ifjúság* is the story of a country lad fleeing from the 1919 battle of Szolnok. This work is interwoven with Illyés's love for the idyllic countryside and with a sensitive, detailed depiction of everyday life in a village. The composition of *Hősökről beszélek* resembles that of an epic poem, but its characters steal from the lord's garden. They are thieves and heroes at the same time: as idealized by Illyés, poverty and misery exempt them from sin. The simple idyll is replaced by an inner struggle in his later volumes *Szálló egek alatt* (Under Flying Skies, 1935) and *Rend a romokban* (Order in the Ruins, 1937). The descriptions, which suggest unbiased objectivity, and the meditative mood indicate that he was constantly struggling with hopelessness and disillusionment. However, the lyrical monologue "Nem menekülhetsz" (You Cannot Escape) most beautifully expresses his *ars poetica*. In the poem he remembers a voyage and describes the upper and lower decks of the ship as a metaphor for social layers. He recollects the memory of his father, who worked as a mechanic for the lord, and suddenly he realizes his place in society and his commitment to the working class. In "A kacsalábon forgó vár" (The Wonder Castle) Illyés uses folktale motifs to depict social division, the conflict between the rich and the poor. "Rend a romokban" represents the poetry of objectivity and loyalty. The poems show a reflective, argumentative lyrical self. In "Ozorai példa" (The Example of Ozora), "Avar" (Leaf Mold), and "Két március" (Two Marches) Illyés analyzes the relationship between man and the universe as well as between the poet and the nation in a stark, disillusioned, and realistic tone.

Beginning in 1933 Illyés regularly published articles on the Transdanubian peasantry. In these articles analyzing society and in diary notes he examined the situation of landless peasants. He concerned himself with Hungary, the Hungarians, and the idea of popular literature, which he defined as a literature that emphasized the unity of social and national development. *Magyarok* (The Hungarians, 1938) is a collection of his diary notes in which he directed public attention toward significant social issues. Probably his most effective essay is "Pusztulás" (Decay, 1933), which analyzes the one-child family model. Especially through decrease of the population he blames the feudal mode of land tenure and the attitude of the political elite for the decay of the Hungarian nation and urges social reforms. He supported the union of the small countries along the Danube in the period of nationalism and during the terror of Nazi Germany. The entire Hungarian literary community responded to "Pusztulás," notably Móricz, Babits, and László Németh. From then on Illyés was known not only as an artist but also as a public figure. In the summer of 1934 he and Lajos Nagy were invited to the First Congress of the Soviet Writers' Association. The leadership in the Kremlin intended to show the postrevolutionary Soviet Union to foreign writers. Illyés reported favorably about his experiences, impressed with the creation of a new society from the aspect of everyday people instead of the official data.

In 1935 the periodical *Válasz* (Answer) began to publish his study of society *Puszták népe* (translated as *People of the Puszta*, 1962), and in the following year *Nyugat* published it in book form. One of the best-known works by Illyés, who was influenced by contemporary documental studies of society as well as Nagy's fiction, rather than the scientific studies of society, *Puszták népe* is a mixture of general statements and personal episodes, objective data, and autobiographical elements. It is at once a poetical psychological study of Illyés and a study of society. It is not only an accusation and a revelation of backward conditions but also a lyrical rejection. The volume depicts the life of the Transdanubian *puszta*, emphasizing a different topic in each chapter—the history of the *puszta*, holidays, family life, discipline and education of children, morals, culture, and religion. It is the combination of autobiography and childhood memories with the authentic, sociological description that makes this work unusual. Illyés's style changes with the topics from objective and threatening to lyrical and passionate to ironic and humorous. He counterbalances the gloomy, frightening facts with comic episodes. This work is a precise description of a period and the confession of the author at the same time.

Published in the same year as *Puszták népe*, Illyés's next work was a biography of the poet Sándor Petőfi, whom Illyés believed embodied the perfect unity of poetry and life. Illyés considered Petőfi a standard for other twentieth-century poets to follow.

After divorcing his first wife, Illyés married Flóra Kozmutza (the muse of Attila József's "Flóra" cycle) in 1939. With the death in 1941 of Mihály Babits, the literary journal *Nguyat* ceased publication. Illyés edited its successor, *Magyar Csillag* (The Hungarian Star), until 1944. When the German Army occupied Hungary, *Magyar Csillag* ceased publication, and Illyés was forced into hiding as his name was on the list of pursued writers.

The poems of *Külön világban* (In a Separate World, 1939) express anxiety for the future of the Hungarian nation. Illyés was primarily concerned with the survival of the country; in spite of the frightening historical reality, he presented ideas to give strength and encouragement to the nation. His concern for his fellow Hungarians is continued in *Ki a magyar?* (Who Is the Hungarian? 1939), which finds the most important reason for belonging together is the attachment to a common spiritual and cultural community. In his autobiographical works he was also concerned with the future of the peasants and the villages, notably in *Lélek és kenyér* (Spirit and Bread, 1940), *Csizma az asztalon* (Boots on the Table, 1941), and *Mint a darvak* (Like the Cranes, 1942). *Kora tavasz* (Early Spring, 1941) can be considered a sequel to *Puszták népe*. The difference between the two volumes is that *Kora tavasz* emphasizes the spiritual events and the relationship between the individual and the revolution instead of the depiction of historical events. The next sequel, *Húnok Párizsban* (Huns in Paris), published after the war in 1946, depicts the years of emigration following the revolution and emphasizes the character-shaping role of the international labor movement and the avant-garde. Illyés is interested in intellectual, moral, and ideological questions; yet, his volume is also an epic work with adventures in Europe and especially in Paris. He characterizes French surrealism and portrays Eluard, Tzara, Marcel Sauvage,and Jean Cocteau. Illyés was the editor and one of the translators of an anthology titled *A francia irodalom kincsesháza* (The Thesaurus of French Literature, 1942).

After the war Illyés was enthusiastic and optimistic for Hungary's future and served as a member of Parliament until 1948. He traveled to France, Italy, and Switzerland to meet literary figures and cultivate cultural relationships. Memories of his travels are revived in the lines of *Tizenkét nap Bulgáriában* (Twelve Days in Bulgaria, 1947). His full-length poem *Két kéz* (Two Hands, 1950) is also a good example of his creativity and innovative power. The five-hundred-line poem is about the hands of his father—a praise of the working man. "Egy mondat a zsarnokságról" (translated as "One Sentence on Tyranny," 1968), also written in 1950, enumerates the features of tyranny. The communist regime led by Mátyás Rákosi is the historical background of the verse. "Egy mondat a zsarnokságról" could not be published in print until 1956. Illyés felt the depressive atmosphere of the 1950s but also realized that history offered a chance to create a new world. Building was a popular theme of the schematic poetry of the period, but Illyés could express his opinions apart from the political expectations and honored the creative work of mankind. Poems of the 1950s were published in the volume titled *Kézfogások* (Handshakes, 1956). These poems deal with the questions of the Hungarian nation and humanity. Illyés shows the completeness and complexity of life: the song of the nightingale, the roaring of the ocean, and a footprint in the snow are as important as the fight of national heroes. The most significant poem of the volume and the era is "Bartók," first published in 1955, in which Illyés tries to show the tragic truths behind the mask of political corruption. In so doing, the poet demands radical social changes and reform. Illyés respected the greatness of Béla Bartók's artistic and moral attitude. The poem refuses illusion and desires a real harmony that can be achieved only by facing the truth. The motif of death and mortality also appears in the poems of the volume. Illyés transforms the motto of Miklós Zrínyi's "Sors bona, nihil aliud" (Good Luck, Nothing More) into "Mors bona, nihil aliud" (Good Death, Nothing More). He sees the preconditions of a good death in a hardworking, complete life. He does not believe in an afterlife—he thinks the memory of a meaningful earthly existence brings salvation.

Illyés's writing for the theater was mainly motivated by the possibility that staging events and heroes of Hungarian history could form and strengthen the national and communal spirit of his audience. *Ozorai példa* (The Example of Ozora, 1952) goes back to the time of the revolution and War of Independence in 1848. The play tells the story of how in a single day patriotism awakened in the hearts of village-dwellers. The real protagonists of the drama are the poor people of Ozora, who seize the land and oppose the indifferent nobility. *Fáklyaláng* (The Flames of a Torch, 1953) revives the debate between Lajos Kossuth and Artúr Görgey. The statesman and the general have to make the right strategical decision for the besieged city of Arad. Kossuth argues for the continuation of the

Illyés (second from left) at a dress rehearsal for a production of his play Különc *(The Freak), a tragedy about the Hungarian writer and politician László Teleki*

fight. He represents a patriot who is ready to face death in order to defend his country. Görgey is a realistic politician who does not see any chance to win the fight. The drama titled *Dózsa György*, published in 1956, deals with the events of the Peasant Revolt of 1514. The work is built on the unity of revolution and patriotism; Dózsa was not only the leader of the peasant revolution but also the protector of his country. However, the revolution failed, and the nation could not take advantage of the historical opportunity. *Kegyenc* (The Minion) and *Különc* (The Freak), published in the volume titled *Másokért egyedül* (Lonely for the Others, 1963), also elaborate on historical events. *Kegyenc* is a drama by

László Teleki that Illyés rewrote and modified. The protagonist is Maximus Petronius, a Roman statesman. Maximus Petronius is the only politician in the troubled Roman Empire who takes everything into consideration. His decisions are determined by the interests of the weakening Empire, and he supports the tyrant because he believes that one must accept absolute obedience if he has accepted the right of autocracy. However, he gradually realizes that his obedience is illogical and becomes disillusioned. The main ideas of the drama are that no one can serve an inhuman cause and that tyranny cannot be tolerated in spite of divine command. *Különc* is about the original writer of *Kegyenc*, László Teleki.

Teleki was a writer, a politician, and a supporter of Kossuth. The Austrian government kept him under surveillance, and when he could bear the pressure no longer, he committed suicide in 1861. In the drama Illyés depicts the tragedy of the isolated statesman who prepares for a new revolution. *Malom a Séden* (The Mill on the Séd, 1960) tells the story of some people who oppose the Germans during World War II and hide refugees in the mill. It is a psychological drama analyzing the moral questions of endurance, survival, and the responsibility to save other people's lives. In *Tiszták* (The Pure Ones, 1971) he is concerned about the future of small nationalities; the plot of the drama is a parable. Kather-Albigens, who are loyally devoted to their ideas and their way of life to the last, fight against the oppression of authority.

In 1962 Illyés published *Ebéd a kastélyban* (Lunch in the Castle), which he intended as the sequel to *Puszták népe.* The conversation between the earl and the writer recalls the past, evaluates the role of the aristocracy before 1945, and delineates the customs and character of the people living on the *puszta.* In his novel titled *Kháron ladikján* (On Kharon's Punt, 1969) Illyés deals with the thoughts of aging and death. He undertakes to analyze sensitively the physical and mental process of aging. In his writing he claims that self-knowledge, consciousness, humor, and a cheerful view of life can ease the fear of death. Even if one cannot accept mortality, literary wisdom acknowledges it. Illyés experiences the approach of his own death as a part of universal law, and this confrontation with death creates an opportunity to remember, to look back on the life behind him. He continues his autobiographical remembrance in his novel *Beatrice apródjai* (Beatrice's Pages, 1979). In it Illyés depicts a subtle picture of the closing years of World War I, the revolution, and the Hungarian Soviet Republic. This book is an historical document, but it can be considered a picaresque as well. Illyés recalls his years as a student, writes about the streets of Budapest and the proletarian houses, just as he writes about the bourgeoisie and the country intelligentsia. The story of this novel is continued in *A szentlélek karavánja* (The Caravan of the Holy Spirit, 1987). This novel is about the two years following his graduation from secondary school, his uncertainty in choosing a profession before his university years, and his illegal organizing activity and subsequent emigration.

His *Új versek* (New Poems, 1961) includes personal confessions. At that time most of his poetry was about love, home, and nature, as in "Bánat tavasszal" (Sadness in Spring), "Erdőben" (In the Forest), and "Elválás" (Separation). These poems are characterized by loveliness and intimacy. The connection between community and the individual seems to loosen. The poet concentrates on himself and his environment, often giving a direct account of his experiences. The poems of *Dőlt vitorla* (Slanting Sail, 1965) bring new lyrical innovations. For example, "Újévi ablak" (New Year's Window) is a representative of pattern poetry, in which the words "snow," referring to the winter, and the admiring "oh" words make up and cover the window itself. "Mozgó világ" (World in Motion)—which, in fact, later became the title of a literary journal—expresses the awakening hope at the sight of the modern, lively, and active world. A new world taking form on the old *puszta* also appears in the poem, which is at the same time a report, a diary, and poetic notes. It shows the images as if the novel were a movie. Confessions and meditations make the pictures richer. As a novelty, Illyés included prose verse in the book, notably "A tenger" (The Sea), "Rokonok" (Relatives), and "Munka" (Work). These are, for the most part, texts of remembrance and confession, and the style reflects closely the everyday use of language.

Illyés also poses questions of poetic importance. The poem titled "Bevezetés egy Kodály-hangversenyhez" (Introduction to a Kodály concerto) can be considered the companion to the former poem titled "Bartók." This poem, besides giving an appreciation of Kodály, also praises the harmony of *Rend* (Order) and *Lét* (Existence). In his volume *Minden lehet* (Everything Is Possible, 1973) Illyés deals with questions of time, history, Hungary's future, mortality, and death. Even while talking about death he propagates the values of life in his poems about love, the young generation, and work, notably in "Párbeszéd új házasok között" (Conversation between a Young Couple), "Hosszú tél" (Long Winter), and "Az idő lebírása" (Wrestling with Time). Both fear and hope appear on the pages: the moody lines of "Pusztuló ország" (Country in Ruins) can be contrasted to the cheerful, intimate atmosphere of "Falusi felvonulás" (Village Procession). The poem "Koszorú" (Wreath) is a confession about the fate and survival of the Hungarian people and their language. Illyés stands up for the basic human right to use the mother language. Illyés's creative urge was further enhanced by the new volumes that were published since 1970—*Különös testamentum* (Strange Will, 1977), *Közügy* (Public Affair, 1982), and *Táviratok* (Telegrams, 1982). These last books do not change basic views expressed in Illyés's earlier poetry; yet, they bring new colors, promising further books to come. Illyés's body of works is the synthesis of Hungarian identity, European identity, and national commitment, and this synthesis is carried out on the level of world literature. Although his death on 15 April 1983 in Budapest prevented his carrying out his new plans, Illyés left behind a body of works that includes novels, poems, essays, and plays, as well as his public role and his efforts to save humanity.

Interviews:

György Nemes, "Beszélgetés a hatvan éves Illyés Gyulával," *Élet és Irodalom*, 44 (3 November 1962): 5–6;

Miklós Béládi, "Magyar irodalom–világirodalom," *Kritika*, 7 (1969): 14–25;

Ervin Mikó, "Illyés Gyulával versről, drámáról, müfordításról," *Utunk* (1970): 6.

Bibliography:

Albert Tezla, "Gyula Illyés," in *Hungarian Authors: A Bibliographical Handbook* (Cambridge, Mass.: Harvard University Press, 1970), pp. 226–232.

Biography:

László Gara, *Az ismeretlen Illyés* (Washington, D.C.: Occidental, 1965).

References:

Imre Bata, "Három vázlat Illyés Gyuláról," *Ívelő pályák* (1964): 182–216;

Miklós Béládi, "A költő felel," in his *Érintkezési pontok* (Budapest: Szépirodalmi, 1974), pp. 263–338;

Béládi, *Illyés Gyula* (Budapest: Kozmosz könyvek, 1987);

Béládi, "Illyés Gyula és a szürrealizmus," *Irodalomtörténeti Közlemények*, 65 (1961): 682–709;

Imre Bori, "Illyés Gyula," in his *A szürrealizmus ideje* (Újvidék: Fórum, 1970), pp. 27–49;

László Csányi, "Illyés Gyula prózája," *Jelenkor* (1970): 932–938;

Matyas Domokos, "Gyula Illyés, a Living Classic," *New Hungarian Quarterly*, 23 (Winter 1982): 9–22;

Domokos, "On Gyula Illyés's Posthumous Journals," *New Hungarian Quarterly*, 29 (Winter 1988): 68–83;

László Fülöp, "Az Illyés-líra újabb fejezetei," in his *Élő költészet* (Budapest: Magvető, 1976), pp. 162–172;

Emery George, "In Memoriam Gyula Illyés (1902–1983)," *Cross Currents: A Yearbook of Central European Culture*, 3 (1984): 321–326;

George Gomori, "Gyula Illyés (1902–1983): An Appraisal," *World Literature Today: A Literary Quarterly of the University of Oklahoma*, 58 (Summer 1984): 344–347;

András Görömbei, "Illyés Gyula és a magyar nyelv," *Tiszatáj*, 9 (1975): 22–28;

József Izsák, *Gyula költői világképe 1950–1983* (Budapest: Szépirodalmi, 1986);

Izsák, *Illyés Gyula költői világképe 1920–1950* (Budapest: Szépirodalmi, 1982);

Thomas Kabdebo and Paul Tabori, eds., *A Tribute of Gyula Illyés* (Washington, D.C.: Occidental Press, 1968);

Zoltán Kenyeres, "Az étlap tartalma," *Kortárs* (1967): 198–205;

Dezső Keresztury, "Költészet és igazság," *Élet és Irodalom* (1972): 29;

Balázs Lengyel, "Mai klasszikusok," in his *Verseskönyvről verseskönyvre* (Budapest: Magvető, 1977), pp. 21–32;

László Németh, "Illyés Gyula: Nehéz föld," *Nyugat*, 22 (16 March 1929): 376–382;

Béla Pomogáts, "Józanság és költészet," *Életünk* (1968): 76–98;

Pomogáts, "Kettős Kötésben," in *Sorsát kereső irodalom* (Budapest: Magvető, 1979), pp. 271–278;

Pomogáts, "Valóság és művészi tudatosság," in his *A tárgyias költészettől a mitologizmusig* (Budapest: Academiai Kiadó, l981), pp. 211–269;

William Jay Smith, "Gyula Illyés: Lyric Realist," *Hollins Critic*, 21 (1984): 1–12;

György Somlyó, "Hommage a Illyés," *Nagyvilág* (1977): 1733–1737;

István Sőtér, "Illyés Gyula," *Négy nemzedék* (1948): 117–118;

László Cs. Szabó, "Illyés Gyula," *Nyugat* (1941): 168–170;

Lőrinc Szabó, "Bevezető Illyés Gyulához," in his *A költészet dicsérete* (Budapest: Szépirodalmi, 1967), pp. 378–382;

Attila Tamás, *Illyés Gyula* (Budapest: Akadémiai Kiadó, 1989);

Tibor Tüskés, *Illyés Gyula* (Budapest: Szépirodalmi Kiadó, 1983);

István Vas, "Újrakezdések korszaka," *Tengerek nélkül* (1978): 259–261.

Wacław Iwaniuk

(17 December 1915 –   )

Elwira M. Grossman
University of Glasgow

BOOKS: *Pełnia czerwca* (Chełm Lubelski: Grupa Literacka "Wołyń," 1936);

Dzień Apokaliptyczny (Warsaw: F. Hoesick, 1938);

Czas Don Kichota. Poezje (London: Wydawnictwo Światowego Związku Polaków z Zagranicy, 1946);

Dni białe i dni czerwone. Dziennik poetycki (Brussels: Klon, 1947);

Szopka polityczna 1952 (Toronto: Konfraternia Artystyczna "Smocza Jama," 1952);

Pieśń nad pieśniami. Poemat (Tunbridge Wells, U.K.: Oficyna Poetów i Malarzy, 1953);

Milczenia: Wiersze 1949–1959 (Paris: Instytut Literacki, 1959);

Wybór wierszy (Paris: Instytut Literacki, 1965);

Ciemny czas. Poezje (Paris: Instytut Literacki, 1968);

Lustro (London: Oficyna Poetów i Malarzy, 1971; New York: A. R. Poray, 1986);

Nemezis idzie pustymi drogami (London: Oficyna Stanisław Gliwa, 1978);

Evenings on Lake Ontario: From My Canadian Diary (Toronto: Hounslow Press, 1981);

Podróż do Europy. Opowiadania i szkice (London: Polska Fundacja Kulturalna, 1982; Wrocław: Oficyna Wydawnicza NZSUWr, 1987);

Nocne rozmowy. Wiersze (London: Polska Fundacja Kulturalna, 1987);

Kartagina i inne wiersze (Lublin: Wolna spółka wydawnicza "Komitywa," 1987);

Trzy spotkania (Toronto: Polski Fundusz Wydawniczy w Kanadzie, 1988);

Moje obłąkanie (Lublin: Stowarzyszenie Literackie "Kresy," 1991);

Zanim znikniemy w opactwie kolorów. Wybór wierszy, selected by Krzysztof Lisowski (Kraków: Wydawnictwo Literackie, 1991);

Kilka wierszy (Berlin: Mordellus, 1994);

Moje strony świata. Poezje (Paris: Instytut Literacki / Warsaw: "Pomost," 1994);

Wiersze wybrane, selected by Edward Zyman (Toronto: Polski Fundusz Wydawniczy w Kanadzie, 1995);

Sceny sądowe. Czyli nasi w Kanadzie (Toronto & Berlin: Polski Fundusz Wydawniczy w Kanadzie, 1997);

W ogrodzie mego ojca. Wiersze z lat 1993–1996 (Toronto & Toruń: Polski Fundusz Wydawniczy w Kanadzie, 1998);

Ostatni romantyk: Wspomnienie o Józefie Łobodowskim (Toronto & Toruń: Uniwersytet Mikolaja Kopernika, 1998).

Collection: *Powrót. Wybór wierszy,* selected by Marek Zieliński (Warsaw: Biblioteka "Więzi" / Kraków: Znak, 1989).

Edition in English: *Dark Times: Selected Poems of Wacław Iwaniuk,* translated by Iwaniuk, Jagna Boraks, and others, edited by John Robert Colombo (Toronto: Hounslow Press, 1979).

OTHER: *Seven Polish Canadian Poets: An Anthology,* edited by Iwaniuk and Florian Smieja (Toronto: Polish-Canadian Publishing Fund, 1984).

TRANSLATIONS: Pawel Mayewski, ed., *Czas niepokoju: Antologia wspólczesnej poezji brytyjskiej amerykanskiej,* includes translations by Iwaniuk of poems by D. H. Lawrence, Archibald MacLeish, and Delmore Schwartz (New York: Criterion, 1958);

Cecil Hemley, "Eurydyka," "Zdobywcy," "Na brzegu rzeki," and "Kaplica śmierci," *Tematy,* 6 (1963): 131–133;

Karl Shapiro, "Burżuazyjny poeta," *Tematy,* 7 (1963): 7–18;

Shapiro, "Esej o rymie," *Tematy,* 9 (1964): 37–106;

Allen Ginsberg, "Skowyt," *Tematy,* 9 (1964): 160–171;

Donald Hall, "Dnie," "Urok śmierci," "Słońce," "Pień," "Morderea," and "Grób kopalnia," *Tematy,* 13 (1965): 94–99;

Anne Sexton, "Gdzieś w Afryce," *Tematy,* 13 (1965): 100–101;

William Dickey, "Trzy mowy po fakcie," *Tematy*, 17 (1966): 95–99;

"Najmniejsza antologia," selected poems by Gertrude Stein, Wallace Stevens, Marianne Moore, Conrad Aiken, Archibald MacLeish, E.E. Cummings, Stanley Kunitz, Robert Penn Warren, W. H. Auden, Theodore Roethke, John Berryman, Thomas Merton, Robert Lowell, Howard Nemerov, James Dickey, Alan Dugan, W. S. Merwin, and Sylvia Plath, *Kultura* (Paris), 8 (1968): 37–70;

Ewa Lipska, *Such Times: Selected Poems*, translated by Iwaniuk and John Robert Colombo (Toronto: Hounslow Press, 1981).

SELECTED PERIODICAL PUBLICATIONS–
UNCOLLECTED: "Dziennik z podróży tropikalnej i wiersze o wojnie. Poemat z lat 1939–1945," *Kultura* (Paris), no. 11 (1950): 45–58;

"Gorycze nocy," *Kultura* (Paris), no. 6 (1951): 81–88;

"Dwie Antologie," *Kultura* (Paris), 7–8 (1966): 204–212;

"Podzwonne," *Kresy*, 2–3 (1990): 118;

"Dziś mogę o tym mówić," "Ja wybrałem miejsce na ziemi," and "Wyskrobek," *Twórczość*, 5 (1997): 49–50.

Wacław Iwaniuk is one of the major postwar émigré Polish poets; he writes in Polish and English and may be considered a Polish-Canadian poet. In the years following World War II his poetry was known only to a limited circle of the Polish émigré community; in Poland his work was virtually unknown until 1987, when the collection *Kartagina i inne wiersze* (Carthage and Other Poems) was published by an underground press. The abolition of censorship in Poland in 1989 made it possible for Iwaniuk's works to be published openly there (with three volumes of his poems appearing between 1989 and 1991). Only at the end of the twentieth century has his work begun to gain wide recognition.

Wacław Iwaniuk was born on 17 December 1915 in Chojny Stare, near Chełm Lubelski, Poland, to Józefina Dyszewska and Szczepan Iwaniuk. While his mother cultivated Iwaniuk's religious beliefs, his father provided a more rational and practical attitude to life; thus, Iwaniuk was exposed to two different ways of perceiving the world, which stirred his imagination from childhood to early youth. He attended a public school in Siedliszcze and later entered a lyceum in Chełm, where—under the influence of his teacher Kazimierz Andrzej Jaworski (also a poet)—Iwaniuk developed his first literary interests. His youthful years in Chełm were among the happiest of his life. Later, the memories of this time became the most recurrent theme in many of his nostalgic poems; his childhood appears as an archetypal image of a lost garden, a burnt Arcadia, and a land of everlasting beauty as well as of strong moral values.

As a pupil in Chełm, Iwaniuk published his early poems and reviews in an ambitious local literary magazine called *Kamena* (Camena), edited by Jaworski. In 1934, with other young poets, Iwaniuk had his first poetry reading. After he graduated from the Chełm school, he continued his education in Szkoła Podchorążych Rezerwy, a military college for reserve officers in Równe. He then left for Warsaw, where he studied journalism briefly. In 1936 he decided to take up economics and international commerce at the Free University in Warsaw. As a university student, he continued his literary interests and joined the poetic group *Wołyń* (Volhynia), which did not have any artistic program per se but gathered young poets from the province of Lublin. The members of the group—Czesław Janczarski, Wacław Michalski, Henryk Domiński, Józef Łobodowski, Stanisław Piętak, Artur Rzeczyca, and Iwaniuk—were largely influenced by Józef Czechowicz, who, next to Bolesław Leśmian, became the most significant poet of the interwar period and a mentor for the younger generation of poets.

During that time Iwaniuk frequently contributed poetry and articles to literary magazines such as *Kamena, Literatura i Sztuka* (Literature and Art), *Okolica poetów* (The Poets' Neighborhood), *Zet* (Zed), *Sygnały* (Signals), the Poznań *Kultura* (Culture), and *Nasz Wyraz* (Our Word), and others. He also published his first collection of poetry, *Pełnia czerwca* (The Fullness of June), in 1936. His poetry from this early period is clearly influenced by Czechowicz and other avant-garde poets who advocated a condensed, elliptic style, free verse, and metaphors based on free association. Iwaniuk's poems teem with such metaphors but are free of empty phrases and purely rhetorical devices. Several critics considered *Pełnia czerwca* an important poetic achievement; it was also awarded a literary prize by the magazine *Kuźnia Młodych* (Youth's Smithy).

Iwaniuk's long poem *Dzień apokaliptyczny* (Day of Apocalypse), written in 1938 during his student training in the Polish Consulate in Pińsk (Polesie), exhibits a strong tendency toward mythological imagery. It is also dominated by the local landscape, which assumes symbolic proportions and conveys prophetic apocalyptic messages. Iwaniuk creates powerful visions that are full of catastrophic themes as well as obscure, yet highly lyrical, images. These images form a lengthy but meaningful pattern of thought born of intuition rather than of logical reasoning; they are thus difficult to interpret. Although the language of Iwaniuk's prewar poetry is original, he still seems to struggle to find his own individual artistic form of expression.

In 1939 the Polish Ministry of Foreign Affairs assigned Iwaniuk (who was then a student specializing in emigration) to consular work in Argentina. His intense duties and training left no time for writing poetry, but his experience of the exotic landscape was later reflected in "Dziennik z podróży tropikalnej i wiersze o wojnie" (Diary from a Tropical Journey and Poems about War, 1950).

With the outbreak of World War II, Iwaniuk left Argentina to join the Polish army in France and to serve with the Polish Mountain Brigade, part of the Allied Expeditionary Corps fighting in Norway. After France capitulated, Iwaniuk attempted to escape to England through Spain. He was caught by the Spanish police and imprisoned, first in Figueras and later in a concentration camp in Miranda, Spain. From there he managed to escape to Great Britain. He then served in the First Polish Armored Division under General Stanisław Maczek in France, Belgium, Holland, and Germany. He remained with the British Occupation Army in Germany until 1946. Echoes of these events found immediate expression in his poetic journal *Dni białe i dni czerwone. Dziennik poetycki* (White Days and Red Days: Poetic Diary, 1947), a collection of war poems published in Brussels. His war experiences are also reflected in a more symbolic and indirect way in *Czas Don Kichota* (The Time of Don Quixote, 1946), which was Iwaniuk's first volume to be published in London.

The title *Dni białe i dni czerwone* alludes to the colors of the Polish national flag and reverberates with patriotic overtones. Even though the work was provoked by deep emotions, Iwaniuk admits that it is more of a document than an artistic achievement. It aims at communicating and preserving the experience of a soldier's life, capturing the mood as well as the painful paradoxes and ethical dilemmas. His war poems written between 1939 and 1945 and published jointly with *Dziennik z podróży tropikalnej* continue these themes.

Czas Don Kichota combines more intimate impressions of the war with philosophical reflections and various allusions to Polish cultural tradition, particularly explicit in the poem "Hymn." In this collection the poet assumes Don Quixote's identity and sets off on a symbolic journey of discovery. The poems account for various "mental adventures" of the traveler, an explorer who grudgingly accepts what he sees. The surrounding world is a fusion of golden ornaments and shattered landscapes, reminiscent of both baroque culture and the violence of the battlefield. Many poems express longings for the lost Arcadia of his idyllic childhood, Romantic models of literature, and prewar order. The poetic style of *Czas Don Kichota* echoes the language of *Pełnia czerwca* and shows that Iwaniuk was still under the influence of his symbolic imagination and still in the process of searching for his own poetic voice.

Dni biate i dni czerwone and *Czas Don Kichota* establish two coexisting tendencies of Iwaniuk's poetic style. The first is the style of reportage in *Dni biate i dni czerwone*, which presents a faithful account of facts, events, and observations couched in a direct and straightforward language of considerable poetic impact. His second literary inclination is the use of natural symbols, shaped by Polish literary tradition and embedded in a style rich in metaphors, allusions, and lyrical images. In the 1960s these two tendencies merged into a highly individual poetic code.

Between 1946 and 1948 Iwaniuk studied English literature at Cambridge and developed an interest in Anglo-Saxon poetry (especially the work of T. S. Eliot), which inspired him to write his first verses in English. He never finished his studies, however. Demobilized as a lieutenant of the First Polish Division, he left England in November 1948 and arrived on his uncle's farm in Edmonton, Canada. After staying briefly in Ottawa and Montreal, he settled finally in Toronto, where he obtained his Canadian citizenship. He worked in a meat-packing factory for more than a year and was subsequently employed by the City of Toronto as a clerk; he was finally engaged by the Ontario Ministry of Justice as a court translator.

While he was slowly adjusting to his new life in a foreign country, his continued sensitivity to current events and the political situation in Poland manifested itself in various forms. He regularly corresponded with other Polish émigré writers such as Józef Wittlin, Kazimierz Wierzyński, Aleksander Janta-Połczyński, Józef Czapski, and Pawel Mayewski exchanging ideas, information, invitations to literary meetings, and opinions about their works. At that time Iwaniuk also was active in many charitable organizations and was influential in having modern medical equipment sent to Poland; further, he organized cultural events for the Polish community of Toronto. During the 1950s he contributed humorous rhymed couplets to a local cabaret called *Smocza Jama* (Dragon's Cave) while composing the major collection of his poems, *Milczenia: Wiersze 1949–1959* (Silences: Poems 1949–1959, 1959), which many critics consider his first fully mature work.

In 1953 his long poem *Pieśń nad pieśniami* (Song of Songs), with drawings by Joseph Czapski, was published in London. It was an indirect reaction to the political and cultural events of that era in Poland. The poem, according to Iwaniuk's preface, was written in a state of national suffering. It is a defense of personal, "symbolist" poetry and may be read, at least in part, as Iwaniuk's poetic response to the concept of ideological poetry, especially Social Realist doctrine.

The volume *Milczenia: Wiersze 1949–1959* made clear that Iwaniuk no longer wished to impress his readers with sublime lyricism but desired to guide them with concise formulas. Thus, succinct phrases and a more direct language took the place of his former ornamental style and the excessively obscure visions of his prewar poems. Themes from previous volumes, such as traumatic war memories and nostalgic feelings for the destroyed Poland of his childhood, are expressed in a more crystallized poetic style. Other themes in this volume include the collapse of Christian ideals, the decay of moral values, the dehumanized nature of life, and the constant struggle to remake the postwar world. The world, according to Iwaniuk, is a lonely and deserted place where war survivors such as himself are predestined to pessimism or nihilism. The agonizing and disturbing imagination he inherited from the war needed a new form of artistic expression, which he struggled to find. Following his inner voice, he concentrated more on intellectual discourse than personal feeling in order to provoke his readers' minds as well as challenge his own poetic craft. This challenge was important to Iwaniuk; he kept writing for virtually nonexistent Polish readers and was never discouraged from publishing in his native tongue. He never succumbed to the temptation to write exclusively in English, even though his volume *Evenings on Lake Ontario: From My Canadian Diary* (1981) proved he was capable of composing skillfully in this new language.

In the 1960s Iwaniuk became fully involved in the intellectual life of the Polish émigré community. Not only did he publish his own works, reviews, and articles on literary topics in the Paris *Kultura*, the London *Wiadomości* (News), and the *Kontynenty* (Continents), but he also translated literary essays and poems of American writers into Polish for the New York journal *Tematy* (Topics). At first, Eliot, W. H. Auden, and Sylvia Plath were his literary models, but soon the list expanded to include such writers as Karl Shapiro, Emily Dickinson, and Allen Ginsberg. His translations of Dickinson were awarded a prize in 1964 by Roy Publishers in New York. Iwaniuk's translations not only helped to familiarize Polish readers with the achievements of American poets and thus broaden the spectrum of poetic styles of émigré poetry, but they also had an influence on his own technique and style, especially in terms of intellectual content, clarity of phrasing, and directness of expression. In fact, Iwaniuk's assimilation of various features of American poetic tradition contributed to the formation of his own distinctive poetic voice.

In 1963 the Poets' and Painters' Press in London awarded Iwaniuk a poetry prize, and a year later he received a prestigious prize from the Literary Institute in Paris for his *Wybór wierszy* (Selected Poems), which appeared in 1965 in the poetry series published by the Institute. In this volume, apart from remembered Polish landscapes, vivid elements of Canadian life begin to fuse with the poet's war-torn imagination as he examines ostensibly ordinary elements of routine existence in order to elucidate hidden and mysterious layers. "Koncert" (A Concert), "O narastaniu życia" (On the Growth of Life), and "Medea" teem with everyday events described by a distant, objective observer who uses his intellect and sense of sight as his main cognitive tools. In addition to the constant elements of his poetic world such as nostalgia, alienation, death, and sensitivity to historical details and political events, Iwaniuk devotes many verses to the problem of compatibility between traditional artistic techniques and the contemporary postwar world. The poem "Ars Poetica" presents this theme in the most explicit way.

In his quest for solutions to modern literature and life, Iwaniuk seems to suggest several things: that restoration is possible through nature, as in "Obrona ziemi" (In Defense of the Earth); that renewal can be attained through language and creativity, as in "Dno" (The Bottom) and "W sprawie wiersza" (Concerning A Poem); that peace can be achieved through a union between the worlds of the dead and the living, as in "Moja epika" (An Epic of My Own); and that works of art have the power of illuminating the meaning of the world. In painting, for Iwaniuk such works include those of Henri Matisse, Vincent van Gogh, Pablo Picasso, and Jan Lebenstein, as evident in "Widziałem obrazy Van Gogha" (I Saw van Gogh's Paintings) and "Lebensztajna portrety wnętrza" (Lebenstein's Interiors). In literature, Iwaniuk finds special value in the writings of Auden, Plath, Thomas Merton, and the nineteenth-century Polish émigré poet Cyprian K. Norwid. He draws a parallel between Norwid's life and his own by emphasizing a

philosophical kinship in the poems "Wariacje na Norwidowskie tematy" (Variations on Norwid's Themes) and "Gdybym był Norwidem" (If I Were Norwid). The poem "Z 'Dziennika' Gombrowicza" (From Gombrowicz's 'Diary') evinces his appreciation for Witold Gombrowicz's ideas, albeit with a slight ironic twist. Although art for Iwaniuk is a powerful means of contemplating existence, his worldview is mostly shaped by an intense belief in the creative and liberating power of the word.

Iwaniuk's process of adjustment to the postwar world is documented in *Wybór wierszy* and in his next collection of poems, *Ciemny czas* (Dark Times, 1968). Suspended between the haunting memories of war and an unknown, unpredictable future, Iwaniuk seems preoccupied with a dark inner vision. He vividly expresses this feeling in the poem "Oto tu jestem jak pasterz bez trzody" (Behold I Am Like a Shepherd without a Flock). Thus *Ciemny czas* becomes a celebration of a fearful yet—for the time being—liberating darkness. At night the acute pain of agonizing war experiences diminishes, and the voices of the dead become clearer and strengthen the poet's inspiration and creativity.

While *Ciemny czas* is in many respects a healing dialogue with the dead, it is also an extended quest for hope and resolution, a search for trust and justice, and a bridge between the past and the present. A lost Arcadia and a destroyed Troy provide the symbolic framework for historical and philosophical reflections. There is an evident tendency in this volume toward elliptic, abbreviated form as well as concise and direct expression. The collection is also an attempt to reconstruct Iwaniuk's own life, comprised of two fundamental components: past memories and his life in Canada. Positive memories preserve the part of Iwaniuk's identity that is associated with the idyllic world of a childhood now lost to everyone but him. On the other hand, nightmarish war memories invade his imagination with fire, snakes, ashes, scars, blood, night, and darkness. As these fragments of identity do not fall into a coherent pattern and are full of nostalgia, alienation, solitude, and sadness, Iwaniuk puts them all under close scrutiny in his next volume of poems, *Lustro* (Mirror, 1971).

Lustro was not only a new phase in the process of establishing Iwaniuk's sense of self, it was also an attempt to describe the world, filtered through his mind and memory. To Iwaniuk, the reflected world appears rather gloomy but also has its brief rewarding moments, intrinsically linked to the creative process. In the opening poem, "Lustro," the poet is like King Lear, who has lost his sense of direction in life because of pain and confusion but gains a painful insight: access to a truth unattainable by others. The poet's confession, "pragnę istnieć, o lustro, pomóż mi wyjść z siebie," (I want to exist, oh mirror, free me from myself), indicates a new stage in his process of self-liberation and self-cognition that continues throughout this volume and the next ones. The poem "Dwa miasta" (translated as "Two Cities," 1979) depicts the background for this process by juxtaposing the dual city of the past (prewar and postwar Chełm) and the dual city of the present (Toronto first ruled by Indians, later by white Europeans). These two cities are permanently connected in Iwaniuk's mind and create the foundation for his identity, which is to be contemplated in solitude and silence.

Basic philosophical questions about the existential situation of the individual, the positing of a system of values, and the nature of human knowledge constitute the second dominant feature of *Lustro*. As the world appears chaotic, orderless, and enigmatic, Iwaniuk's answers to these questions often consist of paradoxes and contradictions. For example, he obsessively presents the past in realistic terms; yet, in poems such as "Statek kosmiczny Apollo 15 w podróży na księżyc. Trzy historyczne dni" (translated as "Spaceship Apollo 15") he also observes that the human sense of time and space is illusive. As he struggles to find the proper words in "Cisza" (Silence), he longs for silence and paradoxically cherishes mute moments as the most sublime form of poetic art. He ostensibly dismisses the Polish Romantic tradition, which emphasized the power of words over deeds, but he is clearly under its influence when he observes in the poem "I zanim oddech opisze jego kształt" (And Before Breath Describes Its Shape) that poets' words preserve the world while people destroy it.

His poems in this volume are also preoccupied with the decay of basic human values, the search for God, and a longing for unattainable clarity and order. Directness, sincerity, and honesty, along with a meditative mood, are the key features of Iwaniuk's best poems in *Lustro*. In 1971, the year of its publication, Iwaniuk won the Kościelski Foundation Prize for literary achievement. In 1975 Iwaniuk received two prizes, one awarded by the University of Toronto and the other (shared with W. A. Zbyszewski) by the jour-nal *Wiadmości* (London) for the best writings published in its 1975 issues.

Iwaniuk's active lifestyle and participation in many sports was interrupted by a heart attack in the mid 1970s, and he was forced to take an early retirement. As his health gradually improved, he resumed some of his artistic and social activities. In the late 1970s he was a member of the jury for *Wiadmości*, which gave annual awards for the best books in Polish published outside Poland. In 1978 he became the managing director (*prezes*) of the Polish-Canadian Publishing Fund and organized readings of well-known poets and writers.

During that time another volume of his poetry, *Nemezis idzie pustymi drogami* (Nemesis Travels Along Empty Roads, 1978), was published in London in an edition of 350 copies, with graphics by Stanisław Gliwa. This volume repeats the topics of previous collections (nostalgia, alienation, death), this time giving priority to the contemplation of the word in general and the significance of the poetic word in particular. Although Iwaniuk admits that words more frequently contaminate than cure, his poetry proves the opposite to be true. He continually illustrates through his verse the power of poetic words to transform: the ordinary becomes the miraculous, as in "Cud na ulicy Yonge" (translated as "Miracle on Yonge Street," 1979); the temporary becomes the timeless and universal, as in "Elegia o cmentarzu w Toronto i słowo o śmierci" (translated as "Elegy in a Toronto Cemetery," 1979); and the banal becomes the profound, as in "Motto."

In poems such as "Mit o Afrodycie powracającej do morza" (translated as "The Myth of Aphrodite Returning to the Sea," 1979), "Przeciw mitologii" (translated as "Against Mythology," 1979), and "Rzeczywistość" (translated as "Reality," 1979) Iwaniuk combines Greek mythology, ancient history, and biblical stories with twentieth-century events in order to reveal parallels and patterns in human history. While his final vision asserts the decline of humanity in the twentieth century, this vision is presented with compassion and acceptance. A collection of witty aphorisms and a short cycle of poetic creations inspired by Barbara Brzozowska's portraits and other paintings conclude the volume. The closing poem, "Elegia o literaturze z Krakowskiego Przedmieścia" (translated as "Conversations in the Warsaw Coffeehouse Spatif" [Stowarzyszenie Polskich Artystów Teatru i Filmu—Society of Polish Theater and Film Artists]) is a satire on the Warsaw literary milieu, which is depicted with black humor and biting sarcasm.

Although no new themes are introduced in this collection, Iwaniuk's constant leitmotivs are developed further. Thus, as his alienation from Canadian culture deepens, his memories of lost Arcadia remain quite vivid; his thoughts on death gain philosophical depth and help to cope with the demands of everyday life; calm expectation takes the place of fear and discomfort; and loneliness becomes a conscious choice that brings fulfillment and is the poet's privilege. The vision of the world as presented in *Nemezis idzie pustymi drogami* is pessimistic but thought-provoking. The language is simple, yet full of ingenious metaphors and skillfully combined, often untranslatable idioms that lead to surprising effects. Polish émigré critics (for example, Maja Cybulska and Adam Czerniawski) have agreed that both *Lustro* and *Nemezis idzie pustymi drogami* are among the greatest poetic achievements in Iwaniuk's literary canon.

The English collection *Dark Times: Selected Poems of Wacław Iwaniuk* (1979) includes poems from *Ciemny czas*, *Lustro*, and *Nemezis idzie pustymi drogami*. Canadian reviewers responded favorably to Iwaniuk's poetry, stressing the high artistic quality of the volume and the fact that it can be read as a history lesson for a nation that never directly experienced a calamity such as World War II.

Evenings on Lake Ontario is a collection of poems written in English, culled from Iwaniuk's diary. The first part of the book, "From My Canadian Diary," is a sort of "report" consisting of twenty-one poems that use numbers in place of titles and that list important episodes of Iwaniuk's life in Canada from 1948 onward, emphasizing major differences between the new society and himself. Here, for the first time, sensitivity to space, not time, is the organizing principle of his poetic imagery.

The second part of the volume follows the same style as the first; but as its subtitle, "Monologues and Dialogues," indicates, it consists of a poetic conversation on existential themes between the poet and an ideal reader. Iwaniuk writes, "Toronto swallowed me like a freshwater fish," suggesting his integration into Canadian society; yet, at the same time, it is clear that his assimilation into that society is far from perfect, as he continues to justify his alienated "self" through his poetry. The poems that conclude the volume—"We Deal with Words," "A Poet and the Poet," and "Birth of a Poem"—are devoted to the creative process, which takes place surprisingly in both spirit and flesh. In a way, both parts of the book allude to the technique of Iwaniuk's previous war "diaries," but, written in English, they also show affinities with the style of some of the American poets he translated.

A passion for polemics is an intrinsic part of Iwaniuk's poetic personality and is well reflected in *Podróż do Europy* (A Trip to Europe, 1982), a prose diary written during the 1960s that consists of stories, light sketches, and more-ambitious essays devoted to issues of art, literature, philosophy, politics, and culture in general. The humorous stories and sketches describe the visit of Iwaniuk's aunt to Canada and various incidents he witnessed while working as a court translator. Apart from being entertaining, they provide many insightful psychological observations on society, human nature, and behavior. Essays inspired by his trips to London, France, and Italy in the 1960s give a detailed account of his impressions and are in addition a perceptive comparative study of European and American cultures. While Iwaniuk respects Europe's intellectual heritage and maturity, his sympathy clearly lies with America's achievements—the vitality and independence and the drive toward perfection and opportunity that the country offers.

The second part, titled "Notatnik poetycki i zapiski" (Poetic Notebook and Jottings), includes essays on the views of particular thinkers (such as José Ortega y Gasset and Polish philosopher Władysław Tatarkiewicz) and works of literary groups and individual writers (Polish, French, British, and American). Sharing his opinions with the reader, Iwaniuk recalls his prewar years in Warsaw and corrects many pieces of misinformation published in various sources on the subject of Polish poetry. This amusing and informative book presents Iwaniuk as an insightful observer, passionate reader, literary critic, reflective thinker, and above all a writer faithful to his inner voice and his own intellectual experience.

The themes of *Nocne rozmowy* (Night Conversations, 1987) are similar to Iwaniuk's previous collections, and their scope is as broad; but they are developed differently and lead to new conclusions. Many nature-based images of a garden, lake, and sea combine his past and present experiences to encourage acceptance of life as it is and to introduce a temporary structure to a chaotic universe. These poems are less pessimistic and rebellious than earlier works, showing that Iwaniuk has absorbed the elements of his current landscape and transformed its foreign components into a universal world of the human condition in which truth is more important than beauty. There is a tendency in this volume, notably in "My plemię Abla" (We, The Tribe of Abel), to speak for a twentieth-century "everyman" who feels confused and abandoned by God but awaits neither revelations nor future happiness.

Several poems in this volume grew out of Iwaniuk's analytical reading of other writers' works and are dedicated to them: Czechowicz, Miron Białoszewski, Bruno Schulz, Franz Kafka, Auden, Merton, Arthur Koestler, and Jerzy Andrzejewski. Other poems, referring to Iwaniuk's biography, comment on the unpredictability of life, human nature, and the passing of time. The deep conviction underlying *Nocne rozmowy* is that art can do justice when people fail; whenever humanity falters, the poet's obligation is to reveal and protect thoughts that are worth preserving and to challenge and intellectually provoke.

Kartagina i inne wiersze was the first volume of Iwaniuk's poetry to appear in postwar Poland; it was published by the Lublin underground printing house "Komitywa." It includes mostly poems on political themes with patriotic overtones, selected from earlier émigré collections. The second such volume, *Powrót* (The Return, 1989), published in official circulation, presented selections chronologically, beginning with *Czas Don Kichota* and ending with *Nocne rozmowy*. Although the volume did not generate many critical responses, it provoked, in the few critical articles that did appear, a deep, analytical exploration of the work. While one critic questioned the intellectual integrity of the poems, others praised their distinctive style and their independent-minded, polemical stance.

Unlike *Powrót*, the collection *Moje obłąkanie* (My Insanity, 1991) is a direct continuation of *Kartagina i inne wiersze* and consists of previously unpublished texts selected by the author. Most of these texts show Iwaniuk's continuing interest in issues such as patriotism, the search for a lost motherland, and Polish identity. Although his vision of the world in this collection is still bitter, the rebellious spirit of his earlier poetry gives way to a world-weary acceptance of life as it is. For Iwaniuk, poetry remains the only remedy for the pain of the incomprehensible nature of the world and the fate of its people.

Zanim znikniemy w opactwie kolorów (Before We Vanish in the Abbacy of Colors, 1991) includes mostly poems from his previous émigré collections and a few new ones, which continue the theme of

nostalgia. The same pattern is apparent in subsequent volumes of poetry published in 1994–1998, with the exception of *Sceny sądowe. Czyli nasi w Kanadzie* (The Court Scenes or Poles in Canada, 1997), Iwaniuk's accounts of humorous situations based on his experiences as a court translator in Toronto.

Ostatni romantyk: Wspomnienie o Józefie Łobodowskim (The Last Romantic: My Memories of Józef Łobodowski, 1998) is Iwaniuk's tribute to a friend and fellow émigré writer. Iwaniuk focuses on the historical background of Łobodowski's poetry and his artistic affiliations with the prewar poetic group Skamander, whose members were known for continuing the Romantic tradition. Iwaniuk describes his friendship with Łobodowski in a personal, occasionally defensive way, rejecting various false accusations directed at his friend by the Polish press and providing substantial background information to justify his opinion. The book is a valuable source of knowledge on literary émigré life, even though the memoir could not be completed because of Iwaniuk's illness.

In addition to working on his memoir, "Toronto and I," Iwaniuk has prepared for publication "Polish Autumn," a long poem devoted to the history of Polish verse, as well as a volume of his translations of American poets.

Iwaniuk's poetry, ostensibly accessible, is in fact complex and allusive. Comprehension of it requires concentration, intellectual effort, and acquaintance with disparate literary traditions. His poems have evoked admiration on the part of readers and critics alike and have been translated into several languages, including English, German, French, Hebrew, and Italian. One of Iwaniuk's major achievements has been the successful transposition of the individual world of a Polish émigré into a truly universal idiom accessible to readers regardless of their ethnic background, experience, and native tongue. Although the artistic quality of his poems is somewhat uneven, varying from one volume to another, his poetry creates a powerful, inspiring, and often poignant vision that, while it disturbs and provokes rather than comforts or delights, cannot leave the reader indifferent.

Interviews:

Marek Zieliński, "'Samotność poety' Rozmowa z Wacławem Iwaniukiem," *Więź*, 4–5–6 (1985): 107–113;

Krzysztof Lisowski, "Gdzie Iwaniuk w Polsce mieszka?," *Kresy*, 2–3 (1990): 119–130;

Florian Śmieja, "Rozmowa siódma: z Wacławem Iwaniukiem," in his *Siedem rozmów o poezji* (Toronto: Polski Fundusz Wydawniczy w Kanadźie, 1990), pp. 99–117;

Lisowski, "O poezji, malarstwie, emigracji czyli druga rozmowa z Waclawem Iwaniukiem, in *London–Toronto–Vancouver: Rozmowy z pisarzami emigracyjnymi*, edited by Andrzej Niewiadomski (Lublin: Stowarzyszenie Literackie KRESY, 1993), pp. 49–54;

Jan Wolski, "Moje strony świata," *Fraza*, 5–6 (1994): 7–13.

References:

Maja Elżbieta Cybulska, "Rozmowa Mistrza Iwaniuka ze śmiercią," in her *Tematy i pisarze* (London: Oficyna Poetów i Malarzy, 1982), pp. 39–44;

Cybulska, *Wacław Iwaniuk: Poeta* (London: Oficyna Poetów i Malarzy, 1984);

Bogdan Czaykowski, *Polish Writing in Canada* (Ottawa: Department of the Secretary of State, 1988);

Adam Czerniawski, "Nowe wiersze Iwaniuka," *Kultura* (Paris), 6–7 (1968): 198–201;

Zbigniew Folejewski, "Wacław Iwaniuk: A Poet of the Dark Time," foreword to *Dark Times:*

Selected Poems of Wacław Iwaniuk, by Iwaniuk (Toronto: Hounslow Press, 1979), pp. 1–6;

Natan Gross, "Ocalić pamięć. Iwaniuk i epoka pieców," *Wiadomości* (London), 1 (1981): 13–14;

Janusz Kryszak, "Wacław Iwaniuk—poeta ciemnego czasu," introduction to *Zanim znikniemy w opactwie kolorów*, by Iwaniuk (Kraków: Wydawnictwo Literackie, 1991), pp. 5–26;

Kryszak, "Wyobraźnia traumatyczna. Próba przybliżenia poezji Wacława Iwaniuka," in *Pisarz na obczyźnie*, edited by Tadeusz Bujnicki and Wojciech Wyskiel (Wrocław: Zakład Narodowy im. Ossolińskich, 1985), pp. 109–121;

Sandi Fleszar Mayewski, "Binary Opposition as the Compositional Feature in the Works of Wacław Iwaniuk," dissertation, Ohio State University, 1984;

Ireneusz Opacki and Zdzisława Mokranowska, eds., *Szkice o twórczości Wacława Iwaniuka* (Katowice: Uniwersytet Śląski, 1992);

Marek Pytasz, "Iwaniuk," *Literatura na Świecie*, 9 (1981): 353–357;

Marek Zieliński, "Iluminacja życia. Próba opisania poezji Wacława Iwaniuka," introduction to *Powrót* (Warsaw: Biblioteka "Więzi," 1989), pp. 5–16.

Jarosław Iwaszkiewicz

(20 February 1894 – 2 March 1980)

Wladimir Krysinski
University of Montreal

BOOKS: *Oktostychy* (Warsaw: Nakładem Redakcji *Pro
  Arte*, 1919);
Zenobia Palmura (Poznań: Biblioteka "Zdroju," 1920);
Legendy i Demeter (Warsaw: Ignis, 1921);
Dionizje (Warsaw: Ignis, 1922);
Ucieczka do Bagdadu (Warsaw: Ignis, 1923);
Hilary syn buchaltera (Warsaw: Ignis, 1923);
Siedem bogatych miast nieśmiertelnego Kościeja (Warsaw:
  Wydawn. Philobiblon, 1924);
Księżyc wschodzi (Warsaw: Wacław Czarski i S-ka,
  1925);
Kasydy, zakończone siedmioma wierszami (Warsaw:
  Wacław Czarski i S-ka, 1925);
Pejzaże sentymentalne (Warsaw: Gebethner i Wolff,
  1926);
*Kochankowie z Werony. Tragedia romantyczna w trzech
  aktach* (Warsaw: Skamander, 1929);
Księga dnia i księga nocy (Warsaw: F. Hoesick, 1929);
Zmowa mężczyzn (Warsaw: F. Hoesick, 1930);
Powrót do Europy (Warsaw: F. Hoesick, 1931);
Lato 1932 (Warsaw: J. Mortkowicz, 1933);
Panny z Wilka (Warsaw: Gebethner i Wolff, 1933);
Czerwone tarcze (Warsaw: Gebethner i Wolff, 1934);
Młyn nad Utratą (Warsaw: Gebethner i Wolff, 1936);
Lato w Nohant. Komedia w 3 aktach (Warsaw: J. Prze-
  worski, 1937); translated by Colina Wien-
  iewaka as *Summer at Nohant: A Play in Three Acts*
  (London: Minerva, 1942);
Dwa opowiadania (Warsaw: Gebethner i Wolff, 1938);
Fryderyk Szopen (Lwów: PWKS, 1938); revised as
  Chopin (Warsaw: Państwowy Instytut Wydawn-
  iczy, 1949);
Pasje błędomierskie (Warsaw: Gebethner i Wolff,
  1938);
Inne życie (Warsaw: J. Przeworski, 1938);
Maskarada. Melodramat w 4 aktach (Warsaw: Gebeth-
  ner i Wolff, 1939);
Nowa miłość i inne opowiadania (Warsaw: Czytelnik,
  1946);
Stara cegielnia, Młyn nad Lutynią (Warsaw: Instytut
  Wydawniczy "Panteon," 1946);

Jarosław Iwaszkiewicz (photograph by B. J. Dorys)

Nowele włoskie (Warsaw: Spółdzielnia Wydawnicza
  "Wiedza," 1947);
Spotkania z Szymanowskim (Kraków: Muzycane, 1947);
Ody olimpijskie (Warsaw: Wiedza, 1948);
Jan Sebastian Bach (Warsaw: Państwowy Instytut
  Wydawniczy, 1951);
Odbudowa Błędomierza. Sztuka w trzech aktach (Warsaw:
  Czytelnik, 1951);

Sprawa pokoju. Wiersze i przemówienia (Warsaw: Czytelnik, 1952);

Cztery szkice literackie (Warsaw: Czytelnik, 1953);

Wycieczka do Sandomierza. Powieść dla młodzieży (Warsaw: Czytelnik, 1953);

Pensja pani Latter, with Jerzy M. Rytard (Warsaw: Czytelnik, 1953);

Warkocz jesieni i inne wiersze (Warsaw: Państwowy Instytut Wydawniczy, 1954);

Listy z podróży do Ameryki Południowej (Kraków: Wydawn. Literackie, 1954);

Ucieczka Felka Okonia. Opowiadanie (Warsaw: Czytelnik, 1954);

Opowieści zasłyszane (Warsaw: Państwowy Instytut Wydawniczy, 1954);

Książka o Sycylii (Kraków: Wydawnictwo Literackie, 1956);

Sława i chwała, 3 volumes (Warsaw: Państwowy Instytut Wydawniczy, 1956, 1958, 1962);

Ciemne ścieżki (Warsaw: Czytelnik, 1957);

Książka moich wspomnień (Kraków: Wydawnictwo Literackie, 1957; corrected, 1968; enlarged edition, Warsaw: Czytelnik, 1994);

Liryki (Warsaw: Państwowy Instytut Wydawniczy, 1959);

Gawęda o książkach i czytelnikach (Warsaw: Czytelnik, 1959);

Tatarak i inne opowiadania (Warsaw: Czytelnik, 1960);

Kochankowie z Marony (Warsaw: Iskry, 1961);

Rozmowy o książkach (Warsaw: Czytelnik, 1961);

Gniazdo łabędzi. Szkice z Danii (Warsaw: Iskry, 1962);

Stanisława Wysocka i jej kijowski teatr "Studya" (Warsaw: Wydawnictwa Artstystyczne i Filmowe, 1963);

Jutro żniwa (Warsaw: Czytelnik, 1963);

Heydenreich. Cienie. Dwa opowiadania (Poznań: Wydawnictwo Poznańskie, 1964);

Dziewczyna i gołębie (Warsaw: Czytelnik, 1965);

Krągły rok (Warsaw: Czytelnik, 1967);

O psach, kotach i diabłach. Opowiadania (Warsaw: Czytelnik, 1968);

Xenie i elegie (Warsaw: Czytelnik, 1970);

Opowiadania muzyczne (Warsaw: Czytelnik, 1971);

Ikar. Staroświecki sklep. Wiewiórka. Opowiadania (Warsaw: Czytelnik, 1971);

Teatr polski w Warszawie, 1938–1949. Szkic (Warsaw: Wydawnictwa Artstystyczne i Filmowe, 1971);

Martwa pasieka. Psyche. Opowiadania (Warsaw, 1973);

Śpiewnik włoski (Warsaw: Czytelnik, 1974);

Sny. Ogrody. Sérénité (Warsaw: Czytelnik, 1974);

Zarudzie (Warsaw: Czytelnik, 1976);

Petersburg (Warsaw: Państwowy Instytut Wydawniczy, 1976);

Album tatrzańskie (Kraków: Wydawnictwo Literackie, 1976);

Mapa pogody (Warsaw: Czytelnik, 1977);

Podróże do Polski (Warsaw: Państwowy Instytut Wydawniczy, 1977);

Podróże do Włoch (Warsaw: Państwowy Instytut Wydawniczy, 1977);

Szkice o literaturze skandynawskiej (Warsaw: Czytelnik, 1977);

Opowiadanie z psem (Kraków: Wydawnictwo Literackie, 1978);

Listy do Felicji (Warsaw: Czytelnik, 1979);

Młodość pana Twardowskiego. Poemat (Warsaw: Czytelnik, 1979);

Biłek (Kraków: Wydawnictwo Literackie, 1980);

Muzyka wieczorem (Warsaw: Czytelnik, 1980);

Utwory ostatnie (Warsaw: Czytelnik, 1981);

Ludzie i książki (Warsaw: Książka i Wiedza, 1983);

Utwory nieznane (Warsaw: Czytelnik, 1986);

Notatki 1939–1945 (Wrocław: Wydawnictwo Dolnośląskie, 1991);

Marginalia (Warsaw: Oficyna Wydawnicza INTERIM, 1993).

Editions and Collections: *Wiersze wybrane* (Warsaw: Czytelnik, 1938);

Wiersze wybrane (Warsaw: Czytelnik, 1946);

Wiersze z różnych epok. 1912–1952 (Warsaw: Czytelnik, 1952);

Opowiadania. 1918–1953, 2 volumes (Warsaw: Czytelnik, 1954);

Dzieła, 10 volumes (Warsaw: Czytelnik, 1958–1959);

Sława i chwała (Warsaw: Państwowy Instytut Wydawniczy, 1963);

Opowiadania wybrane (Warsaw: Czytelnik, 1964);

Wiersze zebrane (Warsaw: Czytelnik, 1968);

Opowiadania zebrane, 3 volumes (Warsaw: Czytelnik, 1969);

Wybór opowiadań (Warsaw: Czytelnik, 1973);

Dzieła, 20 volumes (Warsaw: Czytelnik, 1975–1984)— comprises *Książka moich wspomnień; Hilary syn buchaltera; Księżyc wschodzi; Czerwone tarcze; Pasje błędomierskie; Sława i chwała, t. I–III; Wiersze I–II; Proza poetycka; Opowiadania I–VI; Dramaty I–II; Podróże I–II; Pisma muzyczne; Rozmowy o książkach I–II; Ludzie i książki: Teatralia;*

Wybór wierszy, edited by Jerzy Lisowski (Warsaw: Muza, 1994).

Editions in English: "The Badger," translated by Ilona Ralf Sues, in *Contemporary Polish Short Stories*, selected by Andrzej Kijowski (Warsaw: Polonia, 1960), pp. 169–177;

"A Message," and "The Brotherhood of Man," translated by Adam Gillon and Ludwik Krzyżanowski, in *Introduction to Modern Polish Literature: An Anthology of Fiction and Poetry*, edited by Gillon and Krzyżanowski (New York: Twayne, 1964, pp. 389–393;

"Quentin Matsys," translated by Czesław Miłosz, in *Postwar Polish Poetry*, edited by Miłosz (New York: Doubleday, 1965);

"Autumn Scattering Bitter Cinnamon," translated by Andrzej Busza and Bogdan Czaykowski, in *Durak: An International Magazine of Poetry* 3 (1979) 15;

"Map of Sunshine," translated by Busza and Czaykowski, in *Gathering Time: Five Modern Polish Elegies*, edited by Busza and Czaykowski (Mission, British Columbia: Barbarian Press, 1983);

"The Pope in Ancona" and "How Does the Negative Look . . . ," translated by Magnus J. Kryński and Robert A. Maguire, in *Contemporary East European Poetry*, edited by Emery George (Ann Arbor, Mich.: Ardis, 1983), pp. 103–105.

The voluminous work of Jarosław Iwaszkiewicz should unequivocally be recognized as important, both within its native Polish tradition and within an international context. A canonic figure of twentieth-century Polish literature, Iwaszkiewicz was a versatile and polyvalent writer who expressed his artistic ability in various genres and forms. He achieved his most significant work, however, in prose and particularly in the short-story form, of which he was a great master.

Born on 20 February 1894 in Kalnik near Kiev, Jarosław Iwaszkiewicz stemmed from a family of Polish gentry and intelligentsia and grew up in the cultural climate of three national traditions—Polish, Russian, and Ukrainian. An important event of his youth was his close friendship with the renowned Polish composer Karol Szymanowski, who undoubtedly influenced Iwaszkiewicz's artistic passion and creative interests. Iwaszkiewicz subsequently wrote a libretto for Szymanowski's opera *Król Roger* (King Roger, 1973). The importance of Iwaszkiewicz's friendship with Szymanowski seems undeniable; it was not only crucial to the formation of Iwaszkiewicz's creative process but also to the prevalence in Iwaszkiewicz's work of certain themes, artistic constructions, and a certain vision of the world. Besides imparting a general cosmopolitan dimension to his work, Iwaszkiewicz tended to shape into musical form his prose and his poetry, both of which were strongly permeated with an atmosphere derived from such decadent themes as love-death dialectic, narcissism, the contemplation of beauty, and a quest for perfect artistic form.

Iwaszkiewicz began his education in Elisavetgrad and then went on in 1912 to study law and music in Kiev. At the same time, he began writing, first poetry and later prose. In 1918 he moved to Warsaw, where he became professionally linked with several historic Polish figures, including Maciej Rataj, the Speaker of the Polish Parliament (Sejm), for whom Iwaszkiewicz worked as a secretary (1923–1925). As an employee of the Ministry of Foreign Affairs, Iwaszkiewicz also served as a diplomat in Copenhagen (1932–1935) and in Brussels (1935–1936). In 1922 he married Anna Lilpop, who came from a well-known family of industrialists. The marriage not only enlarged Iwaszkiewicz's circle of literary and artistic friends but also gave him a permanent residence in the beautiful Podkowa Leśna, near Warsaw, where he settled in 1928; his residence, known as Stawisko, became an important meeting place for artists and writers and retained this character both under German occupation and in communist Poland.

Iwaszkiewicz belongs to the generation that gave Polish literature several remarkable poets—notably Kazimierz Wierzyński (1894–1969), Julian Tuwim (1894–1953), Jan Lechoń (1899–1956), and Antoni Słonimski (1895–1976). Along with Iwaszkiewicz, they constituted the literary group called *Skamander*, which published a review under the same name and contributed to the leading literary weekly of interwar Poland, *Wiadomości Literackie* (Literary News). After 1920 these writers participated in the shaping, through the intensity of their work of the literary and social consciousness that evolved in the aftermath of World War I and the recovery of national independence. Although not a typical *Skamandrite*, Iwaszkiewicz throughout his life showed friendship toward and admiration for his fellow poets, and if one can legitimately speak of the "Generation of 1894" in Polish literature, it is thanks to the personal rather than aesthetic cohesion of *Skamander*. Iwaszkiewicz played a paramount role in sustaining the *Skamander* group's status and cohesion.

As a writer, Iwaszkiewicz created a rich and diversified body of work through the use of various, if not all, literary genres. He wrote poetry, novels, short stories, dramas, essays, librettos, and memoirs. He was an excellent translator from various languages. He also developed a specific genre of biographical essay and personal recollections, becoming a sort of chronicler of the lives of many famous and lesser known persons, most of whom were either prominent historical figures (Johann Sebastian Bach, Frédéric Chopin) or his friends (Szymanowski).

Iwaszkiewicz achieved considerable acclaim as a poet, although it would perhaps be an exaggeration to qualify him as a significantly original poet. On the basis of comparative analysis, his poetic

Cover for the 1970 West German edition of Iwaszkiewicz's Matka Joanna od Aniołów, *which was first published in Iwaszkiewicz's 1946 collection of short stories*

work may be accorded the status of classical poetry with strains of personal lyricism. Although quite distinctive, his poetry cannot be situated on a level similar to that of Czesław Miłosz, Tadeusz Różewicz, or Zbigniew Herbert. Still, anyone who intends to describe Iwaszkiewicz's literary work cannot avoid discussing his poetry.

Iwaszkiewicz's poetry is so diversified that one can hear various echoes, not only of the modernist style and themes but also of symbolist and expressionist poetry combined with a specifically personal tone and diction. In placing his poetry within an international system of references and filiations, one notes that Iwaszkiewicz's poetic models were of the highest order. In addition to Paul Valéry, Stefan George, and several Russian symbolists, such Polish masters as Juliusz Słowacki (1809–1849), Adam Mickiewicz (1798–1855), and Cyprian Norwid (1821–1883) influenced his poetry.

The poetic *I* of many of Iwaszkiewicz's poems can easily be identified with the empirical human ego of the enunciating subject, none other than the poet himself, aware that his life and his sensitivity, his travels and his recollections are the sources of his poetry. In this sense Iwaszkiewicz's poetry is significantly personal. At its roots, his poetry is meditative and reflexive, conveying both the passion and the sadness of human existence. The reflexive and autoreflexive stances give a specific dimension to the personal tone and themes of his poetry. To the narcissistic and self-mirroring themes one has to add the constant and ever-growing presence of love and death. As in Iwaszkiewicz's prose, these structures determine both the narrative line and the lyrical enhancement of his poetry.

From the beginning Iwaszkiewicz's poetry is characterized by formal diversity. In the early poems, regular forms are based on traditional oriental poetry. Iwaszkiewicz cultivated the atemporal beauty strongly emphasized in these forms as a means of gaining self-knowledge. Hence, exotic charm pervades all of his poems.

Oktostychy (Octostichs, 1919), published when the poet was twenty-five, is his first book of poetry. He creates a magic aura through a series of images, references, and metaphors based on the recurrence of exotic elements, cultural and literary allusions, and a hedonistic *I*. Through these lyrical exercises Iwaszkiewicz tests the limits of his poetry and reveals his poetic values. In fact, his universe is a pure game of images and sounds. This format may be seen in a poem titled "Deszcz" (Rain), in which the persona demonstrates a range of formal structures:

Whether in joy or in nostalgia—always in love,
I walk intensely listening to your speech.

Good rains, rains so good, laced with gold.
Bright strings, little drops, so beloved.

The poet's suffering and sadness take the form of manneristic images and associations. Similarly, in the poem "Dnie" (Days) the poet, while revealing his solitude, visits his soul contemplatively and without any tragic overtones. The following is his self-revealing vision:

At nightfall I know that sadness will never deceive—
I go out in a dark blanket, dreaming of your mantilla.

In the evening the butterflies of pines move violently
    and weep.
I rage. I would shatter the stars with despair.

Recognized as a strongly expressionistic form of poetry, particularly in the volume *Dionizje* (Dionysiacs, 1922), Iwaszkiewicz's discourse at times tends toward a brutal and crude affirmation of life and at times manifests itself delicately with subjective undertones. The mixture of meditation and sensations constitutes the main resource of his poetry. These features are characteristic of such volumes as *Kasydy, zakończone siedmioma wierszami* (Casidas Completed with Seven Verses, 1925) and *Księga dnia i księga nocy* (The Book of Day and the Book of Night, 1929).

A new vision and innovative formal structures are present in *Powrót do Europy* (The Return to Europe, 1931), a volume that constitutes a crucial moment and a pause in Iwaszkiewicz's poetic development. The meaning of the "return" is symbolically a quest for identity within the European cultural tradition and is paralleled by the identification of the poet as a subjective yet social vehicle of poetry, whose function must be properly and ethically determined. In the opening poem of the collection, titled "Europa" (Europe), Iwaszkiewicz almost ironically scrutinizes exoticism as a potential new territory for a European who finds Europe has become "too narrow." By symbolically denouncing the escape from Europe, the poet imposes as an ethical principle the unconditional attachment to the spiritual heritage of the continent viewed as a land of ancestors and history: "Our dear land, the land across which Mickiewicz used to walk. / We are your servants, your prodigal sons / We will not let you perish, we will not let you die, we will give you new blood." Thus, the "return to Europe" means, above all, faithfulness to the past and to the culture of a common homeland.

In the same volume Iwaszkiewicz published the long poem "Do Pawła Valéry" (To Paul Valéry), in which he probes the question of the objective meaning and the social function of poetry. Valéry, as a representative of pure poetry, is treated as an exemplar and as an interlocutor to whom the poet addresses a series of questions concerning poetry in general and Polish poetry in particular. The opposition between pure poetry and patriotic, socially aware poetry sustains the development of the poem. Having stated toward the end of the poem that the "truth of the word is more important than the truth of beauty," the poet declares: "We will not enter the realm of pure poetry." The poem ends: "Understand, please, what truth is held by the heart of that pilgrim / Who marches above the crowd on the Square of Alma." The conclusion is therefore openly directed toward a poetry of social and national mission. "The pilgrim who marches on the Square of Alma" is an allusion to the monument of Adam Mickiewicz that stands at that location in Paris. Mickiewicz, who is recognized as the most important Polish national poet and is frequently evoked by Iwaszkiewicz, symbolizes the national mission of poetry as opposed to "pure poetry." For Iwaszkiewicz this evocation signifies something essential in terms of poetics and patriotic commitment. His poetics can be defined as constant and imperative awareness that he writes in Polish for Polish readers. On various occasions Iwaszkiewicz systematically evokes the Polish national tradition of patriotism, and his poetry, even though strongly subjective, does not detach itself from love for the homeland. One should therefore read this poetry in a double key—as a desire to convey a message of personal intimacy and individual experiences and as a manifestation of the duty to share in the solidarity of the national destiny proper to the Polish community.

From 1920 until approximately 1934 Iwaszkiewicz published a series of novels that differed considerably in style and theme but had an important feature in common, namely subjective narration. *Zenobia Palmura* (1920), *Ucieczka do Bagdadu* (Escape to Bagdad, 1923), and "Wieczór u Abdona" (An Evening at Abdon's, 1923) are modernist prose works that are essentially expressionistic and strongly marked by an individualistic emphasis and explicit questioning of life versus Art. The sense of this opposition acquires a specific dimension in the two autobiographical novels written subsequently: *Hilary syn buchaltera* (Hilary, Son of an Accountant, 1923) and *Księżyc wschodzi* (The Moon Rises, 1925). In these novels the author succeeds in diminishing the heroic in both life and art. Both acquire a more human and earthly proportion.

In 1932 Iwaszkiewicz moved to Copenhagen as a diplomat. The same year he began publishing a series of short stories. Two are recognized as Iwaszkiewicz's masterpieces: "Panny z Wilka" (Young Ladies from Wilko, 1932) and "Brzezina" (The Birch Grove, 1932). This prolific period of creative activity continued until at least 1942. Other important short stories of the period are "Młyn nad Utratą" (The Mill on the Utrata River, 1936), "Zygfryd" (1936), "Słońce w kuchni" (The Sun in the Kitchen, 1938), "Anna Grazzi" (1938), and "Kongres we Florencji" (Congress in Florence, 1941). "Panny z Wilka" and "Brzezina" deserve particular attention since they epitomize Iwaszkiewicz's narrative art and his vision of the world.

In "Panny z Wilka" forty-year-old Wiktor Ruben revisits Wilko, where he lived as a young man and where he experienced love and the first enthusiastic intensity of life. After a long absence from Wilko, he encounters a group of women still rather young but already changed. Ruben earlier had known some of them erotically. They have now grown older; some have married. One, Fela, has died. These women symbolize the irrevocable loss of intensity and freshness. Trying to approach Jola, Julcia, Kazia, Tunia, and Zosia after a passage of years, Ruben discovers the vanity of recollections and the cruelty of time. No past can be recaptured; the richness of the past cannot possibly be integrated into the present. Between the immediacy of life and the willingness to believe in the eternally positive quality of human relationships there is a gap. Ruben experiences it ironically and irrevocably. He leaves Wilko, intending never to return. The wisdom that he has acquired seems a necessary, though cruel, knowl-

edge of life. In that sense, Iwaszkiewicz's story is an anti-Proustian vision of life. No memory can redeem the past. The cruelty and the cold objectivity of time triumph over recollection.

Strikingly intense in its narrative representation—which combines the simultaneity of perception and the plurality of gestures, words, behaviors, observations, and inner reflections—"Panny z Wilka" is a brilliantly written long short story. (Many of Iwaszkiewicz's texts deserve this name, and he expressed himself best in this literary form.)

"Brzezina" is the story of the agony of Stanisław (Staś), who, after many years spent abroad in Switzerland in a sanatorium in Davos, returns to Poland to await his death in the house of his brother Bolesław. The inevitability of Stanisław's impending death is slowly unveiled by the narrator. Its final announcement takes the form of a short and unequivocal sentence. An atmosphere of strong psychological tension arises between the two brothers and lasts until Staś's death. Bolesław's wife, Basia, had died many years earlier and was buried in the birch grove that lies close to his house. Nonetheless, Bolesław is still living intensely in the recollection of Basia. His brother's presence irritates and vexes him. He closely watches Stanisław, who has a passionate love affair with Malwina, a young and sensual peasant woman. What happens between them becomes the object of Bolesław's jealousy. Staś's farewell to life coincides with his brother's psychological crisis and suicidal thoughts, and the recollections of his wife. Staś's uninhibited behavior casts a light on the ethical choices of human existence and personal relations. In "Brzezina" Eros and Thanatos are ingeniously interwoven throughout the narration, which combines the descriptions of nature with the gestures and feelings of the two brothers. The awesomeness of nature, the desire to escape from time, the intensity of feelings concerning the inevitability of death, and the closeness and distance of human relations constitute the underlying elements on which Iwaszkiewicz based his vision and his artistic project. Playing with the memory and the feelings of his protagonists, the vanity of human condition confronted with nature is subtly and suggestively conveyed by the narrator. He imparts a refined and complex knowledge of life, making the story a literary success in conveying a variety of messages, although the inevitable realization that true intimacy and the knowledge of the Other are doomed to failure is perhaps his main message. The desire to understand the Other stumbles over such feelings as solitude, jealousy, existen-

Iwaszkiewicz receiving the Lenin Prize for the Strengthening of Peace among Nations at the Kremlin on 20 March 1970

tial anguish, and the disproportion between the indifference of nature and the passion of man.

In 1934 the historical novel *Czerwone tarcze* (Red Shields), on which Iwaszkiewicz had been working for a few years, was published. Well received by the public and the critics, this novel occupies a particular place both in Iwaszkiewicz's work and in Polish literature. Iwaszkiewicz's conception of the historical novel is striking in its originality and its stylistic and narrative realization. The specificity of his literary technique resides in the freedom of the narrator vis-à-vis the historic past and his fictional universe. The narrator systematically returns to his own interpretation, inventiveness, and immediate perception of the past, which he puts into a quasi-ironical perspective. For Iwaszkiewicz the historical novel was by no means a reconstruction of events, facts, or language. He saw it as a fiction based on the imaginary and intellectual vision of the presupposed past reality. *Czerwone tarcze* is therefore written in modern, colloquial language. Moreover, it is a novel in which the dominant structures are atmosphere and an individually mediated panoramic vision. They surround the protagonist, Henry from Sandomierz (1127–1166), a young prince and descendant of the first Polish royal Piast dynasty. Henry was one of the five sons of Bolesław III of Crooked Mouth (Bolesław Krzywousty, 1086–1138), who in his testament partitioned Poland by

giving to every son a territory to govern. In a situation in which Poland ceased to exist as a united kingdom, Henry's political project was to reunify a country now feudally divided into antagonistic territories. The symbolic gesture that conveys the national dimension of this obsessive idea is the excavation of the crown from the tomb of King Bolesław the Brave (Bolesław Śmiały). However, the reinstitution of the Kingdom of Poland as an historical project depends on its becoming independent from Germany. When Frederic Barbarossa wants to restore the Kingdom of Poland, but within the realm of the Holy Roman Empire, Henry refuses to accept the crown from the German emperor and commits himself to helping one of his brothers, Bolesław Kędzierzawy; consequently, Henry loses the battle of Krzyszłowice (1157). Henry's doomed resistance is motivated by his refusal to surrender to Germany as the price for including Poland in Western civilization.

Iwaszkiewicz shows Henry to be a divided, if not a split, character. On the one hand, he is a man of vision and of ambitious intention with potentially practical and historically enormous consequences. On the other hand, he is a dreamer, and his way of experiencing the world is primarily aesthetic and passive. In a final symbolic act Henry throws the crown into the Vistula River, a gesture that signifies his definitive refusal to enter Western civilization at the cost of becoming dependent on Germany. This gesture underscores the Polish desire to maintain its national independence.

The substance of the novel consists in presenting the central character through his travels (Germany, Italy, Sicily, and Palestine), encounters (for example, one with King Roger in Sicily), observations, reflections, feelings, and passions. He is the unifying principle, the lens through which pass the intersecting visions, dialogues, comments, landscapes, countries, and kingdoms.

The originality of *Czerwone tarcze* resides in its narrative structure. The narrator constructs the character from the point of view of the present. The narrator is not a historic figure searching for absolute historical truth. Without being an omniscient narrator, he decides upon his characters' actions and intentions. Iwaszkiewicz's writing is an intense, sensitive, visionary, and critical representation of history. It tends to be truth-interrogating and serves to make the history of Poland problematic. Throughout his discourse, the narrator unveils the protagonist's psyche, which is both rich and capricious, exceptionally sensitive, and contemplative.

At the outbreak of World War II, Iwaszkiewicz was in Poland and, unlike most other *Skamandrites*, remained there without interruption until the end of the war in 1945. Stawisko, Iwaszkiewicz's residence since 1928, became almost legendary as the place where the writer and his family sheltered artists, writers, intellectuals, and musicians from possible German persecution. However, after 1945 Iwaszkiewicz's life changed considerably as he aligned himself with the communist regime. During 1945–1946 he was the president of the Union of Polish Writers. In 1947 he was reelected and remained president until 1949. In 1955 he became the chief editor and director of the important literary review *Twórczość* (Creative Work) in Warsaw, a position he held until his death. From 1950 to 1956 he was the vice president of the Union of Polish Writers. In return for his collaboration Iwaszkiewicz received many awards and decorations, including the Lenin Prize for the Strengthening of Peace among Nations in 1970. His unequivocal commitment to the regime and his good relationship with the communist authorities gave rise to many comments and judgments, particularly after his death in 1980. They tended either to be openly negative and ethically condemnatory or to see his activity as relative to the circumstances and give him credit for good intentions under the oppressive communist rule.

Notwithstanding the often critical assessments of Iwaszkiewicz's attitude during communist rule (assessments that sometimes infringe upon the objective evaluation of his work), his work may elicit sincere praise as an important contribution not only to Polish literature but to Polish culture as well. Despite his obviously servile position, one has to acknowledge that Iwaszkiewicz remained faithful to the first inspirations that shaped the development of his artistic prose. Although he did not practice socialist realism in his fiction, he did write some texts that were meant to please the regime. "List do Prezydenta Bieruta" (Letter to President Bierut, 18 April 1952) is a poem in which Iwaszkiewicz indulges in a gesture of self-criticism in line with the Communist Party's requirements. Although some of his literary critics have tried to explain away this act of contrition, the document testifies scandalously to the courtly and opportunist attitude of the writer. However, the value of his work suggests that his behavior should be forgotten.

A systematic writer who worked ceaselessly from the beginning of his career, Iwaszkiewicz created an impressive body of works in terms of volumes, multitude of themes, and literary and artistic perspectives. One is struck by the richness and diversity of his work. He was successful and compelling not only in prose fiction, to which the reception of his later work, such as the three-volume novel *Sława i chwała* (Fame and Praise, 1956, 1958, 1962) and many short stories, testifies, but also in writing travelogues, plays, and critical essays. The plays *Lato w Nohant* (1937; translated as *Summer at Nohant*, 1942) and *Maskarada* (Masquerade, 1939) demonstrate his theatrical talent. *Jan Sebastian Bach* (1951) is a remarkable study of Bach and, more particularly, of Bach's music. *Książka o Sycylii* (Sicily, 1956) testifies both to Iwaszkiewicz's attachment to that splendid island and to his passion for traveling.

Iwaszkiewicz's place in Polish literature is secure. In a way, he became the André Gide of Polish literature, although he was also seeking to realize Balzacian ambitions. His work exemplifies nineteenth-century problems, specifically the situation of the writer who passes from the country to the city and who is faced with both historic pressures and the mutation of values. The literary quality of Iwaszkiewicz's work is undeniable. A master of the representation of the sensitivities of human beings in all their individual and social complexity, Iwaszkiewicz was also the narrator of history. His short stories and his novellas, along with his poetry and his novels, constitute an impressive chronicle of Polish life and culture.

Letters:

Jerzy Andrzejewski, Jarosław Iwaszkiewicz, Listy (Warsaw: Czytelnik, 1991);

Listy z Ostrowa (Ostrów: Muzeum miasta Ostrowa Wielkopolskiego, 1991).

Biography:

V. M. Borisov, ed., *Vospominania o Jaroslavie Iwaszkiewicze* (Moscow: Sovetskii Pisatel, 1987).

References:

Henryk Bereza, "Jarosław Iwaszkiewicz," *Polish Perspectives*, 17, no. 1 (1974): 39–43;

Alicja Brodzka, ed., *O twórczości Jarosława Iwaszkiewicza* (Kraków: Wydawnictwo Literackie, 1983);

Tadeusz Drewnowski, "Jarosław Iwaszkiewicz: An Appreciation," *Polish Perspectives*, 23, no. 5 (1980): 17–19;

Andrzej Gronczewski, *Jarosław Iwaszkiewicz* (Warsaw: Państwowy Instytut Wydawniczy, 1972);

Tadeusz Januszewski, "Z korespondencji Jarosława Iwaszkiewicza po powstaniu warszawskim," *Poezja*, 13, no. 4 (1978): 76–84;

Maria Jędrychowska, "Iwaszkiewicza romans z Czystą Formą: O strukture 'Wieczoru u Abdona,'" *Twórczość*, 32, no. 2 (1976): 80–92;

Jędrychowska, "Jarosław Iwaszkiewicz," *Poezja*, 13, no. 4 (1978);

Jędrychowska, *Wczesna proza Jarosława Iwaszkiewicza* (Wrocław: Zakład Narodowy im. Ossolińskich, 1977);

Jerzy Kwiatkowski, *Eleuter: Szkice o wczesnej poezji Jarosława Iwaszkiewicza* (Warsaw: Czytelnik, 1966);

Kwiatkowski, *Poezja Jarosława Iwaszkiewicza na tle dwudziestolecia międzywojennego* (Warsaw: Czytelnik, 1975);

Eugenia Łoch, *Pierwiastki mityczne w opowiadaniach Jarosława Iwaszkiewicza* (Rzeszów: a Artstystyczne i Filmowe, 1978);

Łoch, *Pisarstwo Jarosława Iwaszkiewicza wobec tradycji i współczesności* (Lublin: Wydawnictwo Lubelskie, 1987);

M. P. Malkov, *Jaroslav Iwaszkiewicz i Aleksandr Blok* (Leningrad: Izdatelstvo Leningradskovo Universiteta, 1988);

Ryszard Matuszewski, *Iwaszkiewicz* (Warsaw: Agencja autorska, 1965);

Matuszewski, "The Work of Jaroslaw Iwaszkiewicz (L'oeuvre de Jaroslaw Iwaszkiewicz)," *Polish Literature/Litterature Polonaise*, 1, no. 1 (1968): 10–15;

Ryszard Przybylski, *Eros i Tanatos: Proza Jarosława Iwaszkiewicza, 1916–1938* (Warsaw: Czytelnik, 1970);

Edward Rothert, "Journeys to Italy," *Polish Perspectives*, 22, no. 10 (1978): 28–35;

Anna Sobolewska, "Jaroslaw Iwaszkiewicz: A Life and an Oeuvre," *Polish Perspectives*, 23, no. 5 (1980): 20–26;

Janusz Stradecki, "Jarosław Iwaszkiewicz a grupa Skamandra," *Teksty*, 50 (1980): 150–164;

Twórczość, special Iwaszkiewicz issue, 2 (1994)—includes correspondence between Iwaszkiewicz and Mieczysław Grydzewski;

Andrzej Wajda, "O fimowaniu prozy Iwaszkiewicza," in A. Brodzka, *O twórczości Jarosława Iwaszkiewicza;*

Wacław Wawrzyniak, *"Sława i chwała" Jarosława Iwaszkiewicza* (Warsaw: Państwowe Zakłady Wydawnictw Szkolnych, 1967);

Helena Zaworska, "Fullness: The Writings of Jaroslaw Iwaszkiewicz," *Polish Perspectives*, 20, no. 9 (1977): 33–41;

Zaworska, *Sztuka podróżowania: Poetyckie mity podróży w twórczości Jarosława Iwaszkiewicza, Julian Przybosia i Tadeusza Różewicza* (Kraków: Wydawnictwo Literackie, 1980);

Zaworska, *"Opowiadania" Jarosława Iwaszkiewicza* (Warsaw: Wydawnictwa Szkolne i Pedagogiczne, 1985).

Jégé
(Ladislav Nádaši)
(12 Februrary 1866 – 2 July 1940)

Vladimír Petrík
Institute for Slovak Literature SAV Bratislava

BOOKS: *Adam Šangala* (Turčiansky Sv. Martin: Matica slovenská, 1925);

Krpčeky sv. Floriána (Žilina: Učiteľské kníhkupectvo a nakladateľstvo O. Trávniček, 1925);

Mia. Komédia v troch dejstvách (Turčiansky Sv. Martin: Kníhtlačiarsky účastinársky spolok, 1925);

Wieniawského legenda (Prague: Leopold Mazáč, 1927);

Z dávnych časov (Žilina: Učiteľské kníhkupectvo a nakladateľstvo O. Trávniček, 1927);

Svätopluk (Prague: Družstevní práce, 1928);

Cesta životom (Turčiansky Sv. Martin: Matica slovenská, 1930);

Itália (Turčiansky Sv. Martin: Matica slovenská, 1931);

Kozinský mlyn (Žilina: Učiteľské nakladateľstvo O. Trávniček, 1931);

Kuruci; historická rozprávka (Turčiansky Sv. Martin: Matica slovenská, 1931);

Alina Orságová (Prague: Leopold Mazáč, 1934);

Medzi nimi (Turčiansky Sv. Martin: Matica slovenská, 1934);

S duchom času (Turčiansky Sv. Martin: Matica slovenská, 1937).

Editions and Collections: *Sobrané spisy L. Nádašiho-Jégého,* 7 volumes (Turčiansky Sv. Martin: Matica slovenská, 1943–1949);

Kuruci a iné rozprávky (Bratislava: Slovenské vydavateľstvo krásnej literatúry, 1955);

Spisy, 6 volumes (Bratislava: Slovenské vydavateľstvo krásnej literatúry, 1956–1960);

Wieniawského legenda (Bratislava: Tatran, 1971);

Výhody spoločenského života (Bratislava: Tatran, 1979);

Medzi nimi (Bratislava: Tatran, 1981);

Človek a literatúra, Spisy VIII (Bratislava: Tatran, 1983), pp. 203–345.

Edition in English: "Wieniawski's Legend," selected and translated by Andrew Cincura, in *An Anthology of Slovak Literature* (Riverside, Cal.: University Hardcovers, 1962).

Jégé (Ladislav Nádaši) in 1928

Jégé is the founder of Slovak historical fiction. His literary identity crystallized in the period of realism and naturalism, but he wrote the overwhelming majority of his works between the two world wars. In his historical novels and novellas he depicted soberly, perhaps even starkly, many stages of Slovak history and, in doing so, indirectly took issue with patriotic historical Romanticism. He was an expert on human nature, and the essence of his art lies in his drawing of characters. His handling of plot and structure is undistinguished, as is his style.

Jégé was born Ladislav Nádaši on 12 February 1866 in the north of Slovakia in the poor region called Orava, which has given the country many of its outstanding writers—including Martin Kukučín (1860–1928), Milo Urban (1904–1982), and the poet Pavol Országh Hviezdoslav (1849–1921). Before the birth of the Czechoslovak Republic in 1918 Slovakia belonged to the Kingdom of Hungary, itself part of the Austro-Hungarian dual monarchy. Hungary was a state composed of many ethnic groups and nationalities, but the Hungarians (Magyars) were dominant and endeavored to make of the kingdom a monolingual state; to that end they stifled the development of the other nations. They abolished the schools of minorities and introduced a unified Magyar educational system throughout the land. For this reason almost the whole of Slovak literature up to 1918 is anti-Hungarian in tone and animated by the idea of nationalism. One of the few exceptions is, in fact, the work of Jégé. (The pseudonym came from the initials of an earlier nom de plume, Ján Grob, under which he had published his early prose endeavors at the turn of the century.)

Ladislav's father, Anton, was a lawyer and, for a long time, mayor of the town of Dolný Kubín (where Jégé was born) and manager of a local bank. He had eleven children, Ladislav being the fifth. Anton Nádaši was a liberal, and although he had changed his original surname of Odrobiňák to the Hungarian Nádaši, he considered himself a Slovak, albeit one who bore no grudges toward the Hungarians. He did not bring up his children in inordinate patriotism but rather encouraged them toward practical skills. He insisted that they—like him—should know foreign languages (Ladislav studied not only Hungarian and German, but also English, French, and Italian). Dolný Kubín was the seat of a župa, or county, and the hub of political life in Orava.

After completing primary and secondary education, Ladislav left home in 1883 to study at the Faculty of Medicine of Charles University in Prague, from which he graduated with a doctorate in 1890. Bohemia was at that time a part of Austria and was suffering the onslaught of Ger-

manization. The Austrian coercion was, however, far more temperate than that of the Magyars, as is suggested, among other things, by the Czechs having had their own schools, from primary level to universities. The Prague university numbered among its students not only Slovaks but also Poles, Serbs, Croatians, and others, for the most part of Slav provenance.

In Prague Jégé became a member of Detvan, a fraternity that brought together Slovak students. Almost all of its members engaged in the study and writing of literature, and Jégé developed his writing talent as a member of this group. He published humorous short stories and novellas set in a small town milieu in the *Národné novíny* newspaper and the *Slovenské pohľady* review. However, on his return to Dolný Kubín, where he became a doctor, his writing ceased. He ascribed this cessation to calamity afflicting his family (his father's bank folded and their house burned down, obliging the family to move elsewhere) and constraining him to attend solely to his medical practice. The nationalist-oriented cultural community, however, suspected him of being drawn into the Magyar fold. After the birth of the independent Czechoslovak Republic in 1918, Jégé returned to literature and became one of the country's most prolific writers.

Even as a member of Detvan, Jégé's literary and intellectual development had taken a different tack from that of the majority of his contemporaries. While they had gravitated toward the close Slavonic literatures, his predilection—not least because of his knowledge of foreign languages—was for the writers of Western Europe. While others were impassioned by the work of Leo Tolstoy and his philosophy of not resisting evil with violence, Jégé's interest was captured by naturalism, which at the end of the nineteenth century was in vogue throughout Western Europe. (Two of Tolstoy's Slovak disciples, Albert Škarvan and Dušan Makovický, emerged from the Detvan circle. Makovický was Tolstoy's personal physician for many years and secretly wrote down Tolstoy's comments, which were published fifty years later.) In 1888 Jégé had given a talk for Detvan on Emile Zola's novel *Thérèse Raquin,* and in 1891 he published an article in the monthly cultural review *Slovenské pohľady* on the same writer. At that time Zola's novels were considered in Slovakia (and in Central and Eastern Europe as a whole) to be little short of pornography and were condemned, above all, on moral grounds. Jégé considered them a literary phenomenon and highly prized the writer's attempt to make an honest statement that embraced those areas of life that had previously been taboo. Jégé's weltanschauung–like that of Zola–had sprung from positivism and philosophical aspects of the natural sciences of the time. Although later he tempered this austere view, Jégé regarded man as the final link of biological development and took pleasure in referring to him as "the king of beasts." Jégé saw people in two groups: in one group were those who surrendered without inhibition to their "natural" essence and allowed themselves to be transported by their instincts and passions; in the other group were those who transcended this essence by dint of will and were guided by reason and conscience. Jégé assigned the first group to the sphere of "nature," the second to the sphere of "culture." This conviction became the intellectual bedrock of his body of works.

In his first works–those written at the turn of the century–Jégé's outlook on life was manifested only in fragments and did not develop fully until his return to literature after 1918. In 1922 he published in *Slovenské pohľady* his historical novella "Wieniawského legenda" (translated as "Wieniawski's Legend," 1962), which appeared in a book with other novellas in 1927. The story is set in Poland in the last third of the seventeenth century at the time when Jan Sobiesky was fighting against the Turks. Jégé says that the work was prompted by his experience of hearing a composition by the Polish violinist and composer Henryk Wieniawski (1835–1880). Its subject is both violence and barbarity (embodied in the hordes of soldiers roaming the land pillaging and killing) and the love between two young people. At the heart of the story are two characters: the brutish soldier Colonel Tomajka and the young and learned aristocrat, Julián. The author instigates between the characters a conflict between feral violence on the one hand and culture and erudition on the other; between inhumanity and humanity. In the story humanity prevails–but the victory fails to ring true in artistic terms. Jégé's view of history is that of a skeptic and pessimist. He sees history on the level of violence; there is no room within it for lofty ideals, patriotism, and higher principles. And if there is, then only as an exception. Critics gave "Wieniawského legenda" a positive reception because it brought a new representation of the past, one more faithful than that provided by other works, which drew mostly on historical background. The critic Štefan Krčméry wrote: "In the first lines you sense that the writer has found his truest genre."

Dust jacket for Jégé's 1925 historical novel set in the Hungarian Kingdom during the seventeenth century

In the novel *Adam Šangala* (1925) Jégé moves forward in time to the beginning of the seventeenth century, a period of feudal lords and serfs and one of religious tension and strife between Catholics and Protestants in the Hungarian Kingdom at the start of a process of re-Catholicization, which brought with it the reconversion of feudal lords through corruption. When his father, who poached in the lord's chase, is hanged, Adam leaves his home and Orava, traverses the whole of Slovakia, and experiences various trials before settling in Trnava (then a center of culture) and working his way up from common village lad to respectable citizen. However, he helps to get a Lutheran pastor, Konôpka, out of prison (the latter having previously rendered him the same service) and dies on the gallows.

For the author, Adam's wanderings are not least a pretext for acquainting the reader with various social milieus, as was customary in the tradition of the picaresque novel or the bildungsroman. The result is a prepossessing tableau of life at the time rendered in dramatic shorthand. The errant Adam is joined by Konôpka, and a relationship of teacher and pupil develops between them. Adam, a child nurtured by life alone, changes under Konôpka's influence, delivering himself from the realm of "nature" and progressing toward the realm of "culture." Illustrative of this change is Adam's altruistic act of liberating Konôpka from prison. Konôpka himself undergoes no change: he is a fixed character. He has studied in Germany and Italy, where he has assimilated a higher culture. Jégé, a disciple of the naturalists and Zola, who ascribed to the material environment a direct influence on human consciousness and intellectual outlook, as a matter of course sent his positive characters where they could achieve a higher level of education and, hence, of culture. The author does, however, engineer a test for Konôpka that he must undergo and pass. Konôpka falls in love with a married woman (who returns his love) with the result that within him the "biological" man is brought into conflict with the moral identity. Jégé resolves the conflict in favor of the moral viewpoint. *Adam Šangala* received the prestigious State Prize for 1925.

The early Middle Ages and the first state of the Danubian Slavs is the setting for *Svätopluk* (1928), which takes its title from the king of Great Moravia in the ninth century. This state extended over an area now occupied by Slovakia, Bohemia, Moravia, and part of Hungary. Svätopluk waged war against the Franks and succeeded in wrestling from them a significant degree of autonomy. He united the Slav tribes in the Danube plain and established an extensive empire that collapsed after his death. For Slovaks, suffering under Hungarian rule, he became an idol and a paragon. From the outset Jégé avoided straightforward history and put ordinary people, rather than historical figures, at the center of his novel. The work was intended to bolster awareness of history in Slovakia. However, Jégé conceived Svätopluk as a cruel feudal lord who employs all means (including murder and treachery) to strengthen his own power and thrust outward the frontiers of his empire. On the other hand, the author also endows him with features of a great reformer and unifier. Jégé sends Svätopluk on what might be termed a *wanderjahr* (year of wandering) to the center of the Byzantine Empire, Constantinople, there to master modern ways of state governance to be applied in Great Moravia. Jégé thus united

in Svätopluk the characteristics of ruthless dictator and rational statesman.

The author conceived the first parts of the novel on a generous, epic scale—studying various historical sources—only then to founder midstream. Aware of the unwieldiness of the subject, he gave the novel the subtitle "tableaux from his life." The conclusion is dramatic: Svätopluk kills his mistress Jarslava, and then he perishes at the hands of his son. But of the crucial historical feats of Svätopluk, there is nothing. Jégé clearly was unable to implant his "history of particular men's lives" into the setting of the traditional historical novel, as readers might have anticipated. The novel fell short of the expectations of its initiator, Štefan Krčméry, who, nevertheless, was among those to evaluate it favorably: "Dr. Nádaši has his own way of looking at the world. In many respects willful, you might say. Well, now he has conjured up from the events of the ninth century a semblance that is individual and willful. It will dazzle you and stun you and you would both caress it and fight it. This is a quality possessed for the most part by works of art that are truly vital." *Svätopluk*, too, was awarded the State Prize.

Historical themes continued to attract Jégé in the 1930s, but in the novel *Cesta životom* (The Journey through Life, 1930) he opted to treat his own life. He returned to the time when he was growing up in Dolný Kubín and to his later practice as a doctor. He captured in the small county town and its surroundings life as it unfolded in the last two decades of the nineteenth century and first decade of the twentieth. Thus, he offered a cross section, once more, via an errant hero, albeit one who, on this occasion, ventures only within the confines of the town through various social environments as he canvasses for votes to the local council. From the recesses of his memory come flooding back people and scenes that Jégé himself experienced as a doctor with access to every household, from the nobility to the peasantry. If he had experienced with *Svätopluk* a difficult gestation, the opposite was true here: "nothing has been as easily written as this. This is something quite different, where I do not have to wrestle with historicity and the like. When I have a scene in my head, I dash it down on paper and it writes itself."

The little town of Dolný Kubín was home to the county administration. In the semifeudal Hungarian Kingdom, where the upper classes had many privileges, the principal holders of administrative functions (from the sheriff down)

Jégé's grave in Dolný Kubín

were members of the lesser aristocracy or gentry. Supposedly unremunerated, in reality they demanded bribes. Corruption assumed the most diverse hues and was accompanied by a blanket demoralization of public life, which left almost no stratum of the populace untouched. The narrator of *Cesta životom* is a young clerk eager to become one of the "masters," a class into which he was not born. He is a moral recreant who scales the bureaucratic ladder with the help of women (individual chapters bear the names of women) and unquestioning obedience. He does not hesitate to disown his nationality if doing so furthers his career, changing his Slovak surname Svoreý to the Magyarized form Szvorényi. As his hero's antithesis, the writer has provided the doctor Búroš, a man of strict principles who is an exception in this moral mire. If in *Adam Šangala* the relationship between Adam and Konôpka was one of pupil and teacher, in *Cesta životom* that between Svoreý and Búroš is one of accused and arbiter. Búroš is, in fact, Svoreý's conscience. The critics called *Cesta životom* the most pessimistic of Slovak books. There is, indeed, little that is uplifting in the image of the decaying world of Magyarized social climbers. The criterion with which the author distinguishes the positive from the negative is not one of rationality, as was the case in the works of others, but of ethics: Jégé evaluates people on the basis of morality. But, in fact, national sentiment is subsumed within this morality: the decent man does not renounce his nationality. As with all Jégé's other works, this novel is a mordant correction to the received view of the past of the nation and a condemnation of other writing for its excessive idealization of reality.

S duchom času (With the Spirit of the Time, 1937) is a loose sequel to *Cesta životom* in which the writer reflects upon the way in which the Slovak gentry integrated itself into the new climate after 1918. He also observes the heightened social problems and sees their solution in good deeds, or altruism. The book of novellas *Medzi nimi* (Among Them, 1934) traces relations between man and wife and within the family as a whole. Here the author engages several delicate subjects—those of so-called free love, including sexual relations between members of the family—that provoked outrage in ecclesiastical circles and in the puritan-minded section of society. Love and eroticism among college students is the theme of the short novel *Alina Orságová*, published in 1934, in which the author drew upon the six months he had spent in Bratislava working in health administration. Among his other historical fiction worthy of note is a collection of novellas titled *Itália* (1931) in which Jégé depicts many love stories against a backdrop of cruel practices in Italian medieval city-republics.

Jégé is also the author of a large number of humorous stories that are set—for the most part—in the village milieu he knew well as a result of his visits as a doctor to the nearby communities. He renders the idiosyncratic village characters with a fond humor but also, occasionally, with irony. These comic pieces—for the most part unpretentious as literature—were published in illustrated magazines and almanacs. Virtually the entirety of Jégé's work from the 1930s reveals an ebbing of his creative powers and frequently a lack of surefootedness. Jégé also wrote two plays of only minor importance and articles on literature in which he was, in particular, critical of young writers.

Jégé died of a heart attack in Dolný Kubín on 2 July 1940. His work constitutes a departure from the canon of realism toward naturalism. In an unpropitious social climate, when literature reflected above all the tragic fate of the nation, a literary stream disposed to the "biological" had no chance of developing fully. In this sense Jégé went against the current. His emphasis on the common human factor led to universalism, and in this pursuit he was ahead of his time—a time that took national particularity as its watchword. Jégé's contribution to Slovak literature is of a distinct stamp.

Biographies:

Ján Gregorec, *Dielo L. N. Jégého* (Bratislava: Slovenský spisovateľ, 1956);

Ivan Kusý, *Mladý Ladislav Nádaši* (Dolný Kubín, 1966);

Vladimír Petrík, *Človek v Jégého diele* (Bratislava: Tatran, 1979).

References:

Mikuláš Gaček, "Rovesník," *Slovenské pohľady*, 82, no. 2 (1966): 60–70;

Peter Huba and Vladimír Petrík, *O diele Ladislava Nádašiho Jégého* (Martin: Osveta pre Oravské múzeum v Dolnom Kubíne, 1987);

Alexander Matuška, ed., *Jégé v kritike a spomienkach (zborník)* (Bratislava: Slovenské vydavateľstvo krásnej literatúry, 1959);

Vladimír Petrík, "Ku genéze svetonázorovej koncepcie Jégého," *Slovenská literatúra*, 23 (1976): 377–404;

Petrík, *Literárne dielo Dr. Ladislava Nádašiho-Jégého* (Martin: Osveta, 1956);

Petrík, "O historizme v Jégého diele," *Slovenská literatúra*, 13 (1966): 113–122;

Viera Zemberová, "Jégého renascimento," *Slovenská literatúra*, 26 (1979): 332–340.

Papers:

Jégé's papers are in the Literárny archív Matice slovenskej, Martin.

Attila József

(11 April 1905 – 3 December 1937)

Ferenc Tóth

Ferenc Kölcsey Pedagogical Institute of the Reformed Church

BOOKS: *A szépség koldusa* (Szeged: Koroknay, 1922);

Nem én kiáltok (Szeged: Koroknay, 1925);

Nincsen apám, se anyám (Budapest: Genius, 1929);

Ki a faluba!, by József and Dániel Fábián (Budapest, 1930);

Döntsd a tőkét, ne siránkozz (Budapest: Új Európa, 1931);

Külvárosi éj (Budapest: A. Szerző, 1932);

Medvetánc (Budapest: Révai, 1934);

Nagyon fáj (Budapest: Cserépfalvi, 1936);

Költészet és nemzet, edited by Pál Sándor (Budapest: Dokumentum Könyvek, 1941);

Irodalom és szocializmus. Válogatott esztétikai tanulmányok, edited by László Forgács (Budapest: Kossuth, 1967);

Szabad-ötletek jegyzéke, edited by Béla Stoll (Budapest: Atlantisz, 1995).

Editions and Collections: *Összes versei és válogatott írásai*, edited by Andor Németh (Budapest: Cserépfalvi, 1938);

Összes versei és műfordításai, edited by György Bálint (Budapest: Cserépfalvi, 1945);

Összes verse, edited by László Kardos (Budapest: Révai, 1950);

Összes művei, 3 volumes, edited by József Waldapfel and Miklós Szabolcsi (Budapest: Akadémiai, 1952–1958)—comprises volume 1, *Versek 1922–1928;* volume 2, *Versek 1929–1937;* volume 3, *Cikkek, tanulmányok, vázlatok;*

Válogatott művei, edited by Erzsébet Szabolcsi (Budapest: Szépirodalmi, 1952);

Összes versei és műfordításai, edited by Szabolcsi (Budapest: Magyar Helikon, 1963);

Összes művei: Novellák, önvallomások, műfordítások. Pótlások az 1–3. kötetekhez, edited by Erzsébet Fehér and Szabolcsi (Budapest: Akadémiai, 1967);

Összes versei, 2 volumes, edited by Béla Stoll (Budapest: Akadémiai, 1984);

Tanulmányok és cikkek 1923–1930, 2 volumes (Budapest: Osiris, 1995)—comprises volume 1, *Mag-*

Attila József

yarázatok, edited by Tverdota; volume 2, *Szövegek*, edited by Horváth.

Editions in English: *Poems*, translated by René Bonnerjea (Budapest: British Embassy Mimeograph, 1965);

Poems, translated by Michael Beevor and others, edited by Thomas Kabdebo (London: Danubia, 1966);

"Behold I Have Found My Land . . .," "I Want to Breathe!," "The Pain Is Sharp," and "Grief," translated by Vernon Watkins, in *New Writing of East Europe*, edited by George Gömöri and

Charles Newman (Chicago: Quadrangle Books, 1968), pp. 161–166;

Selected Poems and Texts, translated by John Bátki, edited by Gömöri and James Atlas (Cheadle Hulme, U.K.: Carcanet Press, 1973);

Poems, translated by Anton N. Nyerges, edited by Joseph M. Ertavy-Baráth (Buffalo, N.Y.: Hungarian Cultural Foundation, 1973);

Winter Night: Selected Poems of Attila József, translated by Bátki (Oberlin, Ohio: Oberlin College Press, 1997).

In his poetry Attila József attempted to reach a synthesis of the most important intellectual, ideological, and lyrical aspirations of his era. Influenced early in his career by the revolutionary vision and symbolist techniques of Endre Ady, the preeminent poet of the first decades of the twentieth century, József emerged as the most prominent voice within Hungarian poetry during the period between the two world wars. Experimenting with a wide variety of poetic styles ranging from expressionism to surrealism, József combined a distinct sensitivity and vivid imagination with a passionate commitment to the ideals of human dignity and social justice. József published his first poems at age seventeen in the prestigious literary journal *Nyugat* (West) and remained a productive and innovative poet despite his intense personal anguish and the gradual deterioration of his mental stability. His popularity continued to increase following his death. His poetry played an instrumental role in the renewal of Hungarian verse after World War II and has since been translated into several languages.

Attila József was born on 11 April 1905 in Budapest to Aron Iosifu, a Hungarian-Romanian soapmaker who changed his name to the Hungarian Áron József, and to Borbála Pőcze, a housemaid and laundress. He had two older sisters, Jolán and Etelka. He was three when his father left for the United States, and for years József believed his father had died there before he was able to reunite the family. József's mother was unable to provide for the children, and in 1910 Etelka and Attila were placed in the care of a peasant family in the countryside for two years. The experience was traumatic for József and resulted in a pronounced sense of isolation and alienation. Afterward, when his mother became seriously ill, she had to ask friends to look after her children, and for a short time József and his sisters were placed in an orphanage. Often without a permanent home, the children attended various schools and regularly had to work to help support the family. József made his first suicide attempt at the age of nine.

Following the death of his mother in 1919 József was placed under the guardianship of his sister's husband, Ödön Makai, a lawyer. This fact made his relative social rise possible, but further distorted his sense of self-worth and importance. Humiliated that his guardian would not allow him to acknowledge his sister as a relative because of her family's higher social status, József retreated into marginality. During the summer of 1920 József worked as a cabin boy; then, with the help of his guardian, he attended the local grammar school in Makó. He proved to be a gifted student and began to pursue his early interest in poetry, often reciting his poems before the literary and debating society. Realizing his talent, József's teachers provided both encouragement and support. In addition, József had the good fortune at the beginning of 1922 to become acquainted with Gyula Juhász, an outstanding lyrical poet who was residing at the time in Makó and with whom József developed a lifelong friendship. Juhász was directly responsible for the publication later that year of József's first volume of poetry, *A szépség koldusa* (Beggar of Beauty), the success of which was partly because of the warm preface written by Juhász, in which he refers to József as "the poet in God's grace" and praises him as an outstanding talent "who will belong to the best and most true of the future generation of poets."

The poems of *A szépség koldusa* show the influence of Juhász as well as other representative poets of the literary journal *Nyugat,* as József adopts and individualizes their voices with maturity and self-assurance. This feature plays an important role in the organization and development of his artistic experience. Most of the poems recall the populist trend in poetry, notably the poems of Sándor Petőfi and the ballads of János Arany, which dominated Hungarian literature of the mid-nineteenth century. Also noticeable in the volume is the influence of Árpád Tóth—for example, both József and Tóth created a poem beginning with the description of a forest at the end of day. However, in "Homály borult az erdőre" (Gloom Covers the Forest, 1921) József interpolates a new motif at the end of the poem: in the middle of the forest a bird and a factory praise a new beginning together. In "Sóhaj" (Sigh, 1921) József imitates the poet Dezső Kosztolányi, and in the intentionally artistic rhymes of "Üdvözlés" (Greeting, 1922) he invites comparison to the poetry of Mihály Babits. "Ösapám" (My Forefather, 1922) is an attempt on József's part to attain the genre technique developed by Juhász; the objective description shows a parallel with Juhász's 1922 sonnet "Berzsenyi." In other poems, for example in "Spleen," József incorporates the manifestations of decadence and the influence of Charles Baudelaire.

In January 1923, following the publication of *A szépség koldusa* and in part as a rebellion against the guardianship of his brother-in-law, József decided to leave school. As a result, he was deprived of all support and was thus forced to become a private tutor. His financial situation worsened over the next several months, and despite the publication in April of three of his poems in *Nyugat*, József became increasingly overwrought and despondent. Finding no solution to his despair, József again attempted suicide.

József once again turned to his writing as a means of solace, and he took part in the May celebration in Szeged of the twenty-fifth year of Juhász's literary career; at the festivities József dedicated his crown of sonnets "A kozmosz éneke" (The Song of the Cosmos) to Juhász. In the following month, for the occasion of a celebration in Makó, József completed the poem "Juhász Gyuláról való nóta" (Folk Song for Gyula Juhász). Afterward, under the guidance of two of his former tutors, he completed his grammar-school studies by passing a private exam, and later that year he graduated from secondary school. Meanwhile, he worked as a book solicitor and bank clerk. In January 1924, however, he was summoned to appear in court for writing the poem "Lázadó Krisztus" (Rebelling Christ), which had been published in the October issue of the journal *Kékmadár* (Bluebird). In the poem he confronts God as a new Christ and blames Him for not being just to people, not being able to understand their suffering. In July he was found guilty of "public abuse of God committed through the medium of the press." He was sentenced to eight months' imprisonment but was later acquitted before he was actually sent to prison. Articles were published both for and against him, and the poem was republished in *Népszava* (People's Voice). József tried to find employment but instead he began studies at the Szeged University, specializing in Hungarian and French literature and philosophy while continuing work on his second collection of poetry.

In January 1925 József published *Nem én kiáltok* (That's Not Me Shouting), which marked a new direction in his poetry. Influenced by Lajos Kassák and other avant-garde writers as well as the populist writer József Erdélyi, József created a type of peasant poetry similar in form and principle to folk ballads. Rebellion against social injustice appears in his poetry for the first time, as do the resentment and

József at age eleven

bitterness of the downtrodden and oppressed, as illustrated in "Szegény ember balladája" (Ballad of the Poor Man, 1924) in which a father decides to drown his newborn child in a pond rather than allow the king to take the child from the father's possession.

Kassák's influence is apparent not only in the peasant poems but also in József's attempts to write expressionistic poetry as well as free verse, but the experimental influences are kept within boundaries of a strict formality. In several poems József incorporated Kassák's technique of interrelated substructures, as in "Keserű" (Bitter, 1924) and "Erőének" (Power Song, 1922). In the title poem (1924; translated as "That's Not Me Shouting," 1973) two basic motifs are combined: the ideals of peacefulness, clarity, and weightlessness, and the realities of anarchist revolt as a means to achieve freedom. First, the individual seeks shelter from change and wants to mingle with the world. The desire for clarity is fulfilled in the act of turning toward others: "You wash yourself in vain, in others shall you be purified of pain." The smallest of all living things and the sphere of cosmic conformity interact: "Be as small as the edge of a leaf / You still won't fall through the sieve of the universal."

In March 1925 József published "Tiszta szívvel" (translated as "With a Pure Heart," 1973), in the daily local paper, *Szeged;* for many critics this poem represented a turning point in József's work and established the motif of a new postwar generation of poets: "Fatherless, Motherless / Godless, Homeless." The bitterness of a demoralized generation and its sense of loss and betrayal is portrayed with an accusatory plainness. The playfulness of the meter and the denotative language, on the other hand, demonstrate a longing for beauty and clarity. One of his professors, however, reacted angrily to the nihilism of this poem and announced that such a man would never become a teacher. So József decided to continue his studies in Vienna, where he became acquainted with leftist intellectual émigrés and avant-garde writers such as Kassák, Lajos Hatvany (who was a literary critic and patron of Hungarian writers), Béla Balázs, György Lukács, and Anna Lesznai (who later supported his studies financially); he also met Andor Németh, who came to have a major role in shaping József's aesthetics and his critical reputation as a poet.

With financial assistance from Lajos and Irén Hatvany, József was able to study at the Sorbonne during 1926 and 1927. Attracted to the ideology of anarchism, József for a short time joined the Union Anarchiste Communiste. He also became acquainted with the works of Karl Marx, and in early 1927 he met some of the leading French surrealists. Influenced by the work of medieval poet François Villon, József wrote poems in French and that summer spent one of the most peaceful periods of his life on the French Riviera. In the autumn of 1927 he returned to Budapest, and soon his poems were appearing in several of the leading literary periodicals, including *Népszava* (Folk's Voice), *A Toll* (The Pen), *Napló* (Diary), *Nyugat,* and the Transylvanian journal *Korunk* (Our Time). He continued his studies at the University of Budapest. However, he was again restricted by financial difficulties and did not take the primary examination.

During this time József also became infatuated with Luca Wallesz, the fifteen-year-old daughter of a painter, for whom he wrote several poems, notably "Tószunnyadó" (Pond Slumber), "Tedd a kezed" (Put Your Hand), and "Ringató" (Dandling), all in 1928. However, in early 1928 he met Márta Vágó, whose father, József Vágó, was a member of the

Hungarian radical Freemason intelligentsia. After a brief courtship during the summer, József asked her father for permission to marry her; her father agreed, but insisted on a period of probation. As a result, Márta was sent to study in London. In January 1929 József began working at the newly formed Hungarian Trading Institute. But the relationship with Márta Vágó broke up as a result of mutual alienation, and shortly afterward József suffered a nervous breakdown and was sent to a private asylum.

At this point József began to formulate his individual aesthetics, outlined initially in his essay "Ady vízió" (Ady Vision, 1929), in which he provides his interpretation of creativity: "Art is neither intuition, nor speculation. It is a different kind of spirituality. Let's call it: inspiration . . . inspiration (poetry) is the spirituality that brings about words and language." For József individual poems are meant to "merge together, as they are one in the whole of the universe. . . . The nation forms some common inspiration. Poetry is the magic of the name in the soul of the nation." József insists that the poet must remain committed to social and political purposefulness. Consequently, poetry and socialist conviction become interconnected.

In February 1929 József published *Nincsen apám, se anyám* (Fatherless, Motherless), a collection of highly charged and kinetic poems merging a broad spectrum of fragmentary elements with emotional intensity. Some of his major, valuable poems were published here for the first time. One of the works most characteristic of the shift in his poetic attitude is the cycle "Medáliák" (translated as "Medallions," 1927), written in 1927 and 1928. Instilled with revolutionary fervor, József's work was praised by Andor Németh and critic Aladár Komlós, but the reception of *Nincsen apám, se anyám* was generally mixed. László Németh wrote an extremely negative review of the volume for *Nyugat,* referring to the poetry as artificial and dishonest. In response József published a series of articles attacking some of the leading literary figures of the day, including Mihály Babits, Kassák, Zsigmond Móricz, and Áron Tamási. In effect, József's poetry reflected a personal transformation as his political views became increasingly radical. Searching for solutions in connection with social and ethnic problems, he desired the organic democracy of the peasantry and the industrious middle class. As a result of his debate with the periodical *Magyar Szemle* (Hungarian Review), József and Dániel Fábián produced a pamphlet titled *Ki a faluba!* (Out Into the Village, 1930), a provocative work that became extremely controversial for its glorification of the peasantry and condemnation of urbanism. In that same year József became a member of the illegal Communist Party, through which he met Judit Szántó. József and Szántó lived together from the autumn of 1930 until the spring of 1936.

At the beginning of 1931 József published an essay titled "Irodalom és szocializmus" (Literature and Socialism), followed shortly thereafter by his fourth volume of poetry, *Döntsd a tőkét, ne siránkozz* (Chop at the Roots). "Irodalom és szocializmus" was meant to be an elaboration of a collectivist aesthetics with the primary focus on the proletariat. The object of class struggle is thus subordinated to the laws of poetry. József advocates the need for political poetry, so that the modern poet can versify political commitment and call attention to revolutionary action. The poet can express social problems in such a way that abstraction blends into the complexity of the work, as illustrated in poems such as "Favágó" (translated as "Woodcutter," 1997) and "Tiszazug" (translated as "Tiszazug," 1973), both written in 1929, and notably in "Füst" (Smoke, 1930), in which personal destiny and cosmic existence intertwine. Incorporating the ancient and profound qualities of folk literature, József transcended the mystical world of the ballads, the minstrels, and the Kalevala, as illustrated in the poems "Regös ének" (Minstrel Song) and "Bánat" (translated as "Grief," 1968) both written in 1930.

The militancy as well as the condescending nature of the poems produced a generally negative critical reaction to *Döntsd a tőkét, ne siránkozz*, even from József's former supporter Andor Németh. Copies of the volume were confiscated, and József was accused in the press of subversive activity and obscenity. Unperturbed by the criticism, József instead began to expand the scope of his personal aesthetics by further exploration of his interest in Freudianism. Interconnecting the ideologies of Marx and Sigmund Freud enabled József to explore the depth of personal experience and the anatomy of revolutionary ideology, as illustrated in the essays "Egyéniség és valóság" (Individuality and Reality, 1932) and "Az ifjúság nemi problémái" (The Sexual Problems of Youth, 1931). At this same time he produced "A halálbüntetés elleni röpirat" (Pamphlet Against the Death Penalty, 1932), in which he objected to the execution of two Communist politicians, Imre Sallai and Sándor Fürst.

In his fifth volume of poetry, *Külvárosi éj* (Night in the Slums), published in October 1932, the full scope of József's poetical methodology emerged. The volume includes powerful poems of

Judit Szántó, with whom József lived from 1930 to 1936

social relevance, such as "Holt vidék" (translated as "The Wasteland," 1973) and the title poem (translated as "Night in the Slums," 1973), as well as poems that reunite man with the beauty of nature, as in "Ritkás erdö alatt" (Under Scanty Woods). Other poems, however, speak of disorientation and man's inability to establish a genuine relationship with the world around him, illustrated in poems such as "Fák" (Trees) and "Háló" (translated as "The Net," 1997), in which the disintegration of life is expressed as the common experience of man.

Andor Németh was among the first to realize the essence of the change in József's poetry and considered *Külvárosi éj* a work of major importance. The volume was also praised by both Zoltán Zelk and Zoltán Fábry, and the critic Jenő Dsida compared József's work to the earlier achievement of Ady. The majority of criticism was negative, however, and did not acknowledge the significance of

DÖNTSD A TŐKÉT, NE SIRÁNKOZZ

JÓZSEF ATTILA UJ VERSEI

új európa könyvtár

k i a d á s a

Title page for József's fourth collection of poetry, which was confiscated by the Hungarian government after the author was accused of subversive activity and obscenity

József's aesthetic awareness of life, ideology, and progression. There was a particularly insulting review in *Társadalmi Szemle* (Social Review), and as a result József began to distance himself from the Communist Party. Meanwhile, it had become increasingly difficult for József to maintain a living. He was living with Szántó, who essentially provided for both of them, but at times she too was out of work, and the odd jobs they did together were hardly enough for bare necessities.

As their relationship deteriorated, József was at the same time preparing his omnibus volume, *Medvetánc* (Bear's Dance, 1934), which comprises eighty-one poems, including what many consider his major poems: "Téli éjszaka" (translated as "Winter Night," 1973) and "Óda" (translated as "Ode," 1973), which were both written in 1933, and "Eszmélet" (translated as "Consciousness," 1973), written in 1934. "Téli éjszaka" brings to perfection the existentialist message of the poems from his previous volume, while "Óda" attempts to restore harmony

within man's troubled existence. "Eszmélet" evolves from the discord between intellect and emotion contrasted with the synthesis between the text of the poem and its signified lyrical self. The depth of József's personal anguish is revealed in the self-accusatory poem "Számvetés" (Account), written in 1933, and his never-ending search for reconciliation with the past is illustrated in poems such as "Egy kisgyerek sir" (translated as "A Child is Crying," 1997), written in 1933, and "Iszonyat" (translated as "Terror," 1997) and "Mama," both written in 1934. Through the process of creation József reaches a level of gentle acceptance and quiet resignation, as illustrated in the poem "Reménytelenül" (1933; translated as "Without Hope," 1973): "On the branch of nothingness sits my heart, shivering lonely without care, surrounded gently by stars that give it an occasional stare."

Although the volume received favorable notice from reviewers for the literary journal *Korunk* (Our Time) and the social-democratic *Szocializmus* (Socialism), it was generally unsuccessful. Again József found himself in financial difficulties that accentuated his hopelessness and depression. In the spring of 1935 he entered psychoanalysis with Edith Gyömrői, who treated József for schizophrenia and with whom he fell hopelessly in love. He was able to obtain some assistance from the Baumgarten Foundation, established by Hungarian-born German benefactor Franz Baumgarten, but it proved inadequate to meet his needs. At the end of 1936 he had a nervous breakdown and for a short time went into a private asylum with the financial support of Hatvany.

In an effort to resume his career József founded and began to publish the literary journal *Szép Szó* (Fine Word) with Pál Ignotus. In addition, he renewed his connections with the urban and radical friends from whom he had earlier distanced himself, as well as with Márta Vágó. He also established a personal acquaintance with the Hungarian composer Béla Bartók. In addition, he was elected a member of the La Fontaine Literary Society. The political and intellectual circumstances of the era, however, as well as József's mental constitution, led to his alienation and to the demand to meditate on a more universal level about his personal condition and the common cause. In his late poetry the struggle with nothingness becomes a primary motif. This period of József's poetry has three essential topics: love, public life, and a dialogue with his own fate—three opportunities to escape from the whirlpool of nonexistence and nothingness. This struggle brought about his most touching and complex poems.

In December 1936 József published the quintessence of the poems from the previous two-year period in the volume *Nagyon fáj* (It Hurts a Lot). The poems of *Nagyon fáj* are cathartic for József, easing the destructive power of his loneliness. "A Dunánál (1936, translated as "By the Danube"), "Thomas Mann üdvözlése" (1937, translated as "Welcome Thomas Mann"), and the sonnet cycle "Hazám" (My Country, 1937) are occasional verses in which individual consideration intervenes in the deliberation of the fate of the community. "Én nem tudtam" (I Didn't Know, 1935), "Mint gyermek" (Like a Child, 1935), and "Bün" (1936; translated as "Guilt," 1973) envision the essence of a failed life in some secret, unfathomable sin. In some poems, reminiscent of Franz Kafka, he relies on the superiority of the autonomous personality who turns away from God. In other poems he finds this secret sin in childhood experiences, notably in the rebellion against the father. In his interpretation, rebellion burns the world to ashes; all one can do in the trap of this incomprehensible world is to wait passively for the miracle of mercy. József unveils the domain of the psyche through Freudianism—waiting for answers from his instincts, dreams, and memories from childhood. He dedicates "Amit szívedbe rejtesz" (What You Hide in Your Heart, 1936) to the then eighty-year-old Freud.

The father motif is connected to József's notion of God, while the mother motif is connected with love. He addresses his dead mother as he would an unfaithful lover in "Kései sirató" (1935; translated as "A Belated Lament," 1973), and he turns to his lovers as he would to a protecting mother. The title poem, "Nagyon fáj" (1936; translated as "It Hurts a Lot," 1973), which he wrote to Gyömrői, also has an abusive yet painfully beseeching tone. In both poems the lyric self becomes infused with the desolation of human existence.

His motifs also include elements of religious poetry. In the first creative period of his art, many of his religious poems were addressed to God with childish directness and playfulness. In his later poetry he again seeks a relationship with God, notably in the poems "Kész a leltár" (1936; translated as "I Have Done My Reckoning"), "Nem emel föl" (1937; translated as "No One Can Lift Me," 1973)—in which the poet, preparing himself for death, cries out for mercy from a God-like figure—and "Bukj föl az árból" (Arise From the Tide, 1937). In his last months József tried desperately to salvage his life; however, all his efforts ended in failure. He unsuccessfully applied for a clerk's job at a private office, and a lecture given with Németh about the psychology of poetic creation was poorly received. He believed that work on poems might rescue his life. "Ars poetica" (1937) unites the individual existence and the domain of poetry. In the poem "Költőnk és kora" (Our Poet and His Time, 1937) the material reality of poetry can be a certainty in the domain of fragmentary Nothingness. In addition, he entered an intense but unrealistic relationship with Flóra Kozmutza, who worked with József doing psychological testing on him. In his last poems—"Majd" (Some Day), "Le vagyok győzve" (I Am Defeated), "Talán eltünök hirtelen" (translated as "I May Suddenly Disappear), "Karóval jöttél" (translated as "You Brought a Stake," 1997), and "Ime, hát megleltem hazámat" (translated as "I Finally Found My Home," 1973)—József seemingly agonized over the meaning of life and the future of his existence in the world.

On 4 November 1937 József's sister Jolán moved him from a private asylum to her boardinghouse at Balatonszárszó. His mental health, however, continued to deteriorate, and he became increasingly detached and withdrawn. Sensing himself a burden to his sister and incapable of overcoming the depth of his despair, on 3 December he jumped to his death in front of a passing freight train. Obituaries praised him as one of Hungary's greatest poets, and, based primarily on the notoriety surrounding his death, József has been elevated to the status of a cult figure in modern Hungarian literature.

Letters:

Válogatott levelezése, edited by Erzsébet Fehér (Budapest: Akadémiai, 1976).

Bibliographies:

Albert Tezla, *Hungarian Authors: A Bibliographical Handbook* (Cambridge, Mass.: Belknap Press of Harvard University Press, 1970), pp. 262–269;

Ernő Reguli, *József Attila. Bibliográfia* (Budapest: Fővárosi Szabó Ervin Könyvtár, 1975);

József Attila kéziratai és levelezése. Katalógus, compiled by Judit M. Róna (Budapest: Petőfi Irodalmi Múzeum, 1980).

Biographies:

László Bányai, *Négyszemközt József Attilával* (Budapest: Körmendy, 1943);

Jolán József, *József Attila élete* (Budapest: Szépirodalmi, 1955);

Judit Szántó and Endréné Kovács, eds. *József Attila* (Budapest: Magyar Helikon, 1958);

Miklós Szabolcsi, *Fiatal életek indulója. József Attila pályakezdése* (Budapest: Akadémiai, 1963);

László Balogh, *József Attila* (Budapest: Gondolat, 1969);

Márta Vágó, *József Attila* (Budapest: Szépirodalmi, 1975);

Miklós Szabolcsi, *Érik a fény. József Attila élete és pályája 1923–1927* (Budapest: Akadémiai, 1977);

Szántó, *Napló és visszaemlékezés* (Budapest: Múzsák Petőfi Irodalmi Múzeum, 1986);

Gyuláné Illyés, *József Attila utolsó hónapjairól* (Budapest: Szépirodalmi, 1987);

Andor Németh, *József Attila* (Budapest: Akadémiai, 1991);

Szabolcsi, *Kemény a menny. József Attila élete és pályája 1927–1930* (Budapest: Akadémiai, 1992);

Szabolcsi, *Kész a leltár. József Attila élete és pályája 1930–1937* (Budapest: Akadémiai, 1998).

References:

Péter Agárdi, *Torlódó múlt. József Attila és kortársai* (Budapest: T-Twins Kiadó, 1995);

Zsuzsa Beney, *József Attila-tanulmányok* (Budapest: Szépirodalmi, 1989);

Antal Bókay, Ferenc Jádi, and András Stark, *Köztetek lettem én bolond* (Budapest: Magvető, 1982);

László Bokor and György Tverdota, eds., *Kortársak József Attiláról 1–3* (Budapest: Akadémiai, 1987);

Dániel Fábián, *József Attiláról* (Budapest: Kossuth, 1974);

György D. Fenyő and György Gelniczky, *Költőnk és korunk. Tanulmányok József Attiláról*, 3 volumes (Budapest: Országos Pedagógiai Intézet, 1983);

László Forgács, *József Attila esztétikája (Tanulmánygyűjtemény)* (Budapest: Magvető, 1965);

László Garai, *Elvegyültem és kiváltam* (Budapest: T-Twins Kiadó, 1993);

Ervin Gyertyán, *Költőnk és kora. József Attila költészete és esztétikája* (Budapest: Szépirodalmi, 1963);

Béla Horváth, *Egy ki márványból rak falut. József Attila és a folklór* (Szekszárd: Babits, 1992);

Iván Horváth and György Tverdota, eds., *Miért fáj ma is? Az ismeretlen József Attila* (Budapest: Balassi Kiadó, Közgazdasági és Jogi Kiadó, 1992);

András Lengyel, *A modernitás antinómiái. József Attila-tanulmányok* (Budapest: Tekintet-könyvek, 1996);

John Lotz, *The Structure of the Sonetti a Corona of Attila József* (Stockholm: Almqvist and Wiksell, 1965);

Tamás Miklós, *József Attila metafizikája* (Budapest: Magvető, 1988);

Béla G. Németh, *7 kísérlet a kései József Attiláról* (Budapest: Tankönyvkiadó);

Sándor Scheiber, *József Attila istenes verseinek tárgy-és képzettörténeti háttere* (Budapest: Magyar Irodalomtörténeti Társaság, 1946);

Miklós Szabolcsi, ed., *József Attila emlékkönyv* (Budapest: Szépirodalmi, 1957);

Szabolcsi and Edit Erdődy, eds., *József Attila útjain. Verselemzések* (Budapest: Kossuth, 1980);

Klára Széles, "*. . . minden szervem óra . . .*" *József Attila motívumrendszeréről* (Budapest: Magvető, 1980);

Lajos Sándor Szigeti, *A József Attila-i teljességigény* (Budapest: Magvető, 1988);

György Szőke, "*Ür a lelkem,*" *A kései József Attila* (Budapest: Párbeszéd, 1992);

József Tasi, ed., *A Dunánál. Tanulmányok József Attiláról* (Budapest: Petőfi Irodalmi Múzeum, 1995);

Tasi, *József Attila és a Bartha Miklós Társaság* (Budapest: Ecriture-Galéria, 1995);

Gábor Török, *József Attila-kommentárok* (Budapest: Gondolat, 1976);

György Tverdota, *Ihlet és eszmélet* (Budapest: Gondolat, 1987);

Tverdota, *A komor föltámadás titka. A József Attila-kultusz születése* (Budapest: Pannonica, 1998).

Papers:

The major collections of Attila József's papers are in the Petőfi Irodalmi Múzeum Kézirattára, the Országos Széchenyi Könyvtár Kézirattára, and the Magyar Tudományos Akadémia Kézirattára, all in Budapest, and in the József Attila Múzeum in Makó.

Frigyes Karinthy

(25 June 1887 – 29 August 1938)

Gábor Palkó
Eötvös University, Budapest

BOOKS: *Ballada a néma férfiakról* (Budapest: Athenaeum, 1912);

Együgyű lexikon (Békéscsaba: Tevan, 1912);

Esik a hó. Novellák (Budapest: Nyugat, 1912);

Görbe tükör (Budapest: Athenaeum, 1912);

Így írtok ti. Irodalmi karikaturak (Budapest: Athenaeum, 1912);

Találkozás egy fiatalemberrel (Budapest: Athenaeum, 1913);

Budapesti emlék. Meséskönyv. Képeskönyv (Budapest: Athenaeum, 1913);

Grimasz. Szatirák és humoreszkek (Budapest: Athenaeum, 1914);

Írások írókról. Kritikák (Békéscsaba: Tevan, 1914);

Beszéljünk másról. Ujabb karcolatok (Budapest: Athenaeum, 1915);

Két hajó. Novellák (Budapest: Athenaeum, 1915);

A repülő ember. Wittman Viktor emléke (Budapest: Athenaeum, 1915);

A vándor katona. Ünnepesti történet (Budapest: Athenaeum, 1915);

Aki utoljára nevet (Budapest: Galántai Gyula, 1916);

Holnap reggel. Tragikomédia három felvonásban (Békéscsaba: Tevan, 1916);

Ó nyájas olvasó! Mindenféle dolog (Budapest: Dick Manó, 1916);

Tanár úr kérem. Képek a középiskolából (Budapest: Dick Manó, 1916); translated by István Farkas as *Please Sir!* (Budapest: Corvina, 1968);

Utazás Faremidóba. Gulliver ötödik útja (Budapest: Athenaeum, 1916);

Így láttátok ti (Budapest: Dick Manó, 1917);

Legenda az ezerarcú lélekről és egyéb elbeszélések (Budapest: Lampel Róbert, 1917);

A bűvös szék. Komédia egy felvonásban (Budapest: Athenaeum, 1918);

Hogy tesz a gránát? (Budapest: Tábori Levél, 1918);

Krisztus és Barabbás. Háboru és béke (Budapest: Dick Manó, 1918);

Gyilkosok. Novellák (Budapest: Dick Manó, 1919);

Kacsalábon forgó kastély (Budapest: Kultúra, 1920);

Frigyes Karinthy, 1918

Kolumbuc tojása. Az álomkép (Budapest: Kultúra, 1920);

Capilláría. Regény (Budapest: Kultúra, 1921);

Hököm-színház. Kis tréfák és jelenetek (Budapest: Athenaeum, 1921);

Jelbeszéd. Válogatott novellák (Budapest: Dick Manó, 1921);

Ne bántsuk egymást (Budapest: Pallas, 1921);

Zsuzsa Berengócziában, by Karinthy and Lajos Kozma (Budapest: Sacelláry, 1921);

Két mosoly (Budapest: Pegazus, 1922);

Visszakérem az iskolapénzt (Budapest: Franklin-Társulat, 1922);

Vitéz László színháza (Bécs: Új Modern Könyvtár, 1922);

Fából vaskarika. A csokoládékirály meséi (Budapest, 1923);

Két álom. Mozgóképjáték három felvonásban és három filmben (Budapest: Franklin-Társulat, 1923);

Kötéltánc. Regény (Budapest: Dick Manó, 1923);

Nevető dekameron. Száz humoreszk (Budapest: Athenaeum, 1923);

Harun al Rasid. Kis novellák (Budapest: Athenaeum, 1924);

Egy tucat kabaré (Budapest: Tolnai Világlapja, 1924);

Drámák ecetben és olajban (Békéscsaba: Tevan, 1926);

Írta . . . Színházi karikaturák (Budapest: Kultúra, 1926);

"Ki kérdezett . . . ?" Cimszavak a nagy enciklopédiáhos (Budapest: Singer és Wolfner, 1926);

Panoráma (Budapest: Grill Károly, 1926);

Heuréka (Budapest: Singer és Wolfner, 1927);

Lepketánc. Fantasztikum egy felvonásban (Budapest: Athenaeum, 1927);

A másik Kolumbusz és egyéb elbeszélések (Budapest: Lampel Róbert, 1927);

Notesze (Budapest: Singer és Wolfner, 1927);

Nem tudom a nevét. Ott ki beszél? Kísérleti módszer (Budapest: Singer és Wolfner, 1928);

Minden másképpen van (Budapest: Athenaeum, 1929);

Nem mondhatom el senkinek. Karinthy Frigyes versei (Budapest: Athenaeum, 1930);

Haditanács Anthroposban (Budapest: Révai, 1933);

Hasműtét. Novellák (Budapest: Athenaeum, 1933);

Vendéget látni, vendégnek lenni . . . (Budapest: Cserépfalvi, 1933);

Még mindig így írtok ti (Budapest: Nyugat, 1934);

100 új humoreszk (Budapest: Nyugat, 1934);

Barabbás (Budapest: Hungária, 1935);

Nevető betegek (Budapest: Athenaeum, 1936);

Mennyei riport. Regény (Budapest: Nova Irodalmi Intézet, 1937);

Utazás a koponyám körül (Budapest: Athenaeum, 1937); translated by Vernon Duckworth Barker as *A Journey Round My Skull* (London: Faber & Faber, 1939; New York: Harper, 1939);

Amiről a vászon mesél. Jegyzetek a filmről (Budapest: Singer és Wolfner, 1938);

Üzenet a palackban (Budapest: Cserépfalvi, 1938);

Az emberke trajédiája Madách Imrike után Istenkéről, Ádámkáról és Luci Ferkóról (Budapest: Új Idők, 1946);

Skarlát. Novellák, edited by Károly Szalay (Budapest: Szépirodalmi, 1972);

Gyermekkori naplok: 1898–1899, 1899–1900, 3 volumes, edited by Szalay (Budapest: Helikon, 1987);

Az elatkozott munkaskisasszony. Válogatas as iro kotetben meg nem publikalt irasaibol, edited by V. Laszlo Urban (Budapest: Aqua, 1992);

Felvesznek a csecsemoklinikara. Kotetben eddig meg nem jelent irasok, edited by Urban (Budapest: Editorg, 1992).

Editions and Collections: *Munkái*, 10 volumes (Budapest: Athenaeum, 1928–1929)—comprises volume 1, *Így írtok ti;* volume 2, *Capillária;* volume 3, *Tanár úr kérem;* volume 4, *Gyilkosok;* volume 5, *Krisztus vagy Barabbás;* volume 6, *Harun al Rasid;* volume 7, *Új görbe tükör;* volume 8, *Színház;* volume 9, *Esik a hó;* volume 10, *Két hajó;*

Kiadatlan naplója és levelei, edited by Oszkár Ascher (Budapest: Nyugat, 1938);

Betegek és bolondok. Elbeszélések (Budapest: Új Idők, 1946);

Martinovics (Budapest: Új Idők, 1947);

Így írtok ti, edited by Imre Szász (Budapest: Szépirodalmi, 1954);

Omnibusz. Humoreszkek, jelenetek, edited by Bela Abody (Budapest: Szépirodalmi, 1954);

Nem nekem köszöntek, edited by Abody (Budapest: Szépirodalmi, 1955);

Cirkusz. Válogatott írások, 2 volumes, selected by Emil Kolozsvári Grandpierre, edited by Miklós Vajda (Budapest: Szépirodalmi, 1956)—comprises volume 1, *Tanár úr kérem; Humoreszkek; Így írtok ti; Kabaré;* volume 2, *Utazás a koponyám körül. "Ki kérdezett . . . ?";*

Hököm-színház, 3 volumes, edited by Andor Kellér (Budapest: Szépirodalmi, 1957);

A lélek arca. Összegyűjtött novellák, 2 volumes, edited by Abody and Károly Szalay (Budapest: Magvető, 1957);

Számadás a tálentomról, edited by Abody (Budapest: Magvető, 1957);

Utazás Faremidóba. Capillária (Budapest: Szépirodalmi / Bucharest: Állami Irodalmi és Művészeti Kiadó, 1957);

Az egész város beszéli. Karcolatek, 4 volumes, edited by Abody (Budapest: Szépirodalmi, 1958);

Kötéltánc, edited by Szalay (Budapest: Magvető, 1958);

Mennyei riport, edited by Endre Illés (Budapest: Magvető, 1958);

Tanár úr kérem (Budapest: Ifjúsági Kiadó, 1959);

Az író becsülete. Válogatott írások, edited by Magda Erdős (Budapest: Magyar Helikon, 1962);

Utazás a koponyám körül, edited by Szalay (Budapest: Szépirodalmi, 1962);

Válogatott művei, edited by László Kardos (Budapest: Szépirodalmi, 1962);

Így írtok ti, 2 volumes, edited by Szász (Budapest: Szépirodalmi, 1963);

Hátrálva a világ körül. Válogatott cikkek, edited by Szalay (Budapest: Szépirodalmi, 1964);

Naplóm, életem, edited by Szalay (Budapest: Magvető, 1964);

Miniatűrök, edited by Szalay (Budapest: Gondolat, 1966);

Följentem as emberiséget, 2 volumes, edited by Matyas Domokos (Budapest: Szépirodalmi, 1967);

A delejes halal. Tudomanyos-fantasztikus elbeszélések (Budapest: Kozmosz, 1969);

Összegyűjtött művei, 10 volumes, edited by Tamás Ungvári (Budapest: Szépirodalmi, 1975–1984);

Így írtok ti, edited by Ungvári (Budapest: Szépirodalmi, 1986).

Editions in English: *Soliloquies in the Bath,* translated by Lawrence Wolfe (London: W. Hodge, 1937);

Voyage to Faremido. Capillaria, translated by Paul Tabori (Budapest: Corvina, 1965; New York: Living Books, 1966);

Grave and Gay: Selections from His Work, selected by Istvan Kerekgyarto (Budapest: Corvina, 1973).

TRANSLATIONS: A. A. Milne, *Micimackó* (Budapest: Kossuth, 1935);

Jonathan Swift, *Gulliver utazásai* (Budapest, 1943);

Milne, *Micsoda négy nap!* (Budapest: Magvető, 1957).

Frigyes Karinthy was one of the most popular Hungarian writers of the first decades of the twentieth century. His life, as well as his work, caught the attention of a wide audience. He wrote in almost every genre and created hybrid genres that are not easily definable, but his most successful pieces were undoubtedly his humorous sketches, travesties, and satires. These texts influenced not only the popular literary genres but also the cultural tastes of Hungarian readers. The complexity of Karinthy's convoluted work generated extensive debate concerning its artistic value, but nonetheless Karinthy remains significant within contemporary Hungarian literature.

One of the best-known commonplaces about Karinthy is that the audience respected only his light works, while his deeper worth remained unappreciated. The author himself described this situation by comparing his artistry to the potato flower—in Europe only the flower is eaten first, and the tuber is tasted later. Yet, in a famous, often cited phrase, Dezsőné Kosztolányi in *Karinthy Frigyesről* (1988) said of Karinthy: "This idiot was the only genius among us."

Frigyes Ernő Karinthy was born on 25 June 1887 in Budapest to József and Karolina (née Engel) Karinthy. His father joined the army, then worked in a bookstore and later became a correspondence clerk; he spoke several languages and was interested in phi-

losophy, science, and art history. His mother was interested in music, literature, and the arts. The family was poor but well educated. Frigyes was the fifth of six children and was only six years old when his mother died. His father, however, managed to ensure that Frigyes and his siblings were provided with higher education. Elza, the firstborn daughter, became a painter; Emília (Mici) learned several foreign languages and assisted Karinthy in his famous translations of A. A. Milne's *Winnie-the-Pooh* (1926) and Jonathan Swift's *Gulliver's Travels* (1726). Karinthy's childhood diary, published in 1987, indicates that he showed early interest in painting and engineering as well as writing. He attended the famous high school of Markó Street and supposedly enrolled at the technological university, but he never completed his studies.

Karinthy's first publication was an explicit imitation of the works of Jules Verne and Mór Jókai, titled "Nászutazás a föld középpontja felé" (A Honeymoon Journey toward the Center of the Earth), which appeared in 1902 in the short-lived newspaper *Magyar Képes Világ*. His first real success, however, was *Így írtok ti* (That's How You Write, 1912), a collection of parodies published from 1908 to 1911 in *Fidibusz*, a popular comic publication—edited by such well-known writers as Jenő Heltai, Ferenc Molnár, Zoltán Ambrus, and Andor Gábor—that focused its humor on cultural life, particularly on literature and art. The parodies have various subjects—including Endre Ady, Mihály Babits, and Kosztolányi, the famous authors of the important journal *Nyugat* (West); Mihály Szabolcska and Ferenc Herczeg, old-fashioned literati; Sándor Petőfi, a great traditional writer; and Oscar Wilde, Henrik Ibsen, and Emile Zola, well-known foreign authors. The genre itself is comparable to Marcel Proust's pastiche or to similar texts by Stephen Leacock, Paul Reboux, and Charles Muller, although at that time Hungarian parody literature was also rather extensive, as in the work of Molnár, Adolf Ágai, and Károly Lovászy. One of the most famous pieces in the collection is a caricature of Szabolcska, titled "Egyszerűség" (Simplicity), in which the obsolete demand for the understandable and simple poem stressed by Szabolcska is contrasted with his hatred of the poetic revolution of the *Nyugat* poets, specifically Ady. Karinthy later published other collections of parodies, notably *Így láttátok ti* (That's How You Saw It, 1917), *Drámák ecetben és olajban* (Drama Is Vinegar and Oil, 1926), *Még mindig így írtok ti* (That's How You Still Write, 1934), and *Amiről a vászon mesél* (About What the Canvas Narrates, 1938). While the reception of the volumes was extremely positive and extensive, there was considerable debate among Karinthy's contemporaries and literary critics about whether the parodies were meant primarily to be entertaining (the

Aranka Böhm, Karinthy's second wife, in 1929

opinion of László Kardos and László Németh) or whether they were understated criticisms of Hungarian literature and society (the opinion of Kosztolányi, Babits, and Gyula Juhász).

Így írtok ti was followed by a collection of short stories titled *Találkozás egy fiatalemberrel* (Encounter with a Young Man), published in 1913, the year of Karinthy's marriage to Etel Judik. In the title story the author-narrator meets his younger self in the street, thus creating a binary opposition: the narrator manifests the accepted norm of everyday life, while the young man confronts him with his own past, filled with childish and wholly unrealistic dreams and aspirations such as inventing the airplane and discovering the North Pole. The narrator becomes frustrated, since he is impatient with the younger self's justification of his chosen lifestyle. In the meantime the self-curtailing author (an educated, working person with a family) is a wholly conscious omniscient narrator with the ability to observe the "true tragedy" of the younger self's situation.

Similar in narrative structure to "Találkozás egy fiatalemberrel" is the famous short story "A cirkusz" (The Circus), published in the volume *Két hajó* (Two

Ships, 1915). In this story the narrator reveals a dream, but the reader does not know if it was a dream from childhood or a dream about childhood. Nevertheless, the subject of the dream is a child who has composed a song on his violin and goes to the circus to perform it; instead, he is forced into the role of a trained acrobat. Later, while performing a stunt on the top of the tension wire, he begins to play the old melody. The song is a metaphor for art, revealing Karinthy's aesthetic principle: art is a timeless entity that comes from the depth of the self, and education, society, and experience merely conceal its creation. The story also emphasizes the negative role of the audience in aesthetic communication. The expectations of the audience create the circus—the inartistic, horrifying place of entertainment, where the role of the artist is to provide amusement for the spectators. In essence, the audience does not care about "real art"—the reaction that Karinthy believed the Hungarian reading public was having to his work.

One of Karinthy's most popular works, *Tanár úr kérem* (1916; translated as *Please Sir!*, 1968), is a collection of satires about schoolchildren, similar in theme to Molnár's novel *Pál utcai fiúk* (Boys from Pál Street, 1907) and Kosztolányi's *A szegény kis gyermek panaszai* (The Laments of a Small Child, 1910). In "Reggel hétkor" (At Seven in the Morning) a young student who cannot get up in the morning is observed in a state between dreaming and wakefulness, consciousness and unconsciousness. "A jó tanuló felel" (The Good Pupil Is Reciting the Lesson) and "A rossz tanuló felel" (The Bad Pupil Is Reciting the Lesson) are monologues on a school assignment. In the preface the author-narrator describes his characteristic approach, in which the world of the children is a separate, unreachable entity opposite from the world of the narrator and the implied reader. This paradox is the main theme of the volume—that the deformed, disproportionate world of inexperienced children is asserted to be more valuable than that of the grown-ups.

Karinthy's first novel, *Utazás Faremidóba* (1916; translated as *Voyage to Faremido*, 1965), was designed as a satirical sequel to *Gulliver's Travels*. In Karthiny's version, the character of Gulliver arrives from World War I at a fantastic world where perfect machines live a better life than human beings. Man is perceived as a disease, and the war is proof of man's inferiority. This satire against the war creates a utopian society in which the pathos of war propaganda and the war itself become ridiculous. The argument is not convincing, however, since the totally conscious, self-controlled machines do not form a consensus of the human vision. The text does manifest two of Karinthy's main themes: critiques of the corrupted human language and of the superiority of the mind (science) over instinct, perhaps best illustrated by the musical "language" of the machines. Karinthy believed that language needed redefinition; his unrealized ambition was to create an "Új/Nagy Enciklopédia" (New/Great Encyclopedia or Dictionary).

In 1920 Karinthy married Aranka Böhm; their son, Ferenc Karinthy, became a well-known writer. In a second Gulliver sequel, *Capillária* (1921; translated as *Capillaria*, 1965), Karinthy treats another sociological or political subject, namely the hegemony of women over men; the book fostered critical comparisons to August Strindberg, Henrik Ibsen, and Otto Weininger. In *Capillária* Gulliver arrives again in a new world—an underwater world where the female creatures terrorize and kill the more intelligent but defenseless male "animals." Both *Utazás Faremidóba* and *Capillária* generated critical debate concerning both the subject matter and Karinthy's utilization of fantasy. Scholars László Kardos and Károly Szalay have asserted an organic, functional connection between the fantastic elements and thematic issues, while other critics, such as Emil Kolozsvári Grandpierre, view the aesthetic structure as decoration that circumvented Karinthy's message. The controversy surrounding his work was further heightened by the publication in 1923 of his novel *Kötéltánc* (Tightrope Walking), which received unilateral rejection by critics, although later scholars have attempted to reevaluate its importance.

The subject of Karinthy's famous last novel, *Utazás a koponyám körül* (1937; translated as *A Journey Round My Skull*, 1939), is the illness of the author, who was diagnosed with a brain tumor. He underwent a successful operation (through which he remained conscious) in Sweden in 1936. The book follows the first-person narrator from the initial symptoms through the medical examinations, the operation, and his partial recovery. The enormous success of the novel derived partly from the public awareness of the author's illness, announced in the newspapers, and partly from the readability of the text, reinforced by the many well-known events of Karinthy's private life. However, the sensationalism of the novel produced a less convincing aesthetic structure than did his more representative fiction. Karinthy died on 29 August 1938.

One of the first truly cosmopolitan writers in modern Hungarian literature, Frigyes Karinthy is nonetheless overshadowed by more noteworthy authors of the first third of the twentieth century—such as Ady, Babits, and Kosztolányi. Generally excluded from the official post–World War I literary canon, Karinthy's work has more recently gained increasing recognition as a result of the political transformation in contemporary Hungary. To what extent Karinthy's reputation will be reevaluated remains to be seen; however, he is acknowledged in Hungarian literature as one of the true masters of the short sketch and satirical essay.

Bibliographies:

Albert Tezla, *Hungarian Authors: A Bibliographical Handbook* (Cambridge, Mass.: Belknap Press of Harvard University Press, 1970), pp. 281–288;

Ferenc Botka and Kálmán Vargha, *A magyar irodalomtörténet bibliográfiája* (Budapest: Akadémiai, 1982), volume 6, pp. 719–730.

Biographies:

Ferenc Karinthy, *Szellemidézés* (Budapest: Hungária, 1946);

Károly Szalay, *Karinthy Frigyes* (Budapest: Gondolat, 1961).

References:

Mihály Babits, "Karinthy, Szellemidézés," *Nyugat*, 31 (October 1938): 233–235;

Babits, "Könyvről könyvre: Karinthy és új novellái," *Nyugat*, 26 (16 April 1933): 486–487;

Zoltán Fráter, *Mennyei riport Karinthy Frigyessel* (Budapest: Magvető, 1987);

Milán Füst, "Néhány fájdalmas szó Karinthy Frigyesről" and "Találkozásom egy fiatalemberrel," in *Emlékezések és tanulmányok* (Budapest: Magvető, 1956), pp. 56–61, 62–69;

Lászlo Kardos, *Karinthy Frigyes. Tanulmány* (Budapest, 1946);

Emil Koloszvári Grandpierre, "Karinthy," *Irodalomtörténet*, 44 (1956): 397–423;

Dezsőnė Kosztolányi, *Karinthy Frigyesről* (Budapest: Múzsák, 1988);

Júlia Levendel, *Így élt Karinthy Frigyes* (Budapest: Móra, 1979);

György Rónay, "Karinthy Frigyes," in his *A regény és az élet. Bevezetés a 19–20. Századi magyar regényirodalomba* (Budapest: Káldor György, 1947), pp. 334–341;

János Szabó, *Karl Kraus és Karinthy Frigyes* (Budapest: Akadémiai, 1982);

Károly Szalay, *"Elmondom hát mindenkinek"* (Budapest: Kossuth, 1987);

Szalay, *Minden másképpen van* (Budapest: Kozmosz, 1987);

Miklós Vajda, "Frigyes Karinthy," *New Hungarian Quarterly*, 3 (April–June 1962): 42–67.

Lajos Kassák

(21 March 1887 – 22 July 1967)

Pál Deréky
University of Vienna

BOOKS: *Életsiratás* (Budapest: Benkő, 1912);

Isten báránykái: Három egyfelvonasos (Budapest: Grill, 1914);

Éposz Wagner maszkjában (Budapest: Hunnia, 1915);

Új költők könyve (Budapest: Ma, 1917);

Egy szegény lélek megdicsőülése és még hét novella (Budapest: Athenaeum, 1918);

Khalabresz csodálatos púpja (Budapest: Táltos, 1918);

Misilló királysága (Budapest: Athenaeum, 1918);

Levél Kun Bélához a művészet nevében (Budapest: Ma, 1919);

Tragédiás figurák (Budapest: Ma, 1919);

Hirdetőoszloppal: 1914–1918 (Budapest: Szellemi Termékek Országos Tanácsa, 1919);

Máglyák énekelnek (Vienna: Bécsi Magyar Kiadó, 1920);

Ma. 1 (Vienna: Elbemühl, 1921);

Novelláskönyv (Vienna: Bán, 1921);

Világanyám (Vienna: Bán, 1921);

Ma-Buch (Vienna: Elbemühl, 1923);

Új versei (Vienna: Írók Könyvtára, 1923);

Álláspont (Vienna: Ma, 1924);

Tisztaság könyve (Vienna: Horizont, 1926)—includes "A ló meghal, a madarak kirepülnek," translated by Kenneth McRobbie and Mária Kőrösy as "The Horse Dies, the Birds Fly Out," in *Arion-Almanach International*, edited by György Somlyó (Budapest: Corvina, 1988), pp. 100–110;

Az új művészet él (Cluj-Kolozsvár: Korunk, 1926);

Napok, a mi napjaink (Budapest: Pantheon, 1928);

Egy ember élete, 8 volumes (Budapest: Dante és Pantheon, 1928–1939)—comprises volume 1, *Gyermekkor* (1928); volume 2, *Kamaszévek* (1928); volume 3, *Csavargások* (1928), translated by Roger Richard as *Vagabondages* (Budapest: Corvina, 1972); volume 4, *Vergődés* (1932); volume 5, *Kifejlődés* (1932); volume 6, *Háború* (1932); volume 7, *Károlyi forradalom* (1935); volume 8, *Kommün* (1939);

Angyalföld (Budapest: Pantheon, 1929);

Lajos Kassák

Marika, énekelj! (Budapest: Pantheon, 1930);

35 verse (Budapest: Munka, 1931);

Megnőttek és elindulnak (Budapest: Pantheon, 1932);

Munkanélküliek (Budapest: Nyugat, 1933);

A telep (Budapest: Pantheon, 1933);

Az utak ismeretlenek (Budapest: Nyugat, 1934);

Menekülők (Debrecen: Nagy Károly és Társai, 1934);

Napjaink átértékelése (Budapest: Munka, 1934);

Földem, virágom (Budapest: Pantheon, 1935);

Három történet (Budapest: Cserépfalvi, 1935);

Akik eltévedtek (Budapest: Cserépfalvi, 1936);

Ajándék az asszonynak (Budapest: Cserépfalvi, 1937);

Anyám címére (Budapest: Cserépfalvi, 1937);

Fújjad csak furulyádat (Budapest: Cserépfalvi, 1939);

Egy kosár gyümölcs (Budapest: Dante, 1939);

Azon a nyáron (Budapest: Dante, 1940);

Sötét egek alatt (Budapest: Hungária, 1940);

Szombat este (Budapest: Kelet Népe, 1941);

Egy emlék hálójában (Budapest: Áchim András, 1942);

Hídépítők (Budapest: Singer és Wolfner, 1942);

Két fiatal élet (Budapest: Áchim András, 1942);

Vallomás tizenöt művészről (Budapest: Popper Ernő, 1942);

Virág Balázs (Budapest: Áchim András, 1942);

Dráma az erdőben (Budapest: Áchim András, 1943);

Egy álom megvalósul (Budapest: Singer és Wolfner, 1943);

Emberek, sorsok (Budapest: Stílus, 1943);

Közelgő viharok (Budapest: Áchim András, 1943);

Karácsonyiék, 2 volumes (Budapest: Új Idők, 1944);

Kis könyv haldoklásunk emlékére (Budapest: Új Idők, 1945);

Összegyűjtött versei (Budapest: Singer és Wolfner, 1946);

Hatvan év összes versei (Budapest: Új Idők, 1947);

Képzőművészetünk Nagybányától napjainkig (Budapest: Magyar Műkiadó, 1947);

Emlékkönyv Kassák Lajos hatvanadik születésnapjára, edited by József Nádas (Budapest: Világosság, 1947);

Egy lélek keresi magát (Budapest: Új Idők, 1948);

Mögötte áll az angyal (Budapest: Új Idők, 1948);

Szegények rózsái (Budapest: Új Idők, 1949);

Válogatott versei 1914–1949 (Budapest: Magvető, 1956);

Csillagok csillogjatok, virágok virágozzatok . . . (Budapest: Móra, 1957);

Boldogtalan testvérek (Budapest: Szépirodalmi Könyvkiadó, 1957);

Azon a nyáron: Hídépítők (Budapest: Magvető, 1958);

Költemények, rajzok. 1952–1958 (Budapest: Szépirodalmi Könyvkiadó, 1958);

Mélyáram (Budapest: Magvető, 1960);

Marika, énekelj! Egy kutya emlékiratai (Budapest: Magvető, 1961);

Misilló királysága: A telep. Éjjel az erdőben (Budapest: Magvető, 1961);

Szerelem, szerelem (Budapest: Szépirodalmi Könyvkiadó, 1962);

Az út vége (Budapest: Magvető, 1963);

Vagyonom és fegyvertáram (Budapest: Magvető, 1963);

A tölgyfa levelei (Budapest: Magvető, 1964);

Mesterek köszöntése (Budapest: Magvető, 1965);

Üljük körül az asztalt (Budapest: Magvető, 1968);

Az izmusok története, by Kassák and Imre Pán (Budapest: Magvető, 1972);

Szénaboglya (Budapest: Szépirodalmi Könyvkiadó, 1988).

Editions and Collections: *Összes versei*, 2 volumes, edited by Klára Kassák (Budapest: Magvető, 1969, 1977);

A fal mögött áll és énekel (Budapest: Magvető, 1974);

Csavargók, alkotók. Válogatott irodalmi tanulmányok (Budapest: Magvető, 1975);

Éljünk a mi időnkben: Írások a képzőmuvészetrűl (Budapest: Magvető, 1978);

Nehéz esztendők (Budapest: Magvető, 1980);

Válogatott művei, 2 volumes (Budapest: Szépirodalmi Könyvkiadó, 1983);

Ahogyan elindultak (Budapest: Kozmosz Konyvek, 1987);

Számozott költemények, edited by Klára Kassák and Ferenc Csaplár (Budapest: Szépirodalmi Könyvkiadó, 1987);

Das Pferd stirbt und die Vögel fliegen aus, edited by Max Blaeulich (Klagenfurt, Austria: Wieser, 1989);

Lesebuch der ungarischen Avantgardeliteratur 1915–1930, edited by Pál Deréky (Budapest & Vienna: Argumentum-Böhlau, 1996), pp. 280–355.

OTHER: *Új művészek könyve / Buch neuer Künstler*, edited by Kassák and László Moholy-Nagy (Vienna: Julius Fischer, 1922);

Összegyűjtött műfordítások, translated by Kassák (Budapest: Magvető, 1986).

Lajos Kassák is the best-known author of Hungarian avant-garde literature, and his works have been translated into many languages. In addition, he created a noteworthy body of artwork that is closely connected with his literary output. Between 1915 and 1939 he edited such important avant-garde reviews as *A Tett* (The Deed), *Ma* (Today), *2 x 2*, *Dokumentum* (Document), and *Munka* (Creative Work). These reviews reported on everything new in the worlds of literature, visual arts, industrial design, music, theater, dance, photography, and motion pictures. Kassák attracted talented young people as contributors to his periodicals, and many poets and novelists describe in their memoirs the large extent to which they were influenced by his free school. During his fifty-year career Kassák consistently stood for his ideals in avant-garde literature and art; just as steadfastly, he refused to strike any compromise with totalitarian ideologies and their representatives, even if doing so condemned him to silence.

Kassák was born on 21 March 1887 into a large and poor family in Érsekújvár (now Nové Zámky), a small town in the Slovak Republic. His father, István Kassák, an assistant apothecary, was Slovak; his mother, Erzsébet Istenes Kassák, a laundrywoman, was Hungarian. At twelve Kassák left school and learned the locksmith trade. In 1904, after a short stay in the western Hungarian city of Győr, he moved to Budapest and found employment as a metalworker in various factories. Kassák became increasingly involved in the workers' wage struggles, and, as a strike organizer, his chances of employment diminished. While taking advantage of the Social Democratic Party's offer of free educational materials for workers, he lived with his mother and sisters, who had moved to Budapest. For the rest of his life he was proud of these years of self-education, which he concluded with a journey on foot from Budapest to Paris in 1909. The poem "A ló meghal, a madarak kirepülnek" (1926; translated as "The Horse Dies, the Birds Fly Out," 1988) is an assessment of this journey. At the beginning of the poem the protagonist is called "Kasi," the diminutive form of Kassák's name, indicating his immaturity; but he develops at the end into "LAJOS KASSÁK," who is aware that the spirit of the technological revolution is in the process of changing the world fundamentally: "fejünk fölött elröpül a nikkel szamovár" (over our heads the nickel samovar flies). After Kassák returned from Paris, he married Jolán Simon, a factory worker with three children who later became a Dadaistic actress.

Kassák's first published volume, the short-story collection *Életsiratás* (Mourning for Life, 1912), shows the characteristics of naturalistic prose, while his sonnets of the time exhibit the influence of the French decadent poetry. Avant-garde ideas reached him in 1913 at a large exhibition of Futurist and Expressionist art held at Budapest's Municipal Art Hall. Carlo Carrà's painting *The Funeral of the Anarchist Galli* (1911) inspired Kassák to write a story with the same title. Concurrently he came across the first works of the Italian Futurists to be translated into Hungarian. The poems of Walt Whitman were a third important influence on Kassák's early avant-garde poetry.

Kassák's first volume of "new poetry," *Éposz Wagner maszkjában* (Epic in Wagner's Mask, 1915), demonstrates his powerful new language. In expressive free verse in such poems as "Az örömhöz" (To Joy) Kassák condemns World War I and dreams of social and aesthetic changes in the postbellum world, the era of *mesteremberek* (craftsmen). In 1917–1918 he experimented with adapting cubist-futurism for poetry and, following the Hungarian composer Béla Bartók's example, attempted to modify Hungarian folk poetry by using the techniques of futurist text formation.

At the end of 1915 Kassák founded the magazine *A Tett*. Seventeen issues were published before it was forbidden by wartime censorship because of its "International Issue." It was immediately succeeded by *Ma*. In the *Ma* free school Kassák and his circle of "Hungarian futurists" developed an alternative design for education, modeled on Kassák's autodidactic background: the "*Ma* method" recommended continuous observation of "new art," "new literature," and "new theater" from Moscow to Paris and from Rome to New York. In the spring of 1919 Kassák named his movement Activism. Derived from Italian Futurism, its art and literature were conceived of as directed to the masses.

After the fall of the short-lived Communist government of Béla Kun on 1 August 1919, Kassák and his family went into exile in Vienna. Most of the Hungarian Activists followed. *Ma* carried on in Vienna and became one of the best-known avant-garde reviews in Europe. The free school was continued, and the group started a publishing house. The Viennese years were, perhaps, the most productive of Kassák's career. In his poetry and the novel *Tragédiás figurák* (Tragic Figures, 1919), published before his exile, he argues that the old bourgeois world cannot be renewed; but in Vienna he admitted that the Communist promise to bring about a workers' paradise could not be fulfilled. Kassák expressed defeat in a book-length poem of about three thousand lines, *Máglyák énekelnek* (Funeral Pyres Sing, 1920). The protagonists of the poem are figures such as the Thick-lipped President, the Bearded Man, the Hunchbacked Student, and the Morphine-Addict Teacher. At the time *Máglyák énekelnek* was thought to be a poem à clef, but later it became clear that Kassák had begun to write abstractly.

In Vienna the literary and artistic paths of the Hungarian Activists diverged. Some became followers of the Soviet proletarian cult and wrote hymns to collective production, while Kassák developed a new form of nonobjective visual art he called *képarchitektúra*, or, in German, *Bildarchitektur* (picture architecture). Its technique was similar to the Suprematism of Russian artists such as Kazimir S. Malevich and Ivan Kliun, but as an ideology it was a continuation of Hungarian Activism. The latter's promise of salvation, however, was replaced in *képarchitektúra* by the optimism-radiating regularity of geometrical forms, an abstract reflection of a harmonious philosophical order. In his poetic work Kassák continued the montage technique and the dissolution of the poetic subject that he had begun in *Máglyák énekelnek*. His collected poems were pub-

Kassák and his wife, Jolán Simon

lished as *Világanyám* (The World, My Mother) in 1921.

Between 1921 and 1931 Kassák wrote his one hundred "Numbered Poems." Underlying this poetry is a digital-analogical principle. From the crushed rubble of reality Kassák shaped arbitrary blocks of meaning—he called them bricks—and pieced them together to form larger linguistic works of art. In the "Numbered Poems" the words *sípláda* and *verkli,* both of which mean "nickelodeon," stand for old, worn-out poetry; *fogak* (teeth) stands for strength, so that toothlessness is the same as weakness. Neither the poetry nor picture architecture met with success at the time; the public found both to be too hermetic.

This failure caused Kassák to search for new forms in literature, as well as in art, that would be more accessible to the general public. In 1922, together with László Moholy-Nagy, he published a pioneering work, the bilingual (Hungarian/German) *Új művészek könyve / Buch neuer Künstler.* An English version, "Book of New Artists," was planned but never published. Illustrated with examples of the new architecture and industrial design, the work was the first comprehensive display of the accomplishments of the artistic avant-garde; El Lissitzky and Hans Arp's *Die Kunstismen*

(The Isms of Art) followed three years later. Also in 1922 Kassák, together with the poet Andor Németh, founded the review *2 x 2.* Kassák's grandiose poem about his walk to Paris was published there for the first time, shaped with great typographic care and illustrated with picture architecture. In 1924 he began to write his eight-volume autobiography, *Egy ember élete* (One Man's Life, 1928–1939). In the early volumes he sketches his development as a poet and artist up to his flight to Vienna and gives a detailed description of the political and intellectual movements of the time. His message is that anyone from the lower classes can rise to the top in art and literature; they need nothing more than an alert intellect, hard work, and courage. Volume 3, *Csavargások* (Roving, 1928; translated as *Vagabondages,* 1972), covers the same period as *A ló meghal, a madarak kirepülnek.* An incident from the prose version characterizes the author splendidly: arriving in Paris after his long walk, Kassák was invited by some artists to go to a restaurant for an evening meal of oysters. Kassák, raised in the middle of the continent, was repulsed by the slippery creatures; but when he saw that the artists were beginning to make fun of the uncouth locksmith, he squeezed lemon juice onto the oysters, as he saw the people at the next table doing, and ate them without batting an eye. His line of reasoning was that if he gave up, not only would he appear ridiculous personally, but so would the working class as a whole. Kassák, who regarded himself all his life as a representative of this class, was determined not to let that happen.

In Vienna, Kassák published *Tisztaság könyve* (Book of Purity, 1926), a selection of poems, stories, and essays with an extremely elegant typographical and pictorial design. In addition to "Numbered Poems" 19 and 41 through 65, the book includes several surrealistic short stories. Kassák and his circle were allowed to return to Hungary at the end of 1926. The juxtaposition of constructivism and surrealism found in *Tisztaság könyve* is also characteristic of the journal *Dokumentum*, which Kassák founded in Budapest in 1926 with several avant-gardists who returned from France and Italy. But *Dokumentum* was discontinued after five issues when its concept of literature was met by a complete lack of understanding in Budapest. In 1928 Kassák founded another review, *Munka*, which featured all that was new in avant-garde art and literature for the young socialist intellectuals he had chosen as the bearers of his movement.

In 1929 Kassák published the novel *Angyalföld;* the title is the name of a working-class district in northeast Budapest where he had settled in 1904. *Angyalföld* tells of the transformation of the villagelike settlement into an industrial suburb at the end of the nineteenth and beginning of the twentieth century, showing the social tensions and struggles accompanying the transformation. The story of the author's development is also related but kept in the background. After the appearance of the last "Numbered Poem" in the volume *35 verse* (35 Poems) in 1931, Kassák's poetry became more simple, direct, and emotional, although traces of constructivism remained. His novel *Anyám címére* (Letters to My Mother, 1937) is an homage to his mother, a "grand old woman" albeit not a "lady," since the struggle she had waged to raise her fatherless children had nothing ladylike about it. But the struggle was crowned with success, and at the age of seventy Kassák's mother still had the desire to be taught to read and write by her son. The backdrop to the story of the mother-son relationship, however, is ominous: the rise of the Nazis.

In 1938 Kassák's wife committed suicide, and in 1939 *Munka* was suppressed. In 1940 he married Klára Kápáti, a teacher. Kassák's faith in the influencing power of literature seems to have been shaken; consequently, he turned to writing essays on art. During World War II he wrote *Vallomás tizenöt művészről* (Portrait of Fifteen Artists, 1942). He reports on his wartime experiences, including the siege of Budapest, in *Kis könyv haldoklásunk emlékére* (Small Book in Memory of Near Death, 1945). Collections of his poems were published as *Összegyűjtött versei* in 1946 and *Hatvan év összes versei* in 1947. In 1947 he also published *Képzőművészetünk Nagybányától napjainkig* (Hungarian Art from the Beginning of Modernism to the Present). That year he received one of the highest literary awards of the time, the Baumgarten Prize. He continued to write novels: *Egy lélek keresi magát* (A Soul in Search of Itself, 1948), *Mögötte áll az angyal* (An Angel behind Him, 1948), *Szegények rózsái* (The Roses of the Poor, 1949), and *Az út vége* (The End of the Road), which did not appear until 1963. Between 1945 and 1948 he edited or co-edited three new literary-artistic reviews: *Új idők* (New Age), *Alkotás* (Creation), and *Kortárs* (The Contemporary).

In 1949, with the Communist takeover of Hungary, Kassák's years of silence began. He was not allowed to publish between 1950 and 1956. He and his wife withdrew to a small house with a garden in a suburb on the northern edge of Budapest, where he began drawing and painting again; his previous nonfigurative style was replaced by large-format oil landscapes and portraits. He kept a diary in which he starkly describes the oppressive intellectual atmosphere of the years of tyranny; it was published posthumously in 1988 as *Szénaboglya* (Haystack).

When tensions lessened, Kassák immediately returned to public literary and artistic life. In 1956 he wrote with Imre Pán an updated history of the avant-garde: "A modern művészeti irányok története" (Schools of Modern Art) was serialized in the Budapest magazine *Nagyvilág* (World Literature) in 1956–1957 and was included in the posthumous *Az izmusok története* (The History of Isms in Art, 1972). Also in 1956 *Válogatott versei 1914–1949* (Selected Poems 1914–1949) was published, and new volumes of verse or novels appeared almost yearly thereafter. Comprehensive exhibitions of Kassák's artwork were held in Budapest in 1957, in Paris in 1960, and in other large European cities in subsequent years. He summarized everyday experiences, remembrances, and feelings of transience in elevated lyrical tones in *Költemények, rajzok. 1952–1958* (Poems, Drawings. 1952–1958, 1958), *Szerelem,*

szerelem (Love, Love, 1962),*Vagyonom és fegyvertáram* (Wealth and Weaponry, 1963), *A tölgyfa levelei* (The Leaves of the Oak Tree, 1964), *Mesterek köszöntése* (Greetings to Great Avant-garde Artists, 1965), and *Üljük körül az asztalt* (Let Us Sit around the Table, 1968). In 1963 László Gara translated a representative collection of Kassák's works into French under the title *Hommage à Lajos Kassák*. In the early 1960s Hungarian literary scholars began arguing against the Hungarian Communist Party's branding of Kassák and his avant-garde cadre as "deviationists"; these efforts were finally successful, and in 1965 Kassák obtained the highest cultural award of Hungary, the Kossuth Prize, for his life's work. On the occasion of his eightieth birthday in 1967 many honors were bestowed on him, including the opportunity to have one of his historic avant-garde reviews reprinted. Kassák chose the ten volumes of *Ma*, the most voluminous of his reviews; the handsome reprint edition appeared in 1971 in four volumes.

Kassák died on 22 July 1967. His *Összes versei* (Complete Poems, 1969, 1977) was edited by his wife in two volumes. Other posthumous editions included *Csavargók, alkotók* (Rovers and Creators, 1975), selected studies of literature; *Éljünk a mi időnkben* (Let Us Live in Our Times, 1978), collected writings on art; and *Összegyűjtött műfordítások* (Collected Translations, 1986). On the centenary of Kassák's birth in 1987 festive events were held across Hungary, as well as in the Slovakian city of his birth, and his most important books were reprinted. The Hungarian National Gallery mounted the Kassák Memorial Exhibition of his artwork; in October the greater part of the exhibition was shown at the Pompidou Center in Paris.

Lajos Kassák is known the world over as one of the founders of the avant-garde movement. His *Képarchitektúra*, reviews, *Új művészek könyve / Buch neuer Künstler*, and graphic poem *A ló meghal, a madarak kirepülnek* are shown at all large exhibitions of the art or literature of the avant-garde. As a poet, novelist, and critic he is of immense importance in Hungary. The literary avant-garde techniques of text formation that he and his circle employed uninterruptedly for more than two decades were taken note of only with great reluctance in the interwar period and were often misinterpreted. After World War II the Hungarian state cultural industry suppressed, or at best barely tolerated, its own avant-garde literature for

Kassák in later years

more than three decades. Despite these adverse circumstances, Kassák's contributions became entwined with native Hungarian literary tradition and became an integral component of Hungarian intellectual and cultural life.

Bibliographies:
Sándor Kozocsa, *Kassák Lajos irodalmi munkássága* (Paris: Magyar Műhely, 1965), pp. 53–60;

Albert Tezla, *Hungarian Authors: A Bibliographical Handbook* (Cambridge, Mass.: Belknap Press of Harvard University Press, 1970), pp. 290–296;

Ferenc Botka and Kálmán Vargha, *A magyar irodalomtörténet bibliográfiája*, volume 6 (Budapest: Akadémiai, 1982), pp. 735–752;

Enikő Molnár Basa, "Hungarian Literary/Critical Survey: Bibliographical Spectrum," in *Review of National Literature*, volume 17: *Hungarian Literature*, edited by Anne Paolucci (New York: Griffon House, 1993), pp. 136–154.

Biographies:
György Rónay, *Kassák Lajos; Alkotásai és vallomásai tükrében* (Budapest: Szépirodalmi Könyvkiadó, 1971);

Miklós Béládi, "Kassák Lajos," in his *Érintkezési pontok* (Budapest: Szépirodalmi Könyvkiadó, 1974), pp. 7–45;

László Ferenczi, *Én Kassák Lajos vagyok* (Budapest: Kozmosz Könyvek, 1987);

Géza Aczél, *Kassák Lajos* (Budapest: Adadémiai, 1999).

References:

Imre Bori and Éva Körner, *Kassák irodalma és festészete*, second edition (Budapest: Magvető, 1987);

Ferenc Csaplár, *Kassák körei* (Budapest: Szépirodalmi Könyvkiadó, 1987);

Pál Deréky, "Lajos Kassák und der ungarische Aktivismus," in *Expressionismus in Österreich: die Literatur und die Künste,* edited by Klaus Amann and Armin A. Wallas (Vienna: Böhlau, 1994), pp. 309–321;

Deréky, ed., *Lesebuch der ungarischen Avantgardeliteratur 1915–1930* (Budapest: Argumentum, 1996; Vienna: Böhlau, 1996), pp. 55–81;

László Ferenczi, "On Lajos Kassák," *Hungarian Quarterly,* 37 (Autumn 1996): 57–62;

Ferenczi, "The Triumph of Will and Conviction," *New Hungarian Quarterly,* 28 (Summer 1987): 73–86;

Endre Gáspár, *Kassák Lajos, az ember és munkája* (Vienna: Julius Fischer, 1924);

Tibor Klaniczay, ed., *A History of Hungarian Literature* (Budapest: Corvina, 1982), pp. 407–411;

"Lajos Kassák, 1887–1967," *New Hungarian Quarterly,* 28 (Summer 1987): 73–124;

Carl Laszlo, *Ma–Kassák* (Basel: Panderma, 1968);

Balázs Lengyel, "The Other Kassák," *New Hungarian Quarterly,* 30 (Autumn 1989): 148–151;

László Moholy-Nagy, "Literature (1947)," in *The Avant-Garde Tradition in Literature,* edited by Richard Kostelanetz (Buffalo, N.Y.: Prometheus Books, 1982), pp. 78–141;

Krisztina Passuth, *Hungarian Art in the European Avantgarde* (Budapest: Corvina, 1969);

György Rónay, "Kassák és az izmusok," *Irodalomtörténet,* 47 (1959): 43–53;

Tomáš Štraus, *Kassák: Ein ungarischer Beitrag zum Konstruktivismus / A Hungarian Contribution to Constructivism* (Cologne: Galerie Gmurzynska, 1975);

Júlia Szabó, "Kassák and the International Avant-Garde," *New Hungarian Quarterly,* 28 (Summer 1987): 117–124;

Szabó, *A magyar aktivizmus művészete 1915–1927* (Budapest: Corvina, 1981);

Ferenc Takacs, "Poems of Lajos Kassák," *Hungarian PEN,* 27 (1986): 57–63;

József Vadas, ed., *Lajos Kassák: Lasst uns leben in unserer Zeit* (Budapest: Corvina, 1989).

Papers:
Lajos Kassák's literary and artistic estate is held by the Kassák Lajos Emlékmúzeum (Lajos Kassák Memorial Museum), founded in the Zichy Palace in Óbuda, a suburb of Budapest, in 1976.

Ivan Krasko
(Ján Botto)
(12 July 1876 – 3 March 1958)

Valér Mikula
Comenius University, Bratislava

Translated by Norma Leigh Rudinsky

BOOKS: *Nox et solitudo* (Martin: Kníhtlačiarsky účastinársky spolok, 1909);

Verše (Martin: Kníhtlačiarsky účastinársky spolok, 1912).

Editions and Collections: *Básne* (Prague & Bratislava: L. Mazáč, 1936);

Básne (Martin: Matica slovenská, 1948);

Dielo (Bratislava: SVKL, 1954);

Lyrické dielo (Bratislava: SVKL, 1956);

Súborné dielo, 2 volumes (Bratislava: VSAV, 1966);

Dielo (Bratislava: Tatran, 1980).

Editions in English: "Solitude," "Jehovah," "Grief," and "The Slave," selected and translated by Paul Selver, in *An Anthology of Czechoslovak Literature* (London: Kegan Paul, Trench & Trubner, 1929), pp. 243–245;

"The Slave," translated by Selver, in *Hundred Towers: A Czechoslovak Anthology of Creative Writing*, edited by Franz C. Weiskopf (New York: Fischer, 1945), pp. 146–147;

"Song," "Ballad," and "The Slave," translated by Edith Pargeter, in *The Linden Tree: An Anthology of Czech and Slovak Literature 1890–1960*, edited by Mojmír Otruba and Zdeněk Pešat (Prague: Artia, 1962), pp. 316–318.

OTHER: Mihail Eminescu, *Tiene na obraze času*, translated by Krasko (Bratislava: SVKL, 1956).

Ivan Krasko is considered the father of modern Slovak poetry. His two collections of symbolist poems from the beginning of the twentieth century extracted Slovak poetry from its esthetic conservatism and thematic preoccupation with the problems of the Slovak nation and brought to it a more universal view of humanity. The dominant theme of Krasko's poetry is the individual in a state of emotional and philosophical crisis, although in part of his work he did not entirely eliminate national and utilitarian tendencies. Evidence of his influence on Slovak poetry is visible throughout most of the twentieth century and emphatically in the 1960s, when the revival of the Krasko line of thinking became one of the possibilities for disrupting socialist realism, which had been installed by the communist regime in the 1950s as the only allowable artistic doctrine.

Ivan Krasko was born Ján Botto on 12 July 1876 in Lukovištia in southern Slovakia as the first of two children (his sister Júlia was born in 1879) of Ján Botto, a farmer, and Rozina Botto (née, Balážová). He was a distant relative of one of the most important Slovak romantic poets, also named Ján Botto (1829–1881), a fact that piqued his interest in literature even as a child. Young Botto finished grade school in his native town and studied at the Magyar gymnasium in Rimavská Sobota from 1887 to 1893 (all Slovak-language gymnasia in Austria-Hungary had been closed in 1875). He spent one year at the German gymnasium in Sibiu in what is now known as Romania and two years (1894–1896) at the Romanian gymnasium in Brašov, from which he graduated.

His first poems dated from the time of his study in Sibiu and followed primarily the traditional national elegiac spirit with expressive elements close to the folk lyric. He received a more significant literary influence in Brašov, where he was introduced to the romantic poetry of Mihai Eminescu and found in Eminescu a strengthening of his own lyrical melancholy, which became a permanent characteristic of his poetry. Krasko later translated Eminescu's poetry into Slovak but published it only in 1956. At the end of 1896, after returning from Brašov, Krasko published his first poem, "Pieseň môjho ľudu" (The Song of My People) in the most prestigious Slovak literary magazine, *Slovenské pohľady* (Slovak Views), under the pseudonym Janko Cigáň (*cigáň* means *gypsy*). Choice of this name reveals in the beginning poet a strong inclination toward music and musicality, characteristics that would become lasting and, in the sense of symbolist doctrine, programmatic characteristics of his poetry. As he explained, his family was said to have a seventeenth-century ancestor who could play the violin "as beautifully as a gypsy." Even during Krasko's childhood, in Austria-Hungary as well as in neighboring countries, itinerant Rom often made their living by playing at rural weddings and similar celebrations.

Krasko's father did not approve of further study, so Krasko spent time at home after graduation before volunteering in 1897 for a year of military service in Trento and Vienna. He returned home again until the fall of 1900, when he could

begin to study chemical engineering at the Czech Technical School in Prague. During that time he had also tried to publish in *Slovenské pohľady* but without success (two poems were printed in 1902).

The period of Krasko's studies in Prague (1900–1905) was decisive for his further literary and personal development. There he met with a mature cultural environment and a self-confident Czech national intelligentsia firmly based in the economically strong middle class. The Czech national emancipation drive as a whole was much more lively and energetic than the provincial Slovak movement, in which Magyarization was succeeding in its gradual assimilation of the Slovak nation into the Magyar nation within the framework of the Hungarian state. The vision of the approaching end of the Slovak nation did not permit Krasko to discard entirely the traditional defensive tone of ethnic protection, even after contact with Czech symbolist poetry that had already mainly emancipated itself from its responsibility for nation-building, and in its best expression (the works of Karel Hlaváček and Jiří Karásek z Lvovic) had already taken up the decadent line of fin-de-siècle art. Though in many respects among Slovak poets Krasko most fully embodied the program of literary modernism, he tried to marginalize and gradually eliminate the decadent elements finding their way into his poems. Apparently playing a role in his attempt was the suggestion of conscious responsibility, or the direct imperative to sacrifice for the nation, still preserved from the period of romanticism in the dominant levels of Slovak culture around the magazine *Slovenské pohľady* in Martin. Also playing a role was the moral rigor of the Protestant environment in which Krasko grew up. On the other hand, the dynamic environment of Prague student circles led him in several poems, notably in "List slečne Ľ. G." (Letter to Miss Ľ. G.), to ironic criticism of Slovak passivity bordering on fatalism.

The environment in which Krasko's social, philosophical, and esthetic beliefs crystallized was primarily Detvan, the Slovak students' club in Prague. By this time Detvan was under the striking influence of Tomáš Garrigue Masaryk, later the first president of the Czechoslovak Republic, who established the so-called realistic or pragmatic policy of persistent small work for the nation. Under his influence was formed the generation of Hlasists, named for the journal *Hlas* (Voice), which criticized the political passivity and esthetic conservatism of the Martin center. With these same motives Krasko actively took part in the work of Detvan, both through his specialized lectures and as an officer (inspector and later treasurer).

Krasko caught the atmosphere of Detvan in mini-portraits of individual participants in his prose piece "Naši" (Ours, 1907), and he wrote three other short prose pieces: "Svadba" (Wedding, 1908), "Almużna" (Alms, 1908), and "List mŕtvemu" (A Letter to a Dead Man, 1911). The chief theme of "Naši" is a sort of ultimate analysis of what broke up the love relations between the student Ján Bánik, who is without doubt an autobiographical character (Bánik is the poet = *básnik*), and the "young woman Ľ. G." (Ľudmila Groeblová, at that time a student of philosophy in Prague, who appears under the name of Mária Hrabáková). Their harmony is broken just at the moment of his profession of love: Bánik confesses his love for Mária in a factual, declarative tone and in the same way proposes that in two years after she graduates they should be married. "He considered this way of proposing as suitable for Mária," since she appeared on the outside as an emancipated feminist. But right at the instant when, under the effect of his proposal, she realized that "the full satisfying life" would be exactly a life in partnership with Bánik and when, in an emotionally exalted mood, she expected from him further "words of love, a hot consuming mad love," his harsh urging of her to answer wounded her and sealed their definitive separation.

"Naši," written during Krasko's studies in Prague, foretold the fundamental theme of his poetry: the aimlessness of human behavior "in harmony with neither the reason nor the heart," the compulsion to emotionally wound one's nearest and dearest and even oneself, the overexalted mood, the stubborn refusal of empathy, the evanescence of any moment of concord with someone near, and the pain-reviving analysis of the causes of disharmony issuing into a series of pangs of conscience and a permanent feeling of guilt. The resulting sense of sadness, nostalgia, and realization of the fragility of life became the leitmotif of the poetic cycle "Lístok" (Little Letter), which was at the same time Krasko's first publishing success. In 1905 the journal *Dennica* published four poems from this cycle, and five more appeared the following year.

The poems drew remarkable attention, especially from the younger generation, because they brought a new type of poetry that basically differed from the dominating Parnassian canon, represented then by the works of the universally venerated Pavol Országh Hviezdoslav. The complex strophic and verse instrumentation of Hviezdoslav was replaced by the simple song form of Krasko,

Ilona Kňazovičová, whom Krasko married in 1912

and in contrast to Hviezdoslav's extensive and rich vocabulary Krasko concentrated upon a narrow group of key words often repeated. In place of highly stylized rhetoric Krasko employed intimate admission, or confession.

The identity of the author, however, was a mystery to readers—he remained hidden by the pseudonym Janko Cigáň. This fact suited the symbolist cult of secrecy as well as the poet's determination not to reveal his civil identity. The editor of the journal *Dennica*, the literary critic František Votruba, outwitted Krasko by a small trick. Since Votruba was also a poet (later he, Krasko, and a small group of other poets were joined under the common name Slovak modernism), he published a poem he had written himself but signed it with the name Janko

Otrok

Som ten, ktorému *v uši* spievala
matka otrokyne.
Tá pieseň v mojej duši nikdy, nikdy
nevyhynie.
Tak smutno znela, drvivým bôľažľivým
bôľom
sa trpko niesla našim úhorným na poľom,
aj chytila sa v detskej trasúcej sa *tváři*.

Som ten, čo dozrieval pod bičom otrokára,
pod bičom, ktorý nestrebené rany denne
znovu podtváral,
že žiadna z nich sa nikdy, nikdy nezahojí.
Môj chrbát skrivený vo naromen sa boji,
však vo sklopenom zraku posiaľ skrytá
iskra horí ...

Som ten, čo čaká na ston poplašného zvona,
do tajka zhynúť otrokovi, pokiaľ povetrie
nevykoná.
Až potom vystrem chrbát, rumeň sfarbí líce.
Povtedy radšej budem stromy, z ktorých
rastú šibenice ...

6. smutno znela pieseň matky-otrokyne.

Ivan Krasko

1911.

Manuscript for a poem in Krasko's 1912 collection, Verše *(from Jozef Benovsky, ed.,* Ivan
Krasko: Vystava z prilezitosti 100, *1976)*

Cigáň. The real Janko Cigáň protested by letter, and the postmark showed where his letter was mailed. The subscription list had only one name from there—the engineer Ján Botto. Votruba wrote to him; Krasko admitted his authorship; and in time they formed a lifelong friendship. Before his death Krasko dedicated a poem to Votruba as the best interpreter of his poetry.

After finishing school in 1905 Krasko went to work as a chemical engineer in a sugar-processing plant in the small town of Klobuky in northern Bohemia. He remained there until 1912, and from this period, his most productive, came a substantial part of both collections of poems. In Klobuky, Krasko lived a solitary, monotonous life sharply contrasting with the lively environment of Prague. The tedious uniformity of his daily rhythm, determined by his departure to the plant and his return home, corresponded to the flat countryside around the town where he strolled in his free time. The wide horizon of the sugar-beet fields was broken only here and there by the vertical rows of poplar trees lining the road.

The scenery of this countryside is suggestively evoked in the collection *Nox et solitudo* (Latin for Night and Solitude, 1909). Its melancholy effect is deepened by situating the "action" of the majority of poems in the autumnal rainy season and the period of dusk, twilight, or full nighttime. The "action" in Krasko's poems consists above all of psychological processes, evocation of tortured memories marked by the failures of his own emotional life, moodiness that from simple nostalgia passes at times into decadent tasting of powerlessness (of "sweet fatigue"), expressed feelings of tedium and melancholy, and above all the leitmotif of solitude, which in its Latin form became part of the title of the collection. Literary criticism has repeatedly found in these poems the psychic context woven into physical nature, as nature in its various forms—such as fog, poplars, the moon, and ravens—symbolizes psychic action or even sometimes philosophical concepts.

Nox et solitudo was published in Martin, and its editor was Svetozár Hurban Vajanský, chief advocate of the so-called conservative center in Martin. The subjective orientation of the poems, pessimistic sense of life, occasional coquetry with Eastern philosophy or evocation of mystical medieval Christianity—all these characteristics contradicted the required esthetics and national ideology of Vajanský, but at the same time he recognized the poet's undoubted talent and published the book. Vajanský provided a foreword urging the poet to

move "from the shadows to the light." Since Vajanský also objected to the pseudonym, he thought of a new one, which the poet definitively accepted as his own, Ivan Krasko. The older generation received the collection with reservation. Hviezdoslav glossed it in one of his poetic cycles, a lyrical diary, and reproved its skepticism, gloominess, emotional uncertainty, and especially its too slight orientation on the nation and its yielding to the "modish spirit" coming from the West. On the contrary, Votruba, who became the chief analyst of Slovak modernism, precisely identified Krasko's poetry as the expression of emotions and thoughts of modern man, full of interior conflicts and anxieties leading to a crisis of consciousness.

In 1912 Krasko published his second collection of poetry, titled simply *Verše* (Verses). In this volume he tried more energetically to clarify his situation in life. Though he reiterated his loss of metaphysical certainties in the poems of the prose pieces "Noc" (Night) and "Ja" (I), the basic clarification came primarily from the fact that Krasko had found happiness in love. The collection is dedicated to his fiancée, and many poems are inspired by his love for her, bringing a positive resolution to life or, more precisely, a determination to seek a positive resolution. This collection, too, continues the genre of short songlike ballads with signs of failed emotions or of sonnets composed as allegories of the poet's hopeless situation in life (described sometimes with almost baroque visualization). This collection, however, is more a matter of symbolist stylization than of confession ruled by interior urgency.

Contrasting this heightened artistry of Krasko's poems and responding to the pressure of domestic tradition, *Verše* includes poems that reflect the national fate—"Otrok" (translated as "The Slave," 1929) and "Otcová roľa" (Paternal Fields). Krasko tried to give his work a nationally and in part socially mobilizing effect in "Baníci" (Miners). Official interpretations during the communist regime praised these poems at the expense of the more advanced and nuanced subjective lyrics.

The year 1912 was an important turning point in Krasko's life in other ways; he married Ilona Kňazovičová (Hviezdoslav was witness at the wedding) and left Klobuky for the small Czech town of Slaný, where he worked as the technical director of a chemical factory until he was mobilized when World War I broke out in 1914. He alternated military service as a lieutenant with frequent hospital stays in Halic, Italy, and Ruthenia in Hungary for his recurring lung trouble. In one of these hospitals he wrote a draft of a long epic verse composition called "Eli, Eli, lama sabachthani," which remained unfinished. With this fragment, which was intended to depict the wartime fate of a village schoolteacher, Krasko's poetic works ended. Later he wrote only a few occasional or dedicatory poems.

After the end of the war and the establishment of Czechoslovakia in 1918 Krasko became a ministerial official in Bratislava. He also served in parliament and later became a senator for the Agrarian Party. In 1920 he became a corresponding member of the Czech Academy of Sciences, and in 1923, a full member. During this time he also attended several lectures at the Philosophical and Law institutes of Comenius University in Bratislava. He remained a state official until 1938, when he retired in protest against the breakup of Czechoslovakia. In 1943 he moved to the spa town of Piešťany, where his home is now a museum. After the end of World War II he became one of the first laureates of the newly established highest state artistic honor, which followed the Soviet model, with the title National Artist. He died on 3 March 1958 in Bratislava and was buried in his native Lukovištia.

The work of Ivan Krasko, though not extensive, belongs to the basic treasury of modern Slovak poetry. Uniting an original stance toward life with esthetic perfectionism, he inspired the direction of the Slovak lyric beginning with the generation immediately following him—Ján Smrek, Valentín Beniak, and Ladislav Novomeský—up to the generation entering literature half a century after *Nox et solitudo* was published. In keeping with this great influence, Krasko's poetry is the subject of many critical interpretations and reinterpretations; he remains the most interpreted Slovak author.

Letters:
Rudo Brtáň, Ludvík Patera, and Jaroslav Voráček, eds., *Z korešpondencie Ivana Krasku, Slovenská literatúra*, 7 (1960): 81–89.

Bibliography:
V. Rečková, *Ivan Krasko. Výberová bibliografia k 100. výročiu narodenia* (Nitra, 1976).

Biography:
Rudo Brtáň, *Poézia Ivana Krasku* (Martin: Matica slovenská, 1933).

References:
Peter Aich, "Ivan Krasko es mi," *Irodalmi Szemle*, 11 (1968): 362–363;
Corneliu Barborica, "Z rumunskych kontaktov Ivana Krasku," *Slovenská literatúra*, 17 (1970): 457–478;
Ján Brezina, *Ivan Krasko* (Bratislava: SAVU, 1946);
Brezina, "Krasko a Novomeský," *Slovenské pohľady*, 92, no. 12 (1976): 31–38;
Vladimir Forst, "Ivan Krasko a Čechy," *Comparative Literature*, 24 (1976): 289–304;
Michal Gáfrik, *Krasko*, in his *Poézia slovenskej moderny* (Bratislava: VSAV, 1965), pp. 132–202;
Ivan Krasko 1876–1976. Litteraria XX–XXI (Bratislava: Veda, 1978);
Cyril Kraus, "O Kraskovej tvorivej ceste," *Slovenské pohľady*, 92, no. 7 (1976): 49–57;
Alexander Matuška, "Krasko," in his *Profily a portréty* (Bratislava: Slovenský spisovateľ, 1972), pp. 313–321;
Stanislav Šmatlák, *Ivan Krasko: 1876–1976* (Bratislava: UV Socialistickej akad, 1978);
Šmatlák, *Vývin a tvar Kraskovej lyriky* (Bratislava: Tatran, 1976);
Štefan Strážay, "V súvislosti s Kraskom," in Krasko, *Plachý akord* (Bratislava: Slovenský spisovateľ, 1980), pp. 7–15;
Miloš Tomčík, "Krasková poézia vo francuzstine," *Slovenské pohľady*, 93, no. 11 (1976): 96–105;
Viliam Turčány, "Rým v období Hviezdoslava a Krasku," in his *Rým v slovenskej poézii* (Bratislava: Veda, 1975), pp. 127–176;
Turčány, "Za hory uz zapadalo," *Slovenské pohľady*, 92, no. 7 (1976): 39–48;
Libuša Vajdová, "Ivan Krasko v rumunčine," *Slovenská literatúra*, 23 (1976): 562–573;
Ján Zambor, *Ivan Krasko a poézia českej moderny* (Bratislava: Tatran, 1981);
Zambor, "Krv poézie," *Slovenské pohľady*, 93, no. 2 (1977): 119–123.

Papers:
Ivan Krasko's papers are in the Múzeum Ivana Krasku in Piešťany and the Matica slovenská in Martin.

Gyula Krúdy

(21 October 1878 – 12 May 1933)

Bònus Tibor
University of Budapest

BOOKS: *Üres a fészek* (Budapest: Országos Irodalmi r.t., 1897);

Szeretlek (Budapest, 1897);

Ifjúság (Budapest: Pesti Könyvnyomda, 1899);

Hamu (Budapest, 1899);

A víg ember bús meséi (Budapest: Légrády Testvérek, 1900);

Az aranybánya (Budapest: Wodianer F. és Fiai, 1901);

Hortobágy (Budapest: Singer és Wolfner, 1901);

Mindenkit érhet baj (Budapest: Méhner Vilmos, 1901);

Utazás a Szepességen (Budapest: Singer és Wolfner, 1901);

Utazás a Tiszán (Budapest: Singer és Wolfner, 1901);

A király palástja (Budapest: Singer és Wolfner, 1902);

Kún László és egyéb történetek (Budapest: Lampel Róbert, 1902);

Letűnt századok (Budapest: Singer és Wolfner, 1902);

Sziklazúzó hajók (Budapest: Singer és Wolfner, 1902);

A komáromi fiú (Budapest: Singer és Wolfner, 1903);

Nyíri csend (Budapest: Lampel Róbert, 1903);

Pogány magyarok s egyéb elbeszélések (Budapest: Lampel Róbert, 1903);

A dévényi fazekas (Budapest: Singer és Wolfner, 1904);

Robinzonok a Kárpátok között (Budapest: Singer és Wolfner, 1904);

Túl a Királyhágón (Budapest: Singer és Wolfner, 1904);

Diákkisasszonyok (Budapest: Singer és Wolfner, 1905);

Előre! (Budapest: Singer és Wolfner, 1905);

Hazám tükre (Budapest: Magyar Kereskedelmi Közlöny, 1905);

Az álmok hőse (Budapest: Rákosi Jenő Budapesti Hírlap, 1906);

A cirkusz-király (Budapest: Franklin-Társulat, 1906);

Pajkos Gaálék (Budapest: Rákosi Jenő Budapesti Hírlap, 1906);

A podolini kísértet (Budapest: Rákosi Jenő Budapesti Hírlap, 1906);

Gyula Krúdy

A szakállszárítón (Budapest: Rákosi Jenő Budapesti Hírlap, 1906);

Hét szilvafa (Budapest: Lampel Róbert, 1907);

Karácsonyest (Budapest: Singer és Wolfner, 1907);

Kék láng (Budapest: Mozgó Könyvtár, 1908);

A szerelem rejtélyei (Budapest: Mozgó Könyvtár, 1908);

Andráscsik öröksége (Budapest: Singer és Wolfner, 1909);

A bűvös erszény és egyéb elbezélések (Budapest: Franklin-Tarsulat, 1909);

A negyvenes évekből (Budapest: Kunossy, Szilágyi és Társa, 1909);

Falu a nádasban (Budapest: Wodianer, 1910);

Mihály csizmája (Budapest: Wodianer, 1910);

A podolini takácsné és a többiek (Budapest: Singer és Wolfner, 1911);

Szindbád ifjúsága (Budapest: Nyugat, 1911);

Francia kastély (Budapest: Singer és Wolfner, 1912);

Kárpáti kaland (Budapest: Eke, 1912);

A magyar Jakobinusok (Budapest: Vári Dezső, 1912);

Szindbád utazásai (Budapest: Nyugat, 1912);

Az arany meg az asszony (Budapest: Országos Monográfia Társaság, 1913);

Csurli és társai (Budapest: Athenaeum, 1913);

De Ronch kapitány csodálatos kalandjai (Budapest: Athenaeum, 1913);

Piros és a többiek (Budapest: Lampel Róbert, 1913);

Az utolsó honvédek (Budapest: Singer és Wolfner, 1913);

Az utolsó vörössapkás és más történelmi elbeszélések (Budapest: Singer és Wolfner, 1913);

A vörös postakocsi (Budapest: Singer és Wolfner, 1913);

Zoltánka (Budapest: Franklin-Társulat, 1913);

Első szerelem (Budapest: Athenaeum, 1914);

Mákvirágok kertje (Budapest: Franklin-Társulat, 1913);

Margit története és egyéb elbeszélések (Budapest: Magyar Kereskedelmi Közlöny, 1914);

Palotai álmok (Budapest: Singer és Wolfner, 1914);

A podolini takacsne (Budapest: Singer és Wolfner, 1914);

A próba-bál (Budapest: Singer és Wolfner, 1914);

Púder (Budapest: Singer és Wolfner, 1914);

Andráscsik örököse (Budapest: Vallalat, 1914);

A 42-ős mozsarak (Budapest: Singer és Wolfner, 1915);

Pest ezerkilencszáz tizenötben (Budapest: Dick Manó, 1915);

A zenélő óra (Budapest: Lampel Róbert, 1915);

Szindbád. A feltámadása (Budapest: Singer és Wolfner, 1916);

Aranykézutcai szép napok (Békéscsaba: Tevan, 1916);

Petit (Békéscsaba: Tevan, 1916);

Szindbád (Budapest: Singer és Wolfner, 1916);

Őszi utazások a vörös postakocsin (Budapest: Singer és Wolfner, 1917);

Pest 1916 (Békéscsaba: Tevan, 1917);

Szindbád ifjúsága és szomorúsága, 2 volumes (Budapest: Táltos, 1917);

Bukfenc (Budapest: Kultúra, 1918);

Kánaán könyve (Budapest: Athenaeum, 1918);

A legszebb mesekönyv (Budapest: Magyar Kereskedelmi Közlöny, 1918);

Napraforgó (Budapest: Kultúra, 1918);

Asszonyságok dija (Budapest: Rácz Vilmos, 1919);

Fehérvári könyv (Budapest: Közoktatási Népbiztossága, 1919);

Havasi kürt (Budapest: Ruszka-Krajna Népbiztossága, 1919);

Á kápolnai földsztás (Budapest: Kultúra, 1919);

Pesti album; Krúdy Gyula feljegyzesei es elbeszélései (Budapest: Franklin-Társulat, 1919);

Tótágas (Budapest: Pallas, 1919);

Az útitárs (Budapest: Franklin-Társulat, 1919);

Álmoskönyv (Budapest: Athenaeum, 1920);

A betyár álma. Kleofásné kakasa és más elbe-szélések (Budapest: Athenaeum, 1920);

A Miatyánk évéből (Budapest: Rácz Vilmos, 1920);

Az oltárterítő. Csillag a Kárpátok felett (Budapest: Hajnal, 1920);

Magyar tükör (Budapest: Athenaeum, 1921);

Nagy kópé (Wien: Pegazus, 1921);

Pesti évkönyv (Budapest: Székási Sacelláry Pál, 1921);

Ál-Petőfi (Budapest: Athenaeum, 1922);

Hét bagoly (Budapest: Athenaeum, 1922);

Egy nemzeti rablóvezér (Budapest: Tolnai Világlapja, 1922);

N. N., egy szerelem-gyerek (Budapest: Athenaeum, 1922);

Az öreg gárdista (Budapest: Tolnai, 1922);

Őszi versenyek (Wien: Pegazus, 1922);

Pesti nőrabló (Budapest: Tolnai, 1922);

Starttól a célig (Budapest: Légrády, 1922);

Szent Margit leánya (Budapest: Eisler G., 1922);

Álom ábécé, 2 volumes (Budapest: Tolnai, 1923);

Liga Gida kalandjai Hollandiában és a világ egyéb tájain (Budapest: Országos Gyermekvédő Liga, 1923);

Rózsa Sándor (Budapest: Béta, 1923);

A fejedelem szolgája és egyéb elbeszélések (Budapest: Magyar Kereskedelmi Közlöny, 1925);

Aranyidő. A templárius (Budapest: Grill Károly, 1925);

Mesemondások Jókai Mórról (Budapest: Franklin-Társulat, 1925);

Szindbád megtérése (Budapest: Athenaeum, 1925);

Jockey Club; het kisregeny (Budapest, 1925);

Mohács vagy két árva gyermek vergődése (Budapest: Pantheon, 1926);

Az alispán leányai (Budapest: Singer és Wolfner, 1930);

Festett király (Budapest: Franklin-Társulat, 1930);

Boldogult úrfikoromban (Budapest: Athenaeum, 1930);

A tiszaeszlári Solymosi Eszter (Budapest, 1931).

Editions and Collections: *Munkái*, 10 volumes (Budapest: Athenaeum, 1925)—comprises volume 1, *A vörös postakocsi*; volume 2, *Őszi utazások a vörös postakocsin*; volume 3, *Szindbád ifjúsága*; volume 4, *Szindbád megtérése*; volume 5, *Napraforgó*; volume 6, *A podolini kísértet*; volume 7, *Aranykézuctai szép napok*; volume 8, *Hét* *bagoly;* volume 9, *N. N., egy szerelem-gyerek;* volume 10, *Az utolsó gavallér, Velszi herceg;*

A szultán rózsája és egyéb elbeszélések (Budapest: Magyar Kereskedelmi Közlöny, 1925);

A tegnapok ködlovagjai (Békéscsaba: Tevan, 1925);

Az élet álom (Budapest: Az Író, 1931);

Az első Habsburg (Budapest: Franklin-Társulat, 1931);

Váciutcai szép napok (Budapest: Révai, 1931);

A magyar sasfiók (Budapest: Fővárosi Könyvkiadó, 1944);

Napraforgó (Budapest: Franklin-Társulat, 1944);

Rezeda Kázmér szép élete (Budapest: Grill, 1944);

Ady Endre éjszakái (Budapest: Fehér Holló, 1948);

Egy pohár borovicska (Budapest: Budapest Székesfőváros, 1948);

A kékszalag hőse (Budapest: Szépirodalmi Könyvkiadó, 1956);

Valakit elvisz az ördög és más kisregények (Debrecen: Alföldi Magvető, 1956);

Az élet álom: elbeszélések, edited by Janos Kass Janos (Budapest: Szépirodalmi Könyvkiadó, 1957);

Írói arcképek, 2 volumes (Budapest: Magvető, 1957);

Rezeda Kázmér szép élete. Nagy kópé. Az utolsó gavallér (Budapest: Szépirodalmi Könyvkiadó, 1957);

Szindbád (Budapest: Magvető, 1957);

Válogatott novellák (Budapest: Szépirodalmi Könyvkiadó, 1957);

Aranykézutcai szép napok (Budapest: Szépirodalmi Könyvkiadó, 1958);

Asszonyságok díja. Napraforgó (Budapest: Magvető, 1958);

Bukfenc.Velszi herceg. Primadonna (Budapest: Szépirodalmi Könyvkiadó, 1958);

Három király: Mohács, Festett király, Az első Habsburg (Budapest: Magvető, 1958);

Pest-Budai séták (Budapest: Magyar Helikon, 1958);

Asszonyságok díja. Napraforgó (Budapest: Racz Vilmos, 1958);

A fehérlábú Gaálné, 2 volumes (Budapest: Magvető, 1959);

Magyar tájak (Budapest: Magyar Helikon, 1959);

Az útitárs; N. N. ket regeny (Budapest: Szépirodalmi Könyvkiadó, 1959);

Az aranybánya. Régi szélkakasok között. Palotai álmok (Budapest: Magvető, 1960);

Aranyidő. A templárius. Két regény (Budapest: Szépirodalmi Könyvkiadó, 1960);

A szerelmi bűvészinas (Budapest: Magvető, 1960);

Az arnany meg az asszony; opera egy felvonasban (Budapest: Zenemukiado Vallalat, 1961);

Éji zene (Budapest: Magvető, 1961);

Mákvirágok kertje (Budapest: Magvető, 1961);

Bella Spiegler, Krúdy's first wife, whom he married in 1899

A tegnapok ködlovagjai (Budapest: Szépirodalmi Könyvkiadó, 1961);

Ki jár az erdőn? (Budapest: Magvető, 1962);

A lőcsei kakas (Budapest: Magvető, 1962);

A magyar jakobinusok. Ál-Petőfi (Budapest: Szépirodalmi Könyvkiadó, 1962);

A podolini kísértet (Budapest: Szépirodalmi Könyvkiadó, 1962);

Hét bagoly. Boldugult úrfikoromban (Budapest: Szépirodalmi Könyvkiadó, 1963);

Pesti levelek (Budapest: Magvető, 1963);

Vallomás (Budapest: Magvető, 1963);

A vörös postakocsi. Őszi utazás a vörös postakocsin (Budapest: Szépirodalmi Könyvkiadó, 1963);

Jockey Club (Budapest: Magvető, 1964);

A kékszalog hőse (Budapest: Szépirodalmi Könyvkiadó, 1964);

A madárijesztő szeretője (Budapest: Magvető, 1964);

A podolini kísértet (Budapest: Szépirodalmi Könyvkiadó, 1964);

Utolsó szivar az Arabs Szürkénél (Budapest: Magvető, 1965);

Almoskonyv (Budapest: Magvető, 1966);

Regi pesti historiak (Budapest: Magvető, 1967);

A szazgalleros: elbeszélésk (Budapest: Mora Ferenc, 1971);

Apam, Szinbád (Budapest: Magvető, 1975);

Az álombeli lovag: válogatott elbeszélések, 1909–1911 (Budapest: Szépirodalmi Könyvkiadó, 1978);

Gordonkazas (Budapest: Szépirodalmi Könyvkiadó; Magyar Helikon, 1978);

Pesti nőrabló (Budapest: Szépirodalmi Könyvkiadó, 1978);

Szerenád: Válogatott elbeszélések, 1912–1915 (Budapest: Szépirodalmi Könyvkiadó, 1979);

Az utolsó gavallér (Budapest: Szépirodalmi Könyvkiadó, 1980);

Királyregények (Budapest: Szépirodalmi Könyvkiadó, 1980);

Etel király kincse (Budapest: Szépirodalmi Könyvkiadó, 1981);

Telihold: Válogatott elbeszélések, 1916–1925 (Budapest: Szépirodalmi Könyvkiadó, 1981);

Delikátesz: Válogatott elbeszélések, 1926–1930 (Budapest: Szépirodalmi Könyvkiadó, 1982);

Almoskonyv: Tenyerjoslasok konyve (Budapest: Szépirodalmi Könyvkiadó, 1983);

Pesti album: Publicisztikai írások, 1919–1933 (Budapest: Szépirodalmi Könyvkiadó, 1985);

A musketas: válogatott elbeszélések (Budapest: Zrinyi Katonai Kaido, 1987);

Irodalmi kalendariom: iroi arckepek (Budapest: Szépirodalmi Könyvkiadó, 1989);

Krúdy Gyula válogatott novellai (Budapest: Szépirodalmi Könyvkiadó, 1990).

Editions in English: *The Crimson Coach*, translated by Paul Tabori (Budapest: Corvina Press, 1967);

The Adventures of Sinbad, translated, with an introduction and notes, by G. Szirtes (London: Central European University Press, 1998).

One of the most versatile and prolific Hungarian prose writers of the first half of the twentieth century, Gyula Krúdy produced an extensive body of works that continues to be appreciated in Hungarian literature. Although his works were relegated to a minor role in the Marxist canon for some decades after World War II, their importance and innovative nature cannot be questioned. As part of the first generation of authors formed around the literary journal *Nyugat* (West), which included Endre Ady (1877–1919), Mihaly Babits (1883–1941), Dezső Kosztolányi (1885–1936), and Milán Füst (1888–1967), among others, Krúdy played a significant role in the development of modernism in Hungarian literature. Krúdy is considered to be an influential innovator in Hungarian prose. His impressionistic and lyrical prose style, especially in his major works of fiction, is characteristic of contemporary European fiction, and Krúdy is often compared by Hungarian literary critics to both Marcel Proust and Virginia Woolf.

Gyula Krúdy was born on 21 October 1878 in Nyíregyháza, inheriting his name from his father, who belonged to provincial nobility but who had been reduced to a middle-class existence as a lawyer. His mother, Csákányi Juliska, was a maid for the Krúdy family, and the poet's father did not marry her until 1895. This heritage of illegitimacy and middle-class upbringing not only impacted Krúdy's life but also appeared as an important theme in his works. He started his elementary studies in Nyíregyháza in 1883. He attended grammar school from 1887 to 1888 in Szatmár, then continued his studies for the next three years (1888–1891) in the Podolin grammar school in Szepesség. In 1891 he became a student in the Protestant Central Grammar School in Nyíregyháza, from which he graduated four years later, thus completing his formal education.

Krúdy's literary progress started strikingly early. He had hardly turned fourteen before he produced his first short story, "Miért ölte meg Káin Ábelt?" (Why Did Cain Slay Abel?). In 1894 he published a series of articles in a Pest newspaper about the hypnosis tragedy in Tuzsér, where a medium had not recovered from the hypnotic state. By the turn of the century Krúdy had written some five hundred short stories. After graduation he undertook a job as an editor, first in Debrecen and then in Nagyvárad. In 1897 he moved to Budapest, where he lived for the remainder of his life. Although the daily and weekly papers as well as tabloids provided a public forum for his writing, Krúdy also published short stories in *A Hét* (The Week), which was considered the forerunner of *Nyugat*. At this same time he became acquainted with Bella Spiegler, who published short stories under the name of Satanella and Bella Bogdán. In 1899 they married, and the couple later had three children: Gyula, Ilona, and Mária.

Krúdy's first volume of short stories, *Üres a fészek* (Empty Nest), was published in 1897, followed in 1899 by a second collection, *Ifjúság* (Youth). The most frequent thematic element in these stories is the contrast between an artistic lifestyle and the accepted norm of society; included in this theme is the opposition between a carefree existence and marriage. The stories in this collection, as with much of Krúdy's fictional body of works, can be interpreted as extended autobiography. Many of

the early stories as well as the early novels—
Szeretlek (I Love You, 1897) and *Hamu* (Ash, 1899)—evolve from the life of the peasantry, which Krúdy depicted with an imaginative sense of affection, humor, and empathy. Well-known folk tales, anecdotes, and legendary narratives are re-created in such stories as "A furfangos kisértet" (The Wily Ghost), "A holt asszony udvarlója" (The Dead Lady's Suitor), "Az öreg gárdista" (The Old Guardsman), "A báróné pipái" (The Baroness's Pipes), "A Gaálok öröksége" (The Heritage of the Gaáls), "A geszterédi agarak" (The Greyhounds of Geszteréd), and "Az utolsó futóbetyár" (The Last Villain), in which an event or incident interrupts—if only temporarily—daily life in the village where the narrative point of view is determined by the perspective of the community. Krúdy often uses metaphoric recognition or simile to form his characters' views of life, as in "A geszterédi agarak," in which the main character, Gaál Sámuel, identifies human life with the world of greyhounds and considers his only daughter, Veronika, his most beloved greyhound. In the story titled "A ló meg a szoknya" (The Horse and the Skirt) the main character is interested only in horses until the widowed Szirákyné explains the importance of a woman in a man's life through the concept of horsebreeding. In the story titled "Szép asszony papucsa" (The Nice Lady's Clogs) Csivik Erzsi turns old when she learns that other people in the village have the same type of clogs, which she had thought were unique and so gave her unrivaled beauty. Primarily anecdotal and striving toward a realism of social consciousness, Krúdy's early stories nonetheless reflect the lyrical prose style that he would later incorporate into his mature fiction.

Krúdy first gained literary recognition with the publication in 1911 of *Szindbád ifjúsága* (Sindbad's Youth), which introduced readers to the adventures of the young Szindbád, perhaps Krúdy's best-known fictional character. Szindbád's further adventures were published in *Szindbád utazásai* (Sindbad's Travels, 1912), *Szindbád. A feltámadása* (Szindbád: The Resurrection, 1916), and *Szindbád megtérése* (Szindbád's Return, 1925). Reminiscent of the tales from the *Arabian Nights*, the Szindbád stories follow the fictionalized alter ego of the author through multiple layers of time that become indistinguishable in chronology. Utilizing the perspectiveless present to heighten the intrinsic value of the past, Krúdy presents the relationship between introspection and retrospection by incorporating outer, natural similes and

Krúdy's second wife, Rózsa-Zsuzsanna Váradi,
whom he married in 1919

allegories to express inner conditions. However, as noted by critic Béla Czére in *Krúdy Gyula* (1987), the escape into the past is also illusory because its direction "does not point towards the real past but towards the situations that bring the promise of fulfilment in the future." Although Krúdy continued writing his Szindbád stories until the end of his life, the narratives after 1925 were never collected by the author in a volume.

Krúdy's popularity was further enhanced by the publication in 1913 of *A vörös postakocsi* (translated as *The Crimson Coach*, 1967), first serialized in 1913 in the literary journal *A Hét;* in this story Krúdy creates an imaginary panorama of Budapest at the turn of the century. The unfinished ending of the novel inspires the reader to think that the work is the reflection of contemporary life in Budapest, while other narrative techniques point out that this world is subjective, fictitious, and a creation of the tyranny of narrative interferences. The present of the novel remains stagnant, while the plot is always interrupted by digressions dealing with the characters' pasts. Szilvia Fátyol and Klára Horváth, unemployed actresses subsisting on the gifts of an elderly landowner, dream of love, wealth, and marriage. Kázmér Rezeda is a failed journalist, who—like Szilvia and Klára—lives

Krúdy and his daughter Zsuzsanna in 1925

in the world of illusions. He can break out of his incapacity only for a brief moment, and even then he turns against himself and tries to escape by committing suicide. Like the character Szindbád, Rezeda serves as an alter ego for Krúdy, who "follows" the fictitious character's life in other novels—*Őszi utazások a vörös postakocsin* (Autumn Journeys on the Red Stagecoach, 1917), *Nagy kópé* (Rascal, 1921), *Rezeda Kázmér szép élete* (The Beauteous Life of Kázmér Rezeda, 1944), and *A kékszalag hőse* (The Hero of the Blue Ribbon, 1956). Krúdy does not strictly adhere to a realistic portrayal of reoccurring characters—the character of Kázmér Rezeda, for instance, who appears in *Őszi utazások a vörös postakocsin*, is not the same Kázmér Rezeda who appears in *Nagy kópé*.

Krúdy's private life changed dramatically in 1917 when he fell in love with the seventeen-year-old Rózsa-Zsuzsanna Váradi, the daughter of a hotel director in Budapest. His marriage to Bella Spiegler had deteriorated, due primarily to Krúdy's overstrained work schedule and bohemian lifestyle. Although he was believed to be one of the best-paid Hungarian writers in the 1910s, he squandered his salary through debauchery and his passion for gambling. In his book titled *Ady Endre éjszakái* (Endre Ady's Nights, 1948) Krúdy re-created the memory of the long nights spent in

the company of the famous poet Ady—and among others, Victor Cholnoky, Sándor Bródy (1863–1924), and Ernö Szép (1884–1953)—exploring the nightlife of Budapest. He left his family many times and eventually moved into one of the exclusive hotels in Budapest. Krúdy lived with Váradi in the Grand Hotel on the Margitsziget in central Budapest beginning in the autumn of 1918, and a year later, after he had divorced Bella Spiegler, they were married. From that time on until 1930, Krúdy lived on the Margitsziget (Margit Island, the island in the Danube that separates Buda from Pest), first in the Grand Hotel and then in the former castle of Joseph Palatine. Only one child was born from Krúdy's second marriage, Zsuzsanna, who would later record her memories of her father in her own work.

Published in 1918, Krúdy's novel titled *Napraforgó* (The Sunflower) incorporates the epic-auctorial principles of the early stories; however, by harmonizing the metaphoric solutions, he creates a more complex structure of merging past with present in which the sunflower becomes symbolic of change: fixed to the ground, the sunflower nonetheless alters its position in relation to the direction of the sun. The fablelike quality of *Napraforgó* is re-created in *Kleofásné kakasa* (Kleofásné's Rooster, published in 1920), which is generally acknowledged as a sequel to the previous novel.

At the outbreak of World War I, Krúdy, like many of his contemporaries, was initially enthusiastic about the participation of Hungary on the side of the Central Powers. However, he soon became disillusioned with the war effort and gradually adopted a pacifist role. Likewise, he welcomed the Astery Revolution and the Council Republic and became a member of the Vörösmarty Academy of "progressive writers." He wrote many articles in support of the revolution, and he edited the leftist newspaper *Néplap*, but his revolutionary zeal later proved disadvantageous to his literary career. In 1920 the National Theater, following the edict of the Theatrical Council, refused to stage the play adaptation of Krúdy's novel *A vörös postakocsi*. In addition, Krúdy encountered a reluctance on the part of publishers to consider his work. However, in 1920 he managed to publish the highly successful *Álmoskönyv* (Book of Dreams), which remains one of his most popular works. In 1921 he published *Nagy kópé*, which reintroduced the character of Kázmér Rezeda; the following year he published *Hét bagoly* (Seven Owls), an imaginative twist on the romantic novel, and the autobiographical novel *N. N., egy szerelem-gyerek*, in which Krúdy evokes a nostalgic remembrance of his childhood.

Following the publication in 1925 of *A templárius* (The Templer), Krúdy began a trilogy of historical novels under the general title of "Királyregények" (The King Novels), consisting of *Mohács vagy két árva gyermek vergődése* (Mohács, 1926), *Festett király* (The Painted King, 1930), and *Az első Habsburg* (The First Hapsburg, 1931). Later collected under the title *Három király* (Three Kings, 1958), the trilogy interprets Hungarian history in the sixteenth century from the wedding of Lajos II and the Hapsburg Mária through the fall of Nándorfehérvár and the Battle of Mohács to the double-king election, the consequences of which determined the course of Hungary's history for centuries.

During this same period Krúdy continued to produce imaginative fiction of critical importance, including his conspicuous short stories on gastronomy. As noted by critic László Fülöp, "The gastronomic motif can be placed well in Krúdy's human- and life-describing epic system. He gives the motif, which seems to be insignificant by itself, an appearance that will enhance his ability to communicate important facts about his characters and their lives." Many of the stories can be read as a treasury of gastronomical knowledge and gourmandism—as illustrated in "Újházi levese" (Újházi's Soup), a story about the protagonist's passion for gastronomy and the chicken soup named after him; "A konyha müvészete" (The Art of Cooking), about the lobster soup of Miklós Szemere; and "Esterházy rostélyosai" (Esterházy's Braised Steak). Krúdy also published a short-story cycle titled "A gyomor örömei" (The Joy of Eating), often choosing one of the restaurants or pubs in Budapest as the scene of the story. The eating scenes are often introduced by the detailed description of the ceremony of ordering. Often the gastronomical experience is introduced as the last act in one's life as a preparation for death, as in "A zsebóra" (The Watch) and "Velszi herceg" (The Prince of Wales). The gastronomical situation is also used to initiate a metaphorical exchange about death, as in Krúdy's well-known story titled "Utolsó szivar az Arabs szürkében" (The Last Cigar at the Grey Arab). Probably Krúdy's best novel, *Boldogult úrfikoromban* (In My Late Lamented Youth), published in 1930, also deals with gastronomy. The novel begins as the narrator is about to tell a story to his friends, two middle-aged gentlemen named Vilmácska and Podolini, but just as he gets started, all three enter an inn and become absorbed in conversation with other companions. As a result, the original story is continuously interrupted, thus raising the reader's expectations by always delaying their fulfillment. The novel describes the happenings of a single day, but the remembrances of the characters help to re-create the intricate layers of the irrecoverable past.

For most of the 1920s Krúdy continued to live on the Margitsziget and seemed to have ensured his critical reputation. The twenty-fifth anniversary of his poetic debut was celebrated in 1925, and on this occasion the Athenaeum publishing house produced an edition of his selected works in ten volumes. In 1925–1926 he spent several weeks in Vienna as the guest of Lajos Hatvany (1880–1961). However, he fell ill in 1926 and was treated in a sanatorium; he never truly recovered from his illness. Facing serious financial difficulties, in 1927 Krúdy was evicted from his flat. In the summer of 1928 he had a partial stroke, and he suffered a nervous breakdown in 1929. As a result he was forced to leave his home on the Margitsziget in 1930 and spent his last years with his family in a house in Óbuda. Although in 1930 he received the Baumgartern Prize, Hungary's most prestigious literary award, it did little to resolve his financial situation, and Krúdy died in virtual poverty on 12 May 1933.

One of the most innovative authors in early twentieth-century Hungarian literature, Krúdy influenced generations of later Hungarian writers. The theme and style of Sándor Márai's novel *Szinbád hazamegy* (Szinbád is Going Home, 1940) resemble those of Krúdy's Szindbád tales. Péter Esterházy's *Termelési regény* (Production Novel, 1979) draws on Krúdy's gastronomic theme, and the modality and motif-structure in the recent stories of László Darvasi can be related to the emotive tone and metaphoric texts of the narrators in Krúdy's prose.

Bibliographies:

Sándor Kozocsa, *Krúdy világa* (Budapest: Fővárosi Szabó Ervin Könyvtár, 1964);

Albert Tezla, *Hungarian Authors: A Bibliographical Handbook* (Cambridge, Mass.: Belknap Press of Harvard University Press, 1970), pp. 356–365;

Mihaly Gedenyi, *Krúdy Gyula: bibliografia, 1892–1976* (Budapest: Petőfi Irodalmi Múzeum, 1978).

References:

Gábor Bezeczky, *Szindbád előtt* (Budapest, 1992);

Béla Czére, *Krúdy Gyula* (Budapest: Gondolat, 1987);

Anna Fabri, "Where Time Stood Still: Images of Upper Hungary in the Work of Mor Jokai, Kalman Mikszath and Gyula Krúdy," *Hungarian Quarterly*, 35 (Winter 1994): 11–22;

László Fülöp, *Közelítések Krúdyhoz* (Budapest: Szépirodalmi Könyvkiadó, 1988);

Gábor Kemény, *Képekbe menekülő élet* (Budapest: Akadémiai Kiadó, 1993);

Kemény, *Krúdy kepalkotasa* (Budapest: Akadémiai Kiadó, 1974);

Sándor Kozocsa, "Utószó," in *Krúdy Gyula: Írói arcképek* (Budapest: Magvető, 1957), II: 535–546;

Zsuzsa Krúdy, *Apam, Szindbád* (Budapest: Magvető, 1975);

László Mátrai, "Krúdy realizmusa," *Magyarok*, 4 (1948): 22–25;

István Sőtér, "Krúdy Gyula," in *Krúdy Gyula: Hét bagoly. Boldogult úrfikoromban* (Budapest: Szépirodalmi Könyvkiadó, 1954), pp. i–xxvi;

Ede Szabó, "Krúdy Gyula," in *Krúdy Gyula: Válogatott novellák* (Budapest: Szépirodalmi Könyvkiadó, 1957), pp. 7–41;

József Szauder, "Szindbád születése," in *A romantika útján. Tanulmányok* (Budapest: Szépirodalmi Könyvkiadó, 1961), pp. 376–396;

Ferenc Takacs, "Gyula Krúdy and Szindbád," *Hungarian P.E.N.*, 23 (1982): 38–43;

Áron Tóbiás, *Krúdy világa* (Budapest: Fővárosi Szabó Ervin Könyvtár, 1964).

Martin Kukučín
(Matej Bencúr)
(17 May 1860 – 21 May 1928)

Ján Gbúr
University P. J. Šafárika Prešov

Translated by Martin Votruba

BOOKS: *Koniec a začiatok. 1. zv. Knižnice časopisu Slovenské pohľady* (Martin, 1892);

Dies irae . . . (Martin: Vyd. Knihkupecko-nakladateľského spolku, 1893);

Rysavá jalovica (Ružomberok, 1903);

Maťvolá: Ohlasy z obce roztratených, 5 volumes (Trnava: G. A. Bežo, 1926–1927).

Editions and Collections: *Zobrané spisy Martina Kukučína*, 32 volumes (Martin: Matica slovenská, 1911–1944)—comprises volume 1, *Z teplého hniezda a iné rozprávky;* volume 2, *Dedinský roman a iné rozprávky;* volume 3, *So stupňa na stupeň a iné rozprávky;* volumes 4–5, *Dom v stráni;* volume 6, *Koniec a začiatok a iné rozprávky;* volume 7, *Rohy a iné rozprávky;* volume 8, *S našej hradskej a iné rozprávky;* volume 9, *Črty z ciest, Dojmy z Francúzska;* volume 10, *Na obecnom salaši a iné rozprávky;* volume 11, *Po deviatich rokoch a iné rozprávky;* volume 12, *Čas tratí–čas platí a iné rozprávky;* volume 13, *Mladé Letá. Poza školu. Zpod školského prachu. Zo studentskych časov. Pred skúškou;* volume 14, *Svadba a iné rozprávky;* volume 15, *Cestopisné črty: V Dalmácii a na Čiernej Hore;* volume 16, *Cestopisné črty: Rijeka–Rohič–Záhreb;* volumes 17–18, *Lukáš Blahosej Krasoň;* volumes 19–22, *Bohumil Valislosť Zábor;* volume 23, *Košútky a iné rozprávky;* volume 24, *Komasácia; obraz zo slovenskej dediny v štyroch dejstvach;* volumes 25–27, *Črty z ciest; Prechádzký po Patagónii;* volumes 28–32, *Maťvolá;*

Zivot (Martin, 1950);

Na dedine (Bratislava, 1953);

Do školy (Bratislava, 1955);

Krátke prózy (Bratislava: Slovenské vydavateľstvo krásnej literatúry, 1955);

Martin Kukučín

Dielo Martina Kukučína, 21 volumes, edited by Marianna Mináriková (Bratislava: Slovenské vydavateľstvo krásnej literatúry, 1957–1971);

Dve cesty (Bratislava: Tatran, 1972);

Martin Kukučín. Výber z diela, 4 volumes (Bratislava: Zlatý fond slovenskej literatúry, 1980);

Keď báčik z Chochoľova umrie (Bratislava: Tatran, 1983);

Kukučín zblizka: vyber z listov (Bratislava: Tatran, 1989).

Editions in English: "The Recruits," selected and translated by Paul Selver, in *An Anthology of Czechoslovak Literature* (London: Kegan Paul, Trench, Trübner, 1929);

"His Imperial and Royal Majesty's Recruits," translated by Selver, in *Hundred Towers: A Czechoslovak Anthology of Creative Writing*, edited by F. C. Weiskopf (New York: Fischer, 1945);

"The Village Story" and "More about the Fair," excerpts from *Dom v stráni*, translated by Andrew Cincura, in *An Anthology of Slovak Literature* (Riverside, Cal.: University Hardcovers, 1976), pp. 104–125;

Seven Slovak Stories, translated by Norma L. Rudinsky (Rome: Slovak Institute, 1980).

Martin Kukučín is one of the most authentic writers of Slovak literary epic realism. His fiction is oriented toward what were originally two marginal literary themes: the general nature of being Slovak and the villager surrounded by his whole environment, speech, and traditions. Through these topics, and through his new language and characteristic humor, Kukučín broadened the horizons of the realistic method in art and inspired the literary awareness of his own and following generations of Slovak fiction writers in a decisive manner.

Kukučín was born Matej Bencúr on 17 May 1860 in the small Slovak village of Jasenová, where he obtained his elementary education. He came from a family of freemen, or so-called *šoltýs*, and according to local custom, as the third son of the family he had to either learn a trade or attend college, and he decided upon the latter. After secondary school in Revuca, Martin, and Banská Bystrica and graduation from a teachers' college in Kláštor pod Znievom, he taught in his home village of Jasenová from 1878 to 1884. During this period Kukučín initiated his career as a writer. His earliest works, written between 1882 and 1884 and published in a variety of Slovak literary journals and periodicals, are stories about the lives of peasant country folk and village life, notably "Na hradskej ceste" (On the County Road, 1883), "Čas tratí–čas platí" (Time Lost–Time Paid, 1883), "Máje" (Maypoles, 1883), "Pán majster Obšival" (Master Sewed-It, 1883); "Na jarmok" (To the Fair, 1883), "Dedinský jarmok" (1883; translated as "A Village Fair," 1980), "Na Ondreja" (On St. Andrew's Holiday, 1883), "Hody" (Feast, 1884), "Hajtman" (Commander, 1884), and "Obecné trampoty" (1884; translated as "Village Squabbles," 1980). While these stories are marked by sentimental literary influences and romantic equivocality, they already partly include stylistic features modeled on folk phraseology and folk poetry. In these early works Kukučín emphasizes his direct relationship to the living prototypes of his characters. At the same time, he makes the stories more interesting with lyrical descriptions in the spirit of Nikolai Vasil'evich Gogol's poetics and of traditional Slovak folk sayings and proverbs. This method of depiction was deliberately aimed at the literary tastes of the common reader, who found himself and his life stories depicted in the author's characters.

Kukučín's literary method is derived from three sources: folklore and folk traditions, Romantic and post-Romantic short fiction, and theories of natural science, particularly Charles Darwin's theory of evolution, Auguste Comte's positivism, and Claude Bernard's experimental physiology. Based on these sources, Kukučín created a type of fiction, the most characteristic feature of which is its colloquial style that uses widely diversified dialogue. Out of this principle grew another characteristic of Kukučín's fiction—his grotesque-humorous stylization of stories with lyrical-optimistic subtext. This trend characterized his writing to the end of World War I. His works after that period acquired a somewhat different character: the employment of lively vernacular was replaced with introspection, and the grotesque-humorous stylization of the stories was replaced by tragic-nostalgic and existential concerns about the destiny of his own nation and mankind.

In 1885 Kukučín received a diploma from the Sopron Gymnasium (located in what is now Hungary). He subsequently studied medicine at Charles University in Prague (1885–1893) and began his medical practice in Selce on the Croatian island of Brač (1894–1907), where on 23 October 1904 he married Perica Didolić. During his studies in Sopron and Prague, Kukučín continued to develop his artistic methodology and published his work on a regular basis in *Slovenské pohľady* and other literary journals and periodicals. The short stories, sketches, satires, and other short pieces of this period—including "Z teplého hniezda" (1885; translated as "From a Warm Nest," 1980), "Rysavá jalovica" (1885; translated as "The Mottled Heifer," 1980), "Panský hájnik" (Master's Forester, 1885),

"Na svitaní" (At Dawn, 1885), "Neprebudený" (1886; translated as "An Unawakened Boy, or the Village Idiot," 1980), "O Michale" (On St. Michael's Holiday, 1886), "Ako sa kopú poklady" (How Treasures Are Dug Out, 1886), "Pozor na čižmy" (Watch Out for Boots, 1886), "Veľkou lyžicou" (With a Large Spoon, 1886), "Sviatočné dumy" (Holiday Musings, 1886), and "Tri roje cez deň" (Three Swarms a Day, 1886)—note how Kukučín names with almost documentary thoroughness the variety of human activities and work and the desires and rhythm of the characters' ordinary working days.

Kukučín delved deeply into the miracles of vernacular, daily routines, folk tales, and holiday celebrations, as well as into the feelings of young villagers and the fantastic delusions of village drunks. The majority of his works have a simple three-part composition in which the comic and tragicomic prevail. Within this context, two short stories—"Rysavá jaľovica" and "Neprebudený"—stand out, since the grotesque serves as the foundation of the comedy and tragedy in both by the deliberate exaggeration and mix of positive and negative features in the central characters. Kukučín derived the topic of "Rysavá jaľovica" from the popular moralistic and abstentionist reading of his day; in it the grotesque mirrors the balance of forces of tradition within the basic societal unit—the family. The protagonist, Adam Krt, uses the occasion of a trip to a country fair to avoid the domestic order embodied in his wife, Eva. Humbled after a series of mishaps that center on his search for a lost calf, Krt resolves to stop drinking and to return to the family hearth and the uneasy certainties of his life. The short story "Neprebudený" counteracts the illusionless aspects of life and death. The unusual nature of the story lies in its depiction of the tragedy of the mentally and physically strapped village shepherd Ondráš Machuľa, who strives in vain to fit into an environment restricted by natural laws and collective traditions. Kukučín's stories "Preháňanky" (Showers, 1888), "Za ženu" (After a Wife, 1888), "Dedina v noci" (Village at Night, 1888), and his memoir "Úvod k vakáciám" (An Introduction to a Vacation, 1888) show an author ultimately moving toward a personal epic style on the level of situation comedy. His most accomplished work of art from the end of the 1880s is the novella "Mladé letá" (Young Years, 1899), in which Kukučín plays out the psychological and lyrical story of an emotional conflict among four young people.

Title page for Kukučín's five-volume fictional chronicle of Croatian immigrant life

At his short-story writing peak (1890–1894) Kukučín paints a wider social picture—in addition to the situation and verbal comedy, with notable depiction of psychological detail—and demonstrates his ability to build an intellectual view of reality. This concept is especially confirmed by the short story "Keď báčik z Chochoľova umrie" (When Uncle from Chochoľov Dies, 1890), in which he utilized the principles of paradox and irony to describe not only the tragedy and comedy of the decline of the impoverished and incompetent landed gentry but also the burgeoning entrepreneurial class and its moral defects. He similarly depicted the emotional emptiness of the petty bourgeoisie, notably in "Na podkonickom bále" (At the Podkoniky Ball, 1891); the philosophical contrast that exists between belief in timeless values and the recognition of their disappearance from human life, as in "Dve cesty"

(Two Roads, 1892); and the sociological ramifications of the destructive power of capitalist money, shown in a miserly farmer during a cholera epidemic in *Dies irae . . .* (1893; translated as *Dies irae . . .*, 1980). In the semidocumentary narrative "Zápisky zo smutného domu" (Notes from a Sad House, 1894), written at the end of his studies in Prague, Kukučín tried to reconstruct his personal and literary experiences up to that point in his life.

On the island of Brač, Kukučín strove as a writer to become one with the local environment, an effort that he realized thoroughly. The first part of this period (1894–1901) was devoted to detailed epic pictures of the environs in Dalmatian villages and towns in such stories as "Svadba" (Wedding, 1896), "Parník" (Steamboat, 1896), "Štedrý deň" (Christmas Eve, 1897), and "Mišo II" (Michael II, 1901) and also to documentary writing, resulting in the extensive travelogue titled *Cestopisne črty* (Travel Features), published in *Slovenské pohľady* in two parts: "V Dalmácii a na Čiernej Hore" (In Dalmatia and Montenegro, 1898) and "Rijeka–Rohič–Záhreb" (Rijeka–Rohič–Zagreb, 1901). The second part of his stay in Brač culminated in the two-volume novel titled *Dom v stráni* (The House on a Hill), which first appeared in *Slovenské pohľady* in 1903–1904 and later in *Zobrané spisy Martina Kukučína* (Collected Works of Martin Kukučín) in 1911–1912. Landscape surroundings and traditions acquire new aspects in this novel; yet, the motives of the characters' actions still have Slovak roots. Furthermore, as is traditional with the author, Darwin's theories about the natural selection of mates and its inevitable consequences are present. The true topic of the novel is the conflict, caused by the influence of the milieu and its traditions upon their parents as well as themselves, that ruins the struggles of patrician son Niko Dubčić to marry the peasant Katica Berac. *Dom v stráni* is a so-called open novel, because the leading characters transcend their societal constraints and are fully accountable for their actions. At the same time, it represents a new perspective (class rather than national) on a traditional motif in Slovak realistic fiction—the conflict between "castle and farm house."

In 1907 Kukučín and his wife moved to South America. In Santiago, Chile, he passed his medical certification exams and went on to become a physician in the remote south Chilean town of Punta Arenas, where he lived within a community of Croatian immigrants until 1922.

There he collected documentary material that later became the basis for his fictional chronicle on Croatian immigrant life, *Mat' volá* (Motherland Calls), published in five volumes in 1926–1927. This novel is of a different type from *Dom v stráni*, primarily because Kukučín develops its literary message through multiple layers of complementary meanings and meditative-reflexive elements of depiction that transcend his previous criteria for realism. In this work the themes of love and death cover a much broader sphere than ever before. As illustrated by its subtitle, *Ohlasy z obce roztratených* (Voices from the Community of the Scattered), the novel deals with love of mankind and love of one's country, as well as with the demise of man, his hopes, and his dreams. The protagonist, Simon Katović—possibly Kukučín's alter ego—is marooned without hope of ever returning to his homeland as he evaluates his idealistic and self-sacrificing but impractical and failed plans. Characteristic of the novel are, on the one hand, a complicated structure that corresponds semantically to the idea of a complex world and, on the other hand, a conclusion filled with the image of lonely pines on the Adriatic coast that symbolizes permanence, the myth of home, and the traditions of the motherland. *Mat' volá* is a so-called closed type of novel, meaning the protagonist's movement through the widely conceived space of the novel is an illusion. In spite of his extensive social contacts, Katović spends most of his time dwelling on his own perceptions, isolated from society. In this sense the novel reflects an overtone of negativism that impacted its mixed critical reception in Slovakia.

Contrary to general expectations, Kukučín did not return to Slovakia after the founding of Czechoslovakia in 1918. Once he did return in 1922, he lived for a time in the Croatian capital of Zagred and then resettled with his wife at the Croatian spa of Lipik in 1926 after she became ill. He only returned to Slovakia as a visitor in order to research material for his novels on Slovak national history. After returning to Europe, Kukučín had difficulty striking a balance between the new reality of life and his old literary methods and stylistic approach. He replaced his original simple and spare expression and dialogue style with expansive meditative monologue, which he tried to use as a narrative principle to express in direct proportion the complexity of problems he undertook to solve. In *Dom v stráni* and *Mat' volá* it became apparent that his change in literary method reduced the semantic interdependencies

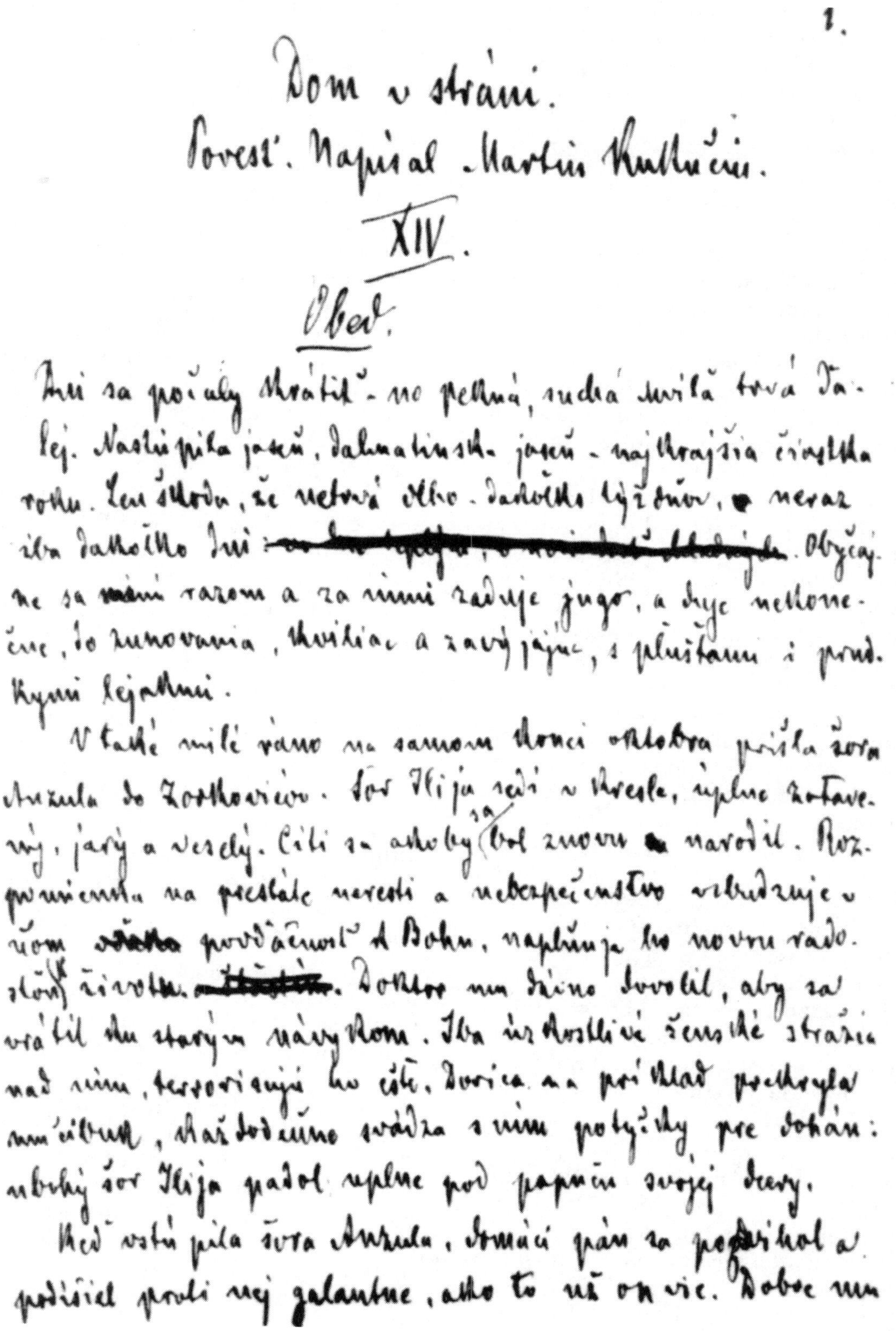

1.

Dom v stráni.

Povesť. Napísal Martin Kukučin.

XIV.

Obed.

Dni sa počaly skrátiť – no pekná, suchá, milá tráva ďa-lej. Nastúpila jeseň, dalmatínska jeseň – najkrajšia čiastka roku. Len škoda, že netrvá dlho – dakoľko týždňov, a neraz iba dakoľko dní [illegible]. Obyčaj-ne sa mení razom a za ňimi zaduje jugo, a duje nekone-čne, do zunovania, kvíliac a zavýjajúc, s pleštanim i prud-kými lejakmi.

V takė milé ráno na samom konci októbra prišla šora Anzula do Zorkovičov. Šor Ilija sedí v kresle, úplne zotave-ný, jarý a veselý. Cíti sa, akoby sa bol znovu narodil. Roz-pomienka na prestaté nerestí a nebezpečenstvo vzbudzuje v ňom [illegible] povďačnosť k Bohu, naplňuje ho novou rado-sťou života [illegible]. Doktor mu dávno dovolil, aby sa vrátil ku starým návykom. Iba úzkostlivé ženské stráže nad ním, terorizujú ho ešte. Dorica na príklad predkypla mu citrón, každodenne vádza s ním potýčky pre dohán: úbohý šor Ilija padol úplne pod papuču svojej dcery.

Keď vstúpila šora Anzula, domáci pán sa pohol a podišiel proti nej galantne, ako to už on vie. Dobre mu

Page from the manuscript for Kukučín's novel Dom v stráni *(The House on the Hill)*

of the narratives, that expression transcended thought, and that quizzical parables obscured the depicted reality. The epic relationships in these novels were removed from their folk foundations and began to latch on to abstract notions. Kukučín's intellectualizing and moralizing approach toward reality even became evident in documentary genres such as the travelogue, illustrated by *Prechádzký po Patagónii* (Walks in Patagonia, 1922) and *Dojmy z Francúzska* (Impressions from France, 1923), but is manifested most in his two novels with national historical themes—*Lukáš Blahosej Krasoň* and *Bohumil Valislosť Zábor*—both of which were published posthumously as part of his *Zobrané spisy* in 1929. With these two works (an unfinished trilogy) Kukučín completed his writing of fiction; especially because of the new inconsistencies in his literary method, he barred himself from ever touching the individual psyche that could mirror the deformed appearance of reality. The philosophy of these novels is aimed toward universality, not toward the authentic human personality, and this characteristic is particularly manifested in his protagonists. For the most part, they are romantically monumentalized and marked by pathos. The protagonist in the novel *Lukáš Blahosej Krasoň*, modeled after the Slovak Romantic poet Samo Bohdan Hroboň and his unhappy love for a Czech nationalist woman, also embodies the language split of Slovak from Czech. He demonstrates a practically magical ability to preach to and persuade people through his arguments and passion. *Bohumil Valislosť Zábor* details the years just before the 1848 revolution in the tense relations of Slovak and Magyar, revealed in individuals, classes, and national differences. Despite their shortcomings, these novels bear witness to the fact that Kukučín did not forego national traditions; consequently, he was driven to focus on the ideal of harmony and not to succumb passively to the pressure of new social phenomena.

Kukučín also devoted himself marginally to drama, writing three plays. He created his first dramatic work as early as the time of his Prague studies. As preparation, he gained practical experience by visiting local theaters and acquired theoretical knowledge through discussions with people in Czech theater and by reading domestic and foreign dramas. This period gave rise to his four-act play *Komasácia* (written in 1889 and published in *Slovenské pohľady* in 1907), which, compared with other contemporary Slovak plays, was remarkable not only because it was the first realis-

tic play with a social theme but also because it was at the same time a play of the highest literary standard, something that had not been reached by other Slovak playwrights. In it he indirectly depicted the theme of *komasácia*—the consolidation of fragmented parcels of land through the intermediation of emotional and family ties. The play begins as a drama and ends as a comedy, and in the space of its dramatic text Kukučín tried to apply his epic method of harmonizing discord in a nonconfrontational manner. Meanwhile, the play *Bacúchovie dvor* (The Bacúchs' Yard), written in 1922 but published only in 1930 as part of his *Zobrané spisy*, does not reach the communicative level of *Komasácia*. The later play sketched an over-idealized picture of Slovak village life at the time Kukučín rediscovered it in 1922. His third play, *Obeť* (Sacrifice), written in 1924 and unpublished until 1964, is less important as a dramatic work; even its theme did not differ from the subject of a nationalist poet, later utilized by Kukučín in the novel *Lukáš Blahosej Krasoň*.

In 1928 Kukučín became seriously ill and died that same year in a hospital in Pakrac, near Lipik, on 21 May. He was buried in a tomb at the Mirogoj Cemetery in Zagreb, Croatia, but his remains were transferred and reburied in the National Cemetery in Martin, Slovakia, on 28 October 1928. The publication of his thirty-two-volume collected works, initiated in 1910, was completed in 1944. Indicative of his importance within twentieth-century Slovak literature, this edition was superseded by the twenty-one volume *Dielo Martina Kukučína*, edited by Marianna Mináriková and published from 1957 to 1971.

Kukučín is the type of author who suppresses in himself the notion that writers hold an elite position in society, instead measuring their importance by the value of their work, which for him was the ability to generate fictions close to real-life models. He initiated and pioneered the most complete type of fiction in the early stage of Slovak literary realism. Kukučín's reputation as a writer of fiction has not waned. His work has been incorporated into modern Slovak fiction as a norm and an aesthetic criterion for the generalized type of Slovak realist fiction, a statement that cannot be made regarding others from his generation.

Bibliography:

Eva Pregnerová, *Martin Kukučín. Výberová bibliografia* (Bratislava, 1980).

Biographies:

Kukučín v kritike a spomienkach. Zborník (Bratislava, 1957);

Ján Juríček, *Martin Kukučín. Život pútnika* (Bratislava: Mladé letá, 1975);

Július Noge, *Martin Kukučín. Život a dielo v dokumentoch* (Martin: Osveta, 1991).

References:

Oskár Čepan, *Kukučínove epické istoty* (Bratislava: Tatran, 1972);

Zlatko Klátik, *Kukučínov román s juhoslovanskou tematikou. Zborník: Literárne vzťahy Slovákov a južných Slovanov* (Bratislava, 1968), pp. 243–257;

Klátik, *Slovenský cestopis vo svetle porovnávacieho skúmania. Zborník: O medziliterárnych vzťahoch* (Bratislava, 1968), pp. 67–76;

Anna Maruniaková, *Martin Kukučín 1860–1928* (Martin: Matica slovenská, 1978);

Pavol Mazák, *Slovenský román v období literárneho realizmu* (Bratislava, 1975), pp. 69–96;

Jozef Mlacek, "Syntax prvych dedinskych poviedok M. Kukučína," *Slovenská reč*, 39 (1974): 149–158;

Andrej Mráz, *Poprevratové literárne dielo Martina Kukučína* (Bratislava, 1953);

Július Noge, *Martin Kukučín tradicionalista a novátor* (Bratislava: Veda, 1975);

Juraj Pado, "Chvile s klasikom," *Slovenské pohľady*, 92, no. 11 (1976): 112–116;

Július Pašteka, *Slovenská dramatika v epoche realizmu* (Bratislava, 1990);

Eugen Pauliny, "Skice k štúdiu formy u Kukučína a Timravy," *Slovenský jazyk*, 1 (1940): 248–249;

Marianna Prídavková, "Kukučínov vzťah k ruskej realistickej literatúre a jeho preklady Gogoľa," in *Jazykovedné štúdie*, 5 (Bratislava, 1961), pp. 223–257;

Marianna Prídavková-Mináriková, *Textologické a štylistické problémy Kukučínovho diela* (Bratislava: SAV, 1972);

Prídavková-Mináriková, ed., *Dielo 21: Listy priateľom a znamym* (Bratislava: Tatran, 1974);

Norma L. Rudinsky, "The Slovak Fairytale Tradition and J. R. R. Tolkien's 'Eucatastrophe,' in the Realistic Stories of Martin Kukučín," *Slovakia*, 30 (1982–1983): 100–111;

Jerzy Slizinski, "Martin Kukučín v Polsce," *Slavica Slovaca*, 3 (1968): 412–415;

Stanislav Šmatlák, "Kukučínova novela Mladé Letá," *Literárnohistorický zborník*, 10 (1953): 60–90;

Ján Števček, *Moderný slovenský román* (Bratislava, 1983), pp. 17–42;

Pavol Števček, "Par vypiskov z Kukučína," *Slovenské pohľady*, 94, no. 5 (1978): 103–109;

Miloš Tomčík, *Literárne dvojobrazy* (Bratislava, 1976), pp. 33–67;

Emil Tvrdon, "Martin Kukučín a slovenčina," *Kultura Slova*, 19, no. 9 (1985): 305–308.

Maria Kuncewicz

(30 October 1895 – 15 July 1989)

Magdalena J. Zaborowska
Århus University

BOOKS: *Tseu-Hi, władczyni bokserów (1836–1909)* (Warsaw: Rój, 1926);

Przymierze z dzieckiem. Powieść (Warsaw: J. Mortkowicz, 1927);

Twarz mężczyzny. Powieść (Warsaw: J. Mortkowicz, 1928);

Miłość panieńska. Sztuka w 4 aktach (Warsaw: Rój, 1932);

Dwa księżyce (Warsaw: Rój, 1933);

Dyliżans warszawski (Warsaw: Rój, 1935);

Cudzoziemka. Powieść (Warsaw: Rój, 1936); translated by B. W. A. Massey as *The Stranger* (London: Hutchinson, 1944; New York: Fischer, 1945);

Dni powszednie państwa Kowalskich. Powieść radiowa (Warsaw: Rój, 1938; revised, 1938);

Kowalscy się odnaleźli. Uzupełnienie powieści radiowej "Dni powszednie państwa Kowalskich" (Warsaw: Rój, 1938);

Serce kraju (Warsaw: Rój, 1938);

Przyjaciele ludzkości (Warsaw: Rój, 1939);

Miasto Heroda. Notatki palestyńskie (Warsaw: Rój, 1939);

W domu i w Polsce (Warsaw: Rój, 1939);

Zagranica (Warsaw: Rój, 1939);

Klucze (London: Nakładem "Nowej Polski," 1943); revised edition (Warsaw: Wiedza, 1948); translated as *The Keys: A Journey through Europe at War* (London & New York: Hutchinson, 1946);

Zmowa nieobecnych. Powieść, volume 1 (London: Światowy Związek Polaków z Zagranicy, 1946); expanded, 2 volumes (Munich: Express, 1950; Warsaw: Pax, 1957); translated by Maurice Michael and Harry Stevens as *The Conspiracy of the Absent: A Novel* (London: Hutchinson, 1950; New York: Roy, 1950);

Leśnik. Powieść (Paris: Instytut Literacki, 1952); translated by Stevens as *The Forester: A Novel* (London: Hutchinson, 1954; New York: Roy, 1954);

Odkrycie Patusanu (Warsaw: Pax, 1958);

Gaj oliwny (Warsaw: Pax, 1961); Kuncewicz's original English version published as *The Olive Grove* (New York: Walker, 1963);

Don Kichote i niańki (Warsaw: Pax, 1965);

Maria Kuncewicz

Tristan 1946 (Warsaw: Czytelnik, 1967); Kuncewicz's original English version published as *Tristan: A Novel* (New York: George Braziller, 1974);

Fantomy (Warsaw: Pax, 1971);

Natura (Warsaw: Pax, 1975);

Fantasia alla polacca (Warsaw: Czytelnik, 1979);

Przeźrocza. Notatki włoskie (Warsaw: Pax, 1985);

Listy do Jerzego (Warsaw: Pax, 1988).

Editions: *Twarz mężczyzny i trzy nowele* (Warsaw: Czytelnik, 1969);

Dzieła. Seria I–II, 13 volumes (Warsaw: Pax, 1978–1986);

Tamto spojrzenie (Kraków: Wydawnictwo Literackie, 1980);

Nowele i bruliony prozatorskie, edited by Helena Zaworska (Warsaw: Czytelnik, 1985);

Dzieła wybrane Marii i Jerzego Kuncewiczów, 8 volumes (Lublin: Wydawnictwo Lubelskie, 1989–1997).

Editions in English: *Polish Millstones*, translated by Stephen Garry (London: P. S. King & Staples, 1942);

"Refugees as World Citizens," *London Times*, 10 March 1949, p. 6a;

"Exile Without Tears," in *The Pen in Exile: An Anthology*, edited by Paul Tabori (London: International PEN Club Center for Writers in Exile, 1954), pp. 14–16.

PLAY PRODUCTIONS: *Miłość panieńska. Sztuka w 4 aktach*, Warsaw, Teatr Mały, 1932;

Thank You for the Rose, London, Teatr Sztuk Czytanych, Scena Klubowa "Ogniska Polskiego," 1956;

Cudzoziemka. Sztuka w 1 akcie z epilogiem, adapted by A. Lutosławska, Kraków, Teatr Miniatura, 1977;

Cudzoziemka, adapted by M. Komorowska, Lublin, Teatr im. J. Osterwy, Scena Kameralna Reduta 70, 1978.

MOTION PICTURE: *Cudzoziemka*, screenplay by Kuncewicz, Zespoły Filmowe, 1986.

RADIO: *Dni powszednie państwa Kowalskich. Powieść mówiona*, 30 segments, Polskie Radio, 1936–1937;

Kowalscy się odnaleźli. Powieść mówiona, 5 segments, Polskie Radio, 1937;

Dialog o zmierzchu. Powieść mówiona, 5 segments, Polskie Radio, 1939;

Polskie żarna, 7 or 8 segments, BBC, Sekcja Polska, 1942;

Oblężenie i obrona Warszawy, BBC, 1949;

Państwo Kowalscy na emigracji: Kowalscy w Anglii, 24 segments, 1956;

Kowalscy w Ameryce, 20 segments, Radio Free Europe, New York, 1956.

OTHER: *Modern Polish Prose*, edited by Kuncewicz (Birkenhead, U.K.: Polish Publications Committee, 1945);

"Avec les réfugies," in *Paris aux yeux du monde*, edited by Boris Metzel (Paris: Deux-Rives, 1951);

The Modern Polish Mind: An Anthology, edited by Kuncewicz (Boston & Toronto: Little, Brown, 1962; London: Secker & Warburg, 1963).

TRANSLATIONS: Jack London, *Gra*, translated by Kuncewicz (Warsaw: Biblioteka Dzieł Wyborowych, 1923);

London, *Podła kobieta*, translated by Kuncewicz (Warsaw: Towarzystwo Wydawnicze Bluszcz, 1923);

London, *Arcybestia*, translated by Kuncewicz (Warsaw: Rój, 1926);

Ilia Erenburg, *Lato. R. 1925*, translated by Kuncewicz (Warsaw: Rój, 1927);

Jean Giraudoux, *Bella*, translated by Kuncewicz (Warsaw: Rój, 1929);

Sigrid Undset, *Pani Hjelde*, translated by Kuncewicz (Warsaw: Rój, 1931);

Undset, *Macierzyństwo*, translated by Kuncewicz (Warsaw: Rój, 1933).

Maria Kuncewicz (in Polish, Kuncewiczowa) was one of the most engaging Polish writers of the twentieth century. In the late 1970s she was nominated for the Nobel Prize in literature, although her reputation has remained more prominent in Poland than internationally. She lived through some of the most profound upheavals of the modern and postmodern period: she came of age when Poland regained independence in 1918; when the German army invaded Poland in September 1939 she went into exile, first in Western Europe and then in the United States; and she returned to her home country in the 1960s as an American citizen. Her works span such genres as the short story, novel, travel notebook, autobiography, radio serial, play, and essay. In their perceptive and subtle treatment of twentieth-century anxieties, her writings can be seen as ahead of their time, especially in their focus on subjects that late-twentieth-century literary critics and readers are "discovering" and hailing as postmodern, feminist, or subversive. In their indefatigable probing into the nature of authorship and the creative process, Kuncewicz's texts are proof that literature often transcends simplistic dichotomies, cultural clichés, and national identity politics.

Kuncewicz came from a family of mixed ethnic origins (German, Russian, Lithuanian, and Polish), and this background had a profound impact on her work. She was born Maria Zofia Szczepańska in Samara, Russia, on 30 October 1895 (some sources say 1897 or 1899; Kuncewicz preferred to give a different year, but documentary evidence indicates 1895). Her parents were, as scholar Barbara Kazimierczyk mentions, "a typical product of [Polish] national history," for they were exiled from the partitioned Poland for political reasons. In addition to ancestors who fought in the insurrection against Russia in 1863 Kuncewicz could also claim almost legendary progenitors who took part in the Napoleonic Wars and migrated as far as Santo Domingo. Her parents came from the intelligentsia or impoverished nobility whose only capital was thorough education: her father, Józef Szczepański, was a teacher of mathematics and a school principal, while her mother, Róża Adela Dziubińska, gave up her career as a violinist to marry and raise a family. Kuncewicz had an older brother, Alexander, who became a prominent diplomat in newly independent Poland.

As was characteristic at that time in middle-class Polish families, the children were given careful schooling. Kuncewicz received an international education that included several languages, music, and the study of French and Polish philology in Nancy, at the Jagiellonian University in Kraków, and the University of Warsaw. She considered a career as a concert singer; some of her studies took place at the conservatories of Warsaw and Paris. Despite her love for music, which often influenced her writings later on, she chose a literary vocation after her debut in the Polish journal *Pro Arte et Studio* in 1918. Three years later she married Jerzy Kuncewicz, a lawyer, populist activist, philosopher, and writer, with whom she had a son, Witold, in 1922.

In the early 1920s Kuncewicz started working at the Polish PEN Club and publishing translations of such authors as Ilia Erenburg, Jean Giraudoux, Jack London, and Sigrid Undset. Her early writings include works for young readers, such as the story *Tseu-Hi, władczyni bokserów* (Tseu-Hi, She-Ruler of Boxers, 1926). In 1927, which Kuncewicz considers the year of her proper debut, she published a volume of short stories titled *Przymierze z dzieckiem* (Covenant with a Child), which biographer Halina Ivaničkova described as "a revolt against deep-seated prejudices and bourgeois prudery." Serialized the year before in *Bluszcz* (Ivy), a widely read journal for women, the title story had caused quite a scandal in 1920s Poland, where the "woman question" debate raged as high as anywhere else in Europe. The story, with its frank depiction of woman's physiology and its unapologetic and emancipated demystification of the sacred Polish myth of motherhood as divine, sublime, and nationalistic, made many critics into Kuncewicz's enemies. As the writer herself humorously suggested after one of the reviews of her next volume, *Twarz mężczyzny* (A Man's Face, 1928), her work evoked "premonitions of blood running in the sewers and the triumph of revolted human female." This work dismantled domestic and European myths of sublime femininity and of mar-

riage as a joining of souls, and it dealt openly with female eroticism, desire, and sexuality.

Kuncewicz's early psychological studies of young women led to her profound and masterful exploration of female identity, creativity, and social roles in her acclaimed first novel, *Cudzoziemka* (1936; translated as *The Stranger*, 1944). Following the staging of her play *Miłość panieńska* (A Maiden's Love) in 1932, Kuncewicz's novelistic debut launched a mature writer and won immediate domestic and international acclaim; it was soon translated into several languages. However, the young writer's preoccupation with woman's place in history, politics, and society, as well as the tone of "public confession" that so disgusted prim and decorous readers of her early stories serialized in *Bluszcz*, are not the only reasons for Kuncewicz's later fame as a major Polish fiction writer of the interwar period.

Before *Cudzoziemka* confirmed some readers' worst expectations about Kuncewicz's morals and values and made others hail her as a master of novelistic narrative and psychological portrayal, she published another volume that contributed to her signature style. *Dwa księżyce* (Two Moons, 1933) is a collection of short stories that are set in Kazimierz on the Vistula, a charming small town with beautiful landscapes and distinctive architecture. In these stories Kuncewicz explores themes of locality, ethnicity, and class. The stories depict two worlds that coexist in Kazimierz: the local community of orthodox Jews, peasants, craftsmen, and impoverished nobility; and the bohemian group of modern painters, models, and writers who descend on the town in search of artistic inspiration in nature and in the "revolting beauty" of its inhabitants. The former group, the poor, goes to sleep under the red moon of those who work until sunset and rise at dawn, while the latter group ventures out to explore the enchantments of the local woods, ravines, and cobblestoned streets under the late, white moon that shines for the ever-nocturnal artist and intellectual. With visual, musical, and even ethnographic sensibility Kuncewicz weaves impressionistic descriptions of nature and poignant portraits of both the natives and the newcomers. There is subtle irony in her depictions of personages from the "worlds on high" and an often touchingly grotesque presentation of small-town Jews, poor craftsmen, and local melodramas, portrayed with frank sympathy and respect. As her husband's nephew Piotr Kuncewicz claims, the volume implies that each individual has a right to his or her own moon, and to some readers the book may seem Kuncewicz's greatest achievement for its "plastic descriptions, humor, thinly directed plot, precision of psychological portrayal, [and] considerable dose of artfulness." The collection enjoyed a significant revival that inspired paintings by young artists and a 1993 motion picture production.

Before publishing her acclaimed first novel, Kuncewicz also produced a collection of what Leon Piwiński, in a 1933 *Wiadomości Literackie* article, called "novelistic pretexts": *Dyliżans warszawski* (Warsaw Stagecoach, 1935). This volume is a series of vignettes and reports from Warsaw that originally appeared in the journal *Gazeta Polska* (Polish Gazette) throughout 1934—impressions of people, streets, private apartments, cafés, and beauty salons. Although considered marginal by some critics, the work may have been an important exercise that enabled Kuncewicz to capture both the psychology and geography of the city with unusual subtlety, complexity, and poignant irony in her first novel. *Cudzoziemka* indeed combines sharp observations of Warsaw (Kuncewicz received a President's Award in the capital for having written the "Warsaw Novel of the Year") with biographical elements taken from her mother's life. By 1932 both of Kuncewicz's parents were dead, and as she admitted years later in an interview, she wrote the novel out of fear that her memory of her mother would disappear unless captured in words. *Cudzoziemka* made the portrait of Kuncewicz's mother immortal, and Kuncewicz won a Golden Laurel from the Polish Academy of Literature in 1938, the same year that another important Polish award—the Gold Cross of Merit of the Second Respublica—confirmed her prominence among leading European artists and intellectuals. As much an homage to the mother as an attempt to exorcise the daughter's complex emotions, *Cudzoziemka* tells a story loosely based on Dziubińska's life and focuses on her sense of displacement and alienation as a woman of mixed ethnicity whose unrequited love and unfulfilled artistic vocation made her into an eternal "foreigner."

The action takes place during an afternoon and late evening, and the setting is first the Warsaw apartment of protagonist Róża Żabczyńska's daughter, to whom Róża pays a tempestuous visit, and then Róża's own bedroom, where she unexpectedly dies of heart failure with her family present just a few hours later. Although the time of action is compressed, the narrative is rich in flashbacks that gradually reveal the heroine's life story. Róża emerges as an exceptionally sensitive and incredibly self-destructive woman, a tormentor of her unloved husband and two children. Róża verges on the absurd and evil or the comical and grotesque at times, but she is constructed as an unmistakably tragic character victimized by repression and her unconscious mind. As fellow writer Bruno Schulz indicated in an enthusiastic review, Róża takes readers,

Róża Adela Dziubinska, Kuncewicz's mother and the model for the protagonist of her first novel, Cudzoziemka *(1936; translated as* The Stranger, *1944)*

"in torment," to the "bottom of the soul," which, once revealed, opens up into a "star-studded firmament." Western European critics were equally enthusiastic and compared *Cudzoziemka* with Leo Tolstoy's *Anna Karenina* (1875–1877) and Gustave Flaubert's *Madame Bovary* (1857), but, as Ivaničkova stresses, they were quick to point out that they saw Róża as "plus artiste, plus aristocratique que l'heroine de Flaubert," not to mention that her tragedy appeared "moins personnel, plus collectif, plus actuel."

Many middle-class white European women at that time were caught between the increasing opportunities to develop their talents and ambitions, and the traditional feminine roles that still held them captive; in embodying these torments Róża was a truly romantic heroine. However, in writing a novel about a woman who felt exiled and alienated even from those closest to her, Kuncewicz also presented an astute study of a thwarted female artist. Róża became embittered because she was deprived of her art; as an unfulfilled concert violinist turned housewife by the force of convention, she proceeded to make other people's lives into the hell that she was experiencing daily as a woman, mother, Pole, and wife. She wages war against those who misunderstood, objectified, or exploited her beauty and sought traditional feminine ideals in her: all men, after her first love betrayed her; and her whole family, after she became pregnant as a result of marital rape. More interesting, Róża also turns her fury against God, a gesture that must have been shocking to some of her readers in Catholic Poland. Equally provocatively, Kuncewicz delves into the erotic and sexual effects of Róża's unfulfilled artistic desires. In a passage narrated with particular brilliance Kuncewicz depicts Róża's moonlit trance as she plays the music of Johannes Brahms to nearly orgasmic fulfillment. The brutal interruption of the scene by her otherwise quiet and weak husband, who turns into a rapist as if in retaliation for her autoerotic musical indulgence, stuns the reader. The novel closes with a scene of lyrical reconciliation and forgiveness in which Róża is finally set free to fully embrace her "music."

Despite her clear focus on women's psychology in this novel, Kuncewicz has not been dubbed a feminist, especially in post–World War II Poland, where many people remain uncomfortable with the term. Although it can boast exceptionally strong women who have challenged the prevailing nationalistic and religious myths of womanhood since the nineteenth century, Poland is still overshadowed by the two romantic types of womanhood that Kuncewicz criticizes with her portrayal of Róża: "Mother Poland," a Virgin Mary–like guardian of tradition, family, and national character; and "chaste maiden," a desexualized creature who, like some Slavic Penelope, faithfully awaits her warrior-lover for years or nurses his wounds until she reaches spinsterhood without a single thought for her own well-being. Róża suffers because of the expectations that these models created for Polish women, but she arrogantly persists in her fierce individualism and rejection of them, no matter what the cost.

After the success of *Cudzoziemka*, Kuncewicz turned to a more popular medium and a genre that made her a pioneer in the history of Polish radio. *Dni powszednie państwa Kowalskich* (Life with the Kowalskis, 1936–1937) was the first radio serial in Europe and depicted the everyday life of a typical Polish couple—a milliner and a teacher—in Warsaw. This project was followed by *Kowalscy się odnaleźli* (The Kowalskis Are Back Again, 1937). Later, during Kuncewicz's stay in the West, came *Państwo Kowalscy na emigracji* (Mr. and Mrs. Kowalski in Exile), which consisted of *Kowalscy w Anglii* (The Kowalskis in England) and *Kowalscy w Ameryce* (The Kowalskis in America), broadcast by Radio Free Europe in New York in 1956. Another of her radio series, one termed "a spoken novel" and titled *Dialog o zmierzchu* (A Dialogue at Twilight), came right on the eve of the war in 1939, as did collections of stories for

young people: *Serce kraju* (The Country's Heart, 1938), *Przyjaciele ludzkości* (Friends of Humanity, 1939), *W domu i w Polsce* (At Home and in Poland, 1939), and *Zagranica* (The World Abroad, 1939).

Also in 1939, as a vice president of the Polish PEN Club, Kuncewicz published an account of her travels to the Holy Land. *Miasto Heroda. Notatki palestyńskie* (The City of Herod. Notes from Palestine, 1939) includes her meditations on the possibility of the emergence of the state of Israel and impressions from her travels to Syria, Egypt, and Palestine in 1936. The book is not only a valuable record by one of the first Polish women writers to ever travel to the Middle East but also an important text that attests to Kuncewicz's craft of reportage, stemming from what Ivaničkova terms her often obsessive curiosity about "the strange and unfamiliar."

World War II began just three years after the completion of Kuncewicz's beloved house in Kazimierz, later named "Kuncewiczówka," which stands on a lush hill overlooking the historic central town square. Ironically, two important PEN congresses that Kuncewicz had attended as a delegate in Paris in 1937 and in Prague in 1938 were both focused on the role and power of intellectuals in countering non-humanitarian world politics. Kuncewicz returned to Prague on the eve of that city's fall to the Germans, as she later described at the beginning of her diary-novel-memoir, *Klucze* (1943; translated as *The Keys: A Journey through Europe at War*, 1946). She realized that her arguments about Polish politics concerning Lithuania sounded as if they were taken "from Hitler's repertoire." In its frank self-examination, pitiless realism, and stark irony, this book is indeed an eye-opener both for the writer and the reader. It sprang from a "whole epoch" that, according to Kazimierczyk, separates Kuncewicz's prewar and wartime writings. *Klucze* uses a metaphor of keys, useless objects that war refugees took with them in flight, clinging to them desperately although the houses and doors that they used to open had been blown away by the bombs in cities and countries that were "deprived of their sky."

Weaving meditations on exile and displacement—what in *Natura* (Nature, 1975) she terms the "commonness of human condition"—Kuncewicz's text records the writer's flight from Kazimierz and Warsaw to Romania and then to France (where she witnessed Philippe Pétain's capitulation) and England, that last European haven, where she lived through the bombings of London and contemplated the ironies of fate. *Klucze* shows, with a good deal of sharp autobiographical insight and astute criticism of the West, that one never knows oneself unless tested by history, and that Poland's naive hopes that France and England would ever come to its rescue were as blind and unfounded as Kuncewicz's earlier belief that good and smart people would prevail over bad ones. (She realized at the Commedie Française, during a performance commemorating Poland's heroic struggle against the German invasion, that her country means to the French no more than "une belle métaphore.") As Margaret Storm Jameson confirmed in her introduction to *The Stranger* in 1945, fate unexpectedly turned Kuncewicz into not only a foreigner but also an exile and political refugee who had to renegotiate her art under extreme circumstances.

Kuncewicz continued to probe the themes of female exile in an interesting futuristic short story, "Dom. Wizja przyszłego fin de siècle'u" (Home: A Vision of a Future Fin de Siècle, 1944). This meditation on a "Global Republic" resulting from a third world war—a world that has disposed of nations, homes, and families, so that "everybody [can] live everywhere"—prefigures Kuncewicz's first novel written in the West, *Zmowa nieobecnych* (1946; translated as *The Conspiracy of the Absent: A Novel,* 1950). Like *Klucze,* this novel focuses on the war and brings together the "home" left behind in Poland and the often meaningless "exile" in England as locations and mythical constructs that connect the characters caught in the war machine in both countries. With a flair for action and imaginative descriptions that made some critics condemn the book as "inauthentic," the narrator presents people in Poland who engage in resistance and love; some die, and some survive. At the same time she offers a perspective on the émigrés in London, who often feel guilty about having fled their country and who try to make up for their sense of uselessness and isolation by showing solidarity with the "absent" ones who face death in Poland. The novel follows the lives of three women: Zofia N., a Polish singer who suffers from depression in London; and Kira and Zuzia, her nieces in Poland, who enter adulthood forced to contemplate and daily witness life and death under Nazi terror.

Writing novels was not Kuncewicz's only concern during her years in England, and she herself never thought highly of *Zmowa nieobecnych.* During this period Kuncewicz devoted much time to working for the Polish PEN Club in exile. One of her main efforts was the PEN Club International War Congress that she organized in London in 1941. It brought together writers and intellectuals from many countries to discuss the ways of resisting fascism; Thornton Wilder and John Dos Passos flew in on a bomber. In the same year Kuncewicz collaborated with Antoni Słonimski on a so-called Black Book of Nazi atrocities that appeared in London in 1941 but may now be lost. She

also worked on several pamphlets translated into English to serve the Polish cause, such as *Polskie żarna* (1941; translated as *Polish Millstones,* 1942) and *Modern Polish Prose* (1945). She collaborated with the BBC and used some of the material from *Klucze* for a radio program, *Oblężenie i obrona Warszawy* (The Siege and Defense of Warsaw), broadcast in 1949. In the same year she took on another, rather utopian initiative: an appeal to the United Nations requesting "world citizenship" for writers and artists who, like herself, became "displaced persons" after the Yalta agreements and the end of the war, and who were arbitrarily assigned countries of residence by international refugee organizations. On 25 February 1949 Kuncewicz sent a letter—also signed by such figures as Bertrand Russell, Thomas Mann, George Bernard Shaw, Aldous Huxley, François Mauriac, and Albert Einstein—to the UN Secretary General. It requested:

> Let the refugees have a say in the cultural reconstruction of the world . . . do not force stateless people, by obstructing their liberty of travel, education, and employment, to apply for new nationalities. By sheer force of events they have acquired the feeling of belonging to a community larger than one nation. . . . history made them citizens of the world, and they should be treated as such.

Predictably, the appeal was ignored; the Iron Curtain fell into place, while the power of the nation-state grew and spread with the booming postwar economies. The International Refugee Organization assigned countries and languages to people such as Jerzy and Maria Kuncewicz in a process that, in an essay included in the collection *The Pen in Exile* (1954), she called the "liquidation as rapid as possible of that awkward monster—the stateless."

Like many exiled Polish authors and artists, Kuncewicz took part in various activities devoted to the Polish cause that were undertaken in London and throughout Britain. She contributed introductions, editorials, and short stories to journals and anthologies, one of which—a volume commemorating the second millennium of Paris, *Paris aux yeux du monde* (1951)—featured a fragment from *Klucze* titled "Avec les réfugies" next to pieces by Fyodor Dostoyevsky, Ernest Hemingway, Gabriele D'Annunzio, and Kate Chopin. Yet, no matter how devoted she was to the causes she was fighting for, Kuncewicz also needed a respite from the themes of the war. The feelings of survivor's guilt haunted her for so long that she wrote in the autobiographical *Natura:* "I will never die in peace because I did not sit in the death chamber." She turned next to interweaving Polish national history and that of her father's family during the second half

Witold Kuncewicz, the author's son

of the nineteenth century in a novel titled *Leśnik* (1952; translated as *The Forester*, 1954).

The book opens with an epigraph from Herman Ould: "we are not real, we crave reality." In the introduction to the 1954 English translation, Kuncewicz explains that the epigraph signifies her focus on the question of representation: "The fact that people are neither what they think they are, nor what anybody else believes them to be, is the book's theme; an ageless problem much alive in modern fiction." Lest she be considered ahistorical and escapist, however, she quickly adds that the book should be read as an historical allegory of sorts; it takes its Western readers into an "unpleasant" foreign past, to the "crossroads of Eastern Europe" marked by revolts against the occupying powers and by the suffering of ethnic minorities under Russian rule.

Leśnik employs a familiar theme in an unfamiliar—perhaps safely remote and "exotic"—setting to show that the "evocations of the past naturally invite analogies with the present." The story follows the life of a young man, Kazimierz (Casimir), in Poland and Lithuania, and its plot is not to be construed as merely

an analogy for the Soviet takeover in Eastern and Central Europe. The young man's story may be read as a direct illustration of the effects of totalitarian oppression, but it may be seen more meaningfully as exploring and anticipating individual people's lives under communism—a system of social repression that in fact may have emerged from the mechanisms of dominance and control in the political regimes of the nineteenth century. As the author makes clear in her introduction:

> Organized violence is still breeding violence, but in the liberal period an imperialistic power had fewer means and less desire to assert its claim to human souls. Under the totalitarian régime Caesar will not be appeased with the face of the coin; and were young Casimir, my hero, to fight his life's battle in our days, neither the forest, nor his mother could afford him a refuge.

Czesław Miłosz, who has not spoken favorably of Kuncewicz's work since her return to Poland, nevertheless praised *Leśnik* in his *History of Polish Literature* (1969) as Kuncewicz's best psychological novel written abroad. He also termed her the most "Western" of Polish women writers for "focusing upon the individual" as well as for her concern with historical detail that allowed her to capture Poland's past.

In 1955 Kuncewicz immigrated to the United States, where she and her husband joined their son, Witold. She continued to write and be active in the PEN Club, taught and lectured on Polish literature at the University of Chicago during the period from 1961 to 1971, had her play *Thank You for the Rose* staged by a Polish club in London in 1956, revived the *Kowalskis* series for Radio Free Europe in New York, and became an American citizen in 1960. She also received prestigious awards: the American Kościuszko Foundation Medal of Merit in 1969 and the Włodzimierz Pietrzak Award in 1971. This period in her life, which resulted in several excellent novels and an autobiographical triptych that bridged her exile and return to Poland, enhanced significantly the unity of her artistic outlook. As she described it later, her writing offered a paradoxical perspective on reality that was a function of two contradictory impulses: a kind of ironic, self-conscious, and somewhat coolheaded realism that emerged in the process of writing; and a pull of unconscious emotions that made her into a fluid and unanchored "phantom," a subject/object in the so-called life outside of her texts. Although she formulated this creed only in her autobiographical *Fantomy* (Phantoms, 1971), it is crucial for the understanding of all the works she produced between 1946 and 1970:

I consider my life to be mostly all that happens in the state of unconsciousness—spinning head, loss of breath, blindness, flight, forgetfulness . . . speed, love trance, vulnerability. I write to bring myself down to earth, to stop the motion I force upon myself: to regain consciousness from un-being . . . in the slow rhythm of writing self-knowledge emerges, I clutch onto an alien element . . . and begin to exist as a separate being. That is the reason for and an aim of my writing—a purely private matter.

Kuncewicz's "purely private" writing during the Cold War remained deeply marked by influences of history and politics while at the same time bearing all the recognizable marks of women's fiction as theorized by feminist critics. It is also crucial to place her art in the context of the "world citizenship" that she claimed for herself in her texts despite the fact that the United Nations Secretary General never answered her appeal of 1949. She felt that she may have given up some of her utopian ideals by having become a citizen of a superpower, but she continued to write like a citizen of the whole world despite her American passport. Having established literature as the only world without borders—what in the introduction to *Gaj oliwny* (1961; Kuncewicz's original English version published as *The Olive Grove*, 1963), she calls the "free-for-all country" of fiction—she then proceeded to prove that "human understanding is not a geographical notion." *Gaj oliwny* is a curious novel that fictionalizes a cause célèbre in the English and French press in 1952: the murder of Sir Jack Drummond and his family by a crazed landowner while they were on vacation in Southern France. The book was begun in England and completed in the United States. Although it was the first novel Kuncewicz wrote in English, it was first published in Polish.

As Kuncewicz explains in the introduction, she was prompted to write this novel by the same obsessive curiosity and commitment to humanism that made her travel in the dangerous Middle East before the war and then to actively promote information about Nazi crimes during the war:

In 1952 only seven years separated us from World War II. But that little girl who had run, under the lovely stars of Provence, from a man who wished to smash her skull, that child's lonely flight through darkness in a strange country, led deeper into human mystery than war itself. Fascinated with this force that can change ordinary breadeaters into murderers, I travelled back home . . . looking attentively at people; the force throbbed under their skins, it worked inside their brains.

The novel indeed probes deeply into the hatreds and feuds between Catholics and Protestants, young and old, rich and poor, men and women. Nevertheless, although the book often reads like a page-turning mystery, Kuncewicz is careful not to pronounce verdicts on the characters. Neither does she blame the evil she analyzes on any one ideology or political system, but instead she elicits the ways in which hatred and the will to destroy others can be taught and inbred. "The time had long passed when I divided humanity into victims and criminals," Kuncewicz says in the preface; "In two world wars I have seen how History was taking charge of individual responsibilities, how Race, Nation, and Church were used to cover up personal obsessions, how the wrong people were slain for the wrong reasons, because love seemed too difficult a solution to human problems."

In 1956, when it still seemed quite unlikely that she would return to the Old World, Kuncewicz was offered contracts by two leading Polish publishers. Because of a post-Stalinist political and cultural "thaw," censorship and the ban on Western publications were relaxed considerably. Two Polish publishing houses, Pax and Czytelnik, promised Kuncewicz that they would "respect the integrity of her texts," although they obviously could not guarantee her freedom from censorship. When the writer announced to PEN members in the West that she had decided to accept these offers, she was forced to resign from the position of honorary president of the international chapter of the club. Some of her colleagues interpreted her decision as a clear indication of her willingness to collaborate with the communists. Although she pleaded that she was simply trying to reach her readers back home and restore some normalcy to a life that for so long had been cut off from family and friends who remained in Poland, she found herself ostracized by some émigré circles.

In *Natura*, however, she recalls slightly different reactions to her decision from those who granted asylum to displaced persons: "An American with whom I had a discussion about this [her decision to publish in Poland] over lunch did not seem either shaken or eager to protest." In contrast, "the so-called Polish Desk [at Radio Free Europe] raised alarm. . . . The demise of 'Kowalscy' [*The Kowalskis*] was suddenly announced and any collaboration with me was immediately dissolved. The latter was implemented so zealously that even two tapes [of the radio novel], already recorded by the actors, were destroyed." Hurt and embittered by this reaction of colleagues, some of whom she ironically called "professional refugees," Kuncewicz decided to visit Poland in 1958 for the first time in nearly twenty years; afterward, having become naturalized in the United States, she returned to Poland regularly and maintained friendly relations with the Polish Consulates in America. This association did not disrupt her "American" activities: travels all over the United States; long visits to Witold's farm, "The Old Kennels," in Flint Hill, Virginia; and lectures at the University of Chicago and University of California, Berkeley, which she greatly enjoyed as they brought back memories of her studies in prewar France and Poland.

It is impossible to determine whether or not the Kuncewiczs' decision to reconnect with People's Poland, and thus renounce the status of political refugees, had anything to do with any concessions on the part of the authorities. It is equally impossible to say how much censorship the writer had to put up with, unless one looks at her third autobiographical volume, post–martial law *Przeźrocza* (Slides, 1985), in which such intrusions are marked in the text. The couple managed to regain their house in Kazimierz, which survived the war because it had been a Gestapo headquarters and remained fairly intact after Soviet "liberation" because it was made into a summer camp base for the children of the members of the *Urząd bezpieczeństwa* (secret police). It is highly unlikely that any serious "betrayal" of loyalties had to take place for the Kuncewiczs to be able to resettle in the old country. In a letter to an American friend the writer explained her view: "I never strove, never strive, to become a national monument; my work is strictly personal." Almost two decades in exile had taught her many lessons about the politicization of the private; to her, simplistic political dichotomies and "us-versus-them" squabbles were a waste of time. In the same letter she added: "Poland is ruled by communists and nationalists, . . . but above all by Russia, and this is not, as everybody knows, the fault of the Polish people so much as of the Yalta agreement. Polish writers have been trained through generations in the art of allusive writing, and the code is clear to every Pole at home and abroad."

Having been forcefully "exiled" from the ranks of her colleagues in the West, Kuncewicz produced an astute study of the postwar mentality of natives and "displaced persons" in England and the United States in her novel *Tristan 1946* (1967; Kuncewicz's original English version published as *Tristan: A Novel*, 1974). As if in response to *Gaj oliwny*, this novel explores the redemptive promises and failures of love and romance. The book was written during a stay in British Columbia and was inspired by memories of Kuncewicz's residence in Cornwall. Using the larger archetypal framework of the battle between good and evil and the medieval romance of Tristan and Isolde, she masterfully narrates a multivocal love story. She presents her characters as inextricably caught between past myths and contemporaneous Cold War politics. More than her other texts, this novel also explores the ambivalence of female authors in exile. Much like her earlier texts, it also openly employs autobiographical elements. The main narrator, Wanda–who may be viewed as a variation on the persona of the author–is a Polish refugee who lives in a quiet Cornwall town and whose life is suddenly disrupted by the return of her traumatized son. The son, Michał, may be (but does not have to be) identified with Kuncewicz's only child. In the novel Wanda has presumed Michał dead in the war and is shocked and scared by the return of the boy who has grown into an estranged adult during their years of separation. The son's romance with a beautiful Irish student who is married to a prominent and much older British scholar and aristocrat follows the pattern of Tristan and Isolde's tale: they cannot help falling in love; they run away and are chased, tested, and punished; later, another woman intervenes, and the lovers are separated as a result of a deathly misunderstanding.

The text is skillfully composed of Wanda's main narrative thread interwoven with sections told in other characters' voices. The book opens with Wanda's charismatic confession about the nature of the exile she has experienced as a Pole and a woman; she explains her belief in the exhaustion of love as a "solution to human problems." Wanda recalls her past in Poland and reevaluates her flight from the war that claimed her heroic husband and dealt her a meaningless life in England. After the romance between a Polish Tristan and an Irish Isolde expires, she visits her son in his new haven in America, where spouses occupy clearly defined conventional spheres and shun mythical passions. Wanda is also telling the story of the romance in much the same manner as Brangien in Tristan and Isolde's tale might: as someone who is bound to recount/write the tragedy that she has brought about by carelessness. In this way she becomes the main character in her own tale. By the end, *Tristan 1946* achieves a shifting stream-of-consciousness viewpoint similar to a musical composition; the true focus is not so much the predictable love story as Wanda's tortured journey to authorship and self-knowledge in exile.

While working on *Tristan* Kuncewicz continued producing travel reportage; she depicted her visit to Spain in a volume titled *Don Kichote i niańki* (Don Quixote and the Nannies, 1965). In the decade following her first visit to Poland she also published three collections of essays and stories—*Odkrycie Patusanu* (The Discovery of Patusan, 1958), another edition of the 1939 work *W domu i w Polsce* (At Home and in Poland), and *Twarz mężczyzny i trzy nowele* (A Man's Face and Three Short Stories, 1969)—that made available to Polish readers her prewar texts together with those written in exile. However, what many critics consider the culmination of her art came with the publication of the autobiographical triptych *Fantomy, Natura,* and *Przeźrocza.* These books appeared over a span of fourteen years that were marked by continued international travels and increasingly prolonged stays in Kuncewiczówka—the beloved home in Poland where the author and her husband collected treasures from their many abodes in exile. *Fantomy, Natura,* and *Przeźrocza* form a logical continuity, although Kuncewicz published other works between the last two volumes, such as *Fantasia alla polacca* (A Fantasy on Polish Airs, 1979), a critical study of the work and phenomenon of notorious Polish modernist Stanisław Przybyszewski. In light of the style employed in the autobiographical series—a mix of fiction, poetic prose, reportage, essay, and diary—one can also consider Kuncewicz's last book, *Listy do Jerzego* (Letters to George, 1988), its logical continuation.

In *Natura* Kuncewicz explains her immigration to the United States as resulting from her insatiable hunger for both familiarity and otherness, which the more homogenous postwar England could not satisfy. A devoted follower of her dream of "world citizenship," she later saw her American naturalization as a "practical step" in that direction. Nevertheless, always quick to reconsider and ever self-critical, she sees in naturalization the symbol of "civilization" as a process of implementing nationalism and cultural imperialism:

> But whose nature was supposed to become adapted to whom? Mine to the new country's? Or the new country's to mine? . . . Before my naturalization in America, a long time ago, Poland had naturalized my ancestors. America wasn't new on Earth either. Long before Columbus it had been naturalized by the native tribes, whose names are dying on the maps and on hotels' neon-signs. Apparently that is the natural sequence of things. . . . The thing I decided to adapt to was: life.

Yet, her new citizenship not only opens the borders for her but also makes her feel guilty about those who remained in Eastern Europe. And even though she grows to like "California magnolias, black dates . . . and crabs from Alaska . . . Faulkner, Gershwin and Marian Anderson, *Moby Dick* . . . the colossal beauty and colossal sadness of America," she discovers that "liking others does not change one's own nature." As she later mentioned in an interview, she saw the very concept of nationhood as flawed and destructive for the self, which has to create its own territories: "No fatherland is a garden without sin. While abroad, I

*Kuncewiczówka, the author's house in Kazimierz,
now a center for Polish culture*

never had the impression that I had been torn away from 'paradise' because in my native environment, too, I had lived through diverse ideological and personal conflicts."

The autobiographies also more clearly draw the authorial persona hinted at in Kuncewicz's novels and earlier prose texts. Kuncewicz openly rewrites and recasts herself and the cultural guises she adopts in different countries, spaces, and linguistic environments. This approach to the art of writing as self-creation recalls Flaubert's famous statement, "Madame Bovary, c'est moi"; Kuncewicz said that her characters "could have been themselves if they hadn't been me." She also reveals her need for confession and introspection, saying that previously, "I disguised my experiences with invented names. . . . Now I throw away the camouflage, I jeopardize myself in relation to Art and people because age has made me invulnerable to the untouchability of authenticity. I feel doubly old: as a person and as a species condemned to extinction amid the nonsenses of hyper civilization. Thus I am confessing for the sake of something that will survive Nonsense."

Przeźrocza continues in the style of the previous autobiographical notebooks and recounts the writer's prolonged visits to Italy, where she and her husband spent winters in the 1970s and early 1980s. Among other events, *Przeźrocza* describes the infamous kidnapping and murder of Aldo Moro, party chairman of the Christian Democrats, by the terrorist Red Brigades. Kuncewicz's detailed analysis of what that event meant to her and others politically and morally coincides with important historical changes in Poland, which at that time witnessed the birth and then the fall of Solidarity under General Jaruzelski's Martial Law. Close reading of the text reveals analogies and painful comparisons that Kuncewicz is making between the situation in Poland, where strikes and food shortages bring the threat of bloodshed and Soviet intervention, and the instability of Italy, which is nonetheless still free from dangers on such a scale. The text was censored before its publication by Pax and includes sections of the law "on the control of publications" in the spaces where parts of Kuncewicz's writing were deleted. Pax took advantage of the provision included in the Law on Censorship to indicate in the text the interventions of the censors. Kuncewicz's accusation of the state in *Przeźrocza* is thus magnified by the totalitarian state's intrusion into her text. As if continuing the meditation that she began in *Gaj oliwny* on nationhood, history, and state as oppressive, destructive, and divisive, she compares it to the kidnappers and murderers of Moro: "But isn't the state a terrorist organization that craves the death of its opponents? What citizen and what country can withstand the terror of the state, if they won't recognize force as the highest tribunal, which some will call God, others civilization, and still others conscience? The names aren't important."

Kuncewicz never seemed to recover from the final disillusionment with the state and with her homeland. After *Przeźrocza* she devoted her time to supervising editions of her works and to tending her house and garden in Kazimierz. She became further isolated from the world when she lost her husband in 1984. After his death she also suffered from recurring ill health and spent the last five years of her life in Kuncewiczówka, where she was visited by her son, friends, and an occasional journalist. She continued writing and arranging bouquets and lived to see a 1986 motion picture version of *Cudzoziemka*, for which she wrote the screenplay; it won Special Prize at the eleventh Festival of Polish Narrative Films in Gdańsk. Her last book, *Listy do Jerzego*, is a moving collection of letters and diary entries, which combine the major themes of her writings with intimate reflections on faith, love, motherhood, sexuality, and, as always, authorship. She died in a hospital in Lublin on 15 July 1989.

After her death Kuncewicz's name remained on the front pages of Polish journals for months, and her work enjoyed a significant renaissance in scholarship. As she requested in her will, Kuncewiczówka became a vibrant center for artistic and creative pursuits for scholars, painters, poets, writers, and actors. In 1990 the Maria and Jerzy Kuncewicz Foundation came into being. Financed by Witold—who retains ownership of the house and its contents but made it available to the foundation under the administration of the Majdanek Museum in Lublin—Kuncewiczówka continues to carefully preserve Maria Kuncewicz's legacy. It is open to visitors and provides a setting for concerts, exhibitions of art, and poetry readings. One of the major missions of the foundation is to fulfill Kuncewicz's dream of promoting Polish culture across boundaries, helping it to act as a bridge between the disparate cultures of the East and the West.

Interview:

Helena Zaworska, ed., *Rozmowy z Marią Kuncewiczową* (Warsaw: Czytelnik, 1983).

Bibliographies:

Anna Palczak, *Maria Kuncewiczowa: Bibliografia* (Opole: Wojewódzka Biblioteka Publiczna, 1989);

Lesław M. Bartelski, *Polscy pisarze współcześni, 1939–1991* (Warsaw: Wydawnictwa Naukowe, 1995), pp. 217–218;

Alicja Szałagan, *Maria Kuncewiczowa: monografia dokumentacyjna 1895–1989* (Warsaw: Instytut Badań Literackich Polskiej Akademii Nauk, 1995);

Współcześni pisarze polscy i badacze literatury. Słownik bibliograficzny, volume 4 (Warsaw: Wydawnictwa Szkolne i Pedagogiczne, 1996), pp. 474–479.

Biographies:

Halina Ivaničkowa, *Kuncewiczowa*, translated by Krystyna Cękalska (Warsaw: Authors' Agency, 1974);

Piotr Kuncewicz, *Agonia i nadzieja. Literatura polska od 1918 r.* (Warsaw: Polska Oficyna Wydawnicza "BGW," 1993), I: 212–216.

References:

Jan Błoński, "Anatomia patriotyzmu," *Przegląd Kulturalny*, 10 (1958);

Michał Głowiński, "Historyzm czy psychologia," *Twórczość*, 12 (1957): 144–147;

Margaret Storm Jameson, introduction to *The Stranger*, by Kuncewicz, translated by B. M. A. Massey (New York: L. B. Fischer, 1945), pp. 7–11;

Maria Janion, "Świat jako pamięć," *Literatura*, 34 (1975): 1–6;

Barbara Kazimierczyk, *Dyliżans księżycowy* (Warsaw: Instytut Wydawniczy Pax, 1977);

Hanna Kirchner, "Klucze wyobraźni," *Literatura*, 40 (1981): 6–11;

Alicja Lisiecka, "Opowieść o miłości i śmierci," *Polityka*, 10 (1968): 6;

Andrzej Z. Makowiecki, "Praca Marii Kuncewiczowej w paru przekrojach," *Argumenty*, nos. 8, 9, 14, 23 (1980);

Marek Pieczyński, "Antypamiętniki Kuncewiczowej," *Polityka*, 45 (1971): 6;

Stefania Podhorska-Okołów, "Maria Kuncewiczowa," *Kobiety piszą . . . Sylwetki i szkice* (Warsaw, 1938);

Bruno Schulz, "Aneksja podświadomości. U wspólnej mety," *Pion*, 17 (1936): 2–3;

Jerzy Skarbowski, "Klęska muzyki—triumf pisarki. O muzycznych motywach prozy Marii Kuncewiczowej," *Literatura*, 3 (1985): 23–25;

Mary C. Smith, "The Stranger: A Study and Note about Maria Kuncewicz," *Polish Review*, 14, no. 2 (1969): 77–86;

Alicja Szałagan, "Cudzoziemka *Marii Kuncewiczowej. Powstanie, dzieje, recepcja*," *Pamiętnik Literacki*, 3 (1986): 241–276;

Anna Tatarkiewicz, "Róża i Barbara," *Życie Literackie*, 42 (1967): 12–13;

Włodzimierz Wójcik, ed., *W stronę Kuncewiczowej. Studia i szkice* (Katowice: Uniwersytet Śląski, 1988);

Magdalena J. Zaborowska, "Ethnicity in Exile in Maria Kuncewicz's Writings," in *Something of My Very Own to Say: American Women Writers of Polish Descent*, edited by Thomas S. Gladsky and Rita Holmes Gladsky (New York: Columbia University Press, 1997), pp. 170–190;

Zaborowska, "In Alien Worlds: Transcending the Boundaries of Exile in the Works of Maria Kuncewicz," in her *How We Found America: Reading Gender through East European Immigrant Narratives* (Chapel Hill: University of North Carolina Press, 1995), pp. 165–221;

Zaborowska, "Writing the Virgin, Writing the Crone: Maria Kuncewicz's Embodiments of Faith," in *Engendering Slavic Literatures*, edited by Sibelan Forrester and Pamela Chester (Bloomington: Indiana University Press, 1996), pp. 174–200;

Stanisław Żak, *Maria Kuncewiczowa* (Krakow: PWN, 1971);

Żak, *Maria Kuncewiczowa*, Seria "Portrety Współczesnych Pisarzy Polskich" (Warsaw: Państwowy Instytut Wydawniczy, 1973);

Helena Zaworska, "Czy można dziś umrzeć z miłości?" *Literatura*, 43 (1974): 12;

Zaworska, "Stylizacja życia," *Twórczość*, 10 (1975): 106–110;

Zaworska, "W stronę utopii. Nad książkami Marii Kuncewiczowej," *Odra*, 9 (1987): 28–36.

Papers:

Maria Kuncewicz's papers are in the Zakład Narodowy im. Ossolińskich, Wrocław, Poland; Fundacja im. Marii i Jerzego Kuncewiczów, ul. Małachowskiego 19, Kazimierz Dolny, Poland; and in the private collection of Witold Kuncewicz, Flint Hill, Virginia.

Bolesław Leśmian

(12 January 1878 – 5 November 1937)

Andrzej Busza
University of British Columbia

and

Bogdan Czaykowski
University of British Columbia

BOOKS: *Sad rozstajny* (Warsaw: J. Mortkowicz, 1912);

Przygody Sindbada Żeglarza (Warsaw: J. Mortkowicz, 1913);

Klechdy sezamowe (Warsaw: J. Mortkowicz, 1913);

Łąka (Warsaw: J. Mortkowicz, 1920);

Napój cienisty (Warsaw: J. Mortkowicz, 1936);

Dziejba leśna, edited by Alfred Tom (Warsaw: J. Mortkowicz, 1938);

Klechdy polskie, introduction by Bronisław Przyłuski (London: Veritas, 1956).

Editions and Collections: *Wybór poezyj*, edited, with an introduction, by Leopold Staff (Kraków: Spółdzielnia Wydawnicza Książka, 1946);

Łąka i Traktat o poezji (London: Stowarzyszenie Pisarzy Polskich, 1947);

Przygody Sindbada Żeglarza (Warsaw: Czytelnik, 1950);

Klechdy sezamowe (Warsaw: Czytelnik, 1954);

Wiersze wybrane, selected, with an introduction, by Mieczysław Jastrun (Warsaw: Czytelnik, 1955);

Szkice literackie, edited, with an introduction, by Jacek Trznadel (Warsaw: Państwowy Instytut Wydawniczy, 1959);

Klechdy polskie, edited by A. Podsiad (Warsaw: Pax, 1959);

Wiersze rosyjskie, translation of Leśmian's Russian poems into Polish by Marian Pankowski (London: Oficyna Poetów i Malarzy, 1961);

Utwory rozproszone. Listy, edited by Trznadel (Warsaw: Państwowy Instytut Wydawniczy, 1962);

Poezje, edited by Trznadel (Warsaw: Państwowy Instytut Wydawniczy, 1965);

Poezje wybrane, edited by Trznadel (Wrocław: Biblioteka Narodowa, 1974);

Niebo, selected poems, bilingual edition in Polish and in Italian translation (Milan: rivista di poesia, 1980);

Skrzypek opętany, edited, with an introduction, by Rochelle Stone (Warsaw, 1985);

Ballady, selected, with an afterword, by Michał Głowiński (Szczecin, 1991);

Samotność i inne wiersze, selected poems, bilingual edition in Polish and in Hebrew translation, with an afterword by R. Loew (Jerusalem, 1992);

Wybór wierszy, selected, with an introduction, by Włodzimierz Bolecki (Warsaw: Świat Książki, 1996);

Wybór poezji, selected, with an afterword, by Stanisław Barańczak (Warsaw: Państwowy Instytut Wydawniczy, 1996).

Editions in English: "Brother," translated by Adam Gillon, and "The Soldier," translated by Gillon and Ludwik Krzyżanowski, in *Introduction to Modern Polish Literature: An Anthology of Fiction and Poetry*, edited by Gillon and Krzyżanowski (New York: Twayne, 1964), pp. 378–381;

"In the Dark," "Brother," "The Cemetery," and "Memories," translated and edited by Jerzy Peterkiewicz and Burns Singer, in *Five Centuries of Polish Poetry* (London: Oxford University Press, 1970), pp. 83–87;

"Metamorphoses," translated by Andrzej Busza and Bogdan Czaykowski, in Czaykowski, ed., *Modern Poetry in Translation: Polish Issue*, 23–24 (1975): 5.

TRANSLATION: Edgar Allan Poe, *Opowieści nadzwyczajne*, 2 volumes (Warsaw: Muza, 1913–1914).

A photograph of Bolesław Leśmian taken around 1925 shows the poet standing small, thin, fragile, almost lifeless, supported by two imposing women dressed in furs and helmet-like hats. His right hand hangs limp; his feet, in polished shoes, do not appear to belong to the rest of the body wrapped in a formal dark coat, above which a lean, pallid, somewhat spectral face peers from under a dark homburg with a vacant and impassive look into an undefined distance. Perhaps there is a touch of a smirk under his tiny moustache. But there is nothing ambiguous about the two provincial society matrons who have taken charge of and seem to be holding upright the unreal poet.

This diminutive, seemingly powerless figure—in ordinary life a notary public in the provincial town of Zamość—was the owner of a prodigious imagination and passionate vitality. While his work embodied all the typical motifs and features of fin-de-siècle Continental modernism (neo-romanticism, symbolism, aestheticism, and the peculiarly Polish variant known as Young Poland), his imagination transcended and transformed them into a highly individual and original poetic vision and expression. It was precisely his passionate vitality that enabled him to overcome the characteristic world-weariness, metaphysical exhaustion, and pessimism of the late symbolist period. At the level of expression three features especially energize traditional poetic form—extensive use of narrative structure, emphasis on the rhythmic quality of versification, and the semantic exploitation of Polish morphology, including the creation of neologisms. His poetic vision combines a fascination with the richness of reality, creationism, and the dynamics of incongruity. Philosophically, his vision finds support in Henri-Louis Bergson's conception of the élan vital and in Friedrich Wilhelm Nietzsche's radical individualism. Further in the background lies the distinction between *natura naturata* and *natura naturans*, which Leśmian apparently derived from John Duns Scotus and Benedict de Spinoza. Literary influences and affinities include Adam Mickiewicz (1798–1855), Juliusz Słowacki (1808–1849), Charles-Pierre Baudelaire, Edgar Allan Poe, the Russian symbolists, and Polish baroque poetry and folklore. The negative matrix of Leśmian's poetic philosophy comprises such typical aspects of modernity as bourgeois mentality, the rise of statistical man, collectivist trends, and the erosion of religious and metaphysical imagination.

Bolesław Leśmian was born in Warsaw on 12 January 1878 (although both the day and the year are in doubt). His real name was Lesman, and both

Boleslaw Leśmian

his parents, Emma and Józef Leśmian, were Polonized Jews. His father was a railway company official and his mother, née Sunderland, came from a middle-class family that owned a porcelain factory in Iłża. Leśmian spent his childhood and youth in Ukraine, where he attended a classical gymnasium in Kiev and took a degree in law at St. Vladimir's University. Equally significant for his poetic development as the grounding in humanist education was Ukraine's lush nature, which imbued him with a permanent fascination with greenness. Late-nineteenth-century Kiev not only was one of the centers of Ukrainian cultural revival but also continued to be at the crossroads of Russian and Polish culture. Leśmian found himself drawn in two directions: on the one hand, there was the revival of Polish Romanticism with its cult of Mickiewicz, emanating from Kraków; on the other hand, there were Russian symbolist thought and poetry and the lyric tradition of Aleksandr Pushkin and Fedor Ivanovich Tiutchev. Leśmian began writing poetry in Polish and published his first poem in 1895. He also wrote some poems in Russian; two cycles of poems in the symbolist manner appeared in *Zolotoje Runo* and *Vesy* (in 1906 and 1907, respectively). His writing in Russian, however, was a passing episode.

Leśmian moved to Warsaw in 1901 and began working, like his father, as a railway official. At the end of 1902, however, he went abroad, visiting first Munich, where there was a large Polish artistic community, and then France, where he stayed, mostly in Paris, until 1907. While in France he married a Polish painter, Zofia Chylińska, and became friends with many writers, including the Russian poet Konstantin Balmont. Between 1907 and 1912 Leśmian lived mostly in Warsaw but returned to France for two years in 1912.

These years were vital for Leśmian's intellectual and literary development. He established close links with the leading representative of the aesthetic trend within "Młoda Polska" (the Young Poland movement), Zenon Przesmycki (pseudonym, Miriam), and became a contributor to the exclusive and sumptuously produced journal *Chimera*, edited by Przesmycki. Leśmian contributed many reviews to other literary magazines and published two seminal essays in which he presented the philosophical basis of his developing poetics: "Z rozmyślań o Bergsonie" (Reflections on Bergson, 1910) and "Znaczenie pośrednictwa w metafizyce życia zbiorowego" (The Significance of Mediation in the Metaphysics of Social Life, 1910). He was also interested in theater, and in 1911 he became both cofounder and a director of the experimental Teatr Artystyczny in Warsaw.

His book publications during this period include his first volume of poetry, *Sad rozstajny* (Crossway Orchard), which appeared in 1912, followed in 1913 by *Przygody Sindbada Żeglarza* (The Adventures of Sindbad the Sailor), ostensibly a story for children but with a philosophical subtext; a collection of oriental narratives, *Klechdy sezamowe* (Sesame Tales); and *Opowieści nadzwyczajne*, two volumes of translations of Poe's tales. He also wrote several highly stylized, quasi folktales, which did not appear until 1956 in London under the title *Klechdy polskie* (Polish Tales). The strangeness of these tales derives from both imagination and its sophisticated poetic treatment. They combine humor and the grotesque, psychological realism and the fantastic, and earthiness and a yearning for wonder. They are in fact modernist re-creations of the fairy tale.

Leśmian spent the war years in Łódź, where he was the literary director of Teatr Polski. After the war he became a notary public, first in Hrubieszów

and then in 1922 in Zamość. Throughout his life Leśmian had financial problems, which assumed critical proportions when in 1929 it became known that his partner in the notary office had been embezzling tax funds. He was saved from financial ruin through the intervention of friends. The other vexing aspect of his later years was growing anti-Semitism; he became one of the main targets of the campaign conducted by right-wing critics and journalists to cleanse Polish culture of "alien toxins." At the same time he gained a measure of recognition in the liberal circles of the literary establishment, and in 1933 he was elected to the Polish Academy of Literature. In 1935 Leśmian moved to Warsaw, where he died on 5 November 1937.

In the interwar period Leśmian published two books of poetry—*Łąka* (The Meadow) in 1920 and *Napój cienisty* (Shadowy Drink) in 1936. A collection of his work titled *Dziejba leśna* (Sylvan Happenings)—which included early as well as later poems, poetic fragments, and a short play—appeared posthumously in 1938. Of his critical writings the most important is his poetic manifesto, "Traktat o poezji" (Treatise on Poetry), which was read posthumously at a meeting of the Polish Academy of Literature and appeared in print for the first time in London in 1947.

In the broadest context Leśmian's thought belongs to the anti-rationalist current that constituted a reaction against nineteenth-century philosophical positivism in its various manifestations—scientism, social determinism, technological mentality, and the rejection of metaphysics and religion. There was a resurgence of metaphysical speculation, a reassertion of the cognitive value of intuition, the emergence of in-depth psychology, the revaluation of subjectivism, and a renewed interest in primitive and mythic modes of thought. All these tendencies are reflected not only thematically but also in the structural and linguistic features of his poetry, especially in the creative transformation of syntactic and lexical forms. The peculiarity of Leśmian's poetics consists in the conjunction of these highly innovative elements with an almost fanatic adherence to traditional, accentual-syllabic versification.

These characteristics, as well as extraliterary factors, made reception of Leśmian's poetry difficult. Following the 1905 revolution, in Polish intellectual life there was a pronounced swing toward social and political activism (reflected, for example, in Stanisław Brzozowski's philosophy of action). In the literary sphere, left-wing, populist, and nationalist ideologies replaced the aestheticism of Young

Manuscript for a poem by Leśmian (from Michał Głowiński, Wiersze Bolesława Leśmiana, *1992)*

Poland. Leśmian's poetic world also became increasingly dynamic but on the plane of vision and metaphysical drama; historical events and sociopolitical issues are conspicuously absent. Moreover, his two major publications came at most inopportune historical moments. *Sad rozstajny* appeared just before the outbreak of World War I, and the publication of *Łąka* coincided with the Polish-Soviet War. In the immediate postwar period, the two dominant poetic movements, *Skamander* and *Awangarda,* differed radically in their attitudes (one traditionalist, the other experimental), but both were essentially anti-metaphysical. Moreover, where Leśmian is in a profound sense a poet of nature, the major preoccupations of the various avant-garde trends are the city, the crowd, and the machine. Similarly, while Leśmian's linguistic innovations can be described as "organic" (often what appear to be neologisms are, in fact, archaic or dialectal forms), avant-garde experimentation with language tends to be schematic and technical. In Leśmian's work the various forms of defamiliarization are an integral part of his vision and metaphysics; they are not simply verbal constructs. Furthermore, in contrast to both the *Skamander* and avant-garde poets, who foreground syntactic structures, Leśmian subordinates syntax to rhythm, which for him is not only a formal but also a metaphysical category. "Thought," he wrote in 1910, "set in motion by rhythm, acquires those elemental vibrations and plasticity, which link it to life itself, reflecting, as in a mirror sensitive to every movement and ray of light, that always elusive 'externality' which is more mysterious than our own psyche." Some years later he wrote: "If a flower could record on its leaf in words that are apt and right the rhythm of its gradual unfolding from the moment it felt the desire to become a flower until it had actually become one, this seemingly insignificant jotting would indeed be a most wonderful poem." In the interwar period few critics could discern the originality behind Leśmian's apparent oddities and diction that harked back to the mannerisms of Young Poland. Although in the 1930s his poetry met with increasing appreciation, especially among poets, the outbreak of war, followed by the imposition of Socialist Realism, delayed the full recognition of Leśmian's poetic achievement until the liberalization of the mid 1950s.

Leśmian's first volume, as suggested by the title, is transitional. On the one hand, it includes poems that thematically still belong to the Young Poland phase and show affinities with the symbolist style; on the other hand, it includes poems that exhibit characteristics of quintessential Leśmian. In a significant departure from symbolist poetics, Leśmian rejects the prevalent practice of treating objects as symbols and seeks to recover the sense of the "thing in itself." Abstractions are not so much banished from his poems as given palpability and concreteness. Above all, Leśmian presents a radically new vision of the world in which the split between nature and man is overcome in a quasi-mystical union; in the cycle of poems "Zielona Godzina" (Green Hour) all entities interrelate and interpenetrate: "Everything sees and is seen. Everything is brimful with the magic of mutual reflection."

In contrast to *Sad rozstajny,* the volume *Łąka* has a unified vision but expresses this vision in various ways. Part of the volume is a continuation and enrichment of the nature theme; several of the poems are not only typical of Leśmian at his best but also have achieved canonical status in modern Polish poetry. There belong "Topielec zieleni" (Drowned in Greenness), "Przemiany" (Metamorphoses), "Wiatrak" (Windmill), and the long title poem, in which the poet and the meadow achieve and celebrate their union in what is, in effect, an epithalamium. The human and the natural worlds interpenetrate: nature is humanized, and metaphors from nature in turn invade human reality. The dynamic character of these processes is often conveyed through an effective use of neologisms, consisting, for instance, in the coining of verbs from substantives that normally do not have verbal forms (for example, *stodola—stodolić się;* barn—to be barning). Present also are extremely graphic, concrete, and sensuous descriptions of the external world, which constitute a kind of hyperrealism that is never an end in itself but always leads to a variety of shifts—ontological, semantic, and discursive. The ballads are another distinctive group of poems that, as many critics have noted, constitute a truly original transformation of the genre. The often ecstatic vision of the nature poems is counterbalanced by the dramatization of the horrific and the hideous, in which the grotesque and macabre are displayed with perverse humor made more aesthetic through the maintaining of balladlike charm and metric virtuosity. Yet a third category, which includes many acknowledged masterpieces, is the erotic poems, a large number of which form the cycle "W malinowym chruśniaku" (In the Raspberry Thicket). While the dominant characteristic of these poems is their passionate sensuality, their formal and intellectual structure recalls the conceptual ingenuity of metaphysical poetry. Finally, a handful of poems in the volume anticipates later developments. For example, the poem "Garbus" (The Hunchback), which belongs to the sequence "Pieśni kalekujące" (Limping Songs), combines a fascination with deformity and the dramatic potential inherent in the ontological diversity of nature, artifice, and fiction. In this poem the hump berates the body of the hunchback for dying on him.

The core of Leśmian's third volume, the last published in his lifetime, *Napój cienisty*, is a cycle of poems called "Postacie" (Beings). Leśmian's principal poetic method in these poems is to spin narratives around a whole spectrum of beings—personified abstractions and natural phenomena; figures from myth, history, legend, literature, and folklore; or concrete objects—and to dramatize their particular worlds as a way of generating a wide range of emotions, imaging the phantasmagoric character of the universe of the mind and commenting with absurdist humor on the mystery of existence. In addition, the volume includes many pure lyrics and several longer poems that offer a synthesis of Leśmian's philosophical and poetic outlook, notably "Słowa do pieśni bez słów" (Words to a Song without Words), "Pan Błyszczyński" (Mr. O'Glimmer), "Dwaj Macieje" (The Two Mathiases), and "Eliasz" (Elijah). The first summarizes Leśmian's view of the existential function of art. In "Pan Błyszczyński" Leśmian conjures up an antiworld in rivalry with God's act of creation but lacks the power to dissolve ontological boundaries: he is unable to make a real girl enter his imagined garden. In the balladlike "Dwaj Macieje" the protagonists, having found the plant of immortality, come upon the melancholy Crygod and give the plant to him on the principle "That God needs immortality and we humans need God." The last poem, "Eliasz," describes the prophet's voyage beyond the world and the otherworld. As he is propelled by the wind on a chariot of fire, he leaves behind him not only the earth, planets, suns, and galaxies but also the entire universe of beliefs, concepts, signs, and symbols. Time, death, immortality, and God recede and vanish; in the end all that remains is "a numb and diligent *Silentium*." With the fire chariot flickering out, Elijah considers " . . . in the clairvoyance of his final breath / The possibility of a dream different from the dream of Existence."

After Leśmian's death the illustrator of some of his books, Alfred Tom, edited *Dziejba leśna*, which included a play of the same name as well as many shorter poems and fragments. This volume adds little that is new: the play, a grotesque necromantic fantasy on the theme of death, lacks the concentrated power and intensity of his best poems on the same topic; as for the poems, most are lyrical sketches; one clear exception is the excellent earlier

Caricature of Leśmian by Edward Glowacki (from Michał Głowiński, Wiersze Bolesława Leśmiana, *1992)*

poem "Sen wiejski" (Rustic Dream, 1916), which is yet another example of Leśmian's exploration of the poetic possibilities of the oneiric.

What future readers will make of Leśmian's poetry is difficult to foresee. The sources of his imagined world and linguistic inventiveness, such as folklore and dialectal diversity, have undergone considerable erosion, and metaphysical imagination is yielding to technologically produced virtual reality. Sensitivity to form has dulled. Humanity is increasingly being separated from nature. In an age of translation and cultural interpenetration the qualities of his poetry seem to make his work almost untranslatable. Yet, in his native Poland there has been a great resurgence of interest in his poetry since the 1960s. His poems have even found their way into popular culture. Set to music and sung by Ewa Demarczyk in a famous Kraków cabaret, his poem "Garbus" reached a mass audience as a recording. What is more important, however, is the universal and perennial character of his themes and philosophical concerns and their linguistically superb embodiment in narrative and symbolic forms, which perhaps have greater staying power than more-discursive writing. In his own words, his type of poetry "flows in the manner of a repeatable melody, one which can be sung again and again from beginning to end with the complete assurance that it will repeat itself as before, retaining, every time it ends, undiminished rhythmical power to become resurrected."

Biography:

Zdzisław Jastrzębski, ed., *Wspomnienia o Bolesławie Leśmianie* (Lublin: Wydawnictwo Lubelskie, 1966).

References:

Paul Coates, *Words after Speech: A Comparative Study of Romanticism and Symbolism* (New York: St. Martin's Press, 1986);

Bogdan Czaykowski, "From Rhythm and Metaphysics to Intonation, Experience and Gnosis: The Poetry of Bolesław Leśmian, Aleksander Wat and Czesław Miłosz," in *The Mature Laurel: Essays on Modern Polish Poetry,* by Adam Czerniawski (Bridgend: Seren Books, 1991), pp. 37–87;

Michał Głowiński, *Wiersze Bolesława Leśmiana* (Warsaw: Wydawnictwa Szkolnel Pedagogiczne, 1992);

Głowiński, *Zaświat przedstawiony. Szkice o poezji Bolesława Leśmiana* (Warsaw: Państwowy Instytut Wydawniczy, 1981);

Głowiński and Janusz Sławiński, eds., *Studia o Leśmianie* (Warsaw: Państwowy Instytut Wydawniczy, 1971);

Ireneusz Opacki, "Uroda i żałoba czasu: Romantyzm w liryce Bolesława Leśmiana," in *Poetyckie dialogi z kontekstem* (Katowice: Śląsk, 1979);

Marian Pankowski, *Leśmian. La révolte d'un poète contre les limites* (Brussels: Presses Universitaires, 1967);

Kajetan Papierkowski, *Bolesław Leśmian. Studium językowe* (Lublin: Wydawnictwo Lubelskie, 1964);

Cezary Rowiński, *Człowiek i świat w poezji Leśmiana* (Warsaw: Państwowe Wydawnictwo Naukowe, 1982);

Rochelle H. Stone, *Bolesław Leśmian. The Poet and His Poetry* (Berkeley & Los Angeles: University of California Press, 1976);

Adam Szczerbowski, *Bolesław Leśmian* (Warsaw: Książnica Literacka, 1938);

Jacek Trznadel, *Twórczość Leśmiana. (Próba przekroju)* (Warsaw: Państwowy Instytut Wydawniczy, 1964).

György Lukács

(13 April 1885 – 4 June 1971)

Gábor Gulyás
University of Debrecen

BOOKS: *A lélek és a formák: Kísérletek* (Budapest: Franklin-Társulat, 1910); expanded as *Die seele und die formen: Essays* (Berlin: E. Fleischel, 1911); translated by Anna Bostock as *Soul and Form* (Cambridge, Mass.: MIT Press, 1974);

A modern dráma fejlődésének története, 2 volumes (Budapest: Franklin-Társulat, 1911);

Esztétikai kultura: Tanulmányok (Budapest: Athenaeum, 1913);

Taktika és etika (Budapest: Közoktatási Népbiztosság Kiadása, 1919); translated by Michael McColgan as *Tactics and Ethics: Political Essays, 1919–1929*, edited by Rodney Livingstone (New York: Harper & Row, 1972);

Die Theorie des Romans: Ein geschichtsphilosophischer Versuch über die Formen der grossen Epik (Berlin: Paul Cassirer, 1920); translated by Bostock as *Theory of the Novel: A Historico-philosophical Essay on the Forms of Great Epic Literature* (Cambridge, Mass.: MIT Press, 1971);

Geschichte und Klassenbewusstsein: Studien über Marxistische Dialektik (Berlin: Malik, 1923); translated by Livingstone as *History and Class Consciousness: Studies in Marxist Dialectics* (Cambridge, Mass.: MIT Press, 1971);

Lenin: Studie über den Zusammenhang seiner Gedanken (Berlin: Malik, 1924); translated by Nicholas Jacobs as *Lenin: A Study on the Unity of His Thought* (London: NLB., 1970; Cambridge, Mass.: MIT Press, 1971);

Pushkin; Gorki: Zwei Essays (Leipzig: Reclam, 1936);

Literaturnii teorii xix veka i marxizma, 3 volumes (Moscow: Khudozhestvennaia literatura, 1937);

Írástudók felelőssége (Moscow: Idegennyelvű Irodalmi Kiadó, 1944);

Balzac, Stendhal, Zola (Budapest: Hungária, 1945);

Deutsche literatur im zeitalter des Imperialismus, eine ubersicht ihrer hauptströmungen (Berlin: Aufbau, 1945);

Irodalom és demokrácia (Budapest: Szikra, 1945);

Goethe és kora (Budapest: Hungária, 1946);

Gottfried Keller: Mit einer Einleitung (Berlin: Aufbau, 1946);

József Attila: A Magyar Kommunista Párt országos székházában 1945 december 2-án elhangzott két előadás (Budapest: Szikra, 1946);

Nagy orosz realisták (Budapest: Szikra, 1946; enlarged, 1949; revised and enlarged, 2 volumes, 1951–1952);

Nietzsche és a fasizmus (Budapest: Hungária, 1946);

A történelmi regény (Budapest: Hungária, 1947); translated by Hannah Mitchell and Stanley Mitchell as *The Historical Novel* (London: Merlin, 1962; Boston: Beacon, 1963);

A polgár nyomában: a hetvenéves Thomas Mann (Budapest: Hungária, 1947); translated by Stanley Mitchell as *Essays on Thomas Mann* (London: Merlin, 1964; New York: Grosset & Dunlap, 1965);

A polgári filozófia válsága (Budapest: Hungária, 1947);

Fortschritt und Reaktion in der deutschen Literatur (Berlin: Aufbau, 1947);

Goethe und seine Zeit (Bern: Francke, 1947; expanded edition, Berlin: Aufbau, 1950); translated by Robert Anchor as *Goethe and His Age* (London: Merlin, 1968; New York: Grosset & Dunlap, 1968);

Der junge Hegel (Zürich: Europa, 1948); translated by Livingstone as *The Young Hegel: Studies in the Relations between Dialectics and Economics* (London: Merlin, 1975; Cambridge, Mass.: MIT Press, 1976);

Essays über Realismus (Berlin: Aufbau, 1948); translated by David Fernbach as *Essays on Realism*, edited by Livingstone (Cambridge, Mass.: MIT Press, 1981); enlarged as *Probleme des Realismus* (Berlin: Aufbau, 1955); translated by John Mander and Necke Mander as *Realism in Our Time: Literature and the Class Struggle* (New York: Harper & Row, 1964);

Karl Marx und Friedrich Engels als Literaturhistoriker (Berlin: Aufbau, 1948); Hungarian version, revised as *Marx és Engels irodalomomelmélete, három tanulmány* (Budapest: Szikra kiadás, 1949);

Schicksalswende: Beiträge zu einer neuen deutschen Ideologie (Berlin: Aufbau, 1948);

Új magyar kulturáért (Budapest: Szikra, 1948);

Ady Endre (Budapest: Szikra, 1949);

Der russiche Realismus in der Weltliteratur (Berlin: Aufbau, 1949);

Existentialismus oder Marxismus? (Berlin: Aufbau, 1951);

Deutsche Realisten des neunzehnten Jahrhunderts (Berlin: Aufbau, 1951);

Balzac und der französische Realismus (Berlin: Aufbau, 1952);

Adalékok az esztétika történetéhez (Budapest: Akadémiai Kiadó, 1953);

Die Zerstörung der Vernunft (Berlin: Aufbau, 1954); Hungarian version, revised as *Az ész trónfosztása: az irracionalista filozófia kritikája* (Budapest: Akadémiai Kiadó, 1954); translated by Peter Palmer as *The Destruction of Reason* (London: Merlin, 1980; Atlantic Highlands, N.J.: Humanities Press, 1981);

Beiträge zur Geschichte der Äesthetik (Berlin: Aufbau, 1954);

Der historische Roman (Berlin: Aufbau, 1955);

Német realisták (Budapest: Szépirodalmi, 1955);

A különösség mint esztétikai kategória (Budapest: Akadémiai Kiadó, 1957);

Wider den missverstandenen Realismus (Hamburg: Claasen, 1958); translated by Mander and Mander as *The Meaning of Contemporary Realism* (London: Merlin, 1963);

Die Eigenart des Ästhetischen, 2 volumes (Neuwied: Luchterhand, 1963);

Über die Besonderheit als Kategorie der Ästhetik (Neuwied: Luchterhand, 1963);

Az esztétikum sajátossága (Budapest: Akadémiai Kiadó, 1965);

Solschenizyn (Neuwied & Berlin: Luchterhand, 1970); translated by William David Graf as *Solzhenitsyn* (Cambridge, Mass.: MIT Press, 1971);

Frühe Schriften zur Ästhetik I: Heidelberger Philosophie der Kunst (1912–1914), edited by György Márkus and Frank Benseler (Darmstadt: Luchterhand, 1974);

Frühe Schriften zur Ästhetik II: Heidelberger Ästhetik (1916–1918), edited by Márkus and Benseler (Darmstadt: Luchterhand, 1975);

A drámaírás főbb irányai a múlt század utolsó negyedében, edited by L. Ferenc Lendvai (Budapest: Akadémiai Kiadó, 1980).

Editions and Collections: *Skizze einer Geschicte der neueren deutschen Literatur* (Budapest: Aufbau, 1953)—comprises *Fortschritt und Reaktion in der deutschen Literatur* and *Deutsche literatur im zeitalter des Imperialismus;*

Schriften zur Literatursoziolgie, edited by Peter Ludz (Neuwied: Luchterhand, 1963);

Lukács György válogattot művei, 3 volumes, edited by Ferenc Fehér (Budapest: Gondolat, 1968–

1970)—comprises volume 1, *Művészet és társadalom: Válogatott esztétikai tanulmányok* (1968); volume 2, *Világirodalom: Válogatott világirodalmi tanulmányok* (2 volumes, 1969); volume 3, *Magyar irodalom–Magyar kultúra: Válogatott tanulmányok*, edited by Fehér and Zoltán Kenyeres (1970);

Történelem és osztálytudat, edited by Mihály Vajda (Budapest: Magvető, 1971);

Zur Ontologie des gesellschaftlichen Seins, 3 volumes (Neuwied: Luchterhand, 1971–1973); translated by David Fernbach as *The Ontology of Social Being*, 3 volumes (London: Merlin, 1978–1980);

Ifjúkori művek, 1902–1918, edited by Árpád Tímár (Budapest: Magvető, 1977);

Moskauer Schriften: Zur Literaturtheorie und Literaturpolitik, 1934–1940, edited by Benseler (Frankfurt am Main: Sendler, 1981);

Napló–Tagebuch (1910–11); Das Gericht (1913), edited by Lendvai (Budapest: Akadémiai Kiadó, 1981);

Esztétikai írások 1930–1945, edited by László Sziklai (Budapest: Kossuth, 1982);

Dostojewski: Notizen und Entwürfe, edited by Janos Kristof Nyiri (Budapest: Akadémiai Kiadó, 1985).

Editions in English: *Studies in European Realism: A Sociological Survey of the Writings of Balzac, Stendhal, Zola, Tolstoy, Gorki, and Others*, translated by Edith Bone (London: Hillway, 1950);

Record of a Life: An Autobiographical Sketch, translated by Rodney Livingstone, edited by István Eorsi (London: Verso, 1983);

Reviews and Articles from Die rote Fahne, translated by Peter Palmer (London: Merlin, 1983).

György Lukács, whose name appeared as Georg Lukács on his English-language publications, was one of the most important philosophers in the twentieth century and an influential theoretician of Hungarian aesthetics and literary criticism. Writing in Hungarian and German, Lukács created an extensive body of critical works over a period of more than a half century. Influenced early in his career by Georg Wilhelm Friedrich Hegel and Karl Marx, Lukács was concerned with the historical, political, and social dynamics of the work of art. His critical works on aesthetics and ethics influenced a generation of philosophical theorists while contributing to the growth and development of modern Hungarian literature.

György Löwinger was born on 13 April 1885 in Budapest, the second child of an assimilating Jewish family; the surname was changed to the Hungarian Lukács five years later. His mother, Adél, née Wertheimer, came from a rich Viennese patrician family; his father, József, was the son of a quiltmaker from Szeged. At the age of twenty-four József Lukács was branch manager of the English-Austrian Bank in Budapest; he then became director of the Hungarian General Credit Bank, one of the largest banks in the Austro-Hungarian Empire. An immensely affluent business magnate, he received noble rank from Emperor Francis Joseph I. József was a generous supporter of the arts and counted among his friends the composer Béla Bartók and the writer Thomas Mann.

Lukács had two brothers and a sister. His elder brother, John, who obtained the degree of doctor of law and later became a director at Machine Factory Láng, died in the Nazi German concentration camp at Mauthausen during World War II. His younger sister, Maria, became a cellist and died in England in 1980. The last-born child, Paul, died at age five.

Lukács was privately tutored until he was nine and then attended the Evangelic Grammar School, from which he graduated in 1902. As a high-school student he was enthusiastic about the modern writers Charles Baudelaire, Paul Verlaine, A. C. Swinburne, Leo Tolstoy, and Henrik Ibsen. Lukács tried his skill at belles-lettres, but after his finals he burned the philosophical plays he had written in the style of Ibsen. His father, however, appreciated his son's efforts. He arranged for a letter of introduction to Ibsen and Bjørnstjerne Bjørnson and paid for a voyage to Norway and Denmark for Lukács and a private tutor. Returning from this Scandinavian journey, Lukács matriculated at the faculty of law of Péter Pázmány University in Budapest, but instead of the seminars on laws he attended lectures on the history of philosophy at the faculty of arts. He published reviews of plays in daily and weekly Budapest newspapers. In 1904 he took part in the foundation of the Thalia Society, which included on its board of directors László Bánóczi, Marcell Benedek, and Sándor Hevesi—who most likely were attracted less by Lukács's talent than by his contacts through his father.

Also in 1904 Lukács traveled to Berlin, where he became increasingly interested in philosophy. In 1905 he returned to the German capital, where he attended lectures by the philosophers Wilhelm Dilthey and Georg Simmel. Although he was in Hungary for a short time in 1906 to take his doctor of law degree, until the fall of 1907 he mostly attended the University of Berlin. In 1907 he submitted a treatise titled *A drámaírás főbb irányai a múlt*

Lukács in Italy with his friend Béla Balázs

század utolsó negyedében (The Main Directions of Dramaturgy in the Final Quarter of the Century, 1980) to the Kisfaludy Society, one of the most respected institutes of Hungarian conservative thinking, and received a prize for it. After significant changes, the study was published in 1911 as *A modern dráma fejlődésének története* (History of the Evolution of Modern Drama). In October 1909, Lukács obtained his second doctorate, in aesthetics, English, and German philology.

Around this time Lukács began a love affair with a prominent artist, Irma Seidler, but their relationship was fraught with difficulty. While Lukács was in Budapest, Berlin, or Dresden, Seidler was working in Nagybánya (Baie Mare), so they could express their feelings only in letters. Seidler soon tired of the situation and decided to marry the painter Károly Réthy. Although her relationship with Lukács revived after he threatened to commit suicide, Seidler was seduced by his friend Béla Balázs, who later became a well-known motion-picture aesthetician. Seidler commited suicide in 1911; whether she jumped into the Danube because of Lukács or Balázs is unknown, but the event had an effect on Lukács's other love relationships. Shortly

after Seidler's death Lukács's closest friend, the aesthetician Leo Popper, also died.

Popper's influence can be seen in essays Lukács wrote between 1908 and 1911 that were published as *A lélek és a formák* (translated as *Soul and Form,* 1974) in Hungarian in 1910 and a year later—with some revision and amplification—in German. The volume became internationally known not only because of its remarkably elaborate analysis but also for its revaluation of the philosophical essay as an artistic form. Lukács posits that while the artist gives the viewer pictures, the essayist or critic—"the Platonist"—goes beyond these pictures to give form abstract meanings. Therefore, for the essayist or critic, the adequate form of experience can only be the parable, the essay, which is about the possibilities of life and fate. At the time of its publication, however, the book was not favorably received.

Meanwhile, Lukács was attempting to found his own newspaper. He had tried unsuccessfully in 1910 to start a German-language philosophical review with Popper. In addition, he wanted to take over the editing of the journal *Renaissance* with Balázs, but the plan failed because Balázs withdrew. Eventually, in 1911, a new philosophical periodical, *Mind,* was published and edited by Lukács, Hevesi, and Lajos Fülep, but after two issues it ceased publication for lack of interest. After this failure Lukács spent the winter of 1911–1912 in Florence to recover his strength. At that time he made friends with the German philosopher Ernst Bloch, with whom he corresponded and frequently exchanged manuscripts.

In the spring of 1912 Bloch visited Lukács in Florence and persuaded him to move to the German university town of Heidelberg, where they could work in an intellectual atmosphere. Lukács moved there in May, and—with short interruptions—he lived in Heidelberg for the next five years. At the time Heidelberg was one of the most important intellectual centers of Europe, the home of the sociologist Max Weber, the poet Stefan George, and the philosophers Wilhelm Windelband, Heinrich Rickert, Emil Lask, and Karl Jaspers. Lukács became a frequent guest at Weber's Sunday tea parties, where he met a distinguished array of people. He began writing a philosophy of art, finishing the first two parts by March 1913. In the summer Lukács visited Balázs, who was in Italy with his wife, his sister, and Ljena Grabenko, an emigrant Ukrainian terrorist who had become Balázs's mistress in the spring of 1912. Lukács fell in love with Grabenko at first sight and married her in May 1914. When World War I broke out at the end of July, military service was not a threat for Lukács because Jaspers worked at a hospital and had given him a certificate saying that he had neurasthenea. He antagonized his German friends, who, being leftist intellectuals, welcomed the war, while Lukács opposed it from the beginning. He tried to write an antiwar pamphlet but did not finish it and also gave up work on his philosophy of art.

Lukács had to return to Budapest to appear before the draft board, but his medical contacts saved him from the front line again. In Budapest he became active in the Sunday Circle, which included prominent representatives of contemporary Hungarian philosophy and sociology. Returning to Heidelberg, he discovered that his wife had moved her lover, a young pianist named Bruno Steinbach, into the flat while Lukács was in Hungary. Steinbach not only exploited Lukács financially, but physically abused Grabenko and threatened Lukács. Lukács allowed the situation to continue while he worked on *Die Theorie des Romans: Ein geschichtsphilosophischer Versuch über die Formen der grossen Epik* (1920; translated as *Theory of the Novel: A Historico-philosophical Essay on the Forms of Great Epic Literature*, 1971). He attempted to become a teacher at Heidelberg University but did not succeed.

Lukács returned to Budapest in November 1917 without completing his aesthetics. Published posthumously as *Frühe Schriften zur Ästhetik* (Early Writings on Aesthetics), the work consists of two parts: *Heidelberger Philosophie der Kunst, 1912–1914* (Heidelberg Philosophy of Art, 1912–1914), published in 1974, and *Heidelberger Ästhetik, 1916–1918* (Heidelberg Aesthetics, 1916–1918), published in 1975. Lukács says in these works that the great work of art, paradoxically, is the paradigmatic form of authentic communication because it does not fix any concrete experience; instead, it forces the reader to recognize the meaning and truth of his or her own experiences. Therefore, the interpretation of a work of art is always new and never reproducible. A genius never attempts to create "the eternal"; instead, he or she tries to create the temporal, the new.

In November 1917 Lukács returned to Hungary. He was not only welcomed enthusiastically by the Sunday Circle, but he also fell in love with Gertrúd Bortstieber. In December 1918 he published an article titled "A bolsevizmus mint erkölcsi problema" (Bolshevism as a Moral Problem), in which he argues that Marx's remarkable sociology has to be separated from his utopian philosophy of history. Lukács recognized "an insolvable moral dilemma in the root of Bolshevik standpoint."

Title page for the German edition of Lukács's first book, translated into English in 1974 as Soul and Form

Shortly after the publication of his article, however, Lukács became acquainted with Béla Kun, the first leader of the Hungarian Communist movement, and as a result underwent a sudden conversion to communism. He took part in illegal organizing work, and in March 1919, after the establishment of the Hungarian Commune, he was appointed the educational commissar, the equivalent of a ministerial rank. After the defeat of the commune a warrant was issued for Lukács's arrest, but in September 1919—after a short period of hiding in Hungary—he escaped to Vienna with the help of his father's contacts. When Lukács arrived in Vienna one of his former compatriots recognized him, reported him to the police, and he was arrested. He would have been interned, but Ferenc Baumgartner organized a public protest in his defense that included Mann. Shortly thereafter Lukács was released.

In 1920 Lukács published *Die Theorie des Romans*, which is not only a philosophical theory of

Gertrúd Bortstieber, who later became Lukács's second wife, at about eighteen

the novel form but also a literary history. Lukács distinguishes two major periods: one is the age of the closed worldview, in which idea and reality are related; the other is the new era, the era of disintegration, loneliness, and ignorance—the time of "transcendental homelessness." In the first period the primary literary form is the epic poem (epos); in the second it is the novel. Lukács also tries to describe the typology of the novel form by analyzing what he considers classical novels.

In 1923 Lukács published *Geschicte und Klassenbewusstsein: Studien über Marxistische Dialektik* (translated as *History and Class Consciousness: Studies in Marxist Dialectics*, 1971), a collection of theoretical works written between 1919 and 1922. For many, this book represented an alternative Marxism, but for the ideologists of emerging Stalinism it was a harmful deviation from the accepted line. In 1924 Lukács published a pamphlet, *Lenin: Studie über den Zusammenhang seiner Gedanken* (translated as *Lenin: A Study on the Unity of His Thought*, 1971), which was received quite negatively in the Soviet Union.

In May 1928 Lukács was arrested again, together with Kun, who was staying illegally in Vienna; but Mann petitioned the Austrian prime minister, who released Lukács a second time. Since

1924 he had been regarded as the deputy leader of the Hungarian Communist emigrants in Vienna. In 1928 he drew up the theses for the Second Congress of the Hungarian Communist Party, which became known as the Blum Theses. (Blum was Lukács's code name in the movement.) The theses were criticized by Lenin and rejected by the party and Lukács was obliged to make a public retraction in the newspaper *New March*. The leaders of the party decided that he should relocate to Moscow.

In Moscow, Lukács began research at the Marx-Engels Institute but soon became discouraged with Soviet intellectual life under Joseph Stalin's terror and had himself transferred to Berlin in the summer of 1931. There he became the leader of the Communist faction of the German Writers Defensive Association and a member of the Imperial Faction. He regularly published critical articles in *Bund* and *Die Linkskurve*.

In March 1933 Lukács returned to Moscow because of the spread of German fascism. Although he remained there for the next twelve years, Lukács found the working conditions poor and was able to write only four books: three volumes of essays in Russian, notably *Literaturnii teorii xix veka i marxizma* (Nineteenth-Century Literary Theory and Marxism, 1937), and a volume in Hungarian titled *Írástudók felelőssége* (The Responsibility of Literary Men, 1944). He was affiliated with the department of literature at the Communist Academy in 1933 and 1934, and with the department of philosophy of the Scientific Academy from 1935 until 1938.

On 22 June 1941 Germany attacked the Soviet Union, and one week later Lukács and his foster son, Ferenc, were arrested. Released after two months, Lukács left Moscow with his wife for Kazan and then Tashkent, where they lived for the most part under deplorable conditions. In 1942 they returned to Moscow, where Lukács's books and manuscripts—among them a monograph on Johann Wolfgang von Goethe—had been "lost." Lukács was, however, able to continue his work at the Scientific Academy. In addition he completed his dissertation on Hegel, published in German as *Der junge Hegel* (1948; translated as *The Young Hegel: Studies in the Relations between Dialectics and Economics*, 1975), to obtain the degree of doctor of sciences from Lomonosov University in Moscow. Toward the end of World War II Lukács decided to return to Hungary, even though Walter Ulbricht had offered him a position as professor of philosophy in Berlin and Ernst Fischer had invited him to the University of Vienna. In August 1945 he arrived in Budapest, where he became a member of the Provisory National Assembly and was appointed professor of aesthetics and philosophy at the University of Budapest. At first Lukács was warmly welcomed by most Hungarian intellectuals, but when, in the preface of his collection of essays *Balzac, Stendhal, Zola* (1945), he rejected his earlier writings and illustrated the extent of his ideological devotion to communism, he was sternly criticized. Between 1945 and 1949, in addition to his articles, Lukács published seventeen books in Hungarian. At that time he was not only the most prominent Hungarian Communist theoretician of art but was also regarded as the leading authority on aesthetics in East Germany. He was becoming increasingly well known abroad through his lectures at international conferences, including a notable 1946 debate with the philosophers Jaspers, Julien Benda, and Maurice Merleau-Ponty; a 1947 congress of Marxist philosophers in Milan; and a 1948 international peace conference in Wroclaw. In 1949 he toured as a lecturer in France and Italy. His books were published in French, German, Italian, Czech, Romanian, Serbo-Croatian, Swedish, Japanese, and Hebrew. In 1948 he received the Kossuth Award, the most important literary award in Hungary. Lukács was responsible for recognition of the Hungarian poet Endre Ady with his monograph *Ady Endre* (1949), which assured Ady's place in the Marxist canon.

In 1948 a Communist dictatorship was established in Hungary, and the progressive intellectual societies were banned. Lukács was demoted in official status. In the summer of 1949 László Rudas, an influential representative of Communist cultural policy, following the directive of party leader Mátyás Rákosi, labeled Lukács anti-Soviet, antiparty, unpatriotic, and a metaphysical idealist whose concepts were compared to those of the executed Bolshevik leader Nikolay Bukharin. Lukács was denounced in the press, and his prestige was greatly diminished. For several years he published nothing in Hungary, and for almost two years he was unable to lecture at the university. In 1953, with the establishment of Imre Nagy's government, the situation was eased somewhat, and Lukács was allowed to publish again.

In 1954 Lukács's monumental *Die Zerstörung der Vernunft* (translated as *The Destruction of Reason,* 1980) was published in both Hungarian and German. In this work he tried to show the historical development of "irrational philosophy." He describes Friedrich Nietzsche as a precursor to Adolf Hitler, while Henri Bergson and Georges Sorel are labeled Benito Mussolini's predecessors. *Die Zerstörung der Vernunft* also includes several criticisms of the Yugoslavian Communist leader Josip Broz Tito, that became official doctrine in the early 1950s in Hungary. The volume was favorably received, and Lukács received the Kossuth

One of the last photographs taken of Lukács (photograph by Demeter Balla, LAK)

Award for a second time. In 1955, with the strengthening of Stalinism, he regained his critical reputation. The press celebrated his seventieth birthday, a book was published in his honor in the German Democratic Republic, and he was elected as a corresponding member of the German Academy.

During the Hungarian Revolution of 1956 Lukács was the minister of culture in Nagy's government, a member of the party central committee, and a member of the Hungarian Socialist Workers' Party's Provisional Executive Committee. After the Soviet invasion he escaped with Nagy and other leading revolutionists to the Yugoslavian Embassy, but they were all deported to Snagov, Romania, by János Kádár, the new pro-Soviet leader of Hungary. Released in April 1957, Lukács was banned from Hungarian intellectual life.

In 1963 Lukács published the two-volume *Die Eigenart des Ästhetischen* (The Specificity of the Aesthetic), which he intended as the first part of his complete aesthetics. In addition to at least two more volumes, he wanted to complete a work on ethics and write his autobiography. At this time a circle of students, called the Lukács or Budapest School and including Ágnes Heller, Ferenc Fehér, György Márkus, and Mihály Vajda, began meeting at Lukács's house. Partly because of the debates at those meetings, Lukács realized that before writing his ethics he needed to produce an ontology of social existence. What initially was conceived as a brief introduction to his ethics developed into a manuscript of more than two thousand pages that was published in German as *Zur Ontologie des gesellschaftlichen Seins* (1971–1973; translated as *The Ontology of Social Being*, 1978–1980).

After learning that he had cancer, Lukács started a race against time. Dissatisfied with his last work, he wanted to rewrite completely the chapters on the history of philosophy and introduce structural alterations. His illness prevented him from completing the project. His final work was a study of Aleksandr Solzhenitsyn, published in 1970 as *Solschenizyn* (translated as *Solzhenitsyn*, 1971). Lukács died in Budapest on 4 June 1971.

From the viewpoint of literary criticism Lukács is most significant for *Heidelberger Philosophie der Kunst (1912–1914)*, *Die Theorie des Romans*, and the essays in *A lélek és a formák*. Until the change of regime in Hungary in 1989, Lukács's late aesthetical and critical conceptions dominated Hungarian literary theory, which turned many contemporary Hungarian intellectuals against him. Despite his problematic political and ideological views, however, Lukács is regarded as the most significant Hungarian philosopher of the twentieth century and the only Hungarian aesthetician who achieved international recognition.

Letters:

"Lukács György és Popper Leó levélváltásából 1909-től 1911-ig," edited by Éva Fekete, *Valóság*, 9 (1974): 16–37;

Paul Ernst und Georg Lukács: Dokumente einer Freundschaft, edited by Karl August Kutzbach (Emsdetten: Lechte, 1974);

Lukács György levelezése (1902–1917), edited by Fekete and Éva Karádi (Budapest: Magvető, 1981).

Interviews:

Leo Kofler, Wolfgang Abendroth, and Hans-Heins Holz, *Gespräche mit Georg Lukács*, edited by Theo Pinkus (Hamburg: Rowohlt, 1967); translated by David Fernbach as *Conversations with Lukács* (London: Merlin, 1974);

István Eörsi and Erzsébet Vezér, *Gelebtes Denken: Eine Autobiographie im Dialog* (Frankfurt am Main: Suhrkamp, 1981).

Biographies:

Erhard Bahr, *Georg Lukács* (Berlin: Colloquium, 1970);

George Lichtheim, *Georg Lukács* (New York: Viking, 1970);

F. László Földényi, *A fiatal Lukács: Egy gondolatkör rekonstrukciójának kísérlete* (Budapest: Magvető, 1980);

István Hermann, *Lukács György élete* (Budapest: Corvina, 1985);

Mary Gluck, *Georg Lukács and His Generation, 1900–1918* (Cambridge, Mass.: Harvard University Press, 1985);

István Szerdahelyi, *Lukács György* (Budapest: Akadémiai Kiadó, 1988);

Árpád Kadarkay, *Georg Lukács: Life, Thought, and Politics* (Oxford: Blackwell, 1991).

References:

Androw Arato and Paul Breines, *The Young Lukács and the Origins of Western Marxism* (New York: Seabury Press, 1979);

Raymond Aron, *Mémoires* (Paris: Julliard, 1983);

Béla Bacsó and F. László Földényi, eds., *A fiatal Lukács dráma és művészetelmélete* (Budapest: Magyar Színházi Intézet, 1979);

József Bayer, "On Lukács's Later Political Philosophy," in *Georg Lukács: Theory, Culture, and Politics*, edited by Judith Marcus and Zoltán Tarr (New Brunswick, N.J.: Transaction, 1989), pp. 181–188;

Julia Bendl and Árpád Tímár, eds., *Der junge Lukács im Spiegel der Kritik* (Budapest: Lukács Archívum, 1970);

Frank Benseler and Werner Jung, eds., *Jahrbuch der Internationalen Georg-Lukács-Gesellschaft 1996* (Bern, Berlin, Frankfurt, New York, Paris & Vienna: Peter Lang, 1997);

Benseler, ed., *Festschrift zum achtzigsten Geburtstag von Georg Lukács* (Neuwied: Luchterhand, 1965);

Eva L. Corredor, *György Lukács and the Literary Pretext* (New York: Peter Lang, 1987);

Isaac Deutscher, "Lukács and Critical Realism," in *Marxism in Our Time* (Berkeley, Cal.: Ramparts Press, 1971), pp. 283–293;

Éva Fekete and Éva Karádi, *Lukács György élete képekben és dokumentumokban* (Budapest: Corvina, 1980);

Lucian Goldmann, *Lukács and Heidegger: Toward a New Philosophy*, translated by William Q. Boelhower (London & Boston: Routledge & Kegan Paul, 1977);

Ágnes Heller, "A kötelességen túl. A német klasszika etikájának paradigmatikussága Lukács György életművében," *Korunk*, 33 (1974): 31–41;

Heller and others, *Die Seele und das Leben: Studien zum frühen Lukács* (Frankfurt am Main: Suhrkamp, 1977);

Heller, ed., *Lukács Reappraised* (New York: Columbia University Press, 1983);

Ottó Hévizi, "A dialógikus Lukács," in *Alaptalanul: Gondolatformák a századfordulón* (Budapest: T-Twins Kiadó, Lukács Archívum, 1994);

Peter Uwe Hohendahl, "The Scholar, the Intellectual, and the Essay: Weber, Lukács, Adorno, and Postwar Germany," *German Quarterly*, 70 (Summer 1997): 217–231;

Fredric Jameson, *Marxism and Form; Twentieth-century Dialectical Theories of Literature* (Princeton: Princeton University Press, 1971);

William M. Johnston, *The Austrian Mind: An Intellectual and Social History, 1848–1938* (Berkeley: University of California Press, 1984);

Ernest Joos, *Lukács's Last Autocriticism: The Ontology* (Atlantic Highlands, N.J.: Humanities Press, 1983);

András Kardos, ed., *A Budapesti Iskola: Tanulmányok Lukács Györgyről. I. Fehér Ferenc–Heller Ágnes* (Budapest: T-Twins Kiadó, Lukács Archívum, 1995);

Béla Királyfálvi, *The Aesthetics of György Lukács* (Princeton: Princeton University Press, 1975);

Harry Levin, *Refractions: Essays in Comparative Literature* (New York: Oxford University Press, 1966);

Michael Löwy, *Georg Lukács: From Romanticism to Bolshevism*, translated by Patrick Camiller (London: NLB, 1979);

Judith Marcus, *Georg Lukács and Thomas Mann: A Study in the Sociology of Literature* (Amherst: University of Massachusetts Press, 1987);

Marcus, "Thomas Mann and Georg Lukács," *New Hungarian Quarterly*, 30 (Spring 1989): 165–175;

Elio Matassi, *Il Giovane Lukács: Saggio e sistema* (Naples: Guida, 1979);

Miklos Mesterházi, *A messianizmus történetfilozófusa: Lukács György munkássága a húszas években* (Budapest: Lukács Archívum, 1987);

István Mészáros, *Lukács' Concept of Dialectic* (London: Merlin, 1972);

Fritz J. Raddatz, *Georg Lukács* (Berlin: Colloquium, 1970);

Raddatz, *Georg Lukács in Selbstzeugnissen und Bilddokumente* (Reinbek bei Hamburg: Rowohlt, 1972);

Tom Rockmore, "Lukács and the Marxist History of Philosophy," in *Georg Lukács: Theory, Culture, and Politics*, edited by Marcus and Tarr (New Brunswick, N.J.: Transaction, 1989), pp. 27–40;

Maynard Solomon, *Marxism and Art* (New York: Knopf, 1973);

Tibor Szabó, ed., *Miért Lukács?: A szegedi Lukács-szimpozion anyaga* (Budapest: Szegedi Lukács-Kör, 1990);

Marzio Vacatello, *Lukács* (Florence: La Nuova Italia Editrice, 1968);

István Varkonyi, "Young Lukács, the Sunday Circle, and Their Critique of Aestheticism," in *The Turn of the Century: Modernism and Modernity in Literature and the Arts*, edited by Christian Berg, Frank Durieux, and Geert Lernout (Berlin: De Gruyter, 1995), pp. 282–290;

Nicholas Vazsonyi, *Lukács Reads Goethe: From Aestheticism to Stalinism* (Columbia, S.C.: Camden House, 1997);

Liliane Weissberg, "Utopian Visions: Bloch, Lukács, Pontoppidan," *German Quarterly*, 67 (Spring 1994): 197–210;

René Wellek, *Four Critics: Croce, Valery, Lukács and Ingarden* (New York: Oxford University Press, 1977);

Raymond Williams, *Marxism and Literature* (New York: Oxford University Press, 1977);

Victor Zitta, *Georg Lukács' Marxism: Alienation, Dialectics, Revolution; A Study in Utopia and Ideology* (The Hague: Nijhoff, 1964);

Lambert Zuidervaart, "Methodological Shadowboxing in Marxist Aesthetics: Lukács and Adorno," in *The Aesthetics of the Critical Theorists: Studies on Benjamin, Adorno, Marcuse, and Habermas*, edited by Ronald Roblin (Lewiston, N.Y.: Mellen, 1990), pp. 244–290.

Papers:

György Lukács left his library and manuscripts to the Hungarian Academy of Sciences in Budapest.

Czesław Miłosz

(30 June 1911 –   )

Bogdan Czaykowski
University of British Columbia

BOOKS: *Poemat o czasie zastygłym* (Wilno: Koło Polonistów Słuchaczy Uniwersytetu Stefana Batorego, 1933);

Trzy zimy (Wilno: Związek Zawodowy Literatów Polskich, 1936);

Wiersze, as Jan Syruć (Lwów: Biblioteka rękopisów wydawnictwa "Brzask," 1939);

Ocalenie (Warsaw: Czytelnik, 1945);

Światło dzienne (Paris: Instytut Literacki, 1953);

Zniewolony umysł (Paris: Instytut Literacki, 1953); translated by Jane Zielonko as *The Captive Mind* (London: Secker & Warburg, 1953; New York: Knopf, 1953);

Zdobycie władzy (Paris: Instytut Literacki, 1955); translated by Celina Wieniewska as *The Seizure of Power* (New York: Criterion, 1955); translation also published as *The Usurpers* (London: Faber & Faber, 1955);

Dolina Issy (Paris: Instytut Literacki, 1955); translated by Louis Iribarne as *The Issa Valley* (New York: Farrar, Straus & Giroux, 1981; London: Sidgwick & Jackson / Manchester: Carcanet New Press, 1981);

Traktat poetycki (Paris: Instytut Literacki, 1957);

Kontynenty (Paris: Instytut Literacki, 1958);

Rodzinna Europa (Paris: Instytut Literacki, 1959); translated by Catherine S. Leach as *Native Realm: A Search for Self-Definition* (Garden City, N.Y.: Doubleday, 1968; Berkeley: University of California Press, 1981; London: Sidgwick & Jackson / Manchester: Carcanet New Press, 1981);

Człowiek wśród skorpionów. Studium o Stanisławie Brzozowskim (Paris: Instytut Literacki, 1962);

Król Popiel i inne wiersze (Paris: Instytut Literacki, 1962);

Gucio zaczarowany (Paris: Instytut Literacki, 1965);

The History of Polish Literature (New York: Macmillan / London: Collier-Macmillan, 1969; revised edition, Berkeley: University of California Press, 1983; translated into Polish by Maria Tarnowska as *Historia literatury polskiej do roku 1939* (Kraków: Znak, 1993);

Czesław Miłosz (photograph by Thomas Victor; from the dust jacket for The Issa Valley, *1981)*

Miasto bez imienia. Poezje (Paris: Instytut Literacki, 1969);

Widzenia nad Zatoką San Francisco (Paris: Instytut Literacki, 1969); translated by Richard Lourie as *Visions from San Francisco Bay* (New York: Farrar, Straus & Giroux, 1982; Manchester: Carcanet New Press, 1982);

Prywatne obowiązki (Paris: Instytut Literacki, 1972);

Gdzie wschodzi słońce i kędy zapada (Paris: Instytut Literacki, 1974);

Emperor of the Earth: Modes of Eccentric Vision (Berkeley: University of California Press, 1977);

Ziemia Ulro (Paris: Instytut Literacki, 1977); translated by Iribarne as *The Land of Ulro* (New York: Farrar, Straus & Giroux, 1984; Manchester: Carcanet, 1985);

Ogród nauk (Paris: Instytut Literacki, 1979; Lublin: Katolicki Uniwersytet Lubelski, 1986);

Nobel Lecture (New York: Farrar, Straus & Giroux, 1981);

Hymn o perle (Paris: Instytut Literacki, 1982; Kraków: Wydawnictwo Literackie, 1983);

Pieśń obywatela (Kraków: Wydawnictwo Świt, 1983);

The Witness of Poetry, Charles Eliot Norton Lectures, 1981–1982 (Cambridge, Mass.: Harvard University Press, 1983); Polish version published simultaneously as *Świadectwo poezji. Sześć wykładów o dotkliwościach naszego wieku* (Paris: Instytut Literacki, 1983; censored edition, Warsaw: Czytelnik, 1987);

Dialog o Wilnie, by Miłosz and Tomas Venclova (Warsaw: Społeczny Instytut Wydawniczy "Młynek," 1984);

Dostojewski i Sartre (N.p., ca. 1984);

Nieobjęta ziemia (Paris: Instytut Literacki, 1984; Kraków: Wydawnictwo Literackie, 1988); translated by Miłosz and Robert Hass as *Unattainable Earth* (New York: Ecco Press, 1986);

Z ogrodu ziemskich rozkoszy, nowe wiersze i epigrafy (N.p., 1984);

Podróżny świata. Rozmowy E. Czarneckiej [Renata Gorczyńska] *z Czesławem Miłoszem* (Kraków: Wszechnica Społeczno-Polityczna, 1984);

The Separate Notebooks, bilingual edition, translated by Miłosz, Hass, Robert Pinsky, and Renata Gorczyńska (New York: Ecco Press, 1984);

Zaczynając od moich ulic (Paris: Instytut Literacki, 1985); translated by Madeline G. Levine as *Beginning with My Streets: Essays and Recollections* (New York: Farrar, Straus & Giroux, 1991);

Kroniki (Paris: Instytut Literacki, 1987; Kraków: Znak, 1988);

Świat/The World, bilingual edition, translated by Miłosz (San Francisco: Arion Press, 1989);

Rok myśliwego (Paris: Instytut Literacki, 1990); translated by Levine as *A Year of the Hunter* (New York: Farrar, Straus & Giroux, 1994);

Dalsze okolice (Kraków: Znak, 1991); translated by Miłosz and Hass as *Provinces* (New York: Ecco Press, 1991; Manchester: Carcanet, 1993);

Szukanie ojczyzny (Kraków: Znak, 1992);

Na brzegu rzeki (Kraków: Znak, 1994); translated by Miłosz and Hass as *Facing the River: New Poems* (Hopewell, N.J.: Ecco Press, 1995);

Polskie kontrasty. On Contrasts in Poland (Kraków: Universitas, 1995);

Jakiegoż to gościa mieliśmy. O Annie Świrszczyńskiej (Kraków: Znak, 1996);

Legendy nowoczesności. Eseje okupacyjne. Listy-eseje Jerzego Andrzejewskiego i Czesława Miłosza, by Miłosz and Jerzy Andrzejewski (Kraków: Wydawnictwo Literackie, 1996);

Abecadło Miłosza (Kraków: Wydawnictwo Literackie, 1997);

Życie na wyspach (Kraków: Znak, 1997);

Piesek przydrożny (Kraków: Znak, 1997); translated by Miłosz and Hass as *Road-side Dog* (New York: Farrar, Straus & Giroux, 1998);

Inne abecadło (Kraków: Wydawnictwo Literackie, 1998).

Editions and Collections: *Dolina Issy* (London: Oficyna Poetów i Malarzy, 1966);

Wiersze (London: Oficyna Poetów i Malarzy, 1967);

Utwory poetyckie. Poems, introduction by Aleksander Schenker (Ann Arbor: Michigan Slavic Publications, 1976);

Widzenia nad Zatoką San Francisco (Warsaw: Krąg, 1979);

Dzieła zbiorowe, 12 volumes (Paris: Instytut Literacki, 1980–1985);

Wiersze zebrane, 2 volumes (Warsaw: Krąg, 1980);

Wybór wierszy (Warsaw: Państwowy Instytut Wydawniczy, 1980);

Gdzie wschodzi słońce i kędy zapada i inne wiersze (Kraków: Znak, 1980);

Poezje (Warsaw: Czytelnik, 1981);

Prywatne obowiązki (Warsaw, 1983; Wydawnictwo Kropka, 1983; Niezależna Oficyna Wydawnicza "Nowa," 1985);

Zniewolony umysł (Warsaw, 1984; Wydawnictwo Wolność, 1986);

Nieobjęta ziemia (Kraków: Wydawnictwo Trzeci Obieg, 1984);

Ogród nauk (Warsaw: Książnica Literacka, 1984);

Gucio zaczarowany. Miasto bez imienia (Warsaw: Wydawnictwo "V," 1985);

Świadectwo poezji (Kraków: Oficyna Literacka, 1985; Wrocław: Oficyna Wydawnicza Constans, 1986);

Poszukiwania. Wybór publicystyki rozproszonej 1931–1983, edited by Konrad Piwnicki (Warsaw: Wydawnictwo CDN, 1985);

Trzy zimy & Głosy o wierszach, edited by Renata Gorczyńska and Piotr Kłoczowski (London: Aneks, 1987);

Metafizyczna pauza, selected and edited by Joanna Gromek (Kraków: Znak, 1989);

Poematy (Wrocław: Wydawnictwo Dolnośląskie, 1989);

Kołysanka (Warsaw: Varsovia, 1990);

Wiersze, 3 volumes (Kraków: Znak, 1993);

Poezje wybrane. Selected Poems, bilingual edition (Kraków: Wydawnictwo Literackie, 1996).

Editions in English: "Not More," translated by Adam Czerniawski, in *San Francisco Review Annual*, 1 (1963): 111–112;

"Campo di Fiori," translated by Adam Gillon, in *Introduction to Modern Polish Literature: An Anthology of Fiction and Poetry*, edited by Gillon and Ludwik Krzyżanowski (New York: Twayne, 1964), pp. 447–449;

Selected Poems, with an introduction by Kenneth Rexroth (New York: Seabury, 1973);

Bells in Winter, translated by Miłosz and Lillian Vallee (New York: Ecco Press, 1978; Manchester: Carcanet New Press, 1980);

The Collected Poems, 1931–1987 (New York: Ecco Press, 1988).

RECORDING: *Fire*, read by Miłosz, Washington, D.C., Watershed Tapes C-200, 1987.

OTHER: *Antologia poezji społecznej*, edited by Miłosz and Zbigniew Folejewski (Wilno: Wydawn. Koła Polonistów Universytetu Stetana Batorego, 1933);

Pieśń niepodległa, edited by Miłosz (Warsaw: Oficyna Polska w Warszawie, 1942);

Kultura masowa, edited by Miłosz (Paris: Instytut Literacki, 1959);

Węgry, edited by Miłosz (Paris: Instytut Literacki, 1960);

Oscar Vladislas de Lubicz Milosz, *The Noble Traveller*, introduction by Miłosz, edited by Christopher Bamford (West Stockbridge, Mass.: Lindisfarne, 1984);

Aleksander Wat, *Mój wiek. Pamiętnik mówiony*, 2 volumes, edited by Miłosz (London: Polonia Book Fund, 1977; Warsaw: Czytelnik, 1990); edited and translated by Richard Lourie, with a foreword by Miłosz, as *My Century: The Odyssey of a Polish Intellectual* (Berkeley: University of California Press, 1988);

Mowa wiązana, edited by Miłosz (Olsztyn: Pojezierze, 1986);

Wypisy z ksiąg użytecznych, edited by Miłosz (Kraków: Znak, 1994);

A Book of Luminous Things: An International Anthology of Poetry, edited by Miłosz (New York: Harcourt Brace, 1996).

TRANSLATIONS: Jacques Maritain, *Drogami klęski* (Warsaw: Oficyna Polska, 1942);

Daniel Bell, *Praca i jej gorycze* (Paris: Instytut Literacki, 1957);

Jeanne Hersch, *Polityka i rzeczywistość* (Paris: Instytut Literacki, 1957);

Simone Weil, *Wybór pism* (Paris: Instytut Literacki, 1958; Kraków: Znak, 1991);

Postwar Polish Poetry: An Anthology (Garden City, N.Y.: Doubleday, 1965; expanded edition, Berkeley: University of California Press, 1983); republished as *Polish Post-War Poetry* (Harmondsworth, U.K.: Penguin, 1970);

Zbigniew Herbert, *Selected Poems*, translated by Miłosz and Peter Dale Scott (Harmondsworth, U.K.: Penguin, 1968);

Aleksander Wat, *Mediterranean Poems* (Ann Arbor: Ardis, 1977);

Księga Psalmów, edited and translated by Miłosz (Paris: Editions du Dialogue, 1979; Lublin: Katolicki Uniwersytet Lubelski, 1982);

Księga Hioba, edited and translated by Miłosz (Paris: Editions du Dialogue, 1980);

Księgi pięciu Megilot, edited and translated by Miłosz (Paris: Editions du Dialogue, 1982; Lublin: RW KUL, 1984);

Ewangelia według Marka. Apokalipsa, edited and translated by Miłosz (Paris: Editions du Dialogue, 1984; Lublin: Katolicki Uniwersytet Lubelski, 1989);

Anna Świrszczyńska, *Happy as a Dog's Tail*, translated by Miłosz and Leonard Nathan (San Diego: Harcourt Brace Jovanovich, 1985);

Apokalipsa, edited and translated by Miłosz (Paris: Editions du Dialogue, 1986);

With the Skin: Poems of Aleksander Wat, translated and edited by Miłosz and Nathan (New York: Ecco, 1989);

Księga mądrości, edited and translated by Miłosz (Paris, 1989);

Haiku, edited and translated by Miłosz (Kraków: Wydawnictwo M. Biblioteka NaGłosu, 1992);

Oscar Milosz, *Storge* (Kraków: Znak, 1993);

Świrszczyńska, *Talking to my Body*, translated by Miłosz and Nathan (Port Townsend, Wash.: Copper Canyon, 1996).

SELECTED PERIODICAL PUBLICATION—UNCOLLECTED: *Robinson warszawski*, by Miłosz and Jerzy Andrzejewski, *Dialog*, 9 (1984): 5–17.

No Polish writer has enjoyed greater renown in the West than Czesław Miłosz. Of the two Polish winners of the Nobel Prize in literature before Miłosz, Henryk Sienkiewicz (in 1905) and Władysław Reymont (in 1924), the former gained enormous popularity in France and the United States, but only briefly; the latter remained virtually unknown and largely untranslated despite the prize. Among the post–World War II writers, several did become well known in the West, most notably Witold Gombrowicz, Tadeusz Różewicz, Zbigniew Herbert; and Wisława Szymborska, winner of the Nobel Prize in 1996. But their recognition in the United States has not equaled that of Miłosz, who has been described on occasion as not only a Polish but also an American poet.

Throughout most of his long literary career, however, Miłosz was virtually unknown to the wider readership. Before World War II his first two volumes of poetry, which had a miniscule circulation, gained him critical recognition as a talented and promising poet who–although he belonged to what was called the Second Vanguard–was not truly avant-garde, having moved rather abruptly from socially committed poetry to a form of incantatory, visionary verse that many critics considered passé. After the war Miłosz quickly made his mark as one of the foremost poets with his volume *Ocalenie* (Rescue, 1945) and was singled out in a major article in 1946 by perhaps the most influential literary critic of the time, Kazimierz Wyka, as the leading poet of the postwar period. By 1951, following his defection to the West, Miłosz came to be regarded by the Communist authorities as a renegade and, except for a brief interlude in 1956–1957, a total ban was imposed on the publication of his writings; in fact, well into the 1970s special permission was required in the Soviet bloc even for his name to be printed or mentioned in the media.

The awarding of the Nobel Prize to Miłosz in 1980 coincided with the considerable relaxation of censorship during the Solidarity period (1980–1981), and his works appeared in print and sold immediately in large numbers. Although stricter censorship was reinstated after the declaration of Martial Law in December 1981, the regime did not find it either possible or politically expedient to reimpose too strict a ban on Miłosz's works, and the collapse of Communist power in Poland in 1989 made it again possible for his works to be published, heard, and discussed extensively. Despite occasional criticism from the nationalist right because of his publicly voiced dislike of nationalism and of what some have regarded as the flaunting of his

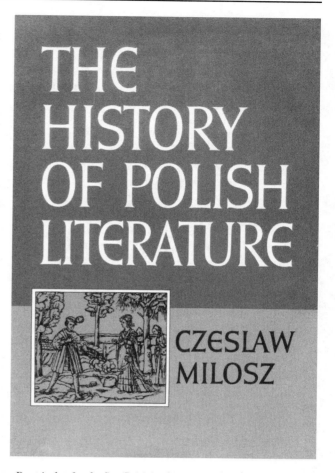

Dust jacket for the first British edition of one of the works Miłosz wrote to introduce English-speaking readers to the literature of his country

Lithuanian roots and sentiments, Miłosz's literary reputation in Poland and his authority as a writer and thinker have remained high among Catholic and left-wing intellectuals, while his books have continued to ensure financial success for their publishers.

Czesław Miłosz was born on 30 June 1911 in the manor house of Szetejnie, in what was then part of the Russian Empire. Historically, the region Miłosz came from is known as Samogitia, one of the major provinces of the medieval Grand Duchy of Lithuania, which joined the Kingdom of Poland in 1386. The nobility of Lithuania gradually adopted the Polish language and culture, but it retained many distinctive characteristics. Both Miłosz's father, Aleksander, and his mother, Weronika (née Kunat), came from Lithuanian stock; his paternal uncle Oscar Vladislas de Lubicz Milosz served as a Lithuanian diplomat in Paris during and after World War I while also writing poetry and mystical prose in French. Samogitia was an ethnically diverse region comprising–in addition to the Lithuanian-speaking Catholic peasantry—a new Lithuanian intelligentsia, Polish-speaking Lithuanian patriots, Polish nationalists, Belorussian peasants and intelligentsia, Russian officials and landowners, and a large, diversified Jewish community with its own traditions, culture, and literature in Yiddish. Miłosz's experience of this diversity was further amplified by the travels of his father, a civil engineer, across Russia during World War I and the 1917 revolution, and also by his father's decision to settle in the territory of independent Poland. Multinational or supranational ideals were reinforced by Miłosz's education from 1921 to 1929 in the King Sigismundus Augustus Secondary School in Vilnius, which gave Miłosz a humanist grounding as well as a realization of the philosophical chasm dividing religious and scientific outlooks.

The religious diversity—not only its Catholic, Orthodox, and Protestant forms but also local propensities for mysticism, Judaic lore, and the pagan substratum, still alive in folklore and various romanticized tales about the Lithuanian lakes, rivers, and forests—proved more important for Miłosz's intellectual development than ideology, whether nationalist (which Miłosz came to regard quite early as pernicious) or Marxist (which he found more convincing, though ultimately unacceptable to his spiritual yearnings). The most significant element of the Christian tradition for Miłosz, however, was Gnosticism, which led him to a starker view of Nature, whose wonders, imbibed from observation and books on animals (including American fauna) were tempered by the realization of the pitiless character of the struggle going on in the natural world. This realization seemed to confirm Miłosz's Manichaean view, derived from some of his readings, of the struggle between the principles of good and evil, and it gave his catastrophist forebodings a metaphysical character.

Despite his early naturalist and literary interests, Miłosz became a student of law at the University of Vilnius in 1930, completing his studies with a degree of master of law in 1934. He did, however, cultivate his literary interests by becoming a member of the Section of Original Writing, affiliated with the Circle of Students of Polish Literature, in which intellectual, literary, and ideological questions were hotly debated. Student life at the university was highly politicized, with left-wing and nationalist ideologies competing against each other, at times in violent forms. Miłosz took active part in social and literary activities and in 1931 joined the poetic group *Żagary* (Tinder or Kindling, referring to the literary review of the same name).

His left-wing leanings found expression in his first volume of verse, *Poemat o czasie zastygłym* (Poem about Congealed Time, 1933); these poems were modeled, at least to some extent, on revolutionary Russian poetry.

The politicized phase, however, was short-lived, as by the time of the appearance of his second volume of poems, *Trzy zimy* (Three Winters, 1936), Miłosz had discovered a dithyrambic mode of versification as well as esoteric lore of mysticism and metaphysics, primarily because of the influence of de Lubicz Milosz, whom the young poet met for the first time in Paris in 1931. Miłosz's reading was quite broad in the decade that followed and during the early years of World War II. As far as his religious ideas of that time were concerned, the most significant influence was perhaps that of Marian Zdziechowski, a profoundly pessimistic Christian thinker, whose lectures Miłosz attended at the University of Vilnius and whose writings contributed to Miłosz's Manichaean tendencies. Another important shaping force of Miłosz's outlook were Russian novelists, poets, and religious thinkers such as Fyodor Dostoyevsky, Leo Tolstoy, Vladimir Sergeyevich Solovyov, and Nikolay Aleksandrovich Berdyayev (and later Lev Shestov).

What is less often realized is the role that French literature, and especially the French novel, from Stendhal and Honoré de Balzac to André Gide, played in shaping Miłosz's views on society and Western culture and his conviction of the influence of literature on popular and ideological beliefs. As far as poetry is concerned, Edgar Allan Poe, Walt Whitman, Robert Browning, and T. S. Eliot were influences once Miłosz learned enough English in occupied Warsaw; he also read modern French and Russian poets, though the earliest and most significant influence in terms of poetic language was undoubtedly the work of Adam Mickiewicz, in which Miłosz discovered, as he later put it, "language in its state of balance." Two contemporary Polish writers also contributed significantly to the formation of Miłosz's intellectual personality: the philosopher and novelist Stanisław Brzozowski, especially with his program of "intellectual deeds," and Stanisław Ignacy Witkiewicz, playwright, philosopher, artist, and precursor of the theater of the absurd, whose deeply pessimistic view of the political and cultural future of European civilization reinforced Miłosz's own catastrophist views.

Upon completion of his studies in 1934 Miłosz obtained a scholarship from the National Culture Fund that enabled him to spend a year in Paris, where he learned French and broadened his artistic and intellectual horizons while continuing to learn from his uncle. Returning to Poland, he obtained a position in the Vilnius Broadcasting Station of the Polish Radio, but he was dismissed by the end of 1936 for his political views and his attempts to promote Belorussian culture. With the help of his left-wing and liberal friends, however, he was soon reappointed to the Warsaw Broadcasting Station, where he worked until the outbreak of World War II. Miłosz made several important new friendships in Warsaw: with the foremost lyrical poet of the time, Józef Czechowicz; the young Catholic novelist Jerzy Andrzejewski; and the future leading critic, Kazimierz Wyka. In addition, he met Jarosław Iwaszkiewicz, whose poetry played a role in Miłosz's later transition to a more classical style. Miłosz also entered the circle of liberal Catholic intellectuals connected with the Laski monastery and the periodical *Verbum* (Word).

The interwar years of Miłosz's intellectual development are portrayed most fully (though still selectively) in two later works, the novel *Dolina Issy* (1955; translated as *The Issa Valley*, 1981) and the essay *Rodzinna Europa* (1959; translated as *Native Realm: A Search for Self-Definition*, 1968). Both may be described as depictions of the growth of awareness. *Dolina Issy* has as its principal theme the development of the sensibility and metaphysical awareness of a boy, Thomas, and is set in the Lithuanian landscape among historical memories, local lore, and the manners of provincial society. *Rodzinna Europa*, overtly autobiographical, includes experiences, observations, and ideas that the poet gathered on his journey to Western Europe and then across redrawn boundaries after the destruction of Poland; it constitutes an attempt, undertaken from the perspective of the 1950s, at a self-definition.

A further insight into Miłosz's early years is offered in his *Rok myśliwego* (1990; translated as *A Year of the Hunter*, 1994). Miłosz developed a lifelong sense of radical alienation and a need to follow his own personal quest; this feeling crystallized during the German occupation, when inessentials became pared down to the existential, human core. Such radical reductionism, rather than leading to despair and abnegation, generated in Miłosz an eruption of creative and intellectual energy, resulting not only in a reorientation of his poetics toward more classical and objective forms but also in a series of penetrating essays that were written in 1942 and 1943 but did not appear in their entirety until 1996 as

Legendy nowoczesności. Eseje Okupacyjne (Legends of Modernity: Occupation Essays).

Except for a still somewhat mysterious journey in September 1939 to Bucharest (where Miłosz managed to obtain a Lithuanian safe-conduct pass) and then through Ukraine and Belorussia to Vilnius, where he stayed briefly during its incorporation into Lithuania and subsequent occupation by Soviet forces, Miłosz spent the war years with Janina Dłuska (whom he married in 1944), principally in Warsaw. His experience of illegally crossing the borders dividing Soviet-occupied Lithuania from Warsaw, an act that required stamina, ingenuity, and courage, is memorably described in *Rodzinna Europa*. Once in Warsaw, Miłosz took part in clandestine literary activity: his *Wiersze* (Poems, 1939), a volume appearing under the pseudonym Jan Syruć, was the first underground publication of its kind, and with the help of his friend Andrzejewski, he edited an anthology of poetry significantly titled *Pieśń niepodległa* (1942; translated as *Invincible Song: A Clandestine Anthology*, 1981). He took a critical view of armed resistance, however, and did not join the underground army. He witnessed the two most tragic events of the German occupation of Warsaw: the final destruction of the Jewish ghetto in 1943, and the long but unsuccessful uprising by the Polish underground army in 1944, followed by the deliberate destruction of most of the city by the Germans. Miłosz managed to escape from the defeated city and eventually went to liberated Kraków, where he took part in literary activity and prepared *Ocalenie* for publication in 1945; it was his first and only volume of poems to appear in postwar Poland between 1945 and 1980.

Miłosz's writings of the war period constitute a watershed in his creative and intellectual development. In witnessing the eruption of genocidal forces that turned the inheritors of one of the most accomplished cultures into instruments of mass destruction, Miłosz acquired a sharp critical perspective on civilization in general and on literature in particular. In *Zniewolony umysł* (1953; translated as *The Captive Mind*, 1953) there is a passage that describes the nature of this dark illumination:

> A man is lying under machine-gun fire on the street of an embattled city. He looks at the pavement and sees a very amusing sight: the cobblestones are standing upright like the quills of a porcupine. The bullets hitting against their edges

Dust jacket for the bilingual text of the speech Miłosz gave when he received the 1980 Nobel Prize in literature

displace and tilt them. Such moments in the consciousness of a man judge all poets and philosophers.

The passage is preceded by a statement of uncompromising severity: "The work of thought should be able to withstand the test of brutal, naked reality. If it cannot, it is worthless."

What preserved Miłosz from nihilistic reductionism or ideological fanaticism (such as, for instance, that of Tadeusz Borowski or of Andrzejewski, both of whom after the war embraced the Communist creed) was the fundamentally religious but at the same time nonideological, highly individualistic nature of his intellectual psyche. Miłosz's writings of the period display a range of theme and perspective, of personae and tones in which mordant and grim feelings are counterbalanced by compassion and affirmation. The burden, if not the guilt, of being an heir to the dark side of Western civilization finds expression in the complex poem "Biedny chrześcijanin patrzy na getto" (translated as "A Poor Christian Looks at the Ghetto"), which is part of a cycle titled "Voices of Poor People" in *Ocalenie*. The insensi-

tivity of people to the suffering and destruction of their fellow human beings is the theme of "Campo di Fiori." In several poems, notably "W malignie" (In Malignant Fever), "Równina" (Plain), and "Rzeka" (River), anger and bitterness are mixed with sadness and pity as the poet addresses the absurdity of interwar Poland, the blindness and irrationality of its politics, and the vulnerability of its inhabitants to the cruel forces of history. Yet, the capacity of human nature to ignore or adapt to the "end of the world," the impossibility of abandoning hope, and the ability to be happy and to find psychological and intellectual alibis in the midst of oppression and naked evil are revealed in poems that range from songlike lyrics to constructs of complex personae, particularly "Piosenka o końcu świata" (translated as "Song of the End of the World"), "Piosenka pasterska" (Shepherds' Song), and "Pieśni Adriana Zielińskiego" (translated as "Songs of Adrian Zieliński").

Miłosz's left-wing leanings underwent a severe test after the war. His catastrophist views predisposed him to regard Soviet Communism as an inevitable phase, perhaps of long duration, in the history of the European continent. Moreover, he was convinced that Poland needed radical social reforms. His close friend in occupied Warsaw and in the immediate postwar years, the Georg Hegel specialist Tadeusz Kroński (called Tiger in *Rodzinna Europa*), influenced Miłosz's attitude toward Marxism as a far-from-spurious theory of societal and historical change and further strengthened his dislike of right-wing ideologies. But at the same time, Miłosz's penchant for sharp observation and his sense of the value of literature as an autonomous mode of cultural activity made him resistant to Socialist Realism, which required of the writer not only to become an instrument of Communist Party policy but also to impose a ready-made and simplistic formula on reality.

Miłosz's knowledge of Soviet reality under Stalin (including his firsthand observations of Soviet Ukraine in the winter of 1939–1940), the materialism of official Communist doctrine, and the gradual but unmistakable Sovietization of Poland, including increasingly severe restrictions on democratic and intellectual freedom, made him gradually recoil from even the limited approval he had initially given to the new regime in Poland. For Miłosz, the real touchstone was poetry: its character, freedom, and future. He could, and did, write journalistic prose that he later judged harshly as an example of the general "descent into abomination"—such as a series of feuilletons in 1945 in *Dziennik Polski* (Polish Daily), edited by Jerzy Putrament, one of the chief cultural functionaries of the Party—but Miłosz could not compromise his poetic principles.

These principles, as his 1946 "List półprywatny o poezji" (A Semi-Private Letter Regarding Poetry, reprinted in *Kontynenty* [Continents, 1958]) shows, were not merely technical. Poetry for Miłosz was a way both of being one's own person and of trying to grasp or clarify the real; it was also a crucial form of societal discourse. In 1950, after working in the diplomatic service for Poland in Washington, D.C., and Paris, Miłosz realized that he could no longer propitiate the cultural apparatchiks by minor concessions (such as "translating" Mao Tse-tung) but would have to conform fully and unambiguously; he decided instead to seek freedom. Early in 1951 he left his job in the Polish embassy in Paris and sought refuge with the editors of the émigré monthly *Kul-*

tura, explaining in an article titled "Nie" (No) his reasons for breaking with Communist Poland.

Three books reveal the intellectual dilemmas Miłosz faced in the immediate postwar years and express his views on Soviet Communism and the political and ideological predicaments of the postwar world. The first of them, *Zniewolony umysł*, in effect launched his literary career in the West while making him a significant moral and ideological influence in Poland. Generically, it is best described as a mixture of essays and biographical sketches; in addition to topical chapters, it includes "portraits" of four Polish writers who collaborated with the Communist regime in Poland. It was intended as a warning to the West (one chapter begins, "Are the Americans really that stupid?") and an attempt to enlighten Western intellectuals about the true nature of the relationship between Communist authorities and intellectuals and the totalitarian character of Soviet Communism. It is a depiction of the lure Communism exerted on the minds of Polish intellectuals (exemplified mainly by the behavior of the Polish literary community) and the frequent "schizophrenia" that characterized their practice of dissimulation or at least mental reservations (which Milosz called *ketman*, borrowing the term from Islamic religious history). On a more personal level, the book is an apology for Miłosz's own collaboration in the diplomatic service and his "Hegelian sting," which made him view Communism as a system willed by history. The book is an eloquent and penetrating document, surpassing in its complexity similar accounts written by Western as well as Eastern authors who became disillusioned with Communism.

The second book, *Zdobycie władzy* (1955; translated as *The Seizure of Power*, 1955, and as *The Usurpers*, 1955), although ostensibly a novel, is of interest mainly as an intelligent presentation of the reasoning and attitudes of those in Poland who experienced Nazi and at times Stalinist evil—people who had to make difficult political and moral choices, faced with the defeat of the prewar Polish political class (symbolized especially in the tragedy of the Warsaw Uprising) and the "betrayal" of the cause of Polish independence by the Western powers.

The third book is entirely different in character. *Światło dzienne* (Daylight, 1953) is a fairly large volume of poems; it includes poems written after Miłosz's break with the regime as well as poems written since *Ocalenie* and mostly published in Poland. The volume opens with "Do

Jonathana Swifta" (To Jonathan Swift), which bitingly sounds the central moral and political themes of the collection:

> I visited the lands of Brobdingnag
> And stopped at the Laputan isles.
> Became acquainted with the Yahoo tribe
> Which worships its own excrement,
> A denunciators' cursed race
> Living in slavish fright.

The volume includes two poetic treatises, "Traktat moralny" (A Treatise on Morals) and "Toast," principally discursive and narrative, respectively. "Dziecię Europy" (translated as "Child of Europe") is a masterpiece of ironic reasoning turned against the fraudulence of Communist dialectics. Several of the poems are about American themes, and there are free renderings of African American spirituals as well as Miłosz's own songlike poems. Two poems deal with contemporary Polish writers. The first, "Do Tadeusza Różewicza, poety" (To Tadeusz Różewicz, Poet), reaffirms Miłosz's view of the importance of poetry: "Fortunate is the nation that has a poet / And in its toil does not walk in silence." The second, "Na śmierć Tadeusza Borowskiego" (On the Death of Tadeusz Borowski), interprets Borowski's suicide (presented as a tragic accident by the Communist authorities) as a flight into death of someone caught between two dead ends: a reactionary Polish ethos and the "smooth wall" of the East: "Borowski betrayed. He fled where he could."

Included also are two poems written during the war, one of which is the cycle "Świat (poema naiwne)" (translated as "The World"), the unquestionable masterpiece of Miłosz's wartime poetry. A "song of innocence" written in the face of and against the horror of experience, it reaffirms—with profound naiveté and serenity and with a mastery of form—the reality of faith, hope, and love, and the beauty of the natural and human world.

Światło dzienne ends with a short poem, "Mittelbergheim," signaling a new turn in Miłosz's poetic preoccupations. The poem, dedicated to Stanisław Vincenz, another of Miłosz's mentors, may be described as the poet's rededication to the pursuit of a quest infinitely more fundamental than politics or ideology: the philosophical and religious search for the nature of reality. It is a poem of the rebirth of the essential Miłosz and of the rediscovery of the concrete world and as such should be read together with another poem

written roughly two years later, "Notatnik: Bon nad Lemanem" (A Notebook: Bon by Lake Leman), the final lines of which read:

> And he who finds repose,
> Order and time eternal in what is,
> Passes without a trace. Do you agree
> To void what is, and to extract from movement,
> Like a gleam from a black river's water,
> The eternal moment? Yes.

With these two poems, Miłosz's poetics entered a phase of epiphany, understood by Miłosz in terms akin to those of James Joyce, who meant by it not only, as he wrote in *Stephen Hero* (1955), a "sudden spiritual manifestation" but the "gropings of a spiritual eye which seeks to adjust its vision to an exact focus. The moment the focus is reached the object is epiphanized."

During the first forty years of his life Miłosz was constantly trying to find his bearings in extremely complex situations, in which personal choices were often tantamount to political acts and ideological declarations, while the sphere of private life was constantly affected by external factors and forces. Once, however, he had made his decision to break with the Communist regime and stay in the West, he gained, after an initial period of hardship, the ability to concentrate on his literary and intellectual pursuits and to deepen and refine his understanding of those forty years of experience.

Miłosz's post-1951 life falls into three periods: his stay in France (1951–1960); his appointment as a lecturer and then professor in the Slavic Department of the University of California at Berkeley (1960–1980); and his post-1980 years, after the award of the Nobel Prize in literature. One of the main problems of the French period was Miłosz's decision to provide for himself and his family (he and his wife had two sons) by writing, which was not easy. Miłosz was regarded as a renegade not only by the Communist authorities in Poland (hence the ban on the publication of his works) but also by a large and influential segment of the French intellectual milieu, while the Polish émigré circles in the West rejected him as a former collaborator of the regime and, in the view of some, a communist agent. An important exception to this ostracism was the support offered Miłosz by the editor of *Kultura*, Jerzy Giedroyc, and his closest associates. Giedroyc not only recognized Miłosz's talent but also provided a considerable portion of Miłosz's earnings between 1953 and 1960 by publishing twelve books either of Miłosz's own writings or of translations. Among these books were two of Miłosz's novels as well as *Zniewolony umysł, Światło dzienne, Rodzinna Europa, Kontynenty* (which included articles on and translations of American poets), and *Traktat poetycki* (A Treatise on Poetry, 1957).

Traktat poetycki is a long poem that constitutes a transition between Miłosz's political phase and his more essential preoccupations. Modeled to some extent on Karl Shapiro's *Essay on Rime* (1945), the poem treats in a major and integrated manner several of Miłosz's earlier themes, such as interwar Poland's ethos and its roots, the meaning of history when judged by extreme human situations, and the nature of Nature; it also includes a brilliantly sketched outline of modern Polish poetry. In a pithy poem titled "Preface" Miłosz formulates his poetic manifesto:

> First, plain speech in the mother tongue.
> Hearing it, you should be able to see
> Apple trees, a river, the bend of a road,
> As if in a flash of summer lightning.
>
> And it should contain more than images. . . .
>
> You often ask yourself why you feel shame
> Whenever you look through a book of poetry.
> As if the author, for reasons unclear to you,
> Addressed the worse side of your nature,
> Pushing aside thought, cheating thought. . . .
>
> One clear stanza can make more weight
> Than a whole wagon of elaborate prose.

The volume that collects most of Miłosz's poems written in France, *Król Popiel i inne wiersze* (King Popiel and Other Poems, 1962), includes a new and, for Miłosz, a rather unusual departure: "Album snów" (translated as "Album of Dreams") is ostensibly a notebook of dreams but is more in the nature of dreamlike recollections of troubling or unclear episodes from the author's life—his only attempt, it seems, at poetically engaging the subconscious. There are also several excellent shorter poems, such as "Nic więcej" (No More) and "Mistrz" (The Master), both of which are ironic, melancholy, but unapologetic reflections on his powers as a poet. The thematically connected "Ballada" (Ballad) is a moving meditation on the fate of Tadeusz Gajcy, a young right-wing poet who perished in the Warsaw Uprising, written from the perspective of his mother. Finally, there are some skillful exercises in the baroque style. The last poem of the volume, "Po ziemi naszej" (translated as "Throughout Our Lands"),

develops further what Aleksander Schenker describes in the introduction to *Utwory poetyckie* (Poems, 1976) as Miłosz's earlier attempts "to fuse" various levels of language or voices "into one poetic idiom" so that, while retaining "their distinctive characteristics and fulfilling distinct stylistic functions," they are "skillfully harmonized into one polyphonic whole." This concluding poem combines not only various styles and voices but also different perspectives to illuminate a major central theme: the universal fate of all human beings, irrespective of their locus, time, culture, gender, or status. It is also the first of Miłosz's major poems that reflects in its imagery and descriptions the impact of the Pacific coast on his poetic mind.

Miłosz's Berkeley years are often referred to as the Californian or American phase of his poetry. Indeed, images of Californian and Pacific Coast nature and cities, especially of San Francisco, often blend or contrast with vividly recollected landscapes of Lithuania. The interplay of the experience of two such different regions enriches not only the evocative and epiphanic powers and scope of Miłosz's poetry but also his sense of the strangeness of human society and civilization. Miłosz made his Californian (and more broadly, North American) experience the subject of a book of short essays, *Widzenia nad Zatoką San Francisco* (1969; translated as *Visions from San Francisco Bay,* 1982) in which, probing the meaning of being in a place, he connected his new experience ("What one feels facing too large a space") to his central preoccupations and already formulated views.

The constant thematic parallelism between Miłosz's discursive prose and his poetry is represented by the poem "Do Robinsona Jeffersa" (To Robinson Jeffers), in which the latter poet's stark vision of an unfeeling and force-driven universe is contrasted with the milder, humanized Nature of "the Slavic poets":

> Thin-lipped, blue-eyed, without grace or hope,
> before God the Terrible, body of the world,
> Prayers are not heard. Basalt and granite.
> Above them, a bird of prey. The only beauty. . . .
>
> And yet you did not know what I know. The earth
>   teaches
> More than does the nakedness of elements. . . .
>
> Better to carve suns and moons on the joints of
>   crosses
> as was done in my district. To birches and firs
> give feminine names. To implore protection
> against the mute and treacherous might
> than to proclaim, as you did, an inhuman thing.

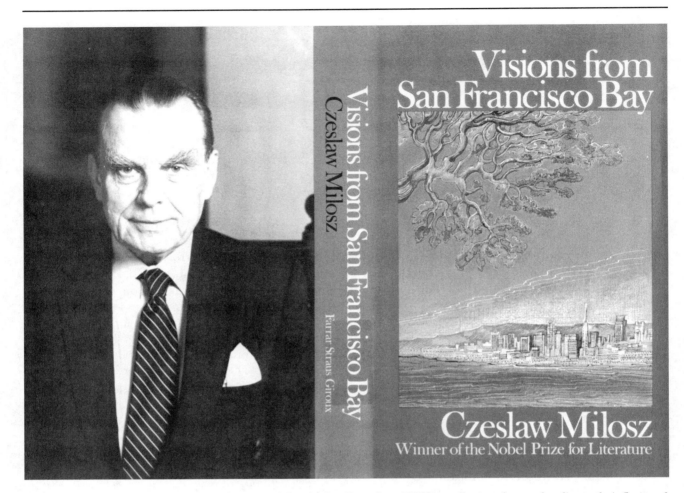

Dust jacket for the 1982 translation of Widzenia nad Zatoką San Francisco *(1969), a collection of essays that discuss the influence of Miłosz's American experiences on his work*

However formally fruitful and enriching in imagery and perspective the Californian phase of Miłosz's poetry is, it cannot be described as thematically American. Miłosz observed with apprehension the turbulence of the American scene in the late 1960s and early 1970s, especially the transformations of the intellectual climate; after all, Berkeley was one of the centers of the student movement, of counterculture, and of political, often Marxist, dissent. These and other developments of American life occasionally find their reflection in Miłosz's poetry, but they function principally as exemplifications of more-general and typically Miłoszian themes.

Miłosz also devoted considerable time and effort to acquainting American readers with Polish literature, especially poetry. The three most important publications in this respect are the anthology *Postwar Polish Poetry* (1965), which met with considerable interest and acclaim; *The History of Polish Literature* (1969); and the post-Nobel Harvard lectures published in 1983 as *The Witness*

of Poetry, which gave Miłosz the opportunity to formulate and argue for his own view of poetry. In the early 1970s Miłosz started presenting his poetry and other writings to English-speaking readers, a process that began with the appearance of *Selected Poems* (1973) and reached its high point with the publication of *The Collected Poems, 1931–1987* (1988), which despite the title is still quite selective. He was helped in the task of crossing the barrier of Polish language by several of his students at Berkeley, who translated his prose and with some of whom, as well as with some American poets, he translated his poems, insisting from roughly the mid 1970s on complete control over the translations of his poetry into English. He also gave many public readings, mostly on university campuses, thus further extending his reading public and the addressees of his writings.

The most important aspect of Miłosz's Californian phase, however, is the intensification of his ontological and metaphysical concerns. In having to resituate himself, Miłosz reevaluated his view of civilization, as illustrated in the poem "Wieści" (translated as "Tidings") in *Gdzie wschodzi słońce i kędy zapada* (From the Rising of the Sun, 1974). He also went deeper than before into his own past and that of his culture, especially in the cycle "Do Heraklita" (To Heraclitus) in *Kroniki* (Chronicles, 1987). He addressed wider anthropological and philosophical concerns and increasingly shed his reticence to reveal his religious (even theological) thinking. In fact, the religious theme becomes the dominant and synthesizing framework for older as well as newer or more overtly treated themes, such as the erotic—as in "Filina," written in 1976, and such relatively late poems as "Ogród ziemskich rozkoszy" (translated as "The Garden of Earthly Delights") and "Annalena" from *Nieobjęta ziemia* (1984; translated as *Unattainable Earth*, 1986). Thus the Californian phase of Miłosz's poetry extended beyond two key events in his life: the Nobel Prize, which transformed him, despite his reluctance, into a public figure and resulted in extensive publication of his work in translation, and the collapse of Communism in Poland and in the rest of Eastern Europe, which made it possible for him not only to spend longer periods of time in Poland but also to visit his native region in Lithuania.

In prose the most important single presentation of the religious theme is *Ziemia Ulro* (1977; translated as *The Land of Ulro*, 1984). Its somewhat meandering form is probably deliberate, though it no doubt also reflects the author's uncertainties about his argument and the putative reactions of his reader. Ostensibly a discussion of the religious views of several writers and thinkers (Mickiewicz, Emanuel Swedenborg, William Blake, Dostoyevsky, de Lubicz Milosz, Gombrowicz, and Shestov), it serves as the central purpose of much of Miłosz's writing since his arrival in Berkeley: to create an intellectual space for religious thought outside of "academic" and confessional theology. In poetry, of the several volumes published between 1962 and the 1990s, the most important in this respect is *Gdzie wschodzi słońce i kędy zapada*, which includes several shorter poems on the religious theme as well as "Nie tak" (translated as "Not this Way"), "Lektury" (translated as "Readings"), "Oeconomia divina," "O aniołach" (translated as "On Angels"), and the long title poem, which directly discloses for the first time some of Miłosz's long-held convictions:

> Yet I belong to those who believe in *apokatastasis*,
> The word promises reverse movement,

> Not the one that was set in *katastasis*,
> And appears in Acts 3, 31.

> It means: restoration. So believed: St. Gregory of Nyssa,
> Johannes Scotus Erigena, Ruysbroeck, and William Blake.

> For me, therefore, everything has a double existence.
> Both in time and when time shall be no more.

The nature of Miłosz's religious quest, and the way in which it has contributed to the character of his poetry, has been well summed up by Aleksander Fiut in his study *Moment wieczny. Poezja Czesława Miłosza* (1987; translated as *The Eternal Moment: The Poetry of Czesław Miłosz*, 1990). Fiut posits that in his religious poetry Miłosz

> tries to rebuild the Christian anthropocentric vision of the world, at the same time (unlike naive traditionalists) acknowledging those theories and experiences that have undermined it. This attempt explains the constant presence in his poetry of antithetical clashes, the dialectic of opposite ideas, and the ambivalence of opinions: all are called into question and reinterpreted. From this point of view, Miłosz's poetry can be read as a hermeneutics of the Christian imagination, one aware of its own limitations.

However, if one takes into account Miłosz's later volumes and such major poetic restatements of the religious theme as his "Sześć wykładów wierszem" (translated as "Six Lectures in Verse"), which pose as problematic the central Christian belief in the Resurrection, it is possible to regard Miłosz's poetic treatment of religious themes as something broader than the hermeneutics of the Christian imagination: as an attempt to revive convincingly religious imagination altogether while subjecting it to severe doubts and tests of experience and philosophical thought.

Miłosz continued to extend and further diversify the already wide range of his poetic form. He worked toward achieving the most effective full line, taut or intonationally hymnic. He wrote aphoristic poems, passages made of unistichs, and whole poems written in dithyrambic versets, such as "Zdania" (translated as "Notes") in *Hymn o perle* (Hymn of the Pearl, 1982); the opening unistichs of another of Miłosz's longer masterpieces, "Gucio zaczarowany" (translated as "Bobo's Metamorphosis"), in a 1965 volume of the same title; and "Na trąbach i na cytrze" (translated as "With Trumpets and Zithers") in *Miasto bez imienia* (City Without a Name, 1969). He wrote short lyrical poems of joy, wonder, adoration, and confession, notably the serene "Dar" (translated as "Gift") in *Gucio zaczarowany* (1965), the poem of paradisiacal happiness "Po wygnaniu" (translated as "After Paradise") in *Nieobjęta ziemia,* and the humorously self-absolving "Wyznanie" (translated as "A Confession") in *Kroniki.* He also mixed prose and verse in longer poems, most notably in "Gdzie wschodzi słońce i kędy zapada," and composed sequences and whole volumes, such as "Osobny zeszyt" (translated as *The Separate Notebooks,* 1984), *Nieobjęta ziemia,* and *Kroniki,* comprising his own poems, passages of discursive prose, reminiscences, epigraphs (his own and translated), and translations of poems. Finally, in *Piesek przydrożny* (1997; translated as *Road-side Dog,* 1998), he included short pieces of prose, poems, and short essays, as well as a sequence subtitled "Tematy do odstąpienia" (Topics for the Taking).

At no point in his long literary career has Miłosz been interested in "mere literature." From at least the mid 1930s he has tried to perfect his language and maintain what he terms its dignity. He has assiduously translated other poets, especially those who either supported his own view of poetic speech "as a more capacious form, that should not be too much like poetry nor too much like prose," or helped him to extend and justify the range of his own poetic form and style (John Milton, William Wordsworth, Whitman, Blaise Cendrars, W. B. Yeats, Eliot, Constantine Cavafy, Chinese poets, and some contemporary American poets of the objectivist school). He has translated religious texts—from the Psalms, the Book of Job, and Ecclesiastes to the Gospel of St. Mark, the metaphysical writings of de Lubicz Milosz, and the essays of Simone Weil. Above all, he has steered clear of vagueness as a mode of symbolism, of the avant-garde tendency to transform language into an antiworld or pure verbal object, and of excessive lyricism, which excluded or "cheated" thought. Finally, he has rejected the worship of poetry as a substitute for religion.

The volume *Nieobjęta ziemia* ends with a short untitled piece of poetic prose, tagged "Berkeley–Paris–Cambridge, Massachusetts, 1981–1983":

> To find my home in one sentence, concise, as if hammered in metal. Not to enchant anybody. Not to earn a lasting name in posterity. An unnamed need for order, for rhythm, for form, which three words are opposed to chaos and nothingness.

The continuously perceived failure to find such a home has led Miłosz to generate a massive body of work that ranks among the most philosophically penetrating and meaningful poetry of the twentieth century.

Letters:

"Wańkowicz i Miłosz w świetle korespondencji," *Twórczość,* 10 (1981);

Listy, by Miłosz and Thomas Merton, translated into Polish by Maria Tarnowska (Kraków: Znak, 1991);

Striving Towards Being: The Letters of Thomas Merton and Czesław Miłosz, edited by Robert Faggen (New York: Farrar, Straus & Giroux, 1997);

Zaraz po wojnie. Korespondencja z pisarzami 1945–1950, edited by Jerzy Illg (Kraków: Znak, 1998).

Interviews:

Aleksander Fiut, *Rozmowy z Czesławem Miłoszem* (Kraków: Wydawnictwo Literackie, 1981);

Ewa Czarnecka (Renata Gorczyńska), *Podróżny świata: Rozmowy z Czesławem Miłoszem. Komentarze* (New York: Bicentennial Publishing, 1983; expanded edition, Kraków: Wydawnictwo Literackie, 1992);

Czarnecka and Fiut, *Conversations with Czesław Miłosz,* translated by Richard Lourie (San Diego: Harcourt Brace Jovanovich, 1987);

Fiut, ed., *Czesława Miłosza autoportret przekorny. Rozmowy przeprowadził A. Fiut* (Kraków: Wydawnictwo Literackie, 1988).

Bibliography:

Rimma Volynska-Bogert and Wojciech Zalewski, *Czesław Miłosz: An International Bibliography, 1930–1980* (Ann Arbor: University of Michigan Press, 1983).

Biography:

Andrzej Zawada, *Miłosz* (Wrocław: Wydawnictwo Dolnośląskie, 1996).

References:

Stanisław Barańczak, "Miłosz's Poetic Language: A Reconnaissance," *Language and Style,* 4 (1985): 319–333;

Stanisław Bereś, *Ostatnia wileńska plejada* (Warsaw: PEN, 1990);

Jan Błonski, *Miłosz jak świat* (Kraków: Znak, 1998);

Bożena Chrząstowska, *Poezje Czesława Miłosza* (Warsaw: Wydawnictwo Szkolne i Pedagogiczne, 1982);

Bogdan Czaykowski, "From Rhythm and Metaphysics to Intonation, Experience and Gnosis: The Poetry of Bolesław Leśmian, Aleksander Wat and Czesław Miłosz," in *The Mature Laurel: Essays on Modern Polish Poetry,* edited by Adam Czerniawski (Bridgend, Wales: Seren Books, 1991), pp. 37–87;

Adam Czerniawski, "Poezja Czesława Miłosza," *Kultura,* 6 (1963): 25–49;

Donald Davie, *Czesław Miłosz and the Insufficiency of Lyric* (Knoxville: University of Tennessee Press, 1986);

Helen De Aguilar, "A Prince Out of Thy Star: The Place of Czesław Miłosz," *Parnassus: Poetry in Review,* 2 (1983–1984): 127–154;

Terrence Des Pres, "Czesław Miłosz: The Poetry of Aftermath," *Nation,* 30 December 1978, pp. 741–743;

Jolanta Dudek, *Europejskie korzenie poezji Czesław Miłosza* (Kraków: Księgarnia Akademicka, 1995);

Aleksander Fiut, *Moment wieczny. Poezja Czesława Miłosza* (Paris: Libella, 1987); translated by Theodosia S. Robertson as *The Eternal Moment: The Poetry of Czesław Miłosz* (Berkeley: University of California Press, 1990);

Zbigniew Folejewski, "Czesław Miłosz: A Poet's Road to Ithaka Between Worlds, Wars, and Poetics," *Books Abroad,* 43 (1969): 17–24;

Witold Gombrowicz, *Przeciw poetom. Dialog o poezji z Czesławem Miłoszem,* edited by Francesco M. Cataluccio (Kraków: Znak, 1995);

Ironwood, special Miłosz issue, 8 (1981);

Konstanty A. Jeleński, "Poeta i historia," *Kultura,* 1–2 (1954): 179–185;

Jeleński, "Poeta i przyroda," *Kultura,* 11 (1968): 3–22;

Bożena Karwowska, "Czesław Miłosz's Self-Presentation in English-Speaking Countries," *Canadian Slavonic Papers,* 3–4 (1998): 273–295;

Jerzy Kwiatkowski, ed., *Poznawanie Miłosza. Studia i szkice o twórczości poety* (Kraków: Wydawnictwo Literackie, 1985);

Zdzisław Łapiński, *Między polityką a metafizyką. O poezji Czesława Miłosza* (London: Odnowa, 1981);

Madeline G. Levine, "Czesław Miłosz: Poetry and Ethics," in her *Contemporary Polish Poetry, 1925–1975* (Boston: Twayne, 1981), pp. 36–54;

Literatura na Świecie, special Miłosz issue, 6 (1981);

Edward Możejko, ed., *Between Anxiety and Hope: The Poetry and Writing of Czesław Miłosz* (Edmonton: University of Alberta Press, 1988);

Leonard Nathan and Arthur Quinn, *The Poet's Work: An Introduction to Czesław Miłosz* (Cambridge, Mass.: Harvard University Press, 1991);

Nils Ake Nilsson, ed., *Czesław Miłosz: A Stockholm Conference* (Stockholm: Kungl. Vitterhets Historie och Antikvitets Akademien, 1992);

Ryszard Nycz, *Sylwy współczesne* (Wrocław: Zakład Narodowy im. Ossolińskich, 1984);

Józef Olejniczak, *Czytając Miłosza* (Katowice: Szkoła języka i kultury polskiej, 1997);

Pamiętnik Literacki, special Miłosz issue, 4 (1981);

Partisan Review, special Miłosz issue, 66 (Winter 1999);

Poezja, special Miłosz issue, 7 (1981);

A. Staniszewski, ed., *Studia i szkice o twórczości Czesława Miłosza* (Olsztyn: WSP, 1995);

Beata Tarnowska, *Geografia poetycka w powojennej twórczości Czesława Miłosza* (Olsztyn: WSP, 1996);

Teksty, special Miłosz issue, 4–5 (1981);

Twórczość, special Miłosz issue, 6 (1981);

Tomas Venclova, "Poetry as Atonement," *Polish Review,* 4 (1986): 265–271;

Helen Vendler, "Czesław Miłosz," in her *The Music of What Happens: Poems, Poets, Critics* (Cambridge, Mass.: Harvard University Press, 1988), pp. 209–223;

Andrzej Walicki, *Spotkania z Miłoszem* (London: Aneks, 1985);

Walicki, *"Zniewolony umysł" po latach* (Warsaw: Czytelnik, 1993);

World Literature Today, special Miłosz issue, 3 (1978);

Kazimierz Wyka, "Ogrody lunatyczne i ogrody pasterskie," *Twórczość,* 5 (1946): 135–147.

Papers:

Some of Czesław Miłosz's papers are in The Beinecke Rare Books and Manuscripts Library, Yale University.

Ferenc Molnár
(Ferenc Neumann)
(12 January 1878 – 2 April 1952)

András Veres
Institute of Literary Studies of MTA, Hungarian Academy of Sciences

BOOKS: *Magdolna és egyéb elbeszélések* (Budapest: Ranschburg Gusztáv, 1898);

A csókok éjszakája és egyéb elbeszélések (Budapest: Kunosy Vilmos, 1899);

Ne mondj igazat! Monológ (Budapest: Singer és Wolfner, 1900);

Az éhes város (Budapest: Révai & Salamon, 1901);

Egy gazdátlan csónak története (Budapest: Magyar Hírlap, 1901);

A doktor úr. Bohózat 3 felvonásban (Budapest: Róbert Lampel, 1902);

Józsi és egyéb kis komédiák (Budapest: Pallas, 1902);

Éva (Budapest: Magyar Hírlap, 1903);

Józsi. Bohózat 3 felvonásban (Budapest: Franklin-Társulat, 1904);

Egy pesti lány története (Budapest: Magyar Kereskedelmi Közlöny, 1905);

Gyerekek. Rajzok (Budapest: Róbert Lampel, 1905);

A Pál utcai fiúk. Ifjúsági regény (Budapest: Franklin-Társulat, 1907); translated by Louis Rittenberg as *The Paul Street Boys* (New York: Macy-Masius, 1927);

Az ördög. Vígjáték 3 felvonásban (Budapest: Franklin-Társulat, 1907); translated by Oliver Herford as *The Devil* (New York: Kennerley, 1908);

Rabok (Budapest: Franklin-Társulat, 1907); translated by Joseph Szebenyi as *Prisoners* (Indianapolis: Bobbs-Merrill, 1925);

Muzsika. Elbeszélések (Budapest: Franklin-Társulat, 1908);

Ketten beszélnek. Tárcák, rajzok (Budapest: Franklin-Társulat, 1909);

Pesti erkölcsök. Humoros rajzok (Budapest: Róbert Lampel, 1909);

Liliom. Egy csirkefogó élete és halála. Külvárosi legenda hét képben (Budapest: Franklin-Társulat, 1910); translated by Benjamin F. Glazer as *Liliom* (New York: Boni & Liveright, 1921);

Ferenc Molnár

A testőr. Vígjáték 3 felvonásban (Budapest: Franklin-Társulat, 1910); translated by Grace I. Cobron and Hans Bartsch as *The Guardsman* (New York: Boni & Liveright, 1924);

Hétágú síp. Tréfák, karcolatok, tárcák (Budapest: Franklin-Társulat, 1911);

A farkas. Vígjáték 3 felvonásban (Budapest: Franklin-Társulat, 1912); translated as *The Tale of the Wolf* (London: S. French, 1973);

A ferencvárosi angyal. Karácsonyi játék egy felvonásban (Budapest: Róbert Lampel, 1912);

Ma, tegnap, tegnapelőtt. (Vasárnapi krónikák) (Budapest: Róbert Lampel, 1912);

Báró Márczius és egyéb elbeszélések (Budapest: Róbert Lampel, 1913);

Kis hármaskönyv. Elbeszélések (Budapest: Franklin-Társulat, 1914);

Egy haditudósító emlékei, 2 volumes (Budapest: Franklin-Társulat, 1916);

Az aruvimi erdő titka és egyéb szatírák (Budapest: Légrády Testvérek, 1916);

A fehér felhő. Mirákulum egy felvonásban, öt változásban (Budapest: Franklin-Társulat, 1916);

Az óriás és egyéb elbeszélések (Budapest: Franklin-Társulat, 1917);

Ismerősök. Feljegyzések, krónikák (Budapest: Franklin-Társulat, 1917);

Farsang. Színmű 3 felvonásban (Budapest: Franklin-Társulat, 1917);

Úri divat. Vígjáték 3 felvonásban (Budapest: Franklin-Társulat, 1917);

Vacsora és egyéb jelenetek (Budapest: Érdekes Újság karácsonyi melléklete, 1917);

Andor (Budapest: Athenaeum, 1918);

Széntolvajok. Elbeszélés (Budapest: Népszava, 1918);

A hattyú. Vígjáték 3 felvonásban (Budapest: Franklin-Társulat, 1921); translated by Melville Baker as *The Swan* (New York: Longmans, Green, 1924);

Színház. Három egyfelvonásos (Budapest: Franklin-Társulat, 1921);

Égi és földi szerelem. Dráma 5 felvonásban (Budapest: Pantheon, 1922);

A vörös malom. Színjáték két részben, 26 képben (Budapest: Franklin-Társulat, 1923);

Az üvegcipő. Vígjáték egy felvonásban (Budapest: Franklin-Társulat, 1924);

Csendélet. Vígjáték 2 felvonásban (Budapest: Franklin-Társulat, 1925);

A gőzoszlop (Budapest: Franklin-Társulat, 1926);

Játék a kastélyban. Anekdota 3 felvonásban (Budapest: Franklin-Társulat, 1926); translated by P. G. Wodehouse as *The Play's the Thing* (New York: Brentano's, 1927);

Riviera. Vígjáték 2 felvonásban (Budapest: Franklin-Társulat, 1926);

A csók és egyéb elbeszélések (Budapest: Tolnai, 1927);

Olympia. Vígjáték 3 felvonásban (Budapest: Franklin-Társulat, 1928); translated by Sidney Coe Howard as *Olympia* (New York: Brentano's, 1928);

Toll. Rövid igaz történetek, megjegyzések, feljegyzések, kuriózumok (Budapest: Franklin-Társulat, 1928);

Egy, kettő, három. Vígjáték egy felvonásban (Budapest: Franklin-Társulat, 1929);

A jó tündér. Vígjáték 3 felvonásban, utójátékkal (Budapest: Franklin-Társulat, 1930); translated by Jane Hinton as *The Good Fairy* (New York: Long & Smith, 1932);

Harmónia. Családi idill karénekkel 3 felvonásban (Budapest: Athenaeum, 1932);

Valaki. Vígjáték 3 felvonásban (Budapest: Franklin-Társulat, 1932);

Csoda a hegyek közt. Legenda 4 felvonásban (Budapest: Athenaeum, 1933);

A zenélő angyal. Egy fiatal szerelem regénye (Budapest: Athenaeum, 1933); translated by Victor Katona and Peggy Barwell as *Angel Making Music* (New York: H. Smith & R. Haas, 1935);

Az ismeretlen lány. Drámai történet 3 felvonásban, 7 képben (Budapest: Athenaeum, 1934);

A cukrászné. Menyegző. Két egyfelvonásos (Budapest: Athenaeum, 1935); *A cukrászné* translated by Gilbert Miller as *Delicate Story* (New York & Los Angeles: S. French, 1941);

Nagy szerelem. Vígjáték 3 felvonásban (Budapest: Athenaeum, 1935);

Delila. Vígjáték 3 felvonásban (Budapest: Athenaeum, 1937);

A zöld huszár (Budapest: Athenaeum, 1937);

Őszi utazás (Budapest: Athenaeum, 1939);

A Dohány-utca és a Körút-sarok. "Aszfalt-regény" (Budapest: Borka, 1943);

Farewell, My Heart, translated by Elinor Rice (New York: Simon & Schuster, 1945); Hungarian version published as *Isten veled szívem* (Budapest: Káldor György, 1947);

Az aruvimi erdö titka (Budapest: Magveto, 1957);

A kekszemü (Budapest: Magveto, 1957).

Editions and Collections: *Összes munkái*, 20 volumes (Budapest: Franklin-Társulat, 1928);

Utitárs a száműzetésben. Jegyzetek egy önéletrajzhoz, foreword by Adorján Stella (Budapest: Táncsics, 1958);

Színművei (Vienna: Rudolf Nowak, 1972);

Pesti napló. Vezércikkek, tárcák, edited by Péter Gál Molnár (Budapest: Nyilvánosság Klub-Századvég, 1993);

A férfi szíve. Novellák, edited by László V. Urbán (Budapest: Argumentum, 1994).

Editions in English: *Fashions for Men and The Swan: Two Plays*, translated by Benjamin J. Glazer (New York: Boni & Liveright, 1922);

Éva and The Derelict Boat, translated by Emil Lengyel (Indianapolis: Bobbs-Merrill, 1924);

Plays of Molnar, translated by Glazer (London: Jarrolds, 1927);

The Plays of Ferenc Molnár, introduction by David Belasco, edited by Louis Rittenberg (New York: Vanguard, 1929);

The Captain of St. Margaret's, translated by Barrows Mussey (New York: Duell, Sloan & Pearce, 1945);

Companion in Exile: Notes for an Autobiography, translated by Mussey (New York: Gaer, 1950);

Stories for Two (New York: Horizon, 1950);

Romantic Comedies: Eight Plays by Ferenc Molnár (New York: Crown, 1952).

PLAY PRODUCTIONS: *A doktor úr*, Budapest, Vígszínház, 28 November 1902;

Józsi, Budapest, Vígszínház, 5 January 1904;

Az ördög, Budapest, Vígszínház, 10 April 1907;

Liliom, Budapest, Vígszínház, 7 December 1909;

A testőr, Budapest, Vígszínház, 19 November 1910;

A farkas, Budapest, Magyar Színház, 9 November 1912;

A fehér felhő, Budapest, Nemzeti Színház, 25 February 1916;

Farsang, Budapest, Népszínház, 28 October 1916;

Úri divat, Budapest, Nemzeti Színház, 23 November 1917;

A hattyú, Budapest, Vígszínház, 18 December 1920;

Színház, Budapest, Magyar Színház, 22 October 1921;

Égi és földi szerelem, Budapest, Magyar Színház, 3 November 1922;

A vörös malom, Budapest, Magyar Színház, 9 October 1923;

Az üvegcipő, Budapest, Vígszínház, 15 November 1924;

Csendélet, Budapest, Vígszínház, 26 February 1925;

Riviéra, Budapest, Renaissance Színház, 12 January 1926;

Játék a kastélyban, Budapest, Magyar Színház, 27 November 1926;

Olympia, Budapest, Magyar Színház, 2 March 1928;

Egy, kettő, három, Budapest, Vígszínház, 5 October 1929;

A jó tündér, Budapest, Vígszínház, 11 October 1930;

Valaki, Budapest, Belvárosi Színház, 25 February 1932;

Harmónia, Budapest, Magyar Színház, 7 October 1932;

Az ismeretlen lány, Budapest, Vígszínház, 3 November 1934;

A cukrászné és a Menyegző, Budapest, Andrássy úti Színház, 18 April 1935;

Nagy szerelem, Budapest, Vígszínház, 11 October 1935;

Csoda a hegyek között, Budapest, Vígszínház, 8 May 1936;

Delila, Budapest, Pesti Színház, 17 September 1937;

Carousel, New York, Majestic Theater, 19 April 1945;

A császár, Budapest, Vígszínház, 20 April 1946;

Panoptikum, Budapest, Nemzeti Színház, 7 October 1994;

Nászinduló, Budapest, Játékszín, 10 May 1996.

OTHER: "A császár. Színmű előjátékkal, 3 felvonásban," *Színház*, 25, no. 9 (1992).

TRANSLATIONS: Gerhart Hauptmann, *Henschel fuvaros* (Budapest, 1898);

Gaston-Blum Serpette and Paul Ernest-Ferrier, *Félfordult virág* (Budapest, 1900);

Anatole France, *A vörös liliom* (Budapest, 1901);

Alfred Hennequin and Paul Billhaud, *Szívem* (Budapest, 1901);

Hennequin and Billhaud, *A korbács* (Budapest, 1903);

Paul Gavault and Robert Charvay, *A csodagyermek* (Budapest, 1903);

Paul Lincke and Heinz Bolten, *Makrajcos hölgyek* (Budapest, 1903);

Robert de Flers and Gaston Armand de Caillavet, *Az erény útjai* (Budapest, 1903);

Jerome K. Jerome, *Miss Hobbs* (Budapest, 1904);

Georges Feydeau, *Kézről kézre* (Budapest, 1905);

Flers and Caillavet, *Az őrangyal* (Budapest, 1905);

Flers and Caillavet, *Buridán szamara* (Budapest, 1909);

Henry Bataille, *A botrány* (Budapest, 1909);

Flers and Caillavet, *A szent liget* (Budapest, 1909);

Bruno Granichstädten, Alfred Maria Willner, and Robert Bodanszky, *Ábrahám a mennyországban* (Budapest, 1912);

Henry Meilhac and Ludovic Halévy, *Frou-Frou* (Budapest, 1924).

Ferenc Molnár, an outstanding representative of Hungarian literature before the turn of the century, became a journalist a year after the millennial anniversary of the foundation of the Hungarian nation, and his meteoric rise to fame seemed to justify the miraculous expectations about the millennium. He realized one of the most daring Hungarian dreams by creating the Hungarian version of the modern bourgeois comedy and put Hungarian playwrights on the map of the world. His body of works is considered almost the sole representative of Hungarian literature for Western public opinion.

Ferenc Molnár was born Ferenc Neumann on 12 January 1878 in Budapest, and his career was closely connected to the evolution of his birthplace (which he liked to call, with loving irony, his "native village") into a metropolis. As Budapest, in the matter of a few decades, grew into a large city of European significance, Molnár also became first a well-known prose fiction writer and then a successful playwright who was the best-known figure of European theatrical life. He was the first to depict Budapest in a literary work—in his novel titled *Az éhes város* (The Hungry City, 1901). Using Budapest as his setting was a pioneering effort on his part in turn-of-the-century Hungarian literature, which was still mostly centered in the provinces.

Molnár's father, Mór Neumann, was a physician with a large number of patients. Apart from being a general practitioner, he also worked as a company physician for Ganz Factory and was among the founders of the workers' sick-relief fund in the 1870s. He was a friend of Max Nordau, the future "apostle" of the Zionist movement. Molnár's mother, Józsa Neumann (née Wallfisch), was a sensitive, neurotic woman who passionately loved her son and encouraged him to become an artist. According to the reminiscences of Molnár's sister, Erzsébet, who was three years his junior, the two children had a carefree childhood despite the illnesses and the long absences of their mother.

Molnár was fourteen when he first tried his hand at literature: he produced a journal of his own called *Haladás* (Progress), and, with his friends, he staged his first attempt at a play, *Kék barlang* (Blue Cavern). Having graduated from the Protestant secondary school on Lónyai Street, he started reading law on his father's insistence but soon became more interested in journalism. In 1896 he offered his services to *Pesti Hírlap* (Pest Newspaper), and when in the fall of the same year he moved to Geneva to study, he began to send home articles and sketches from there. At this point he changed his name to Molnár.

In 1897 Molnár returned to Budapest and decided that he would take journalism seriously by joining the liberal *Budapesti Napló* (Budapest Daily). The editor, József Vészi, intended to make a star reporter out of Molnár since he spoke excellent German and French. Vészi sent Molnár to Vienna in 1898 to cover the funeral of Queen Erzsébet, who had been assassinated, and also to Geneva to cover the trial of her assassin. During the same time Molnár also wrote for other periodicals—first of all, for *A Hét* (The Week)—and became assistant editor of the comic periodical *Kakas Márton* (Martin Rooster).

Apart from the weekly assignments, he averaged almost a novel and a play every year, along with a few additional pieces of short prose fiction and many translations. He was the first to translate Gerhart Hauptmann's *Henschel fuvaros* (Carter Henschel) in 1898 and Anatole France's *A vörös liliom* (Red Lily) in 1901. At first Molnár received assignments from the Magyar Színház (Hungarian Theater) and then from the Vígszínház (Comedy Theater) to translate sixteen farces, comedies, and operettas—mostly French pieces written around the end of the century. These works provided good practice for him to master stage effects and punch-line-based dialogues.

Molnár was also enthusiastic about delving into the bohemian lifestyle that at the time was regarded as a pertinent aspect of journalism; this life included constant reveling and drinking sprees in the world of coffeehouses, music halls, and brothels. Molnár, who was called both "Molináry" and "Muli," was the life and soul of the company nicknamed "cúgoscipősök" (the ones wearing elastic-sided boots). Among his friends were two of the future masters of the operetta genre, Viktor Jacobi and Imre Kálmán. The head of this group was Sándor Bródy, the most successful Hungarian writer of the turn of the twentieth century besides Kálmán Mikszáth. Molnár considered Bródy an example to follow both as a writer and as a human being. Molnár's fast and successful start as a man of letters (he was already an author who had made his mark when his peers were just starting out) and his secessionist-naturalist view of the world made him a contemporary of the previous generation.

Time and again, the extremely hard work and the endless nightlife undermined his health and made escape necessary, most often to Paris. He was in Geneva when he wrote his novel titled *Egy gazdátlan csónak története* (The Story of a Derelict Boat, 1901), the heroine of which, a sensitive teenager, falls in love with a talented but dissipated journalist and is finally driven to suicide by her hopeless love. In fact, Molnár tried to take stock of his own life as a journalist, since he was concerned about its inherent ambiguity. According to this ambiguity, every journalist was supposed to have been influenced by the German poet and critic Heinrich Heine to be profane and cynical on the one hand and a naive believer on the other hand. What appears for the first time in *Egy gazdátlan csónak története* later becomes a leitmotif of Molnár's body of work: literature and the love propagated by it represent a dangerous challenge to life because they undermine conventions; yet, conventions are the source from which life gets its strength. "All the bad things women do must have been learned by them from poets," thought the writer at the age of twenty-two.

Even the best of Molnár's early works are marred by journalistic superficiality and overemphasized didacticism. Aladár Schöpflin, a contemporary critic, denounced *Az éhes város* for including simply condensed public vices that were the talk of young journalists at the time. As if it were a pamphlet, the novel describes a "hungry" city that suffers from a lack of capital and is built on credit. A greedy excitement takes over the city, however, when it has a chance to acquire some money by accident. The accident is embodied in the daughter of an American multimillionaire who marries an undistinguished but ambitious bank clerk from Budapest. The city resembles a huge revolving stage on which everyone is motivated and moved by money and love (and these two notions are interchangeable). The ruling elite, including the nouveau riche Jews, who emulate the Hungarian gentry's aristocratic manners, is at the forefront of this vicious rivalry. Molnár, from the viewpoint of the honest, and thus endangered, Jewish intellectuals, accuses the newly rich Jews of an attitude that engenders anti-Semitism. However, this critique does not unfold from the plot but is given by the more likable characters, who behave as mouthpieces for the author. The only character portrayed in a positive light is the American multimillionaire railroad baron, who is the embodiment of the sympathetic self-made man and who, through his puritanism and charity, represents the American mentality idealized by Molnár.

The farce titled *A doktor úr* (1902; translated as *The Lawyer*, 1929) was called a typical "journalistpiece" by the poet Endre Ady. Although the consecutive misunderstandings at the backbone of the piece follow the recipe of the French "well-made play," the central conflict is not created by the conventional love intrigue but by a social anomaly. When a burglar, who has been repeatedly acquitted by the star lawyer as his favorite client, breaks into the lawyer's home and is caught red-handed, he pretends to be the owner of the place. He performs the role with such skill that the real owner gets arrested by the police instead of the thief. The roles of the burglar and the lawyer prove to be interchangeable not only in the incredible situations but also at the level of values, since both "professions" are based on crime. This lesson, then, which disentangles all the ambiguities, is assessed by the burglar in the last act as a reproach to the lawyer. At first Molnár had been encouraged by László Beöthy, the director of the Nemzeti Színház (National Theater), to write

this farce, but by the time Molnár managed to complete it, Beöthy had been dismissed from his position, and the Vígszínház was ready to sign Molnár, after his successful debut, as their private dramatist.

In 1906 *Budapesti Napló* was transformed into a tabloid, and Molnár began to write for *Pesti Napló* (Pest Daily). He also contributed to the editing of *A Hét*, and in 1910 he was instrumental in founding the new daily called *Az Est* (The Evening), assisting its fast-growing popularity with his ideas for advertisements. The year 1906 was pivotal for Molnár, both professionally and in his private life. On 20 May he married Margit Vészi, daughter of József Vészi, who had been courted by Endre Ady as well. (Margit's younger sister, Jolán, was proposed to by Lajos Bíró. Bíró was also an editor and a playwright who, in the 1930s, became the best-known screenwriter for English movies.) Molnár's marriage deteriorated in a few months; he and Margit soon moved to separate homes, and despite the birth of a daughter, Márta, in March 1907, they could never reconcile their differences. They were divorced in 1910.

Beginning in 1908 Molnár was entranced by actress Irén Varsányi, and the relationship was literally captivating for him since she could not decide between him and her husband and children. She kept putting off the decision for years. Finally, after the opening night of *A testőr* (translated as *The Guardsman*, 1924) in 1910 (Molnár wrote the female lead part of the play specifically for her), she gave in. However, her husband started to blackmail her with the children, and she had to go back on her word. As a result, Molnár, gravely humiliated, tried to commit suicide on 13 May 1911.

These years were when Molnár wrote his first outstanding works. In 1906 he published the short masterpiece titled *Széntolvajok* (Coal Thieves), and in the following year he published *A Pál utcai fiúk* (translated as *The Paul Street Boys*, 1927), a gem of Hungarian juvenile literature. His former teacher Kornél Rupp asked him to write it for a Budapest student paper named *Tanulók Lapja* (Students' Paper), in which it was published in installments before it was published in book format in 1907. *Széntolvajok* introduces in one symbolic scene a large number of destitute characters: the thieving coal delivery workers and the other poor people who expose them out of convention, compulsion, or ill will. Their motivation is that "the lies of the rich they had had to experience for millennia" had taught them to take care of each other. Through the use of wryly ironic comments, Molnár made the tone moralizing; he finely counterbalanced and reduced the weight of social injustice through a warning about the finiteness of human existence. *Széntolvajok* is rightly regarded as Molnár's most popular short-fiction piece.

Almost from the beginning of his career, Molnár had been interested in depicting the mentality of teenagers. He immortalized the figure of Józsi, the inquisitive Budapest urchin, first in a series of booklets (1902) and then in a farce (1904). In the sketches of *Gyerekek* (Children, 1905), he foreshadows the characters to appear in his most famous novel. The world of *A Pál utcai fiúk*, with the settings of the *grund* (a vacant lot), the Füvészkert (Botanical Garden), and the whole Józsefváros (Joseph City, a district of Budapest) ambience, is based on Molnár's childhood experiences, and his reminiscences add both a nostalgic and an ironic light to the novel. This atmosphere benevolently counterpoints the adventurous turns of the plot borrowed from the then-popular *Leatherstocking Tales* of James Fenimore Cooper.

On the surface the novel is the story of the struggle between two groups of children, one from Pál Street and the other from Füvészkert, in which the Füvészkert gang tries to seize the Pál Street boys' favorite playground, a vacant lot they call *grund*. The gangs truly wage war against each other, with a declaration of war clarifying the rules of the game, shrewd strategies, and mutual espionage activities. The Pál Street boys, who are defending their territory, are almost defeated and ousted. Yet, with the help of their companion who has escaped from his sickbed, the emaciated and despised Ernő Nemecsek (the only private in the group), they manage to turn the tables. However, Nemecsek's heroic deed, knocking the enemy leader to the ground, costs Nemecsek his life. Retroactively, then, not just his fellow companions make due apology to him, but also the members of the *gittegylet* (Glazier-Putty Association)—whose association is based on the chewing of the jointly owned glazier's putty. The term has become a dictionary entry since, meaning "a small association busying itself with unimportant/irrelevant matters." The group's members had previously accused Nemecsek of treason and registered his name written in lowercase all the way through the minute book of the association.

In the attempts of the boys to imitate adults as they learn about their world, Molnár emphasizes both the strong and the weak points of the emulated world. The novel provides a detailed description of the different values of the various social organizations. These values range from the formal and official regulations of the school to the partly feudal-

Scene from a 1924 Theater Guild production of Molnár's A testőr *(1910; translated as* The Guardsman, *1924), with Alfred Lunt and Lynn Fontanne (photograph by Francis Bruguiere)*

military norms of the two boys' groups based on voluntary organization. Included is the voluntary organization of the *gittegylet*, which is based on a democratic value system and copies the principles at work in various associations in "civil society." Molnár does not conceal his resignation concerning the ways of the world. He reveals his attitude through the Pál Street crowd, which least appreciates the one person who is the noblest among them; moreover, he questions the immense effort and sacrifice through indicating after the victory that the vacant lot is to be developed. Nevertheless, through the glorification of a noble objective similar to the love of one's country and of the sacrifice made for it, Molnár questions this resignation to some extent. *A Pál utcai fiúk* was translated into German soon after its publication, and since then it has been translated into twenty different languages. It has been adapted for the stage several times, and the film version directed by Frank Borzage (titled *No Greater Glory*) won a prize at the Venice Film Festival in 1934, while the Hungarian-American movie version directed by Zoltán Fábry in 1968 was nominated for an Academy Award.

These two masterpieces of fiction earned Molnár international recognition, which was enhanced by the succession of plays written and produced from 1907 to 1910: *Az ördög* (1907; translated as *The Devil*, 1908), based on reversing the principle at work in the French genteel comedies; *Liliom* (1909; translated as *Liliom*, 1921), the Budapest version of the nineteenth-century Hungarian plays about peasants with popular music; and *A testőr*, the first instance of the so-called comedy of character, invented by Molnár, which is based on the similarity between stage roles and real life. From this time Molnár devoted himself to the theater. He was not only a master of writing plays but also of producing them. *Az ördög* became popular under his direction, but he often played an important role behind the scenes when others were identified as official directors. He was probably the best director of his own plays.

The idea for *Az ördög* occurred to Molnár after seeing a performance of Johann Wolfgang von Goethe's *Faust*. He wondered about making Mephistopheles the protagonist of a modern sexual comedy. The fall into sin in this case is made not the starting but the final point of the plot, when the rekindled love of the fashionable painter and the society belle gets confused by the intrigues of the devil. They had once been poor and, consequently, they had had to give up their love. Now, the devil first moves them out of the well-built trenches of decorum and repression to have them end up in each other's arms. Molnár's devil appears to be a ratiocinator and a villain in the same person and, at that, a villain who means well. His figure may be regarded as symbolic of the desires relegated into the subconscious. Molnár might well have been the first to use Sigmund Freud's theories on the stage at a time when the exciting and spicy news about the new tenets had just begun to spread around literary salons and coffeehouses in Pest. This instance of a momentous desire being satisfied in a sweeping fashion is almost singular in Molnár's works, since he otherwise relied mostly on the safety provided by literary conventions. The success of the play, which has been the greatest in the history of Vígszínház to date, was overwhelming. The Italian Ermete Zacconi, who was on tour with his company in Hungary at the time, went to see the play and liked it so much that soon afterward he staged it in Italy, thus starting the worldwide success of both the play and the playwright. During the winter season of 1908 the play was running simultaneously in four New York theaters.

In January 1908 the first issue of the periodical *Nyugat* (West) came out, which opened a new chapter in the history of Hungarian literature. The circle around *Nyugat* regarded Molnár as more or less belonging to them. However, the playwright was careful not to be associated with the new direction represented by them. This attitude obviously made his acceptance in high-ranking but more conservative literary societies easier. He became a member of the Petőfi Society in 1908, while the Kisfaludy Society admitted him to membership in 1911.

The "legend of the outskirts" of *Liliom* takes the readers into the milieu of an amusement park located on the edge of the big city, a fictional world of openhearted ruffians and amorous servant girls, imagined in a slightly sentimental way. The title character, who deserves a better lot, is a barker of the merry-go-round in the amusement park. He leaves his work behind for the sake of Julika, a young servant girl. Since Liliom considers himself an "artist," he cannot take up a janitor's job, so he tries robbery instead. However, he is not particularly good at it, and he ends up committing suicide out of shame. The detectives of God question him at the heavenly precinct station, but even there he remains the same stubborn and warmhearted Liliom. After sixteen years spent in limbo, he is at last allowed to return to earth for one day to pay a visit to Julika and their daughter, who has since grown up. His intention is to help them for once, but he is unable to use this opportunity to their advantage.

Molnár put much of himself into *Liliom;* in the unhappy fate of the barker protagonist, he probably was partly mourning his own bohemian youth. The contemporary Budapest audience did not appreciate this play much, and it had an unsuccessful first night. Nevertheless, it became a success abroad and is regarded as Molnár's most popular play. Even its musical version, titled *Carousel*, first produced in New York in 1945, has been a hit ever since.

The most peculiar characteristic of *A testőr* is that its setting is the world of the theater, where undetectable illusions are produced professionally. Its protagonist is an actor who tries to seduce his actress wife in the disguise of a guardsman, courting her while pretending to be a dashing officer. He almost manages to seduce his own wife when, frightened by the potential outcome, he deliberately gives himself away. The play leaves readers in the dark about whether the actress tells the truth when she contends at the end of the play that she saw through the attempt from the first minute. She argues that she feigned interest only to teach her jealous husband a lesson. The amplification of the interchangeability of appearance and reality could just as well have led to serious consequences if the playwright had let the events evolve into a tragedy. While in his early works and in *Az ördög*, Molnár did not consider old, hypocritical conventions a serious difficulty to overcome and thought the rules could be rewritten at least partially, in *A testőr* and in his later plays, he opted for maintaining these conventions. Although he presented them as transparent and deceptive, he could not seem to offer a better solution.

By this time a special understanding of love can also be discerned in Molnár's works (perhaps because of the long uncertainty of his love affair with Irén Varsányi). The dramatist equates love and jealousy. The title character of *A testőr* nearly becomes a split personality when he experiences the duality of his suffering from the betrayal by his wife and his apparent success in the attempt to prove his wife's adultery.

In the last 1910 issue of *Nyugat*, Endre Ady, the most influential Hungarian poet of the beginning of the century, published an article titled "Molnár Ferenc színpada" (The Stage of Ferenc Molnár), in which he suggested that the dramatist should choose between the two extremes of cheap fame and the glory of an apostle, because the two together (which the playwright was apparently after) would not work. The upcoming decade seemed to justify Ady's warning, as Molnár mostly just repeated himself; the standard of his plays from this period is far below that of his previous ones.

A farkas (1912; translated as *The Tale of the Wolf*, 1973) is also a comedy based on jealousy, just as was *A testőr*. In *A farkas* a Budapest lawyer is jealous of his wife's former lover and, in the scene at a party in the second act, the look-alikes of the one-time lover, including a victorious officer and a famous artist, actually appear on the stage. Later, it turns out that the woman only dreamed that they were present, and she has been recounting their appearances in order to enjoy her secret desires and unfaithfulness. As a surprise ending, the real former suitor also appears; he is but a simple clerk and an idiot to boot. Thus, the play shows that breaking of conventions is a futile idea, and the situation exposed in *Az ördög* gets turned upside down in this play.

The outbreak of World War I in 1914 influenced Molnár's career in an unfavorable way. In November 1914 he was working as a war correspondent in Galicia. His best writings were collected and published in 1916 in two volumes called *Egy haditudósító emlékei* (The Memories of a War Correspondent), for which he received the Order of Franz Joseph (Ferenc József-rend). Molnár's sentimental mystery play about the sad fate of war orphans, *A fehér felhő* (1916; translated as *The White Cloud*, 1929), was awarded the Vojnits Prize of the Hungarian Academy. Through the two comedies he wrote in 1917 Molnár wanted to compete with Ferenc Herczeg, another popular contemporary dramatist, and he also meant to provide good parts for his new love, Sári Fedák, who was a celebrated star of the stage at the time.

Two works of prose fiction stand out among Molnár's works in this period: *Az aruvimi erdő titka* (The Secret of Aruvim Forest, 1916), a satirical "gothic novel" (as he himself called it), and his novel titled *Andor*, written in 1917, which was somewhat rightly dubbed by his critics the Hungarian version of Ivan Goncharov's *Oblomov*. Both pieces attest to the disillusionment of their authors and their concern about the age they lived in. *Az aruvimi erdő titka* introduces readers to the world of financial rackets. The company called Egyenruha Vegytisztító Rt. (Dry Cleaners of Uniforms) wants to bribe Lajos Tisztességes (Louis Incorruptible), a father of nineteen children who is a deputy sniffer in the government office established for locating stench. The company runs a booming business, as they do not even have to touch the uniforms of the government clerks, since the latter are so careful that their clothes remain immaculate. Lajos Tisztességes wants to return the bribe, but in order to be able to do so he has to undergo many tribulations (for example, he needs to cut his way through a thick forest, because the head of the company has had his office surrounded by an exact replica of the forest of Aruvim in Africa).

With the title character of *Andor*, Molnár wanted to present the so-called superfluous man of the turn of the century. Molnár endowed his character with events taken from his own life. Just like the dramatist, Andor Aradi begins as a law student and switches to journalism later. What is missing in him, though, is the stamina that could provide him with stature. Andor aspires to gain a vocation, but he is unable to find satisfactory engagements. His attempts to break out fail and repeatedly become distorted (for example, he becomes separated from his fiancée so as to avoid a petty, bourgeois way of life that "smells of onions" only to use his recovered freedom to get bogged down in the swamp of cheap joints and night-haunts). He remains lonely to the end, a state that predestines him for suicide. At the end of the novel the whole background turns dark, and Molnár mourns for the good old times before the war. *Az aruvimi erdő titka* was a complete success; *Andor* was much less so. The most arduous critic of *Andor* was Georg Lukács, who later, even in his communist period, frequently referred to Molnár's works as negative examples.

Molnár was in Budapest at the end of the war in 1918 and during the revolutions in 1918 and in 1919. He had always been apolitical; nevertheless, during the term of the bourgeois government headed by Count Mihály Károlyi, he accepted the position of chairman of the Otthon Kör (Home Circle), considered the most esteemed club of journalists, and in the company of Mihály Babits and Zsigmond Móricz he edited the "revolutionary textbook" prepared for the workers. During the dictatorship of the proletariat in 1919, Molnár consistently turned down every assignment, and he was regularly attacked by *Vörös Újság* (Red News) as a bourgeois writer. He was filled with awe by the period of white terror at the end of 1919 and at the beginning of 1920, not in the least because his name also came up during the anti-Semitic campaign. Nevertheless, it did not take long for him to find his voice again. In December of 1920 the audience of the Vígszínház applauded the premiere of *A hattyú* (1921; translated as *The Swan*, 1924). In his new comedy Molnár used the already tested scenario, but for the first time ever he picked a Prussian aristocratic location for the setting, and the conflict around the flirting of the archduchess and the family governess provides him with an opportunity to make fun of the blue-blooded class. (Only after all the historical events of the period did Molnár dare to give a value judgment about the aristocracy, and even then he disguised his characters as Prussians.)

At the beginning of the 1920s Molnár's old friends seemed to disappear, and he felt less and less at home in Budapest. He spent more and more time abroad, and in 1925 he finally moved to Vienna. From that time on his new plays were produced there—the first one was the comedy *Riviéra*, the director of which was the famous Max Reinhardt—in Vienna's Josefstadter Theater in 1926. Molnár quit journalism and wrote plays exclusively. In 1926 he was nominated for the Nobel Prize in literature; in 1927 he received the Legion of Honor in Paris (mostly for his translations of French literature to Hungarian); and in 1928 he celebrated his fiftieth birthday in the United States, where he also had the honor of meeting President Calvin Coolidge, and a twenty-volume collection of his works was published in Budapest. The 1930 premiere of *A jó tündér* (translated as *The Good Fairy*, 1932) also marked the 750th performance of a Molnár play in the Vígszínház. These successes had their shady sides as well. Jealous Hungarian writers tried to do their best to alienate him from his country; one of the milder jokes spread about him was the nickname "Csekkszpír" (Checkspeare), alluding to his alleged money-mindedness.

The beginning of the 1920s also meant another crisis for him emotionally. In 1922 he fell in love with Lili Darvas, the young, beautiful, and talented ingenue. He wrote the lead role in *Égi és földi szerelem* (1922; translated as *Heavenly and Earthly Love*, 1929) for her. In order to placate his former sweetheart, Sári Fedák, Molnár married her. However, Fedák was reluctant to divorce him later, and the divorce cost him a huge sum of money, not to mention a long delay. Molnár had to wait until 1926 to be able to marry Lili Darvas. When Sári Fedák was touring the United States after their divorce and decided to have herself called "Molnár Ferencné" (Mrs. Ferenc Molnár) in the hope of gaining more popularity, the irate Molnár placed the following disclaimer in *The New York Times*: "I consider it my duty to inform the highly esteemed audiences of New York City that the woman who appears in different plays on Broadway under the name of Molnár Ferencné is neither my wife nor my mother. Ferenc Molnár."

The plays Molnár wrote during the 1920s fall into two distinct categories. The first half of the decade is marked by a series of failures, while the second half represents new peaks in Molnár's art. *Égi és földi szerelem* and *A vörös malom* (1923; translated as *Mima*, 1929) are less successful because they try to update their sentimental messages in the cloak of the abstract parables typical of German expressionist theater. After these two plays Molnár abandoned further experimentation to return to the type of comedy in *Az üvegcipő* (1924; translated as *The Glass Slipper*, 1929) and to the milieu of *Liliom*, but his efforts produced less than convincing results. Finally, he re-staged *Az ördög* and *A testőr*, and these revivals became fabulous hits.

Játék a kastélyban (1926; translated as *The Play's the Thing*, 1927), just as *A testőr*, takes readers into the realm of the theater. All the characters in the play are connected to the theater: Annie, a young, pretty, and popular actress; Ádám, a young and talented composer who is Annie's fiancé; Turai and Gál, a famous dramatist duo, the patrons of Ádám; and Almády, an aging former *jeune premier*. The conflict in the play occurs when all the characters are in a castle by the seaside, and Ádám and his two patrons accidentally overhear a confession of love between Annie and Almády, who are in the adjacent room.

What the play suggests is that, in both the theater and in life, one experiences mere illusions; the only difference is that on stage, the parts are played better, since the actors and actresses (and even the dramatists) are professionals. A special effect is achieved by Molnár when the section taken from real life in the one-act play actually seems stilted and artificial as compared to the rest of the play; moreover, because Turai is totally absorbed by his profession, playwriting is included in the play. In the opening scene Turai discusses the difficulties of writing an opening scene with his partners; in the dénouement he discusses a closing scene. In some of his utterances Turai sounds much like an alter ego of Molnár. Molnár's comedies probably are not compared to Luigi Pirandello's by mere chance. Although their messages are totally different, their structures are similar. While Pirandello's *Sei personaggi in cerca d'autore* (Six Characters in Search of an Author, 1921) points out that appearance and reality cannot be considered the same, because the stage cannot bear the gravity of life, *Játék a kastélyban* suggests there is no real difference between appearance and reality. In other words, life functions the same way the theater does. This play became as great a hit as Molnár's most popular pieces had before, and in P. G. Wodehouse's translation it also conquered the English-speaking world.

Two plays by Molnár, *Olympia* (1928; translated as *Olympia*, 1928) and *Egy, kettő, három* (One, Two, Three, 1929), also belong to the same type of comedy of character as *Játék a kastélyban*. Although the characters are not representatives of the histrionic arts, they still command the same skill of producing make-believe effects as if they were actors and actresses.

Olympia presents a conflict that is similar to the one in *A hattyú*, but in this work the characters are members of the aristocracy of the prewar monarchy. Duchess Olympia flirts with a captain of the Hussars, until rumors spread about the relationship. The aristocratic family demands that the pair end the relationship, because the family is afraid of what will happen if the emperor finds out about the affair—the title originally planned for the play was *A császár hideg kék szeme* (The Cold Blue Eyes of the Emperor). The duchess offends the officer by calling him a peasant; he, in turn, takes revenge on her by disguising himself as a confidence man. As such,

he is not supposed to be a nobleman, and, consequently, he is not bound by his promise. He demands one night with the duchess in return for his keeping the affair a secret, a request which she finally grants him. However, the plot reveals that he is really a captain, and the duchess's family has to face humiliation.

Molnár's *Egy, kettő, három*, a one-act comedy of character, is definitely better than *Olympia*, despite that the central conflict is based on business and not on love. Norrison, a wealthy banker, entertains the daughter of his rich American client in his home for a year. The daughter, Lydia, is about to return home when she confesses that she has secretly married a taxi driver and is expecting a child. Lydia's parents are due to arrive in an hour, and Norrison must extricate himself from the predicament. He has barely an hour to create a presentable gentleman with a comfortable job and a nobleman's background out of the poor and ignorant taxi driver. The machinery behind Norrison gets busy, and a miracle happens: by the time the parents arrive the young man has become a managing director, a consul, a talented inventor, and a well-dressed socialite.

Egy, kettő, három is based on the same shrewd magician's trick as *Játék a kastélyban*. Norrison is a master of creating illusions (he puts his trickster's ability to good—or at least ambivalent—use) just like Turai or the devil. Yet, Norrison seems to stand for more than the earlier two characters. Although he has to solve a problem in the private personal sphere, he can take care of other problems with the help of the administrative apparatus he has at his disposal. Since he is the one pulling the strings, he is situated above the servile human puppets, whose crowd might as well be called the world. At the end of the play Norrison does not miss the chance to express his condemnation of humankind, a species that bows and scrapes to money. The play reveals the extent of Molnár's criticism.

As one of the most successful dramatists of Europe, Molnár had become a citizen of Europe by the 1930s. He did not stay in one place long. As Lili Darvas was working on her own career, sometimes they had to spend weeks or even months away from one another. In 1932 Molnár met Vanda Bartha in Budapest, and in her he found an ideal partner for his wanderings, since she had just gotten out of an unhappy marriage. Officially, she was his secretary, but in reality she was his proofreader, maid, and general servant. Lili Darvas accepted this situation and remained Molnár's wife until his death.

After *Egy, kettő, három* Molnár wrote seven more plays but none even approached his previous successes. *Valaki* (Someone, 1932), a comedy of character, could have become a masterpiece on the strength of the basic idea. In the play a rich and independent society belle would like to have a husband who supported her in public but lacked those unpleasant features that husbands are prone to have. The lady's father, who is an experienced con man, is willing to help his daughter in this respect and creates a phantom figure of a count for the purpose. With the help of false papers as well as rumors about and souvenirs from the alleged count, the father manages to bring the figure of a kind-hearted, active, and busy husband to life. People everywhere get to know about the count, despite the fact that he does not exist. The problem is that, by this time, the phantom figure seems to have reached a kind of independence from his creators (for example, he gets sued for alimony payments), so they need to dispose of him. Unfortunately, Molnár's interest in the potential complications of the plot seems to have lasted only as long as the first act. When the phantom really comes to life and the comedy is about to gather momentum, the story comes to an abrupt ending.

Among Molnár's works written in the 1930s, the novel *A zöld huszár* (The Green Hussar, 1937) seems to be the only outstanding piece. It is perhaps his best prose fiction work. The book is based on autobiographical details; despite this nostalgic air about the years he spent as a journalist, Molnár makes his novel a ruthlessly precise diagnosis of the times when people could still carelessly indulge in their passions and sufferings. A Budapest journalist tells the story of his ill-fated love affair with a streetwalker he meets when he goes to a small provincial town to make a report. He experiences simultaneous attraction to and repulsion from her and decides to turn down her advances since he is engaged; he longs for a happy family life with children. However, when he later finds out that she has moved to Budapest and is working as a chorus girl (having the part of a hussar in the musical play *János vitéz*, dressed in green), he can no longer resist the temptation of her love. Consequently, the more he tries to suppress his love, the stronger it becomes. They finally meet at a party, but he manages to reject her pleas to lift her out of the gutter and take her with him. The next thing he hears about her is the news of her suicide (after having been brutally beaten by her jealous lover, the girl has taken her own life), and the news has a devastating effect upon him. In order to repress his twinges of remorse, he has to live under the influence of alcohol and narcotics until eventually he takes an overdose. On his deathbed he briefly regains consciousness to complete his story.

The protagonist of the novel tries to recall the events of the past with exact preciseness, and his narrative, so typical of the toned-down passion of the obsessed, is without pathos. No matter how well he is aware of the cheap sensuality offered by the girl, he cannot withstand its elementary force. Thus, both of them become puppets in the hands of fate. Critics received *A zöld huszár* favorably. Menyhért Lengyel—the most popular contemporary Hungarian dramatist abroad besides Molnár—considered it the pinnacle of Molnár's achievement, and he wrote a script for a movie based on it. Later, however, the novel fell into oblivion.

The last time Molnár stayed in Budapest for any length of time was in September 1936, on the opening night of *Delila*. He was to leave Vienna in 1937 because of the imminence of the *Anschluss*. When World War II broke out, he was in Geneva again; from there he left for the United States. He arrived in New York on 12 January 1940 (on his sixty-second birthday). Although he could relocate himself into the New World, his penchant for writing must have gotten lost on the way. He worked until the end of his life—writing plays, novels, movie scripts, or editing his old works for republication—but the majority of the yield of the last ten to twelve years of his life was generally dispirited.

Molnár received his American citizenship in 1947. In the following year Lajos Dinnyés, the Hungarian prime minister, asked him in a letter to return home, but Molnár was discouraged by the ominous news about political prospects. Shocked upon learning about the suicide of Vanda Bartha in 1947, he wrote a piece titled *Utitárs a száműzetésben* (translated and published in English as *Companion in Exile*, 1950). By the time of the first Hungarian publication (1958) the original manuscript was missing, and his last work had to be translated from English for its Hungarian publication. Ferenc Molnár died of cancer on 2 April 1952.

Interviews:

"Az Ördögről," *Világ*, 12, no. 246 (1921): 5–6;

"A Nobel-díj jelöltjeként," *Színházi Élet*, 21, no. 45 (1926): 8–9;

Sándor Hunyady, "Molnár Ferencnél," *Színházi Élet*, 29, no. 15 (1934): 28–29.

Bibliographies:

Albert Tezla, *Hungarian Authors: A Bibliographical Handbook* (Cambridge, Mass.: Belknap Press of Harvard University Press, 1970), pp. 404–412;

Elizabeth M. Rajec, *Ferenc Molnár: Bibliography* (Wien: Bohlaus, 1986).

Biographies:

Adorján Stella, "Molnár Ferenc," in his *Beszélő házak* (Budapest: 1957), pp. 176–181;

Molnár Erzsébet, *Testvérek voltunk* (Budapest: Magvető, 1958);

László Bóka, "Molnár Ferenc," in his *Arcképvázlatok és tanulmányok* (Budapest: Akadémiai, 1962), pp. 994–995;

Kálmán Csathó, "Molnár Ferenc," in his *Rótársak között* (Budapest: Szépirodalmi, 1965), pp. 278–322;

Gyula Krúdy, "Molnár és közönsége," in his *A szobrok megmozdulnak* (Budapest: Gondolat, 1974), pp. 251–253;

Menyhért Lengyel, *Életem regénye* (Budapest: Gondolat, 1987);

Péter Gál Molnár, "Molnár Ferenc Amerikában," *Színház,* 25, no. 9 (1992): 1–10;

Mátyás Sárközi, *Színház az egész világ* (Budapest: Osiris-Századvég, 1995).

References:

Endre Ady, "Molnár Ferenc színpada," *Nyugat,* 3, no. 2 (1910): 1909–1910;

János Barta, "A Molnár Ferenc-probléma," *Debreceni Szemle,* 2 (1928): 153–160;

Tamás Bécsy, "Modern cselvígjáték," *Színház,* 25, no. 9 (1992): 24–29;

László Gerold, "Lehetőség és korlát. Molnár Ferenc: Valaki," *Literatura,* 3–4 (1980): 353–357;

Clara Györgyey, *Ferenc Molnár* (Boston: Twayne, 1980);

Bódog Halmi, *Molnár Ferenc, az író és az ember* (Budapest: Szerző kiadása, 1929);

Lajos Hatvany, "Molnár Ferenc halhatatlansága," *A Toll,* 6, no. 76 (1934): 254–256;

Ignotus, "A testőr," *Nyugat,* 3, no. 2 (1910): 1723–1725;

Endre Illés, "Játék, játék, játék," in his *Krétarajzok* (Budapest: Magvető, 1970), pp.107–113;

Frigyes Karinthy, "Játék a kastélyban," *Nyugat,* 20, no. 1 (1927): 218–220;

Aurél Kárpáti, "Molnár Ferenc," in his *Tegnaptól máig* (Budapest: Szépirodalmi, 1961), pp. 185–220;

Dezső Kosztolányi, "Liliom," in his *Színház* (Budapest: Nyugat, 1948), pp. 103–106;

Georg Kőváry, *Der Dramatiker Franz Molnár* (Innsbruck: Wagner, 1984);

György Lukács, "Molnár Ferenc Andorja," *Huszadik Század,* 19, no. 2 (1918): 253–257;

Péter Gál Molnár, "Molnár Ferenc, a fordító," *Színház,* 26, no. 1 (1993): 40–48;

Zsigmond Móricz, "Az Ördög," *Nyugat,* 5, no. 1 (1912): 704–709;

Péter Nagy, "Molnár Ferenc," in his *Drámai arcélek* (Budapest: Szépirodalmi, 1978), pp. 87–124;

Béla Osváth, "A Molnár-legenda," *Kritika,* 1, no. 1 (1963): 40–46;

György Rónay, "Az éhes város," in his *A regény és az élet* (Budapest: Magvető, 1947), pp. 203–210;

Aladár Schöpflin, "Molnár Ferenc," *Pesti Napló,* 68, no. 224 (1917): 17–19;

Schöpflin, "Molnár Ferenc," *Nyugat,* 31, no. 2 (1928): 497–500;

Jenő J. Tersánszky, "Liliom," *Nyugat,* 22, no. 1 (1929): 770–771;

Delfino Tinelli, *Molnár* (Brescia: La Scuola, 1971);

István Varkonyi, *Ferenc Molnár and the Austro-Hungarian "Fin de Siècle"* (New York: Lang, 1991);

Irén Vécsei, *Molnár Ferenc* (Budapest: Gondolat, 1966).

Zsigmond Móricz

(2 July 1879 – 4 September 1942)

Péter Bényei
Institute of Hungarian Philology, Kossuth University

BOOKS: *A szép asszony dombja* (Budapest: Vilmos Méhner, 1904);

Erdő-mező világa. Állatmesék (Budapest: Róbert Lampel, 1906);

Két biblia (Budapest: Viktor Hornyánszky, 1906);

Mikor a part szakad (Budapest: Viktor Hornyánszky, 1907);

Hét krajczár. Elbeszélések (Budapest: Nyugat, 1909);

Csitt-csatt és több elbeszélés (Budapest: Róbert Lampel, 1910);

Munkácsy Mihály (Budapest: Róbert Lampel, 1910);

Sári bíró. Vígjáték (Budapest: Nyugat, 1910);

A sasfia, meg a sasfióka (Budapest: Róbert Lampel, 1910);

Tragédia (Budapest: Nyugat, 1910);

Vas Jankó (Budapest: Vilmos Méhner, 1910);

Falu (Budapest: Nyugat, 1911)—comprises *Mint a mezőnek virágai*, *Magyarosan*, and *Kend a pap?*;

Sárarany (Budapest: Nyugat, 1911);

Az Isten háta mögött. Regény (Budapest: Nyugat, 1911);

Boldog világ. Összes állatmeséi (Budapest: Nyugat, 1912);

A galamb papné. Regény (Budapest: Franklin-Társulat, 1912);

Harmatos rózsa (Budapest: Nyugat, 1912);

Magyarok. Elbeszélések (Budapest: Nyugat, 1912);

Tavaszi szél. Elbeszélések (Budapest: Nyugat, 1912);

Kerek Ferkó. Regény (Budapest: Athenaeum, 1913);

Szerelem, 3 volumes (Budapest: Nyugat, 1913–1917);

A kárpáti vihar (Budapest: Az Érdekes Újság, 1915);

Mese a zöld füvön. Elbeszélések (Budapest: Athenaeum, 1915);

Nem élhetek muzsikaszó nélkül. Regény és elbeszélések (Budapest: Légrády Testvérek, 1916);

Pacsirtaszó (Budapest: Az Érdekes Újság, 1916);

A tűznek nem szabad kialudni. Novellák e háborus időkből (Budapest: Légrády Testvérek, 1916);

Árvalányok. Regény (Budapest: Légrády Testvérek, 1917);

Karak szultán (Budapest: Nyugat, 1917);

Pacsirtaszó. Színdarab (Budapest: Légrády Testvérek, 1917);

Szegény emberek. Elbeszélések (Budapest, Nyugat, 1917);

Vidéki hirek és más elbeszélések (Budapest: Táltos, 1917);

A fáklya (Budapest: Légrády Testvérek, 1918); translated by Emil Lengyel as *The Torch* (New York: Knopf, 1931);

Fortunátus (Budapest: Az Érdekes Újság, 1918);

Szerelem. Egyfelvonások, 7 volumes (Budapest: Légrády Testvérek, 1918);

A szerelmes levél. Kis regény (Budapest: Légrády Testvérek, 1918);

Vérben, vasban. Kis képek, a nagy háboruból (Budapest: Légrády Testvérek, 1918);

A földtörvény kis kátéja. Az 1919: XVIII. néptörvény magyarázata és utasítása a földmíves nép földhöz juttatásárról (Budapest: Néplap Kiadása, 1919)—comprises *A földtörvény kis kátéja*, *Népszavasás a földreformról*, and *A somogymegyei földmíves szovetkezetek*;

Légy jó mindhalálig (Budapest: Athenaeum, 1921); translated by Susan Körösi as *Be Faithful unto Death* (Budapest: Corvina, 1962);

Tündérkert. Szépasszonyok hosszú farsangja (Budapest: Athenaeum, 1922);

Egy akol, egy pásztor. Elbeszélések (Budapest: Athenaeum, 1923);

Házasságtörés. Kisregény (Budapest: Athenaeum, 1923);

Jószerencsét. Regény (Budapest: Athenaeum, 1923);

Búzakalász. Színdarab három felvonásban (Budapest: Athenaeum, 1924);

A vadkan. Színdarab három felvonásban (Budapest: Athenaeum, 1924);

Pillangó. Idill (Budapest: Athenaeum, 1925);

Kivilágos kivirradtig. Regény (Budapest: Athenaeum, 1926);

Baleset. Elbeszélések (Budapest: Athenaeum, 1927);

Az ágytakaró. Kisregények (Budapest: Athenaeum, 1928);

Arany szoknyák. Ebbeszélések és jelenstek (Budapest: Athenaeum, 1928);

Úri muri. Regény (Budapest: Athenaeum, 1928);

Forró mezők. Regény (Budapest: Athenaeum, 1929);

Esőleső társaság. Kisregények, Elbeszélések (Budapest: Athenaeum, 1931);

Forr a bor (Budapest: Athenaeum, 1931);

Barbárok. Elbeszélések (Budapest: Athenaeum, 1932);

Rokonok. Regény (Budapest: Athenaeum, 1932);

Az asszony beleszól. Regény (Budapest: Athenaeum, 1934);

A boldog ember. Regény (Budapest: Athenaeum, 1935);

Erdély. Móricz Zsigmond történelmi regénytrilógiája (Budapest: Athenaeum, 1935)—comprises *Tündérkert, A nagy fejedelem,* and *A nap árnyéka;*

Bál. Regény (Budapest: Az Est-Lapkiadó és a Magyarország Napilap, 1936);

Komor ló. Ebbeszélések (Budapest: Athenaeum, 1936);

Rab oroszlán. Regény (Budapest: Athenaeum, 1936);

Betyár (Budapest: Athenaeum, 1937);

Tiborc, by Móricz and Iván Boldizsár (Budapest: Cserépfalvi, 1937);

Míg új a szerelem (Budapest: Athenaeum, 1938);

Pipacsok a tengeren (Budapest: Athenaeum, 1938);

Életem regénye (Budapest: Athenaeum, 1939);

Kemény Zsigmond: A rajongók. Regény Moricz Zsigmond átírásában (Budapest: Athenaeum, 1940);

Árvácska. Regény (Budapest: Athenaeum, 1941);

Rózsa Sándor a lovát ugratja (Budapest: Athenaeum, 1941);

Rózsa Sándor összevonja szemöldökét. Regény (Budapest: Athenaeum, 1942);

Kapitalista a tanyán (Budapest: Stádium, 1942);

A fecskék fészket raknak (Budapest: Athenaeum, 1943);

Házasság a vége (A csillagszemú lány) (Budapest: András Áchim, 1943);

Kisiklott élet (Budapest: András Áchim, 1943);

Nosza rajta . . . (Budapest: András Áchim, 1943);

Veszélyes vállalkozás (Budapest: András Áchim, 1943);

Csibe. Elbeszélések (Budapest: Athenaeum, 1948);

Shakespeare (Budapest: Holló Fehér, 1948).

Editions and Collections: *Művei,* 12 volumes (Budapest: Athenaeum, 1938–1939)—comprises volume 1, *A nap árnyéka;* volume 2, *Az asszony beleszól;* volume 3, *A boldog ember;* volume 4, *Életem regénye;* volume 5, *Esőleső társaság;* volumes 6–7, *Forr a bor;* volume 8, *Forró mezők;* volume 9, *Míg új a szerelem;* volume 10, *A nagy fejedelem: A Tündérkert virágbaborul, Bethlen Gábor dicsősége, Zsuzsanna fejedelemasszony szenvedése eljő;* volume 11, *Rab oroszlán;* volume 12, *Tündérkert;*

Tündérkert, A nagy fejedelem, A nap árnyéka, 3 volumes (Budapest: Athenaeum, 1939);

Összes művei, 20 volumes (Budapest: Athenaeum, 1939–1949)—comprises volume 1, *A fáklya;* volume 2, *A galamb papné;* volume 3, *Harmatos rózsa;* volume 4, *Hét krajcár;* volume 5, *Az Isten háta mögött;* volume 6, *Kerek Ferkó;* volume 7, *Kivilágos kivirradtig;* volume 8, *Légy jó mindhalálig;* volume 9, *Magyarok;* volume 10, *Nem élhetek muzsikaszó nélkül;* volume 11, *Pillangó;* volume 12, *Sárarany;* volume 13, *Szegény emberek;* volume 14, *A tűznek nem szabad kialudni;* volume 15, *Úri muri;* volume 16, *A boldog ember;* volume 17, *Csibe;* volume 18, *A galamb papné;* volume 19, *Barbárok;* volume 20, *Rokonok;*

Válogatott elbeszélései, edited by Péter Nagy (Budapest: Szépirodalmi, 1951);

Gyalogolni jó. Ripartok, edited by Endre Illés (Budapest: Szépirodalmi, 1952);

Válogatott irodalmi tanulmányok, edited by Kálmán Vargha (Budapest: Művelt Nép, 1952);

Összegyűjtött művei, 44 volumes, edited by Illés, Pál Réz, Mátyás Durkó, László Oláh, Péter Nagy,

and others (Budapest: Szépirodalmi, 1952–
1959)—comprises volume 1, *Rózsa Sándor a
lovát ugratja;* volume 2, *Rózsa Sándor összevonja
a szemöldökét;* volume 3, *Betyár;* volume 4, *A
boldog ember;* volume 5, *Elbeszélések, 1900–1912;*
volume 6, *Elbeszélések, 1913–1915;* volume 7,
Elbeszélések, 1916–1919; volume 8, *A fáklya;* volume 9, *Kivilágos kivirradtig. Úri muri;* volume
10, *Elbeszélések, 1920–1929;* volumes 11–13,
Erdély; volume 14, *Légy jó mindhalálig;* volume
15, *Pillangó. A fecskék fészket raknak;* volume 16,
Rokonok; volume 17, *Az asszony beleszól. Rab oroszlán;* volume 18, *Elbeszélések, 1930–1933;* volume 19, *Elbeszélések, 1934–1936;* volume 20,
Elbeszélések, 1937–1942; volume 21, *Forró mezők;*
volume 22, *Kerek Ferkó;* volume 23, *Sárarany. Az
isten háta mögött;* volume 24, *Forr a bor;* volume
25, *Jobb, mint otthon;* volumes 26–27,
Kisregények; volume 28, *Színművek, 1909–1913;*
volume 29, *Színművek, 1913–1923;* volume 30,
Színművek, 1924–1926; volume 31, *Színművek,
1927–1928;* volume 32, *Színművek, 1929–1933;*
volume 33, *Színművek, 1934–1940;* volume 34,
Harmatos rózsa. A galamb papné; volume 35,
Ifjúsági írások; volume 36, *Riportok, 1910–1942:
1910–1919;* volume 37, *Riportok, 1910–1942:
1920–1929;* volume 38, *Riportok, 1910–1942:
1930–1935;* volume 39, *Riportok, 1910–1942:
1936–1940;* volume 40, *Életem regénye;* volume
41, *Irodalomról, művészetről, 1899–1923;* volume
42, *Irodalomról, művészetről, 1924–1942;* volume
43, *Míg új a szerelem;* volume 44, *Tanulmányok,
cikkek;*

Új világot teremtsünk, edited by Durkó (Budapest:
Művelt Nép, 1953);

A kis vereshajú. Elbeszélések, edited by Nagy (Budapest:
Szépirodalmi, 1954);

Benyus, edited by Piroska D. Szemző and Sándor
Kozocsa (Budapest: Móra, 1957);

Este a tűz mellett. Elbeszélések, cikkek, rajzok, edited by
Dezső Szalatnai (Bratislava: Szlovákiai Szépirodalmi, 1957);

Versei, edited by Oszkár Gellért (Budapest: Magyar
Helikon, 1958);

Az Isten háta mögött. A fáklya (Budapest:
Szépirodalmi, 1959);

Betyár. Árvácska. Regények (Budapest: Szépirodalmi,
1960);

Hagyatékából, edited by Réz (Budapest: Magyar
Tudományos Akadémia Irodalomtörténeti
Intézete, 1960);

Kenyéren és vizen, edited by Edgár Balogh (Bukarest:
Irodalmi, 1962);

Regényei és elbeszélései, 12 volumes, edited by Magda
Erdős, Michály Caine, Kálmán Vorgha, and
Nagy (Budapest: Magyar Helikon, 1962–1965)—
comprises volume 1, *Sárarany; Harmatos rózsa;
A galamb papné; Árvalányok; Az Isten háta mögött;
Kerek Ferkó; Nem élhetek muzsikaszó nélkül;* volume
2, *Jószerencsét; A fáklya; Légy jó mindhalálig;
Házasságtörés; A kis vereshajú;* volume 3,
Tündérkert; A nagy fejedelem; A nap árnyéka; vol-
ume 4, *Kivilágos kivirradtig; Pillangó; Kamaszok;
Úri muri; Az ágytakaró; Forró mezők;* volume 5,
Forr a bor; Rokonok; volume 6, *A fecskék fészket
raknak; A boldog ember; Az asszony beleszól; Jobb
mint otthon;* volume 7, *Rab oroszlán; Betyár; Míg
új a szerelem; Életem regénye; Árvácska;* volume 8,
*Rózsa Sándor, 1940–1941; Rózsa Sándor a lovát
ugratja; Rózsa Sándor összevonja a szemöldökét;*
volume 9, *Elbeszélések, 1900–1914;* volume 10,
Elbeszélések, 1915–1925; volume 11, *Elbeszélések,
1926–1934;* volume 12, *Elbeszélések, 1934–1942;*

Összes Munkái, 20 volumes, edited by Caine, Ferenc
Szabó, Réz, Vargha, and Nagy (Budapest:
Szépirodalmi, 1973–1990)—comprises volumes
1–4, *Elbeszélések* (1973–1974); volumes 5–11,
Regények (1975–1987); volumes 12–14, *Tanulmányok* (1978–1980); volumes 15–16, *Drámák*
(1980–1981); volumes 17–18, *Kisregények* (1985–
1986); volumes 19–20, *Riportok* (1989–1990).

Editions in English: *Seven Pennies and Other Short
Stories,* translated by George F. Cushing (Budapest: Corvina, 1988);

Be Faithful unto Death, translated by Stephen Vizin-
czey (Budapest & New York: Central European
University Press, 1995).

PLAY PRODUCTIONS: *Sári bíró,* Budapest, Nemzeti Szinház, 17 December 1909;

Búzakaldse, Budapest Renaissance Színház, 19 January 1924;

A vadkan, Budapest, Vígszénház, 24 October 1924;

Nemélhetek muzsikaszó nelküb, Budapest, Nemzeti
Szinház, 12 September 1928;

Lágy só nindhaláig, Budapest, Nemzeti Szinház, 29
November 1929;

Rokonok, Budapest, Nemzeti Szinház, 16 February
1934.

OTHER: *Mai dekameron. Az uj irók,* edited by Móricz
(Budapest: Nyugat, 1932);

Magvető. A magyar irodalom élö könyve, compiled by
Móricz (Budapest: Kelet Népe, 1940).

Zsigmond Móricz is one of the outstanding figures of twentieth-century Hungarian prose writing.

The author's parents, Erzsébet and Bálint Móricz

He continued some valuable trends of the nineteenth-century realist tradition; his works are characterized by the vivacity of the realist approach and by social commitment. His poetics and the worldview evident in his works, however, show him to be a typical twentieth-century writer.

Móricz was born on 2 July 1879 in Tiszacsécse, a small village on the banks of the Tisza River in Szatmár County. One of the recurrent motifs in his work is the representation of this rustic world and the peasant view of life, and it is largely because of Móricz that this world was presented in a new manner on an artistic level in Hungarian literature. His father, Bálint Móricz, was an ambitious, enterprising smallholder, while his mother, Erzsébet Pallagi, was the daughter of a clergyman of noble birth; they married in spite of the strict social boundaries of the village. Later, in his autobiographical novel, *Életem regénye* (The Novel of My Life, 1939), Móricz interpreted his background as legitimizing his artistic mission: since he belonged to both of the fundamental classes of Hungarian society, he felt entitled to interpret the entire spectrum of Hungarian reality.

Although the family often had financial difficulties, they ensured a good education for Móricz, mostly at the behest of his sophisticated mother, who had a thorough knowledge of the Hungarian literary tradition. From 1891 until 1896 he attended two ancient colleges of the Reformed Church (Debrecen and Sárospatak), and he graduated in Kisújszállás in 1898.

Móricz studied theology, law, philology, linguistics, and literary history at Debrecen and at the University of Budapest, where he moved in 1900; however, he did not complete an advanced degree. In 1903 he became a contributor to the Liberal daily *Az Újság* (News). Although at the turn of the century writing for the press was an almost inseparable part of being an artist, Móricz was on the periphery of the literary world. He was far removed from the teeming life of the societies and cafés where the new generation of artists rallied with the demand for radically new social and literary institutions. He had little initial success with his short stories, which lacked originality and reflected the influence of such popular nineteenth-century Hungarian writers as Kálmán Mikszáth and Mór Jókai.

Two events in Móricz's life had a crucial impact on his career as a writer. The first was his marriage in 1905 to Eugénia Holics, which, at least at the beginning, brought some regularity into his life. This peace was soon overshadowed by the early deaths of their two sons, although they later had three surviving daughters: Viréy (born 1909), Gyöngyi (born 1911), and Lili (born 1915). The second event was his participation between 1903 and 1906 in collecting folk poetry in Szatmár County on behalf of the Kisfaludy Társaság literary society. Returning to his native land had a liberating effect on his art. The observation of the social conditions of rural communities and the natural order of peasant life transformed Móricz's artistic approach and facilitated the creation of his first significant works.

Móricz's first four books were all unsuccessful. He was twenty-nine when "Hét krajczár" (Seven Pennies), the short story that brought him the fame he had long desired, was published in the most important journal of the emerging new literature, *Nyugat* (West). He was already a permanent member of its staff. His collection of short stories, also titled *Hét krajczár*, was published in 1909 and was received with unanimous approval. Endre Ady, the most influential Hungarian poet of the turn of the century, appreciated Móricz's works and became a close friend; the young writer, in turn, regarded Ady as an example to follow. Another of his contemporaries, the poet Dezső Kosztolányi, greeted Móricz as the one to fulfill some long-standing expectations in Hungarian literature.

Móricz renewed the nineteenth-century genre of the anecdotic short story that often gave a sentimental and idyllic representation of the Hungarian village. He enriched it with a new meaning and form of expression: his realistic approach focused on the presentation of the psychological background and the tragic aspects of events hidden under the anecdotic surface. "Hét krajczár" is about a poor mother who, together with her son, starts a playful search in their house for seven pennies—the price of a piece of soap. A beggar who comes to their house for alms and sees their poverty gives them the final penny. The novelty of the story lies mostly in the terse dialogues, the closed structure, and the turning of the anecdotal scene into a scene of tragedy—the mother's laughter turns into tubercular coughing, and she dies.

"Tragédia" (Tragedy), the important title story of his next significant volume, published in 1910, opens a different world before the reader. To express a kind of instinctive rebellion against his poverty, the "hero" of the story eats himself to death at the wedding of a rich peasant. The fate of János Kiss, who is practically an embodiment of the Russian archetype of the "superfluous man" in the specific environment of the Hungarian village, reflects a basic tenet of the twentieth-century perception of the world: tragedy is no longer possible. His last thoughts ("Die, you son of a bitch") remind the reader of the depictions in Franz Kafka's novels of the inessentiality and absurdity of human existence.

Móricz's next two publications—*Sárarany* (Gold Nugget, 1911) and *Az Isten háta mögött* (The Back of Beyond, 1911)—brought him lasting fame and generational commitment. Some basic motifs of his art and some distinctive features of his style became prominent in *Sárarany*, his first novel. The story takes place in a rural setting where life is totally determined by social differences. The talented hero is Dani Turi, a "peasant Don Juan" who is eager to break free of the boundaries of social determination; his burning eroticism enchants even a countess whose husband he later kills. However, it is not exclusively social criticism that guided Móricz either in the creation of his hero or in the naturalistic presentation of his fictional world. The predominant value and aim of his art is the psychological approach: Móricz explores the depths of the human psyche and the altered situation of the individual in the twentieth century. Dani Turi assumes mythic dimensions in the course of the novel; he experiences both a subhuman, beastly existence and a transcendental experience in his vital instinctiveness and later in the decadent ecstasy of killing. The closing lines of the novel suggest that divine creation is a failure and that all of human existence is meaningless.

Az Isten háta mögött shows a different aspect of the impossibility of any metaphysical guarantees of existence. The story, which follows a well-known literary scheme, takes place in the depressing atmosphere of a small town and is plotted around the characters of an old husband (a teacher), his sensual and unsatisfied wife, and some clerks who desire her. The behavior of these characters, who sublimate their desires into speech, exposes the inessentiality of their world. The Madame Bovary-like heroine, who is presented with a slightly bitter irony, does not succeed in her attempts to commit adultery or suicide: both scenes turn into a farce. The dispassionate presentation of this world is achieved by the use of free indirect speech, a technique Móricz used consistently in almost all of his major works. It allows the fictional world of his novels to unfold directly and saves Móricz, who interpreted writing as a moral act, from direct moralizing.

These two works, although they did not give rise to such heated debate as Ady's first volumes of poetry, divided contemporary critics. The conservatives, who had been used to a "genteel" literary tra-

dition, were appalled by these works of overt
sensuality that explore the domain of instincts. At
the same time, one of the most outstanding critics
of the period, Aladár Schöpflin, in his influential
essay of 1912, "Az új magyar irodalom" (The New
Hungarian Literature), characterized Móricz as a
leading figure of the new generation of artists on
the altering Hungarian literary scene.

Móricz's lifestyle changed in accordance with
this new role. From 1909 he earned his living solely
by writing, and financial difficulties sometimes
forced him to work too quickly and superficially. He
tried his hand at almost every literary genre. His
desire to create the new Hungarian drama led him
to write a new play for the Hungarian theater almost
every year; although he did not create any masterpieces in this genre, his plays *Sári bíró* (Magistrate
Sári, 1910), *Búzakalász* (Ear of Wheat, 1924), and *A
vadkan* (Wild Boar, 1924) were moderately successful. His short stories and essays were regularly published in *Nyugat* and in other journals, notably *Az
Újság* and *Vasárnapi Újság* (Sunday News). His other
novels written in this period, such as *Kerek Ferkó*
(1913) and *Nem élhetek muzsikaszó nélkül* (I Cannot
Live Without the Sound of Music, 1916), can be
interpreted as early versions of a theme that became
more significant in his later works: the problems of
the anachronistic layer of impoverished medium
landowners of noble birth, the gentry.

Móricz, like many other Hungarian intellectual leaders, welcomed the outbreak of World War I
in 1914, hoping that it would bring about the collapse of the Austro-Hungarian monarchy and initiate radical social changes. In 1915 he was a war
correspondent reporting from the eastern front,
but he soon lost all his illusions about the war. Apart
from Ady's and Mihály Babits's poetry, some of
Móricz's short stories, such as "A tűznek nem szabad
kialudni" (You Must Not Let the Fire Go Out, 1916)
and "Szegény emberek" (Poor People, 1917), provide the strongest protests in Hungarian literature
against the war.

The main character of "Szegény emberek" is a
soldier returning from the front after twenty-six
months of service. He is forced to steal in order to
help his family, which fell into debt while he was
away. He is discovered, however, by two little girls,
whom he kills with soldierly self-discipline. The tension between the impersonal, mechanical killing, to
which he is conditioned, and some retained human
feelings, such as fatherly love and responsibility,
results in the splitting of his self. A schizophrenic
vision, in which present events intermingle with
memories of the front, reveals to him that the prime

*Title page for Móricz's 1928 novel about the self-destructive
behavior of the Hungarian gentry*

mover of the war machine is nothing else but the
interests of "the rich." Móricz's contemporaries living in the atmosphere of patriotic war propaganda
were truly shocked by this story.

During the war Móricz also wrote a novel titled
A fáklya (1918; translated as *The Torch*, 1931). The
story, as Schöpflin puts it, "is built around the struggling of the human soul bound by strict limits," but
as a result of an altered perspective it gains an ironic
overtone. The protagonist, Miklós Matolcsy, becomes
the parson of a small village. Although he tries to
see himself as a prophet whose mission is to reform
the world, all his efforts are in vain, and he later lays
the blame for his failure on the backward rural environment. The real reasons for his failure are his
doubts and the weakness of his character: he cannot
subdue his desires for money and women. At the
end of the novel a fire in the village is symbolically

kindled by his petty rancor: his "responsibility" is not diminished even by his subsequent death. The unbalanced structure of the novel, which was criticized even by Móricz's contemporaries, is a result of his personal involvement. The writer, who lost his belief in the certainty of any human order in life during the war, raises one of his most fundamental ontological questions in Matolcsy's character: what guarantees the unity of the personality in this altered reality?

The utter defeat and ruin of Hungary in World War I, the bourgeois-democratic revolution in 1918, and the dictatorship of the proletariat in 1919 connected the already influential writer with the practical organization of Hungarian literary life for the first time. Móricz became the deputy chairman of Vörösmarty Academy, which was founded with the guidance of such outstanding poets as Babits, Kosztolányi, and Ady. Though Móricz was characterized by a basically apolitical mentality, he temporarily took part in the political events of the period, mostly through his writings. Although he did not agree with the aims of the extreme left, he wrote articles admitting the necessity of social change, and he was persecuted when their dictatorship collapsed. Móricz, who had a sensitive character, fell into a state of depression as a result of this injustice. He overcame this deep intellectual and existential crisis only by "writing it out"—by creating *Légy jó mindhalálig* (1921; translated as *Be Faithful unto Death*, 1962), a novel based on his experiences as a student in Debrecen.

The main character of *Légy jó mindhalálig*, Misi Nyilas, is a conscientious, diligent, twelve-year-old Debrecen schoolboy who takes a job as a private tutor and steps out from the closed world of the college into the unknown world of adults. He is unjustly accused of stealing a winning lottery ticket he was entrusted to keep. His teachers humiliate him with empty moral platitudes and almost find him guilty; then his uncle turns up unexpectedly and reveals the truth: the ticket was stolen from him by one of his relatives, a "man of the world." The novel gives a parabolical interpretation of the alienness and unfamiliarity of the adult world as revealed through the innocent and vulnerable child's perspective. The novel becomes a naive expression of the writer's concept of art and writing, which he regarded as his duty and mission, and his concept of love as the most important principle of human life. *Légy jó mindhalálig* is Móricz's most popular novel, and it has been translated into more than twenty languages. He became well-known to the interna-

tional reading public primarily because of this novel.

Despite the political difficulties, Móricz's writing career remained undiminished. His authority and international reputation grew to the point that Thomas Mann, during a trip to Hungary, went to visit him at his home. Móricz turned toward new directions in his art in the 1920s: he focused on the problems of the nation's future and the artistic interpretation of the relationship between men and women.

The Treaty of Trianon signed after World War I had harsh consequences for the Hungarian nation: Hungary lost two-thirds of her territory, which resulted in a shaken national self-esteem. This fact was reflected in Móricz's works as an urge for the writer to take the responsibility of facing the fundamental questions of the fate of the nation. He tried to answer these questions by renewing the genre of the historical novel and representing the behavior of outstanding Hungarian historical personalities in critical moments of the past as examples worth following. His next novel, *Tündérkert* (Fairyland, 1922), is based on thorough background research: it describes the political events that took place in Transylvania at the beginning of the seventeenth century, when it was a battlefield for the clashing interests of two neighboring great powers, the Hapsburg and the Turkish empires. (After the Treaty of Trianon in 1920, Transylvania became a part of Romania.) Móricz's evaluation of the contemporary political situation is reflected in the relationship and conflicts of the two main characters, whose portrayal is far from one-sided. Prince Gábor Báthory desperately wants to turn Transylvania into "fairyland," even by launching wars of conquest that endanger the very existence of his country; he has an unshakable belief in the omnipotence of will. As opposed to Báthory's almost mythical figure of ungovernable sensuality and Oriental wildness, the Puritanic Gábor Bethlen, who is an adherent of political realism, stands for what can be perceived as the only valid alternative for the Hungarian nation: flexibility, the objective evaluation of possibilities instead of wishful thinking and the preservation of national identity. Móricz's use of the power of language and style to create characters and weltanschauung, a characteristic feature of his entire canon, is especially prominent in this novel: the archaic Hungarian vernacular and Móricz's naturalistic style (which is, however, rich in symbols) have a special role in the representation of the distant past.

At the beginning of the 1920s Móricz's marriage was failing: his wife was a good mother and a faithful companion, but she had a willful character and expected Móricz to devote himself fully to his family, which he felt was a limitation of his spiritual and intellectual freedom. One of the recurrent motifs of his work is the artistic interpretation of the mysterious relationship between men and women. He used the archetype of the dual nature of the feminine principle that irresistibly attracts men: one of her faces is that of the Virgin Mary, who can bring her mate's life to perfection in marriage but who imprisons him at the same time; the other is the attractive and seductive femme fatale who creates both insuppressible desires and destruction, since it is her essence that she cannot be possessed by anybody. Móricz's main characters suffer constantly, as he did, from having to choose between these two opposites, between faithfulness and the desire for another woman. One of his contemporaries, Milán Füst, said that Móricz's novella *Házasságtörés* (Adultery, 1923), one of the less successful versions of this theme, was "the portrayal of painful, spasmodic convulsions," but the same could be said about all his works addressing this topic. The only exception may be *Pillangó. Idill* (The Butterfly: An Idyll), a novel written in 1925, in which Móricz is in search of an essence of love that may be beyond suffering.

Pillangó uses the national vernacular to tell the story of a couple who get acquainted with each other during harvest season in a rustic setting. The relationship of Zsuzsi Hitves and Jóska Darabos, however, cannot be fulfilled: they are tied not only by the expectations of their families, who object to marriage between poor people, but also by their own hesitation between repulsion and yielding to their desires. Móricz's philosophy of love is summed up in the unexpected turn of the novel that resolves the tension of this painful passion: Jóska Darabos leaves behind a rich fiancée and sets out like a "butterfly" with his beloved Zsuzsi toward some kind of eternal happiness. This ending transfers the entire story into the irrational world of fairy tales and legends.

Móricz's sensitive and neurotic wife committed suicide in the spring of 1925. To ease this loss, in 1926 Móricz hastily married an actress, Mária Simonyi, but his private life remained unhappy. In his work he turned again toward the current social problems. He was interested in the fate of the gentry, a layer of Hungarian society that had lost its historical mission as a result of the disintegration of the social hierarchy at the end of the nineteenth century and had been unable to develop a bourgeois mentality. This issue was already a central theme in some novels written at the end of the nine-

teenth century. In two of his novels, *Kivilágos kivirradtig* (Till the Day Breaks, 1926) and *Úri muri* (Gentry Revelry, 1928), Móricz not only continues this nineteenth-century tradition but also rewrites it.

The main characters of *Kivilágos kivirradtig* are presented at the beginning of the novel from an ironic, diminishing point of view: they are like fleas seen from an upper, "celestial" perspective. The grotesque metaphor of the parallel between the levels of animals and human beings appears throughout the entire novel. An ardent criticism of the gentry unfolds in the presentation of the night-long revelry of a group of gentlemen celebrating the name day of a freshly dismissed land steward, the host. Instead of facing their reality, they escape into drunken partying, telling anecdotes, and speaking degradingly about the Jews, who gradually take on bourgeois habits and begin assuming the only social role that could be available for the gentry at all. As in the novels of Móricz's contemporary, Gyula Krúdy, telling anecdotes acquires a new function: they become expressions of a superficial and meaningless human existence.

The story of *Úri muri* takes place, symbolically, in 1896, the millenium of Hungarian history, in the ecstatic atmosphere of national pride and glory. The main character, Zoltán Szakhmáry, in contrast with the characters of *Kivilágos kivirradtig*, is portrayed as a many-sided, active personality. He endeavors to step out of the self-deceptive, beastly mentality of the gentry. His efforts to carry out an agrarian reform on his estate, however, end in failure, and his wavering between his cold wife and a peasant girl who fulfills his sexual desires results in the splitting of his personality. He sets his house on fire and commits suicide in a spectacular way, though these actions are nothing but theatrical gestures revealing his helplessness. Concerning the current social issues, the novel carries the message that the gentry cannot be expected to support national causes or initiate a national revival.

From 1929 Móricz again took an active part in the shaping of Hungarian literary life. Ernő Osvát, the editor in chief of *Nyugat*, committed suicide, and the journal almost went bankrupt. Móricz then became the editor of its prose column as well as a joint proprietor, together with Babits, who edited the poetry column. Babits was an advocate of "organic" art, or art for art's sake, while Móricz believed in socially and morally committed literature. He endeavored to broaden the circle of writers publishing in *Nyugat* along these lines and encouraged the development of young writers of talent by

Móricz with his second wife, actress Mária Simonyi

title *Erdély* (Transylvania); it included *Tündérkert* and two additional novels, *A nagy fejedelem* (The Great Prince) and *A nap árnyéka* (The Shadow of the Sun). Although his view of history and style unite the three novels, the author is no longer as interested in the historical question of the future of the nation as he is in the personality of the primary character, Bethlen. Móricz focuses on the loneliness of the prince, who fulfills his tasks as a ruler perfectly according to his principles and brings prosperity to his country, and on Bethlen's hesitation between his barren wife, Zsuzsanna Károlyi, and his demonic lover, Anna Báthory, the sister of Gábor Báthory.

Prose writer László Németh remarked, in his *Két nemzedék*, that while the short stories Móricz wrote in the 1920s were mostly "by-products" of his novels, his short stories of the 1930s can be perceived as the culmination of his writing career. The title story of the volume *Barbárok* (Barbarians, 1932) takes readers to the world of the *puszta* (prairie) and recounts a robbery and murder, the victim of which is a shepherd. The novelty of this story lies mostly in the fact that the core of its meaning is not the moral judgment passed over the murderer but the clashing of two totally different views of life: that of the "civilized" world and that of the world of the *puszta*. In the latter "barbarian" world, one's perception of life is determined by the *puszta* and the infinity of the sky: all of man's activities fall into the unchanging rhythm of nature, which is apparent in the regular changes of seasons. Murder is still a sin in this world, but it cannot be judged according to the standards and laws of the "civilized" world, nor can the murderer be made to confess his crime with "civilized" methods. He breaks down only at the trial, when he is shown the murdered shepherd's belt, which he stole. Even then the reason for his breakdown is that, according to his archaic concept of the world, the object and its owner are perceived as one.

Móricz's next volume of short stories, *Komor ló* (Somber Horse, 1936), is characterized by a similar worldview. The novelty of this collection lies in the balladlike tone and terseness of the stories and in the fact that the unfolding of the plots is determined not by the narrative voice but practically by the rhythm of nature. As Kosztolányi put it in his appreciative review in *Nyugat* (1932) of Móricz's short stories "he does not explain what life is like but shows it in an enchanting way."

The aim of Móricz's next novel, *A boldog ember* (The Happy Man, 1935), was exactly this direct representation of life. It was a truly different direction for his work: having done away with his wavering,

publishing the anthology *Mai Dekameron* (Nowadays Decameron, 1932). He traveled in the country frequently and widely, writing reports and sketches about his experiences in order to call attention to current social problems. He was forced to withdraw from his editorial position because of unfavorable literary and political criticism, however, and he resigned in 1933.

Móricz did not give up his own writing while he was the editor of *Nyugat:* apart from some works of lesser importance, such as the volumes *Forró mezők* (Hot Fields, 1929) and *Forr a bor* (Fermenting Wine, 1931), he wrote some successful novels in which he both returned to earlier themes and turned in new directions. In *Rokonok* (Relatives, 1932), for example, he treats the issue of the gentry in a more ironic and satiric tone than he had previously: he portrays the corrupt world of the 1920s, in which everything depended on family connections.

From the middle of the 1920s Móricz was working on a monumental plan: he wanted to continue the story of the Transylvanian prince Gábor Bethlen and develop *Tündérkert* into a trilogy. In 1935 this completed project was published with the struggling, suffering heroes, Móricz presents the life of a peasant, György Joó, in a journalistic, biographical form. Although György Joó is a fictional character, Móricz based the novel on the real-life peasant Michály Papp, to whom he was related. György Joó makes a reckoning with his experiences: though his life has been hard and full of suffering, he reconciles himself to his lot. In this novel Móricz diminished the distance between fiction and sociology, setting an example for the so-called populist writers who saw the improvement and education of the peasantry as the only possible means of the survival of the Hungarian nation. During the last decade of his life Móricz became increasingly allied with their movement.

After writing some minor novels, such as *Rab oroszlán* (The Caged Lion, 1936), which elaborates the marriage theme again in an urban environment, and *Míg új a szerelem* (Till Love is New, 1938), which records the failure of his second marriage, Móricz wrote his confessions in the 1939 autobiographical novel, *Életem regénye*. Although the aging writer had three attentive and loving daughters from his first marriage, he was becoming increasingly lonely (he and Simonyi were divorced in 1939), and a need for self-analysis as well as his increasingly objective artistic approach turned his attention toward his recollections of youth. In *Életem regénye* the writer "relives" his life up to the age of twelve: he is searching for the roots of his personality among his childhood memories, the traditions of his family, and the world of the village, of which he gives a detailed presentation with almost sociographic thoroughness. The retrospective, systematizing, interpretative point of view of the narrator, however, incorporates the turning points and fundamental questions of his entire life.

In 1939 Móricz began an even more daring enterprise: he took over the periodical *Kelet Népe* (People of the East), which rallied mostly populist artists and included the work of such writers as Németh and Gyula Illyés. Móricz's working capacity can be well characterized by the fact that in addition to editing this periodical (which prospered for a while under his editorship) he also modernized some nineteenth-century novels for the purposes of popular education and wrote three novels of his own between 1940 and 1942.

In 1941 Móricz returned to the restylized perspective of a child with his novel *Árvácska* (in Hungarian this word means "pansy" and "orphan"; the writer uses it as the name of the main character). The story of a child who is mistreated by inhuman foster parents goes far beyond the boundaries of realist documentary prose, which aims mostly at exposing social injustices. The novel achieves an almost biblical and definitely lyrical tone through its structure (it is divided into "psalms") and through the reflection of the child's desperate longing for love, which penetrates the superficial surface of the brutal events. The closing lines, which describe how Árvácska and her family perish in a fire that breaks out in their house on Christmas Eve, elevate this story beyond the level of realistic events: the fire becomes the apocalyptic fire that purifies and saves the world.

Móricz sought escape from the horrible experience of World War II and the depressing state of his health by working on another monumental project he had planned for a long time. Before his death from apoplexy on 4 September 1942, he wrote the novels *Rózsa Sándor a lovát ugratja* (Sándor Rózsa is Putting His Horse at a Jump, 1941) and *Rózsa Sándor összevonja a szemöldökét* (Sándor Rózsa is Frowning, 1942), the first two books of an intended trilogy about the famous outlaw. In these last works the writer expresses his fears for his mother country, which had just entered World War II, and his desire for independence by writing about the life of the highwaymen, which recalls the historical past and the world of legends at the same time, and by elevating the representation of nineteenth-century outlaws to an artistic level.

Zsigmond Móricz made a significant impact on the development of Hungarian literature in the first part of the twentieth century. His multifaceted career encompassed nearly every sphere of Hungarian letters: as a writer, he published novels, short stories, plays, and essays; as a journalist, he wrote articles, reports, and reviews; as an editor, he played an important part in the popularization of literature and the nurturing of literary talent.

Letters:

Móricz Zsigmond levelei, 2 volumes, edited by Dóra F. Csanak (Budapest: Akadémiai Kiadó, 1963);

Kedves Mária! Móricz Zsigmond levelei Simonyi Máriához, compiled by Lili Móricz (Budapest: Magvető, 1973; expanded, 1979);

A nyugat szerkesztője: Levelek, edited by Jószef Tasi (Budapest: Petőfi Irodalmi Múzeum, 1984).

Interviews:

Aladár Schöpflin, "Magyar írók otthonukban," *Vasárnapi újság*, 44 (1917): 704–705;

"Előszó a Fáklya kiadásához," *Nyugat*, 1 (1921): 398;

"Beszélgetés az 50 éves Móricz Zsigmonddal," *Az Est*, 144 (1929): 5;

"Győtrdés," *Kelet Népe*, 11 (1940): 2–3.

Bibliographies:

József Pintér, "Bibliográfia és repertórium," in *Móricz Zsigmond ébresztése. Emlékkönyv,* edited by József Darvas (Budapest: Sarló, 1945), pp. 243–291;

Sándor Kozocsa, *Móricz Zsigmond irodalmi munkássága* (Budapest: Művelt Nép, 1952);

Albert Tezla, *Hungarian Authors: A Bibliographical Handbook* (Cambridge, Mass.: Belknap Press of Harvard University Press, 1970), pp. 419–432;

Ernő Pesti, *Móricz Zsigmond Bibliográfia* (Budapest: Fővárosi Szabó Ervin Könyvtár, 1979).

Biographies:

Virág Móricz, *Apám regénye* (Budapest: Szépirodalmi, 1953; expanded, 1954);

Miklós Móricz, *Móricz Zsigmond indulása* (Budapest: Magvető, 1959);

Lili Móricz, *Fecskék a verandán* (Budapest: Magvető, 1966);

Miklós Móricz, *Móricz Zsigmond érkezése* (Budapest: Szépirodalmi, 1966);

Virág Móricz, *Móricz Zsigmond szerkesztő úr* (Budapest: Szépirodalmi, 1967).

References:

Endre Ady, "Móricz Zsigmond," *Nyugat,* 2 (1909): 169–171;

Imre Bori, *Móricz Zsigmond prózája* (Újvidék: Fórum, 1983);

Mihály Czine, *Móricz Zsigmond* (Budapest: Gondolat, 1968);

Géza Féja, "Boldog ember," *Magyar Írás,* 9 (1935): 48–50;

László Fülöp, "Emberszemlélet és lélekábrázolás," *Alföld,* 7 (1979): 54–73;

Milán Füst, "Házasságtörés," *Nyugat,* 1 (1923): 503–506;

Gábor Halász, " A magyar regény problémája," *Magyar Szemle,* 3 (1929): 283–288;

Gyula Herczeg, *Móricz Zsigmond stílusa* (Budapest: Tankönyvkiadó, 1982);

Miklós Hubay, "A drámaíró Móricz," in his *A dráma sorsa* (Budapest: Szépirodalmi, 1984), pp. 399–446;

Ignotus, "Arcképvázlat Móricz Zsigmondról," *Nyugat,* 1 (1918): 109–113;

Géza Juhász, *Móricz Zsigmond* (Budapest: Studium, 1928);

Frigyes Karinthy, "Szegény emberek," *Nyugat,* 1 (1924): 274–275;

János Kodolányi, "A tűznek nem szabad kialudni," *Nyugat,* 1 (1924): 267–268;

Dezső Kosztolányi, "Barbárok," *Nyugat,* 1 (1932): 235–238;

Kosztolányi, as Lehotai, "Hét Krajcár," *Hét,* 30 (1909): 499–500;

Kálmán Kovács, "Móricz Zsigmond művészetéről," in his *Eszmék és irodalom* (Budapest: Szépirodalmi, 1976), pp. 217–240;

Géza Laczkó, "A történelmi regény és Móricz Zsigmond," *Nyugat,* 2 (1922): 1255–1260;

Péter Nagy, *Móricz Zsigmond* (Budapest: Művelt Nép, 1953);

Nagy, "Zsigmond Móricz the Novelist," *New Hungarian Quarterly,* 3 (1961): 32–46;

László Németh, "Baleset," *Napkelet,* 2 (1927): 812–813;

Németh, "Erdély, Rózsa Sándor eposza," in his *Két nemzedék* (Budapest: Magvető, 1970), pp. 530–533, 708–712;

Németh, *Móricz Zsigmond* (Budapest: Turul, 1943);

Aladár Schöpflin, "A fáklya Amerikában," *Nyugat,* 1 (1932): 97–100;

Schöpflin, "Az új magyar irodalom," *Huszadik Század,* 26 (1912): 624–644;

Schöpflin, *Móricz Zsigmondról,* edited by Ádám Réz (Budapest: Szépirodalmi, 1979);

Schöpflin, "Úri muri," *Könyvbarátok lapja,* 3 (1928): 227–229;

István Sőtér, "A Sáraranytól az Úri muriig," in his *Tisztuló Tükör* (Budapest: Gondolat, 1966), pp. 73–79;

János Szávai, "Életem regénye," in his *Magyar emlékírók* (Budapest: Szépirodalmi, 1988), pp. 172–179;

Kálmán Vargha, *Móricz Zsigmond és az irodalom* (Budapest: Akadémiai, 1962);

Vargha, ed., *Kortársak Móricz Zsigmondról* (Budapest: Akadémiai, 1958).

Zofia Nałkowska

(10 November 1884 – 17 Deczmber 1954)

Hanna Kirchner
Institute of Literary Research, Polish Academy of Sciences

BOOKS: *Kobiety* (Warsaw: Księgarnia Powszechna, 1906); translated by Michael Henry Dziewicki as *Kobiety (Women): A Novel of Polish Life* (New York & London: Putnam, 1920);

Książę. Powieść (Warsaw: Gebethner i Wolff, 1907);

Rówieśnice (Warsaw: Gebethner i Wolff, 1909);

Koteczka czyli białe tulipany (Lwów: Księgarnia B. Kołonieckiego, 1909);

Narcyza (Kraków: Książka, 1911);

Noc podniebna (Warsaw: Książnica Literacka, 1911);

Lustra (Kraków: Książka, 1913);

Węże i róże (Kraków: Książka, 1915);

Moje zwierzęta (Warsaw: J. Mortkowicz, 1915);

Tajemnice krwi (Warsaw: Gebethner i Wolff, 1917);

Hrabia Emil. Romans nowoczesny (Warsaw: Towarzystwo Wydawnicze, 1920);

Charaktery (Warsaw: Ignis, 1922);

Na torfowiskach (Warsaw: Biblioteka Dzieł Wyborowych, 1922);

Romans Teresy Hennert. Powieść dzisiejsza (Warsaw: Ignis, 1924);

Małżeństwo (Warsaw: Biblioteka Dzieł Wyborowych, 1925);

Dom nad łąkami. Powieść (Warsaw: Wacław Czarski, 1925);

Choucas. Powieść internacjonalna (Warsaw: Gebethner i Wolff, 1927);

Księga o przyjaciołach, by Nałkowska and Maria Jehanne Wielopolska (Warsaw: Gebethner i Wolff, 1927);

Niedobra miłość. Romans prowincjonalny (Warsaw: Gebethner i Wolff, 1928);

Dom kobiet. Sztuka w 3-ch aktach (Warsaw: Gebethner i Wolff, 1930);

Dzień jego powrotu. Dramat w 3-ch aktach (Warsaw: Gebethner i Wolff, 1931); translated by M. C. Słomczanka as *The Day of His Return* (London, 1933);

Ściany świata (Warsaw: Gebethner i Wolff, 1931);

Między zwierzętami (Lwów: Państwowe Wydawnictwo Książek Szkolnych, 1934);

Zofia Nałkowska

Granica (Warsaw: Gebethner i Wolff, 1935);

Renata Słuczańska. Sztuka w trzech aktach na tle powieści "Niedobra miłość" (Warsaw: Gebethner i Wolff, 1936);

Niecierpliwi. Powieść (Lwów: Książnica-Atlas, 1939);

Medaliony (Warsaw: Czytelnik, 1946);

Charaktery dawne i ostatnie (Warsaw: Państwowy Instytut Wydawniczy, 1948);

Węzły życia. Powieść (Warsaw: Czytelnik, 1948; revised, 2 volumes, 1950, 1954);

Mój ojciec (Warsaw: Nasza Księgarnia, 1953);

Widzenie bliskie i dalekie, edited by T. Breza and others (Warsaw: Czytelnik, 1957);

Dzienniki czasu wojny, edited by Hanna Kirchner (Warsaw: Czytelnik, 1970);

Dzienniki, 6 volumes, edited by Kirchner (Warsaw: Czytelnik, 1975–1999)—comprises volume 1, *1899–1905* (1975); volume 2, *1909–1917* (1976); volume 3, *1918–1929* (1980); volume 4, *1930–1939* (1985); volume 5, *1939–1944* (1996); volume 6, *1945–1954* (1999).

Editions and Collections: *Pisma wybrane*, edited by Wilhelm Mach (Warsaw: Czytelnik, 1954; enlarged edition, 1956);

Dzieła, 17 volumes, edited by Zofia Mycielska-Golik (Warsaw: Czytelnik, 1976–1990).

Editions in English: "PPC," translated by Else C. H. Benecke and M. Bunsch in *Polish Tales* (London & Edinburgh, 1921);

The Day of His Return, translated by M. C. Słomczanka (London, 1933);

"Medallions" [excerpts], translated by Jadwiga Zwolska, and "Characters," translated by Christina Cekalska, in *Introduction to Modern Polish Literature. An Anthology of Fiction and Poetry*, edited by Adam Gillon and Ludwik Krzyżanowski (New York: Twayne, 1964), pp. 129–142;

"Beside the Railroad Track," in *Stories from the Literary Review*, edited by Charles Angolf (Rutherford, N.J.: Fairleigh Dickinson University Press, 1969), pp. 221–227;

"At the Railroad Track" and "Rock Bottom," translated by Helena Goscilo in *Russian and Polish Women's Fiction*, edited by Goscilo (Knoxville: University of Tennessee Press, 1985), pp. 334–343.

PLAY PRODUCTIONS: *Dom kobiet*, Warsaw, Teatr Polski, 21 March 1930;

Dzień jego powrotu, Warsaw, Teatr Narodowy, 11 April 1931;

Niedobra miłość, Warsaw, Teatr Narodowy, 29 January 1936.

MOTION PICTURE: *Granica*, screenplay by Nałkowska, Józef Lejtes, S. Urbanowicz, and Krystyna Severin Zelwerowicz, Parlo-film, 1938.

RADIO: "Noce Teresy," Polskie Radio, 1935.

The writings of Zofia Nałkowska are an important contribution in twentieth-century Polish prose. Nałkowska introduced into Polish fiction the modern question of personality; she abandoned traditional realism in favor of the novel of analysis with its philosophical interests and its goal of uncovering the laws governing "character." Many of her works combine features of the novel and the essay, with the author becoming one of the characters. This practice distinguishes her from the stream-of-consciousness trend in modern psychological fiction. At the same time, she followed closely the historical and social transformations of her nation, deriving material for broad generalizations concerning the individual and the collective consciousness. She was a grand figure of Polish literature during the first half of the twentieth century and an example of the emergence of women authors in Polish culture.

Zofia Nałkowska was born on 10 November 1884 in Warsaw to Wacław Nałkowski, a distinguished geographer and social publicist, and Anna Šafranek. Her father came from the impoverished petty nobility and was related to the Italian family of Scipio del Campo. Her mother came from a family of civil servants in Czech Moravia (she was the daughter of a Frenchman and a Moravian). Nałkowska's younger sister, Hanna, became a sculptor. When Zofia was one year old, her parents took her to Leipzig, where her father was a student; later she returned to Warsaw. Initially she received her education at home, and from 1898 to 1901 she attended a private school for girls; toward the end of her secondary education she also attended some lectures of the clandestine Flying University. Her talent and intellectual abilities became apparent early under the influence of her parents. At twelve she read with her father the works of Friedrich Nietzsche, and starting in 1897 she wrote verse; her first poem, "Pamiętam" (I Remember), was published in *Tygodnik Ilustrowany* (Illustrated Weekly) in 1898. She continued publishing poems until 1908, when she abandoned the genre.

Beginning in 1895 she lived alternately in Warsaw and in a modest suburban wooden house on a forested hill in Górki; this home appears as a setting in her later fiction. As was typical of large segments of the Polish intelligentsia, her family was too poor to finance her further studies; but the influence of her father and his friends—writers and scientists—kindled in Nałkowska the desire for self-education and a strong interest in philosophy, psychology, the history of culture, and the natural sciences as well as Polish and foreign literature, which she could read in four languages. Her father's milieu, that of the radical and progressive intelligentsia centered around the periodical *Głos* (Voice), shaped Nałkowska's basic outlook, which was secular, monistic, and uncompromisingly democratic, though somewhat modified by the neoromantic ideas that had influenced her youth.

Besides her early poetry, Nałkowska's literary apprenticeship was her diary, which she kept from 1896 (though its preserved manuscript dates back to 8 September 1899) until the year of her death. She published her first short story when she was nineteen, and at the end of that year she began writing her first novel, *Lodowe pola* (Ice Fields), based to a large degree on her diary entries. Published in the weekly periodical *Prawda* (Truth) in 1904, it became part of the novel *Kobiety* (1906, translated as *Kobiety (Women): A Novel of Polish Life*, 1920); it was also published separately in 1927. In February 1904 she married a minor writer, Leon Rygier, who was also a well-regarded pedagogue. Together they wrote the novella "Dalecy" (The Distant Ones), published in 1906 in the periodical *Młodość* (Youth); this work became the nucleus of Nałkowska's novel about the revolution of 1905, *Książę* (Prince, 1907). She spent the next year with her husband in the provincial town of Kielce, where he edited the daily *Echa Kieleckie* (Kielce Echoes), in which she published articles, translations, and stories. She was also involved in educational activities.

In the spring of 1907 Nałkowska gave an address at the All-Polish Congress of Women, "On the Ethical Tasks of the Women's Movement," which met with a stormy response. In the address she called for the liberation of women from ethical norms established by men to suit their own interests and based on social and moral hypocrisy. At the beginning of 1909 she traveled with her father to Kraków (then in the Austrian part of Poland) as a witness for the defense in the highly publicized case of the writer and philosopher Stanisław Brzozowski, who had been accused by the leaders of the Polish Socialist Party of being an agent of the tsarist political police. She also published reports of the proceedings.

After moving back to Warsaw from Kielce in the fall of 1907, Nałkowska had begun her novel *Rówieśnice* (Contemporaries, 1909), a reflection of the dark times that followed the defeat of the revolution, and a volume of short stories, *Koteczka czyli białe tulipany* (The Kitten or White Tulips, 1909). In the fall of 1909 she divorced her husband and moved to Kraków; in the spring of 1910 she traveled as a *dame de compagnie* to Italy. In 1911 her father died suddenly, and Nałkowska became responsible for the financial well-being of the family. Until 1914 she lived with her mother and sister in Górki, contributing to many magazines and writing books.

In Nałkowska's early works the most important characters are the heroines. These highly autobiographical works are both self-portraits and manifestos. Nałkowska represents an interesting form of feminism that derives its inspiration from the writings of Nietzsche, Arthur Schopenhauer, Henri-Louis Bergson, and William James. Nałkowska's women follow the principle of the "will to power": they cultivate individualism and are liberated from conventions and subordination to men. They are conscious of themselves and others, and the intellectual element is the single most important part of their personalities. Another feature that characterizes them is aestheticism—they want, like the nineteenth-century dandy, to be the artists of life. Against the background of traditional women characters in Polish fiction, their novelty is striking.

These early works, apart from their programmatic model of womanhood and their stylistic qualities, are important in another way. They pose questions that Nałkowska tried to answer in all of her later works: what shapes human character; how much of that shaping is done by nature and how much by culture; and how one should cope with the constant tension between these two forces. In this respect her works are close to Sigmund Freud's problematics. No doubt these interests of the writer derived, at least partly, from her early literary readings: Stendhal and other French writers, eighteenth-century moralists, and especially Fyodor Dostoyevsky.

After World War I broke out, Nałkowska moved back to Warsaw. The war became for her a school of reality. The egocentrism of the autobiographical elements in her works and the sophisticated psychological themes became superseded by an interest in the ordinary and the simple. The earliest indication of this change is to be found in *Charaktery* (Characters, 1922), a collection of short prose pieces (a genre to which she gave a new energy in Polish literature) written since 1915. In 1916 she taught Polish literature in a course designed to prepare students for university entrance. Her first war experiences are recorded in the volume of short stories *Tajemnice krwi* (Secrets of Blood), published in 1917. During that same year she worked on the war novel *Hrabia Emil. Romans nowoczesny* (Count Emil: A Modern Romance, 1920) and drafted the first version of a book about the family property in Górki; the latter project was published in 1922 under the title *Na torfowiskach* (On the Peatbog) and revised in 1925 as *Dom nad łąkami* (The House by the Meadows). In *Dom nad łąkami* there is an interesting interweaving of the points of view of a child and an adult.

Nałkowska (seated, second from left) at the premiere of her play Dom kobiet *(The House of Women) at the Teatr Polski, 1930*

The novel is an homage to the country house of the Nałkowskis, the landscapes of the Mazovian countryside around Warsaw, and the neighbors, who were simple folk with dignity and moral principles.

Hrabia Emil, a novel about the war and the legions that took part in it under the leadership of Józef Piłsudski, is first and foremost an analysis of the response of the protagonist's sensitive psyche to the horrors and the phenomenon of war. A complete contrast to the writings of the time, which celebrated Polish military deeds and *wojenka* ("little war," as it was called in a popular song) as male adventure, this book depicts war as a consequence of barbaric instinct, made palatable with the help of nationalistic ideas and the models of behavior that serve them.

At the end of World War I, Nałkowska worked in the Office of External Propaganda of the Presidium of the Council of Ministers, where she edited publications promoting Polish culture. She also participated in the establishment of the Professional Union of Polish Writers.

When Poland regained her independence in 1918, enormous changes in social and individual life accompanied the effort of establishing statehood and uniting the inhabitants of the former Prussian, Russian, and Austrian empires. Nałkowska was one of the first to give these developments expression in literary form. In the novel *Romans Teresy Hennert* (The Romance of Theresa Hennery, 1924) that expression is bitter and critical, since she depicts the heroism of the freedom fighters becoming degenerate in conditions of peace: the demonic Colonel Omski, a "military psyche," kills his love, Teresa Hennert, the wife of another. A milieu novel, *Romans Teresy Hennert* is nevertheless a penetrating depiction of new social relations and of the changing mores that had undermined the identity of many ("life and the entire soul had undergone a radical change"). The title of the novel, seemingly chosen to entice the reader, is in fact ironic, and it expresses one of the constant motifs of her writing: the love story as a metaphor for personal, existential, and social relations.

In 1916 Nałkowska met Jan Gorzechowski (pseudonym Jur), a Piłsudski legionary and fighter for the Polish Socialist Party during the 1905 revolution as well as the prime actor in the valiant freeing of ten socialist fighters from a tsarist prison. She and Gorzechowski fell in love but could not marry until 1922, after his divorce. Once married, they settled near Wilno in Lithuania, and then in Grodno, where Gorzechowski was the commander of military gendarmes. The characteristics of her husband's male psyche and marital role appear in many of Nałkowska's writings.

In Grodno, although basically reduced to the role of an officer's wife, Nałkowska nevertheless worked on *Romans Teresy Hennert*, depicting the first years of independent Poland. She was also a member of Patronat (Relief Committee), a society devoted to the welfare of prisoners—an activity that did not please her gendarme husband. Many of these prisoners were Byelorussian peasants, often badly mistreated and dying from tuberculosis. Her prison observations were later used in a cycle of short stories, *Ściany świata* (Walls Separating Worlds, 1931). The striving after authenticity in Nałkowska's documentary prose, including this cycle, gives it elements of the essay. The narrator not only recounts events but also subjects them to philosophical reflection, asks questions, draws conclusions, and coins aphorisms (some of which have acquired wide currency). Thus *Ściany świata* is not merely reportage from the prison and its hospital in Grodno; the work is also a meditation on crime, penance, death, madness, unhappiness, suffering, and first and foremost on the sources and the meaning of evil.

In 1925 Nałkowska spent some time with her husband in a sanatorium in Leysin-Feydey in Switzerland, which gave her the idea of writing an "international novel" titled *Choucas* (Jackdaws, 1927). In 1926, after painful instances of her husband's infidelity, she left Grodno. These experiences, as well as those of life in a provincial town, found expression in two of her novels: *Niedobra miłość* (Bad Love, 1928), which was awarded the 1929 literary prize of the city of Łódź, and *Granica* (Border, 1935).

In *Choucas, Niedobra miłość,* and *Granica* Nałkowska traces parallels between the destruction of personal bonds and the falling apart of social groups. She tries to show that human beings are shaped, above all else, by the pressure of conventional forms, social roles, and cultural "schemas" that have been created in human intercourse. For instance, in *Choucas* the visitors of a Swiss sanatorium are creatures of nationalistic prejudices and stereotypes, and their attitudes are reinforced by religion, which on both sides of the front line serves chauvinism and militarism. In the later novels the same phenomenon of the determinism of social roles is shown through close-up as well as distancing images of the "society" of a border town and of the neighboring landed gentry. There is an additional motif, that of betrayal, both as infidelity in love and as betrayal of ideals and the changes in personality that result from them. Love is depicted as a social role: a woman who is loved is not the same to herself and to her milieu as a rejected woman is. Thus the main characters of *Niedobra miłość* undergo change: Renata Słuczańska, who reappears in Nałkowska's 1936 play, is at first a woman replete with domestic virtue and faithful to her much older husband, but she suddenly becomes a ruthless and triumphant lover and steals Blizbor from Agnieszka, his wife, the magnificent daughter of a dignitary and a woman of the world.

In 1928 Nałkowska traveled to Italy and France, and then to Zagreb and Prague in connection with the staging of her successful play *Dom kobiet* (The House of Women, 1930), which was also performed in Italy, Estonia, Denmark, and Norway. In 1931 another of her plays, *Dzień jego powrotu* (The Day of His Return), was staged in England, Yugoslavia, Austria, and Estonia. In that same year, she visited Greece and Yugoslavia with a group of women intellectuals.

In *Dom kobiet* conflict arises from the lack of correspondence between the way an individual is perceived by others and the mystery of that individual's true personality. The heroines of the play (a grandmother, a mother, two aunts, two daughters, a divorcée, and a widow) constantly revise their images of their dead loved ones and live with their myths of the others. Reality interferes for one of the women, Joanna, when the illicit daughter of her beloved and lamented dead husband appears, destroying Joanna's inner myths. Perhaps the most acute statement is made by the grandmother: "Between one human being and another there is darkness," which is an assertion of cognitive powerlessness. In an otherwise commonplace plot the author managed to present a wealth of psychological insight.

The question of the origin of the criminal instinct in human beings is the theme of *Dzień jego powrotu*. Ksawery leaves prison and returns to his wife, who disappoints his hopes in the steadfastness of her feelings; this betrayal leads Ksawery to another crime, the killing of her lover. In the tradition of Henrik Ibsen the play reveals the fateful influence of the past on human action, but at the same time it subtly shows how crime can arise out of a lack of emotional support among one's closest circle (a father's absolute condemnation, a wife's unfaithfulness) and a lack of hope. This play, as well as *Dom kobiet*, continues to be performed with success in Polish theaters and on radio and television.

By 1929 Nałkowska broke completely with her husband. She often stayed in her house in Górki (which she eventually sold in 1937), worked in the Union of Writers as president or vice president several times, and was active in the Polish PEN Club, representing the Polish literary milieu at international congresses. She became one of the leading personalities in the cultural life of the interwar period; she was famed not only for her beauty and personal charm but also for being a master of the art of conversation. She held a literary salon frequented by writers, artists, scholars, politicians, and diplomats. She was a patron of young literary talents, including Bruno Schulz and Witold Gombrowicz. Her works also influenced several younger writers, and critics spoke of "Nałkowska's school of writing," characterized by a socio-psychological approach and authenticity of setting. She frequented the salons of government figures and, especially after 1926, she signed and organized protests in defense of persecuted left-wing activists and political prisoners, against the use of torture in investigative proceedings, and against police repression of workers, peasants, and national minorities.

In the spring of 1932 Nałkowska began working on *Granica*, one of her most important books; it was awarded the State Prize in 1936 and made into a film in 1938. In *Granica* the effect of a panoramic analysis of contemporary society is achieved through a sparse and near-parabolic narration. The plot concerns the public career of Zenon Ziembiewicz, a member of the intelligentsia who has studied abroad and imbibed socialist ideals but who becomes, through the pressure of his social position, a conformist. He transgresses, one after another, the boundaries of moral, social, personal, and ideological obligations. Ziembiewicz is torn between his wife, Elżbieta, and his lover, the servant Justine, and this personal drama is also a social one. His aunt's house—a middle-class apartment building in which unemployed paupers, dying of hunger and disease, live under the floor of the well-appointed apartment of its owner—is symbolic of the social stratification of Poland.

Ziembiewicz is accused of shooting at demonstrating workers (the order was given without his knowledge). He is also blinded by his lover, who becomes demented after the abortion of their child. Ziembiewicz eventually understands (but only when it is too late) what has happened to him: "that one is the way one's place is." Finally realizing the extent of his defeat and guilt, he ends by committing suicide. This novel is, among other things, a permanently relevant treatise on power. The debate that develops in the novel about secular and religious concepts of existence gives it an additional philosophical interest.

Also during 1932 Nałkowska met the prominent Croatian writer Miroslav Krleža, who was then visiting Warsaw; she had a short but passionate love affair with him. Krleža, a leftist, had an indirect but radicalizing influence on *Granica*. In 1933 Nałkowska became the only female member of the newly established Polish Academy of Literature. At the same time, she joined *Przedmieście* (Suburbia), a group of populist writers who wanted literature to focus on social themes: the unemployed, the homeless, the proletariat, and the "loners" vegetating on the outskirts of cities. In 1936 and 1937 she helped to edit the monthly *Studio*, in which she also anonymously published literary and theater reviews. A year earlier, fellow *Studio* editor and prose writer Bogusław Kuczyński had become Nałkowska's unofficial husband. In 1936 she began work on a new novel, which appeared in January 1939 under the title *Niecierpliwi* (The Impatient Ones).

The sum of Nałkowska's probing into the nature of man and of his place in the world and among others can be found in *Niecierpliwi*, which was written during the first manifestations of existentialism. A panorama of death, madness, suicides, and crimes delineates the chronicle of the Szpotawa family, who represent the human family expressing in these ways their "impatience" with the pain and evil of existence. Nałkowska depicts the basic situations and the meaning of the human condition, in which the individual is condemned to biological insignificance and the tortures of consciousness. In the foreground are Jakub and Teodora, a married couple whose difficult love ends in murder. After their torturous marriage, Teodora finds solace in a new love, which is as natural as nature itself; but Jakub kills her. The symbolic background to this plot is provided by fish ponds and the cycle of the growth of

Page from the manuscript for Węzły życia (Life's Knots, 1948), Nałkowska's attempt to write a political novel analyzing the downfall of Poland in September 1939 (from Ewa Pienkowska, Zofia Nałkowska, 1975) fish to the point when they are ready for the catch. The motif of fish, a symbol of silent suffering and the innocence of nature, recurs in Nałkowska's fiction (together with other animal analogues).

Niecierpliwi is well crafted, oscillating between reality—which, however, carries with it symbolic meanings—and the dark aura of Franz Kafka, of existential despair and contemporary knowledge of intuitive psychology; moreover, it makes use of what were then fairly new ideas of fictional time and the poetics of the dream. The contemporary receptivity to a novel of this kind was fairly low; the critics were ill prepared to interpret it properly and they failed to see its innovative features. It was the first time that a novel by Nałkowska met with a negative reception from the critics. The situation was even less favorable after World War II, during the Socialist-Realist phase. *Niecierpliwi* received its due only after 1956.

When World War II broke out in September 1939 Nałkowska joined the mass exodus of refugees fleeing to eastern Poland; she thus parted with Kuczyński, who crossed the border into Romania. Nałkowska returned to her mother and sister in Warsaw, where she lived throughout the German occupation of Poland, supporting herself and her family with the modest earnings of a tobacco shop she had set up and later with advanced payments from an underground publisher. As a result of various decisions of the German authorities, she had to move from place to place, and on the eve of the Warsaw Uprising in 1944 she was living in the corner of her sister's studio. She participated in underground literary activity, but living conditions prevented her from writing anything else except her diary. Toward the end of the German occupation she returned to literary work in the house of a friend near Warsaw, where she worked on "Życie Wznowoine" (Life Revived), a book about her father, and began work on the novel *Węzły życia* (Life's Knots, 1948). In 1944 she was contacted by representatives of the Polish Workers Party, who tried to persuade her to join the Home National Council, a kind of underground parliament organized by the Communists; however, she refused. Just before the Warsaw Uprising broke out she left the city and eventually lost all her belongings.

In February 1945 she moved to the city of Łódź, where she was assigned an apartment in a house for writers. She then became a member of the Home National Council and participated in the work of the Main Commission for Investigating German War Crimes. She visited sites, attended court proceedings, and talked to survivors. The result was her masterpiece, *Medaliony* (Medallions, 1946), a slim volume of documentary reports transformed into a work of poignant symbolism and acute moral probing. The shattering depiction of Nazi crimes, and the story of those who managed to survive extermination camps and other places of suffering, is told with maximal simplicity and without commentary. The work constitutes not only a testimony to martyrdom but also an attempt to fathom the incomprehensible moral sense of the events, to look into the abyss of evil. The author-narrator is present in these accounts as someone who observes and writes things down, asks questions, but herself says nothing. Only the often-quoted epigraph to the book—"Ludzie ludziom zgotowali ten los" (Human beings prepared such fate for other human beings)—conveys stunned disbelief and is perhaps the deepest insight in the work.

Right after the end of the war Nałkowska began publishing various chapters of *Węzły życia* in literary magazines such as *Odrodzenie* (Renaissance). The novel was an attempt at a political diagnosis of the prewar period and of the causes of Poland's defeat in September 1939. The retrospective presentation of the fate and attitudes of members of the prewar ruling elite is juxtaposed against the author's personal experiences as a refugee, with material taken from her intimate journal of 1939. However, the ambitious attempt at writing a political novel, alien to her talent and interests, at best proved a partial success. The novel was badly received by the critics of the Communist establishment as insufficiently critical of the prewar regime, but it found favor with the reviewer of the oppositionist Catholic weekly *Tygodnik Powszechny* (Universal Weekly). Responding to the criticism, Nałkowska worked on a revised and enlarged version that would satisfy the ideological critics, although ultimately she changed surprisingly little.

Nałkowska became a contributor to the Marxist weekly *Kuźnica* (The Smithy), but her increasingly critical attitude toward the cultural policies of the ruling Communist Party led her to write polemical articles that expressed oppositionist views and to reject Socialist Realism. On the other hand, she put much enthusiasm into the Polish-French Friendship Society over which she presided, trying to develop cultural contacts with France, for which she always had a special sentiment. She headed delegations of Polish writers to France, Czechoslovakia, and Yugoslavia in 1946, and to Moscow a year later. From 1947 she was a member of Parliament and participated in the work of the Parliamentary Commission for Culture and Art. In 1948 she took part in the World Congress of Intellectuals in Defense of Peace, which met in Wrocław, and the following year she was a delegate to the World Congress of Defenders of Peace in Prague. Having moved back to Warsaw in 1950, Nałkowska became the vice president of the Polish PEN Club and a member of the League to Fight Racism; she also participated in the Polish Writers' Union, evaluated the works of young authors, and gave support and assistance to various writers and artists. In 1953 she was awarded the State Prize for her lifetime achievements.

Nałkowska completed a popular young-people's biography of her father, titled simply *Mój ojciec* (My Father), which appeared in 1953. She was, however, unable to finish a more substantial book about him, "Życie wznowione" (Life Revived), although a few of its chapters appeared in the literary journals. She died in Warsaw on 17 December 1954.

Some additional works appeared posthumously: a volume of essays (which she herself had put together) titled *Widzenie bliskie i dalekie* (Close and Distant Vision, 1957), and *Dzienniki czasu wojny* (Journal of the Time of War, 1970), based on the manuscripts of her diary. Later there were consecutive volumes of the scholarly edition of the diary, which renewed interest in Nałkowska's other writings. Her journal was recognized as a work of excellent prose, a novel-like story of an intellectual Polish woman told against the rich panorama of national culture. The life of this unusual heroine reflects three consecutive epochs in Polish history: the last years under Russian rule and resistance to it; the state-building and wartime period between the sudden gaining of independence in 1918 and the Warsaw Uprising in 1944; and finally an era of revolutionary change in the shadow of Soviet tanks, and at the same time the spontaneous striving of the nation to rebuild the homeland, its institutions, and culture. The last words of the journal were written a few days before the author's death, at a time when there appeared the first signs of an ideological thaw.

Nałkowska influenced a significant group of young writers who began their literary careers in the 1930s. Her works have appeared in translation in many countries, including Britain, the United States, Russia, Slovakia, Germany, France, the Czech Republic, Ukraine, Bulgaria, Croatia, Italy, Denmark, Norway, Romania, and Portugal. Her writing is a model of crystalline prose, concise to the point of aphorism. Her place in Polish literature is that of a master of psychological analysis, an intellectual who at the same time was aware of the role of feelings and instinct, and a writer who saw clearly and who was always sensitive to human injustice and suffering.

Bibliography:

Jan Zenon Brudnicki, *Zofia Nałkowska. 1884–1954. Poradnik Bibliograficzny* (Warsaw: Biblioteka Narodowa. Instytut Bibliograficzny, 1965).

Biographies:

Wspomnienia o Zofii Nałkowskiej (Warsaw: Czytelnik, 1965);

Hanna Kirchner, *Zofia Nałkowska*. Polski Słownik Biograficzny, 22 (Wrocław: Zakład Narodowy im. Ossolińskich, 1977).

References:

Grażyna Borkowska, "Cztery drogi: regres, narcyzm, walka, sztuka" and "*Dzienniki* Zofii Nałkowskiej i *Dzienniki* Marii Dąbrowskiej," in her *Cudzoziemki. Studia o polskiej prozie kobiecej* (Warsaw: Wydawnictwo IBL, 1994), pp. 201–231, 239–248;

Wanda Chylicka, "W węzłach życia," *Więź*, 14, no. 4 (1971): 82–90;

Ewa Frąckowiak-Wiegandtowa, *Sztuka powieściopisarska Nałkowskiej* (Wrocław: Zakład Narodowy im. Ossolińskich, 1975);

Michał Głowinski, "Trzy poetyki *Niecierpliwych*," *Twórczość*, 3 (1959): 141–148;

Witold Gombrowicz, "O stylu Zofii Nałkowskiej," *Świat*, 5 (1936), pp. 8–9;

Krystyna Jakowska, *Międzywojenna powieść perswazyjna* (Warsaw: Wydawnictwo Naukowe PWN, 1992);

Jakowska, "Zofia Nałkowska. (Narrator autorski funkcją stylistyki i kompozycji)," in her *Powrót autora. Renesans narracji auktorialnej w polskiej powieści międzywojennej* (Wrocław: Zakład Narodowy im. Ossolińskich, 1983);

Hanna Kirchner, "O *Granicy* Zofii Nałkowskiej," in *Z problemów literatury polskiej XX wieku*, volume 2, edited by Stefan Żółkiewski, Henryk Wolpe, and Henryk Markiewicz (Warsaw: Państwowy Instytut Wydawniczy, 1965), pp. 330–367;

Kirchner, "Modernistyczna młodość Zofii Nałkowskiej," *Pamiętnik Literacki*, 1 (1968), pp. 67–109;

Kirchner, "'Najściślejsze zależności.' (Koncepcja osobowości w książce Zofii Nałkowskiej *Niedobra miłość*," in *O prozie polskiej XX wieku*, edited by A. Hutnikiewicz and H. Zaworska (Wrocław: Zakład Narodowy im. Ossolińskich, 1971), pp. 71–94;

Kirchner, "Nałkowska–prolegomena do Gombrowicza," in *Gombrowicz i krytycy* (Kraków: Wydawnictwo Literackie, 1984), pp. 573–586;

Ewa Kraskowska, "Niebezpieczne związki. Jeszcze raz o prozie Zofii Nałkowskiej," *Teksty Drugie*, 4 (1996): 71–91;

Maciej Podgórski, "Główne problemy analizy *Medalionów* Zofii Nałkowskiej," *Roczniki Humanistyczne*, 13, no. 1 (1966): 151–180;

Bogdan Rogatko, *Zofia Nałkowska* (Warsaw: Państwowy Instytut Wydawniczy, 1980);

Bruno Schulz, "Zofia Nałkowska na tle swojej nowej powieści," *Skamander*, no. 108–110 (1939): 166–176;

Bogdan Wojciechowski, "Niedobra miłość: Romans eksperymentalny," *Przegląd Humanistyczny*, 19, no. 8 (1975): 67–74;

Włodzimierz Wójcik, "Praca Nałkowskiej nad powieściami w świetle *Dzienników*," *Pamiętnik Literacki*, 58 (1967): 555–576;

Wójcik, *Zofia Nałkowska* (Warsaw: Wiedza Powszechna, 1973);

Danuta Zawistowska, "Elementy psychologizmu w neoromantycznej prozie Zofii Nałkowskiej," *Roczniki Humanistyczne*, 16, no. 1 (1968): 67–87;

Ewa Pienkowska, *Zofia Nałkowska* (Warsaw: Wydawnictwa Szkolne i Pedagogiczne, 1975);

Helena Zaworska, *"Granica" Zofii Nałkowskiej* (Warsaw: Wydawnictwa Szkolne i Pedagogiczne, 1991);

Zaworska, *"Medaliony" Zofii Nałkowskiej* (Warsaw: Państwowe Zakłady Wydawnictw Szkolnych, 1961);

"Zofia Nałkowska," in *Literatura polśka 1918–1975*, 2 volumes, edited by Alina Brodzka, Helena Zaworska, and Stefan Żółkiewski (Warsaw: Wiedza Powszechna, 1975, 1993), I: 639–644, II: 620–634.

Papers:
Zofia Nałkowska's manuscripts are housed in the Biblioteka Narodowa and the Muzeum Literatury im. Mickiewicza in Warsaw, and in the Biblioteka Jagiellońska in Kraków.

László Németh

(18 April 1901 – 3 March 1975)

István Chován
University of Debrecen

BOOKS: *Ortega és Pirandello* (Debrecen: Nagy Károly
 és Társai, 1933);
Ember és szerep (Kecskemét: Tanú, 1934);
Magyarság és Európa (Budapest: Franklin-Társulat,
 1935);
Gyász (Budapest: Franklin-Társulat, 1936);
Villámfénynél (Budapest: Tanú, 1937);
Bűn, 2 volumes (Budapest: Franklin-Társulat, 1937);
 translated by Gyula Gulyás and Anna Tauber
 as *Guilt* (Budapest: Corvina / London: Owen,
 1966);
Kocsik szeptemberben (Budapest: Franklin-Társulat,
 1937);
A Medve-utcai polgári (Kecskemét: Első Kecskeméti
 Hírlapkiadó, 1937);
Alsóvárosi búcsú, 2 volumes (Budapest: Franklin-Tár-
 sulat, 1938);
Berzsenyi (Budapest: Franklin-Társulat, 1938);
Kisebbségben (Budapest: Első Kecskeméti Hírlapki-
 adó, 1939; enlarged edition, 4 volumes,
 Budapest: Magyar Élet, 1942);
Szerdai fogadónap, 2 volumes (Budapest: Franklin-
 Társulat, 1939);
Magyar ritmus (Budapest: Mefhosz, 1940);
A minőség forradalma, 6 volumes (Budapest: Magyar
 Élet, 1940–1943);
Szekfű Gyula (Budapest: Bolyai Akadémia, 1940);
Téli hadjárat (Kecskemét: Első Kecskeméti Hírlapki-
 adó, 1940);
Készülődés a Tanu elótt, 2 volumes (Budapest: Magyar
 Élet, 1941);
A másik mester, 2 volumes (Budapest: Franklin-Társu-
 lat, 1941);
Cseresnyés (Budapest: Exodus, 1942);
Széchenyi: Vázlat (Budapest: Bolyai Akadémia, 1942);
Lányaim (Budapest: Turul, 1943);
Magam helyett: tanulmány az életemröl (Budapest:
 Turul, 1943);
Móricz Zsigmond (Budapest: Turul, 1943);
Emberi színjáték, 2 volumes (Budapest: Franklin-Tár-
 sulat, 1944);

Az értelmiség hivatása (Budapest: Turul, 1944);
A tanügy rendezése (Budapest: Sarló, 1945);
Széchenyi (Budapest: Misztótfalusi, 1946);
Eklézsia-megkövetés (Budapest: Misztótfalusi, 1947);
Iszony (Budapest: Nyugat, 1947); translated by Kath-
 leen Szász as *Revulsion* (London: Eyre & Spot-
 tiswoode, 1965; New York: Grove, 1966);

Égető Eszter (Budapest: Magvető, 1956);

II. József (Debrecen: Alföldi Nyomda, 1956);

Történeti drámák, 2 volumes (Budapest: Szépirodalmi, 1956)—comprises volume 1, *VII. Gergely, Husz János, Galilei, II. József;* volume 2, *Apáczai, Eklézsia megkövetés, Petőfi Mezőberényben, Széchenyi; Galilei*, translated by Ilona Duczynska as *Galileo* in *The Plough and the Pen: Writings from Hungary, 1930–1956*, edited by Duczynska and Karl Polanyi (London: Owen, 1963), pp. 142–165;

Társadalmi drámák, 2 volumes (Budapest: Szépirodalmi, 1958)—comprises volume 1, *Bodnárné, Villámfénynél, Papucshős, Cseresnyés, Erzsébetnap;* volume 2, *Győzelem, Mathiász-panzió, Szörnyeteg, Pusztuló magyarok, Sámson;*

Sajkódi esték (Budapest: Magvető, 1961);

Változatok egy témára (Budapest: Szépirodalmi, 1961);

A kísérletező ember (Budapest: Magvető, 1963);

Mai témák (Budapest: Szépirodalmi, 1963);

Irgalom, 2 volumes (Budapest: Szépirodalmi, 1965); excerpts translated as "Compassion," *Hungarian Survey* (1966): 125–136;

Újabb drámák (Budapest: Szépirodalmi, 1966);

Puskin (Budapest: Gondolat, 1967);

Kiadatlan tanulmányok, 2 volumes (Budapest: Magvető,1968);

Életműsorozat, 23 volumes (Budapest: Magvető-Szépirodalmi, 1969–1989);

San Remo-i naplo, edited by Szigethy Gabor (Budapest: Magvető, 1981);

Akasztofavirag: Aurel a Kekesre megy (Budapest: Magvető, 1985).

Edition in English: "The Faith of the Pedagogue," translated by Irving Dennis, in *Landmark: Hungarian Writes on Thirty Years of History*, edited by Miklos Szabolcsi and Zoltán kenyeres (Budapest: Corvina, 1965), pp. 243–246.

PLAY PRODUCTIONS: *Villámfénynél*, Budapest, Nemzeti Színház Kamaraszínháza, 30 March 1938;

VII. Gergely, Budapest, Nemzeti Színház, 13 May 1939;

Papucshős, Budapest, Nemzeti Színház, 4 November 1939;

Cseresnyés, Budapest, Nemzeti Színház, 10 January 1942;

Galilei, Budapest, Katona József Színház, 20 October 1956;

Széchenyi, Budapest, Madách Kamara, 14 May 1957;

A két Bólyai, Budapest, Katona József Színház, 20 April 1961;

Utazás, Budapest, Katona József Színház, 11 May 1962;

Nagy család, Veszprém, Petőfi Színház, 25 October 1963;

II. József, Budapest, Nemzeti Színház, 7 February 1964;

Mathiász-panzió, Budapest, Madách Kamara, 13 February 1965;

Petőfi Mezőberényben, Budapest, Irodalmi Színpad, 26 March 1966;

Szörnyeteg, Budapest, Katona József Színház, 30 September 1966;

Csapda, Miskolc, Nemzeti Színház, 7 October 1966;

Az áruló, Budapest, Madách Színház, 22 December 1966;

Apáczai, Veszprém, Petőfi Színház, 17 January 1969;

Gandhi halála, Győr, Kisfaludy Színház, 19 October 1969;

Az írás ördöge, Szeged and Hódmezővásárhely, Nemzeti Színház, 6–7 February 1970;

Bodnárné, Budapest, Madách Színház, 28 January 1971;

Erzsébet-nap, Debrecen, Csokonai Színház, 11 November 1971;

Győzelem, Veszprém, Petőfi Színház, 17 March 1972;

Sámson (opera), Budapest, Magyar Állami Operaház, 26 October 1973;

József és testvérei, Veszprém, Petőfi Színház, October 1974;

Négy próféta, Veszprém, Petőfi Színház, 29 October 1974;

Colbert, Budapest, Madách Kamara, 6 February 1976;

Bethlen Kata, Veszprém, Petőfi Színház, 25 February 1977;

Pusztuló magyarok, Veszprém, Petőfi Színház, 24 February 1978;

Eklézsia-megkövetés, Budapest, József Attila Színpad, 1 April 1978;

Husz János, Budapest, Nemzeti Színház, 28 March 1980;

Harc a jólét ellen, Veszprém, Petőfi Színház, 18 September 1981.

TRANSLATIONS: Thornton Wilder, *Caesar* (Budapest: Révai, 1948);

Alois Jirásek, *A kutyafejűek* (Budapest: Szépirodalmi, 1951);

Leo Tolstoy, *Anna Karenina* (Budapest: Szépirodalmi, 1951);

Vitalij Zahruthin, *Az úszó falu* (Budapest: Új Magyar, 1951);

Fjodor Gladhov, *Szabad élet* (Budapest: Új Magyar, 1952);

Maxim Gorky, *Nyaralók: Drama* (Budapest: Új Magyar, 1952);

Vaszilij Groszman, *Sztepan Kolcsugin* (Budapest: Új Magyar, 1952);

Ivan Alekszandrovics Goncsarov, *Oblomov* (Budapest: Új Magyar, 1953);

Jirásek, *Sötétség* (Budapest: Új Magyar, 1953);

Aleksey Tolstoy, *Első Péter. Regény* (Budapest: Új Magyar, 1953);

Jirásek, *Mindenki ellen* (Budapest: Szépirodalmi, 1954);

William Shakespeare, *V. Henrik. VI. Henrik* (Budapest: Új Magyar, 1955);

Leo Tolstoy, *Kreutzer-szonáta* (Budapest: Új Magyar, 1956);

Frederico García Lorca, *Yerma* (Budapest: Európa, 1957);

Henrik Ibsen, *A társadalom támaszai. Nóra. Rosmersholm* (Budapest: Európa, 1957);

Heinrich von Kleist, *Az eltört korsó* (Budapest: Európa, 1957);

Gotthold Ephraim Lessing, *Emilia Galotti* (Budapest: Táncsics, 1957);

Groszman, "Az igaz ügyért," *Nagyvilág* 1 (1958), pp. 5–18;

Thomas Middleton and William Rowley, *Átváltozások* (Budapest: Európa, 1961);

Aleksandr Pushkin, *Borisz Gosunov* (Budapest: Európa, 1964);

Martin Andersen Nexø, *Daangardi emberek* (Budapest: Gondolat, 1968).

SELECTED PERIODICAL PUBLICATIONS—UNCOLLECTED: "The Two Bolyais," *New Hungarian Quarterly*, 3 (1960): 115–138;

"If I Were Young Today," *New Hungarian Quarterly*, 5 (1962): 3–18;

"A Translator's Report," *New Hungarian Quarterly*, 1 (1964): 23–32;

"Small Nation, Great Soul," *Mosaic* (October 1967): 39–51.

László Németh, whose career spanned the period from the mid 1920s to the 1970s, was an outstanding figure in Hungarian intellectual and literary life. His novels have been translated into many languages, and his dramas are among the best of Hungarian dramatic literature. Németh was also important as a thinker and essayist.

Németh was born on 18 April 1901 in Nagybánya, Hungary (now Baia-Mare, Romania), to József Németh, a teacher, and Vilma Németh, née Gáal. Soon after his birth the family moved to Szolnok; in 1905 they moved to Budapest. Németh spent his summer vacations in the peasant household of his paternal relatives in Szilasbalhás; traces

Dust jacket for Németh's 1947 novel (translated as Revulsion, *1965) about a woman forced to marry a man who disgusts her*

of everyday peasant life appear in many of his short stories, novels, and dramas. Németh started his intellectual career after the Treaty of Trianon, one of the treaties that concluded World War I and resulted in the loss of two-thirds of Hungary's land and people. The loss of his birthplace shocked him, as it did many of his contemporaries, and anxiety over the fate of the nation was a theme of many of his essays.

In 1919 Németh began Hungarian and French studies at the University of Pest. A year later he registered in the Faculty of Medicine. After finishing his studies in 1925 he started a medical practice and married Ella Démusz.

Németh began his literary career the same year. His realistic short story about a peasant community, "Horváthné meghal" (The Death of Mrs. Horváth, 1925), was awarded first prize in a competition sponsored by the influential literary magazine *Nyugat* (West) and was published in the Christmas issue. (It was republished in the first volume of Németh's collected works in 1969.) This success opened his way to publication in many other periodicals, and his stories and critical pieces appeared in *Nyugat, Protestáns Szemle, Erdélyi Helikon*, and *Napkelet*. In his criticism he recognized the merits of such young Hungarian writers as Áron Tamási, Lőrinc Szabó, and Gyula Illyés; he also published essays on Luigi Pirandello, André Gide, James Joyce, and Aldous Huxley. He became friends with Mihály Babits, the most distinguished Hungarian writer of the time. He visited France and Italy in 1928 and began studying Greek culture.

In 1929 Németh's first novel, *Emberi színjáték* (The Human Comedy), was serialized in the literary magazine *Napkelet;* it was not published in book form until 1944. Like the author, the protagonist of the lengthy novel, Zoltán Boda, is a thinker, an eccentric, a lonely, rebellious hero who goes down to defeat—a modern Don Quixote.

In 1932 Németh founded, at his own expense, the periodical *Tanú* (Witness), for which he wrote all of the material. The journal ran for seventeen issues, ceasing publication in 1936. Németh also founded, with Pál Gulyás and Lajos Fülep, the periodical *Válasz* (Answer) in 1934; in addition, during this period he headed the literary department of Hungarian radio. Németh's essays in *Tanú* detailed his utopian social reform ideas. He believed that the decaying Hungarian nation could be saved by elevated spirituality, which would be achieved first by the intellectuals. He promoted a "third way," a Hungarian path independent of both socialism and capitalism. He argued that Hungary had to become a model for surrounding Eastern European countries.

In 1936 Németh lost his faith in government promises to introduce reforms. Recognizing the utopian nature of his ideas, without giving them up, he turned to literature, producing mostly novels and dramas. The novel *Gyász* (Mourning, 1936) and a drama, *Bodnárné* (Mrs. Bodnár), written around the same time but not published until 1958 and not staged until 1971, evoke the world of the peasantry. *Gyász* is a masterpiece that revolutionized the Hungarian novel. The heroine is a young widow, Zsófi Kurátor, who misses the opportunity for a happy life with a second husband because of her exaggerated mourning for her first husband. Zsófi becomes an unhealthy eccentric and recluse and ultimately goes insane. When her son becomes seriously ill, she is unable to realize the peril; his death only deepens her sorrow and solitude. Németh had created a new type of Hungarian novel, mixing psychological profundity and stream of consciousness narration with a realistic picture of social conditions. At the same time he creates a mythological resonance for his heroine, who resembles Sophocles' Antigone. The text is dominated by motifs of coffins, old age, stiffness, and blackness. *Bodnárné* is about the struggle of two brothers, one of whom remains a peasant while the other becomes an intellectual.

In *Villámfénynél* (By Lightning, 1937), *Papucshős* (Henpecked Husband, 1939), *Cseresnyés* (Cherry Orchard, 1942), and *Mathiász-panzió* (Mathiász Boarding House, 1965) noble intentions conflict with the unworthy environment that prevents their realization. Dramatic heroes, representing some noble ideas, rise above their community. Being aware of their calling they come into antagonism with their families and communities. These heroes are plain, everyday people who become valuable because of their sense of vocation. The main character of *Villámfénynél*, Dr. Imre Nagy, is a rural-district physician who after not finding happiness in his private practice decides to found a public clinic for those in need. His utopian attempt does not succeed, however, and his efforts are defeated.

VII. Gergely (Gregory VII, 1939) is one of Németh's most successful dramas. Pope Gregory is a typical Némethian hero. He pardons Emperor Henry at Canossa, and as a result he has to leave Rome. At the end of the drama Gregory is exiled at Salamanca and has to face his failure.

Németh was also a prolific novelist in the 1930s. *Bűn* (1937; translated as *Guilt*, 1966) depicts the world of the poverty-stricken people of Budapest. Lajos Kovács, a manservant, is given shelter by Dr. Endre Horváth, an intellectual who attempts to rise above the ills of society but is tormented by inner conflicts. As a result, he commits suicide, leaving Kovács to face an uncertain future. The novel is written in the realist tradition of Roger Martin du Gard, whose eight-volume novel series *Les Thibault* (1922–1940) inspired Németh to write his own novel series with the aim of providing a comprehensive social picture. Four novels of the planned seven were published: *Kocsik szeptemberben* (Wagons in September, 1937), *Alsóvárosi búcsú* (Downtown Parish Feast, 1938), *Szerdai fogadónap* (Reception Day on Wednesday, 1939), and *A másik mester* (The Other Master, 1941). The work was to follow the life of Peter Jó from his student days to his death. The published volumes describe his struggle with his father for his education, his studies and intellectual maturation, and his loves.

Németh's *Kisebbségben* (In Minority, 1939) gave rise to much heated debate. A survey of the history

Németh (right) with the Hungarian author Gyula Illyés

of Hungarian literature, it divides the authors into two groups: writers who expressed the spirit of the Hungarian nation and had tragic fates, and those who wrote shallow works and had successful careers. Németh stresses the importance of works that take upon themselves the teaching of the national heritage.

During the Soviet siege of German-occupied Budapest in 1944–1945, Németh stayed with Illyés. In March 1945 he and his family moved to Békésat at the invitation of the publisher Sándor Püski. Between the autumn of 1945 and December 1948 Németh taught at the Bethlen Gábor Reformed Secondary School at Hódmezővásárhely. In 1945 he worked for the journal *Válasz*. His novel *Iszony* (translated as *Revulsion*, 1965), which he had worked on since 1942, appeared in 1947 and brought him international fame. The heroine of the novel, Nelli Kárász, is the puritanical daughter of an impoverished tenant farmer. She is compelled to marry Sanyi Takaró, a rich, good-natured peasant. Nelli finds her husband's sexual advances revolting; only work gives meaning to her life. She creates a nice, neat home but is unable to accept the moral values of the society of their town, Fáncs. Her noble character grows coarse in the hell of her marriage, and in a struggle she kills her husband.

Égető Eszter, written in 1948 but not published until 1956, shows that Németh's faith in humanity had revived. This novel is his greatest epic venture, covering a fifty-year period. It is the story of Eszter Égető, who at the start of the century is an elementary-school student, up to 1948, when she is a grandmother deprived of her family. The most important elements in Eszter's life are her father, husband, and son. She is a submissive, self-denying creature, who finds the meaning of life in sacrifice willingly undertaken for others. The "hero" (Zoltán Boda) and "monster" (Zsófi Kurátor and Nelli Kárász) figures of Nemeth's earlier works are now joined by a new character, that of the "saint."

Németh's dramas written between 1945 and 1955 are mainly characterized by social struggle transferred into history. While *Erzsébetnap* (Celebrating Elisabeth, 1971) and *Pusztuló magyarok* (Perishing Hungarians, 1978), both written in 1946, turn again to peasant themes, *Széchenyi* (1957), *Husz János* (Jan Hus, 1980), *Eklézsia-megkövetés* (Public Penance, 1978), *Galilei* (1956; translated as *Galileo*, 1963), *II. József* (Joseph II, 1964), and *Apáczai* (1969) explore the secrets of historical figures. Németh's heroes are people such as Jan Hus or the tragic figure of Hungarian history, Count Istvál Széchenyi, whose rebellions are hopeless.

One of Németh's outstanding dramas is *Galilei*, which was performed on 20 October 1956, three days before the Hungarian revolt against the Soviets. The historical Galileo was compelled by the

Inquisition to recant his heliocentric teachings, but Németh's play has two endings: one shows a rebellious Galileo, the other a resigned compromiser who withdraws his teachings and reproaches himself for doing so. Still, even the tortured and struggling Galileo is not without hope: the young physicist Evangelista Torricelli continues his work.

In the late 1940s and for much of the 1950s Németh produced translations of foreign literature. The first, *Caesar*, by Thornton Wilder, appeared in 1948. He translated Leo Tolstoy's *Anna Karenina* (1874–1877) in 1951, for which he received the Attila József Prize. In the mid 1950s Németh began to suffer from recurrent illnesses.

In the last phase of his career Németh conducted a literary workshop in Sajkód. The repercussions of the 1956 revolution did not affect him, and in 1957 he was awarded the Kossuth Prize. He received the Herder Prize in 1965 and the Batsányi Prize in 1968.

Németh's last novel, *Irgalom* (excerpts translated as "Compassion," 1966), appeared in 1965. Its heroine, Ágnes Kertész, is a "saint" figure who succeeds in fulfilling her life, like Eszter Égető. The novel was the realization of an old theme Németh had worked on as early as the 1920s and 1930s. He does not try to evoke the age and the entire society in this psychological novel; it is a portrait of an individual. His dramas written in the 1960s are primarily biblical allegories. *Négy próféta* (The Four Prophets, 1974), written in 1964, and *József és testvérei* (Joseph and His Brothers, 1974), written in 1967, compare the savagery and vengefulness of Old Testament books with modern barbarism. The prophet—according to Németh's faith in morality and goodness—is the genius of love and humaneness. His last drama, *Az írás ördöge* (The Devil of Writing) was performed in 1970 by the Szegedi Nemzeti Színház. Németh died of a stroke on 3 March 1975.

Interviews:

Imre Monostori, *Beszélgetések Németh Lászlóval* (Budapest: Argumentum, 1992).

Bibliographies:

Albert Tezla, *Hungarian Authors: A Bibliographical Handbook* (Cambridge, Mass.: Belknap Press of Harvard University Press, 1970), pp. 442–448;

Németh László-Bibliográfia, compiled by István Hartyáni and Zoltán Kovács (Budapest: Petőfi Irodalmi Múzeum, 1992).

Biography:

László Vekerdi, *Németh László alkotásai és vallomásai tükrében* (Budapest: Szépirodalmi, 1970).

References:

Mihály Babits, "Könyvről könyvre: Tanú," *Nyugat*, 26 (1 February 1933): 187–189;

Babits, "Pajzzsal és dárdával," in *Írók két háború közt* (Budapest: Nyugat, 1941), pp. 213–239;

Ferenc Grezsa, *Németh László háborús* (Budapest: Szépirodalmi, 1985);

Grezsa, *Németh László Tanu-korszaka* (Budapest: Szépirodalmi, 1990);

Grezsa, *Németh László vásárhelyi korszaka* (Budapest: Szépirodalmi, 1979);

Lajos Hopp, "Németh László és a 'régi magyarság,'" *Irodalomtörténeti Közlemények*, 63 (1959): 287–306;

Géza Juhász, "Németh László regényei," *Protestáns Szemle*, 47 (September–October 1938): 461–466;

János Komlós, "Németh László: Bűn," *Új Hang*, 4 (April 1955): 105–108;

Péter Nagy, "Németh László történelmi drámái," *Iradolmtörténet*, 2 (1957): 179–182;

Károly Pap, "Németh László és a Tanú," *Nyugat*, 26 (16 May–1 June 1933): 646–649;

Péter Rényi, "Németh László: A két Bolyai," *Új Írás*, 1 (June 1961): 555–560;

György Rónay, "A kísérletező ember. Jegyzetek Németh László új könyvéről," *Új Írás*, 4 (April 1964): 242–249;

István Sőtér, "Egy klasszikus regény," *Válasz*, 8 (June–July 1948): 441–450;

Sőtér, "Németh László tanulmányai. (Készülődés; A minőség forradalma; Kisebbségben)," *Magyar Csillag*, 2 (15 November 1942): 344–350;

Gábor Szabolcsi, "A Magyar műhely' és a történelem parancsa," in *Író és valóság* (Szeged: Tiszatáj Irodalmi Kiskönyvtár, 1960), pp. 129–140;

Sophie Török, "Önéletrajz, generációs probléma, vagy amit akartok," *Nyugat*, 28 (March 1935): 201–212.

Vítězslav Nezval

(26 May 1900 – 6 April 1958)

Jiří Holý
Charles University, Prague

BOOKS: *Most* (Brno: Bedřich Kočí, 1922);
Pantomima (Prague: Ústřední studentské knihkupectví a nakladatelství, 1924);
Wolker (Prague: Ústřední studentské knihkupectví a nakladatelství, 1925);
Falešný mariáš (Prague: Jan Fromek, 1925);
Abeceda (Prague: Jan Otto, 1926);
Básně na pohlednice (Prague: Aventinum, 1926);
Diabolo (Prague: Vaněk & Votava, 1926);
Karneval (Prague: Jan Fromek, 1926);
Menší růžová zahrada (Prague: Jan Fromek, 1926);
Akrobat (Prague: Rudolf Škeřík, 1927);
Blíženci (Prague: Rozmach, 1927);
Dobrodružství noci a vějíře (Plzeň: V. Žikeš, 1927);
Nápisy na hroby (Prague: Jan Otto, 1927);
Edison (Prague: Rudolf Škeřík, 1928);
Manifesty poetismu, by Nezval and Karel Teige (Prague: Jan Fromek, 1928);
Židovský hřbitov (Prague: Jan Fromek, 1928);
Hra v kostky (Prague: Rudolf Škeřík, 1929);
Kronika z konce tisíciletí (Prague: Bohumil Janda, 1929);
Smuteční hrana za Otokara Březinu (Litomyšl: Josef Portman, 1929);
Sylvestrovská noc (Prague: Sfinx, 1929);
Básně noci (Prague: Aventinum, 1930);
Chtěla okrást lorda Blamingtona (Prague: Jan Fromek, 1930);
Jan ve smutku (Prague: Bohumil Janda, 1930);
Posedlost (Prague: Bohumil Janda, 1930);
Slepec a labuť (Prague: Ústřední studentské knihkupectví a nakladatelství, 1930);
Snídaně v trávě (Prague: Aventinum, 1930);
Strach (Prague: Ústřední studentské knihkupectví a nakladatelství, 1930);
Dolce far niente (Prague: Bohumil Janda, 1931);
Schovávaná na schodech (Prague: František Borový, 1931);
Sexuální nokturno (Prague: J. Štyrský, 1931);
Signál času (Prague: František Borový, 1931);
Tyranie nebo láska (Prague: František Borový, 1931);

Vítězslav Nezval

Milenci z kiosku (Prague: František Borový, 1932);
Pan Marat (Prague: Melantrich, 1932);
Pět prstů (Brno: B. Kilian, 1932);
Skleněný havelok (Prague: František Borový, 1932);
Jak vejce vejci (Prague: Družstevní práce, 1933);
Zpáteční lístek (Prague: František Borový, 1933);
Monaco (Prague: Mánes, 1934);
Sbohem a šáteček (Prague: František Borový, 1934);
Neviditelná Moskva (Prague: František Borový, 1935);
Anička skřítek a Slaměný Hubert (Prague: Dědictví Komenského, 1936);

52 hořkých balad věčného studenta Roberta Davida, anonymous (Prague: František Borový, 1936);

Frivolní báseň pro slečnu Marion (Prague: Vítězslav Nezval, 1936);

Praha s prsty deště (Prague: František Borový, 1936);

Řetěz štěstí (Prague: Václav Čejka, 1936);

Ulice Gît-le-coeur (Prague: František Borový, 1936);

Žena v množném čísle (Prague: František Borový, 1936);

Absolutní hrobař. Básně 1937 (Prague: František Borový, 1937);

Josef Čapek (Prague: František Borový, 1937);

Moderní básnické směry (Prague: Dědictví Komenského, 1937);

100 sonetů zachránkyni věčného studenta Roberta Davida, anonymous (Prague: František Borový, 1937);

Matka Naděje (Prague: František Borový, 1938);

Pražský chodec (Prague: František Borový, 1938);

70 básní z podsvětí na rozloučenou se stínem věčného studenta Roberta Davida, anonymous (Prague: František Borový, 1938);

Historický obraz (Prague: František F. Müller, 1939; expanded edition, Prague: Melantrich, 1945);

Pět minut za městem (Prague: František Borový, 1940);

Manon Lescaut: hra o sedmi obrazech podle románu Abbé Prévosta (Prague: Melantrich, 1940);

Loretka (Prague: Melantrich, 1941);

Balady Manoně (Prague: Melantrich, 1945);

Švábi (Prague: Svoboda, 1945);

Valérie a týden divů (Prague: František F. Müller, 1945);

Stalin (Prague: Československý spisovatel, 1949);

Veliký orloj (Prague: František Borový, 1949);

Zpěv míru (Prague: Československý spisovatel, 1950); translated by Jack Lindsay and Stephen Jolly as *Song of Peace* (London: Fore, 1951);

Z domoviny (Prague: Československý spisovatel, 1951);

Antonín Slavíček (Prague: Orbis, 1952); translated by Ilse Gottheiner as *Antonín Slavíček, a Great Czech Painter* (Prague: Artia, 1955);

Křídla (Prague: Československý spisovatel, 1952);

Tři mušketýři (Prague: Československý spisovatel, 1953);

Věci, květiny, zvířátka a lidé pro děti (Prague: SNDK, 1953);

Chrpy a města (Prague: Československý spisovatel, 1955);

Dnes ještě zapadá slunce nad Atlantidou (Prague: Československý spisovatel, 1956);

O některých problémech současné poesie (Prague: Československý spisovatel, 1956);

Veselá Praha (Prague: Dilia, 1957);

Z mého života, edited by Vlastimil Fiala (Prague: Československý spisovatel, 1959).

Editions and Collections: *Dílo Vítězslava Nezvala*, 38 volumes edited by Milan Blahynka and Jiří Taufer (Prague: Československý spisovatel, 1950–1990);

Nedokončená, edited by Fiala (Prague: Československý spisovatel, 1960);

Nový Figaro (Prague: Československý spisovatel, 1962);

Kůň a tanečnice, edited by Blahynka and F. Dvořák (Prague: SNKLU, 1962);

Jak se z klubíčka ježek vyklubal (Prague: SNDK, 1962);

Scénické básně, hry, scénária a libreta, 1920–1932, edited by Blahynka (Prague: Československý spisovatel, 1964);

Hry, rozhlasové hry a libreta (1935–1940), edited by Blahynka (Prague: Československý spisovatel, 1965);

Manifesty, eseje a kritické projevy z poetismu, 1921–1930, edited by Blahynka (Prague: Československý spisovatel, 1967);

Manifesty, eseje a kritické projevy z let 1931–1941, edited by Blahynka (Prague: Československý spisovatel, 1974);

Eseje a projevy po osvobození 1945–1948, edited by Blahynka (Prague: Československý spisovatel, 1976);

Kniha básní v próze. Básně v próze. Věci, květiny, zvířátka a lidé pro děti. Juvenilie. Náměty k filmům, edited by Blahynka (Prague: Československý spisovatel, 1985);

Veselá Praha. Překlady libret. Pásma. Písně, edited by Blahynka (Prague: Československý spisovatel, 1986);

Nezařazené básně. Balady Manoně. Kůň a tanečnice, edited by Blahynka (Prague: Československý spisovatel, 1988);

Pozůstalé básně. Melancholičtí upíři. Jitro. Říkadla. Štyrský a Toyen. Pražská domovní znamení, edited by Blahynka (Prague: Československý spisovatel, 1990).

Editions in English: "Night of Acacias" and "Panorama of Prague," translated by Ewald Osers, in *Heart of Europe: An Anthology of Creative Writing in Europe, 1920–1940*, edited by Klaus Mann and Hermann Kesten (New York: L. B. Fischer, 1943), pp. 521–522;

"Prague in the Mid-day Sun," "Night of Acacias," "Lilac," "Panorama of Prague," and "Better a Life of Toil. . . ," translated by Osers, in *Modern Czech Poetry*, selected by Osers and J. K. Montgomery (London: Allen & Unwin, 1945), pp. 53–58;

"Three Poems of Prague," translated by Osers, in *Hundred Towers: A Czechoslovak Anthology of Creative Writing*, edited by Franz C. Weiskopf (New York: Fischer, 1945), pp. 37–39;

"Hiss goes the rain in the rushes!" and "A Farewell—A Handkerchief," edited and translated by Alfred French, in *A Book of Czech Verse* (London: Macmillan, 1958; New York: St. Martin's Press, 1958), pp. 86–91;

"A Goodbye with a Scarf," "Sonnet from Krkonose," and "On the Limestone Highbroad," translated by Edith Pargeter, in *A Handful of Linden Leaves: An Anthology of Czech Poetry*, edited by Jaroslav Janů (Prague: Artia, 1960), pp. 28, 33, 40;

"The Batavian Tear," "A Goodbye with a Scarf," and "Edison (Part III)," translated by Pargeter and others, in *The Linden Tree: An Anthology of Czech and Slovak Literature, 1890–1960*, edited by Mojmír Otruba and Zdeněk Pešat (Prague: Artia, 1962), pp. 156–163;

"City of Spires," "Walker in Prague," "St. Wenceslas Square at Evening," "The Lilac by the Museum on St. Wenceslas Square," "The Bells of Prague," "Strangers' Faces," "The Clock in the Old Jewish Ghetto," "Balconies," "The Suburb," "Covered Market," "Panorama of Prague," "Old Prague in the Rain," "Obscure Hotels," "The Little City Square," "Four P.M. on a Certain Day in Spring," "Night of Acacias," "Chimneys," "Prague in Winter," "Prague in the Midday Sun," "Moon over Prague," and "Prague with Fingers of Rain," translated by Osers, in *Three Czech Poets: Vítězslav Nezval, Antonín Bartušek, Josef Hanzlík* (Harmondsworth, U.K.: Penguin, 1971), pp. 25–63;

Two poems for Roman Jakobson, *Cross Currents: A Yearbook of Central European Culture*, 2 (1993): 203–204.

PLAY PRODUCTIONS: *Depeše na kolečkách*, Prague, Osvobozené divadlo, 1926;

Pan Fagot a Flétna, Prague, Osvobozené divadlo, 1926;

Schovávaná na schodech, Prague, Stavovské divadlo, 1931;

Milenci z kiosku, Prague, Stavovské divadlo, 1932;

Strach, Plzeň, Studio Městského divadla, 1932;

Tři mušketýři, Prague, Městské divadlo na Král. Vinohradech, 1934;

Věštírna delfská, Prague, Nové divadlo, 1935;

Nový Figaro, Prague, Komorní divadlo, 1936;

Le petit riens, Prague, Stavovské divadlo, 1937;

Veselohra s dvojníkem, Brno, Dramatická konzervatoř, 1938;

Hlas lesa, Prague, Divadélko pro 99, 1940;

Zlověstný pták, Prague, Divadélko pro 99, 1940;

Manon Lescaut, Prague, D 40, 1940;

Loretka, Prague, D 41, 1941;

Dnes ještě zapadá slunce nad Atlantidou, Prague, Tylovo divadlo, 1956;

Jak se z klubíčka ježek vyklubal, Liberec, Severočeské loutkové divadlo, 1963.

MOTION PICTURES: *Varhaník u svatého Víta*, conceived by Nezval, directed by Martin Frič, 1929;

Ze soboty na neděli, script by Nezval, directed by Gustav Machatý, 1931;

Extase, script by Nezval and others, directed by Machatý, 1932;

Na sluneční straně, script by Nezval, Miroslav Disman, and Roman Jakobson, directed by Vladislav Vančura, 1933;

Za tichých nocí, script by Nezval, directed by Gina Hašler, 1941;

Bajaja, texts by Nezval, directed by Jiří Trnka, 1950.

TRANSLATIONS: Edgar Allan Poe, *Básně* (Prague: Rudolf Škeřík, 1928);

Dílo J. A. Rimbauda (Prague: Odeon-Družstevní práce, 1930);

Stéphane Mallarmé, *Poesie* (Prague: Rudolf Škeřík, 1931);

André Breton, *Spojité nádoby*, translated by Nezval and Jindřich Honzl (Prague: Mánes, 1934);

Breton, *Nadja*, translated by Nezval, Miloš Hlávka, and Bedřich Vaníček (Prague: František F. Müller, 1935);

Paul Éluard, *Veřejná růže*, translated by Nezval and Vaníček (Prague: Mánes, 1936);

Breton, *Co je surrealismus?*, translated by Nezval and Karel Teige (Brno: Joža Jícha, 1937);

Dora Gabe, *Dávno* (Prague: Dědictví Komenského, 1938);

Aleksandr Pushkin, *Povídky veršem a prózou* (Prague: Melantrich, 1938);

Nezami, *Příběh panice*, translated by Nezval and Jan Rypka (Prague: Evropský literární klub, 1939);

Raniero da Calzabigi, *Orfeus a Eurydika* (Prague: František F. Müller, 1940);

Heinrich Heine, *Kniha písní. Výbor z poezie* (Prague: Svoboda, 1950);

Pablo Neruda, *Juliu Fučíkovi* (Prague: Československý spisovatel, 1953);

Nezval in 1933

Mao Tse-tung, *Osmnáct básní na staré nápěvy*, translated by Nezval and Josef Hejzlar (Prague: Československý spisovatel, 1958);

Charles Baudelaire, *Květy zla*, edited by Blahynka (Prague: Mladá fronta, 1964);

Překlady 1, edited by Blahynka and Václav Kubín (Prague: Československý spisovatel, 1982);

Překlady 2, edited by Blahynka (Prague: Československý spisovatel, 1984).

Vítězslav Nezval was the most important Czech avant-garde poet of the period between the two world wars. Like fellow writers of that time, he combined literary modernism with revolutionary communist tendencies. Nezval was a prolific writer and his extensive body of work includes poems, plays, prose, and essays. His output was unequal in quality. His best works were his poems of the 1920s and 1930s. After World War II he became the official cultural agent of the communist regime in Czechoslovakia and the quality of his work deteriorated.

Nezval came from the countryside in south Moravia. He was born on 26 May 1900 in Biskoupky, where his father, Bohumil, a former pupil of the well-known composer Leoš Janáček, was a primary-school teacher; his mother's name was Emilie. In 1903 the Nezval family moved to the village of Šamikovice, where Nezval spent a large part of his childhood and to which he often returned on holiday. From 1922 to 1932, Nezval's parents lived in Dalešice and then later moved to Brno.

After graduating from secondary school in 1919, Nezval enrolled in the faculty of law in Brno. In 1920 he transferred to the faculty of arts at Charles University in Prague to study modern languages. He never finished his studies. In 1924 and 1925 he helped to edit *Masarykův slovník naučný* (Masaryk's Encyclopaedia, 1925–1933), and in 1927–1929 he was a literary adviser for the *Osvobozené divadlo* (The Liberated Theater). Otherwise, until 1945, he made his living by writing, translating, and scriptwriting.

Nezval made his debut as a poet in his secondary-school magazine in February 1919. He modeled himself on the Brno poet Jiří Mahen, who later became a friend. Nezval's poem "Podivuhodný kouzelník" (The Amazing Magician), published in the anthology *Devětsil. Revoluční sborník* (Devětsil. The Revolutionary Collection, 1922) and later in Nezval's *Pantomima* (Pantomime, 1924), helped establish him as the leading poet of his generation. A new artistic movement, poetism, took shape in *Devětsil. Revoluční sborník*. Nezval was its chief representative, along with the poets Jaroslav Seifert and Konstantin Biebl, the prose writer Vladislav Vančura, the essayist and theoretician Karel Teige, and the graphic artists Josef Šíma, Jindřich Štýrský, Toyen (Marie Čerminora), and František Muzika. Poetism, whose devotees associated themselves with the group Devětsil, was connected with a vision of communism that attracted the younger generation in the unsettled atmosphere of society after World War I. Nezval was a member of the Communist Party from 1924 until his death. Poetism, however, was not an attempt to speak for the poor but rather to provide a blueprint for a happy life. Trying to use poetic lyricism to come nearer to everyday life—to develop a new style of life, these artists were inspired not only by related avant-garde movements, such as Dadaism, and the poetry of Guillaume Apollinaire but also by the dynamism of their time and place and by big-city pleasures—the circus, jazz, silent movies, and modern civilization. Nezval's writings are not based on logical constructions; they rely on startling combinations and free association. The source of his stream of metaphors and memories is often the experiences and fantasies of childhood. Erotic images are also important. In this spirit Nezval wrote several books of poetry, including *Menší růžová zahrada* (A Small Rose Garden, 1926) and *Dobrodružství noci a vějíře* (Romantic Nights and Fans, 1927); stage plays such as *Milenci z kiosku* (Lovers in a Kiosk, 1932); prose works depicting the magic world of childhood such as *Dolce far niente* (1931); and imaginative stories for children, notably *Anička skřítek a Slaměný Hubert* (The Brownie Anička, and Hubert, the Straw Man, 1936), reminiscent of Lewis Carroll's *Alice in Wonderland* (1865). In addition, Nezval wrote screenplays for movies, most of which were never made. A few movies that were based on his ideas were conventional pieces, except for *Erotikon* (1929), directed by Gustav Machatý, for which Nezval did not receive screen credit. Nezval also wrote literary manifestos and essays, including the collection *Falešný mariáš* (A Sham Game of Cards, 1925). He led a bohemian life and was involved in various scandals. He enjoyed "dráždění měšťáků" (scandalizing the bourgeoisie) and later wrote, "This was a particularly happy time. I reveled in life. I was carefree in the pursuit of love."

Toward the end of the 1920s, Nezval's work, and poetism itself, changed. His long poem *Edison*, dedicated to the American inventor Thomas Alva Edison, was symptomatic of this change. It was published separately in 1928. The events of Edison's life provided the stimulus for Nezval to express the anxiety that comes with knowledge, as well as the risks and courage required for any creative work. The enthralling melody of the work comes from its rhythm, changes of intonation, and precise cyclic structure. Two refrains—"here there was something beautiful that crushes / courage and joy from life and death" and "here there was something burdensome that crushes / sadness, longing, angst from life and death"—express not only joy, but also a tragic outlook previously unknown in Nezval's work.

At the beginning of the 1930s a split developed in the avant-garde generation of artists. The great economic crisis, as well as the rise of Stalinism in the Soviet Union and fascism in Italy and Germany, created a more oppressive social atmosphere. Enthusiasm for revolution waned, and aesthetic poetism lost its initial impact. Some poets, including Seifert, returned to traditional poetry while others, such as Nezval and the theoretician Teige, tried to keep art "modern" and "revolutionary." In the poems of Nezval's collection *Sbohem a šáteček* (Farewell and Handkerchiefs, 1934), inspired by a journey through Europe, he restored poetic magic by introducing exotic faraway places. In the 1930s Nez-

val and Teige adopted surrealism and created the nucleus of the Czech surrealist school (founded in 1934). They cooperated closely with the French surrealists André Breton and Paul Éluard, whose highly successful visit to Prague in the spring of 1935 Nezval organized. He also translated their poetry. Surrealism, like poetism, was seen as a revolt against bourgeois society. Its aim was to free the imagination from the straitjacket of rational control; to shed light on the unconscious and repressed, mainly sexual, impulses; and to give free rein to "the principle of pleasure." The poems in Nezval's collections *Žena v množném čísle* (Woman in the Plural, 1936) and *Absolutní hrobař* (The Absolute Gravedigger, 1937) are darker, more staccato, and more full of sudden twists than his work of the 1920s: "The absolute gravedigger / Old as that granite country / from whose crib the tethered donkey drinks / the remainders of yesterday's storm. / He lifts up his head, hair like a burned steak / a mushroom has grown through his hat / He hangs his head over a hoe of a great bee sting."

Nezval also produced "antilyrical," militant poems that revealed his commitment to communism, including those in *Skleněný havelok* (The Glass Cloak, 1932). Socialist motifs also appear in the Robert David cycle, *52 hořkých balad věčného studenta Roberta Davida* (52 Bitter Ballads of the Eternal Student Robert David, 1936), where the lyrical hero is stylized as an unemployed intellectual. Nezval wrote the cycle in a strictly regular verse, in ballad and sonnet forms. He published the cycle anonymously, for in writing these poems he was at odds with surrealist doctrine. The Robert David poems caused a sensation, and the author was eagerly sought. Karel Čapek identified Nezval as the author on the basis of an analysis of the poems.

Between 1936 and 1938, after news of the Stalinist purges and trials in Russia, there were bitter quarrels between leftist and communist men of letters in Czechoslovakia. There was also a split in the surrealist group. Nezval, loyal to Stalinism, officially "disbanded" the group, but it continued to function under Teige's leadership. When he broke with the surrealists, Nezval's work lost some of its explosive sensuous quality. He resorted more and more to regular versification, using well-tried figures of speech and sentiment—as in his popular play *Manon Lescaut*, published in 1940, which was based on Antoine-François Prévost's novel of the same name (1731). In *Historický obraz* (A Historical Picture, 1939) Nezval began expressing his ideas in nonfigurative language.

During the repressive era of the German occupation (1942–1945) Nezval, like many other writers, could not publish his work. After the war he launched himself into public life with great enthusiasm. He became an important political activist and headed the motion picture department of the Ministry of Information from 1945 to 1950, when he suffered a heart attack. Nezval fully supported the Communist Party line, even after February 1948, when the communists took full power and introduced a totalitarian order in Czechoslovakia. The level of his poetic output visibly declined, becoming mere skillful rhetoric transforming political ideas into verse, as in *Stalin* (1949) and *Zpěv míru* (1950; translated as *Song of Peace*, 1951). In the mid 1950s Nezval attempted to return to his avant-garde style with *Chrpy a města* (Cornflowers and Cities, 1955). These late poems, and some of Nezval's public performances, when he refuted descriptive, didactic socialist realism, were an inspiration to a younger generation of writers—including Milan Kundera and Jiří Šotola—who cited Nezval in their fight against the deadening literary forms then in vogue. At the end of his life Nezval returned to the themes and avant-garde style of his stormy youth in *Z mého života* (From My Life), a memoir that appeared in the magazine *Kultura* (Culture) in 1957 and 1958 and in book form in 1959. He did not complete this memoir. In spring 1958, soon after returning to Prague from a trip to Italy, he suffered a fatal heart attack.

Letters:

Depeše z konce tisíciletí: korespondence Vítěslava Nezvala, edited by Marie Krulichová, Milena Vinařová, and Lubomír Tomek (Prague: Československý spisovatel, 1981).

Bibliography:

Vítězslav Nezval, edited by Milan Blahynka and Jaroslav Nečas (Prague: Mír, 1960).

Biographies:

Vlasta Fischerová-Nezvalová, *Kouzelná říše dětství Vítězslava Nezvala* (Prague: SNDK, 1962);

Jiří Svoboda, *Přítel Vítězslav Nezval* (Prague: Československý spisovatel, 1966);

František Hrubín, "Naše životy jsou jako noc a den," in his *Lásky* (Prague: Československý spisovatel, 1967), pp. 54–60;

Zdeněk Kalista, "Vítězslav Nezval," in his *Tváře ve stínu* (České Budějovice: Růže, 1969), pp. 195–216;

Jaroslav Seifert, "Láhev burgundského," in his *Všecky krásy světa: příběhy a vzpomínky* (Prague: Československý spisovatel, 1985), pp. 294–296;

Igor Inov, *Sud'ba i muzy Vitezslava Nezvala: po stranitsam vospominanii, dnevnikov, pisem, rukopisei . . .* (Moscow: Khudozhestvennaia literatura, 1990);

Julius Firt, *Knihy a osudy* (Brno: Atlantis, 1991);

Bedřich Fučík, "Svítání," in *Čtrnáctero zastavení,* edited by Vladimír Binar and Mojmír Trávníček (Prague: Melantrich, 1992), pp. 171–181.

References:

Milan Blahynka, *Nezval dramatik* (Prague: Divadelní ústav, 1972);

Blahynka, *Vítězslav Nezval* (Prague: Československý spisovatel, 1981);

Ljudmila Norayrovna Budagova, *Vítězslav Nezval: ocherk zhizni i tvorchestva* (Moscow: Nauka, 1967);

Peter Drew, *Devětsil und Poetismus* (Munich: Otto Sagner, 1975);

Vratislav Effenberger, "Tragédie básníka Vítězslava Nezvala," in his *Realita a poezie* (Prague: Mladá fronta, 1969), pp. 252–263;

Alfred French, "The Czech Lyric Poet Vítězslav Nezval," *Melbourne Slavonic Studies,* 2 (1968): 21–38;

French, "Nezval's Amazing Magician," *Slavic Review,* 32 (1973): 358–369;

French, *The Poets of Prague: Czech Poetry Between the Wars* (London: Oxford University Press, 1969);

Mojimír Grygar, "Nezval," in *Jak číst poezii,* second edition, expanded, edited by Jiří Opelík (Prague: Československý spisovatel, 1969), pp. 83–113;

Antonín Jelínek, *Vítězslav Nezval* (Prague: Československý spisovatel, 1961);

Jaromír Kabíček, ed., *Vítězslav Nezval–spolutvůrce pokrokové kulturní politiky* (Brno: Státní vědecká knihovna, 1986);

Marie Kubínová, "Vítězslav Nezval—představitel poetismu," in her *Proměny české poezie dvacátých let* (Prague: Československý spisovatel, 1984), pp. 37–80;

Milan Kundera, ed., *Podivuhodný kouzelník* (Prague: Československý spisovatel, 1963), pp. 7–30;

Graham Martin, introduction to *Three Czech Poets: Vítězslav Nezval, Antonín Bartušek, Josef Hanzlík,* translated by Ewald Osers and George Theiner (Harmondsworth, U.K.: Penguin, 1971), pp. 11–22;

Josef Vojvodík, "Proměny těla. K sémiotice tělesnosti v surrealistické lyrice Vítězslava Nezvala," in *Český surrealismus 1929–1953,* edited by L. Bydžovská and Karel Srp (Prague: Galerie hlavního města Prahy-Argo, 1996), pp. 170–199.

Papers:

Vítězslav Nezval's papers are in the Memorial to Czech Literature, Prague.

Laco Novomeský

(27 December 1904 – 4 September 1976)

Štefan Drug
Institute for Slovak Literature SAV

BOOKS: *Nedeľa* (Bratislava: DAV, 1927);

Romboid (Bratislava: Edícia Záhrada, 1932);

Marx a slovenský národ (Bratislava: DAV, 1933);

Otvorené okná (Prague: L. Mazáč, 1935);

Svätý za dedinou (Prague: Melantrich, 1939);

Pašovanou ceruzkou (Bratislava: Obroda, 1948);

Hviezdoslav (Bratislava: Tatran, 1949);

Výchova socialistického pokolenia (Bratislava: Pravda, 1949);

T. G. Masaryk (Bratislava: Pravda, 1950);

Vila Tereza (Bratislava: Slovenský spisovateľ, 1963);

Do mesta 30 minút (Bratislava: Slovenský spisovateľ, 1963);

Dobrý deň vám (Bratislava: Slovenský vydavateľstvo krásnej literatúry, 1964);

Nezbadaný svet (Bratislava: Slovenský spisovateľ, 1964);

Stamodtiaľ a iné (Bratislava: Slovenský spisovateľ, 1964);

Publicistika, 5 volumes, edited by Karol Rosenbaum (Bratislava: Epocha, 1969–1972)—comprises volume 1, *Znejúce ozveny. 1924–1932. Výber z politických statí a článkov* (1969); volume 2, *Čestná povinnosť. 1933–1944. Výber z politických statí a článkov* (1969); volume 3, *Manifesty a protesty. 1924–1937. Výber zo statí a príspevkov o kultúre a umení* (1970); volume 4, *Slávnosť istoty. 1938–1944. Výber zo statí a príspevkov o kultúre a umení* (1970); and volume 5, *Zväzky a záväzky. 1945–1950. Výber zo statí a článkov* (1972);

O literatúre (Bratislava: Slovenský spisovateľ, 1971);

Z piesní o jednote (Bratislava: Matica slovenská, 1971);

Moderní česká literatura a umění (Prague: Československý spisovatel, 1974);

Nový duch novej školy (Bratislava: SPN, 1974);

Z úrodných podstát človečích (Bratislava: Smena, 1975).

Editions and Collections: *Nedeľa. Romboid* (Prague: L. Mazáč, 1935);

Otvorené okná (Bratislava: Slovenský spisovateľ, 1964);

Laco Novomeský

Časová nečasovost, edited by Karol Rosenbaum (Prague: Československý spisovatel, 1967);

Znejúce ozveny, edited by Rosenbaum (Bratislava: Epocha, 1969);

Básnické dielo, 2 volumes, edited by Rosenbaum (Bratislava: Slovenský spisovateľ, 1971);

Básne (Bratislava: Slovenský spisovateľ, 1973);

Svätý za dedinou (Bratislava: Tatran, 1974);

Pašovanou ceruzkou (Bratislava: Slovenský spisovateľ, 1974);

Nedel'a (Bratislava: Smena, 1977);

Panychída za Ladislavom Novomeský, edited by Rosenbaum and Stanislav Šmatlák (Bratislava: Pravda, 1977);

Analyza (Bratislava: Slovenský spisovatel', 1979);

Desatročia do chivil' skl'bene (Bratislava: Smena, 1984);

Dielo, 2 volumes (Bratislava: Tatran, 1984);

Splátka vel'kého dlhu. Publicistika, volumes 1–2, 1963–1970 (Bratislava: Nadácia V. Clementisa, 1994).

OTHER: Vladimír Clementis, *Listy z väzenia*, edited by Novomeský (Bratislava: Tatran, 1968).

Ladislav (Laco) Novomeský was born on 27 December 1904 in Budapest to Samuel Novomeský, a tailor, and Irma Novomeský, née Príkovopová; they had gone there in search of work from Senica, a small town in western Slovakia. In 1918 the family, which included Novomeský's sister, Mária, returned to Senica. Novomeský studied at the teachers' college in Modra, taking the exit examination in June 1923. He became a teacher at a junior school in Bratislava, where he also enrolled at the Faculty of Arts of Comenius University. In the spring of 1924 he began editing the student literary monthly *Mladé Slovensko* (Young Slovakia); he turned it into a platform for the socialist-inclined intellectuals of the DAV group, of which he was a member. (The word *dav* means "masses"; the name also referred to the first initials of the founders of the group, Daniel Okáli, Andrej Sirácky, and Vladimír Clementis.) As a result, he was soon dismissed from the journal. In May 1925 he joined the staff of the Communist newspaper *Pravda chudoby* (Truth of the Poor) in the mining town of Ostrava in the Czech Republic.

Novomeský's debut poetry collection, *Nedel'a* (Sunday, 1927) documents the social problems of the day—including unemployment, poverty, tuberculosis, prostitution, and suicide—but its prevailing tone is the yearning for happiness of a melancholy young man who "so terribly, so boundlessly" loves life and "the things and trifles of this world." Novomeský's socially critical poetry was without precedent in Slovakia; older critics deemed it unfitting for a young state still finding its feet—the Czechoslovak Republic had been formed in 1918 from territories that had previously been part of the Austro-Hungarian Empire. They also upbraided the poet for the

Russian and French influences in his poetry and for shunning domestic traditions. *Nedel'a* fared better with the younger generation, which valued the poems for their "love of the world," "rare humanity," and melancholic timbre.

For almost four years—and on a minimal salary—Novomeský edited a workers' paper and was frequently imprisoned for violating press laws. He also found himself in conflict with dogmatic Communist Party officials who took exception to his bohemian leanings, "meek" poetry, and independence of thought. When he concocted an "interview" in which he suggested facetiously that he was "more devoted to wine than anything," "had never looked upon anything with reason," was constantly "hopelessly in love," and "lived only at night" and that the only Slovak literature he read was "the doggerel on lavatory walls," attempts were made to excommunicate him from the party. In a letter to a friend Novomeský compared himself to a certain fourteenth-century Turkish pasha to whom the sultan sent a silken rope so that he might hang himself.

Novomeský's next collection, *Romboid* (1932), brought accusations that he had betrayed revolutionary ideals. The collection represents the apex of experimental endeavors in Slovak poetry of the time, which were inspired by Czech "poetism" with its playfulness of form and joyous sentiments. Novomeský plays with words, metaphors, and verse forms and discovers unexpected associations and beauty in nature and everyday life, but an undertone of nostalgia and melancholy is present throughout. The work paved the way for surrealism in Slovak poetry.

In the spring of 1929 Novomeský started work in Prague as an editor in the Communist press, making his mark as an incisive political commentator. He took an active part in the nationwide L'avý front organization of intellectuals; he was a cofounder of the League of Proletarian Writers of Czechoslovakia but engineered its demise when he became convinced that such an association was an anachronism. In Prague he became friends with Czech avant-garde artists and scientists, including the poets Karel Teige, Jaroslav Seifert, and Vítěslav Nezval; the actors Jiří Voskovec and Jan Werich; and the linguists Jan Mukařovsky and Roman Jakobson. On 19 March 1932 Novomeský married Karla Marešová.

In his journalism Novomeský rejected nationalist passions and urged the necessity of making Slovaks equal with Czechs within Czechoslovakia. He warned of the danger of Nazism as

Adolf Hitler rose to power in Germany. In August 1934 he took part in the first Congress of Soviet Writers in Moscow. After his return home his articles and talks promulgated the ideas of Nikolay Bukharin and Karl Radek—who were executed in Russia a few years later—advocating a synthesis of socialist humanism and artistic avant-gardism. He championed and later translated the poetry of Boris Pasternak.

A new combined edition of *Nedel'a* and *Romboid* in 1935 was followed by the collection *Otvorené okná* (Open Windows, 1935). Novomeský here deepens his perception of the complexity of human existence, the beauty and the woes of life. He illuminates both the fleeting instant and the wisdom of the centuries. In the cyclical composition "Stretnutie" (Encounter) he employs epic elements, setting forth in poetic shorthand the tragic fate of victims of World War I and the migration of Slovaks to other lands. He sees beauty and pain as inseparable and highlights the moral strength of the ordinary suffering mortal. He does not pretend that poetry can change the course of the world; rather, the poet must rise above the grinding chaos of the world to see "purely the pure and beautiful." Critics praised Novomeský for closing his eyes neither to the horrors of the past nor to those of the present; he was declared the most Slovak poet and the most international, for he was able to link "the plains with the summits . . . volatility with melancholy, irrationalism with realism."

After the success of *Otvorené okná* Novomeský continued his political and journalistic work. He edited the Communist *L'udový denník* (People's Daily) and campaigned against international fascism and its domestic followers. In his essays he opposed isolationism, demanded contacts with the art world at large, and proposed a gathering of Slovak literati that took place at the end of 1936. He delivered the principal speech at the meeting, calling for a synthesis of "the humanism of the East and the refined form of the West."

In the autumn of 1936 Novomeský planned to make a lecture tour of the United States and Canada with a group of leftist intellectuals but was refused a passport. In January of the following year he took part in an international conference of artists and writers in aid of Republican Spain, and in the summer he attended a series of meetings of writers in Paris, Barcelona, Valencia, and Madrid. A visit to members of the International Brigade in Spain spawned a cycle of reports and antimilitarist poems. He warned unflaggingly

Title page for Novomeský's 1964 collection, which includes poems written while he was in prison

of the danger of a new world war. Although appalled by Joseph Stalin's show trials, he was persuaded of the need to support the Soviet Union as the only safeguard against fascism, a view to which he endeavored to win the participants at a gathering of PEN clubs in Prague in the summer of 1938.

When Hitler dismembered Czechoslovakia—the Germans occupied Czech lands in 1939 and compelled Slovak politicians to declare an "independent" state—Novomeský remained in occupied Prague. In July his son, Daniel, was born. At the end of November, Novomeský returned to Slovakia, no longer able to sustain the effort required to elude the Gestapo.

In *Svätý za dedinou* (Saint behind the Village, 1939) Novomeský presents himself as a journalist and politician who wants to help the suffering and the imperiled but sees that his efforts are futile, for humanity will not learn. The horrors occurring in the Soviet Union under Stalin show that a communist society is not the solution. The collection has a concentration of harrowing images from the Spanish Civil War—the graves of children, bombed towns—that few other poets have equaled. The speaker does not lose hope, however, but argues that the "wretched time of guns, daggers and lamenting" must pass. In almost every current fact he discovers ancient mythical echoes.

During World War II Novomeský was unemployed, then worked briefly as a clerk before returning to journalism. From the summer of 1943 he was a clandestine leader of the Communist Party and later of the underground Slovak National Council, which prepared armed resistance against the Germans and the collaborationist Slovak government. In April 1944 his daughter, Elena, was born. In October he flew to London as a member of a delegation of insurgents to negotiate with Czechoslovak president-in-exile Edvard Beneš and to inform the British public of the aims and significance of the uprising. In the meantime the Germans quashed the rebellion, and not until January 1945 was Novomeský able to return, through Moscow, to a liberated eastern Slovakia. In April he was appointed deputy chairman of the Slovak National Council and minister of education and information. In November 1946 his son died.

In 1948 the Communists took over the Czechoslovakian government and, at the behest of Moscow, began to hunt in their own ranks for "enemies and traitors" who were allied with "Western imperialists." Novomeský was accused—along with the minister of foreign affairs, Vladimír Clementis, and the future president, Gustav Husák—of bourgeois nationalism and was sentenced to ten years in prison. He was conditionally released after five years; forbidden to return to Bratislava or to publish, he took a job as an exhibition adviser at the Prague museum of literature. After confessing under torture to trumped-up crimes, he had been permitted to write poems in prison; he had been required to hand them over to the warden, in whose office they were typed out. Although Novomeský received copies, he and his fellow inmates used them as cigarette papers. The originals were not returned to him. After his release he reconstructed some of the works from memory.

When restrictions were relaxed in the 1960s, Novomeský published *Vila Tereza* (Villa Teresa, 1963), *Do mesta 30 minút* (Thirty Minutes to Town, 1963), and *Stamodtial' a iné* (From There and Others, 1964). *Vila Tereza* is a poetic account of the

celebrations at the Soviet embassy in Prague marking the anniversary of the Bolshevik revolution in Russia; the event brought together the flower of the Czech artistic and literary avant-garde. The work also promotes modern art, which the Czechoslovakian Communist regime had proscribed. *Do mesta 30 minút,* dedicated to the memory of Novomeský's friend Clementis, praises the poet's cherished hometown, Senica, and pays homage to simple people who have lived admirable lives in adverse conditions. *Stamodtial' a iné* includes the prison poems he was able to reconstruct, together with works written during his period of conditional release. Novomeský rejects the wiles of Galileo, who recanted before the Inquisition only to retain his views in private, seeing greater wisdom in the fairy-tale character who alone shouts out that the emperor is naked.

Novomeský died on 4 September 1976. His poetry is an artistic testimony to the cruel destiny of Slovakia in the twentieth century and provides a way for the Western world to understand what has happened in Central and Eastern Europe. Novomeský was a poetic virtuoso and a seer who experienced and expressed the suffering of modern humanity.

Letters:

Listy o DAVe, edited by Štefan Drug (Bratislava: Tatran, 1975);

Umenie politiky, politika umenia: Z listov Laca Novomeského, 3 volumes, edited by Drug (Bratislava: Tatran, 1988–1990).

Bibliographies:

Blažej Belák, *Ladislav Novomeský* (Martin: Matica slovenská,1976);

M. Zemánková, *Ladislav Novomeský* (Senica: Okresná knižnica,1984).

Biography:

Štefan Drug, *Dobrý deň, človek . . . Životopisné rozprávanie o mladosti Laca Novomeského* (Bratislava: Slovenský spisovateľ, 1983).

References:

Albin Bagin, "Epické prvky v poezii Laca Novomeského," *Slovenská literatúra,* 21 (1974): 596–613;

Ján Brezina, *Básnické dielo Laca Novomeského* (Bratislava: Veda, 1982);

Štefan Drug, "Z prazskych liet Laca Novomeskeho," *Slovenske pohľady,* 97 (December 1981): 15–22;

Viera Dubcová, "Dve podoby socialistickej poézie: N. Guillén – L. Novomeský," *Litteraria,* 22 (1980): 258–280;

Mária Hagárova, *Ladislav Novomeský: 1904–1976* (Martin: Matica slovenská, 1979);

Zdenka Holotíková, *Ladislav Novomeský* (Bratislava: Pravda, 1981);

Ivan Kamenec, "Historizmus v diele Ladislava Novomeského," *Historický časopis,* 25 (1977): 159–186;

Zlatko Klátik, "Príbuznost typov socialistickej poézie. S. Kosovel– J. Wolker–L. Novomeský," *Litteraria,* 22 (1980): 136–157;

Kochol, "Novomeský a Wolker," *Slovenská literatúra,* 21 (1974): 583–595;

Alexander Matuška, "Úsilie o celistvý obraz človeka v poézii L. Novomeského," *Slovenská literatúra,* 22 (1975): 248–260;

Matuška, "Vyznam Novomeskeho pre formovanie socialistickej literatury," *Slovenská literatúra,* 18 (1971): 340–348;

S. V. Nikol'skij, "J. Wolker a L. Novomeský," *Slovenská literatúra,* 21 (1974): 624–631;

Ludvik Patera, "Neznamy prispevek L. Novomeského k problematice vztahu česke a slovenske literatury," *Slovenská literatúra,* 27 (1980): 80–87;

Vladimír Reisel, *Poézia Laca Novomeského* (Bratislava: SAVU, 1946);

Karol Rosenbaum, "Zapas o osobnost," *Slovenske pohl'ady,* 98 (January 1982): 100–106;

Rosenbaum and Stanislav Šmatlák, *Panychida za Ladislavom Novomeskym* (Bratislava: Pravda, 1977);

Rosenbaum and Šmatlák, eds., *Nenáhodné stretnutia: Zbornik o diele Laca Novomeského v socialistickom svete* (Bratislava: Slovensky spisovatel', 1974);

Šmatlák, *Básnik Laco Novomeský,* second edition (Bratislava: Slovenský spisovatel', 1984);

Šmatlák, ed., *Keď nevystačia slová: State o Lacovi Novomeskom* (Bratislava: Vydavateľstvo SAV, 1964);

Šmatlák and Michael Daehne, "Poézie jako umeni videt," *Literarni mesičnik,* 9 (1980): 70–77;

František Štraus, "Veršová kompozícia v poézii Laca Novomeského," *Slovenská literatúra,* 31 (1984): 484–501;

Viliam Turčány, "Na okraj rýmu v poézii Laca Novomeského," *Slovenská literatúra,* 12 (1965): 32–63;

Papers:

Laco Novomeský's papers are in the Slovenský národný archív, Bratislava, and the Archív literatúry a umenia Matice slovenskej, Martin, Slovakia.

Jiří Orten

(30 August 1919 – 1 September 1941)

Jiří Holý
Charles University, Prague

BOOKS: *Čítanka jaro,* as Karel Jílek (Prague: Václav Petr, 1939);

Cesta k mrazu, as Jílek (Prague: Václav Petr, 1940);

Jeremiášův pláč, as Jiří Jakub (Prague: Privately printed by Zdeněk Urbánek, 1940);

Ohnice, as Jakub (Prague: Melantrich, 1941);

Elegie (Prague: Čin, 1946); translated by Lyn Coffin and Eva Eckert as *Elegie–Elegies* (Washington, D.C.: SVU Press, 1980);

Dílo Jiřího Ortena, edited by Václav Černý (Prague: Václav Petr, 1947);

Deníky Jiřího Ortena: Poesie, myšlenky, zápisky, edited by Jan Grossman (Prague: Československý spisovatel, 1958);

Eta, Eta, žlutí ptáci, edited by Marie Rút Křížková and Karel Svátek (Liberec: Severočeské nakladatelství, 1966);

Pro děti: Knížka naslouchajícím, edited by Křížková and Karel Svátek (Liberec: Severočeské nakladatelství, 1967);

Převleky, edited by Křížková and Svátek (Liberec: Severočeské nakladatelství, 1968);

Tisíc nahých trápení, edited by Jan Adam (Prague: Československý spisovatel, 1985);

Veliké stmívání, edited by Jiří Holý (Prague: Odeon, 1987);

Červený obraz, edited by Marie Langerová (Prague: Československý spisovatel, 1991);

I v blátě snít, edited by Jaromír Hořec (Prague: Votobia, 1999).

Editions and Collections: *Ohnice,* edited by Bohuslav Březovský (Prague: Československý spisovatel, 1964);

Čemu se báseň říká, edited by Josef Kocián and Marie Rút Křížková (Prague: Československý spisovatel, 1967);

Hrob nezavřel se: Výbor z díla, edited by Jana Štroblová (Prague: Mladá fronta, 1969; enlarged, 1994);

Verše, edited by Křížková and Jitka Vrbová (Prague: Odeon, 1970);

Citový průvodce po Kutné Hoře (Prague: Privately printed by Jiří Franěk, 1991);

Spisy, 6 volumes published, edited by Křížková and Ota Ornest (Prague: Český spisovatel, 1992–1998);

Čechy za oknem smutných duší, edited by Ornest and Marie Borešová (Prague: Paseka, 1993).

Although Jiří Orten was only twenty-two when he died in 1941, he left behind a significant body of work, especially poetry. Orten belonged to the "war generation," writers who began working at the end of the 1930s and set themselves in opposition to the previous generation of avant-garde writers. Partly because of the author's early death, Orten's poetry was regarded with almost cultlike devotion after World War II; young poets used it as a source of inspiration into the 1970s.

Orten was born Jiří Ohrenstein on 30 August 1919 in the ancient town of Kutná Hora in central Bohemia to Eduard and Berta Orten, née Rosenzweig. His father was a middle-class businessman, and his mother was an actress in the local amateur theater. Orten's uncle on his mother's side, Josef Rosenzweig-Moir, had been an anarchist poet at the beginning of the twentieth century. Orten's older brother, Ota, wrote poetry, acted, and directed plays under the pseudonym Ota Ornest; his younger brother, Zdeněk, became a well-known actor after World War II, using the stage name Zdeněk Ornest.

When he was sixteen and seventeen Orten published poetry and essays in the periodicals *Haló noviny* and *Mladá kultura.* He did not complete secondary school but followed Ota to Prague to study drama at the Prague conservatory in 1937, supporting himself as an archivist. He also acted in experimental theater and published poetry and essays. In the summer of 1938 he spent a month in Paris. It was his only trip abroad; after Bohemia and Moravia were occupied by German

Jiří Orten

troops in March 1939, he was no longer allowed to travel because he was Jewish. Ota and some of Orten's friends escaped to Great Britain in the summer of 1939; Orten refused to go with them, probably afraid that he would lose his poetic inspiration if he left his homeland.

Orten's point of view was quite different from that of avant-garde poets such as Vítězslav Nezval, Jaroslav Seifert, and Konstantin Biebl, who had started writing in the 1920s. Admiring the Russian Revolution and predicting a glorious future, the avant-garde poets aimed to conquer and transform the world with their poetry. Orten and other war generation poets—including Kamil Bednář, Zdeněk Urbánek, Ivan Blatný, Josef Kainar, and Jiří Kolář—were deeply affected by the catastrophe of World War II. They did not trust

"great ideas" or universal truths and did not believe that they could see into the future. They concentrated on the present as they experienced it and on the actual plight of human beings. The poet was no longer an adventurer, an explorer, or a joyful conqueror but a perceptive, anxious, and attentive "witness." On 19 March 1939 Orten wrote in his diary, "I have been born on this earth for nothing else except to bear witness, being tied down by my weight, by my heaviness and by my lightness."

Published posthumously in 1958 as *Deníky Jiřího Ortena: Poesie, myšlenky, zápisky* (Diaries of Jiří Orten: Lyrics, Ideas, Notes), Orten's diaries are his most extensive and significant work. They were kept in three volumes, which he named according to the colors or designs of their covers:

"Modrá kniha" (The Blue Book) covers the period from early 1938 to December 1939; "Žíhaná kniha" (The Striped Book) extends from December 1939 to December 1940; and "Červená kniha" (The Red Book) covers the period from December 1940 to 29 August 1941, the day before the traffic accident that ended his life. The diaries include all of Orten's poems, both those in the three collections published during his lifetime and those in two volumes he had readied for publication that came out after his death. They also include excerpts from books he had read and records of his dreams, conversations, and letters.

Among the personal matters described in the diaries is Orten's stormy relationship with the actress Věra Fingerová. In the summer of 1938 Orten, who did not believe that he had fathered the child she was expecting, refused to marry her, and Fingerová had an abortion. The relationship ended in late 1940 with what Orten saw as her "betrayal." Thenceforth Orten tormented himself and those around him with his grief over his lost love.

The diaries do not include some of Orten's attempts at prose and dramatic works, such as the novel "Malá víra" (Little Faith), written in 1938–1939 and published in 1966 in the collection *Eta, Eta, žlutí ptáci,* (Eta, Eta, Yellow Birds [*Eta* is a nonsense word]) or the horrifying, dreamlike title story of that collection, written in December 1938. Orten's unpublished play *Blahoslavení tiší* (Blessed Are the Quiet, 1941) was inspired by the story "Florián" in his friend Urbánek's *Úžeh tmou* (Sunstroke from Darkness, 1940).

Orten's poems are tuneful, make use of suggestive repetitions, and always lead to a climax. A statistical analysis has shown that *smrt* (death), *láska* (love), *Bůh* (God), *sen* (dream), and *bolest* (pain) are the most often repeated nouns in Orten's diaries, and they are frequent themes in his poetry. His first work, *Čítanka jaro* (Reader of Spring, 1939), published under the patronage of his older friend and fellow war generation poet František Halas, as well as some of the poems in *Cesta k mrazu* (The Journey toward Frost, 1940) and *Ohnice* (Charlock, 1941), are characterized by a sense of an intimate relationship to all living creatures. Love is seen as total fulfillment, repose, and security; the beloved merges with the image of the mother. Death is projected through images of destruction, passing, and parting. The lyrical hero defends himself from the insensitive "big world" by enclosing himself in a small one that is permeated by a feeling of security.

In the summer of 1940 Orten worked as a laborer on a farm in Kutná Hora. When he returned to Prague, he was not allowed to leave again because he was Jewish. He was increasingly isolated: he was expelled from the conservatory and could only rarely meet with his friends; his father had died in 1936; his mother had remained in Kutná Hora; his brother Zdeněk was placed in a Jewish orphanage in Prague; and his relationship with Fingerová had ended. He took odd jobs, such as shoveling snow, and for a time was on the staff of the periodical *Židovské listy* (The Jewish Newsletter); but it was risky for him to publish, even under a pseudonym. Nevertheless, he went on writing feverishly, mainly poetry. He found inspiration in the Old Testament, as illustrated in the long poem *Jeremiášův pláč* (The Lamentations of Jeremiah, 1940). His poems became more dissonant, harsh, and aggressive, especially the series "Scestí" (Led Astray), included in the posthumously published *Dílo Jiřího Ortena* (Jiří Orten's Works, 1947). The motif of death emerges with terse and cruel insistence, as in "Černý obraz" (A Black Picture) in *Ohnice*: "Hle, pomatení biřici / jdou bohaprázdnou ulicí / životy zhasínat" (Look, lunatic bailiffs / going along a godless street / to snuff out lives). The poet carries on dialogues with himself as a child, with his former girlfriend, and with God in the nine extensive poems in *Elegie* (1946; translated as *Elegies*, 1980). Ultimately he finds only one solution: to accept the desperate situation without any consoling illusions, to hold out in spite of everything, and to "sing until the end." In July 1940 Orten wrote in his diary: "Miluji velmi slepce, kteří se učí chodit bez bílé hole. At' padají, at' klopýtají, ale chodí, podepřeni sami o sebe" (But I adore those blind people, who try to walk without a white stick. They may keep falling over, they may keep stumbling, but they do manage to walk, supporting themselves).

On 30 August 1941, his twenty-second birthday, Orten was hit by a German ambulance in a Prague street. A friend took him to the public infirmary; but Orten could not be admitted because he was Jewish, and he had to be moved to a different hospital. He died two days later.

In 1945 Orten's friends and some younger poets formed a group that they named for his collection *Ohnice*. After the beginning of Communist totalitarianism in February 1948 Orten's works were judged unacceptable; his poems were seen as "poetry of the dying upper classes" and "degenerative muck." These condemnations were similar to statements made in the anti-Semitic newspapers during World War II, which had characterized Orten's poetry as "Jewish perversion" and "degeneration of morality." Nevertheless, Czech poets of the 1960s such as Josef Hanzlík, Jiří Gruša, Antonín Brousek, and Ivan Wernisch admired Orten for his emphasis on morality, personal responsibility, and purity. His poetry became a model for the work of many young Czech authors in the 1960s and the 1970s.

Letters:

Sám u stmívání: Básníkova korespondence s matkou, doplněná básněmi, prózou, výpisky z deníků a citáty, edited by Zdeněk Ornest (Prague: Mladá fronta, 1982);

Hořký kruh: Korespondence s Věrou Fingerovou, edited by Jarmila Víšková and Jaroslava Jiskrová (Prague: Torst, 1996).

Biographies:

Ota Ornest, "O bratrovi," in Orten's *Deníky Jiřího Ortena: Poesie, myšlenky, zápisky,* edited by Jan Grossman (Prague: Československý spisovatel, 1958), pp. 459–468;

Ornest, "Nebudu dobrá píšťalka!" in Orten's *Červená kniha,* edited by Marie Rút Křížková (Prague: Český spisovatel, 1994), pp. 261–281;

Zdeněk Urbánek, "Podoba Jiřího Ortena," in Orten's *Deníky Jiřího Ortena,* pp. 33–42.

References:

Kamil Bednář, ed., *Za Jiřím Ortenem* (Prague: Václav Petr, 1945);

Antonín Brousek, "Hrst kamínků na nepřítomný hrob Jiřího Ortena," in Orten's *Čemu se báseň říká,* edited by Josef Kocián and Marie Rút Křížková (Prague: Československý spisovatel, 1967), pp. 9–26;

Václav Černý, "Básnický profil Jiřího Ortena," in his *Tvorba a osobnost I,* edited by Jan Šulc (Prague: Odeon, 1992), pp. 701–709;

George Gibian, "Jiří Orten's *Elegies,*" in Orten's *Elegie–Elegies,* translated by Lyn Coffin and Eva Eckert (Washington, D.C.: SVU Press, 1980), pp. v–ix;

Jan Grossman, "Deníky Jiřího Ortena," in his *Analýzy,* edited by Jiří Holý and Terezie Pokorná (Prague: Československý spisovatel, 1991), pp. 201–224;

Holý, "Smrt proměněná v poezii," in Orten's *Veliké stmívání,* edited by Holý (Prague: Odeon, 1987), pp. 189–196;

Kocián, *Jiří Orten* (Prague: Československý spisovatel, 1966);

Křížková, "Nad knihami Jiřího Ortena," in Orten's *Červená kniha,* edited by Křížková (Prague: Český spisovatel, 1994), pp. 282–321.

Papers:

Jiří Orten's papers are in the Memorial to Czech Literature, Prague.

Teodor Parnicki

(5 March 1908 – 5 December 1988)

Wojciech Skalmowski
University of Louvain

BOOKS: *Aecjusz, ostatni rzymianin* (Warsaw: Rój, 1937);

Srebrne orły: Powieść z przełomu wieków X i XI, 2 volumes (Jerusalem: W drodze, 1944, 1945; Wrocław: Książnica-Atlas, 1949);

Koniec "Zgody Narodów": Powieść z roku 179 przed narodzeniem Chrystusa, 2 volumes (Paris: Institut Littéraire, 1955);

Opowiadania (Warsaw: Instytut Wydawniczy PAX, 1958);

Słowo i ciało: Powieść z lat 201–203 (Warsaw: Instytut Wydawniczy PAX, 1959);

Twarz księżyca, 3 volumes (Warsaw: Instytut Wydawniczy PAX, 1961–1967)—comprises volume 1, *Powieść z wieków III–IV* (1961); volume 2, *Opowieść bizantyńska z roku 450* (1961); volume 3, *Część trzecia* (1967);

Nowa baśń, 6 volumes (Warsaw: Państwowy Instytut Wydawniczy, 1962–1970)—comprises volume 1, *Robotnicy wezwani o jedenastej* (1962); volume 2, *Czas siania i czas zbierania* (1963); volume 3, *Labirynt* (1964); volume 4, *Gliniane dzbany* (1966); volume 5, *Wylęgarnie dziwów* (1968); volume 6, *Palec zagrożenia* (1970);

Tylko Beatrycze: Powieść historyczna (Warsaw: Instytut Wydawniczy PAX, 1962);

I u możnych dziwny. Powieść z wieku XVII (Warsaw: Instytut Wydawniczy PAX, 1965);

Koła na piasku: Powieść z roku 160 przed narodzeniem Chrystusa (Warsaw: Instytut Wydawniczy PAX, 1966);

Śmierć Aecjusza: Powieść z lat 451–457 (Warsaw: Instytut Wydawniczy PAX, 1966);

"Zabij Kleopatrę" (Warsaw: Instytut Wydawniczy PAX, 1968);

"Inne życie Kleopatry": Powieść z wieku XIX (Warsaw: Instytut Wydawniczy PAX, 1969);

Muza dalekich podróży: Powieść (Warsaw: Instytut Wydawniczy PAX, 1970);

Tożsamość: Powieść (Warsaw: Czytelnik, 1970);

Przeobrażenie: Powieść (Warsaw: Instytut Wydawniczy PAX, 1973);

Staliśmy jak dwa sny (Warsaw: Instytut Wydawniczy PAX, 1973);

Rodowód literacki (Warsaw: Instytut Wydawniczy PAX, 1974); enlarged as *Historia w literaturę przekuwana* (Warsaw: Czytelnik, 1980);

Hrabia Julian i król Roderyk: Powieść historyczna (Poznań: Wydawnictwo Poznańskie, 1976);

Sam wyjdę bezbronny: Powieść historyczno-fantastyczna w trzech częściach (Warsaw: Instytut Wydawniczy PAX 1976);

Szkice literackie (Warsaw: Instytut Wydawniczy PAX, 1978);

Dary z Kordoby: Powieść na tle przełomu lat 1018 i 1019 (Poznań: Wydawnictwo Poznańskie, 1981);

Rozdwojony w sobie (Warsaw: Instytut Wydawniczy PAX, 1983);

Sekret trzeciego Izajasza (Warsaw: Czytelnik, 1984);

Kordoba z darów: Powieść na tle dziejów XI wieku (Poznań: Wydawnictwo Poznańskie, 1988);

Opowieść o trzech Metysach, 2 volumes (Warsaw: Noir sur blanc, 1992)—comprises volume 1, *Raczej jednak oni;* volume 2, *Raczej ja.*

PLAY PRODUCTION: *Mandżukuo (Walka o Wschód): Sztuka w 6 odsłonach,* Łódź, Teatr Popularny, 28 September 1934.

SELECTED PERIODICAL PUBLICATION— UNCOLLECTED: "Trzy minuty po trzeciej," *Lwowski Kurier Poranny* (1929–1930).

Teodor Parnicki is regarded in Poland as one of the country's most original and important twentieth-century novelists, but he is virtually unknown in the West, and none of his books have been translated into English, French, or German. His genre is conventionally described as the historical novel, but this designation is not wholly adequate because of the elements of science fiction and fantasy in his works—especially the later ones. His writing has affinities with that of Jorge Luis Borges and Vladimir Nabokov, but without the elegant brevity of the first or the dazzling brilliance of the second. His early novels impart a feeling of the complexity and ambiguity of history and of existence in general; his later works embody a nearly solipsistic vision of the world as a reflection of the consciousness of the author, in which his personal experiences, reconstructions of historical events, and reminiscences of other literary works are blended. Only his earlier books are popular in Poland; his later novels discourage many readers with their obscurity and longueurs. Parnicki has, however, a small but devoted following of readers who enjoy immersing themselves in this strange literature.

Parnicki's paternal ancestors came from Wielkopolska, a northwestern province of Poland that had belonged to Prussia since the end of the eighteenth century. Parnicki's grandfather August Parnitzki was a noncommissioned officer in the Prussian army during the Franco-Prussian War in 1870; later he settled in Russia, where he worked as a technician. Parnicki's father, Bronisław Parnicki, studied engineering at Kiev University but was dismissed for social-democratic political activity. He married his Jewish fiancée from Kiev, Augustyna Piekarska, and completed his studies in Berlin, where Teodor Parnicki was born on 5 March 1908. The family returned to Russia at the beginning of 1911, and Bronisław Parnicki obtained work as an engineer in Moscow. Since his German citizenship could have led to his internment during World War I, the family moved to the provincial town of Ufa to escape the attention of the authorities. After the death of his wife in 1918 Bronisław married a Russian woman, who resented Teodor and his younger brother. For that reason Parnicki was sent in 1919 to a military preparatory school in Omsk that was soon evacuated to Vladivostok because of the civil war. He never saw his father again; Bronisław Parnicki died in 1928.

In 1920 Parnicki ran away from the school and went to Harbin in Manchuria, where he expected to meet a friend of his father. Although Parnicki did not find this individual, the large Polish colony adopted the boy and sent him to the local Polish high school, from which he graduated in 1927. This was the period of his reintegration into Polish language and culture (at home he had spoken Russian almost exclusively). He became fascinated with Polish literature, espe-

Teodor Parnicki

cially poetry of the Romantic period. Reading historical novels by the popular Polish author Henryk Sienkiewicz led Parnicki to resolve at the age of fifteen to become a Polish-language writer of historical fiction.

After graduation from high school Parnicki received, on the recommendation of his teachers and the Polish consul in Harbin, a scholarship from the government of the newly independent Poland. In 1928 he enrolled at Jan Kazimierz University in Lwów (now L'viv, Ukraine) to study literature; he also took courses in English and Oriental philology. He never formally completed his studies. In 1929–1930 he published his first novel, a thriller titled "Trzy minuty po trzeciej" (Three Minutes Past Three), in installments in

Dust jacket for Parnicki's historical "quasi-novel," published in 1970, which consists of fragments of two historical fictions linked by reminiscences of his childhood in Russia

the local journal *Lwowski Kurier Poranny* (Lwów Morning Courier); it was never published separately. He wrote book reviews, short stories on historical subjects, and studies of historical fiction and Russian literature for other Polish periodicals; the stories were collected in *Opowiadania* (Short Stories, 1958), and a selection of the literary studies appeared in *Szkice literackie* (Literary Essays, 1978). Between 1933 and 1939 the University of Lwów, which had no Russian department, regularly invited him to lecture on Russian literature. In 1933 he was admitted to the Lwów branch of the Zawodowy Związek Literatów Polskich (Professional Union of Polish Writers). His play, *Mandżukuo (Walka o Wschód)* (Manchukuo [Struggle for the East]), was staged by the Teatr Popularny in Łódź in 1934; it was a spectacular failure. That same year he entered an historical novel, *Hrabia Julian i król Roderyk* (Count Julian and King Roderick), about Visigoth Spain just before the Muslim conquest in the eighth century, in a literary competition organized by the journal *Ilustro-*

wany Kurier Codzienny (Illustrated Daily Courier); he did not receive a prize, and the novel was not published until 1976. He was married in the spring of 1934. In 1936 he was elected secretary of the Zawodowy Związek Literatów Polskich, and in 1938 he became a member of its executive committee.

Parnicki's first literary success was his historical novel *Aecjusz, ostatni rzymianin* (Aetius, the Last Roman, 1937); the work depicts the struggle of the Romans against the Huns, concentrating on the Roman emperor Valentinian III's military commander and dictator Aetius. The book was highly acclaimed by critics and scholars and was short-listed for the Prize for Young Writers of the Polish Academy of Literature in 1938. Although it did not win, it earned the author the academy's scholarship for a voyage abroad. He traveled through Romania, Bulgaria, Turkey, and Greece to Italy, where he stayed for about three months.

Parnicki returned to Poland on 26 August 1939. Five days later Poland was invaded by Germany; on 17 September the Soviet Union also invaded the country. With eastern Poland occupied by the Soviets, about one million Polish citizens were expelled from the country; among them was Parnicki, who was deported to Kazakhstan in January 1940. After the Germans invaded the Soviet Union in June 1941, the Polish government in exile of Władysław Sikorski was recognized by the Soviet dictator Joseph Stalin. Parnicki was freed in August and joined the staff of the Polish embassy in the Soviet Union as an aide to the press attaché; later he became cultural attaché. In this position he came into contact with such notable Russian writers as Aleksey Tolstoy and Ilya Ehrenburg. In the spring of 1943 Stalin broke relations with Sikorski's government in exile, and embassy personnel were evacuated to Tehran.

From Iran, Parnicki was sent to Jerusalem, where he was allowed to serve in a semiofficial capacity while he finished his two-volume novel *Srebrne orły: Powieść z przełomu wieków X i XI* (Silver Eagles: A Novel of the Turn of the Tenth and Eleventh Centuries, 1944, 1945). The work, which was published in Jerusalem, describes the newly Christianized Poland under the rule of Bolesław the Brave against the vast background of medieval Europe. It was an immediate success among Polish soldiers and civilians displaced by the war. In 1949 *Srebrne orły* was reprinted in Poland and became widely known there, even though it was soon suppressed by the Communist Party for political reasons. It remains Parnicki's most popular book.

At the beginning of 1944 Parnicki was transferred from Palestine to England; after six months he was sent as a cultural attaché to the Polish legation in Mexico. He had asked for the assignment because he had become interested in Aztec civilization and was planning a book on the subject.

In June 1945 the Western Allies withdrew recognition of the Polish government in exile; as a consequence, Parnicki's diplomatic status and salary ended. A group of well-to-do Polish expatriates, however, established a modest private scholarship that freed him from the necessity of looking for a job. In 1954 he was divorced from his wife, whom he had not seen since his deportation from Lwów in 1940. A year later he was married by proxy to a Polish divorcée living in England.

The Aztec project was never completed; instead, the first novel Parnicki wrote in Mexico

was set in ancient Central Asia. *Koniec "Zgody Narodów": Powieść z roku 179 przed narodzeniem Chrystusa* (The End of the "Concord of Nations"; A Novel from the Year 179 B.C., 1955), was published by an émigré firm in Paris. In this work Parnicki started to stray from strict historical fiction by deliberately introducing an anachronism: a steamship in the second century B.C.

A political thaw in the Soviet bloc in 1956 made it possible for Parnicki's books to be published again in Poland. In the 1960s a Communist-backed but partly autonomous Polish organization of "socially progressive Catholics" called PAX, which had its own publishing house, embraced Parnicki as "its" writer. The group republished his earlier books, published his new ones, and brought the writer and his wife to Poland for two long visits in 1963 and 1965. The group induced the Parnickis to return for good in 1967 and provided an apartment for them in Warsaw.

Parnicki's writing became increasingly idiosyncratic and divergent from traditional historical fiction. For example, a character known as "Z" appears in two novels set in the seventeenth century: *Gliniane dzbany* (Earthen Jugs, 1966)—the fourth part of the six-volume cycle *Nowa baśń* (The New Fable, 1962–1970)—and *I u możnych dziwny* (And for the Mighty Ones Astonishing Too, 1965), whose title is a quotation from the sixteenth-century Polish author Piotr Skarga. Z is the illegitimate son of the English playwright Christopher Marlowe, who, in Parnicki's version, is not killed in Deptford in 1593 but exchanges his "life role" with a Pole named Boniecki, who dies in his place. The reader is expected to recognize in Z a younger embodiment of Jan Onufry Zagłoba—a Falstaffian fictional character in Sienkiewicz's historical trilogy *Ogniem i mieczem* (1884; translated as *With Fire and Sword*, 1898), *Potop* (1886; translated as *The Deluge*, 1898), and *Pan Wołodyjowski* (1887; translated as *Pan Michael*, 1898). Such trickery occurs in most of Parnicki's novels, so that practically all of his characters are related to each other and often to historical and fictional personalities throughout the world. Pursuing this notion to the extreme, Parnicki wrote all of his later books, beginning with *"Zabij Kleopatrę"* ("Kill Cleopatra," 1968) as parts of a huge cycle. Consequently, his later novels are virtually incomprehensible to readers unacquainted with all of the preceding ones.

Parnicki deliberately mixed history, fantasy, autobiography, and metaphysics. His characters may be historical, vaguely historical (his favorites), imaginary, personifications of abstract notions, or even himself. Abandoning realistic conventions, he finally abolished the constraints of time and space, so that his characters can appear anywhere in more than two thousand years of history and move freely from Central Asia to America. He also includes much theological and mythological material, which provides a source of interminable conversations and reflections by the characters. Parnicki was much more interested in the history of religious, philosophical, and political ideas, including the extremely complicated conceptual schemes of his own characters, than in the tangible aspects of the past. He suggests that ancient myths and literary works contain, in coded form, such knowledge as the Copernican system of astronomy and the existence of America.

The quasi novel *Muza dalekich podróży* (The Muse of Far Voyages, 1970)— the title is a quotation from the Russian poet Nikolay S. Gumilyov— consists of fragments of two historical fictions: one concerning the imaginary Fourth Kingdom of Poland, which came into being after the (counterfactual) Polish victory in the uprising against Russia in 1830, and the other about the vaguely historical Slavic state of King Samo in the seventh-century Balkans; a unifying third plot comprises seemingly random reminiscences of the author's childhood in Russia.

Parnicki had begun substituting direct speech for traditional narration as early as *Słowo i ciało: Powieść z lat 201–203* (Word and Flesh: A Novel from the Years 201–203, 1959)—an epistolary novel set in Alexandria, Egypt, in the third century. In his later works readers increasingly confront characters—whose "official" identity is, moreover, often put into question or denied by other characters—exclusively through their internal monologues or documents such as memoirs, protocols, and letters. His novels are often staged as interrogations, conferences, or trials. *Palec zagrożenia* (Finger of Menace, 1970), the final part of *Nowa Baśń*, presents the trial of the author; the proceedings have been organized by the characters of the preceding novels in the cycle. The deliberate ambiguity of Parnicki's books, which is enhanced by a peculiar stylized language based on Polish prose of the Baroque period, was originally intended as an imitation of the difficulties one confronts in trying to discover the truth in incomplete or unreliable sources. Later, however, it began to serve as a means of transforming his

writings into a self-sufficient, hermetic puzzle requiring the reader's full attention. After 1970 Parnicki's books openly declare that their entire "action" is only a projection of the imagination of the author, stimulated by his experiences and his studies of the past. Consequently, the question the reader should ask is not "Why did this historical event happen?" but "Why is this event described by the author in this way?" The autobiographical asides in the novels are intended as clues to the answer.

From this perspective one can see that Parnicki's earlier, more conventional novels were also motivated by his personal preoccupations. They usually center around two concerns: *mieszańcy* (half-breeds) and political power. His favorite characters are of mixed ethnic, cultural, or religious origin, while the settings are on the borders between different cultures and societies, such as the Roman Empire endangered by the "barbarians," the Hellenized Middle East of the late antiquity, or the Slavic countries where Western and Eastern Christianity meet. Political power embodied in well-established institutions, such as states, churches, or monastic orders, is presented as an opportunity for the powerful to dominate and manipulate the weak—especially the "half-breeds," who remain eternally vulnerable because they do not belong. Problems of this kind must have affected him personally as a half-Jewish, Russian-speaking, German-born Pole living in Palestine, Iran, and Mexico; transforming them into literary texts was one of the ways he coped with the traumatic experiences of his uncommon life. Reading Parnicki's works gives one the feeling of sharing with him the fear and excitement of confronting an impenetrable universe characterized by incessant struggles for power, where suspicion and deception reign supreme, and any interpretation of the underlying dynamics must remain subjective and uncertain.

From 1967 until his death on 5 December 1988 Parnicki lived in Warsaw; he never went abroad again. He did not involve himself in the dubious political activities of his PAX sponsors, and his increasingly obscure and self-contained novels remained free from allusions to contemporary conditions in Poland. The only public activity in which he engaged after his return to Poland was a series of lectures about his creative work given at Warsaw University in the early 1970s that was published as *Rodowód literacki* (Literary Genealogy, 1974) and enlarged as *Historia w literaturę przekuwana* (History Forged into Literature,

1980). His final novel was the largely autobiographical *Opowieść o trzech Metysach* (A Tale of Three Metis), written between 1982 and 1986 and published posthumously in 1992.

References:

Antoni Chojnacki, *Parnicki: W labiryncie historii* (Warsaw: Państwowe Wydawnictwo Naukowe, 1975);

Teresa Cieślikowska, *Pisarstwo Teodora Parnickiego* (Warsaw: Instytut Wydawniczy PAX, 1965);

Małgorzata Czermińska, "Autotematyczność i dystans czasowy w powieściach Parnickiego," *Z Dziejów Form Artystycznych w Literaturze,* 24 (1971): 311–331;

Czermińska, *Czas w powieściach Parnickiego* (Wrocław: Ossolineum, 1972);

Czermińska, "Parnicki Teodor," in *Literatura polska: Przewodnik encyklopedyczny,* edited by Julian Krzyżanowski and others, 2 volumes (Warsaw: Państwowe Wydawnictwo Naukowe, 1984–1985), I: 147–148;

Czermińska, *Teodor Parnicki* (Warsaw: Państwowy Instytut Wydawniczy, 1974);

Krzysztof Dybciak, "Krytyczna działalność powieściopisarza: O krytyce literackiej Teodora Parnickiego w latach 1928–1939," *Pamiętnik Literacki,* 3 (1979): 115–151;

Wojciech Jamroziak, "The Historical SF of Teodor Parnicki," *Science Fiction Studies,* 5 (1979): 130–133;

Mieczysław Jankowiak, *Przemiany poetyki Parnickiego* (Bydgoszcz: Wydawnictwo uczelniane WSP w Bydgoszczy, 1985);

Jankowiak, "Sztuka narracji w powieściach historycznych Parnickiego," *Z Dziejów Form Artystycznych w Literaturze,* 24 (1971): 333–360;

Anna Łebkowska, *Fikcja jako możliwość* (Kraków: Universitas, 1991);

Zygmunt Lichniak, "Collage urodzinowy (na siedemdziesięciopięciolecie Teodora Parnickiego)," in his *Kopa lat* (Warsaw: Instytut Wydawniczy PAX 1985), pp. 440–467;

Jacek Łukasiewicz, "Teodor Parnicki," *Polish Perspectives,* 9 (1966): 41–44;

"Parnicki Teodor," in *Słownik współczesnych pisarzy polskich,* volume 2, edited by Ewa Korzeniewska and others (Warsaw: Państwowe Wydawnictwo Naukowe, 1964), pp. 619–621;

Wacław Sadkowski, *Parnicki: Wprowadzenie w twórczość powieściopisarską* (Warsaw: Agencja Autorska i Dom Książki, 1970);

Wojciech Skalmowski, "History as Fiction: The Novels of Teodor Parnicki," in *East European Literature: Selected Papers from the Second World Congress for Soviet and East European Studies,* edited by Evelyn Bristol (Berkeley, Cal.: Berkeley Slavic Specialties, 1982), pp. 69–84;

Maciej Szybist, "Parnicki i sprawa polska," *Teksty,* 4 (1973): 67–72;

Stefan Szymutko, *Zrozumieć Parnickiego* (Katowice: Gnome Books, 1992).

Karel Poláček
(22 March 1892 – January 1945)

Ondřej Hausenblas
Charles University, Prague

BOOKS: *Povídky pana Kočkodana* (Brno: Polygrafie, 1922);

Mariáš a jiné živnosti (Prague: Obelisk, 1924);

35 sloupků (Prague: V. Horák a spol., 1925);

Na prahu neznáma: Satirické romanetto–Kouzelná šunka. První pražská pohádka (Prague: František Borový, 1925);

Pásky na vousy (Prague: Moderní knihkupectví a nakladatelství E. Rosendorfa, 1925);

Čtrnáct dní na vojně (Prague: Obelisk, 1925);

Lehká dívka a reportér (Prague: František Topič, 1926);

Povídky izraelského vyznání (Prague: Pokrok, 1926);

Okolo nás (Prague: Čin, 1927);

Život ve filmu (Prague: Pokrok, 1927);

Bez místa (Prague: A. Synek, 1928); republished as *Pan Selichar se osvobodil* (Prague: A. Synek, 1933);

Dům na předměstí (Prague: Čin, 1928); translated by Peter Kussi as *What Ownership Is All About* (Highland Park, N.J.: Catbird Press, 1993);

Muži v offsidu. Ze života klubových přívrženců (Prague: František Borový, 1931);

Hráči. Obrazy ze života. Humoristický román (Prague: František Borový, 1931);

Hedvika a Ludvík (Prague: František Borový, 1931);

Hlavní přelíčení. Román (Prague: František Borový, 1932);

Židovské anekdoty (Prague: Orbis, 1933);

Edudant a Francimor (Prague: František Borový, 1933);

Žurnalistický slovník (Prague: František Borový, 1933);

Michelup a motocykl. Román (Prague: František Borový, 1935);

Okresní město. Román (Prague: František Borový, 1936);

Hrdinové táhnou do boje. Román (Prague: František Borový, 1936);

Podzemní město. Román (Brno: Lidové noviny, 1937);

Vyprodáno. Román (Prague: František Borový, 1939);

Hostinec U kamenného stolu, published under the name Vlastimil Rada (Brno: Lidové noviny, 1941);

Bylo nás pět. Povídka (Brno: Svobodné noviny, 1946);

Otec svého syna. Veselohra o 4 jednáních (Prague: Československý kompas, 1946).

Karel Poláček (courtesy of the National Library of the Czech Republic)

Editions and Collections: *Knihy Karla Poláčka,* 9 volumes (Prague: František Borový, 1931–1948);

Dílo Karla Poláčka, 11 volumes (Prague: Československý spisovatel, 1954–1961);

Ze soudní síně, selected and edited by Jan Řezáč, with assistance by Zdeňka Fraňková (Prague: Vydavatelství ROH-Práce, 1956);

Z Lidových novin 1936–1939 (Prague: Vydavatelství ROH-Práce, 1956);

Se žlutou hvězdou. Deník z roku 1943, edited by Z. K. Slabý (Hradec Králové: Nakladatelství krajského domu osvěty, 1959);

O humoru v životě a v umění, selected and edited by Slabý (Prague: Československý spisovatel, 1961);

Paměti o válce rychnovské (Rychnov nad Kněžnou: Okresní lidová knihovna, 1962);

Doktor Munory a jiní lidé, selected and edited by Slabý (Havlíčkův Brod: Východočeské nakladatelství, 1965);

Vše pro firmu, edited by Slabý (Hradec Králové: Východočeské nakladatelství, 1967); originally published in the literary supplement of *Lidové noviny,* 10 (1933–1934);

Metempsychóza čili Stěhování duší, edited by Slabý (Prague: Československý spisovatel, 1970);

Hedvika a Ludvík a jiné povídky, edited by Jarmila Víšková (Prague: Odeon, 1970);

Spisy Karla Poláčka, 16 volumes to date (Prague: Nakladatelství Franze Kafky, 1994–).

Edition in English: "The Reformation of Felix Piskora," selected and translated, with an introduction, by Jeanne W. Nemcova, *Czech and Slovak Short Stories* (London & New York: Oxford University Press, 1967), pp. 119–130.

PLAY PRODUCTIONS: M. Glass and S. Klein, *Firma,* Prague-Vinohrady, Municipal Theatre, 1922;

Pásky na vousy, Prague, National Theatre, 31 December 1925;

Sven Rindom, *Premiéra,* Prague-Vinohrady, Municipal Theatre, 1928;

Fyodor Mikhaylovich Dostoyevsky, *Ves Štěpančikovo,* Prague, Theatre D-40, 1940;

Otec svého syna. Veselohra o 4 jednáních, Prague, Divadlo kolektivní tvorby (Theater for Collective Creative Work), 13 October 1945.

MOTION PICTURES: *Muži v offsidu,* libretto by Poláček, script by Josef Neuberg, František Tichý, and Vladimir Rýpar, 1931;

Obrácení Ferdyše Pištory, script by Poláček with Josef Kodíček, 1 January 1932;

Načeradec, král kibiců, libretto by Poláček, script by Gustav Machatý, 12 February 1932;

Dům na předměstí, script by Poláček in cooperation with Hugo Haas and director Josef Kodíček, 1933;

U nás v Kocourkově, libretto by Poláček, script by Jaroslav Mottl, Václav Wasserman, and Miroslav Cikán, 23 November 1934;

Včera neděle byla, libretto by Poláček (based on the play by Václav Skutecký, *Malé štěstí*).

OTHER: *Almanach Kmene,* edited by Poláček (Spring 1937).

PERIODICAL PUBLICATIONS–UNCOLLECTED: Fragment of the fifth volume of Poláček's pentalogy, edited by Z. K. Slabý, in *Plamen,* 10, nos. 3 and 4 (1968);

Karel Poláček is, along with Karel Čapek and Jaroslav Hašek, one of the most important Czech novelists between the two world wars. Like Čapek, Poláček is an interpreter of everyday life, and like Hašek he is a great antiwar writer. Poláček's style and language are also distinctive, not through literary affectation but by his use of lively everyday speech beside bookish expressions.

Since Poláček's death, publication has been limited more or less to his smaller humorous works for reasons that have nothing to do with literature—that is, for ideological, financial, personal, or racial motives. Thanks to his popular humorous books, especially the novel of his boyhood memories, *Bylo nás pět* (There Were Five of Us, 1946), and the short novels *Muži v offsidu* (Men Offside, 1931) and *Hostinec U kamenného stolu* (The Stone Table Inn, 1941), Poláček, his language, his typical characters, and his subjects have become an indelible part of the national culture.

Karel Poláček was born on 22 March 1892 into the family of a small Jewish merchant who lived in the East Bohemian town of Rychnov nad Kněžnou. Karel was one of four children. His mother died when he was seven. His father did not have time to take care of the children, so they were brought up by his second wife. Poláček came from one of the Jewish families that had assimilated with Czech society—Czech was spoken at home. As an adult in Prague, unlike many contemporary writers, he did not count himself one of the so-called Prague Jewish authors; yet, his work remained eternally Jewish, especially his writing revolving around trade and tradespeople. Jewish themes are sometimes prominent, notably in the play *Pásky na vousy* (Moustache Mask, 1925), and the novels *Lehká dívka a reportér* (The Tart and the Reporter, 1926), *Povídky izraelského vyznání* (Stories of the Israelite Faith, 1926), and *Židovské anekdoty* (Jewish Anecdotes, 1933). In other works Jewish themes are just part of the wider scene, as in *Muži v offsidu* and in the novels of his tetralogy; sometimes they can just be sensed, as in

Dust jacket for the 1993 English translation of Poláček's first novel, Dům na předměstí *(1928), which depicts the arrogance of insignificant people who gain power under fascism*

Michelup a motocykl (Michelup and the Motorcycle, 1935).

Poláček went first to the secondary school in Rychnov (where he once repeated a year) and finished his schooling in Prague in 1912. He completed a year of study at the German Commercial Academy and also matriculated in the Faculty of Law at Charles University. Before being called up for service in World War I, he worked as a typist. During the war he saw four years of service on two fronts—Galicia and Serbia, both of which appear in the novel tetralogy. In Serbia he was taken prisoner. After the war, with some difficulty he found a job in Prague as an ordinary clerk in a Czechoslovakian commercial import and export company, where he worked until 1922. The rest of his personal and family life has little to do with his work. He had no strong attachment to family. He preferred spending his time alone or with his friends playing cards, and

his marriage, from which he had a daughter, broke up in the 1930s. After long legal wrangling, in 1940 Poláček disinherited his former wife. However, he did take care of his daughter, Jiřina, and his children's book *Edudant a Francimor* (Edudant and Francimor, 1933) developed from stories he made up for her. In 1938, in order to protect his seventeen-year-old daughter from possible danger, he sent her to England. To judge from letters that have been preserved, Poláček did not change his habits even during the German occupation while he was having an affair with Dora Vaňáková.

By 1920 Poláček was publishing in the satirical weekly *Nebojsa* (Dreadnought). In 1922 he joined the staff of *Lidové noviny* (The People's Paper) as legal reporter and columnist, but that same year he left the paper. The first of his collections of short stories, *Povídky pana Kočkodana* (Mr. Kočkodan's Tales), was published in 1922. These stories, printed first in various newspapers under the pseudonym Kočkodan (Long-Tailed Monkey), made Poláček popular with readers and caused a great demand for newspapers in which they appeared. Poláček's works focus on trivial, everyday human concerns from the viewpoint of a small tradesman. In that way he brings out the comedy in the pettiness and limitations of the people, their problems, and their solutions. The reader finds the subjects of the stories and Poláček's outlook familiar and understandable: the problems are the kind that fill a person's life sometimes to the exclusion of all else. Occasionally, Poláček also uses this outlook on life when he writes about the Jews that have assimilated into Czech society, as in *Povídky izraelského vyznání*.

Until the end of the 1920s Poláček wrote mainly smaller pieces. These works were mostly for newspapers and were chiefly courtroom reports and so-called columns—something between short literary articles and news reports. All his work as a journalist and fiction writer is connected with his intense interest in understanding both everyday life and stock responses to situations. In *O humoru v životě a v umění* (1961), he said "I am not attracted by topical events if they do not repeat themselves, if they do not occur all the time . . . the routine, ordinary, daily life is the greatest task."

Poláček's stories have been criticized for having no plot and no point. Critics have said that they are nothing but padded-out news items. The attraction of these stories, however, lies elsewhere. Poláček creates interest by bringing banal events to life. He demonstrates typical situations in which people of little importance seek to come to terms with their own insignificance by assuming superior airs or by making a great drama out of their not very serious worries. The motivating force in Poláček's stories is not the plot but the delving into the minutiae of everyday life. In so doing, Poláček disdains soulless realism or "realistic consistency," constructing in contrast a creatively stylized image of reality that his critics were unable to detect in his work: "if you copy life as it is, you will have a very unclear idea of what it is all about."

Poláček collected his stories and articles into books. In 1924 he published *Mariáš a jiné živnosti* (Whist and Other Trades). In writing of the activities, fads, and social aspirations so fervently pursued by his characters, Poláček adopts a literary style that makes even an apparently factual description enough to bring out the comedy in these characters and their activities. He gives his texts an impression of objectivity by setting out before the reader a kind of scholarly (in reality, of course, a false and ridiculous) study of tradespeople and their obsessions. Poláček's meticulous descriptions of these typical, insignificant details direct the reader's attention to the discrepancy between the importance a given trade has for the tradesman and the importance usually accorded it. This "tradesman's" philosophy of life—regarding the world primarily from the point of view of self-interest and never looking beyond the horizons of one's own life—is one of the basic themes to which Poláček constantly returns in his work, both in his short stories and in his humorous novels.

In certain works Poláček treats his subjects as if they were scientific studies. In *Mariáš a jiné živnosti* he deals with trade; in *Muži v offsidu* he deals with football fans; and in *Hráči* (Gamblers, 1931) he deals with professional cardplaying. In *Hedvika a Ludvík* (Hedvika and Ludvík, 1931) and in the children's book *Edudant a Francimor* he lampoons the making of a profession out of marriage. His more serious works—*Michelup a motocykl* and the tetralogy about provincial town life—also include these spurious studies. Another book of short stories, *Bez místa* (Unemployed), was published in 1928. In 1933 these stories were published in another arrangement as *Pan Selichar se osvobodil* (The Emancipation of Mr. Selichar). Poláček, speaking of what interested him and what finally decided the format of his novellas, said: "The psychology of the individual does not interest me as much as the psychology of the crowd and class."

For five years Poláček worked on the newspaper *Tribuna* (Tribune), for which he became chief column writer. In these articles he worked out his contemplative, ironic style. Like Čapek he criticized the use of clichés in journalism. While Čapek explained and explicitly rejected clichés, Poláček used a different method; he highlighted the idiotic way clichés function in language. Some of his characters speak almost exclusively in clichés—for example, Deputy Fábera in *Okresní město* (A Provincial Town, 1936). Thus, Poláček's highly individual style came into being. Poláček wrote *Žurnalistický slovník* (Dictionary of Journalese, 1933), which was printed for the first time in installments in the humorous fortnightly paper *Dobrý den* (Hello!), which Poláček edited from 1927 to the seventh issue of 1930. From 1928 to 1933 Poláček was on the staff of *České slovo* (The Czech Word), to which he contributed humorous short stories in addition to courtroom reports and articles. He also contributed articles, columns, and essays to Ferdinand Peroutka's magazine *Přítomnost* (Here and Now) from its inception in 1924 until its demise in 1939.

Besides the collections of newspaper articles—*35 sloupků* (35 Columns, 1925), *Čtrnáct dní na vojně* (A Fortnight in the Army, 1925), *Okolo nás* (Around Us, 1927), and *Život ve filmu* (Life in Films, 1927)—Poláček began writing fairy tales. In 1925 he published a little book with two satirical fairy tales—*Na prahu neznáma* (On the Threshold of the Unknown), subtitled *Satirické romanetto* (A Satirical Horror Story), and *Kouzelná šunka* (The Magic Ham), subtitled *První pražská pohádka* (A First Prague Fairy Tale). Fantastic events occur in both stories. Poláček uses these events to lampoon contemporary political and public life and the fairy tale itself—already a declining branch of literature. In the first story a comet appears and is about to destroy the earth. As the end of the world is forecast, a bizarre fight breaks out among all the political parties. This story develops concurrently with that of two men who are trapped into marrying two ugly women desperate to be married. All these occurrences are the fault of the comet. The comet itself turns out to be an advertisement in lights created by an ad agency. The second fairy tale lampoons social life and trade. It is the story of a poor man to whom God gives a miraculous ham that can never be consumed because it constantly grows back to its original size. The unimportant man becomes rich and famous and gets completely entangled in political scandals.

In 1925 Poláček's play *Pásky na vousy* was staged unsuccessfully in the National Theatre under the direction of Karel Želenský. The second of Poláček's plays, *Otec svého syna* (The Father of his Son, 1946), adapted from the story "Vše pro firmu" (All for the Firm), was not staged until 1945. The latter play is worthy of notice because of the paradoxical reversal of roles—just as in the original story. The serious-minded, reliable son saves the firm from his debauched father. This explicit reversal of roles and values is one of Poláček's favorite ploys. It is his typical way of unsettling his readers by turning their values upside down. Likewise, in *Hráči* he makes the gamblers act like honest, hardworking people, and in the novel *Hrdinové táhnou do boje* (Heroes Go Off to Fight, 1936) a father forces his beloved son to ruin his health by smoking and drinking for the sole purpose of preventing him from having to go to war. In the novel *Podzemní město* (The Underground City, 1937) the relationship of subordinate to superior (between traveling salesman Raboch and his assistant Růžička) is reversed when they are both drafted into the army.

Of course, the "small tradesman's view of the world" is also a reversal of values, because the tradesman cannot see the great for the small. So in the world of the "little man," great abstract concepts of life must not be treated directly. Poláček achieves indirection by means of clichés. Clichés can give a name to a social phenomenon without the speaker's really understanding it. A cliché allows the user to believe he can master the world both by what he actually does and by his general thinking, but at the same time it prevents his understanding the essence of matters and closes his mind to self-examination and wider horizons. In a phrase from *Bylo nás pět*, Poláček's characters often "act by speaking" simply to retain the illusion that life is an orderly, controllable process.

The great task that Poláček set himself as a novelist was to discover to what extent people's stereotyped speech patterns, aims, and values make up the basic elements in human society. Consequently, he cannot be considered simply a critic of narrow-minded philistinism. He was conscious of the banality, yet at the same time of the greatness and nobility that reside in repetitive behavior, stereotypes, and clichés.

Before Poláček began writing novels, he had accumulated in his short stories and short novels many favorite themes and characters with typical patterns of speech that he could use again and again. *Lehká dívka a reportér* is full of such material. Just as *Kouzelná šunka* does, *Lehká dívka a reportér* includes a parody of a political career. With the unintentional help of the editor of a minor tabloid newspaper, an ordinary prostitute becomes the grande dame of the Czech political world. Thus, the defeatism of the Jewish editor is set against the easy adaptability of a person "without scruples." This

minor work is unpretentious and not a piece of particularly polished writing; however, that it was not republished from the year it first came out until 1995 had more to do with its criticism of the political scene and its astringent Jewish humor than with its literary qualities.

Not until 1928 did Poláček publish his first novel, *Dům na předměstí* (The House in the Suburbs; translated as *What Ownership Is All About*, 1993). The main character, police officer Jan Faktor, the domineering owner of a block of rented flats, was taken as an example of how, when fascism was rising in Germany, limited and insignificant people grew in arrogance as they acquired property and official power. Until recently critics overlooked that the people Faktor treated so cruelly and spitefully were not exactly admirable characters either. Syrový, a clerk, is a creature who cannot stand up for himself. He is timid and helpless in the face of much weaker aggression than that of a bullying landlord. The neighbors and the small local shopkeepers reveal the cowardice, timidity, and inability of ordinary people, the "tenants of life," to take a stand against evil. The landlord and his unhappy tenants make pronouncements about their fates in set phrases that they use to persuade themselves of both the justifiability and the inevitability of their situations. In so doing they lose any power they might have had to solve their own problems. Although this book is classified as humorous, it is more grotesque than amusing and so is rather sad.

The short novel *Muži v offsidu* brought Poláček unprecedented fame. This notice was undoubtedly due to the motion picture made from the novel in the same year. Despite Poláček's loathing for football and football fans, he managed in the book to produce a perfect study of the ordinary citizen, of the football-mad individual and of mass football mania—and he made it funny. He put colorful descriptions of Jewish and non-Jewish businessmen and tradesmen side by side but in no way at odds with each other. Poláček's comedy, however, does not rely only on descriptions of farcical figures and situations. His humor comes from high-flown clichés and platitudes in the mouths of ordinary characters and from commonplace events being described in incongruous bookish or scholarly language. He includes literal quotations of stock phrases. He also associates unconnected objects and incongruous elements of language in an unusual way: bizarre phenomena such as the sleeping, clairvoyant "besserwisser" in *Hráči*, completely incongruous epithets in *Okresní město* such as "flaking old men," and tongue-in-cheek associations of ideas such as "white curls covered his head like whipped cream on a cup of iced coffee." The conversations in Poláček's stories achieve their comic effects in the same way. Objects in daily use or parts of the body speak for their owners in *Muži v offsidu* and in *Hostinec U kamenného stolu*—for example:

> Eman the father stood up from the table with his hands in his pockets and with his face to the window he pronounced to the acacia in the yard the following idea: "Some might think they can fill their stomach free of charge and be entertained by some other's playing the fool, on the top of it!"

> Eman the son responded toward the stove: "Some might think they should be thanked for a piece of grub!"

> Eman the father raised his voice as he answered to the acacia: "If my lunch is a grub to someone, it need not be eaten, right?"

> The stove heard this response: "One need not be reproached."

> And the acacia: "Let someone go out to lunch at the hotel, there the cuisine for lords is served, isn't here."

The dialogue between the acacia and the stove went on this way until the acacia sent a message to the stove that it is going to put things in order. When the stove was curious what kind of order that should be, the acacia winked its eye meaningfully that "one will see." The stove shook its mop of hair and said, "OK."

The story *Hráči*, also dating from 1931, is in a certain sense a study in fiction of a "trade." In it Poláček uses the career of a lifelong "professional" cardplayer to demonstrate his firm belief in the virtues of honesty and mutual help. This belief is, of course, a paradox in the world of people unashamedly mad about cards. In the world of this novel, playing for money is regarded as an honest way of earning a living. A fair, honest game is the criterion for measuring family and national fortunes. Using this method of upholding certain moral values unobtrusively, even though ambivalently, was a master stroke on Poláček's part. At the same time, he presented these values so entertainingly amid the absurdity that he avoided both didacticism (which he categorically lampoons) and pathos.

In the same year, Poláček published another parody, the story *Hedvika a Ludvík*, in which he reduces to the absurd the popular sentimental story of a wedding with a "happy ever after" ending. The

KAREL POLÁČEK

HLAVNÍ PŘELÍČENÍ

ROMÁN

1932

NAKLADATELSTVÍ FR. BOROVÝ

PRAHA

Title page for Poláček's novel about a murder committed from the most banal of motives (courtesy of the National Library of the Czech Republic)

main characters are children of a first marriage. One parent dies, and the children find a stepparent; then the other parent dies, and so on, many times over. More and more stepparents marry new partners, so that in the end, the children are much older and wiser than their stepparents, who have hardly come of age.

Poláček did not produce his first really serious novel, *Hlavní přelíčení* (Trial for Murder) until 1932. It is the story of a railwayman dissatisfied with his family's hand-to-mouth existence. Waking and sleeping, he is obsessed by his rather poor conception of the ideal woman and by some stereotypical notions of a better life. The hero, Maršík, cheats an older servant girl out of her life savings with false promises of marriage and in the end, driven to despair, kills her. *Hlavní přelíčení* is the story of a merciless crime told without using traditional means of creating tension and excitement. The novel was not meant to be an interesting exposition of crime and punishment. Instead, it was intended to show how lack of self-control, meanness of spirit, and the more or less subconscious, unexpressed desire for a better lifestyle begets crime. After years of reporting court proceedings, Poláček knew the real, nonliterary motives for crime and in typical fashion showed how an exceptionally terrible act can result from an unexceptional life.

At the beginning of the 1930s Poláček worked at the AB movie studios for a time, but he later left of his own accord. He had gained some insight into scriptwriting when he wrote the articles collected in *Život ve filmu* (Life in Films, 1927), in which he revealed the inauthenticity of the contemporary movie scene by objectively presenting the clichés of concept and composition in Czech movie production. He also wrote the dialogue for some quite successful comic movies and collaborated in script writing for movies. He wrote dialogue for several other movies, possibly even for *Hostinec U kamenného stolu* (with a script by Otakar Vávra and Vlastimil Rada, and directed by Josef Gruss), first released in 1949 and banned by the censors.

In 1937 Poláček edited the spring issue of the important literary anthology *Almanach Kmene*. In 1939, because he was a Jew, he was dismissed from the newspaper *Lidové noviny*, to which he had returned in 1933 as an acclaimed journalist and author. Poláček managed in both his journalism and his writing and in his private life to cultivate self-irony and detachment from problems—his own and other people's. His ability to remain uninvolved in passion and suffering was legendary. His colleagues on the editorial staff and he himself built up many anecdotes about it. These tales appeared with other items in the column "Pražský film" (Prague Films) in *Lidové noviny*. A great deal of this detachment can also be discerned in *Židovské anekdoty*, a collection of Jewish anecdotes published by Poláček in 1933. However, when Poláček's marriage broke up in the late 1930s and he started an affair with Dora Vaňáková, his colleagues on the editorial staff jeered at him as he had jeered at them for years over their emotional crises.

Poláček's children's books retained their popularity even during the decades when not much of his work was published and he was given little publicity. Only its subject, however, makes *Edudant a Francimor* a children's story; the book includes much of the author's characteristic style. The two young sons of the witch Halabába fly aboard a magic broom on an outing with their school class, into which they do not fit because of their ages and because of their knowledge of magic. The class becomes involved in various adventures but are res-cued either by coincidences or by the magic of Edudant and Francimor. Madame Halabába's magic "trade" resembles a provincial firm. The brothers are models for the Štědrý brothers in *Okresní město*—they use typical catch phrases. The school world has features that anticipate the atmosphere of the novel *Bylo nás pět*. The topsy-turvy values in some passages from the fairy tales, notably in "Město psů" (Dogs' Town), are reminders of the unifying principle already used by Poláček in *Hráči*, as are situations also frequently to be found in many novels and short stories.

The novel *Michelup a motocykl* is often considered a humorous work but is so only in plot. A gray-haired clerk has a fetish—he longs for a magnificent motorcycle. However, when he does acquire one for his family, he gets himself and them into bizarre difficulties stemming from his ungenerous, narrow-minded approach to life: consequently, Michelup, who had longed for a motorcycle as a symbol of personal freedom from financial and spiritual poverty, is unable to learn to use it properly. Certainly the novel is humorous in the details of the everyday life and posturing of the characters, but it deals sharply with their provinciality. Poláček puts his characters into embarrassing situations—thus foreshadowing by many years the trend set by Milan Kundera and the movie director Miloš Forman.

In 1936 publication began on Poláček's four-part novel, his greatest work. The first two volumes—*Okresní město* and *Hrdinové táhnou do boje*—have always produced quite different reactions. Contemporary critics showed they did not understand Poláček's building his view of life and literature on repetitive, routine actions and occurrences. Moreover, those who recognized themselves in the novel greeted it with fury and indignation. There was an absolute outcry in Poláček's native town because he did not use poetic license to spare either private individuals in his accurate caricatures or the citizens' professed moral standards.

Not until 1937 did Pavel Trost write an article in *Slovo a slovesnost* pointing out that the deplorable provinciality and obduracy of the people of pre–World War I Austria-Hungary, a comic characteristic of the culture of the time, was actually Poláček's great literary discovery. Poláček highlighted his belief both in the thematic structure and the language of his fiction. He saw the stagnation as extending to both natural phenomena and human life. The provincial town lives by ever-repeated words and events. In the family of the businessman Štědrý, the main character in the first two parts of Poláček's tetralogy, the fact that the same things are said every day, every passing season, and every year forms almost a ritual. In the fixed hierarchy among the town's inhabitants everyone knows his place, even the local beggars. Nobody rebels against this pecking order. The beginning of the world war strikes the town like a thunderbolt. The people react as if they do not realize that their traditional values and social order are about to be destroyed: in spite of all the confusion, the beginning of the war, when the main characters of the novel go to the front, is just another event within the established order of provincial Austria-Hungary.

The third part of the tetralogy, *Podzemní město*, shows the heroes at the front and in the trenches. The characters, torn from the tranquility of their small town, come to terms in various ways with the unnatural conditions under which they are living. They try to act in accordance with their places in the old social order, but this pattern is now just a memory, something unreal that they are afraid to lose and about which they argue. Here Poláček makes a point of showing how in the army, civilian social standing means nothing; positions in society can be reversed and relations between people degraded, a fact that became important in the social and political life of the nation after the war. The people in the provincial town try to keep up the old customs, but the destruction of the prewar civilization has made them irrelevant. The worst human qualities come to the surface. Poláček had intended to write a political novel, and if statements that he wanted the action to extend to the rise of the Czech fascist movement Vlajka can be trusted, then the reason he thought the influence of army life on the individual was important is obvious: in the army, attitudes were being fostered that would one day destroy democracy in the postwar republic. At the same time, however, Poláček felt he had to show that not even war "can in the end change forever the human being and his class loyalty."

In the fourth volume of the tetralogy, *Vyprodáno* (Sold Out, 1939), Poláček shows no mercy when he describes this situation. Some of the characters' lifetime values have been shattered, and these individuals just vegetate, as illustrated by the businessman Štědrý. People obtain subsistence in all kinds of ways; dishonesty becomes the norm. At home there are huge numbers of single women in the population; the proportion of men to women is reversed, and a man is a valuable commodity. Many people's lives are reduced simply to moneymaking, anti-Semitic diatribes, and dominating other people. Signs of political disintegration appear. Poláček turns the literal meaning of the words "sold out" into a metaphor; the commonly accepted social standards in the lives of individuals and families to which the characters cling

KAREL POLÁČEK

OKRESNÍ MĚSTO

ROMÁN

1936
NAKLADATELSTVÍ FR. BOROVÝ
PRAHA

Title page for Poláček's novel that shows how clichés can be used in an ironic way to reveal character (courtesy of the National Library of the Czech Republic)

and that readers found repeated in *Okresní město* are now clearly meaningless.

That Poláček did not choose a sensational plot with triumphant heroes for a tetralogy on a grand scale is typical. Nevertheless, the tetralogy has its important characters; the three sons of Štědrý the businessman repeatedly return to the fore throughout the novel to show in detail how the world has changed. The almost fairy-tale structure was certainly deliberately chosen. The three sons, completely different in temperament, go out into the world and return with their trophies. The trophies are metaphorical; they represent change or strengthening of character. The prewar world order was an allegory—a kindly providence allocated a place to everyone and everyone duly played his part. However, Poláček in typical fashion gives the fairy tale a twist. The sons return, each with experiences not shared by the others. The most obvious example is the youngest, the introverted Jaroušek. The prewar world was just as strange to him as the wartime world, but he finds his identity in the war: his search for self-knowledge takes him back to the Italian front and to his death from artillery fire. The wartime experiences of the eldest, Viktor—a placid, unimaginative fellow—reinforce his pragmatism. For the middle son, Kamil, the most typical representative of his social class, the end of the monarchy meant the collapse of his personal life, because its values were strongly rooted in him. Since Kamil was completely dependent on the fleshpots of the big city, Poláček dropped him from the story after his first unsuccessful struggles with the wartime environment. In the fragment of the unfinished fifth part, however, Kamil suddenly returns after the war, almost unchanged.

The fragmentary work did not turn up until 1967; it was in the possession of Oleg Malevich, the specialist in Czech studies from Petrohrad, to whom the poet Josef Palivec had entrusted it. Although there has been a vigorous search at home and abroad for the manuscript or for some of the copies of the complete text of the fifth part, none has been found. It could have been lost during the German Occupation or later during Communist rule, while people who might have preserved it were emigrating or being imprisoned. It might still be discovered among the papers of someone to whom it was given for safekeeping.

Until the German Occupation, Poláček's literary, journalistic, and social life was not particularly dramatic. As a skeptic and realist he lampooned all political movements. He utterly condemned fascism and communism. The horror story *Na prahu neznáma* (On the Threshold of the Unknown, 1925) could not be republished under communism. Poláček was a friend of Čapek and belonged to the group of democratic intellectuals, the so-called Friday Club, which met on Fridays in Čapek's home and in whose discussions President Tomáš Garrigue Masaryk sometimes took part. However, Poláček never had any political leanings and was not attracted to Masaryk's politics. The great number of short stories, novels, and newspaper articles bear witness to his having been hardworking, in spite of describing himself as the opposite. As he said, distancing himself from his namesake, a member of the staff of the publishing house "Družstevní práce" (Cooperative Work), "I am not Cooperative Work Poláček, but Poláček Laziness Personified."

From 1939 Poláček was employed by the Jewish Council of Elders. He catalogued books from the libraries of the Jewish religious communities. He recorded his experiences from this sad period in a diary from 1943, published in 1959 under the title *Se žlutou hvězdou* (With a Yellow Star) and in letters published in Toronto as *Poslední dopisy Doře* (Last Letters to Dora, 1984). Even during the cheerless era of the German Occupation, Poláček managed to write humorous books such as *Hostinec U kamenného stolu* and *Bylo nás pět*. Thanks only

to the willingness of Vlastimil Rada, the humorist and painter, to take the risk of having it published under his own name, *Hostinec U kamenného stolu* was published in 1941. A certain number of Poláček's most typical features had to be removed from the text and some elements of Rada's style added, but the changes were not made consistently. The publisher's paperwork also needed to be faked. The text strongly reflects Poláček's style, especially the method used to create comic situations and comedy from language, but considering the circumstances at the time, *Hostinec U kamenného stolu*, of all Poláček's work, is the least typical example of the author's creating lives and history from ordinary and uninspiring matters. In *Bylo nás pět* Poláček uses boyish escapades to give a picture of a small town as the boys see it. The novel was hidden during the occupation and was not published until 1946 after the author's death.

Poláček was sent to the Theresienstadt concentration camp on 3 June 1943. There is little information about what he did there. He may well have been relatively better treated than the other prisoners. The memoirs of other prisoners have established that he gave a few lectures. In the 1990s came the first news and proof of the existence of short humorous sketches that Poláček wrote at Christmas even after being transported on 19 October 1944 to the labor camp at Hidenburg near Auschwitz. According to witnesses, Poláček appears to have died during a death march, perhaps around 21 January 1945. The last survivors corroborate the claim that even in the misery of the transports the ordinary prisoners recognized Poláček as a famous writer.

Poláček's journalism, reports from the law courts, and stories in newspapers were not only well received by his readers but also had a marked influence on the development of Czech writing. The great prose writers of the 1960s such as Bohumil Hrabal and Josef Škvorecký learned from his concentration on the commonplace and from his narrative style. Poláček can be considered as carrying on the tradition of Jan Neruda (1834–1891)—seeing the magic and the curse of the unsophisticated, provincial outlook on life or of a world whose values are restricted to "trade." This style and kind of subject are now prominent in modern literature. Poláček found much inspiration in the nineteenth-century Russian writers, especially Anton Chekov and Fyodor Dostoyevsky.

Poláček's language and style, especially in *Bylo nás pět* and in the dialogues in *Muži v offsidu*, not only influenced other writers but also brought into common usage some literary expressions that were becoming slightly archaic, as well as expressions taken from the speech of Jewish tradesmen. Poláček's tendency to use themes from ordinary life to a certain extent blinded critics and readers alike to the fact that his style, especially in the tetralogy, is highly sophisticated, that it is consistent in every detail of language and subject matter. Poláček's often repeated descriptions—for example, of the buildings in the small town, the decor of homes or brothels, the physical appearance of several characters—draw attention to themselves for a good reason. Through these descriptions the author builds up effective visual concepts. In the course of these repetitions Poláček can see every theme from more than one point of view; he can look at it through the eyes of the beggar and the gentleman, or the individual, or take a general perspective. The vast extent of the tetralogy—in fact, all of Poláček's work—in which he repeats similar themes and uses them as a unifying device, offers the reader the chance to become aware of the interconnection in complicated relationships.

Poláček has brought other values to Czech culture. By using football mania as a theme in *Muži v off-sidu*, Poláček made it a subject for the public to think about. The book made it more difficult for people to be carried away by popular crazes. His sympathetic and humorous description of everyday Jewish and Czech society contributed to clarifying the ideal of cultural tolerance in the first Republic. He established the world of children before the world wars in *Bylo nás pět* as an archetype in Czech culture, thanks also to the splendid radio readings of the work by actor František Filipovský, broadcast from 1953 to 1954. That the serialized television adaptation of 1995, produced by Karel Smyczek, could create a new range of situations and interpretations based on the book testifies to the firm place this work has in Czech culture.

Poláček is unusual among Czech authors: he combines Jewish humor and realism with Czech skepticism and irony. He did not belong to any contemporary movement or literary group. In form and subject matter he was never part of any fashion or exclusive literary trend. Above all, he can take credit for bringing new life to Czech fiction and giving the commonplace and unchanging patterns of life greater cultural significance.

Letters:

Poslední dopisy Doře, edited by Martin Jelinowicz (Toronto: 68 Publishers, 1984).

Bibliographies:

Z. K. Slabý, "Karel Poláček," compiled by Helena Winklerová, *Kulturně-politický kalendář* (1961–1962): 201–202;

Boris Mědílek, *Bibliografie Karla Poláčka* (Prague: Nakladatelství Franze Kafky, 1998).

References:

Alena Hájková, *Komika jako nástroj kritiky maloměšťáctví v díle Karla Poláčka* (Prague: Academia, 1985);

Karel Hausenblas, "O jazyce humoristické prózy (na materiálu děl Karla Poláčka)," in *Knížka o jazyce a stylu soudobé české literatury*, edited by Lubomír Doležel and Jaroslav Kuchař (Prague: Orbis, 1961), pp. 86–96;

Jaroslav Kolár and Jan Tydlitát, eds., *Sborník příspě-vků ze sympózia Karel Poláček a historie židovské kultury ve východních Čechách* (Boskovice: Albert, 1995);

Helena Korecká, "Geneze a proměny opakovaných motivů v díle Karla Poláčka," *Česká literatura*, 3–4 (1971): 278–293;

Jan Lopatka, "Biografie šosáka?" *Kritický sborník*, 6, no. 2 (1986); 48–60;

Lopatka, *Ptáci vítají jitro zpěvem, poddůstojníci řvaním. Záznam sympózia ke stému výročí narození Karla Poláčka* (Prague & Rychnov nad Kněžnou, 1992);

Tomáš Pěkný, as (f. w.), "Karel Poláček," *Kalendář 1, Alef 1986* (samizdat); also published in *Židovská ročenka 5752*, 191–192 (1991): 266–282;

F. X. Šalda, "Karel Poláček, Okresní město, neboli Co s maloměstským románem?" *Šaldův zápisník*, 9, no. 1 (1936–1937): 63–67;

Z. K. Slabý, "Torzo? Prozatím . . . ," *Plamen*, 10, no. 4 (1968): 150–151;

Pavel Trost, "Poláčkův román maloměstský," *Slovo a slovesnost*, 3, no. 3 (1937): 166–172;

Trost, "Poslední próza Karla Poláčka," *Slovo a slovesnost*, 10, no. 2 (1947): 107–109;

Jan Tydlitát, *100 let Karla Poláčka 1892–1992. Retrospektivní sborník připomínající semináře a vzpomínky věnované Karlu Poláčkovi v letech 1962, 1967, 1982 a 1984. Vydáno u příležitosti celostátního sympózia s mezinárodní účastí uspořádaného k 100. výročí narození Karla Poláčka.* (Rychnov nad Kněžnou: The Municipal Council in cooperation with the District Library, 1992).

Miklós Radnóti

(5 May 1909 – 8 or 9 November 1944)

Ákos Czigány

Pázmány Péter Catholic University, Budapest–Piliscsaba

BOOKS: *Pogány köszöntő. Versek* (Budapest: Kortárs, 1930);

Újmódi pásztorok éneke. Versek (Budapest: Fiatal Magyarország, 1931);

Lábadozó szél (Szeged: Szegedi Fiatalok Művészeti Kollégiuma, 1933);

Ének a négerről, aki a városba ment (Budapest: Gyarmati Könyvnyomtatóműhely, 1934);

Kaffka Margit művészi fejlődése: Doktori értekezés (Szeged: Szegedi Fiatalok Művészeti Kollégiuma, 1934);

Újhold: Versek (Szeged: Szegedi Fiatalok Művészeti Kollégiuma, 1935);

Járkálj csak, halálraítélt! (Budapest: Nyugat, 1936);

Meredek út. Versek (Budapest: Cserépfalvi, 1938);

Ikrek hava (Budapest: Almanach, 1940);

Naptár (Budapest: Hungária, 1942);

Tajtékos ég. Versek (Budapest: Révai, 1946); translated by Steven Polgar, Stephen Berg, and S. J. Marks as *Clouded Sky* (New York: Harper & Row, 1972);

Bori notesz: Radnóti Miklós utolsó versei (Budapest: Magyar Helikon, 1970).

Editions and Collections: *Válogatott versek 1930–1940* (Budapest: Almanach, 1940);

Versei, edited by Imre Trencsényi-Waldapfel (Gyoma: Kner Izidor, 1948);

Válogatott versei, edited by György Somlyó (Budapest: Szépirodalmi, 1952);

Versek és műfordítások, edited by Sándor Koczkás (Budapest: Szépirodalmi, 1954);

Tanulmányok, cikkek, edited by Pál Réz (Budapest: Magvető, 1956);

Ikrek hava: Napló a gyerekkorról (Budapest: Magyar Helikon, 1959);

Sem emlék, sem varázslat (Budapest: Szépirodalmi, 1961);

Eclogák (Budapest: Magyar Helikon, 1961);

Összes versei és műfordításai, edited by Sándor Koczkás (Budapest: Szépirodalmi, 1963);

Miklós Radnóti

Próza: Novellák és tanulmányok, edited by Réz (Budapest: Szépirodalmi, 1971);

Naptár (Budapest: Magyar Helikon, 1975);

Művei, edited by Réz (Budapest: Szépirodalmi, 1976);

Eclogák, edited by Réz (Budapest: Magyar Helikon-Szépirodalmi, 1979);

Költeményei, edited by Réz (Budapest: Helikon, 1982);

Összes versei és versfordításai, edited by Réz (Budapest: Szépirodalmi, 1984);

Napló, edited by Fanni Radnóti (Budapest: Magvető, 1989);

Nem bírta hát . . .: Utolsó versei (Békéscsaba: Kner, 1989);

Meredek út (Budapest: Cserépfalvi, 1990);

Versei és versfordításai (Budapest: Unikornis, 1996).

Editions in English: *Postcards,* translated by Stephen Polgar, Stephen Berg, and S. J. Marks (West Branch, Iowa: Cummington, 1969);

Forced March: Selected Poems, translated by Clive Wilmer and George Gömöri (Manchester, U.K.: Carcanet New Press, 1979);

The Complete Poetry, edited and translated by Emery Edward George (Ann Arbor, Mich.: Ardis, 1980);

Under Gemini: A Prose Memoir and Selected Poetry, translated by Kenneth and Zita McRobbie and Jascha Kessler (Athens: Ohio University Press, 1985);

Foamy Sky: The Major Poems of Miklós Radnóti, selected and translated by Zsuzsanna Ozsvath and Frederick Turner (Princeton: Princeton University Press, 1992).

OTHER: "Vészes sorály-sikollyal ha fölsikoltok," in *Jóság: Antológia* (Budapest: Hoffmann és Társany, 1929), p. 63;

"Önéletrajz," "Télre leső dal," "Októberi vázlat," "Eső," "Boldog hajinali vers," "Tavaszi vers," and "Szélesen," in *Azért is! Harc az öregek ellen,* edited by Sándor Hangay (Budapest, 1931), pp. 145–149;

"Táj, változással," "Beteg a kedves," "Emlékező vers," and "Köszëntsd a napot!," in *Új magyar líra: Fiatal költők antológiája,* edited by Aurél Kárpáti (Budapest: Vajda János Társaság, 1934), pp. 49–51;

Korunk. Tizenkét fiatal költő, edited by Radnóti and Béla Dénes (Budapest: Független Szemle, 1935);

"A könyv és az ember," in *Az új Könyvek könyve: 173 író, művész, tudós vallomása olvasmányairól,* edited by Béla Kőhalmi (Budapest: Gergely, 1937), pp. 265–268;

Margit Kaffka, *Összes versei,* edited by Radnóti (Budapest: Franklin-Társulat, 1940);

Foreword to appendix, in *Makói évek: József Attila élete nyomában,* edited by Ödön Galamb (Budapest: Cserépfalvi, 1941), volume 1, pp. 107–113;

"Montenegrři elégia," "Himnusz a békéről," "Harmadik ecloga," "Huszonnyolc év," "Huszonkilenc év," "Nyugatalan órán," "Járkálj csak,

halálraítélt," and "Apró versek," in *Mai magyar költők: A fiatal magyar költőnemzedék negyven lírikusának versei,* edited by László Vajthó (Budapest: Dante, 1941), pp. 135–139;

Margit Kaffka, *Összes versei,* edited by Radnóti (Budapest: Magyar Helikon, 1961).

TRANSLATIONS: Bertolt Brecht, "Részlet a Mahagonnyból," *A Színpad,* 1, nos. 1–3 (1935): 27–31;

Jakob Bidermann, "Cenodoxus, Páris doktora: Színjáték három részben. Jakob Bidermann után írta Joseph Gregor," *A Színpad,* 2, nos. 7–8 (1936): 378–389;

Imre Trencsényi-Waldapfel, ed., *Pásztori Magyar Vergilius: Publius Vergilius Maro eclogáinak teljes szövege,* translated by Radnóti and others (Budapest: Magyar Officina, 1938);

Guillaume Apollinaire, *Válogatott versei,* edited and translated by Radnóti and István Vas (Budapest: Vajda János Társaság, 1940);

Szerelmes versek: Világirodalmi antológia két ezredév költészetéből, edited and translated by Radnóti and others (Budapest: Szukits, 1941);

Henri de Montherlant, *Lányok* (Budapest: Cserépfalvi, 1942);

Orpheus nyomában: Műfordítások kétezer év költôiből, edited and translated by Radnóti (Budapest: Pharos, 1943);

Miguel de Cervantes, *Don Quijote,* edited and translated by Radnóti (Budapest: Cserépfalvi, 1943);

Jan Huizinga, *Válogatott tanulmányok: Tudomány, irodalom, művészet* (Budapest: Pharos, 1943);

Jean de La Fontaine, *Fables choisies / Válogatott mesék* (Budapest: Franklin-Társulat, 1943);

Conrad Ferdinand Meyer, *Ausgewählte Gedichte / Válogatott versei,* translated by Radnóti and others (Budapest: Franklin-Társulat, 1944);

Kende István, ed., *Karunga a holtak ura: Néger mesék* (Budapest: Pharos, 1944);

William Shakespeare, *Drámái: Vízkereszt, vagy amit akartok,* translated by Radnóti and others (Budapest: Európa, 1960).

Influenced by the generation of writers who in the first decades of the twentieth century embraced European modernism as a means to revolutionize Hungarian literature, Miklós Radnóti emerged in the late 1920s as a gifted poet possessed of the ability to transcend the depth of personal despair with dignity and compassion. He himself became a victim of World War II atrocities: after being sent to forced labor, he was executed and buried in a mass

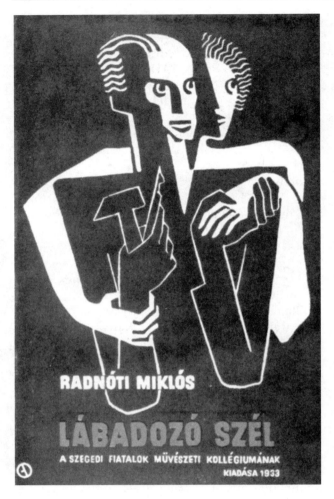

Dust jacket for Radnóti's 1933 collection of poetry, in which the wind is a prominent image

attended commercial school and was tutored by Károly Hilbert, a teacher of mathematics, who first realized and encouraged the young man's affinity toward literature. During this time Radnóti also established his first "literary" friendships with Antal Forgács and György Tamássi (Wágner) and began to publish in such junior periodicals as *Mindnyájunk Lapja* (Everyone's Magazine) and *Haladás* (Progress). In 1927 and 1928 Radnóti studied textile manufacturing in Reichenberg (now Liberec, Czech Republic), and for the next two years he worked as an assistant in his uncle's textile business.

Beginning in Reichenberg, Radnóti became increasingly influenced by avant-garde Czech and Hungarian poetry and biographies of Jesus, and after returning to Budapest he began to actively pursue his literary interests. He contributed to *1928*, a short-lived magazine of the young leftist generation, and published twelve poems in the anthology *Jóság* (Goodness). In 1929 he helped edit *Kortárs* (Contemporary), a new magazine influenced by Lajos Kassák, the major figure of the Hungarian avant-garde. Radnóti also published a poem in *Remény* (Hope), a journal of Jewish youth, even though he was apathetic about his religious origin. Influenced by modernist poets such as Kassák, Endre Ady, and Attila József, the majority of Radnóti's early poetry incorporates a variety of avant-garde techniques such as surrealist imagery, expressionist language, and free verse. Yet, in a poetic self-reflection published in 1931 titled "Most fölfújom . . ." (translated as "Now I Inflate . . . ," 1980), Radnoti recognized that his claim for a radical poetry could not be satisfied by imitating literary trends. Radnóti was searching for his own methodology of expression, and as illustrated in the memoir-like "Szerelmi ciklus 1927–28-ból" (translated as "Love Cycle from 1927–28," 1980), he was capable of deep emotional and spiritual exploration.

In *Pogány köszöntő* (Pagan Salute), published in April 1930, Radnóti creates a strongly hermetical world in which the triumph of the poetic will serves to unify opposite poles of existence—love and nature, body and universe, dream and reality. The poems represent a rite of purification, merging the pagan and biblical as a means of sanctification. For Radnóti, the rite is both symbolic and cathartic, reflecting his own sense of personal anguish in realizing the nature of his own identity. The truth about his birth had been concealed from him by his father and stepmother; only after his father's death did he learn from a relative that the woman he accepted as his mother was really a stepmother and that his natural mother and brother had died because of—or

grave. Although Radnóti produced only a limited body of work, he is generally acknowledged as one of the most significant writers in twentieth-century Hungarian literature.

Miklós Radnóti was born on 5 May 1909 in Budapest to Jakab Glatter, a clerk, and Ilona Grósz. Like many others of Jewish origin who abandoned their foreign-sounding—mostly German—surnames, the poet changed Glatter to Radnóti, drawing upon Radnót, his father's place of birth. Radnóti's mother and twin brother died during childbirth, and his father remarried a year later; his stepmother gave birth to Radnóti's half sister, Ágnes Erdélyi, who was killed by Nazis in the same year as the poet. Radnóti attended elementary and secondary school in Budapest. In 1921 his father died, and his stepmother and half sister moved to Nagyvárad (now Oradea, Romania), but Radnóti remained in Budapest with his maternal uncle, Dezső Grósz, a prosperous textile merchant. From 1923 to 1927 he had been "killed" by—Radnóti himself. The poetic self therefore feels like a modern Cain, murderer of his brother, and the matricide replaces the biblical Original Sin committed by Eve, the mother of humankind. In addition, the somewhat contradictory desire for both home and freedom is closely related to another aspect of the purification, that is, to the search for pure poetic autonomy free from other literary influences.

Following the publication of *Pogány köszöntő* Radnóti left his uncle's textile business and enrolled at the University of Szeged, where from 1930 to 1935 he studied Hungarian and French language and literature. He formed close and lasting friendships with Dezső Baróti and Gábor Tolnai, future literary historians, and Gyula Ortutay, folklorist-ethnologist; together with them, Radnóti enjoyed the patronage of their professor, Sándor Sík, a Catholic priest, literary scholar, and poet. In addition, he became involved with the newly formed Szegedi Fiatalok Művészeti Kollégiuma (Szeged Youth Arts College), a leftist intellectual movement, through which Radnóti met graphic artist György Buday, poet and playwright Károly Berczeli Anzelm, and stage director and theoretician Ferenc Hont. By way of these intellectual circles Radnóti was exposed to a broad spectrum of experiences ranging from readings of surrealist and leftist authors to ethnology, psychoanalysis, folk music, and stances of political opposition from bourgeois liberalism to communism. Szegedi Fiatalok Művészeti Kollégiuma later published Radnóti's third and fourth volumes of poetry and his doctoral dissertation on renowned woman poet and prose writer Margit Kaffka.

Újmódi pásztorok éneke (Song of New-Fashioned Shepherds), published in April 1931 in Budapest, includes poems written in the months before he moved to Szeged as well as those of his early university years. Influenced by his association with the Szegedi Fiatalok Művészeti Kollégiuma, the volume assumes an intellectual stance in relation to the plight of humanity while creating a bucolic world defined by social consciousness. The role assumed by the poet is that of a modern-day shepherd whose flock is the poor, the derelict, and the oppressed. Tropes based on nature are detached from the substance of the poems, and landscapes become more concrete, embodied in pictures of rural life that draw on the traditional genres of folk poetry (song, ballad) and on ethnographic knowledge, which makes new—grotesque and tragic—qualities possible. The first cycle of poems, "Táj, szeretőkkel" (Landscape, with Lovers), is mostly descriptive,

omitting the extensive use of apostrophe that dominated the previous volume. The main poetical tendencies in *Pogány köszöntő* underline the pagan voice, which marked the second volume as a provocative target for official censorship. The title of the third cycle, "Aprószentek" (Holy Innocents) is again a hint, taken from the New Testament, at Radnóti's birth trauma; but the first poem of the volume, "Arckép" (translated as "Portrait," 1980), elaborates the comparison of the poetic self-image to that of the twenty-two-year-old Christ, in a gently erotic tone: "girls / dreamed about him at night!" On this pretext, the volume was banned the same month it was published, and Radnóti was accused of sacrilege and offense against public modesty. As a result of the trial in December 1931, the poet was acquitted of the second charge but condemned for the first crime to eight days' imprisonment. However, after an appeal on his behalf by Sík and others, in May 1932 the decision was confirmed but its execution suspended so that Radnóti would not have to leave the university.

Paradoxically, the proceedings against him reinforced Radnóti's decision (made in 1927 or 1928) to convert to Christianity, so as to make it impossible for anyone to accuse him of exploiting symbols of an "alien" religion, since the New Testament faith was no more alien to him than that of the Old Testament. The inner certainty of this decision, however, was more important for Radnóti than its actual realization. Living in a country governed by an anti-Semitic rightist régime, Radnóti had long feared that his conversion would be seen as nothing more than a means to escape the consequences of his Jewish descent. Apart from the official anticommunist censorship and the realization that the leftist clichés in his early avant-garde poems were uncomfortable for his otherwise individualistic sense of artistic quality, his modest and deep religious faith led him to omit from the collections those socially tuned poems that could be mistaken for signs of socialist or communist political engagement.

After staying with a friend in Nogent-sur-Marne from July through August 1931 Radnóti traveled to Paris for the first time, where he was deeply impressed by the Exposition Coloniale Mondiale, which contributed toward the formation of his humanist conviction and a sense of the exotic. That experience is reflected in a lengthy, rebellious poem showing some expressionist attraction to primitivism: *Ének a négerről, aki a városba ment* (translated as "Song of the Black Man Who Went to Town," 1980), which appeared as the final poem in his subsequent collection and as a separate work a year later in 1934.

In 1933 Radnóti brought out *Lábadozó szél* (Convalescent Wind), which includes ten poems from the previously confiscated collection. In the prologue the poet establishes analogies among poetic speech ("my words / march, in the distance, raising / dust among cockfeathers!"), the daybreak, and an approaching storm, introducing the central element of the wind as an agent of change and transformation. In the poem "1931. December 8 (Főtárgyalás)" (translated as "8 December 1931 [Public hearing]," 1980) the "convalescent" wind is called forth to carry the essence of poetic language "all over into poems." In a later poem, "1932. május 5 (Huszonharmadik évem)" (translated as "5 May 1932 [My twenty-third year]," 1980), the poet discovers in his lover a faithful partner, and the wind leitmotiv turns to an erotic extension of breath itself. In effect, *Lábadozó szél* is a farewell to Radnóti's childhood and juvenile poetical aspirations, expressed in a startlingly pert manner as he declares that he and his lover are ready to go forth in life together.

In the autumn of 1933 Radnóti was invited to contribute to the prestigious literary journal *Nyugat* (West), in which he began publishing poems, critical essays, and reviews. For Radnóti, this activity represented a reconciliation with the editor, the prominent poet Mihály Babits, who had published a devastating review of *Lábadozó szél* in the same journal. In 1934 Aurél Kárpáti edited an anthology, *Új magyar líra* (Recent Hungarian Poetry), featuring Radnóti's work along with that of such writers as István Vas, Sándor Weöres, Zoltán Zelk, Antal Forgács, and Anna Hajnal. In his review of the anthology Babits termed the participants the "third generation" of *Nyugat*, giving rise to a lasting critical discussion. The following year Radnóti worked on another significant anthology of twelve poets, *Korunk* (Our Age), with Béla Dénes. Radnóti felt it important to belong to a literary group but later rejected the "generational" point of view for eliminating the most important divergences between individual authors while assimilating them into a so-called movement.

In *Újhold* (New Moon), published on 5 May 1935, Radnóti brought closure to the first stage of his literary development and simultaneously established the tone and quality of his mature poetry. Constituting a poetical manifesto, the opening poem, "Mint a bika" (translated as "Like a Bull," 1980), provides the poetic self with a surprisingly masculine and animal image: a bull about to be martyred during an attack by wolves. This image, in turn, is contrasted with the image of a solitary wolf—the representation of Adam and God, the creator of Genesis—trying day by day to tear or "create" a she-wolf out of his own side. The brutal imagery of this manly solitude issues from introspection—certainly reactivated also by external threat—driven by the circumstances of Radnóti's own birth, which is suggested by the conceit of "the slowly glancing knife" in "És kegyetlen" (translated as "And as Cruel," 1980). As with poems in *Lábadozó szél*, Radnóti creates scenes that are equally susceptible to the possibilities of tranquility or sudden change, as illustrated in "Vihar előtt" (translated as "Before a Storm," 1980). Most striking are the poems inspired by Radnóti's relationship with Fanni Gyarmati, whom he had known since 1926 and married on 11 August 1935, a few months after *Újhold* was released. The closing poem, "Kortárs útlevelére" (translated as "Into a Contemporary's Passport," 1980), claiming that poetic survival is granted only by revolt, is partly a farewell to the "nurturing community" of the Szegedi Fiatalok Művészeti Kollégiuma.

Having earned a certificate for high school teaching, Radnóti moved to Budapest with his wife. Nevertheless, his decisive Szeged friendships remained alive even after the Szegedi Fiatalok Művészeti Kollégiuma ceased to exist in 1938. Because of his Jewish origin, Radnóti was not allowed to obtain employment as teacher, so he had to earn his living by tutoring and by freelance writing. He contributed a lecture on Margit Kaffka as well as poems and translations to the János Vajda Society and joined the *Irodalomtudományi Társaság* (Society of Literary Studies), founded by, among others, Gábor Halász, Antal Szerb, and Miklós Szentkuthy. Radnóti also worked for such leftist papers as *Gondolat* (Thought), *Népszava* (People's Word), and *Szocializmus* (Socialism) and published translations in Kassák's periodical *Munka* (Labor).

Published in 1936, *Járkálj csak, halálraítélt!* (Keep Walking, Condemned to Death!) represented a further refinement of Radnóti's poetic transition while serving as a prophetic announcement of the poet's own death. The title poem, placed at the end of the collection, returns to the image of animal martyrdom found in the previous volume. The new element in this work is a fine separation of the poetic soul—as a synecdoche of earthly life—from the body. Several significant poems display Radnóti's fondness for the diary format; and as in the previous collection, poems devoted to his wife, Fanni, provide the volume with a gentle and elegant grace. As noted in contemporary reviews by critics such as György Bálint and Gábor Tolnai, *Járkálj csak, halálraítélt!* illustrates Radnóti's control of tone and imagery characterized by a rich simplicity. In the following year Radnóti was awarded the prestigious Baumgarten Prize in Poetry, despite the animosity and over the objection of the political establishment, indicating his developing status as a poet.

Radnóti further enhanced his critical reputation with the publication in 1938 of *Meredek út* (Steep Road). Some of the poems reflect his second trip to France, which he made with his wife, critic Aladár Schöpflin, and his family in the summer of 1937 to attend an international writers' congress and take part in a mass demonstration declaring solidarity with the victims of Fascism in Spain. At the beginning of the volume Radnóti placed "Huszonnyolc év" (translated as "Twenty-Eight Years," 1980) inspired by his birthday; this poem is addressed to his mother, who died at the same age Radnóti had reached when he wrote the poem. In other poems the reader encounters recollections as well as dirges about deceased fellow poets such as Gyula Juhász, József, and Federico García Lorca. In several poems, influenced in part by Guillaume Apollinaire and by József's "Párizsi anzix" (1927; translated as "Parisian Postcard"), Radnóti employs a *carte postale* (postcard) technique in which details of visual reality are presented as fragmented and suggestive elements to be deciphered by the reader. The volume also includes disquieting premonitions about the future, culminating in the two final and most powerful poems, "Első ecloga" (translated as "First Eclogue," 1980) and "Huszonkilenc év" (translated as "Twenty-Nine Years," 1980).

In the summer of 1939 Radnóti returned with his wife to France. In Paris he was hosted by the French PEN Club, and he and his wife also visited Rouen, Chantilly, Senlis, and Ermenonville. In the following year Radnóti published a selection of his poems written from 1930 to 1940 and edited a volume of verse by Apollinaire, which he translated with his friend and fellow poet István Vas. Radnóti's most important publication in 1940 was *Ikrek hava* (Month of Twins; translated as *Under Gemini*, 1985), subtitled "Journal on Childhood." This memoir, written soon after the return from France, is Radnóti's longest and most significant work of prose, and its scope is far wider than that suggested by the subtitle. A series of personal memories about the poet's life, *Ikrek hava* provides insight and understanding into Radnóti's complex self-image and the relationship between the nature of existence and the birth of creativity.

Radnóti and his wife, Fanni, in 1938

Following the outbreak of World War II, Radnóti was drafted into forced labor, and for the final months of 1940 he worked in Transylvania before he was allowed to return to Budapest and resume his career. In 1941 he contributed an important note to a new edition of poems by József, and in that same year—with Vas, Géza Képes, and Ferenc Szemlér—he helped edit and translate *Szerelmes versek* (Love Poems), an anthology of world poetry. After the demise of *Nyugat* following the death of Babits, Radnóti continued to publish in its successor, *Magyar Csillag* (Hungarian Star), edited by Gyula Illyés.

In 1942 Radnóti's last volume of poetry published during his lifetime was released as *Naptár* (Calendar), a thin chapbook consisting of twelve short lyrics, one for each month of the year. In July of that same year Radnóti was again drafted into forced labor but was allowed to remain in Budapest. Anxious for his well-being, many representative figures of Hungarian intellectual life—writers, artists, scholars, and politicians—signed a petition presented to the Minister of National Defense, and in May 1943 the poet was exempted from that term of forced labor. In the same month, Sík baptized Radnóti and his wife in the Roman Catholic faith.

During the early 1940s—the poet's last years—Radnóti continued to write poetry while producing an extremely rich harvest of translations, notably works by poets of classical antiquity, Apollinaire, and Henri de Montherlant. In 1943 he edited his own anthology of foreign poetry, *Orpheus nyomában* (In Orpheus's Footsteps), translated selections from essays by Jan Huizinga and fables of Jean de La Fontaine, and reworked a version of Miguel de Cervantes's *Don Quixote* (1605). In the following year he published *Karunga, a holtak ura* (Karunga, Lord of the Dead), a collection of his translations of African folk poetry, and he also contributed to a bilingual edition of the work of Conrad Ferdinand Meyer.

In May 1944, when he received a third and final draft notice for another term of forced labor, Radnóti was busy translating William Shakespeare's *Twelfth Night* (ca. 1601 or 1602). He was taken to Lager Heidenau, not far from Bor, Yugoslavia, where he worked in copper mines and on railroad construction. Alarmed by the partisan and Soviet advance on the Balkans, the fascist military force relocated the prisoners to Bor in August. Several weeks later Radnóti and his fellow prisoners were moved again to northwest Yugoslavia. In the end, half-dead because of the long forced march, sickness, and brutal treatment, Radnóti and twenty others were shot and thrown into an anonymous grave on 8 or 9 November 1944 near Abda, western Hungary. During the exhumation of the mass grave in the summer of 1946, a small notebook, later published as *Bori notesz* (Bor Notebook, the facsimile of which was not edited until 1970), was found in one of his pockets; it comprised the poet's last poems. On the first page he had written a note in five languages giving information on himself and his last will as to the future destination of the booklet. After giving his name, the poet asked the finder of the notebook to send it to the address of his close friend Ortutay. Radnóti was buried again in the Jewish cemetery of Győr, and then, after a re-exhumation, in Budapest.

The bulk of Radnóti's posthumous *Tajtékos ég* (translated as *Clouded Sky,* 1972), published in 1946, had been formerly collected and prepared by the poet himself, but it was also complemented with lyrics written during the forced labor and march, copies of which had been sent home by the poet. It is

much more voluminous than any of his previous collections, comprising almost all of his late poetry. The most celebrated of the poems are the "Eclogues," in which Radnóti adapted the *Eclogues* of Virgil to serve as a medium for the emotional and psychological conflict emerging in his late poetry. The form offered by Virgil was dialogic and dramatic, referring to poetry endangered by war, so the situation was appropriate for Radnóti.

Because of the anti-Semitic climate and Hungary's involvement in World War II, only an ever-decreasing circle of friends and intellectuals could properly estimate Radnóti's merit during his lifetime. In addition, the idiosyncratic nature of the late poetry and the circumstances surrounding his death resulted in a symbolic interpretation in which the poet and poetry became interchangeable, further exploited by the dominance of Marxist ideology for nearly a forty-year period following 1948. Like many others, most notably Attila József, Radnóti became an anti-Fascist sacrificial hero. His social sympathies have been exaggerated as socialistic, and his religious concerns were consistently underplayed. Later interpretations, however, allow for a more appropriate appreciation of his poetic nature and purpose. He managed to solve the contradiction of poetic memory and liberty by a visionary inner independence. The poet's devotion to translation and to his professional craft led him to an unparalleled economy of expression. Radnóti thus occupies a distinctive position in the mainstream of Hungarian literary history as a poet of extraordinary achievement.

Letters:

Négy Radnóti-levél (Budapest: Magyar Iparművészeti Főiskola, 1973).

Bibliographies:

István Vasvári and Gyula Batári, eds., *Radnóti Miklós: Bibliográfia* (Budapest: Fővárosi Szabó Ervin Könyvtár, 1966);

Albert Tezla, *Hungarian Authors: A Bibliographical Handbook* (Cambridge, Mass.: Belknap Press of Harvard University Press, 1970), pp. 481–486;

Emery Edward George, *The Poetry of Miklós Radnóti: A Comparative Study* (New York: Karz-Cohl, 1986), pp. 537–552, 699–785;

Mariann Nagy, ed., *Radnóti Miklós: Bibliográfia* (Budapest: Petőfi Irodalmi Múzeum, 1989).

Biographies:

Dezső Baróti, ed., *Radnóti Miklós 1909–1944* (Budapest: Magyar Helikon, 1959);

Ábel Kőszegi, *Töredék: Radnóti Miklós utolsó hónapjainak krónikája* (Budapest: Szépirodalmi, 1972);

József M. Pásztor et al., *A 2 X 2 józansága: Emlékezések Radnóti Miklósról* (Budapest: Magvető, 1975);

Baróti, *Kortárs útlevelére: Radnóti Miklós 1909–1944* (Budapest: Szépirodalmi, 1977);

Béla Pomogáts, *Radnóti Miklós* (Budapest: Gondolat, 1977);

László Z. Szabó, ed., *Radnóti koszorúja: Magyar költők versei Radnóti Miklósról* (Győr: Győr-Sopron Megyei Tanács, 1979);

Pomogáts, ed., *Emlék és varázslat: Vallomások Radnóti Miklósról* (Budapest: Kozmosz Könyvek, 1984);

Szabó, ed., *Radnótitól Radnótiról* (Budapest: Tankönyvkiadó, 1985);

Béla Bognár, *Gyötrelmek útja: Dokumentum-regény* (Győr: Győr-Sopron Megyei Tanács–Radnóti Miklós Emlékbizottság és Irodalmi Társaság, 1987);

Ernő Hulesch, *Stációk: Dokumentumriport Radnóti Miklósról* (Győr: Győr Megyei Lapkiadó Vállalat, 1989).

References:
Marianna D. Birnbaum, *Miklós Radnóti: A Biography of His Poetry* (Munich: Veröffentlichungen des Finnisch-Ugrischen Seminars an der Universität, 1983);

Imre Bori, *Radnóti Miklós költészete* (Novi Sad: Forum, 1965);

Edit B. Csáky, ed., *Radnóti tanulmányok* (Budapest: TIT-Magyar Irodalomtörténeti Társaság, 1985);

Emery Edward George, *The Poetry of Miklos Radnoti: A Comparative Study* (New York: Karz-Cohl, 1986);

István Nemes, *A képszerűség eszközei Radnóti Miklós költészetében* (Budapest: Akadémiai Kiadó, 1965);

Nemes, *Radnóti Miklós költői nyelve* (Pécs: Pécsi Tanárképző Főiskola Tudományos Bizottsága, 1974);

János Pilinszky, "Radnóti Miklós," in his *Összegyűjtött művei: Tanulmányok, esszék, cikkek,* volume 2, edited by Zoltán Hafner (Budapest: Századvég, 1993), pp. 265–266;

Áron Tóbiás, "Késői beszélgetések Radnóti Miklósról," *Tiszatáj,* 31 (1977): 39–60.

Bruno Schulz

(12 July 1892 – 19 November 1942)

Bożena Shallcross
Indiana University

BOOKS: *Sklepy cynamonowe* (Warsaw: Towarzystwo Wydawnicze Rój, 1934);

Sanatorium pod Klepsydrą (Warsaw: Towarzystwo Wydawnicze Rój, 1937);

Druga jesień (Kraków: Wydawnictwo Literackie, 1973);

Xięga Bałwochwalcza (Warsaw: Interpress, 1988); translated by Bogna Piotrowska as *The Book of Idolatry* (Warsaw: Interpress, 1989);

Republika marzeń: utwory rozproszone, opowiadania, fragmenty, eseje, rysunki, edited by Jerzy Ficowski (Warsaw: Chimera, 1993).

Editions and Collections: *Sklepy cynamonowe. Sanatorium pod Klepsydrą. Kometa* (Kraków: Wydawictwo Literackie, 1957);

Proza (Kraków: Wydawnictwo Literackie, 1964);

Sklepy cynamonowe, Sanatorium pod Klepsydrą (Kraków: Wydawnictwo Literackie, 1978);

Sklepy cynamonowe (Kraków-Wrocław: Wydawnictwo Literackie, 1984);

Opowiadania; Wybór esejów i listów, edited by Jerzy Jarzębski (Wrocław: Ossolineum, 1989).

Editions in English: *Cinnamon Shops and Other Stories,* translated by Celina Wieniewska (London: MacGibbon & Kee, 1963); republished as *The Street of Crocodiles,* translated by Wieniewska (New York: Walker, 1963);

The Sanatorium Under the Sign of the Hourglass, translated by Wieniewska (New York: Walker, 1978; London: Hamilton, 1979);

The Fictions of Bruno Schulz, translated by Wieniewska (London: Picador, 1988);

The Complete Fiction of Bruno Schulz, translated by Wieniewska (New York: Walker, 1989);

The Collected Works of Bruno Schulz, edited by Jerzy Ficowski (London: Picador, 1998).

Bruno Schulz was one of the most innovative Polish writers of the twentieth century. The two slim volumes of short stories on which his reputation is based are a significant contribution to European expressionism in their evocation of an intensely phantasmagorical world in which the simplest objects are made to reveal their hidden, magical side. Schulz was also an accomplished draftsman and printmaker who remained faithful to the figurative mode of expression at a time when abstraction, in its various styles, all but dominated the visual arts.

Schulz was born on 12 July 1892 in a town of Drohobycz, located in eastern Galicia, then a part of the Austro-Hungarian Empire. He was the third child of Henrietta Hendel (née Kuhmarker) and Jakub Schultz; the couple also had a daughter named Hania, their firstborn, and a second son, Izydor. Jakub Schulz was a textile merchant and a shop owner. The Schulz family was Jewish but not religious and spoke Polish at home.

After receiving an elementary education, Schulz was enrolled in the Emperor Franz Joseph Gymnasium in Drohobycz in 1902. In 1907 his father proudly published a postcard of young Bruno's sculpture, the first indication of his son's artistic inclinations. Although the future fiction writer had dreams of becoming a visual artist, he deferred to his father's and brother's advice and enrolled in 1910 in the Department of Architecture at Lwów Polytechnic. However, his lack of interest in architecture, coupled with his father's bankruptcy and failing health, compelled young Schulz to abandon his studies three years later. At the outbreak of World War I, Schulz, along with several members of his family, left Drohobycz for Vienna, where for a while he had an opportunity to study painting at the Viennese Academy of Fine Arts. In 1915 his father died, and for the next nine years Schulz eked out a living working as a visual artist. Few of his works from this period have survived, except for his main accomplishment, *Xięga Bałwochwalcza* (1988; translated as *The Book of Idolatry,* 1989), a series of erotic prints that idealized femininity and represented man as masochistically debased. The technique he employed was a method called *cliche-verre*, in which an image was scratched on a glass plate covered by a black gelatin.

In the early 1920s Schulz developed a rather intense intellectual relationship with a talented student of Polish literature named Władysław Riff. In their correspondence they shared literary ideas; it was at this time that Schulz began his first attempts at creative writing. Unfortunately, not a single letter survived—all of Riff's archives were destroyed after the latter died of consumption in 1927. During this same period Schulz became an avid reader; bilingual, he was fully cognizant of German literature, in particular the poetry of Rainer Maria Rilke, whom he greatly admired.

Difficult financial circumstances forced Schulz to seek a steadier source of income. In 1924 he accepted a position as a teacher of drawing at the King Władysław Jagiełło State High School. He also temporarily taught a class in woodwork and was an instructor in mathematics. Since Schulz lacked both pedagogical experience and a degree, his position was not permanent, and in 1928 he found himself without a job. Not until 8 March 1932 was he offered a tenured position by a special decree of the Board of Education of the Lwów School District. Besides his teaching duties at the state high school, he also taught occasionally at the elementary and private high schools in that district. These additional duties were necessary, for after the death of his brother, Schulz became the sole provider for his mother; his sister, Hania Hoffmanowa; and her son. Although reclusive and shy by nature, Schulz was genuinely liked by his pupils and was well remembered long after his death due, in part, to the manner in which he engaged his students in his drawing class and entertained them with his fascinating tales.

During his frequent visits to Zakopane, Schulz became acquainted with the avant-garde playwright and painter, Stanisław Ignacy Witkiewicz. At his house the playwright introduced Schulz to his circle of like-minded friends. Among them, Schulz met Debora Vogel, a young and well-educated poet from Lwów. A correspondence ensued. As a postscript to his letters to Vogel, Schulz incorporated drafts of short stories that later comprised the collection *Sklepy cynamonowe* (1934; translated as *Cinnamon Shops and Other Stories*, 1963; also translated as *The Street of Crocodiles*, 1963). Vogel and her friend Rachela Auerbach made an effort to introduce Schulz to publishers, but they were not successful. In the spring of 1933, Schulz met another interesting woman, Józefina Szelińska, who was, like him, a

Bruno Schulz in the mid 1930s

teacher in Drohobycz and who later became his fiancée.

Shortly after meeting Szelińska, Schulz became acquainted with Zofia Nałkowska, a prominent writer and a member of the literary and political establishment at the time. Her admiration for his prose became a turning point in Schulz's career. A noted writer herself, she was able to interest the Warsaw publishing house Towarzystwo Wydawnicze Rój in Schulz's work, and in December 1934 Rój published his *Sklepy cynamonowe*, which was financed by his older brother Izydor just before he died. Shortly after publication of *Sklepy cynamonowe*, the intensely private school instructor became a rather well-known literary figure.

The first cycle of his short stories is permeated by a lyrical quality that transformed the world of a sleepy, provincial Galician town before World War I into an imaginary reality. This collection of separate

Dust jacket for Schulz's first book (1934), a collection of short stories

incidents is unified by a narrator assuming the role of protagonist; other main characters include the father, the mother, several family members, and Adela, their servant.

The most elusive aspect of the volume is its thematic line. On the surface *Sklepy cynamonowe* whimsically describes odd facts that are of seemingly minor significance; however, these diverse descriptions convey the narrator's inner life, colored by his father's idiosyncratic philosophy and unpredictable behavior. The motif of initiation is introduced in the volume by the opening story, "Sierpień" (translated as "August"), thus preparing the reader for the overall design of the work. The rite of initiation, in which a cataclysmic change of consciousness occurs in conjunction with a dramatic shift from one level of existence to another, is accompanied in Schulz's short stories by a constant process of metamorphosis. His fluctuating world is not only apparent in the visible changes of the weather and other natural phenomena, but most importantly, in a series of transformations to which the father, the central character, is subjected. Thus, the father, a failed businessman, evolves into an inspired prophet, who becomes a madman obsessed with birds, and who, in the end, becomes a bird himself. But the father's obsessions are not focused on birds alone, for he has other fixations, such as a fetish with the female foot and being fascinated with the Creator's eternal struggle with matter, its constant mutation, and its aborted or degraded forms. The latter fascination is the basis of his idiosyncratic aesthetic theories, which he propounds to a female audience.

The method of composition of this cycle of stories has been described as resembling that of a nonlinear, loosely structured novel. As a matter of fact, the generic character of the volume is quite complex, and it owes some of its diversity to the use of various genres in the crafting of individual stories. In some of the stories, Schulz places emphasis on a rather well-developed plot (notably "Ptaki," translated as "Birds"); in other stories he relies on description ("Nemrod" and "Pan"); while in others he employs the genre of an essay or a treatise ("Traktat o manekinach," translated as "Treatise on Mannequins").

The success of Schulz's first volume of short stories brought him new friends throughout Poland—mostly young writers and critics, such as Tadeusz Breza, Kazimierz Truchanowski, and Leon Piwiński. In 1933 Nałkowska introduced Schulz to a literary circle that called itself "Przedmieście" (The Suburbs), of which he soon became a member. Although not particularly active, he supported the group's initiatives, even as he harbored artistic ideas that were quite different from theirs. Yet, despite his growing fame, Schulz remained closest to his own small group of Polish Jewish artists and intellectuals. In 1934 Schulz began to work on a novel tentatively titled *Mesjasz* (The Messiah). In it he depicts the second coming of the messiah (to Drohobycz). *Wiadomości Literackie* (The Literary News) published a portion of that work as a short story titled "Genialna epoka" (translated as "The Wondrous Age") and provided it with a cryptic footnote that read: "from the novel 'The Messiah.'" In this short story, Schulz—as had Walter Benjamin and Franz Kafka before him—formulated his vision of modernity by reviving the old Judaic lore in its specific Messianic form derived from the Cabala.

As the novel progressed, Schulz attempted to normalize his private life. He spent the summer of

1934 in Zakopane in the company of Witkiewicz and Jósef Wittlin; there he and his fiancée made plans to marry. Several obstacles, however, threatened their union. Szelińska, who had left her teaching post and moved to Warsaw, was a Catholic whose family converted from Judaism. Schulz, however, was not interested in converting to Catholicism. Instead, the couple considered a Protestant wedding ceremony in Silesia, but to marry there required residency in the province. Schulz, although basically a passive man, tried to save the relationship by traveling to Silesia on the chance that he might grow to like it; he also elicited advice from their mutual friends, but nothing came of his attempts—for despite his love for Józefina, he had grown attached to Drohobycz, and to leave the familiar sanctuary of his hometown was a sacrifice he was unwilling to make.

In 1935 a group of prominent poets and critics—Julian Tuwim, Adolf Nowaczyński, and Antoni Słonimski—nominated Schulz for an award sponsored by *Wiadomości Literackie*, the leading literary weekly. However, this highly distinguished honor was accompanied by a negative reception to his work by both right-wing and left-wing critics, who deplored the author's refusal to address the pertinent political issues of the time. That Schulz was also attacked for his disjointed narrative within an experimental temporal frame showed the critics' poor understanding of modern aesthetics. Schulz's approach toward the avant-garde is a complex matter in itself. Briefly, he was its adherent only in the purely aesthetic sense of the term, rejecting the sociopolitical and historiosophic ideas of the modern trend—in particular, the notion of progress.

At this point in his career, the writer felt compelled to begin a series of essays meant to clarify his artistic vision and to produce new work to bolster them, but his time-consuming pedagogical duties—of which he often complained in his letters—precluded his completing his projects. Not until 1936 did his superiors on the school board recognize him as a gifted writer and grant him the title "professor." In addition, they gave him a six-month sabbatical. Schulz used this time to write several short stories, including "Wiosna" (translated as "Spring"), "Jesień" (translated as "Autumn"), and "Republika marzeń" (translated as "The Republic of Dreams"), as well as many critical essays, mostly book reviews, for such periodicals as *Wiadomości Literackie, Skamander, Pion, Tygodnik Ilustrowany*, and *Studio*. In the same year, in the periodical *Studio* he exchanged open letters with Witold Gombrowicz, whom he had met on previous occasions. Gombrowicz's letter was aggressive, criticizing Schulz's fiction as pretentious. Schulz responded by defending the purity of the spiritual life from which his work derived.

The whole episode is a sad footnote to the history of their friendship, especially in light of Schulz's genuine admiration for Gombrowicz's prose.

In 1936 Szelińska's translation of Franz Kafka's *The Trial* appeared with a foreword by Schulz. Szelińska received no credit, since it has been generally accepted that for the book's commercial success it was agreed between them that only Schulz's name should appear on the cover. In 1937 Szelińska broke off her engagement to Schulz; according to Schulz, she could not accept the unresolved state of their relationship. After the separation, he never attempted to marry another woman.

Before the year ended, Schulz wrote a short story in German titled "Die Heimkehr" (translated as "The Return Home"). With the hope of seeking a wider audience and in interesting Western publishers, he sent the manuscript to Thomas Mann, then living in Switzerland. According to the authorities who conducted a search in Mann's Swiss archives, the story was lost, thereby sharing the fate of most of Schulz's manuscripts. Meanwhile, his second book of prose, titled *Sanatorium pod Klepsydrą* (1937; translated as *The Sanatorium Under the Sign of the Hourglass*, 1978), was brought out by the same publishing firm (Towarzystwo Wydawnicze Rój) that published his first collection. This second collection was comprised of both old and new short stories; they further testified to his lyricism and inventive use of poetic language, but Schulz introduced ideas quite different from those in his first collection. If the first volume can be described as the narrator's "song of innocence," the second cycle can rightly be considered his "song of experience." Although both works have a narrator named Józef, the position this character holds in the second book is that of the main protagonist. Schulz replaced the figure of the father, central to *Sklepy cynamonowe*, with Józef. In *Sanatorium pod Klepsydrą* such quixotic adventures as the visit Józef pays to his father in the underworld amount to a reinvention of old myths, especially the myth of loss. "The old semantics," as the author called them—that is, myths that defined his creative consciousness—became much more apparent in *Sanatorium pod Klepsydrą* than in his previous book. His goal in this volume was to return to mythical reality, accessible in modern times only in fragments, and to reinvent it as the primary substance of the world. His belief in the mythical and textual nature of reality led him to reinvent the myth of the Book conceived as the World in the opening short story, "Księga" (translated as "The Book"); thus, the Book became the symbol of his fundamental belief in the textual nature of reality, time, and space. In the short story "Wiosna" (translated as "Spring") he textualized time as follows: "This is the

*Dust jacket for Schulz's second collection of short stories (1937),
which reinterpret myth in modern context*

story of a certain spring that was more real, more dazzling and brighter than any other spring, a spring that took its text seriously: an inspired script written in the festive red of sealing wax and of calendar print, the red of colored pencils and of enthusiasm, the amaranth of happy telegrams from far away."

That Schulz included in this work portions from his novel *Mesjasz* added a religious dimension to the book. Undoubtedly, Schulz yearned for a religious nature, but his religiousness was the tributary of two main traditions—Christianity and Judaism, with its Judaic component only recently recognized by scholars.

Once again the reception of Schulz's prose was mixed. Critics were polarized between those who praised the work for its originality—among them the young Artur Sandauer—and those such as Kazimerz Wyka and Stefan Napierski who attacked him for being unnecessarily complex. Yet, in 1938 in the midst of controversy, the forty-six-year-old author was honored with the Gold Laurel of the Polish Academy of Literature, the most prestigious literary award of that time. The last published works of his career were two

short stories: "Kometa" (translated as "The Comet") and "Ojczyzna" (translated as "Fatherland"), both of which appeared that same year in the press. Up until the outbreak of World War II Schulz was working on yet another volume of short stories, but these were subsequently lost (as were his archives) during the Holocaust.

As war clouds gathered, Schulz's friend, the pianist Maria Rey-Chasin, in an attempt to break the writer's isolation, urged him to visit Paris. Reluctant to leave his hometown, he finally conceded and left for Paris for a brief period in the summer of 1938. Writing to another friend, Romana Halpern, Schulz indicated that his sojourn in the City of Lights was not entirely successful. He saw great works of art in the galleries and museums, but he failed to establish contacts with the French art dealers and to show them the samples of his own work that he had brought with him. Equally unsuccessful were his few attempts at having his short stories translated into other languages. Soon after he returned to Poland, Schulz learned that Mendel Neugroschel, who was his sole liaison with an Austrian publishing house, was arrested after the *Anschluss* (annexation) of the country by the Nazis. Early in 1939, eager for new contacts, Schulz met in Warsaw the Italian writer Massimo Bontempelli, who showed interest in his work, but nothing of consequence came of their meeting.

In September 1939 Poland was invaded by the German and Russian armies, and its eastern territories, including Drohobycz, were annexed by the Soviets. Though Schulz kept his position as a teacher, the new rulers imposed a socialist realist style of fiction that did not at all appeal to him. In 1941 Hitler invaded the Soviet Union, and Drohobycz fell under Nazi rule. After a short period, its Jewish inhabitants were herded into a section of the town designated as a ghetto, Schulz among them. For a time, the writer was protected by a Gestapo officer, a certain Feliks Landau, who recognized Schulz's talents and used him for various light jobs. Meanwhile, his friends in Warsaw prepared false papers for him and organized an escape. Schulz again procrastinated, ever apprehensive of leaving the town in which he grew up and that provided him ample material for his artistic endeavors. Whether he decided to leave Drohobycz is not known, for on the eve of the planned escape—Thursday, 19 November 1942—he was shot dead on a street by another Gestapo officer, Landau's adversary, during a random pogrom during which the writer had, only moments before, bought a loaf of bread. His friends found his body at night and buried him in the Jewish cemetery. Whatever belongings he left behind,

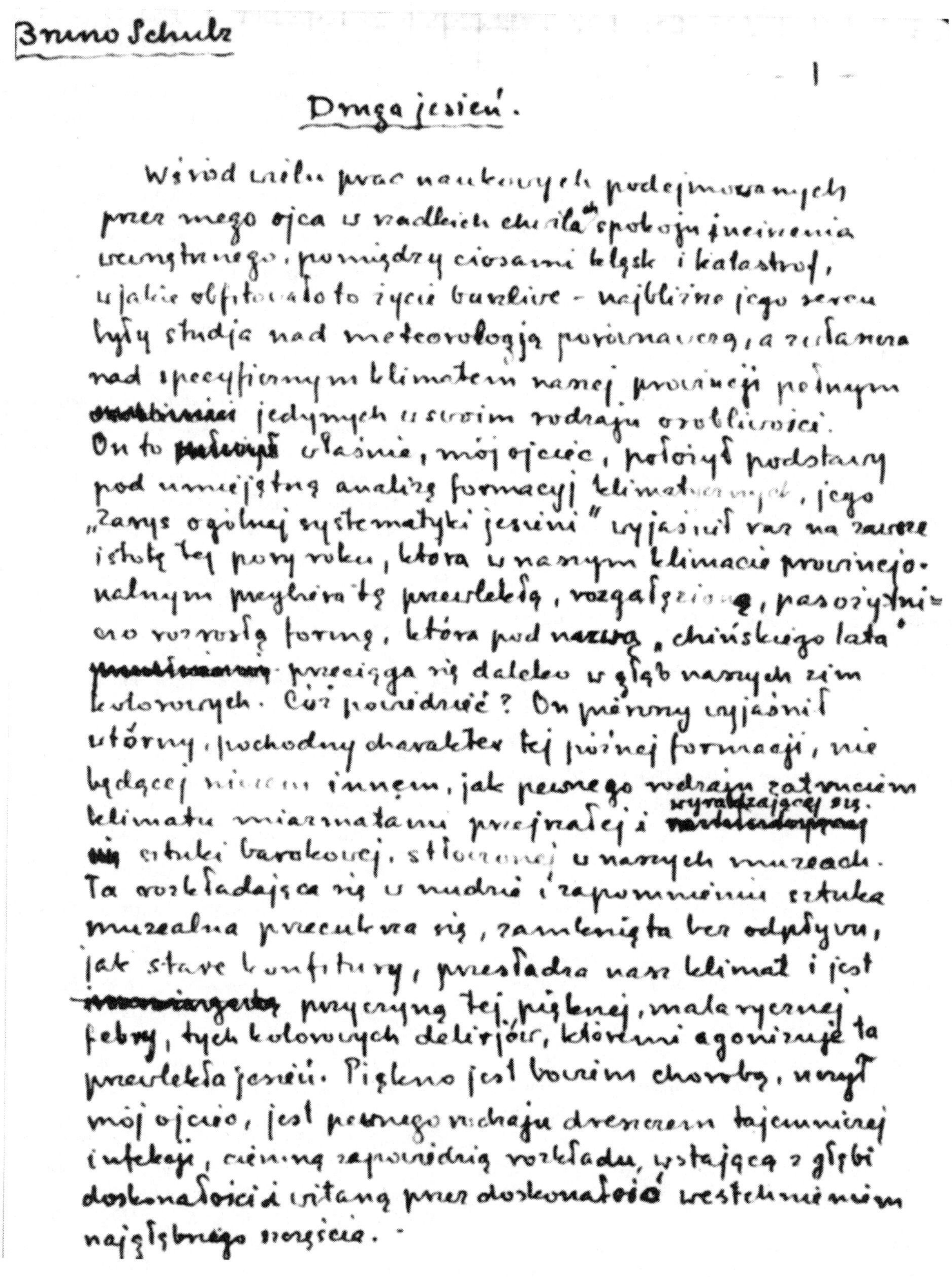

Bruno Schulz

– 1 –

Druga jesień.

Wśród wielu prac naukowych podejmowanych przez mego ojca w rzadkich chwilach spokoju i wytchnienia wewnętrznego, pomiędzy ciosami klęsk i katastrof, w jakie obfitowało to życie burzliwe – najbliższe jego sercu były studja nad meteorologją porównawczą, a zwłaszcza nad specyficznym klimatem naszej prowincji pełnym jedynych w swoim rodzaju osobliwości. On to właśnie, mój ojciec, położył podstawy pod umiejętną analizę formacyj klimatycznych, jego „Zarys ogólnej systematyki jesieni" wyjaśnił raz na zawsze istotę tej pory roku, która w naszym klimacie prowincjonalnym przybiera tę przewlekłą, rozgałęzioną, pasożytniczo rozrosłą formę, która pod nazwą „chińskiego lata" przeciąga się daleko w głąb naszych zim kolorowych. Cóż powiedzieć? On pierwszy wyjaśnił wtórny, pochodny charakter tej późnej formacji, nie będącej niczem innem, jak pewnego rodzaju zatruciem klimatu miazmatami przejrzałej i wyradzającej się sztuki barokowej, stłoczonej w naszych muzeach. Ta rozkładająca się w nudzie i zapomnieniu sztuka muzealna przecukrza się, zamknięta bez odpływu, jak stare konfitury, przesładza nasz klimat i jest przyczyną tej pięknej, malarycznej febry, tych kolorowych delirjów, któremi agonizuje ta przewlekła jesień. Piękno jest bowiem chorobą, uczył mój ojciec, jest pewnego rodzaju dreszczem tajemniczej infekcji, ciemną zapowiedzią rozkładu, wstającą z głębi doskonałości i witaną przez doskonałość westchnieniem najgłębszego szczęścia.

First page of the manuscript for the short story "Second Fall" in Sanatorium pod Klepsydrą, *the only extant manuscript for any of his fiction (Collection of Jerzy Ficowski)* which were kept on the "Aryan side" of town, have disappeared.

In the thirty-two short stories that constitute his entire body of works, Schulz offered his readers an original presentation of a world whose character transcends politics, psychology, or philosophy. The vision of subtle spirituality that he created owes a great deal to a sublime imagination that reveals and evokes, through kaleidoscopic change and metaphoric language, hidden realms of reality. In addition to being a writer, Schulz was also an artist. His many drawings and sketches can thematically be divided into Drohobycz sketches, self-portraits, erotic scenes, and illustrations for his short stories. Though these works share certain elements with his fiction, the latter far surpasses them in pure imagination and originality.

Letters:

Księga listów, edited by Jerzy Ficowski (Kraków: Wydawnictwo Literackie, 1975);

Listy, fragmenty. Wspomnienia o pisarzu, edited by Ficowski (Kraków: Wydawnictwo Literackie: 1984);

Letters and Drawings by Bruno Schulz with Selected Prose, edited by Ficowski, translated by Walter Arndt with Victoria Nelson (New York: Fromm International, 1990).

Bibliography:

Russell E. Brown, "Bruno Schulz Bibliography," *The Polish Review,* 2 (1994): 231–253.

Biographies:

Jerzy Ficowski, *Regiony wielkiej herezji. Rzecz o Brunonie Schulzu* (Kraków: Wydawnictwo Literackie, 1967);

Ficowski, *Okolice Sklepów cynamonowych. Szkice, przyczynki, impresje* (Kraków-Wrocław: Wydawnictwo Literackie, 1985).

References:

Russell E. Brown, *Myth and Relatives: Seven Essays on Bruno Schulz* (Munich: Verlag Otto Sagner, 1991);

Bohdan Budurowycz, "Galicia in the Work of Bruno Schulz," *Canadian Slavonic Papers,* 28 (1986): 359–368;

Wojciech Chmurzyński, ed., *Bruno Schulz 1892–1942. Rysunki i archiwalia ze zbiorów Muzeum Literatury im. Adama Mickiewicza* (Warsaw: Muzeum Literatury im. A. Mickiewicza, 1992);

Jan Ciechowicz and Halina Kasjaniuk, eds., *Teatr pamięci Brunona Schulza* (Gdynia: Władze Miasta Gdyni, Teatr Miejski w Gdyni and Uniwersytet Gdański, 1993);

Jerzy Ficowski, ed., *The Drawings of Bruno Schulz,* with an introduction by Ficowski (Evanston: Northwestern University Press, 1990);

Elisabeth Goślicki-Baur, *Die Prosa von Bruno Schulz* (Bern: Herbert Lang / Frankfurt: Peter Lang, 1975);

Jerzy Jarzębski, "Wstęp," in *Bruno Schulz. Opowiadania, wybór esejów i listów* (Wrocław: Zakład Narodowy im. Ossolińskich, 1989);

Jarzębski, ed., *Czytanie Schulza* (Kraków: Instytut Filologi Polskiej, 1994);

Czesław Karkowski, *Kultura i krytyka inteligencji w twórczości Brunona Schulza* (Wrocław: Zakład Narodowy im. Ossolińskich, 1979);

Małgorzata Kitowska-Łysiak, ed., *Bruno Schulz. In memoriam* (Lublin: Wydawnictwo Fis, 1992);

Henri Lewis, *Bruno Schulz ou Les strategies messianiques* (Paris: La Table Ronde, 1989);

Susan Miron, "Bruno Schulz redux," *Partisan Review,* 59, no. 1 (1992): 161–166;

Leonard Orr, "The 'Kafkaesque' Fantasie in the Fiction of Kafka and Bruno Schulz," *Newsletter of the Kafka Society of America,* 6 (1982): 34–40;

Sandford Pinsker, "Jewish-American Literature's Lost-and-Found Department: How Philip Roth and Cynthia Ozick Reimagine Their Significant Dead," *Modern Fiction Studies,* 35 (1989): 223–235;

Andreas Schoenle, "*Cinnamon Shops* by Bruno Schulz: The Apology of Tandeta," *Polish Review,* 36, no. 2 (1991): 127–144;

Krzysztof Stala, *Na marginesach rzeczywistości. O paradoksach przedstawiania w twórczości Brunona Schulza* (Warsaw: Instytut Badań Literackich, 1995);

Stala, *On the Margins of Reality: The Paradoxes of Representation in Bruno Schulz's Fiction* (Stockholm: Almqvist & Wiksell International, 1993);

Colleen M. Taylor, "Childhood Revisited: The Writings of Bruno Schulz," *Slavic and East European Journal,* 13 (1969): 455–472;

Wojciech Wyskiel, *Inna twarz Hioba: Problematyka alienacyjna w dziele Brunona Schulza* (Kraków: Wydawnictwo Literackie, 1980).

Jaroslav Seifert

(23 September 1901 – 10 January 1986)

Miroslav Zelinský
Academy of Sciences of the Czech Republic

See also the Seifert entry in *DLB Yearbook 1984*.

BOOKS: *Město v slzách* (Prague: Komunistické knih-
kupectví a nakladatelství, R. Rejman, 1921);
Samá láska (Prague: Večernice, 1923);
Na vlnách TSF (Prague: Václav Petr, 1925; revised
and published as *Svatební cesta* (Prague: Melan-
trich, 1938);
Slavík zpívá špatně (Prague: Odeon, 1926);
Hvězdy nad rajskou zahradou (Prague: Pokrok, 1929);
Poštovní holub (Prague: Rudolf Škeřík, 1929);
Jablko z klína (Prague: Melantrich,1933);
Ruce Venušiny (Prague: Melantrich,1936);
Zpíváno do rotačky (Prague: Melantrich, 1936);
Jaro, sbohem (Prague: Melantrich, 1937);
Osm dní (Prague: Melantrich, 1937);
Zhasněte světla (Prague: Melantrich, 1938);
Vějíř Boženy Němcové (Prague: František Borový,
1940);
Světlem oděná (Prague: František Borový, 1940);
Kamenný most (Prague: František Borový, 1944);
Přílba hlíny (Prague: Práce, 1945);
Mozart v Praze (Prague: Picka, 1948);
Ruka a plamen (Prague: František Borový, 1948);
Koulelo se, koulelo (Blansko: Karel Jelínek, 1948;
expanded edition, Prague: Státní nakladatel-
ství dětské knihy, 1955);
Šel malíř chudě do světa (Prague: Družstevní práce,
1949);
Píseň o Viktorce (Prague: Československý spisovatel,
1950);
Maminka (Prague: Československý spisovatel, 1954);
Chlapec a hvězdy (Prague: Československý spisovatel,
1956);
Praha a věnec sonetů (1956); translated as *A Wreath of
Sonnets* (Toronto: 68 Publishers, 1987);
Prague (Prague: Československý spisovatel, 1964);
Koncert na ostrově (Prague: Československý spisova-
tel, 1965);
Halleyova kometa (Prague: Státní nakladatelství
dětské knihy, 1967);

Jaroslav Seifert

Odlévání zvonů (Prague: Československý spisovatel,
1967); translated by Paul Jagasich and Tom
O'Grady as *The Casting of Bells* (Iowa City: The
Spirit that Moves Us Press, 1983);
Morový sloup (Czechoslovakia, 1973; augmented edition, 1977; Koeln am Rhein: Index, 1977);
translated by Ewald Osers as *The Plague Column*
(London & Boston: Terra Nova Editions, 1979);
Deštník z Piccadilly (Munich: Poeziemimo domov,
1979; Prague: Československý spisovatel,
1979); translated by Osers as *An Umbrella from
Piccadilly* (London: London Magazine Editions, 1983);

Všecky krásy světa (Koeln am Rhein: Index / Toronto: 68 Publishers, 1981; Prague: Československý spisovatel, 1982).

Editions and Collections: *Dílo* (Prague: Československý spisovatel, 1954–1970; expanded edition, 1957–1959), edited by A. M. Píša—comprises volume 1: *1921–1926* (1954; expanded edition, 1956); volume 2: *1929–1944* (1954; expanded edition, 1957); volume 3: *1937–1952* (1955; expanded edition, 1958); volume 4: *1937–1953* (1956; expanded edition, 1959); volume 5: *1929–1954* (1957); volume 6: *1945–1956* (1964); volume 7: *1965–1968*, edited by Rudolf Havel (1970);

Zápas s andělem (Prague: Československý spisovatel, 1981);

Býti básníkem (Prague: Československý spisovatel, 1983);

Knížka polibků (Curych: Konfrontace, 1984);

Koncert na ostrově, Halleyova kometa, Odlévání zvonů, edited by Jarmila Víšková (Prague: Československý spisovatel, 1986);

Vějíř Boženy Němcové, Přilba hlíny, Ruka a plamen, Píseň o Viktorce, edited by Víšková (Prague: Československý spisovatel, 1989);

Město v slzách, Samá láska, Svatební cesta, Slavík zpívá špatně, Poštovní holub, edited by Víšková (Prague: Československý spisovatel, 1989);

Jablko z klína, Ruce Venušiny, Jaro, sbohem, edited by Víšková (Prague: Československý spisovatel, 1990).

Editions in English: "Town in Tears," "Discourse with Death," "Factories in a Spring Landscape," and "At the Vault of the Kings," selected and translated by Ewald Osers and J. K. Montgomery, in *Modern Czech Poetry: An Anthology* (London: Allen & Unwin, 1945), pp. 47–52;

"Of All the Songs I Heard Men Sing," translated and edited by Albert French, in *A Book of Czech Verse* (London: Macmillan / New York: St. Martin's Press, 1958), pp. 92–93;

"The Mountain of Rip," "The Wallenstein Garden," and "At the Window," translated by Edith Pargeter, in *A Handful of Linden Leaves: An Anthology of Czech Poetry*, edited by Jaroslav Janů (Prague: Artia, 1960), pp. 13, 18, and 38;

"Glowing Fruit," "Put Out the Lights," and "Mozart in Prague," translated by Pargeter, in *The Linden Tree: An Anthology of Czech and Slovak Literature 1890–1960*, edited by Mojmír Otruba and Zdeněk Pešat (Prague: Artia, 1962), pp. 169–179;

"A Song of a Mirror," translated by Pargeter, in *New Writing in Czechoslovakia*, edited by George

Theiner (Harmondsworth, U.K.: Penguin, 1969), pp. 130–133;

Morový sloup–The Plague Monument, bilingual edition, translated by Lyn Coffin (Silver Spring, Md.: SVU, 1980); republished in *Cross Currents: A Yearbook of Central European Culture* (Ann Arbor: University of Michigan Press, 1984), pp. 135–145;

"Russian bliny," excerpt from *Všecky krásy světa*, translated by Mark Suino, in *Cross Currents: A Yearbook of Central European Culture* (Ann Arbor: University of Michigan Press, 1983), pp. 197–202;

"A Garland on the Wrist" and "Fingerprints," translated by Osers, in *Contemporary East European Poetry: An Anthology*, edited by George Emery (Ann Arbor, Mich.: Ardis, 1983), pp. 201–202;

"Enough of Wolker!" chapter 12 of *Všecky krásy světa*, translated by Ruth Leadbetter, in *Scottish Slavonic Review*, 3 (1984): 119–126;

Eight Days: An Elegy for Thomas Masaryk, translated by Jagasich and O'Grady (Iowa City: The Spirit that Moves Us Press, 1985)—includes Seifert's 1985 acceptance speech for his honorary doctorate from Hampden-Sydney College in Virginia;

Mozart in Prague: Thirteen Rondels–Mozart v Praze: třináct rondelů, bilingual edition, translated by Jagasich and O'Grady (Iowa City: The Spirit that Moves Us Press, 1985);

"Paradise Lost," in *Cross Currents: A Yearbook of Central European Culture* (Ann Arbor: University of Michigan Press, 1985), pp. 291–293;

The Selected Poetry of Jaroslav Seifert, translated by Osers, edited and with additional translations by George Gibian (New York: Macmillan, 1986).

OTHER: *Devětsil. Revoluční sborník*, edited by Seifert and Karel Teige (Prague: V. Vortel, 1922);

Komunistické večery, edited by Seifert and Stanislav Kosta Neumann (Prague: R. Rejman, 1922).

Jaroslav Seifert, the first Czech winner of the Nobel Prize in literature, was primarily a poet, but he was also a journalist, translator, and prose writer. His influence on Czech literature has been felt throughout the twentieth century. Seifert was the leading representative of avant-garde art and a member of the group Devětsil (Nine Forces). First, he wrote proletarian poetry. In the 1920s Seifert and Vítězslav Nezval were the chief exponents of poetism, a major original school of poetry in Czech literature of the 1920s. During World War II Seifert became a fearless defender of Czech national culture. In his declining years, he was an outstanding representative of the democratic trend in Czech arts. As early as the mid 1950s Seifert took a courageous stance within the writers' opposition challenging the Communist totalitarian regime.

Jaroslav Seifert was born 23 September 1901 in Žižkov, a suburb of Prague, to working-class parents, Antonín and Marie Seifertovi. His thorough knowledge of his own working-class background later led him to produce proletarian poetry. Unlike his fellow poets of the day, he had no need to discover this milieu. He attended secondary school in Žižkov but did not complete his studies and began to concentrate on journalism and literature. In the 1920s he was a notable contributor to left-wing and communist journals and newspapers such as *Červen* (June), *Proletkult* (Proletarian Culture), and *Rudé právo* (Red Rights). As one of the founding members of Devětsil, he associated with writers, playwrights, and graphic artists such as Karel Teige, Vladislav Vančura, Jiří Wolker, Emil F. Burian, Jindřich Honzl, Jiří Voskovec, František Muzika, Jindřich Štyrský, and Toyen (Marie Čermínová). He collaborated in the translation of the poetic works of Guillaume Apollinaire and of Alexandr Blok collected in *Dvanáct* (Twelve). With Karel Teige he edited a volume of work by the members of Devětsil titled *Devětsil. Revoluční sborník* (Devětsil. The Revolutionary Collection, 1922). He and Stanislav Kostka Neumann prepared the collection of poetry readings *Komunistické večery* (Communist Gatherings, 1922), and he edited the special issue of *Červen* devoted to Devětsil. Later he worked in the Communist Bookshop and Publishing House in Prague. In 1923 he visited France, Italy, and Switzerland, and in 1925 he went to the Soviet Union. He married Marie Ulrichová in 1928, and the couple had two children, Jana and Jaroslav. From 1927 to 1929 Seifert edited the communist illustrated weekly *Reflektor*. In 1929 with six other communist writers he signed a document expressing disagreement with the views and practices of the new pro-Stalinist leadership. As a result these writers were expelled from the Communist Party.

Over time Seifert edited many periodicals, notably *Nová scéna* (The New Scene, 1930), *Pestré květy* (The Bright Flowers, 1930–1932), *Panorama* (1940–1941), *Kytice* (The Garland, 1945–1948), and *Práce* (Labor, 1945–1949). In the *Práce* publishing house he was responsible for editing *Klín* (Wedge), a series of books of poetry between 1945 and 1948. He also prepared a selection from the works of Jaroslav Vrchlický and Neumann. In 1966 he was named national artist, and in 1984 his body of works

brought him the Nobel Prize in literature; he was, however, too ill to journey to Stockholm to receive it.

Seifert's first collections of poetry from the 1920s anticipated much of what was to come in his later works. First, there is a dynamic force, resulting from the juxtaposition of discord and harmony that are parallel themes in the poet's work. These themes developed between the first and the fourth collections; the character of individual books relates in some way to what has gone before but at the same time presents opposing points of view. His second book, *Samá láska* (Nothing but Love, 1923), argues against points made in his first book, *Město v slzách* (A City in Tears, 1921). In *Město v slzách*, still under the influence of the revolutionary postwar era, the poet is expressing faith in radical social change. His verses have the characteristic ring of passion of the foremost contemporary exponent of proletarian poetry. To fit in with this kind of poetry Seifert uses colloquial expressions and popular songs. One of the main themes throughout his poetry is grief and anger at the "harsh picture of suffering" that the modern city is to the poet. In *Samá láska*, the second collection, the poet is more bewitched and intoxicated by the city than aware of its dark side.

If the first two books had a revolutionary ring to them or at least expressed sorrow in varying degrees over the state of contemporary society, there was absolutely no trace of these sentiments in the third book, *Na vlnách TSF* (On the Air, 1925). It was an expression of official poetism, the original Czech literary movement, and it has all the hallmarks of that movement—playfulness in form and content, association of images, and intoxication with life and its beauty. "Black thoughts and a heavy heart" are consigned to oblivion. The poet also made significant experiments with the graphics of the text, using various types of letters and calligraphy.

In the next collection, *Slavík zpívá špatně* (The Nightingale Is Out of Tune, 1926), he is already arguing the idea that the world needs its good and bad sides. Under "all the beauties of the world" lies "Weltschmerz." The poet is now duty-bound to communicate this idea and give it form. In the collections *Poštovní holub* (Carrier Pigeon, 1929), *Jablko z klína* (An Apple in the Hand, 1933), *Ruce Venušiny* (The Hands of Venus, 1936), and *Jaro, sbohem* (Farewell, Spring, 1937) Seifert's poetry takes on a new tone. Reverberations from current events and the realization that youth is gone, never to return, create a mood not unlike the poetry of his final creative period. The unifying theme in these collections is

Title page for the 1980 illustrated edition of Seifert's best-known poem (National Library of the Czech Republic)

the awareness of the shortness of life and the swift passage of time. At this point the poet begins to be interested in childhood as a subject and as the source of moral values and literary inspiration.

The events of history were of critical importance in influencing Seifert's poetry during the German occupation during World War II. His poetry from this period offered the reader traditional stable national values. First among those constants is Prague as a symbol of national independence, pride, and liberty. Some poems in *Zhasněte světla* (Put Out the Lights, 1938) had already featured this theme. Later, however, Seifert's poetry became directly committed in character. In the polyphonic poetic composition *Světlem oděná* (Arrayed in Light, 1940) the dominant features are images from history and memories of childhood together, creating faith in a bright future for the city, nation, and homeland. The author elaborates this theme in five poems in another book dedicated to Prague, *Kamenný most* (The Stone Bridge, 1944).

The writer Božena Němcová, a veritable national institution through the human and literary qualities of her work, was the inspiration for Seifert

in *Vějíř Boženy Němcové* (Božena Němcová's Fan, 1940). In the book *Přílba hlíny* (A Helmetful of Earth, 1945) the theme of liberty and thanksgiving reappears and with it condemnation of war.

The thirteen rondeaux in *Mozart v Praze* (Mozart in Prague, 1948) are lyrical impressions of the tragic life of the famous composer. The author's friends, mostly writers and artists, on the other hand, are the subjects of *Ruka a plamen* (Hand and Flame, 1948). This book consists of serious, not occasional poetry; Seifert had lived through too much and his ties of friendship were too strong to allow him any superficial outpourings. The collection *Šel malíř chudě do světa* (A Pauper Artist Braved the World, 1949) was inspired by paintings of Mikoláš Aleš. The composition of the book is based on the changing seasons and closely corresponds to the principle Aleš often used in his work. With this collection Seifert changed from being a poet of the city to being a poet of the Czech countryside. At this time he had a tendency to turn for inspiration to works of art and personalities. So it was with the next book, *Píseň o Viktorce* (The Story of Viktorka, 1950), a heartfelt variation on a well-known tragic story of ill-fated love featured in Němcová's classic work *Babička* (Grandmother, 1855). At the beginning of the 1950s, authoritarian conservative critics such as Ivan Skála used this book as a pretext to attack Seifert for not devoting his work to building a new communist society and other socially committed subjects. For a time he was also ostracized by the literary community. However, at the Second Congress of Czechoslovak writers in 1956, Seifert made a triumphant comeback when, in a paper stating his principles, he demanded that the creative arts should be free and be responsible for themselves. Most important, he expressed his support for writers in prison for all kinds of artistic or political reasons.

In the collection *Praha a věnec sonetů* (1956; translated as *A Wreath of Sonnets,* 1987) Seifert does not focus his attention on the tragic city solely because of its historical and geographical associations. The city also brings back to the author many personal memories. Next, in *Maminka* (Mother, 1954) Seifert goes back to the surroundings and objects of his childhood days and all the people he loved. He continued to find inspiration from the same source for the 1955 expanded edition of *Koulelo se, koulelo* (Round and Round, first published in 1948) and for *Chlapec a hvězdy* (The Boy and the Stars, 1956). In the first of these, there are portraits painted of Božena Vejrychová-Solarová and in the second, portraits of Josef Lada. For nine years after these books were written, the poet wrote nothing because of a serious illness.

In the mid 1960s, Seifert started writing poetry again, but his poetry had changed radically. All his previous verse had been regular, rhyming, and melodious, each work a harmonious whole even when the subject matter was darker in mood. Now the poet used colloquial language and direct nonmetaphorical expressions and free verse. In the eleven parts of the first work from this new and final period of his creative activity, *Koncert na ostrově* (Island Concert, 1965), Seifert takes stock of his life to date. He takes into account two extremes—the inevitability of death and the unassuming celebration of the regenerating power of poetry. Memories of actual historical events, mainly from World War II, play the most important part in this work. The struggle between the "black" angel of death, surrender, and sorrow and the "white" angel of love and vibrant life sets the tone for all Seifert's succeeding work. Only Seifert's imagery changes from one book to another. The next collection, *Halleyova kometa* (Halley's Comet, 1967), testifies to the poet's increasing serenity—his return to childhood when the sighting of this celestial body was an experience of special significance for him within his native city, Prague. From another angle the book is also the poet's highly individual guided tour of the capital city and places indelibly imprinted on his memory. The long interval before he returned to poetry was also somehow connected with his longevity, foretold sometime in his youth by a gypsy reading his palm. After predicting, correctly, the early deaths of the poet's friends František Halas and Artuš Černík, she turned to Seifert: "She seized my hand / and shouted angrily, You will have a long life! And it sounded like a threat!" Initially noting this incident in *Morový sloup* (1973; translated as *The Plague Column*, 1979), Seifert later elaborated on the prediction in his book of memoirs *Všecky krásy světa* (All the Beauties of the World, 1981). In *Halleyova kometa* yet another subject appears, one that is also connected with the anthology that immediately followed, *Odlévání zvonů* (1967; translated as *The Casting of Bells*, 1983), and with poems from *Morový sloup*, written between 1968 and 1970. (In the late 1970s Seifert signed a human rights manifesto, Charter 77, and his later work was banned from publication for a few years by the Communist authorities.) These books constitute a triptych "of love, women, and death" (Zdeněk Pešat). The first of them records the raptures of first love and the fascination with a woman's body. The second concentrates more on that moment of crisis, when besides being aware of

"grace and mercy" in the world, the poet becomes increasingly aware of the "judgments" meted out to human beings in the form of death, illness, and sorrow. In the last part of the triptych Seifert appears to feel this end of the scale of human experience with greater intensity. It also forms the longer part of the work.

Deštník z Piccadilly (1979; translated as *An Umbrella from Piccadilly*, 1983) is the author's penultimate collection, and although it includes memories and confessions as is usual with Seifert, it seems to reveal a certain change in position. The author concentrates his attention on events from his childhood, visits to artists' studios and so on, and this narrative element, already evident in the titles of individual poems—"Vlastní životopis" (Autobiography), "Hrob pana Casanovy" (Mr. Casanova's Grave), and "U malíře Vladimíra Komárka" (Vladimír Komárek's Studio)—supports the contention that his poetry has changed direction. Seifert moves his poetry another step away from his previous works by sudden breaks or interruptions in the structure of the poems, and by introducing unrelated ideas within a single poem, when the thematic plan and its emotional appeal suddenly change in accordance with the time shifts mentioned by the narrator. In his last collection, *Býti básníkem* (To be a Poet, 1983), with its markedly harmonizing tone, Seifert returns to the kind of poetry he wrote before the publication of *Koncert na ostrově*.

The extensive collection of memoirs *Všecky krásy světa* is quite different in character from the rest of Seifert's work of that time. His tendency to see his life and the lives of his friends through rose-colored spectacles creates an atmosphere similar to the poetry of his final creative period.

Seifert was awarded the Nobel Prize in literature in 1984. He was too ill to compose his acceptance speech and authorized Dalibor Plichta to write it for him. The lecture was published in 1985 as *O patetickém a lyrickém stavu ducha* (On Passion and Lyricism). Seifert died 10 January 1986 in Prague of an apparent heart attack. The two states in the title *O patetickém a lyrickém stavu ducha* are for him bound together by inseparable elements in poetry and in art in the wider sense of the word, but perhaps above all they are united by the natural principles governing human society:

> Is not passion an attempt to step beyond one's own shadow, an attempt to return to Arcadia where reason, justice and natural instincts are as one? Is not passion nothing but an attempt to return to that idyllic state where we feel no alien power over us

and where discord between what is and what should be fades away, when reason and power, morality and politics can sit together at the same table? Is not, after all, the world of lyricism that Lost Paradise that passion strives to regain? After all, is not Poetry, Lyricism, one of the main architects and interpreters of the vision of this paradise? When I say this, I, a lyrical poet by instinct, am tempted to become a lyrical poet by conscious choice.

Biography:
Zdeněk Pešat, *Jaroslav Seifert* (Prague: Československý spisovatel, 1991).

References:
Jiří Brabec, "Jaroslav Seifert," *Nový život*, 3 (1957): 251–266;

Václav Černý, *Jaroslav Seifert. Náčrt k portrétu* (Kladno, 1954);

Alfred French, *The Poets of Prague. Czech Poetry Between the Wars* (London & New York: Oxford University Press, 1969);

František Götz, "Jaroslav Seifert," in *Jasnící se horizont* (Prague: V. Petr, 1926), pp. 207–217;

Igor Hájek, "All the Beauty of the World—or What's Left of It," *Scottish Slavonic Review*, 3 (1984): 115–119;

William E. Harkins, "Jaroslav Seifert," in *Anthology of Czech Literature* (New York: Columbia University Press, 1953), pp. 198–203;

Harkins, "On Jaroslav Seifert's *Morový sloup*," in *Cross Currents: A Yearbook of Central European Culture* (Ann Arbor: University of Michigan Press, 1984), pp. 131–135;

Marie Kozlíková, "Úloha oblasti všedního v lyrice Jaroslava Seiferta," *Česká literatura*, 14 (1966): 273–292;

Marie Kubínová, "Seifertova poezie plynoucího času, *Česká literatura*, 35 (1987): 306–319;

Vladimír Macura, "Jaro, sbohem," in *Rozumět literatuře 1: Interpretace základních děl české literatury* (Prague: SPN, 1986), pp. 308–315;

Macura, "Jaro, sbohem," "Město v slzách," "Na vlnách TSF," "Slavík zpívá špatně," "Zhasněte světla," in *Slovník básnických knih* (Prague: Československý spisovatel, 1990), pp. 79–81, 163–165, 276–277, 374–376;

Zdeněk Pešat, "Čtyři básníkovy poetiky," in *Dialogy s poezií* (Prague: Československý spisovatel, 1985), pp. 101–120;

Pešat, "Koncert na ostrově," in *Česká literatura 1945–1970* (Prague: SPN, 1992);

Pešat, "Morový sloup," in *Český parnas: Vrcholy literatury 1970–1990* (Prague: Galaxie, 1993), pp. 62–67;

Pešat, "Ruce Venušiny," in *Slovník básnických knih* (Prague: Československý spisovatel, 1990), pp. 254–256;

A. M. Píša, "Jaroslav Seifert," *Čin*, 2 (1930–1931): 29–34;

F. X. Šalda, "O nejmladší poezii české," in *Studie z české literatury. Soubor díla F. X. Šaldy, 8* (Prague: Československý spisovatel, 1961), pp. 158–168;

Josef Škvorecký, "Jaroslav Seifert—the good old drinking poet," in *Cross Currents: A Yearbook of Central European Culture* (Ann Arbor: University of Michigan Press, 1985), pp. 283–290;

Alexander Stich, *Seifertova Světlem oděna* (Prague: Argo, 1998);

Richard Svoboda, "Všecky krásy světa," in *Slovník české prózy 1945–1994* (Ostrava: Sfinga, 1994), pp. 343–345;

Ludvík Vaculík, "A Recreational River-Boat," in *Cross Currents: A Yearbook of Central European Culture* (Ann Arbor: University of Michigan Press, 1985), pp. 279–281.

Lőrinc Szabó
(31 March 1900 – 3 October 1957)

Lóránt Kabdebó
University of Miskolc

BOOKS: *Föld, erdő, isten* (Gyoma: Kner Izidor, 1922);
Kalibán! (Budapest: Athenaeum, 1923);
Fény, fény, fény (Budapest: Kultúra, 1926);
A Sátán műremekei. Versek (Budapest: Pandora, 1926);
Te meg a világ. Versek (Budapest: Pantheon, 1932; Gyoma: Kner Izidor, 1932);
Válogatott versei (Budapest: Nagy Károly és Társai, 1934);
Különbéke. Versek (Budapest: Athenaeum, 1936);
Reggeltől estig. Egy repülőtazás emléke (Budapest: Magyar Bibliofilek Szövetsége, 1937);
Harc az ünnepért (Budapest: Királyi Magyat Egyetemi Nyomda Konyvesboltjanak bízománya, a Bartha Miklós Társaság kíadása, 1938);
Válogatott versei (Budapest: Singer és Wolfner, 1939);
Régen és most (Budapest, 1943);
Tizenkét vers. Tiz rajz (Budapest: Singer és Wolfner, 1943);
Tücsökzene. Rajzok egy élet tájairól (Budapest: Magyar Élet, 1947; revised edition, Budapest: Szépirodalmi, 1957);
Válogatott versei (Budapest: Magvető, 1956);
A huszonhatodik év. Lirai rekviem százhúsz szonettben (Budapest: Magvető, 1957);
Szavakkal nő a gyász. Posztumusz szonettek, edited by Lóránt Kabdebó (Budapest: Szépirodalmi, 1975).

Editions and Collections: *Összes versei*, edited by Szabó (Budapest: Singer és Wolfner, 1943);
Összegyűjtött versei (Budapest: Magvető, 1960);
Kicsi vagyok én . . . . Gyermek versek (Budapest: Móra, 1961);
Válogatott versei, edited by György Somlyó and László Szíjyártó (Budapest: Móra, 1963);
A költészet dicsérete. Válogatott cikkek, tanulmányok, edited by István Simon (Budapest: Szépirodalmi, 1967);
Homlokodtól fölfelé. Válogatott versek, edited by Mátyás Domokos (Budapest: Szépirodalmi, 1971);
Könyvek és emberek az életemben. Prózai írások, edited by Ágota Steinert (Budapest: Magvető, 1984);

Lőrinc Szabó, 1925

Bírákhoz és barátokhoz, edited by Kabdebó (Budapest: Magvető, 1990);
Vers és valóság, 2 volumes, edited by Kabdebó (Budapest: Magvető, 1990);
Magyar sors és fehér szarvas, edited by József Bognár (Budapest: Magyar Fórum, 1994);
Összes versei, 3 volumes, edited by Kabdebó and Kristina Lengyel Tóth (Budapest: Unikornis, 1998).

TRANSLATIONS: Charles Baudelaire, *Kis költemények prózában* (Budapest: Lantos, 1920);
Omár Khayyám, *Rubáiját* (Budapest: Táltos, 1920); revised (Gyoma: Kner kiadás, 1930); revised

341

again (Budapest: Uj Idűk Irodalmi Intézet Rt, 1943);

Paul Verlaine, *Nők*, anonymous translation, (N. p., 1920); as Szabó (Budapest: Helikon, 1983);

William Shakespeare, *Szonettek* (Budapest: Genius, 1921); revised (Budapest: Franklin, 1948);

Adalbert Stifter, *A pusztai falu*, in *Monumenta Literarum*, first series, volume 9 (Gyoma: Kner Izidor kiadása, 1921);

Samuel Taylor Coleridge, *Ének a vén tengerészről*, in *Monumenta Literarum*, first series, volume 10 (Gyoma: Kner Izidor kiadása, 1921); revised as *Rege a vén tengerészről*, illustrated by Gustave Doré (Budapest: Magvető, 1957);

Baudelaire, *A romlás virágai*, translated by Szabó, Mihály Babits, and Árpád Tóth (Budapest: Genius, 1923);

Verlaine, *Válogatott versei* (Budapest: Pandora, 1926);

Johann Wolfgang von Goethe, *Az ifjú Goethe. 1749–1776; A férfi Goethe. 1777–1800; Az öreg Goethe. 1801–1832*, 3 volumes, translated by Szabó and József Turóczi-Trostler (Gyoma: Kner, 1932);

Goethe, *Werther* (Budapest: Az Est-lapok Filléres Klasszikusai, 1933);

Shakespeare, *Athéni Timon* (Budapest: Athenaeum, 1935);

Heinrich von Kleist, *Amphitryon* (Budapest: Singer és Wolfner, 1938);

Shakespeare, *Ahogy tetszik* (Budapest: Singer és Wolfner, 1938; revised edition, Budapest: Művelt Nép, 1956);

Shakespeare, *Macbeth* (Budapest: Singer és Wolfner, 1939);

François Villon, *A szegény Villon tíz balladája és A szép fegyverkovácsné panasza* (Budapest: Singer és Wolfner, 1939);

Villon, *Nagy testámentuma* (Budapest: Singer és Wolfner, 1940);

Gottfried Keller, *Tükör, a cica* (Berlin: Niels Kampmann Verlag, 1941); revised (Budapest: Magvető, 1957);

Anette von Droste-Hülshoff, *Zsidóbükk* (Berlin: Niels Kampmann Verlag, 1941);

Theodor Storm, *Aquis submersus* (Berlin: Niels Kampmann Verlag, 1941); revised (Budapest: Magvető, 1957);

Örök barátaink. Kisebb műfordításai (Budapest: Singer és Wolfner, 1941);

Baudelaire, *A Romlás Virágai*, translated by Szabó, Mihály Babits, and Árpád Tóth(Budapest: Révai, 1943);

Villon, *Nagy testámentuma. Hat balladával bővített második kiadás* (Budapest: Új Idők Irodalmi Intézet Rt, 1944); revised as *Összes versei* (Budapest: Európa, 1957);

Arthur Conan Doyle, *Rejtelmes világ a tenger alatt* (Budapest: Fehér-holló könyvek, 1947);

Shakespeare, *Troilus és Cressida*, in *Összes drámai művei*, 4 volumes (Budapest: Franklin, 1948), IV: 313–446;

Örök barátaink. Kisebb műfordításainak második kötete (Budapest: Egyetemi Nyomda, 1948);

Aleksandr Sergeevich Pushkin, *Bahcsiszeráji szökőkút*, in *Költemények és egyéb verses munkák*, edited by Andor Gábor and Endre Gáspár (Budapest: Szikra-Új Magyar, 1949), pp. 201–208;

Jean Racine, *Andromaché*, in *Összes drámai művei*, edited by Gyula Illyés (Budapest: Franklin, 1949), pp. 135–208;

Szabó Lőrinc válogatott műfordításai (Budapest: Franklin Könyvkiadó N. V., 1950);

Thomas Hardy, *Egy tiszta nő* (Budapest: Szépirodalmi, 1952);

Ivan Andreevich Krilov, *Válogatott mesék* (Budapest: Ifjúsági, Budapest, 1952);

Vladimir Mayakovsky, *150.000.000*, in: *Elbeszélő költemények*, edited by Gábor Devecseri, Gáspár, and István Simon (Budapest: Szépirodalmi, 1953), pp. 21–73;

Jean de La Fontaine, *Mesék*, edited by Albert Gyergyai (Budapest: Szépirodalmi, 1954);

Fedor Ivanovich Tiutchev, *Versek* (Budapest: Fordította Szabó Lőrinc / Új Magyar, 1954);

Molière, *Embergyőlölő* (Budapest: Új Magyar, Világirodalmi kiskönyvtár, 1956);

Molière, *Nők iskolája* (Budapest: Új Magyar, Világirodalmi kiskönyvtár, 1956);

De Coster, *Thyl Ulenspiegel*, translated by *Szabó* and Illyés (Budapest: Európa, 1957);

Heinrich von Kleist, *Az eltört korsó, Amphitryon*, translated by Szabó and László Németh (Budapest: Európa, 1957);

Örök barátaink: A költő kisebb lirai versforditásai, 2 volumes (Budapest: Szépirodalmi, 1958).

Lőrinc Szabó's poetry and his translations are outstanding products of Hungarian lyricism. His works not only capture the experience of a certain historical present but also provide a poetic occasion to consider existence in its entirety. In his poetry Szabó portrays a century in which every effort turns into its opposite; the poet himself stands at a crossroads, as does humanity of the twentieth century. In his poem "Tao Te King" (1931) he writes, "your self can be true only with your opposites," and one of his powers as a poet is his ability to bring together such diversity in his compositions. His poetic irregularities, many times praised by his critics, are all attacks on the seemingly unchangeable order. There exist various readings of his lyric works; nevertheless, the simultaneous validity of these different approaches indicates the greatness of his poetry and its place in world literature.

Lőrinc Szabó was born on 31 March 1900 in Miskolc, one of the county seats of the Austro-Hungarian monarchy—a town that, as a result of the incomes from Greek merchants in the eighteenth century, became an industrial and railway center by the turn of the century. He was born in a small house on Újvilág Street (now Vörösmarty Street); although the houses have since disappeared, in the tower block of Vörösmarty Street there is a little street named after the poet. His father—also named Lőrinc Szabó—was a railroad engineer and did not like the surroundings, so soon after Szabó's birth the family began moving almost every year from place to place.

Szabó's ancestors were Calvinist ministers and teachers. Gábor Bethlen, the Transylvanian prince who defended Protestantism and the Hungarians during the Thirty Years' War, granted nobility to the family, and they took the name Gáborjáni (of Gáborján). Since in Hungarian the name "Szabó" (Tailor) is relatively common, these ancestors decided upon the rare Lőrinc (Lawrence) as a first name; often, they used their noble name, too. For this reason, the poet used the name Lőrinc G. Szabó on his first publications. Szabó's father, who did not want to learn Latin and failed secondary school, left the family tradition and became an honored craftsman. Szabó's mother, Ilona Panyicky, was a descendent of a poor, noble Polish family that had escaped to Hungary because of political reasons. The poet describes the history of his mother's family in his poem "Anyám mesélte" (Mother Told Me, 1943); he recalls that his grandfather was a "jack-of-all-trades" whose ancestors

> came from Poland somehow
> they were even related to the throne and he himself
> still spoke Polish
> . . . .
> a long time ago
> they had silver-pieces even in the dough-basket
> but it's all gone now, as all the land's gone,
> because our father liked to make merry.
> . . . .
> He oversaw the estate
> . . . .
> and under him there were
> labourers and tobacco farmers,
> and then we got burnt, the machines and the thresher,
> we lost it all, and we went to Miskolc
> and your grandfather ended up on the railways.

FÖLD, ERDŐ, ISTEN

*

SZABÓ LŐRINC
VERSEI

1 9 2 2.
KNER IZIDOR KIADÁSA
GYOMA

Title page for Szabó's first book, a collection of poems that reflect the general mood in Hungary after World War I

Szabó's brother also became an engineer and worked for the railway in Miskolc his entire life. His sister Rózsika died soon after her birth; his other sister, Hajnalka, also died at a young age of tuberculosis. The poet lamented her death, considering also the controversy of desires and limitations of human existence, in "Halott húgom könyvei" (Books of My Dead Sister, 1937).

Szabó inherited his sensitivity to the arts from his mother. He excelled in primary school, which he began in Miskolc in 1906 and continued from 31 March 1907 at another county seat, Balassagyarmat; at the time they lived in 10 Templom Street, now renamed Szabó Lőrinc Street. He finished school in 1909 in Debrecen, the center of Calvinism in Hungary. In Debrecen, at one of the most important Calvinist secondary schools, the Református Főgimnázium, he became acquainted with Hungarian and world literature, natural sciences, and the rules of the social life of the intelligentsia. Among his schoolmates were significant representatives of the next era:

poets, such as Pál Gulyás, later a close friend of the writer László Németh; literature scholars and later professors of the universities of Debrecen and Budapest, such as Géza Juhász, Pál Kardos, and László Kardos; and scientists, such as Imre Törő, professor of biology and medicine, and the internationally famed nuclear physicist and radar scientist Zoltán Bay. Another classmate and early love was Katalin Dienes, who was from an intelligent and wealthy family.

Szabó completed his final school exams on 8 March 1918; then, on 15 March, he had to join the army. He had been in the officer's school in Debrecen, and as he said later, in order to escape the front he had become first in his class; thus, he was taken to the artillery regiment of Lugos as cadet-corporal. The news that the front had collapsed reached him there, and he immediately returned to the capital and registered at the University of Polytechnics and then at Pázmány University in the departments of Hungarian, German, and Latin at the Faculty of Arts. After the revolt against the Austro-Hungarian monarchy, led by Count Mihály Kárelyi in the autumn of 1918, Szabó lived with Ferenc Gráf, a wine merchant, and his sister at their flat in Podmaniczky Street, beginning in early 1919. He became a tutor to the children of their business partner. Later, when the Gráfs had to flee to Vienna during the Hungarian Bolshevik Revolution of 21 March–1 August 1919, also know as the Commune, they trusted him to guard their flat. The friendship lasted after their return; after 1945, Gráf had to leave again for Sao Paulo, but he remained throughout his life a parental supporter of the poet.

During the revolution, Katalin's brother, László, took Szabó as a colleague to the Office of National Libraries and Bibliography, but only for a short time, because with Dienes's emigration Szabó also had to leave. At the end of the war, Romanian troops pushed up to the line of the Danube River, occupying the capital; when on 16 November 1919 they conceded power to the Hungarian national army of Admiral Miklós Horthy, the Romanians retreated only as far as the river Tisza, thus cutting off the eastern parts of the country from the capital. This move meant for Szabó that he lost contact with his family living in Debrecen, and as a result he had no money and began to starve. He sent his first poems, still in the Parnassian style, to Mihály Babits, chief editor of Nyugat (West), the most important Hungarian literary magazine of the time. Although Babits did not publish the poems, he decided to help Szabó: he introduced him at the famous literary café Centrál, took him as his teaching assistant at the university, and from July 1920 shared his own flat with the young poet who, at this time, had been living in the most miserable lodgings.

Szabó in his youth had paid great attention to Nyugat, the literary magazine of the reformist movement in Hungarian literature, and to the works of Babits, who was a poet of deep philosophical insight with a thorough European education and a strong sense of style. Szabó was also reading and studying the works of German author Stefan George. By the time he became involved with literary life at the end of the war—still as a university student in Budapest—he had already translated works from Latin, Greek, German, and French, including Paul Verlaine's Femmes (Women, 1890) and Charles Baudelaire's Petits Poëmes en Prose (Little Prose Poems, 1868). As a close disciple of Babits, he soon began to translate from English—works such as Omar Khayyám's poems, William Shakespeare's sonnets, and Samuel Taylor Coleridge's ballad The Rime of the Ancient Mariner (1798). Preparing for the Baudelaire centenary, Szabó and two other renowned poets, Babits and Árpád Tóth, translated Baudelaire's volume of poetry Les Fleurs du mal (The Flowers of Evil, 1857). This translation, A romlás virágai, published in 1923, not only introduced Hungarian readers to Baudelaire's poetry but also provided a comprehensive monument to the poetical language of the time. (When the volume was republished in 1943, Szabó significantly revised his own translations in order to assimilate them to the more mature style characteristic of his later period.) The documents of his translations from these early years are discussed in Érlelő diákévek (Maturing School Years), a 1979 collection of letters and other papers.

During the Commune, Babits and Dezső Szabó, author of Az elsodort falu (The Village Swept Away, 1919), an influential novel that opposed the revolution, organized the Society of Hungarian Writers in opposition to the cultural politics of the Communist revolutionary leader Béla Kun. After the fall of the Commune in August 1919, Babits proposed Szabó for the position of secretary of the society. Since Babits, conservative in his views, broke with Dezső Szabó, who by this time had become a radical nationalist, Lőrinc Szabó resigned in early September from this post, not willing to give up his leftist political views.

Szabó's first poems were published in Nyugat in June 1920, including "Novus nascitur ordo" (A New Order being Born), which was also published in his first volume of poetry. By that time he was completely familiar with contemporary European literature and the emerging avant-garde movements. His first volume, *Föld, erdő, isten* (Earth, Forest, God, 1922), received unusual recognition. It was handsomely printed by the famous Kner Press; its physical appearance was praised in *Nyugat*. As to its literary merits, in a period tormented by historical catastrophes, this volume succeeds in simultaneously conveying—in a poetically authentic voice—human defenselessness, a young man's pan-eroticism, and a sense of orientation in the order of existence.

After the "maturing school years" Szabó's life and poetical focus entered a different phase, summed up in the first line of one of his best-known poems, "Semmiért egészen" (All for Nothing, 1931): "It is terrible, I admit that, but this is how it's true" (translated by Edwin Morgan). An overpowering feeling of revolt and helplessness accumulated in the wake of World War I because of the subsequent waves of revolutions and counterrevolutions, the fall of the defeated Austro-Hungarian monarchy, the Treaty of Versailles (in which Hungary was reduced to a third of its previous size), inflation, and a resulting loss of ground for the intelligentsia. Szabó's first volume represents a stylistic synthesis of expressionism and classical evenness, and in its theme it conveys the historical, emotional, and ontological endangerment of the modern personality. The volume was written under Babits's protective friendship; however, by the time the book was published, this relationship was already disintegrating. Szabó's fiancée, Ilona Tanner, later known as poetess Sophie Török, married Babits instead, and the initial friendship of the three became a lifelong source of personal conflicts.

On New Year's Eve in 1921 Szabó married Klára Mikes, a widow who was four years his senior. Her father, Lajos Mikes, strongly opposed this marriage, though later he accepted the young poet. Mikes was at the time the editor of the newspaper conglomerate *Az Est-lapok* (The Evening-Conglomerate); where Szabó had undertaken a post in August 1921. This conglomerate had been founded after World War I: Andor Miklós, the owner of a tabloid, *Az Est*, had bought the two most renowned liberal daily papers of the period, *Pesti Napló* (Pest Journal) and *Magyarország* (Hungary), as well as the Athenaeum Press. As a result of this merging, Miklós had become the most important press baron in the capital. Szabó first worked for *Az Est*, until 1 July 1926, then after an interval of about eighteen months, for *Pesti Napló* from 15 October 1927, and finally for *Magyarország* from the autumn of 1928 until the end of 1944. For a long time *Az Est* provided for him not only a post but also a venue for publication.

On 23 April 1923 Szabó's first child was born—a daughter who later became an actress known as Klára Gáborjáni. During this time he also began a series of

Klára Mikes, whom Szabó married in 1921

romantic entanglements, including one with Zorka, the famous model of Mihály Rippl-Rónai, one of the most renowned painters of the time. In 1925 Szabó began a lifelong involvement—kept in secret until 1928—with a young woman named Erzsébet Korzáti, who was married at the time and was also his wife's best friend. The posthumous publication in 1989 and 1993 of the letters of the poet and his wife, *Harminchat év*, acquainted readers with the story of their marriage. His love story with Korzáti is commemorated in his cycle of poems *A huszonhatodik év. Lirai rekviem százhusz szonettben* (The Twenty-Sixth Year. A Lyrical Requiem in One Hundred Twenty Sonnets), written in 1950–1951 and published in 1957.

In 1924 Szabó traveled to Italy and returned there the following year with his wife. The two also made an Austro-German trip in September 1928, and Szabó and his brother traveled to Austria again in 1929. There was also a trip in July and August 1927 to Transylvania after its annexation to Romania to report on the situation of the Hungarian ethnic minority to send to the *Az Ezt* publications—the documents of this travel were published in the correspondence collection titled *Utazás Erdélyben* (1992). Friends from Slovakia occasionally invited the Szabós to spend some days or weeks at Újtátrafüred, in the new Hotel

Palace. These trips are commemorated in two of his expressionist poems: "Óda a genovai kikötőhöz" (Ode to the Geneva Harbor, 1925) and "Grand Hotel Miramonti" (1926).

In the course of every generation there is a master and a literary magazine against which younger artists revolt. Babits and *Nyugat* became the targets for Szabó's generation in 1923, and in 1927 Szabó helped to found *Pandora*, a magazine for which he became the chief editor. The history of *Pandora* was similar to other new magazines: after its sixth number it ceased publication because of financial and personal problems. As a result Szabó had serious debts and one and a half years of unemployment. The years between 1926 and 1930 were difficult for Szabó: he had terrible conflicts in his love life, and his wife attempted suicide on the night of 26 October 1928. Later they reconciled, and he unwillingly broke up with Korzáti for several years. According to his memoirs he was also experimenting with drugs.

During this period he produced *Kalibán!* (1923), *Fény, fény, fény* (Light, Light, Light, 1926), and *A Sátán műremekei. Versek* (Satan's Masterpiece. Verses, 1926). In these works there is a tone of expressionistic social criticism and an unrestrained but stumbling wish for individuation, especially in the title poems and in "Isten" (God), "Klió" (Clio), "Ujsághírben a végtelen" (The Infinite in a Newspaper Article), "Mérget, revolvert" (Poison, Revolver), and "Negyedóra Isten és a Hivatal közt" (A Quarter of an Hour between God and the Office). These poems, however, are different from the other expressionist poems of the time: they do not express belief in the redeeming, messianic role of the revolt, and they are written with the postulation of the unchangeable. In 1927 and 1928 Szabó published poems in *Az Est-lapok*, including "Vezér" (The Leader). These poems devastated him: although he could have published a volume in 1928 from the poems written in the previous two years, he decided not to; he felt he had reached an artistic crisis. He did, however, return later to these poems and make alterations to them, and they were published in his 1943 collected poems. Nevertheless, the poems of this period added to Szabó's poetical renewal, and the contradictions in them linked him to contemporary world lyricism.

In 1916 Babits had translated Shakespeare's *The Tempest* (circa 1611), calling it a fable-play as an antiwar gesture, with a peacemaking and balancing Prospero in the center of his interpretation. This historically significant act induced the emergence of a certain kind of humanist pathos in the Hungarian literature of the century. Szabó disturbed the tradition with his *Kalibán!* Some of his interpreters read it as a manifesto of a generation's rebellion, others as the constitutional

and political self-portrait of a young poet. As the poet later testified in his own commentary on the poem, it was inspired by Caliban's suggestive stage rendering as well as by Ernest Renan's play *Caliban: Suite de La tempete: drame philosophique* (1878; translated as *Caliban: A Philosophical Drama Continuing "The Tempest" of William Shakespeare*, 1896). Babits's aim was to register a traditional interpretation at a time when history was shattering the traditional order of cultural symbols in world literature. Seeing this change, Szabó was pointing to its inevitability.

Szabó's *Kaliban!* displays features that characterized his early work between 1920 and 1928. Influenced by the classical poetry of Stefan George, the avant-garde, and Greek choral songs, he developed a kind of monologue in which he united the figures of Leader and Poet in order to transcend the social tensions and the cultural decline of the age. From the ars poetica of "Legyen a költő hasznos akarat" (Let the Poet Be a Useful Will) he arrives at the extremity of "Kellenek a Gonosz fegyverei!" (We Need the Arms of Evil!). In this poem, with admiration as well as horror, Caliban is quoted as the modern technician who burns books. Through him, in first-person singular, the Poet-Leader's program to gain world power is declared.

The second phase of classical modernity beginning in the 1920s broke up the traditional system of cultural symbols and introduced the new language of the literary treatment of myths. A poem of Szabó's from 1935, "Szun Vu Kung lázadása" (Sun Wu Kung's Rebellion), with its ballad-like frame-work, illustrates this development in Hungarian poetry. It depicts Sun Wu Kung, the monkey-king, whose ambition is to rule the world, in opposition to the cultural symbol of the peace-bringing Buddha. The dialogue is not between the personas (which would only shift the poem toward a latent monologue) but within them. Sun Wu Kung's journey to the end of the world and his "will to power" distort traditional ideals. Buddha, on the other hand, presents not only a redeeming goodness but also the ever-restricting power of his "sparingly" cruel punishment. "Szun Vu Kung lázadása" was later included in the 1936 volume *Különbéke* (Private Truce).

Te meg a világ (You and the World, 1932) is about the fight for individuation and is considered by many a climactic achievement of twentieth-century Hungarian poetry. The volume is a stubborn and consistent poetic attempt at grasping truth, which, however, arrives at the questioning of a single Truth: the longing for God is rejected with a cold respect for the facts. In this volume Szabó establishes the practice of the dialogical poetic paradigm. Tradition and renewal, the main notions of time (as a series of independent "points of present," or as authentic time), the collective human and personal experience, and finally the series of personal and historical coincidences are the ideas that define a characteristic poetic order.

Szabó's poetry is relatively easy to understand, which is why it can be easily dismissed; nevertheless, the dialogic quality of his discourse brings the oppositions in his poetry to the surface. His sentence structure, his choice of words, and his narrative technique make his works close to everyday speech. Nevertheless, this seemingly plain style, grammatically precise sentences, and traditional form simultaneously present statement, doubt, and negation.

From the 1930s Szabó's personal and professional lives were full of controversies. His poetry, advocating the truth of the individual, was suspicious both to the Hungarian nation preparing for war on the side of Nazi Germany and later to that of the Soviet-Communist world behind the Iron Curtain. In such a continuously changing world, Szabó had to take care of his family and be able to carry out his artistic work at the same time. After the marital crisis of 1928 and the compromise that followed, Szabó and his wife moved to a new apartment in Budapest where their son, the "Lóci" of Szabó's later poems, was born on 14 December 1929. In 1935 they moved to 8 Volkmann Street, where his library was constructed and still remains in its original form.

Following the deaths of Mikes in 1930 and Miklós in 1933, Szabó's employment and publication possibilities changed. Though Szabó had supporters, such as the famous actress Frida Gombaszögi, *Magyarország* was sacrificed to political interests: Gyula Gömbös, who was prime minister from 1932, began to organize reforms similar to those in Germany, and he wanted *Magyarország* to be the propagator of this new orientation after 1934. Gömbös met the editors and writers of the paper, but when it became clear that his program, the "New Intellectual Front," was not exactly along the lines of a Rooseveltean New Deal, they quit and organized the opposition publication *Márcinsi Front* (March Front) on 15 March 1937. *Az Est-lapok* ceased to exist in 1939 as a result of this political trap; only *Magyarország*, the oldest newspaper of the concern, could survive, but it lost its independence, its profile becoming defined by the new prime minister, Pál Teleki. Szabó was allowed to remain editor of the paper, but he hardly ever wrote for it.

During this time Szabó received a favorable proposal from the painter-proprietor István Farkas, who tried to push the idea that the literary magazine *Új Idők* and the Singer and Wolfner Literary Institute should become more open to contemporary trends. As a part of this project, Farkas made a lifetime contract with Szabó, and the first poem published in *Új Idők* in 1939

was "Ima a gyermekekért" (A Prayer for the Children). Szabó tried to continue his earlier lifestyle: he spent his vacations traveling, sometimes with his wife or his children, and in order to cover the expenses he wrote reports or poems about the memorable moments of these trips. He was also occupied with translations for the National Theatre. In 1934 he traveled to Paris with his wife, then to Dalmatia three times: once alone, then with his wife and his daughter, finally with his son; these travels are commemorated in the ontological poems "Mosztári tücsök" (A Cricket of Mostar), "A ragúzai leánderhez" (To the Leander in Ragusa), "Beszélgetés a tengerrel" (Conversation with the Sea), and "Lóci és a szakadék" (Lóci and the Abyss). He translated Shakespeare's *Timon of Athens* (circa 1605–1608) in July 1935 in the mountains of Transylvania, where he had been invited by his friend Ferenc Bisztrai Farkas (later minister of the 1956 revolutionary government). In July 1938, in the Black Forest by the Titisee, he translated Heinrich von Kleist's *Amphitryon* (1807) and Shakespeare's *As You Like It* (circa 1599–1600). *Macbeth* (circa 1606) was translated in the Tatra mountains in 1939.

He had official travels as well: in early July 1931, he went as a representative of *Az Est* to Trieste, Venice, Brindisi, Alexandria, and Cairo on a voyage organized for the press. En route he saw the pyramids, described in "Sivatagban" (In the Desert), a poem discussing history, ethics, and ontology. In 1933, with the help of the Czechoslovakian Cultural Attaché, because of his translations of Czech and Slovak poets, he spent several weeks in Czech and Moravian towns with his lover, Korzáti; they even went to Dresden. On the postcard he sent to his wife from Prague, there are the signatures of the most prominent contemporary Czech and Slovak poets—Josef Hora, František Halaš, Ján Šmrek, and Vilém Závada. In 1936 he participated in a flight organized for the press from Budapest to Switzerland. In 1941 with a cultural delegation he went to Belgrade, then with the same purpose to Bulgaria in 1942. He also traveled frequently to Germany.

In October 1940 Szabó tried to write "still-life" poems from the rough material of a soldier's life, but attacks in the extreme right-wing periodical *Szózat* (Declaration, 18 November 1940) and in *Katonaújság* (Soldier's Journal, 23 November 1940) forced him to stop publishing poems on this theme and to explain himself in an article published in *Katonaújság* (30 November 1940). The publication of an extract of his *Macbeth* translation in a liberal daily, *Esti Kurír* (Evening Courier), was prevented by wartime censorship: "the piece is so much interwoven with the conspiracies against state leaders and attacks that the publication in today's circumstances of any of its parts

Page from the manuscript for "Semmiért egészen" (All for Nothing, 1931), one of Szabó's best-known poems (from Lóránt Kabdebó, Szabó Lőrinc, 1985) is not desirable." He presented his controversial political experiences at the Lillafüred Conference, which was organized in November 1942 to discuss Hungary's political role. Although he was not publishing war poems, he defended the war theme:

> What is needed is the plasticity of life and reality, with its thousands and millions of colors and contrasts; for true elucidation there has to be exposure to light and shadow. The war is something terrible; still, Shakespeare's and Schiller's bloodsheds are beautiful on the scene. Without the freedom of representation it is impossible to represent. . . .Today's official opinion would not allow the existence of a new Hungarian Shakespeare. . . . Well, let's have the proper palette, because Dante's Hell cannot be painted with Heaven's colors.

This speech was to be published in *Magyar Csillag* (Hungarian Star), but its publication was finally banned; only the proof sheets remain.

After the war the authorities detained Szabó several times because he had visited Germany and had German friends; on 25 September 1945 he was censured as a journalist. He wrote about the adversities of this period in his *Napló* (Diary), later published in *Bírákhoz és barátokhoz* (To Judges and Friends, 1990). In his trials he made two defense speeches in which he summed up the earlier facts of his life. The documentation of the trials, together with the speeches, were published in 1990 in *Bírákhoz és barátokhoz*. Though he was cleared, he did not undertake further employment, because the newspaper where he had been working as editor ceased publication. From this time on, he supported his family through translations. His wife went to work in an office; his daughter became an actress for Hungarian Radio; and his son was an internationally renowned volleyball player who went to the Film Academy of Budapest and earned a degree in directing.

After the war all of the magazines and presses in which Szabó used to publish his poems had ceased to exist. From the autumn of 1946 he edited the poetry column of *Válasz* (Response), the literary magazine of the so-called rural poets; here he could publish some of his poetry, but after 1949, in the years of the dictatorship, for political reasons and because of his "individualistic lyricism," as his poetry was labelled by socialist realist critics, he remained without any possibility of publication. His lifestyle became simple: as the guest of friends, he spent his summers by Lake Balaton and translated the classics of world literature. He revised his translation of Shakespeare's sonnets, then translated Shakespeare's *Troilus and Cressida* (circa 1601–1602) and *Twelfth Night* (circa 1601), Jean

Racine's *Andromaque* (1667), Molière's *Le Misanthrope* (1666) and *L'Ecole des femmes* (1662), Aleksandr Pushkin's *Bakhchisaraiskii fontan* (The Fountain of Bakhchisarai, 1824), Vladimir Vladimirovich Mayakovsky's poem *150.000.000* (1921), a volume of poems by Fedor Ivanovich Tiutchev, animal fables by Ivan Andreevich Krylov and Jean de La Fontaine, and Thomas Hardy's *Tess of the d'Urbervilles* (1891).

On 12 February 1950 Korzáti committed suicide, ending a twenty-five year relationship with Szabó and beginning for him a year of mourning that resulted in the cycle of 120 sonnets, *A huszonhatodik év.* From the different perspectives of the three people involved (himself, his lover, and his wife), the poet reconsiders the story of a quarter of a century as well as the recurring and unanswerable question of why his lover decided to terminate her life.

As a result of the strenuous work of that year, on 10 October 1951 Szabó had a heart attack in Tihany. A second, more serious one occurred on New Year's Eve in 1954. In the winter of 1956 he suffered from polyarthritis. In 1957 he became ill again in Tihany; a third heart attack was suspected, but it turned out to be lung cancer which had already spread to other parts of his body.

Throughout his life Szabó's status as a poet and a translator had been acknowledged in the forms of literary awards: he won the distinguished prize, the Baumgarten Award for Poetry, three times (in 1932, 1937, and 1944). In 1937 he was elected a member of Kisfaludy Társaság (Kisfaludy Society), a literary society. In 1940 he was granted the Arany János Medal of Budapest, and in 1943 he received the Csokonai Award of the Debrecen Literary Societies and the award of the Society for Literature (Irodalompártolók Társasága). He was nominated for the most distinguished scientific and literary award of the Horthy era as well, the "Corvin chain." This nomination, however, came to nothing because of the German Occupation. In 1947 he was elected to the Society of Hungarian Writers, and before and during the 1956 revolution he was elected to the presidency of the society. On 2 July 1956 in Budapest there was a literary evening organized in his honor, and his native town celebrated him on the eve of the 1956 revolution. For his translations he was granted the Attila József Award in 1954, and in March 1957 he received the highest national award for the arts, the Kossuth Award (other recipients of the prize of that year were Zoltán Kodály and László Németh).

On 13 May 1957 in Tihany, Szabó saw the lunar eclipse, about which he wrote his last finished poem. He died on 3 October 1957; his funeral was at the

Kerepesi Út Cemetery on 8 October, and his death was mourned nationally.

Letters:

Érlelő diákévek. Napló, levelek, dokumentumok, versek Szabó Lőrinc pályakezdésének éveiből, emlékezések az 1915–1920-as évekről, edited by Lóránt Kabdebó (Budapest: Petőfi Irodalmi Múzeum és Népművelési Propaganda Iroda, 1979);

Harminchat év. Szabó Lőrinc és felesége levelezése, 2 volumes, edited by Kabdebó (Budapest: Magvető, 1989, 1993);

Utazás Erdélyben, edited by Kabdebó (Salgótarján: Mikszáth Kiadó, 1992).

Interviews:

Napló, levelek, cikkek, edited by Lóránt Kabdebó (Budapest: Szépirodalmi [Műhely sorozat], 1974).

Bibliography:

Albert Tezla, *Hungarian Authors: A Bibliographical Handbook* (Cambridge, Mass.: Belknap Press of Harvard University Press, 1970), pp. 529–533.

Biographies:

Lóránt Kabdebó, *Szabó Lőrinc lázadó évtizede* (Budapest: Szépirodalmi, 1970);

György Rába, *Szabó Lőrinc* (Budapest: Akadémiai [Kortársaink sorozat], 1972);

Kabdebó, *Útkeresés és különbéke* (Budapest: Szépirodalmi, 1974);

Kabdebó, *Az összegezés ideje* (Budapest: Szépirodalmi, 1980);

Judit Sándor, *'Szeressétek a gyermekeimet!'. Szabó Lőrinc, a költő-apa* (Budapest: Móra, 1982);

Kabdebó, *Szabó Lőrinc* (Budapest: Gondolat [Nagy magyar írók sorozat], 1985);

Kabdebó, *"A magyar költészet az én nyelvemen beszél." A kései Nyugat-líra összegződése Szabó Lőrinc költészetében* (Budapest: Argumentum [Irodalomtörténeti Füzetek sorozat], 1992);

Kabdebó and Anna Menyhért, eds., *Újraolvasó. Tanulmányok Szabó Lőrincről* (Budapest, 1997).

References:

Mihály Babits, "Egy fiatal költő," in his *Írók két háború közt* (Budapest: Nyugat, 1941), pp. 40–43;

György Bálint, "Szabó Lőrinc válogatott versei," *Nyugat*, 1 (1934): 341–343;

László Baránszky-Jób, "Tücsökzene," *Diárium* (1947): 62–63;

Tibor Déry, "Vers-és önelemzés. 'A huszonhatodik év' 104. szonettje kapcsán," *Kortárs* (1965): 1621–1626;

László Ferenczi, "The Poet as Egoist (Lőrinc Szabó)," *New Hungarian Quarterly*, 29 (1967): 156–160;

Gábor Halász, "Te meg a világ. Szabó Lőrinc új verskötete," *Nyugat*, 1 (1933): 133–135;

Gyula Illyés, "Szabó Lőrinc, vagy: boncoljuk-e magunkat elevenen?" *Alföld*, 7 (March–April 1956): 55–72;

Lóránt Kabdebó, "On the Borderline of Nineteenth and Twentieth Century Poetic Discourses: The Appearance of the Dialogical Poetic Paradigm," *Neohelicon*, 21 (1994): 61–83;

Béla Katona, "Szabó Lőrinc és Szabolcs-Szatmár," *Iradalomtörténeti Közlemények*, 67 (1963): 492–509;

Aladár Komlós, "Szabó Lőrinc," *Új Hang*, 5 (1956): 58–61;

Ákos Moravánszky, *Szabó Lőrinc lírája 1926-ig* (Debrecen: Lehotai Pál, 1943);

László Németh, "Szabó Lőrinc," *Nyugat*, 24 (16 August 1931): 236–240;

Németh, "Szabó Lőrinc (1957)," *Tiszatáj*, 1 (1975): 72–78;

János Pilinszky, "Összegyűjtött versek (Collected Poems by Lőrinc Szabó)," *Hungarian P.E.N.*, 3 (1963): 28–29;

Miklós Radnóti, "Különbéke. Szabó Lőrinc új verseskönyve," *Nyugat*, 2 (1936): 47–51;

György Rónay, "Szabó Lőrinc: Tücsökzene," *Iradalomtörténeti Közlemények*, 67 (1963): 492–509;

Zoltán Simon, "Szabó Lőrinc költészetének keleti vonatkozásai," *Iradalomtörténeti Közlemények*, 68 (1964): 162–170;

György Somlyó, "Szabó Lőrinc összegyűjtött versei," *Élet és Irodalom* (1961): 4–6;

István Sőtér, introduction to *Négy nemzedék* and "Szabó Lőrinc portréja," *Parnasszus* (1948): 5–27, 96–97;

Pál Szegi, "Szabó Lőrinc. Teremtő nyugtalanság és klasszicizmus," *Magyar Csillag*, 2 (1943): 57–65;

Miklós Szentkuthy, "Szabó Lőrinc. Szenvedély és értelem," *Magyar Csillag*, 2 (1943): 66–77;

Gáspár Miklós Tamás, "A rendszerváltás zimankója (Szabó Lőrinc: Bírákhoz és barátokhoz, Vers és valóság)," *Élet és Irodalom* (5 April 1991): 10.

Magda Szabó

(4 October 1917 –   )

Lóránt Kabdebó
University of Miskolc

Bibliography compiled by Attila Buda

BOOKS: *Bárány* (Budapest: Egyetemi Nyomda, 1949);

Vissza az emberig (Budapest: Egyetemi Nyomda, 1949);

Neszek (Budapest: Szépirodalmi, 1958);

Freskó (Budapest: Magvető, 1958);

Mondják meg sófikának (Budapest: Magvető, 1958);

Bárány Boldizsár (Budapest: Móra, 1958); translated by Kathleen Szász as *The Fawn* (London: Jonathan Cape / New York: Knopf, 1963);

Sziget-kék (Budapest: Magvető, 1959);

Az őz (Budapest: Szépirodalmi, 1959);

Disznótor (Budapest: Szépirodalmi, 1960);

Álarcosbál (Budapest: Móra, 1961);

Születésnap (Budapest: Móra, 1962);

Pilátus (Budapest: Magvető, 1963);

A Danaida (Budapest: Szépirodalmi, 1964);

Tündér Lala (Budapest: Móra, 1965);

Hullámok kergetése (Budapest: Szépirodalmi, 1965);

Eleven képét a világnak (Budapest: Magvető, 1966);

Mózes egy, huszonkettő (Budapest: Magvető, 1967);

Alvók futása (Budapest: Szépirodalmi, 1967);

Zeusz küszöbén (Budapest: Szépirodalmi, 1968);

Katalin utca (Budapest: Szépirodalmi, 1968);

Ókút (Budapest: Magvető, 1970);

Abigél (Budapest: Móra, 1970);

A szemlélők (Budapest: Magvető, 1973);

Szilfán halat (Budapest: Magvető-Szépirodalmi, 1975);

Az órák és a farkasok (Budapest: Magvető, 1975);

Régimódi történet (Budapest: Szépirodalmi, 1977);

Erőnk szerint (Budapest: Magvető, 1980);

Kívül a körön (Budapest: Szépirodalmi, 1980);

Megmaradt Szobotkának (Budapest: Magvető, 1983);

Béla Király (Budapest: Magvető, 1984);

Az ajtó (Budapest: Magvető, 1987);

Az öregség villogó csucsain (Budapest: Magvető, 1987);

Záróvizsga (Budapest: Református Zsinati Iroda Sajtóosztálya, 1987);

Magda Szabó

A pillanat (Creusais) (Budapest: Magvető, 1990);

A Félistenek szomorúsága (Budapest: Szépirodalmi, 1992);

Az a szép, fényes nap (Budapest: Magvető, 1994)

A lepke logikája (Budapest: Argumentum, 1996);

Ne félj! (Debrecen: Csokonai, 1997);

Csekei monolog (Budapest: Europa, 1999);

Mézes sók Cerberus nak (Budapest: Osiris, 1999).

Editions in English: *Tell Sally*, translated by Ursala McLean (Budapest: Corvina, 1963; New York: Knopf, 1966);

Night of the Pig-Killing, translated by Szász (London: Cape, 1965);

"At Cockcrow," in *Twenty-Two Hungarian Short Stories*, translated by Lily Halápy (Budapest: Corvina, 1967);

The Door, translated by Stephan Draughton (New York: Columbia University, 1994).

TRANSLATIONS: William Shakespeare, *A két veronai nemes*, translated by Szabó (Budapest: Új Magyar Könyvkiadó, 1955);

Mariana Alcoforado, *Portugál levelek*, translated by Szabó (Budapest: Móra, 1959);

John Galsworthy, *A Forsyte-Saga*, translated by Szabó and Tibor Szobotka (Budapest: Európa, 1960);

Galsworthy, *Modern komédia*, translated by Szabó and Szobotka (Budapest: Európa, 1960);

Thomas Kyd, *Spanyol tragédia*, translated by Szabó, in *Angol reneszánsz drámák* (Budapest: Európa, 1961), pp. 385–495.

Magda Szabó began her career as a poet but is also acknowledged as a successful playwright, essayist, and travel writer. She is, moreover, an astute and elegant translator, notably of William Shakespeare and John Galsworthy, but she has established her reputation primarily as a writer of fiction. Her novels have been translated into thirty-three languages, including Danish, Dutch, Finnish, French, German, Greek, Italian, Polish, Russian, Spanish, and English. Several of her novels have been translated in more than one version—*Az ajtó* (The Door), for example, was published in 1987, translated into German in 1990 as *Die tür*, and then translated into English as *The Door* in 1994; the French translation of *Mózes egy, huszonkettő* (Moses One Twenty-Two, 1967), titled *1 Moses 22* (1968), was published nine times. Szabó is now recognized as one of the most popular writers in contemporary Hungarian literature.

Szabó has continued a tradition that regards writing as an act of moral resolve; what is observed and experienced elicits a moral response in the writer and turns her rage into narrative. In her early works, written in the 1940s but not publishable during the oppressive regime of Mátyás Rákosi—*Freskó* (Fresco), published only in 1958, and *Az őz* (translated as *The Fawn*, 1963), published only in 1959—the moral impulse is at the center. In her later work, however, her traditional, realistic rendering of the world has turned into a self-examination of varying

orientations, as in *Az ajtó* and, especially, in *A pillanat (Creusais)* (The Moment [Creusa], 1990), in which she relies on postmodern tools to do away with history itself.

She belonged to a group of writers who began writing during World War II, discovering each other in the first days of peace after the war, and who took the Bloomsbury writers as their exemplar. Despite all the horrors and violence of the German and Russian occupations of Hungary in 1944 and 1945, these writers claimed Europe to be their spiritual home. The group was named after a short-lived literary journal of the late 1940s called *Újhold* (New Moon). Indeed, this word symbolized a secret bond implied by their internal exile during the years of Stalinist dictatorship; it also became the target of attacks against them. Among those who belonged to this loosely knit circle were Ágnes Nemes Nagy (1922–1991), János Pilinszky (1921–1981), Géza Ottlik (1912–1990), Iván Mándy (1918–), and Miklós Mészöly (1921–), all of whom have achieved international reputations.

When the writers of the Újhold group first began to publish in 1946–1947, their works were well received and garnered the most prestigious literary awards established before and still existing for a time after the war. Their elders and such literary critics whose judgments have since stood the test of time praised them. In 1948, however, there came the political turn that swept away prize givers and recipients. As a result, the group dissolved as an emerging influence in postwar Hungary. Owing to the upheavals they lived through, their careers can hardly be called typical; for they did not—or rather, did not *only*–have to struggle to express their talent but also had to persuade others to accept their integrity in a political atmosphere that promoted a contrary set of expectations and that also made use of brute force to realize them. As testimony to her commitment and determination to survive, Szabó has since received the highest literary honor in Hungary, the Kossuth Prize; is a member of both the Hungarian Academy of Art and the European Academy of Art, Literature, and Humanities; and received an award in 1992 from the Getz Corporation of the United States for services rendered to Hungarian writing.

Throughout her career, Szabó has conscientiously associated herself with her origins—with the images of family and native town that define her own moral countenance. Magda Szabó was born on 5 October 1917 in Debrecen, an old town of peasant citizens right in the center of the Hungarian plain, the Alföld, without the protective surroundings of marshes, mountains, or city walls—which, during the century and a half of Turkish domination, had to pay tribute by turns to the prince of Transylvania, to the Hapsburg king, and again to the Turkish sultan—to escape the state of political acclimatization, that today is called "Balkanization." It was with a strong sense of duty that the conservative, Calvinist burghers of the town guarded their rich Eurocentric culture and civic liberties. "It was an honor to be a citizen of Debrecen. One had to take an oath as a citizen, the law demanded that, and those accepted as citizens could have 'Citizen of Debrecen' inscribed on their coffins. They had rights, but duties as well," writes Szabó.

The city has a monument to the memory of those Hungarian Calvinist preachers who were sent to the galleys in the seventeenth century by the Hapsburgs, the Catholic kings of Hungary, and in fact one of Szabó's ancestors was among those condemned. She herself is a warden of her church, and in 1992 on her seventy-fifth birthday she was awarded an honorary doctorate by the Calvinist Theological Seminary in Debrecen.

In this city in the first half of the twentieth century, the alderman in charge of the theater and the arts conversed in Latin at mealtimes with his daughter Magda; when her parents, rightly or wrongly, forbade her to go to the cinema she, familiar with stills of the movie, would compensate by writing down the story of the movie as she imagined it. In the course of her childhood Szabó also learned the regimen by which she and her husband later, when the Iron Curtain had descended, spent the weeks: a day speaking German, then English, and then French. This habit was of value not only in terms of practice but also in affirming their intellectual freedom. Known as "The City of Durability," Debrecen is today both praised and mocked by the phrase. This durability, however, may have sustained Szabó when, as a student, she witnessed Germany's occupation of Vienna and later when, as a young teacher, she lived through both the German and the Soviet occupations of Hungary.

She began by writing poetry and changed to writing novels only in the "reticent years," knowing that her work would not be accepted for publication in the post-1948 political climate. Indeed, the poet taught the novelist how to write. Through poetry Szabó acquired the experience essential to her craft as a novelist—personal involvement in her themes and the awareness that the fate of the individual has to be put into perspective. Everyone's personal history is at the same time a repetition of the histories of others, Szabó maintains: "It is a general mistake, I

think, to regard any one of us as an original, a hitherto never seen phenomenon; the most that can be said is that we don't know our predecessors, that we haven't yet come across the documentation of the relationship. We have all appeared previously, whether in our details or in our manifestation, or in the themes voiced by certain artists of centuries past, it is simply that we do not know our grandfathers." Just as Szabó the poet recorded her wartime experiences in two volumes, *Bárány* (Lamb, 1947) and *Vissza az emberig* (Return to Man, 1947), Szabó the novelist was to continue in this vein when reflecting upon the countless and often hellish situations posed by life.

Szabó as a novelist appears to stand in a literary tradition whose members include Thomas Hardy, François Mauriac, László Németh, and perhaps Nikos Kazantzakis—either as immediate precursors or as fellows—related not in their style but rather in expressing a common view of the relationship between the author and the work. Szabó steps out of history and, in analyzing her own stories, conveys both to herself and to the reader the message that what is happening has happened before. On a first reading, her novels seem hastily written, not in form, which is always precise and bound by classicism, but in terms of the enthusiasm with which the author appears to approach the given theme. Her style suggests she has come across her subjects while writing and cast them onto paper while they were still fresh so as to record and understand them. A reading of her life work, by contrast, leaves one with the impression that each of her novels has fallen into a preordained place, as if this type of literary career had been predestined at the moment of her birth. Equally characteristic are her virtually random choices of themes and the archetypal certainty in the twists and turns of a novel. Each novel is an idiosyncratic—almost capricious—direct hit, a hit with inevitable results. One critic has referred to the "ancient formula" of the typical Szabó novel, which, like the Oedipus tale, moves to ever-deeper and more-complicated mysteries, focusing attention on increasingly frightening traps. Her novels develop like clockwork: each word uttered and each gesture enacted is a necessary part of the whole.

Szabó is a tough writer expecting retribution; in her novels sin enfolds the transgressor and elicits a compulsion to admit to sinning. Rather than await justice from the outside world, she lays her trust in the power of inner accountability within the soul. She is essentially a Calvinist. It is not the liberating sensation of a Roman Catholic confession that resounds in her novels but rather the somber

Szabó as a child

Szabó reflects on the passing of the years, on adulthood, with the consequent loss of the island of childhood and the happiness that was once to be had in togetherness. Nonetheless, as *Mózes egy, huszonkettő* (Genesis I:22) underscores, the members of each new generation yearn for this island, where they can live without fear alongside one another in mutual respect. But relationships cannot be rationally planned, nor can behavior toward each other be programmed; these truths are the themes of both *Pilátus* (Pilate, 1963) and *A Danaida* (The Danaid, 1964).

All the same, her novels ultimately acknowledge the need for intimate relationships; it is precisely the absence of such relationships that leads to tragedy. This conviction, too, nourishes the ideal whereby the past is revived to new life. The past, however, retains and avows its pastness. Such is the case with the reenacted past portrayed in *Katalin utca*, in *Ókút* (The Ancient Well, 1970), in *Régimódi történet* (An Old-Fashioned Story, 1977), and in *Megmaradt Szobotkának* (He Remained Szobotka, 1983). Indeed, such is also the case in *Abigél* (Abigel, 1970), a novel Szabó wrote for a young adult audience.

Mutual attraction and even a sexual bond are not enough to sustain a relationship; the breakdown of the relationship between the Western diplomat and the highly educated, humanist Central-European woman in *A szemlélők* (The Spectators, 1973) is evidence of the truth of this statement. The miracle occurs when two individuals do break through the wall between them and go back and forth into each other's worlds as in *Régimódi történet, Megmaradt Szobotkának,* and *Az ajtó*. The tragedy, however, is that not even then can they really help each other—whether the causes are external or internal differences—and they finish by tying each other's helping hands. In the end, the individual is still left to his own devices. The question that lingers is whether this result, too, is inevitable.

Even in distilling individual histories from biographical events, mosaics of memories—indeed, documentable events—and turning them into narrative, as in *Régimódi történet,* her mother's history, and *Megmaradt Szobotkának,* her husband's history, Szabó shows that behind the thrill of discovery an historical model or archetype is always found. That which happens has happened before. Even the titles of her novels allude to this belief—*Pilátus, A Danaida,* and *Mózes egy, huszonkettő.* Beyond its literal meaning, *Ókút* is an allusion to Thomas Mann's "infinitely deep" well, the idea that history as it progresses repeats itself even on the individual level. In the titles of her other novels, one finds the possibility

catharsis entailed in accounting to a congregation through public confession and through self-incrimination. Her novels are the drawing up of accounts of distorted individuals; all around her, at the time of various dictatorships, generations were compelled to act without regard to what their hearts and beings told them. A great deal of hurt and self-destructive passion surges within her characters, who are nourished less and less by their own beings and more and more by motives embedded in the collective subconscious.

Szabó's novels describe the various states of malevolence between individuals. They are full of mutual fear, furtive mutual observation, accumulated injuries, and premeditated injury, as illustrated in *Freskó*. Eventually, the moment comes when the characters open up: confessions flow out like lava, and individuals try to redress what can no longer be salvaged and to put an end to their years of reticence. In *Katalin utca* (Katalin Street, 1968) of repetition and, as a consequence, of comparison.

Szabó's most distinguished novels may well include two early ones, the two apotheoses of otherness, *Freskó* and *Az őz*; the pillar of her mid career, *Régimódi történet*, in which she retrieves the individual living entirely in the confines of family and history; and her two more-recent works, *Az ajtó* and *A pillanat (Creusais)*. The first two novels recount torrid personal vengeance, involving two heroines ostracized because of different circumstances. In one case, the ostracism results from middle-class pretensions, the gap between a family's well-to-do past and the reality of poverty; in the other, ostracism results from "socialism," precisely because of an upper-class past. The two women break with their respective families and move into the distinctive province of art. Corinna, in *Freskó*, prevails as a painter, and Eszter Encsy, in *Az őz*, triumphs as well, as an actress. Corinna's victory is exclusively of a moral nature. Her art has value only in her own eyes; it was disowned by the cultural policy of the dictatorship. Her triumph in the face of her disintegrating, indolent, conformist family is indeed real. Eszter Encsy, meanwhile, has seen success as an artist and with the appearance of her autobiography, a pack of lies rewritten in keeping with the formula prescribed by the regime, but her success destroys her inner world, including her love. The demon of destruction possesses her and, in spite of herself, she destroys everything that she wants to preserve. *Régimódi történet*, by contrast, represents a retrieval of the past that Corinna and Eszter have discarded; in this work the individual cannot live without the past of her family and community. This book presents the resurrection of the Hungarian professional middle class, its existence denied under socialism. The play based on the book, as well as the series produced for Hungarian television, are true to the theme of the novel. The work is not, however, the uncritical creation of something heroic; it is simply the documented discovery of a lost social ambience. Perhaps in translating Galsworthy's *The Forsyte Saga* into Hungarian with her husband, Szabó realized the virtual absence of the middle-class family in Hungarian fiction. *Abigél*, her "novel for young people," presents a similar realization; the novel describes the apotheosis of a Calvinist secondary school during the German occupation of World War II. As a television series it educated generations of Hungarian viewers as a cautionary tale.

A short précis would make *Az ajtó* seem meaningless. As against the heroines of her previous novels, a servant has the lead role in *Az ajtó*, as if Szabó had chosen to redirect the spotlight from Hamlet to Rosencrantz and Guildenstern. The novel relates the confidential relationship between a successful woman author and Emerenc, her charwoman. Emerenc earnestly hopes that the lady writer is worthy of her trust; Emerenc wants to reveal to the author more and more about her life, past and present. The writer is on the defensive, however, and becomes increasingly inclined to isolate herself—even though curiosity consumes her as well. Emerenc's secret is that none may enter her home. Both writer and servant began their lives in surroundings where mutual responsibility was something given, pure and simple. This memory yields the tact with which the writer-protagonist, after all rebuffs, misgivings, and attempts at retaining distance, nonetheless returns to Emerenc's confidence—indeed, to an ever-more-intimate circle of trust.

By this time, Emerenc has become a maid of all work and adviser to those living on a well-to-do street. Yet, she increasingly withdraws from the outside world. She allows no one into her home, into which she gathers cats she takes in out of pity—all in immaculate cleanliness. The novel actually begins at this point. What would happen, however, if Emerenc were to become ill, perhaps terminally, and could no longer look after herself? She wants to die alone in her spotless lair, even if it means rotting away; for her symbolic secret—the cats she has cared for out of compassion—is not to be seen by anyone while she is still alive. Trust leads her to share her secret, to let the writer see her sanctuary.

Emerenc even serves as an example for the writer to follow. She has allowed a wretched, vain old maid, whom she has taken under her wing, to die; indeed, she has helped her prepare for suicide. Emerenc, too, expects to be treated this way. She wants to live only as long as there is meaning to her life, not in miserable humiliation at another's mercy. And here is her real secret: Emerenc wishes to live in the sight of others only as long as she can retain her dignity. She does not want to be tormented while sick or dying. She wants her relationship with the outside world to last only while every one of her words—rare though they are—actions, and gestures are resolute acts, while every manifestation of her being is a meaningful and useful complement to her surroundings. Others can demonstrate their real concern by leaving her alone. This response is what she wants, and she has entrusted the writer with the responsibility of seeing that her wish is granted.

Once Emerenc does become ill, she shuts herself in, and her spotless home becomes infested with stench and filth. Her neighbors want to rescue her, and the writer joins in the effort. At the writer's request Emerenc finally opens the door; as a result, the neighbors storm her lair, take her to be disinfected, and then put her in the hospital. The writer does not even have the time to keep track of further developments; she is busy with a television appearance, a presentation of awards, and an official journey to Greece. As for Emerenc's home, that too is fumigated, and the furniture burned; the cats scatter in all directions. All that she has feared has occurred: she has been humiliated. The writer, nonetheless, acts out one more torturous scene. She calms Emerenc down in the hospital by telling her that nothing has happened—that her home awaits her, safe and sound. Emerenc, however, recovers and prepares to go home. She must be told the truth. The writer dares not do so and entrusts a helpful acquaintance with the task. Emerenc cannot and does not survive this breach of faith. All the trials the writer has come through successfully count for nothing, for she fails the real test. Because she has feared to let another person live and die according to her own maxims, the writer's triumphs are annulled. She is left with a recurrent dream, that of the opening door, which is to be her eternal punishment and suffering—the fate of a traitor.

Az ajtó describes the linking of two different personalities. The first, that of the writer, is explosive and passionate but nonetheless in need of understanding; the other, that of the servant, is introspective and doggedly insistent on sticking to her own decisions. The novel may be said to measure two types of intellect: civilized humanism and ancient-archaic integrity. Ultimately, however, the novel represents more than the struggle of two individuals to understand each other; the conflict veiled by the plot actually amounts to an inner struggle. Emerenc is a moral genius—in the Kantian sense—who is part of all. She goes through the hells of human experience, recollects the barbaric and tragic events of fate, is capable of essential movements only, is generous, and in her every relationship seeks to defend and develop her own dignity. The novel is more than the struggle of two types of persons for mutual

understanding; it is a duel that is really an inner struggle. Emerenc and the fiction writer are then two sides of the same person. A human fragmented into roles searches for the self, for the Emerenc that lives in all. With *Az ajtó*, Szabó took a thematic step away from heroines wrestling with history to the articulation of a moral phenomenon that exists outside history. Prior to this novel, an historical precedent was to be found behind each of Szabó's narratives. Emerenc, however, represents archaic morality; her story is of necessity one of pathos. Yet, Szabó has had enough of history; it has trampled over her more than once and has brought her no consolation. Therefore, she breaks her relationship with history; the break means she can tell every story in as many ways as there are characters. Her historical works essentially encompass such new interpretations. The creation of the Hungarian nation-state and the conversion to Christianity previously were written about heroically or with pathos. Szabó begins simply to create frivolous stories: her situations must be accepted because nothing else can be done.

Her novel *A pillanat (Creusais)* confronts every kind of stylized history. Szabó, turning the story of Aeneas inside out, takes merciless revenge on every kind of power and gives the reader occasion to roar with laughter. In playful mien, but with unyielding hatred, Szabó looks back upon a mendacious world. Considering Szabó's ethical and poetic orientation, she has validly articulated every sort of lie, as well as the inner and outer forces behind the humiliation of human dignity. Both the poetic radiance of the work and the enlivening beauty evident as the writer formulates her thoughts attest to her success.

Her Creusa—contrary to legend—does not die in Troy but rather kills her husband, Aeneas, and lives through adventures in her husband's name. She is a woman in the role of a womanizing hero. Indeed, she becomes a merciless and methodical adventurer, a triumphant cheat given to resolute action—and an unhappy woman. The moment referred to by the title of the novel is that in which destiny offers a human being something other than the *status quo*—the chance to turn a schematically preordained, doomed life into a success. The circumstances of this moment, however, offer not completeness and self-fulfillment but a triumph that is merely a path of escape. In return, Creusa must drag about her own unhappiness; she can realize success only by patronizing and taking advantage of others, by regarding

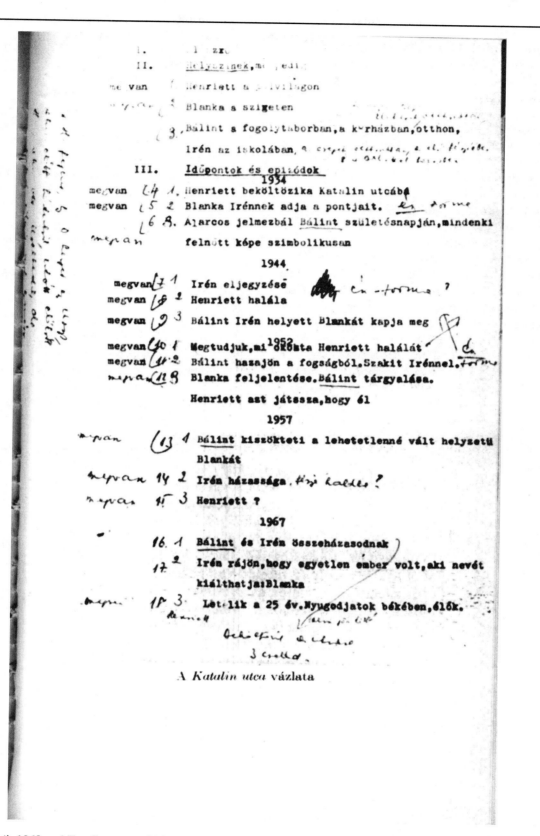

I.
II. Helyszínek, m. ,ed.

me van   Henriett a 1. világon

4.   Blanka a szigeten

3. Bálint a fogolytáborban,a k~rházban,otthon,

Irén az iskolában, a cre.

III.   Időpontok és epizódok
1934
megvan   4 1. Henriett beköltözik a Katalin utcába

megvan   5 2 Blanka Irénnek adja a pontjait.

6 3. Álarcos jelmezbál Bálint születésnapján,mindenki

felnőtt képe szimbolikusan

1944

megvan 7 1 Irén eljegyzése   én -forme ?

megvan 8 2 Henriett halála

megvan 9 3 Bálint Irén helyett Blankát kapja meg

megvan 40 1 1952 Megtudjuk,mi okozta Henriett halálát

megvan 41 2 Bálint hazajön a fogságból.Szakit Irénnel.

megvan 42 3 Blanka feljelentése.Bálint tárgyalása.

Henriett azt játssza,hogy él

1957

13 1 Bálint kiszökteti a lehetetlenné vált helyzetű
Blankát

14 2 Irén házassága.

15 3 Henriett ?

1967

16 1 Bálint és Irén összeházasodnak

17 2 Irén rájön,hogy egyetlen ember volt,aki nevét
kiálthatja:Blanka

18 3 Letelik a 25 év.Nyugodjatok békében,élők.

A *Katalin utca* vázlata

Notes for Szabó's 1968 work Katalin utca, *which contemplates the loss of the sense of togetherness that one feels in childhood (from Judit Kónya,* Szabó Magda, *1977)* them as objects to be used. A woman seeking love, she finds herself doing not what she wants to do but for the rest of her days playing the role of a man who can offer no love. The ultimate consequence is that she scorns the means of her success and, likewise, herself. Hell is not the underworld where Aeneas sought her but the life of the liberated Creusa. Her successes are merely illusions; each new success is simultaneously a new defeat.

With this novel, Szabó has liberated herself from all that formerly bound her art. In it, history ceases to exist; heroes and heroines are nonessential; and, as a result, pathos also disappears. There remains a bitter disillusionment, of such basic force that it resounds with the ecstasy implied by the freedom of play, the deconstruction of history, and the riddance from the story. The author, whose impulse toward vengeance had until now compelled her to write classical works in a particular national tradition, has cast away every forced constraint. If Szabó had donned earlier the realist mask of the mythical heroine in her struggle for individual freedom, now she has concealed her despair behind the ardor of postmodern playfulness.

Interview:

Judit Aczél, *Beszélgetések Szabó Magdával* (Debrecen: Csokonai Kiadó, 1997).

Biography:

Judit Kónya, *Szabó Magda* (Budapest: Szépirodalmi, 1977).

References:

Endre Bajomi-Lázár, "Hungarian Works in French," *New Hungarian Quarterly*, 8 (1962): 251–253;

Pal Belohorszky, "A Magyar Romlas Viragai: Szabó Magda: Rigimodi tortenet," *Irodalmi es Kritikai Folyoirat*, 1054, no. 22 (1978): 626–634;

Jean Chalon, "La romanciére hongroise Magda Szabó," *Le Fiagro Littéraire* (2 June 1962);

Irodalomtőrténet, no. 3, special Szabó issue (1997);

Lóránt Kabdebó, "Heroines, of Self-Salvation," *New Hungarian Quarterly*, 130 (1993): 14–23;

Louise Mamiac, "Une romanciére de notre temps, Magda Szabó," *Revue France-Hongrie*, 80 (1964): 55–58;

Ivan Nagel, "Die Wirbel die in die Vergangenheit," *Die Zeit* (11 December 1964);

Péter Nagy, "On Modern Hungarian Novels," *New Hungarian Quarterly*, 1 (1961): 45–53;

Margarete Pirich, "Ich liebe alles Lebendige," *Rheinische Post* (26 October 1965);

Béla Pomogáts, "Les trois decennies de Magda Szabó," *Hungarian PEN*, 16 (1975): 66–69;

Pomogats, "Szabó Magda harom alkoto evitzede," *Alfold: Irodalmi es Muvelodesi Folyoirat*, 27, no. 4 (1976): 52–58;

Else Schmücker, "Zwischen den Zeiten. Zu drei Büchern Magda Szabó," *Frau und Beruf*, 7–8 (1965): 16–20;

Zoltan Simon, "Egy varos buvoleteben: Szabó Magda," *Szuletesnapjara*, 28, no. 10 (1977): 66–69;

Tamas Ungvari, "Irok a szinpadon. Szabó Magda Regimodi tortenete," *Irodalmi es Kritikai Folyoirat*, 1054, no. 22 (1978): 800–802.

Áron Tamási

(20 September 1897 – 26 May 1966)

Péter H. Nagy
Loránd Eötvös University of Budapest

Translated by Zsuzsa Duray

BOOKS: *Lélekindulás* (Kolozsvár: Fraternitás, 1925);
Szűzmáriás királyfi: Regény, 2 volumes (Kolozsvár: Erdélyi Szépmíves Céh, 1928);
Erdélyi csillagok (Kolozsvár: Minerva, 1929);
Hajnali madár (Budapest: Athenaeum, 1929);
Címeresek: Regény (Kolozsvár: A Szerző, 1931);
Helytelen világ: Novellák (Kolozsvár: Erdélyi Szépmíves Céh, 1931);
Ábel a rengetegben: Regény (Kolozsvár: Erdélyi Szépmíves Céh, 1932); translated by Mari Kuttna as *Abel Alone* (Budapest: Corvina, 1966);
Ábel az országban: Regény (Kolozsvár: Erdélyi Szépmíves Céh, 1934);
Ábel Amerikában: Regény (Kolozsvár: Erdélyi Szépmíves Céh, 1934);
Énekes madár: Székely népi játék három felvonásban (Budapest: Kazinczy, 1934);
Jégtörő Mátyás: Regény (Kolozsvár: Erdélyi Szépmíves Céh, 1935);
Rügyek és reménység (Budapest: Székely Egyetemi és Főiskolai Hallgatók Egyesülete, 1935);
Ragyog egy csillag: Regény (Kolozsvár: Erdélyi Szépmíves Céh, 1938);
Virágveszedelem (Budapest: Révai, 1938);
Szülőföldem (Budapest: Révai, 1939);
Három játék (Budapest: Révai, 1941)—comprises *Énekes madár, Tündöklő Jeromos,* and *Vitéz lélek;*
Magyari rózsafa: Regény (Kolozsvár: Erdélyi Szépmíves Céh, 1941);
Csalóka szivárvány: Színjáték három felvonásban (Budapest: Révai, 1942);
Téli verőfény. Elbeszélések (Kolozsvár: Erdélyi Szépmíves Céh, 1942);
Virrasztás (Budapest: Révai, 1943);
A legényfa kivirágzik (Budapest: Misztótfalusi Közművelődési Szövetkezet, 1945);

Áron Tamási

Szivbéli barátok: Ifjúsági regény (Budapest: Révai, 1946);
Hullámzó vőlegény: Színpadi játék 3 felvonástan (Budapest: Révai, 1947);
Zöld ág (Budapest: Révai, 1948);
Kikelet: Válogatott elbeszélések (Budapest: Révai Könyvkiadó Nemzeti Vállalat, 1949);

Bor és víz. Szüreti játék (Budapest: Népművészeti Intézet, 1951);

Búbos vitéz (Budapest: Művelt Nép, 1952);

Kossuth nevében: Toborzási jelenet (Budapest: Művelt Nép, 1952);

Bölcső és bagoly: Regényes önéletrajz (Budapest: Szépirodalmi Könyvkiadó, 1953);

Hazai tükör: Krónika, 1832–1853 (Budapest: Ifjúsági Könyvkiadó, 1953);

Szegénység szárnyai: Félszáz elbeszélés (Budapest: Szépirodalmi Könyvkiadó, 1954);

Kakasok az Édenben: Két színpadi játék (Budapest: Szépirodalmi Könyvkiadó, 1956)—comprises *Énekes madár* and *Ördögölő Józsiás;*

Hegyi patak (Budapest: Szépirodalmi Könyvkiadó, 1959);

Szirom és Boly: Magyar rege (Budapest: Szépirodalmi Könyvkiadó, 1960);

Játszi remény: Új novellák és egy költői elbeszélés (Budapest: Szépirodalmi Könyvkiadó, 1961);

Világló éjszaka (Budapest: Magvető, 1966);

Vadrózsa ága (Budapest: Szépirodalmi Könyvkiadó, 1967).

Editions and Collections: *Összes novellái* (Budapest: Révai, 1942);

Jégtörő Mátyás; Ragyog egy csillag (Budapest: Szépirodalmi Könyvkiadó, 1957);

Elvadult Paradicsom: Összegyűjtött novellák, 1922–1936 (Budapest: Szépirodalmi Könyvkiadó, 1958);

Világ és holdvilág: Összegyűjtött novellák, 1936–1957 (Budapest: Szépirodalmi Könyvkiadó, 1958);

Ábel, 3 volumes (Budapest: Szépirodalmi Könyvkiadó, 1960)—comprises volume 1: *Ábel a rengetegben;* volume 2: *Ábel az országban;* volume 3: *Ábel Amerikában;*

Akaratos népség: Színpadi művek, 2 volumes (Budapest: Szépirodalmi Könyvkiadó, 1962)—comprises volume 1: *Énekes madár, Tündöklő Jeromos, Vitéz lélek, Csalóka szivárvány;* volume 2: *Hullámzó vőlegény, Ördögölő Józsiás, Hegyi patak, Boldog nyárfalevél;*

Hétszínű virág (Budapest: Magvető, 1963);

Czimeresek (Budapest: Szépirodalmi Könyvkiadó, 1964);

Összegyűjtött novellái, 2 volumes (Budapest: Szépirodalmi Könyvkiadó, 1967);

Valogatott művei, 2 volumes, edited by Géza Féja (Budapest: Szépirodalmi Könyvkiadó, 1974);

Szinpadi művek (Budapest: Szépirodalmi Könyvkiadó, 1978);

Összes novellái, 2 volumes (Budapest: Szépirodalmi Könyvkiadó, 1982);

Tamási Áron szinjatekai, 2 volumes (Budapest: Szépirodalmi Könyvkiadó, 1987, 1988);

Tamási Áron szinjatekai, 1924–1942 (Budapest: Szépirodalmi Könyvkiadó, 1989).

PLAY PRODUCTIONS: *Énekes madár: Székely népi játék haróm feluonásban,* Budapest, Royal Theater of Pest, November 1935;

Tündöklő Jeromos, Kolozsvár, Hungarian Theater of Kolozsvár, 1936;

Vitéz lélek, Budapest, National Theater, 1940;

Csalóka szivárvány, Budapest, National Theater, 1942;

Hullámzó vőlegéy, Budapest, Studio Theater, 30 January 1947;

Ősvígasztalás, Pécs, Hungary, 1976.

Known primarily as a novelist, the Transylvanian writer Áron Tamási was also an accomplished short-story writer, dramatist, essayist, and literary historian. Influenced by historical folk ballads, Tamási captured in his body of work the rustic tone and creative imagination of the Szekler peasantry of southwestern Transylvania.

János Áron Tamási was born on 20 September 1897 in Farkaslaka, Transylvania, which was then part of Hungary. His mother gave birth to eleven children, but six died young. Tamási attended the primary school in Farkaslaka from September 1904 until June 1910. After one of his thumbs was mutilated in an accident, his parents, assuming that he would be unable to work in the fields, enrolled him in the Catholic grammar school in Székelyudvarhely; the cost was covered in part by an uncle. Tamási entered military service in 1916, attended the Academy of Officers in Gyulafehérvár (now Alba Iulia), fought in the Piave offensive from 15 to 24 June 1918, and was awarded the Grand Silver Medal of Heroism and the Károly Cross Medal. After leaving the army in the autumn of 1918 Tamási began to study law at the University of Kolozsvár (today Cluj-Napoca, Romania). That year, with the Austro-Hungarian Empire having been defeated in the war, the Romanians of Transylvania declared the region to be united with Romania; the union was ratified in the Treaty of Trianon in 1920. In 1921 Tamási transferred to the Academy of Trade in Kolozsvár, graduating in 1922.

Tamási's first literary success came in the summer of that year, when he won a prize in a short-story competition sponsored by the journal *Keleti Újság.* "Szász Tamás, a pogány" (Tamás Szász, the Pagan) was published in the 23 July issue. At that time Tamási was working at the Credit Bank of Kolozsvár; later he worked at the Peoples' Bank of Brassó. In 1923 he was one of eleven young Transylvanian authors whose work was published in a literary anthology, *The Eleven*. Three of his stories were included: "Megnyitom a földnek száját" (I Open the Mouth of the Earth), "Föld embere" (The Man of the Earth), and "Vigadjatok ügyesen" (Rejoice Carefully).

In July 1923 Tamási traveled to the United States at the invitation of his brother. He obtained temporary jobs in New York and worked as a bank clerk in Gary, Indiana, and Welch, West Virginia. Meanwhile, he sent feuilletons, short stories, and essays to *Keleti Újság* and other Hungarian literary journals, such as *Vasárnapi Újság, Pásztortűz*, and *Ellenzék*. He wrote his first play in 1924, answering a call for submissions from the Hungarian Theater in Kolozsvár. The "Szekler tragedy" *Ősvígasztalás* (Primeval Consolation) was submitted, under the pseudonym Siculus, by his fiancée. The jury was impressed by the work, but the manuscript disappeared; a copy was discovered only after the author's death, and the play was finally staged in Pécs in 1976. In 1925, again with the assistance of his fiancée, Tamási published a volume of short stories, *Lélekindulás* (Soul Moving), in Kolozsvár. The following year he left the United States and returned to Kolozsvár, where he worked as a journalist. He was one of the founding members, with Erdélyi Helikon, of the "Free Writers' Company," which published the political journal *Hitvallás* (Faith).

Tamási's first novel, *Szűzmáriás királyfi* (The Virgin-Mary King), was published at the beginning of 1928. In January 1929 Tamási received the Baumgarten Prize; he won the same prize the following year for his second volume of short stories, *Erdélyi csillagok* (Transylvanian Stars, 1929). In 1931 he published a second novel, *Címeresek* (The Escutcheoned), as well as a third collection of short stories, *Helytelen világ* (Incorrect World). The following year he was invited to an eight-day conference of Hungarian writers at Lake Balaton, where he gave a speech in the name of the representatives from Transylvania at a reception after a banquet for Archduke Albert.

During the next few years Tamási produced his "Ábel" trilogy, consisting of *Abel a rengetegben* (Ábel in the Wilderness, 1932; translated as *Abel Alone*, 1966), *Ábel az országban* (Ábel in the Country, 1934) and *Ábel Amerikában* (Ábel in America, 1934). An extended bildungsroman, the trilogy has a circular plot: in each volume Ábel is forced to undergo change, and at the end of each he returns home to rediscover himself. The reception of the trilogy was

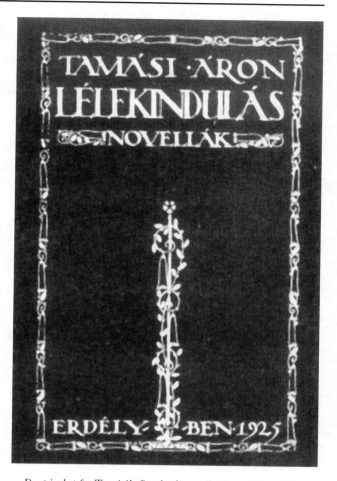

Dust jacket for Tamási's first book, a collection of short stories published in Romania while he was living in the United States

extremely favorable; the first volume earned Tamási a third Baumgarten Prize in 1933.

Responding to Tamási's popularity, the newspaper *Brassói Lapok* hired him to write a column titled "Tiszta beszéd" (Clear Speech), in which he discussed current public issues. In 1935 he began writing a new trilogy, of which only two volumes were completed: *Jégtörő Mátyás* (Matthias the Icebreaker, 1935) and *Ragyog egy csillag* (The Star Is Shining, 1938). *Jégtörő Mátyás* concerns two young people who fall in love, have a child, and struggle against life-threatening forces. The novel maintains a balance between realistic and fantasy elements.

In November 1935 the Új Thália Company performed Tamási's *Énekes madár* (Singing Bird, published 1934) at the Royal Theater of Pest. A Szekler peasant play about the love affairs of three sisters, the work has elements of mythology and fantasy. Tamási published a collection of short stories, *Rügyek és reménység* (Buds and Hope), in 1935, and his peasant play *Tündöklő Jeromos* (Glittering Jeremy, published 1941), was performed the following year. Written in less than a month, the play won a competition sponsored by the publishing house Erdélyi Szépmíves Céh and the Hungarian Theater of Kolozsvár.

Tamási's study of Hungarian literature in Romania, *Szülőföldem* (My Homeland), appeared in 1939; the publication of new editions was prohibited for several decades in Central and Eastern European countries struggling with the problem of restive ethnic minorities. His play *Vitéz lélek* (Gallant Soul, published 1941), was performed at the National Theatre in Budapest in 1940. His radio play "Székely karácsony" (Szekler Christmas) was broadcast several times but never published, and the manuscript is lost. In 1942 his play *Csalóka szivárvány* (Deceptive Rainbow) was produced at the National Theater; it was also performed in Kolozsvár, where it was a huge success. In 1943 the Révai firm in Budapest published a collection of Tamási's essays, *Virrasztás* (Staying Up), and he was awarded the Great Prize of the Baumgarten Foundation. On 14 May he was elected a corresponding member of the Hungarian Academy of Sciences.

Tamási escaped from Transylvania to Hungary with his second wife and father-in-law when the Soviet Union invaded Romania in October 1944. He was an honorary representative in the Hungarian parliament from 1945 until 1947. On 30 January 1947 the Studio Theater of the National Theater of Hungary presented his *Hullámzó vőlegéy* (Surging Bridegroom), which received such an outstanding response that the play was twice broadcast on radio.

In 1948 the Hungarian coalition government banned *Mezei próféta* (Field Prophet)—a movie version of *Vitéz lélek*—and Tamási's *Bölcső és bagoly: Regényes önéletrajz* (Cradle and Owl: Fictional Autobiography); the latter did not appear until 1953. In August 1949, however, a selection of his short stories, *Kikelet* (Spring), was allowed to be published. In July 1953 the newly formed government of Imre Nagy awarded Tamási the Kossuth Prize, and he was elected to the National Council of the Patriotic People's Front. Fifty of his short stories, collected as *Szegénység szárnyai* (The Wings of Poverty, 1954), were published by the Budapest house Szépirodalmi Könyvkiadó, to which Tamási entrusted the publication of almost all of his later works. In 1955 he trav-

eled to his hometown for the first time in eleven years, and in the fall of 1956 he was elected to the board of directors of the Association of Hungarian Writers. Tamási's play *Világi zsoltár* (Secular Psalm), later retitled *Hegyi patak* (Mountain Stream, 1959), was completed by the end of 1957 for the Theater of the People's Army; but its successor organization, the Theater of Comedies, and the Madách Theater both refused to produce the play. In 1960 Tamási published the nationalistic novel *Szirom és Boly* (Szirom and His Anthill), in which he describes the difficult transition of Szekler peasants from Romanian Bukovina to life under Hungarian rule.

At the end of 1963 Tamási's health began to deteriorate from heart disease. He was treated at the János Hospital in the autumn of 1965. During this time, with the assistance of his third wife, Ágota Bokor, he struggled to complete his autobiography. Shortly before his death on 26 May 1966 he published a collection of short stories, *Világló éjszaka* (Lighting Night).

Bibliography:

Albert Tezla, *Hungarian Authors: A Bibliographical Handbook* (Cambridge, Mass.: Belknap Press of Harvard University Press, 1970), pp. 558–562.

Biographies:

Géza Féja, *Tamási Áron alkotásai és vallomásai tükrében* (Budapest: Szépirodalmi Könyvkiadó, 1967);

József Izsák, *Tamási Áron* (Bucharest: Ifjúsági Könyvkiadó, 1969);

Ernő Taxner-Tóth, *Tamási Áron* (Budapest: Gondolat Kiadó, 1973);

Sándor Z. Szalai, *Hit a harcban, remény a bajban: palyakep Tamasi Aronrol* (Budapest: Szépirodalmi Könyvkiadó, 1991).

References:

László Bóka, "Tamási Áron novellái," *Magyar Csillag*, 2 (1 October 1942): 237–240;

Mihály Czine, "Tamási Áron újabb műveiről," *Csillag*, 8 (1954): 516–527;

László Németh, "Tamási játékai," *Magyar Csillag*, 2 (1 December 1942): 403–407;

György Poszler, "Tamási Áron újabb regényei," *Irodalomtörténet*, 43 (1955): 242–248.

Timrava
(Bożena Slančeková)
(2 October 1867 – 27 November 1951)

Marcela Mikulová
Institute for Slovak Literature SAV, Bratislava

Translated by Norma L. Rudinsky

BOOKS: *Tá zem vábna* (Martin: Kníhtlačiarsky účastinársky spolok, 1907);
Márnosť všetko (Martin: Kníhtlačiarsky Účastinársky Spolok, 1908);
Dedinské povesti (Prague: F. Topič, 1920);
Chudobná rodina (Martin: Matica slovenská, 1921);
Páva (Martin: Matica slovenská, 1923);
Hrdinovia (Prague: L. Mazáč, 1929);
Všetko za národ (Prague: L. Mazáč, 1930);
Dve doby (Martin: Żivena, 1937);
Novohradská dedina (Martin: Żivena, 1937);
Výber z rozprávok (Martin: Matica slovenská, 1937);
Výber z diela (Martin: Matica slovenská, 1937);
Prvé kroky (Martin: Żivena, 1938).
Editions and Collections: *Sobrané spisy*, 12 volumes (Martin: Lipa, Matica slovenská, 1921–1945);
Skúsenosť (Martin: Matica slovenská, 1952);
Hrdinovia (Bratislava: Slovenský spisovateľ, 1953);
Zobrané spisy, 7 volumes (Bratislava: SVKL, 1955–1959);
Za koho ísť? (Bratislava: Smena, 1956);
Mojžík a iné rozprávky (Bratislava: Smena, 1956);
Ťapákovci a iné poviedky (Bratislava: Mladé letá, 1960);
Ťažké položenie (Bratislava: Smena, 1964);
Veľké šťastie (Bratislava: Tatran, 1967);
Hrdinovia (Bratislava: Tatran, 1968);
Dielo, 2 volumes (Bratislava: Tatran, 1971);
Bez hrdosti (Bratislava: Tatran, 1973);
Timrava Božena Slančíková, edited by Ivan Kusý, 2 volumes (Bratislava: Tatran, 1985);
Hrdinovia (Bratislava: Tatran, 1985);
Za koho ísť? (Liptovský Mikuláš: Tranoscius, 1997).
Editions in English: "The "Ťapák Family," excerpt from *Ťapákovci*, translated by K. Kornel, in *The*

Timrava (Bożena Slančeková)

Linden Tree: An Anthology of Czech and Slovak Literature, edited by Mojmír Otruba and Zdeněk Pešat (Prague: Artia, 1962);
"The Tapak Family," translated by Andrew Cincura, in *An Anthology of Slovak Literature*, compiled by

Cincura (Riverside, Cal.: University Hardcovers, 1976);

That Alluring Land, edited and translated by Norma L. Rudinsky (Pittsburgh, Pa.: University of Pittsburgh Press, 1992).

PLAY PRODUCTIONS: *Chudobná rodina,* Bratislava, Národné divadlo, 14 December 1921;

Páva, Prešov, Slovenské divadlo, 16 February 1952.

Timrava is the culminating representative of late realism in Slovak literature. In her prose works by original tragicomic means she caught human relations and destinies against the background of social changes at the end of the nineteenth century and the first decades of the twentieth century. Because of her themes and technique of presentation her works had a provocative effect on Slovak literature, and from the first they were interpreted contradictorily. On the one hand, critics praised their great empathy, but on the other hand, they rejected their aesthetics. Timrava's position among prose writers was felt then and is still felt today to be unique. This position resulted not by accident but from her deliberate literary stance.

Timrava was born Bożena Slančíková on 2 October 1867 with her twin brother Bohuslav in the village of Polichno in Novohrad County in central Slovakia. She lived in Polichno and in the neighboring village of Ábelová most of her life. Her father, a national activist and Lutheran pastor, was Pavel Slančík; her mother was Eva-Mária Honétzy. They had eleven children, six of them growing to adulthood. In her short autobiography (written in 1922, not published until 1958 in *Timrava v kritike a spomienkach*) Timrava wrote, "Our father taught his daughters himself because his small stipend did not allow sending them away to school. Only for our 'finishing' they sent us for a year to city schools. They sent me to a girls' school in Banská Bystrica. I began to write as a twenty-three-year-old. Almost as a joke and for fun. In this way I passed the dull hours in Polichno." Her father's teaching was of high quality, and all the children passed their tests. The boys went on to study in the higher grades of the gymnasium, but there were no means for the four girls to study further. Nevertheless, all four developed culturally, and the eldest, Irena, eventually published some of her writing in newspapers and magazines.

In the year 1887 Timrava, together with Irena, began to "publish" a household serial "Ratolest'" (Branch)—only one number now extant—to which she contributed a poem of the same name and a tale, "Na vrchoch" (On the Hilltops). Her literary talent began to develop with versifying doggerel—140 verses are extant in a notebook titled "Pesničky na Żigúra, Bacúra, Oľgu Pe, a na iných" (Little Poems on Żigúr, Bacúr, Oľga Pe, and Others), written between 1887 and 1897. Timrava's simple little verses, begun as a family joke sung to the melodies of well-known songs, took on gradually a sharply ironic character toward herself and a sarcastic attitude toward her prototypes. Their motifs foretold the basic thematic complex of Timrava's later tales of the village intelligentsia; the dominant theme that emerged was the relations between women and men, in which already resounded the bitter emotional tones of lost illusions resulting from disharmony in love.

Writing verse did not fulfill Timrava's creative ambition, and the most natural field of her literary activity became prose, in which the thematic differentiation of her stories into village and middle-class corresponded to an ambiguity in her personality. The equal proportion of these themes evinces how her interest passed at regular intervals from herself as subject and from the village intelligentsia to the wider nature of the village itself. In the first of her published stories, *Za koho íst'?* (Whom to Marry?, 1893), she drew attention to a theme provocative for that period (later developed many times)—that is, how to make a good match. The relations between men and women, untraditionally conceived as a naive young girl's loss of illusions and her acceptance of hard realities, formed the main theme of most of Timrava's middle-class stories, and their autobiographical elements enlarged the reader's experience. In almost all her long stories the author seemed bitterly sure that the single life was the best resolution (she herself never married). This point of view also generally determined her pictures of male figures as unimpressive weaklings, ridiculous in their self-satisfaction.

Timrava drew the content of stories published before 1896 chiefly from events in the Novohrad countryside she knew so intimately: "Darmo" (No Use), "Kandidát żenby" (A Candidate for Marriage), "Bude dačo" (Something Will Happen), and "Na Jurkovej svadbe" (At Jurko's Wedding) were all published in 1893. However, these stories also seemed to polemicize with the sentimental presentation of love found in literature contemporary with hers. In her longer stories—"Pomocník" (The Assistant Teacher), "Ťažké položenie" (A Hard Status), "Tak je darmo" (So There's No Help), "Pozde" (Too Late), "Nemilí" (Unpleasant People), "Bál" (The Ball), and "Boj" (Battle)—written from 1896 to 1900,

ODTLAČOK ZO „SLOVENSKYCH POHĽADOV"
ČISLO 6.

PÁVA.

ĽUDOVY DIVADELNY KUS V 4 DEJSTVACH

NAPISALA

TIMRAVA.

TLAČOL MATICE SLOVENSKEJ A KNIHTLAČIARSKIHO ÚČ SPOLKU
V TURČIANSKOM SV. MARTINE
1913

Title page for the published version of one of Timrava's four plays. The title means "Peacock" or "Proud Woman."

there emerged a psychologically elaborate type of heroine with feelings of vague sadness, disenchantment, and moodiness that directly related to the social atmosphere at the turn of the century but were then unusual in Slovak literature. These stories were also characterized by Timrava's effort at new textual expression by an almost poetically conceived use of a vocabulary of multiple meanings. The longer stories were surprisingly original and formally differed from the rest of Slovak realistic prose. Thus, they were provocative not only in content but also in their effort to disrupt the clichés of realism. Through translations of Hungarian, German, and Russian literature and also through modernist Slovak works, Timrava perceptively caught the immediate stimuli of current European literature and sensitively implanted them into her stories. These stimuli were always worked out strikingly with wide understanding and precise indications of the radicalness of the artistic changes arriving with the new century. Timrava also knew the original domestic

canon, and her best texts challenged it with their own complex authority.

Evidence of the polemical response of the contemporary literary establishment appears in the reaction to the magazine publication of Timrava's novella *Skúsenosť* (Experience, 1902). The openness with which Timrava revealed her experiences in Dolný Kubín, where she lived as a paid companion to an insensitive Slovak widow, was generally interpreted as a subjective distortion because her analysis did not suit the most significant representatives of Slovak literature and culture. Disgusted by editorial cuts in *Skúsenosť*, Timrava for a while gave up on open self-expression and in 1904 wrote a village story, "Na jednom dvore" (In One Courtyard/ Household).

The years from 1904 to 1906 became for Timrava a phase of creative exploration and resulted in stories with differing thematic goals and artistic weight. She gave a sarcastic view of a realistic artist's relation to his spring of inspiration in "Veľký

Manuscript for the first page of Timrava's brief autobiography (from Ivan Kusý, Bożena Slančeková-Timrava, *1967)*

majster" (The Great Master, 1904). In this same year she published the first story of the trilogy *Pódi*, which deliberately destroyed the established stereotype of the Jewish village tavernkeeper as a merciless usurer. Timrava created Pódi as a tragicomic, miserable fellow, a slave of his ambitious wife. The novellas *Bez hrdosti* (Without Pride, 1905) and *Veľké šťastie* (Great Happiness, 1906) in a fundamental way surpassed the traditional realistic aesthetics by the high degree of the heroines' subjective involvement, their freer structure, and their preference for literary stylization over realistic imitation. *Bez hrdosti*

indirectly condemned Slovak indifference to the national plight, but its plotline rested on the hopeless love of the autobiographical heroine Milina for a self-satisfied Magyarone (a Slovak who had renounced his faith). The emphatic self-irony leads almost to the self-degradation of the heroine. Despite everything, the novella is not tragic and from a certain aspect can even be considered a parody—on love, friendship, human relations, "serious" literature, and "patriotism." With the novella *Veľké šťastie*, Timrava broke down the accustomed criteria for composition of realistic works, and by transferring the focus to the serious interior problems of the characters she completed this synthesizing period of her writing career.

Timrava's works reveal no extraordinarily outstanding personalities. Among all the characters of the social stories, Šaba in *Nemilí* (Unkind People) is a typical example; she "is neither interesting, nor pretty, nor rich." Timrava's works show almost a "cult of the average," which she emphasized as a worthy measure. This approach was somewhat risky, since the ordinary and banal were not loved by the preceding generation of Parnassians. Her generation of later realists, however, found that the only possible way to picture reality in their own time was the path of little steps and modest desires.

Oľga Krčméry, Timrava's closest friend, remembered years later:

> I felt the depth of Božena's intellect, and told her many times that if I were a young man ready to marry, I would certainly choose her alone. But she already had a premonition that she would never get married. She said to me: "You'll see, Irenka will marry, and all of you, except me. Not from principle. But with my nature I don't know how to get close to anyone, and maybe not even to someone I want to get close to."

Despite all of Timrava's interior melancholy, she was sociable and witty. She made peace with her fate as an unmarried woman, especially since she strongly loved her parents and felt best in their home. In 1909 her father's death was a cruel blow emotionally and also meant the loss of her and her mother's material security. In that same year she and her mother moved to the village of Ábelová, dependent on the financial help of Timrava's brother, the Lutheran pastor there. His low salary did not suffice to take care of them, and Timrava, though feeling psychically exhausted, worked as a teacher in the local nursery school. She stayed on in Ábelová after the death of her mother in 1923 until 1945, when she went to live with a niece in the small city of Lučenec.

Timrava's village prose also shows her effort to be original. In the novella *Tá zem vábna* (1907; translated as *That Alluring Land*, 1992) she reinterpreted and in the end cast doubt upon even such a theme as immigration to America, which Slovak literature and politics then regarded simplistically. The village, caught up in immigration, was disoriented, and Timrava artistically coded arguments for and against immigration as rivalry between the masculine (rational) and the feminine (emotional). Timrava often reduced her village characters to puppets (for example, the self-important road repairman Ondro Karman in the 1896 story of the same name), as if she wanted to point out that the new capitalist period was revealing itself in the village by its deformation of the human character. The new social situation brought with it the breakup of the old village society and a decline in the human personality, as the village lost its wholeness.

The novella *Márnosť všetko* (The Vanity of All, 1908), a monumental tale of basic human values in the dimensions of life and death, presented the tragic fate of a village servant woman who was wrapped up in her ownership of money. The culmination of Timrava's creative phase in village prose is the great novella *Ťapákovci* (The Ťapák Clan, 1914), in which she deliberately enclosed the village reality as a model to allow herself an artistic abbreviation, showing in the relations of a single family the end of one social formation and the tragicomic establishment of the new capitalism in rural Slovakia. At the end Timrava emphasized the anthropological constants of history—human envy, joy, and misfortune—which always remain the same, though society changes.

The novella *Strašný koniec* (An Awful Ending, 1912) demonstrated that Timrava was beginning more and more to focus on serious social questions, though the differences between the village and other classes were steadily becoming less relevant. In the pacifist novella with the ironic title *Hrdinovia* (Heroes, 1929), she linked the two classes, but the result was a little uncertain. Her desperate financial situation drove her to enter a literary competition sponsored by the women's magazine *Živena* with the subject of the ongoing of World War I. Timrava correctly guessed that the judges would favor a direct and single-minded position, but she won the prize by giving up her characteristic implicit method. To this creative period also belongs the masterful fresco depicting human misery, weakness, and suffering, the novella *Skon Paľa Ročku* (The Death of Paľo Ročko, 1921), which in its universal theme evinced Timrava's expressionistic sensitivity.

One of the most significant of Timrava's works is the novelistic *Všetko za národ* (Everything for the Nation, 1930). This synthesizing work is the result of the author's polemic throughout her life with the Slovak literary establishment and its official national conception of literature, which seemed rigid to Timrava with its too sentimental relationship to the nation, the common people, and folklore. Timrava's permanent inner dialogue is played out in a stylized form by the two female protagonists (the autobiographical Viera and her alter ego, Hana). Though it is indeed an autobiographical novel, the factual parts are built into a highly stylized and mystified text. Love is the chief focus—and love for three men. This rectangle must inevitably collapse, a fact that sufficiently explains the single life of the autobiographical heroine in the tragic or grotesque epilogue. The long interval from the original experiences brushed off unflattering characteristics and unpleasant memories, but they survived in the harsh polemical nature of the author.

The novella *Skon Paľa Ročku* showed clearly that in her culminating creations Timrava escaped from her previously established borders of realistic determinism to more-universal levels. On the other hand, in her two final prose works, *Dve doby* (Two Periods, 1937) and *Záplava* (Flood, 1938), both critically reflecting the actual social problems of the first Czechoslovak Republic, Timrava narrowed the distance between reality and her picture of it.

Timrava's four plays—*Chudobná rodina* (A Poor Family, 1921), *Páva* (Peacock/Proud Woman, 1923), *Odpoveď* (Answer, 1934), and *Prekážky* (Barriers, written, 1949)—belong in a place outside the context of her other works. Timrava wanted to communicate with the general population for whom books and literary magazines were unavailable, and she was drawn to the theater because it concentrated upon the human being. Timrava's implicit artistic method, however, was unsuited to dramatic construction of dialogue, and her plays were not favorably received by the critics.

The dominant approach of Timrava's mature works about the village can be called constructive modeling and generalizing. In her autobiographical novellas, by contrast, decomposition, the breakup of reality, and individualized relations dominate. Timrava's prose ended one period of Slovak literary goals and opened new possibilities for presenting the human—on the one hand, highly individualized Slovak modernism and, on the other hand, universalized literary expressionism.

Letters:

Ivan Kusý, ed., *Korešpondencia Timravy a Šoltésovej* (Bratislava: Nakladateľstvo SAVU, 1952);

Pavol Petrus, ed., *Listy Boženy Slančíkovej Timravy* (Prešov: Filozofická fakulta UPJŠ, 1994).

Bibliography:

Mária Mališová and Magda Drugová, *Božena Slančíková Timrava (1867–1951)* (Lučenec: Okresná knižnica, 1976).

Biographies:

Hana Ponická, *Ábelovský dom* (Bratislava: Slovenský spisovateľ, 1959);

Ivan Kusý, "Pramene k životu a dielu Timravy," *Literárny archív,* 2 (1965): 5–22.

References:

Oskár Čepan, "Timravina ironická deziluzia," in his *Stimuly realizmu* (Bratislava: Tatran 1984), pp. 179–241;

Michal Gáfrik, "Timrava a slovenská moderna," *Slovenská literatúra,* 15 (1968): 174–179;

Michal Kocák, ed., *Božena Slančíková-Timrava, Koloman Banšell* (Martin: Matica slovenská, 1990);

Ivan Kusý, *Božena Slančeková-Timrava* (Martin: Matica slovenská, 1967);

Kusý, "Božena Slančeková-Timrava," in his *Dejiny slovenskej literatúry IV* (Bratislava: Veda, 1975), pp. 386–417;

Daniela Lehutová, *Hrdinovia* (Bratislava: Tatran, 1973);

Alexander Matuška, "Timrava," in his *Profily a portréty* (Bratislava: Slovenský spisovateľ, 1972), pp. 329–334;

Ján Menšík, "Úvod," in *Dedinské povesti,* by Timrava (Prague: F. Topič, 1920), pp. 5–18;

Marcela Mikulová, *Próza Timravy medzi realizmom a modernou* (Bratislava: Ústav slovenskej literatúry SAV, 1993);

Pavol Palkovič, "Dráma v Timravinom diele," *Slovenské divadlo,* 7 (1959): 521–528;

Eugen Pauliny, "Skice k štúdiu formy u Kukučína a Timravy," in his *O jazyku a štýle slovenskej prózy* (Bratislava: Slovenský spisovateľ, 1983), pp. 44–52;

Ján Števček, "Román psychologického naturalizmu," in his *Dejiny slovenského románu* (Bratislava: Tatran, 1989), pp. 223–235;

Timrava v kritike a spomienkach (Bratislava: SVKL, 1958).

Papers:

Timrava's papers are in the Literárny archív Matice slovenskej, Martin.

Milo Urban

(24 August 1904 – 10 March 1982)

Braňo Hochel
Comenius University

BOOKS: *Jašek Kutliak spod Bučinky (Črta zo života oravských horalov)*, as Milko U (Ružomberok: Lev, 1922);

Za vyšným mlynom (Bratislava: Slovenský národ, 1926);

Živý bič: Román vo dvoch dieloch (Bratislava & Prague: Vydáva Sväz slovenského študentstva, 1927);

Výkriky bez ozveny (Bratislava: Academia, 1928);

Hmly na úsvite: Román (Prague: Družtevní práce, 1930; revised edition, Turčiansky svätý Martin: Kompas, 1941; revised again, Bratislava: Slovenský spisovateľ', 1970);

S tichého frontu (Časové rozprávky) (Bratislava: Ústredie slovenského katolickeho študentstva, 1932);

Česká literatúra a Slováci (Prague: Družtevní práce, 1934);

V osídlach: Román (Turčiansky svätý Martin: Kompas, 1940);

Zhasnuté svetlá (Bratislava: Slovenský spisovateľ', 1957);

Kto seje vietor (Bratislava: Slovenský spisovateľ', 1964);

Zelená krv: Spomienky hájníkovho syna (Bratislava: Tatran, 1970);

Kade-tade po Halinde: Neveselé spomienky na veselé roky (Bratislava: Slovenský spisovateľ', 1992);

Na brehu krvavej rieky: Spomienky novinara (Bratislava: Slovenský spisovateľ', 1994);

Sloboda nie je špás: Spomienky dôchodcu, edited by Ján Medvęd (Bratislava: Slovenský spisovateľ', 1995);

Železom po železe (Bratislava: Slovenský spisovateľ', 1996).

Editions and Collections: *Novely* (Martin: Kompas, 1943);

Výkriky bez ozveny (Bratislava: Slovenský spisovateľ', 1965);

Roztopené srdce (Bratislava: Tatran, 1984);

Vybrané spisy Mila Urbana, 9 volumes (Bratislava: Slovenský spisovateľ', 1989–1995).

Milo Urban

PLAY PRODUCTION: *Beta, kde si?* Prešov, Divadlo Jonáša Záborského, 1991.

The writing of Milo Urban has been acknowledged by many literary critics and historians as a unique type of expressionism and the highlight of literary realism. His works are among the most frequently read and published Slovak literature of the twentieth century. His major books have been translated into many languages (but none into English), and his influence on later Slovak prose writers is significant.

Milan August Urban was born on 24 August 1904 in the village of Rabčice in Orava, a region in northern Slovakia near the border with Poland. Urban's father, also named Milan, was a forester; his mother, Anna, née Lachová, was the father's second wife. There were two children from the father's first marriage: Jozef, who became a Catholic priest and died during World War I, and Ilona. Urban also had a younger brother and sister, František and Mária. He knew little of city life: the closest town, Námestovo, was about twelve miles away. In the first volume of his memoirs, *Zelená krv: Spomíenky hájníkvho syna* (The Green Blood: Memories of a Forester's Son, 1970), he recalled his reaction when he was first enrolled in primary school in Zázrivá, a village in a distant part of Orava where his maternal grandparents lived: "School? What is it? . . . I have never known a pupil or a teacher. I have never seen a blackboard, a pencil, a textbook, or a school building."

Urban attended lower high school in Trstená and started upper high school in Ružomberok. In January 1920 his father drowned during an unexpected thaw in the mountains. His mother remarried in September—much too soon, according to Slovak tradition. Urban dropped out of school at that time.

Urban published his first short stories in *Vatra*, a nationalistic Catholic-oriented student journal, when he was sixteen. They were clearly influenced by his reading of such writers as the realists Pavol Országh Hviezdoslav, Martin Kukučín, and Svetozár Hurban Vajanský; the symbolist Ivan Krasko; the Czech poets Petr Bezruč and Jiří Wolker; and the Magyar poet Endre Ady. The same is true of his novel *Tiene* (Shadows), written in Ružomberok several months after his father's death and published in the daily *Slovak* from October 1922 to March 1923. At the same time, he was contributing pieces to other literary magazines and newspapers, and—using the pseudonym Milko U—he published his first book, *Jašek Kutliak spod Bučinky (Črta zo života oravských horalov)* (Jašek Kutliak from under Bučinka [Sketches from the Life of Orava Foresters], 1922). Although written early in his career, this novella incorporates many of the principles he developed in his later works. For Urban, plot was less important than the inner conflicts and psychological motivations of his characters. Jašek is physically strong but, like Urban's later protagonists, emotionally pliable and, consequently, defenseless.

In 1921–1922 Urban was employed as an assistant editor at the magazine *Slovák* and then as a clerk in the Catholic St. Vojtech Union in Trnava. In September 1922 he began studies at the secondary school for foresters in Banská Štiavnica. He left after two years and worked for the magazine *Slovenský národ* until it went bankrupt. Unemployed, Urban devoted his full energies to writing. In 1926 he published the novella *Za vyšným mlynom* (Behind the Upper Mill); seven shorter works were collected in *Výkriky bez ozveny* (Shrieks with No Echo, 1928).

Za vyšným mlynom takes place in the village of Malkov, where Jano Štetina, the lover of Katrena Zalčíková, is found murdered. Ondrej Zimoň is accused of the crime but is released for lack of evidence. Zimoň marries Katrena, and they have a son in whose features Zimoň sees his murdered rival. The novella concentrates on the psychological duel between Zimoň and Peter Štetina, the dead man's father, and ends with Zimon admitting his guilt. Zimoň's inner struggle is similar to that of Raskolnikov in Fyodor Dostoyevsky's *Crime and Punishment* (1866): neither character is able to keep the secret of his "perfect crime."

Psychology is also dominant in the novellas collected in *Výkriky bez ozveny*. In "Svedomie" (Conscience), for example, a village priest refuses to give last rites to a dying girl because she is unmarried and pregnant. He is shunned for his action by the other villagers. In "Staroba" (Old Age) the elderly Pavol Duchaj's use of a walking stick is interpreted by the villagers as a sign of his impending death; they, and even the old man's closest relatives, are offended when he does not die. His lonely death finally provides satisfaction to the village.

In 1927 Urban published the long novel *Živý bič: Román vo dvoch dieloch* (The Living Scourge: A Novel in Two Sections); it went through sixteen editions and has been translated into German, Slovenian, Serbo-Croatian, Magyar, Czech, Romanian, Bulgarian, and Russian. (The German translation was one of the books that were burned by the Nazis.) In the poor mountain village of Ráztoky, Eva Hlavajová, whose husband, Adam Hlavaj, is away fighting in World War I, has an affair with a lawyer named Okolický. The villagers discover her sin, and the pregnant Eva commits suicide. When Adam returns home, his decision not to seek revenge against Okolický gains him the respect of the villagers, and he becomes their leader in the struggle for a better way of life.

The success of *Živý bič* led Urban to write, at his publisher's instigation, *Hmly na úsvite* (Fog at Dawn, 1930), in which Adam is again the main char-

Urban with his wife, Žofia Paňáková

acter. The episodic plot is set not only in a rural milieu but also in small Slovak towns and in the capital, Prague, which is full of political intrigue. Even there Adam continues to believe in archetypal country truths. Another character, the worker Sedmik, is a revolutionary; but a building collapses on him, and he has a vision of Christ shortly before his death. Urban rewrote the novel in 1941 and again in 1970.

In 1935 Urban married Žofia Paňáková, who was also from Orava. They had three children: Ol'ga, born in 1935; Cyril, born in 1940; and Katarina, born in 1944. In October 1938 Urban signed an antifascist manifesto, but in 1940 he accepted the post of editor in chief of the fascist daily *Gardista;* he held the position until 1945. A few days before the end of World War II he moved his family to Austria, where he was imprisoned by the American armed forces. In 1947 he was taken back to Czechoslovakia and put on trial. Thanks to the testimony of people he had helped during the war and to the intervention of the Soviet writer Ilya Ehrenburg, he was freed on 16 December 1947; but a year later he was sentenced to "public condemnation." At that time he moved to Chorvátsky Grob, a village in southwest Slovakia.

Urban's next novel, *Zhasnuté svetlá* (Turned-off Lights), was published in 1957; it was the first part of a trilogy, which also included *Kto seje vietor* (Who Sows the Wind) in 1964 and *Železom po železe* (To Beta Iron by Iron), which appeared posthumously in 1996. *Zhasnuté svetlá* depicts the time between the great mobilization in Czechoslovakia in autumn 1938 and the creation of the Slovak state in March 1939; *Kto seje vietor* deals with events up to the antifascist Slovak national uprising in August 1944; and *Železom po železe* describes the social and political chaos in Czechoslovakia during the final months of World War II. Slovak critics generally contend that the trilogy has more documentary than artistic value.

While living in Chorvátsky Grob, Urban wrote his four-volume memoirs. The first volume, *Zelená krv: Spomíenky hájníkovho syna*, published during the Czechoslovak political thaw in 1970, is an impressionistic picture of the author's childhood. In 1974 Urban moved to Bratislava, where he lived until his death on 10 March 1982. The Communist government did not allow the other volumes of the memoirs to be published; they appeared only after the collapse of the Soviet bloc and, therefore, posthumously: *Kade-tade po Halinde: Neveselé spomienky na veselé roky* (Walking about Halinda: Unhappy Memories of Happy Years) in 1992, *Na brehu krvavej rieky: Spomienky novinara* (On the Bank of a Bloody River: Memories of a Journalist) in 1994, and *Sloboda nie je špás: Spomienky dôchodcu* (Freedom Is No Fun: Memories of a Pensioner) in 1995. The memoirs depict the same events as Urban's later novels, and they do so more vividly. A noteworthy feature of the memoirs is Urban's account of the diverse political and ideological streams in twentieth-century Slovakia.

Milo Urban is one of the most important prose writers in twentieth-century Slovak literature. His penetrating insights into the psychological makeup of his characters and his highly artistic style set high standards for Slovak fiction; in his major novels and novellas one can discover and appreciate the true character of the nation.

Bibliography:

Marta Mikitová, *Milo Urban: Personálna bibliografia* (Martin: Matica slovenská, 1994).

References:

Jozef Bžoch, "O niektorých znakoch Urbanových noviel," *Slovenská literatúra*, 16 (1969): 586–599;

Zděnek Eis, "K počátkum konkretizace Urbanova románu *Živý bič*," *Slovenská literatúra*, 15 (1968): 445–464;

Eis, "Konkretizace Urbanova románu *Živý bič* v českem tisku," *Česká literatura*, 16 (1968): 534–548;

Július Noge, "Milo Urban," in his *Heimkehr und andere slowakische Erzählungen aus acht Jahrzenten* (Prague: Artia, 1960);

Noge, "Urbanov *Živý bič*, román sociálneho sebauvedomovania sa dediny," *Slovenská literatúra*, 28 (1981): 128–149;

Daniel Okáli, "Slovo o Živom biči a jeho autorovi," *Slovenské pohľady*, 95 (1979): 93–98;

Peter Petro, *A History of Slovak Literature* (Montreal: McGill-Queen's University Press, 1995), pp. 130–136;

Ján Stevcek, *Lyrízovaná próza* (Bratislava: Tatran, 1973), pp. 63–81;

Stevcek, *Nezbadané prózy* (Bratislava: Slovenský spisovateľ, 1971), pp. 10–30;

Jožo K. Šmálov, *Život v slove: Esej o diele Mila Urbana* (Bratislava: Unia 1939);

Miloš Tomčík, "Dva romány na jednu tému: Zo vzťahov medzi modernou slovenskou a českou prózou," *Slovenská literatúra*, 20 (1973): 325–348;

Tomčík, "M. Urban," in his *Na prelome epoch* (Bratislava, 1961), pp. 436–437;

František Vsesticka, "Umění Urbanovy povidky," *Slovenská literatúra*, 29 (1982): 150–155.

Papers:

Milo Urban's papers are in the Matíca Slovenská in Martin.

Vladislav Vančura

(23 June 1891 – 1 June 1942)

Jiří Poláček
Masaryk University, Brno

BOOKS: *Amazonský proud* (Prague: Čin, 1923);
Dlouhý, Široký a Bystrozraký (Prague: Kniha, 1924);
Pekař Jan Marhoul (Prague: Družstevní práce, 1924);
Pole orná a válečná (Prague: Jan Fromek, 1925);
Rozmarné léto: humoristický román (Prague: Jan Fromek, 1926);
Učitel a žák (Prague: Rudolf Škeřík, 1927);
Nemocná dívka (Prague: Rudolf Škeřík, 1928);
Poslední soud (Prague: Jan Fromek, 1929; third revised edition, Prague: Melantrich, 1935);
Hrdelní pře anebo Přísloví (Prague: Aventinum, 1930);
Kubula a Kuba Kubikula (Prague: Adolf Synek, 1931);
Markéta Lazarová (Prague: Sfinx, 1931);
Útěk do Budína (Prague: Melantrich, 1932);
Luk královny Dorotky (Prague: Melantrich, 1932);
Alchymista (Prague: Družstevní práce, 1932);
Konec starých časů (Prague: Melantrich, 1934);
Jezero Ukereve (Prague: Melantrich, 1935);
Tři řeky (Prague: Družstevní práce, 1936);
Rodina Horvatova (Prague: Evropský literární klub, 1938);
Obrazy z dějin národa českého, 3 volumes (Prague: Družstevní práce, 1939, 1940, 1948);
Josefina (Prague: Umění lidu, 1950).

Editions and Collections: *Knihy Vladislava Vančury*, 4 volumes (Prague: Družstevní práce, 1929–1936);
Spisy Vladislava Vančury, 8 volumes (Prague: Melantrich, 1932–1936);
Dílo Vladislava Vančury, 8 volumes (Prague: Družstevní práce-Melantrich-Svoboda, 1946–1950);
Spisy Vladislava Vančury, 16 volumes (Prague: Československý spisovatel, 1951–1961);
Vědomí souvislostí, edited by Alena a Jindřich Santarová (Prague: Československý spisovatel, 1958);
Rozmarné novely, edited by Milan Kundera (Prague: Mladá fronta, 1959);
Řád nové tvorby, edited by Milan Blahynka and Štěpán Vlašín (Prague: Svoboda, 1972);

Vladislav Vančura

Zvony mého kraje, edited by Havel (Prague: Albatros, 1976);
Spisy Vladislava Vančury, 7 volumes to date (Prague: Československý spisovatel, 1984–   ).

Editions in English: "In My End Is My Beginning," translated by M. Weatherall, in *Heart of Europe: An Anthology of Creative Writing in Europe, 1920–1940*, edited by Klaus Mann and Hermann Kesten (New York: Fischer, 1943), pp. 524–526;
"All's Well That Ends Well," translated by M. and R. Weatherall, in *Hundred Towers: A Czechoslovak*

Anthology of Creative Writing, edited by F. C. Weiskopf (New York: Fischer, 1945), pp. 181–203;

"The Honest Pint," translated by Erika Vilímová, in *The Linden Tree: An Anthology of Czech and Slovak Literature 1890–1960,* edited by Mojmír Otruba and Zdeněk Pešat (Prague: Artia, 1962), pp. 185–196;

The End of the Old Times, translated by Edith Pargeter (New York: Vanous, 1965).

PLAY PRODUCTIONS: *Učitel a žák,* Prague, Osvobozené divadlo, 14 October 1927;

Nemocná dívka, Prague, Osvobozené divadlo, 26 September 1928;

Alchymista, Prague, Národní divadlo, 18 November 1932;

Jezero Ukereve, Prague, Stavovské divadlo, 8 February 1936;

Poklad na ostrově, adapted from *Treasure Island,* by Robert Louis Stevenson, Prague, National Theater, 16 October 1936;

Pražský žid, adapted from the play by Josef Jiří Kolár, Prague, National Theater, 23 February 1946;

Josefina, Prague, Národní divadlo, 23 February 1949.

MOTION PICTURES: *Před maturitou,* with Julius Schmitt, Josef Neuberg, and Svatopluk Innemann, Prague, A-B, 9 September 1932;

Na sluneční straně, with Schmitt, Vítězslav Nezval, Roman Jakobson, and Miloslav Disman, Prague, A-B, 1 December 1933;

Marijka nevěrnice, with Karel Nový, Ivan Olbracht, and Bohuslav Martinů, Prague, Ladislav Kolda, 2 March 1934;

Láska a lidé, with Václav Kubásek and Jaroslav Martínek, Prague, Favoritfilm, 25 December 1937;

Naši furianti, with Kubásek, Prague, P.D.C.-Musil, 4 March 1938.

OTHER: Robert Louis Stevenson, *Poklad na ostrově,* adapted by Vančura (Prague: Universum, 1935);

Josef Jiří Kolár, *Pražský žid,* adapted by Vančura (Prague: ČDLJ, 1957).

Vladislav Vančura is one of the great Czech writers, who, according to František Xaver Šalda, "moved Czech prose into a whole new sphere." He was also an important dramatist, essayist, movie director, scriptwriter, and public figure. In all his works, Vančura used rich poetic language in a highly personal way. He was a leading representative of the Czech avant-garde between the world wars,

and he was an uncompromising opponent of fascism.

Vladislav Vančura was born 23 June 1891 in Háj near Opava. His parents were Václav Vojtěch, a business manager at a sugar refinery, and Marie Vančura (née Svobodová). Vančura had four sisters and many relations, among whom was the author Jiří Mahen (the pseudonym of Antonín Vančura). Vančura's childhood was spent in various places, including Davle near Prague and Prague itself. He attended grammar school in Benešov but interrupted his schooling to learn bookselling and to study at the college of applied arts. In 1915 he took his final secondary-school examinations in Prague. After his final school examinations he worked briefly as a clerk. He spent a term in the faculty of law at Charles University and then changed to the faculty of medicine. In 1921 he took his degree and that same year married a fellow medical student, Ludmila Tuhá. Together they set up a medical practice in Zbraslav near Prague. They had one daughter, Alena, who wrote books for children and young people.

Vančura produced chiefly prose, mostly short stories and novels. He wrote about issues relevant to his own time and about the history of Czechoslovakia. Several of his works were criticisms of contemporary society from the avant-garde point of view and included a search for a new social order. He glorified working together, community spirit, and love, but he also dealt with the problems of individuals, guilt and punishment, and national character. He created many remarkable literary characters; in describing them and their fates he reveals his idea of the ideal man and the ideal life—a life of action in which people are free, natural, and passionate. The stories are sometimes told in the first person, the narrator expressing Vančura's own ideas and judgments; his individual impassioned style is characteristic of all his writing. Often experimental, he employed elements of colloquial speech, poetic metaphors, archaic vocabulary and sentence structure, and wordplay. His works are characterized by lyricism, eloquent graphic vision, and humor.

Vančura began his literary career with short stories that were published in magazines. The first of them, titled "V aleji" (In the Avenue), appeared in *Horkého týdeník* (Horký's Weekly) in 1909. However, he did not publish any other stories until the late teens; then stories appeared in various journals—*Červen* (June), *Proletkult* (Proletarian Culture), *Kmen* (Stem), *Lumír, Nebojsa* (Dreadnaught), *Orfeus,* and *Země* (The Earth). At that time Vančura took a particular interest in the graphic arts. When he was young, he had wanted to be a painter. Now he could at least work as an art critic for *České slovo* (The Czech Word), where he worked from 1919 to 1920. At the same time he became interested in the theater and tried his hand at drama—writing the short plays *Několikerá zasnoubení* (Multiple Betrothals), *Satyrské komedie* (Satyr's Comedies), and *Latinští klasikové* (The Latin Classics). In 1959 these plays were published in a volume titled *Hry* (Plays), and in 1985 they were included in *První prózy a první pokusy* (First Efforts) as part of *Spisy Vladislava Vančury*. In 1924 he was writing theatrical reviews for the newspaper *Národní osvobození* (The National Liberation). He also began to write original essays, studies on various themes, and commentaries on current events, art, and culture and to give papers at conferences. The texts of these papers were published in many journals, including *Host* (The Guest), *Plán* (The Plan), *Panorama, Odeon, Tvar* (Form), *Literární noviny* (The Literary Gazette), *Tvorba* (Creative Work), and in newspapers such as *České slovo* (The Czech Word), *Národní osvobození* (National Liberation), and *Lidové noviny* (The People's Newspaper). In 1958 some of his essays were included in the anthology *Vědomí souvislosti* (Awareness of Continuity); in 1972 his collected essays, together with his art and theater reviews, were published in the volume *Řád nové tvorby* (The Rules of the New Creative Method).

In the course of the 1920s Vančura gradually stopped practicing medicine and concentrated on literature and public life. He was the first president of Devětsil, the "artists' union," which brought together young writers, painters, architects, and actors. He also contributed to *Devětsil. Revoluční sborník* (Devětsil. The Revolutionary Anthology, 1922) and wrote the foreword to *Město v slzách* (A City in Mourning, 1921), the first work of Jaroslav Seifert, who later received the Nobel Prize in Literature. Besides being engaged in these projects, Vančura also made several journeys abroad. In 1924 he was in Paris; two years later he was in Cairo; and in 1927 he was in Moscow. From 1921 he was a member of the Czech Communist Party, although he had certain reservations about it. When the new leadership under Klement Gottwald defended the increasing influence of Russian communism at the fifth party congress in 1929, Vančura and six other writers opposed these efforts; Vančura was then expelled from the party and never returned to it.

In 1923 Vančura published his first book, *Amazonský proud* (The Current of the Amazon River). It included fourteen short stories that had already been published in journals. Most of them are characteristic of the avant-garde program; their out-

standing features are revolutionary ideology, lyricism, unfettered imagination, dreams, and exoticism. In them Vančura depicts the greatness and poetry of everyday life, glorifying cooperative work, love, and community spirit. He criticizes contemporary social conditions, using extravagant exaggeration, parody, and satire. He peoples his stories with small tradesmen, solitary daydreamers, workmen on the Panama Canal, and even animals and fairy-tale characters.

Vančura's second book, *Dlouhý, Široký a Bystrozraký* (Long, Broad, and Hawkeyes, 1924), includes three short stories that had also been published in journals. All are ambiguous and present an original picture of contemporary society and the cultural movements of the day. They are full of poetic imagination and extravagant hyperbole, which might even be called Dadaistic absurdity. There are also elements of folktale and movie techniques. The first story, "Cesta do světa" (Journey into the World), is about two young daydreamers, Jan Kylich and Ervín Weil, who run away from home. As the story unfolds, their flight takes on several different meanings: it is a way to self-knowledge, a realization of boyish dreams, and a criticism of avant-garde exoticism. The heroes of the next story, "Havraní křídlo" (A Raven's Wing)—František Dlouhý, Alexandr (San) Široký, Josef Bystrozraký, and the cobbler—are lighthearted drinking cronies who roam the world in their imagination. Their imaginary travels owe much to movie techniques and are full of poetic symbolism, but they are also a further criticism of the avant-garde obsession with exoticism. In the last story, "F. C. Ball," the main characters are the members of a strange football team, who—like the heroes of Eduard Bass's *Klapzubova jedenáctka* (Klabzuba's Eleven, 1922)—are celebrating worldwide success. However, the story of the team is a metaphor for the contemporary avant-garde culture, in particular Devětsil.

Both books met with a relatively lukewarm reception; not until 1924 did Vančura arouse interest, with the publication of his first novel, *Pekař Jan Marhoul* (Jan Marhoul, Baker). This tragic, timeless story of the gradual proletarianizing of the eponymous hero and his family ends with Marhoul's death. The novel was meant as a condemnation of contemporary society, but to a great extent Marhoul is the cause of his own downfall. Vančura portrays him as a good-hearted fellow, generous to a fault—in fact, several times downright foolish—but also convivial, hardworking, optimistic, honest, and unspoiled. The strength of this novel about a quixotic baker lies in its striking metaphors and out-

VLADISLAV VANČURA

ROZMARNÉ LÉTO

1926

ODEON – J. FROMEK – PRAHA

Title page for Vančura's 1926 novel about six characters who meet at a summer resort

standing passages of almost biblical passion. The first paragraph offers a typical example:

> The vast canopy of night is silent, not a voice to be heard, the universe flies through frost and darkness. Men, like seeds sown in secret, sleep in their houses. If poverty and pain were to shout out, their crying would be whipped up into a pillar rising to the outer reaches of darkness. If death were not a gloomy, terrible and great event, it would thunder through midnight with every stroke of time.

Vančura's second novel, *Pole orná a válečná* (Plowed Field and Battlefield, 1925), is similar in character. The hero is František Řeka, a peasant "lacking in judgment," who for no good reason kills another peasant. Then Řeka is caught up in the maelstrom of war, gets killed, and is given a solemn burial as the country's unknown soldier. Through this absurdity Vančura exposes the obscenity of war when even a murderer can be honored. Other characters, notably Baron Maximilián Danowitz and his

sons, Ervín and Josef, suffer equally absurd fates. Vančura presents pictures of degenerate humanity, rottenness, corruption, and frustration, counterbalanced by the straightforward honesty of the narrator and by visions of a future peaceful time when "the workers would come into their own." This novel was rejected by some contemporary critics because of the naturalistic characterizations while other reviewers thought highly of it because of the beauty of the writing and its antiwar emphasis.

Vančura's fifth book, *Rozmarné léto: humoristický román* (Capricious Summer: A Humorous Novel, 1926), was illustrated by Josef Čapek, the brother of the writer Karel Čapek. *Rozmarné léto* is different from both previous novels. As its subtitle indicates, it is "an entertaining novel," and of course it is highly individual. Closely related to poetism, the artistic movement of the Czech avant-garde of the 1920s, *Rozmarné léto* has six main characters—the manager of the swimming pool, Antonín Důra; his wife, Kateřina; Major Hugo; Canon Roch; the magician Arnoštek; and his partner, Anna. The action takes place in a little summer resort called Krokovy Vary. The arrival of Arnoštek and Anna causes quite a stir in the quiet little town. Důra, Roch, and Hugo all gradually attempt to seduce the lovely Anna, and Kateřina makes a play for the magician. All these attempted conquests end unsuccessfully. In addition to creating comic situations, Vančura projected his own opinions and his philosophy of the contented life into the conversations of his amiable heroes. He insisted one should enjoy all the gifts life has to offer. At the time critics paid little attention to *Rozmarné léto*. They saw it as nothing more than a kind of deviation in the development of its author. Yet, it is one of Vančura's most successful works. It has been reprinted many times and has been adapted for the theater. In 1967 Jiří Menzel made it into a popular motion picture of the same name.

In the latter half of the 1920s Vančura wrote two plays; in 1927 he produced *Učitel a žák* (Teacher and Pupil) and in 1928, *Nemocná dívka* (The Sick Girl). These plays include many lyrical passages and might well be termed poems for the stage. The first play is about the conflict of ideas of a young man, Jan, and his teacher, Doktor. Vančura meant this play to be a parable of the character and development of avant-garde art. He had the same ideas in mind with *Nemocná dívka*. This play, the story of the successful treatment of the ailing Ida by three doctors—the professor, Kolovrat, and Křikava—is Vančura's metaphor for dealing with the question of Czech national character.

The setting of the next novel, *Poslední soud* (The Last Judgment, 1929), is Prague in the 1920s. In it Vančura portrays the harsh existence of people from the poorer sections of Prague society—Weil, Odeta, Dejm, Nikodém, and Zajíc on the one hand and Pilipaninec, Mejgeš, and Iliadora, emigrants from sub-Carpathian Ukraine, part of Czechoslovakia until World War II, on the other hand. On the literal level Vančura contrasts the modern big city and a backward mountainous region; on a higher plane he sets civilization and nature in opposition to each other. He also deals with the question of love through the relationship of Pilipaninec to Iliadora and Odeta and with the problem of guilt and punishment with Mejgeš's killing of the forester and Pilipaninec's arson. At the same time, Vančura celebrates the spirit of loyalty and harmony among men. In the year *Poslední soud* was published, it was awarded the state prize and was favorably received by the critics. Some reviewers, however, with some justification, found it much too metaphorical. Perhaps that is why Vančura rewrote this novel in 1935.

By the mid 1930s he had brought out several other works. The novel *Hrdelní pře anebo Přísloví* (Investigating Murder or Proverbs, 1930), partly continues the theme of *Poslední soud*. The chief characters are four elderly cronies—the narrator, who is unnamed; a former judge, Skočdopole; a retired teacher, Vyplampán; and a doctor, Zazaboucha. Other characters are Skočdopole's wife, son, and daughter-in-law and the brothers Josef and Jiří Půlpytl. The four friends attempt after some time to clear up the mystery of the death of the wife of Josef Půlpytl. They are unsuccessful, so they come to terms with the situation and give themselves up to life in the present. Vančura thus offers a solution to the topical problems of guilt and punishment and the potential for self-knowledge. (Other writers, including Karel Čapek, were concerned with similar problems.) Vančura, partially because of the influence of François Rabelais, pays homage to a full earthy life, human solidarity, and joy. He attaches an important role to humor, which he understands as a wise outlook on life, maintaining that "laughter is the highest form of wisdom." *Hrdelní pře anebo Přísloví* is remarkable for the frequent use of colloquial speech and folk sayings that form an independent layer of general truths in the text. The novel was well received by the critics of the day.

In 1931 the fairy tale *Kubula a Kuba Kubikula* (Kubula and Kuba Kubikula) began a new stage in Vančura's work, which was characterized by a more narrative style. Vančura often told stories to his daughter, Alena, and this custom led his wife and his publisher, Adolf Synek, to urge him to write the book. It is a series of lighthearted adventures of the bear leader, Kuba Kubikula; the teddy-bear Kubula; the ghost Barbucha; and several villagers, both adults and children. Here Vančura gently satirizes traditional folktales and permeates reality with fantasy. The emphasis in the book is on humor, action, cheerful comradeship, and the vigorous speech of his heroes. *Kubula a Kuba Kubikula* is one of the most original and popular tales for children and young people in Czech literature.

In 1931 Vančura also published the balladlike novel *Markéta Lazarová*. The work, dedicated to Jiří Mahen, was inspired by the history of Vančura's own family. He set the action in the Middle Ages, but he did not intend the work to be an historical novel, for he interpreted the past imaginatively, disregarding accuracy of time and place. The story is about two quarreling robber families, the Kozlíks and Lazars. It tells of their fights with each other and with the king's army. Vančura also introduces two love stories. The entire novel is a glorification of love, a full life, passion, and courage. It is a polemic aimed at the lifestyle of the author's own time and the "delightful complexity" of its literature. Contemporary journals gave the novel favorable, even enthusiastic, reviews. The awarding of the state prize and winning the readers' poll in the renowned *Lidové noviny* newspaper drew even more attention to the originality of this work. In 1967 the director František Vláčil made *Markéta Lazarová* into an equally excellent movie with the same title.

The theme of love is just as important in the next two works, published in 1932—the novel *Útěk do Budína* (Escape to Buda) and the collection of short stories *Luk královny Dorotky* (Queen Dorothy's Bow). The novel is the tragic story of the love of a Czech woman, Jana Myslbeková, and a Slovak, Tomáš Bárány. It is set in post–World War I Prague, Budapest, and Slovakia. Vančura confronts not only Czech and Slovak national character but also two different lifestyles, one with a city and one with a country background. Contemporary critics had nothing but praise for this book. Of the six stories in *Luk královny Dorotky,* two take place in the past and four at the beginning of the 1930s. The characters are two pairs of lovers, people of a small town, rival doctors, tramps, and even the French writer Guy de Maupassant. The stories are mostly love stories, their charm reminiscent of Renaissance tales. In his stories Vančura takes the part of love, youth, comradeship, and simple humanity. However, he also deals with economic crisis and at times allows a note of social criticism to creep in. In 1970 Jan Schmidt made a successful motion picture of the work.

In 1932 Vančura wrote the play *Alchymista* (The Alchemist). The action takes place in Prague in the reign of Rudolf II (1576–1611). As in his stage poems of the 1920s, Vančura is concerned with Czech national character and life. The play makes its point through the confrontation of several Czech characters with the Italian scholar Alessandro del Morone. It also examines the relationship between poetry and science.

At the beginning of the 1930s Vančura devoted much of his time and energy to moviemaking. It was not the first time he had taken an interest in this branch of art. From 1920 he had been writing about motion pictures for the newspapers, and in 1926 and 1927 he had written the movie scripts *Nenapravitelný Tommy* (Inveterate Tommy) and *Host 6* (Guest 6). Vančura left behind more than a dozen incomplete movie scripts and other movie projects. Elements of movie techniques are also found in his prose; in his own movie work Vančura was influenced by that of the contemporary Soviet and French avant-garde.

In 1932 Vančura helped to make a fairly successful motion picture, set in a grammar school, *Před maturitou* (Before the Exams). In 1933 he directed a short motion picture, *Na sluneční straně* (On the Sunny Side), the story of children growing up without parents. In 1934, in collaboration with Karel Nový and Ivan Olbracht, Vančura made a movie in the Sub-Carpathian Ukraine. Called *Marijka nevěrnice* (Marijka Adultress), it is the story of an unfaithful wife, but it is above all a valuable documentary picture of the life of the people of the Carpathian Ukraine and the Jews. In spite of its original artistic effects and the impressive music of composer Bohuslav Martinů, this movie was not successful with audiences. Today, however, it is considered one of the most remarkable Czech motion pictures made between the world wars. In the later 1930s Vančura again collaborated in a movie; released in 1937 and set in the world of sport, it was called *Láska a lidé* (Love and the Human Race). In 1938 he adapted for the screen the well-known nineteenth-century play *Naši furianti* (The Braggarts) by Ladislav Stroupežnický.

Vančura had intended to film the story of a modern Baron Münchhausen. However, he did not manage to bring it to the screen, so in 1934 he turned his script into a novel, *Konec starých časů* (The End of the Good Old Days). The action takes place at the beginning of the 1920s in the fictional south Bohemian castle Kratochvíle. The action centers on a mysterious Russian emigrant, Prince Alexandr Megalrogov, who has traces not only of Baron Münchhausen but also of Don Quixote and Don Juan. He and his servant Váňa represent the old feudal world that Vančura satirizes by opposing it to the postwar world of the Czech parvenus. Critics at the time rated *Konec starých časů* highly; however, some reviewers considered it simply a sociological novel and, as such, judged it as unsatisfactory. In 1989 Jiří Menzel made a motion picture of the same name based on the book.

The year after the publication of *Konec starých časů* in 1934, Vančura wrote the script for a crazy comedy, *Nedorozumění* (Misunderstanding). Vančura's parodies, *Výstřel* (The Gunshot) and *Začátek povídky zvané Gilotina* (The Beginning of the Story Called Guillotine), published in 1935 and 1937 respectively, deal with the world of motion pictures. In 1961 these two works were reprinted in *Občan Don Quijote a jiné prózy* (Don Quixote and Other Tales). Another play, *Jezero Ukereve* (Lake Ukereve), was produced in 1936; in it Vančura returned to the subject of his movie script of 1929, *Lethargus. Jezero Ukereve* was set in Africa, and the central theme was the fight against a dangerous disease, which Vančura meant as a metaphor for the threat of fascism. In writing this play Vančura also intended to honor the work of scientists and to protest against colonialism and racism. In 1935 he dramatized Robert Louis Stevenson's *Treasure Island* (*Poklad na ostrově*) and adapted Josef Jiří Kolár's 1871 play *Pražský žid* (The Jew from Prague, which, however, was not staged until 1946). At the same time he contributed to the anthology *10 let Osvobozeného divadla* (Ten Years of the Liberated Theater), published in 1937.

After this interlude of playwriting Vančura went back to writing novels. In 1936 he published the novel *Tři řeky* (Three Rivers), a vast panorama of the world in which he juxtaposed home life to public life. *Tři řeky* takes place in Bohemia and Russia from the end of the 1880s to 1918. The hero, Jan Kostka, the son of a peasant, studies and later takes part in war and revolution. Other important characters are a peasant farmer, Emanuel Kostka; a farm laborer, Štěpán Černohus; a Jewish doctor, Hugo Mann; and a Russian revolutionary, Lev Eberdin. All strata of society are represented by other characters, among whom are several historical figures such as Tsar Nicholas II and Franz Ferdinand d'Este. In the construction of this novel Vančura used elements of the fairy tale and movie techniques. Contemporary opinion was divided; the novel received many unfavorable reviews.

Besides his literary, dramatic, and motion picture work Vančura was active in the Levá fronta (The Left Front) organization. He supported the demands of the workers (for example, during the miners' strike in northern Bohemia in 1932), but above all he took a firm stand against fascism and Nazism. He signed several antifascist manifestos, spoke at public meetings, and condemned fascist tyranny in print. He was spurred to greater antifascist activity by the growing danger of German Nazism and the Spanish Civil War, to which he reacted in 1937 by writing the stories "Občan Don Quijote" (Citizen Don Quixote) and "Kněz Gudari" (Priest Gudari). He supported those who had fled from Germany and was a member of the board of the German Cultural Union of Czechoslovakia. In 1938 he signed the famous proclamations "Věrni zůstaneme" (We Shall Be Faithful), "Na obranu kultury" (In Defense of Culture), and "K svědomí světa" (Appealing to the Conscience of the World). In the latter half of the decade Vančura also worked for the Czech motion-picture society, which attempted to raise the artistic standards of the

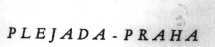

VLADISLAV VANČURA

UČITEL A ŽÁK

SCÉNICKÁ BÁSEŇ

1927

PLEJADA - PRAHA

Title page for Vančura's 1927 play, which presents the story of a conflict between a pupil, Jan, and his teacher, Doktor

movie industry. Vančura became the first president of this organization in 1936. He also took part in drafting plans for a people's theater, and in 1937 he became president of the editorial board of the publishing firm Družstevní práce (Cooperative Work) with which he previously had collaborated closely.

In the years between the world wars Vančura became friends with many well-known personalities in Czech cultural life—notably the writers Karel Nový, Ivan Olbracht, Vítězslav Nezval, Jaromír John, and Jaroslav Seifert—and language specialists from the Prague Linguistic Circle such as Jan Mukařovský and Roman Jakobson. He also attended the famous Friday meetings at the house of the Čapek brothers, which President Tomáš Garrigue Masaryk occasionally attended. Many of these well-known writers—including Jaroslav Seifert, Vítězslav Nezval, and Bedřich Fučík—recorded their friendship with Vančura in their memoirs. In *Všecky krásy světa* (All the Beauty of the World, 1982), a collection of what he calls "tales and memories," Seifert writes of Vančura: "He was a man who was acutely aware of the glory and the beauty of the world and also of the tremendous power of art. He was courageous and had great nobility of mind. . . . He was an aristocrat with the heart of a democrat."

At the end of the 1930s Vančura contemplated writing a trilogy titled "Koně a vůz" (Horses and Carriage), but by 1933 he had written only the first part—the novel *Rodina Horvatova* (The Horvat Family, 1938). In it he portrayed Czech society on the threshold of World War I but also brought in some descriptions of life in the nineteenth century. Vančura intended the work as a sociopolitical novel with a love story. He peopled it with many outstanding individual characters from different walks of life. The most important were the members of the family of the estate owner Vojtěch Horvat, his wife, five children, and his uncle, Edvard Horvat. The action takes place chiefly on the Horvat estate, Jankov, and Vančura tells the story soberly, objectively, and dispassionately with emphasis on the joy of everyday life.

Vančura gave up the idea of finishing the trilogy and also abandoned plans for the novel he had thought of on the subject of the sixteenth-century creator of many fish ponds in South Bohemia, Jakub Krčín of Jelčany. Instead he concentrated his efforts on the historical cycle *Obrazy z dějin národa českého* (Pictures from the History of the Czech Nation), which he believed was needed at the time. Originally he intended this cycle to be an eight-volume work by a team of writers. In the end Vančura wrote it alone but relied heavily on the work of historians Václav Husa, Jaroslav Charvát, and Jan Pachta. The first part of the work was published in 1939, the second was published a year later, and the unfinished third part was not published until 1948, after Vančura's death.

Obrazy z dějin národa českého is, as its subtitle says, "the true story of the life, warlike deeds and the education of the spirit," a record of the development of the Czech nation from its mythical beginning to the time of the last Přemyslide rulers—that is, to the end of the thirteenth century. Many fictional characters come into the story, but there are also many historical figures, mostly rulers. The historical character of the greatest interest is the medieval chronicler and diplomat Kosmas. Vančura wrote the work in response to the threat to the existence of the Czech nation from Adolf Hitler's Germany. Through this work Vančura heightened national awareness and gave people belief in the indomitable spirit of the nation and the endurance of its language and its culture.

In the difficult times after 1938 when Czechoslovakia lost part of its territory and after 1939 when the remaining country was occupied by Germany, Vančura continued writing his history. He also wrote the play *Josefina* (Josephine, 1950), a delightful comedy on a subject much like that of George Bernard Shaw's *Pygmalion* (1913), and several stories for magazines, which were later collected into a book, *Povídky a menší prózy* (Tales and Shorter Pieces), as part of the collected works. He also wrote a few short essays and many academic papers.

During the same period Vančura, as the president of the National Revolutionary Committee of the Intellectuals, was engaged in the struggle against the Nazis. Among other accomplishments, he helped to edit illegal printed matter and prepare for cultural life after the war. Artists, scientists, and even politicians looked to him as a brave man capable of leading, planning, and carrying out resistance. At the beginning of May 1942 further repression was threatened, and Vančura suggested halting resistance activities. Early on the morning of 12 May, Vančura was arrested, imprisoned, and then cruelly tortured. He betrayed nothing to his captors. On 1 June 1942—five days after the assassination of the German governor of Bohemia and Moravia, Reinhard Heydrich, by Czech rebels—Vančura was condemned to death in Prague and shot. "He died because he was the most important one of us," Ivan Olbracht wrote in 1946 in the journal *Lidová kultura* (Culture for the People); "with him the entire Czech nation was supposed to be struck down."

Vladislav Vančura was not only an author and cultural activist of prime importance but also an unusual personality who had considerable influence in society. The popularity of his work, which covered so many spheres, continued with only a little fluctuation well into the postwar decades, as evidenced by many translations and reprints of his prose works, movies, and adaptations for the theater.

Letters:

Adresát Jiří Mahen, edited by Jiří Hek and Štěpán Vlašín (Prague: SNKLU, 1964);

Polohy srdce (Z korespondence Jaromíra Johna), edited by Marie Krulichová and Milena Vinařová (Prague: Československý spisovatel, 1982).

Bibliography:

Miroslav Laiske, "Bibliografie Vladislava Vančury," in *Vladislav Vančura mezi dramatem a filmem* (Opava: Slezské muzeum, 1973).

Biographies:

Vítězslav Nezval, *Z mého života* (Prague: Československý spisovatel, 1959);

Ludmila Vančurová, *Dvacet šest krásných let* (Prague: Československý spisovatel, 1967);

Jaroslav Seifert, *Všecky krásy světa* (Prague: Československý spisovatel, 1982);

Bedřich Fučík, *Čtrnáctero zastavení* (Prague: Melantrich-Arkýř, 1992);

Václav Černý, *Paměti,* volume 2 (Brno: Atlantis, 1992).

References:

Luboš Bartošek, *Desátá múza Vladislava Vančury* (Prague: Filmový ústav, 1973);

Milan Blahynka, *Vladislav Vančura* (Prague: Melantrich, 1978);

Blahynka, *Vladislav Vančura* (Prague: Horizont, 1981);

Lubomír Doležel, "Karel Čapek and Vladislav Vančura: An Essay in Comparative Stylistics," in *Narrative Modes in Czech Literature* (Toronto: University of Toronto Press, 1973), pp. 91–111;

Vladimír Dostál, *Slovo a čin* (Ostrava: Profil, 1972);

Mojmír Grygar, *Rozbor moderní básnické epiky. Vančurův Pekař Jan Marhoul* (Prague: Academia, 1970);

Alena Hájková, *Humor v próze Vladislava Vančury* (Prague: Academia, 1972);

Luboš Hlaváček, "Výtvarné složky Vančurova díla," *Estetika,* 13, no. 3 (1976): 153–179;

Jiří Holý, *Práce a básnivost. Estetický projekt světa Vladislava Vančury* (Prague: Československý spisovatel, 1990);

Zdeněk Kožmín, *Styl Vančurovy prózy* (Brno: UJEP, 1968);

Milan Kundera, *Umění románu. Cesta Vladislava Vančury za velkou epikou* (Prague: Československý spisovatel, 1960);

Alena Macurová, *Výstavba a smysl Vančurova Rozmarného léta* (Prague: Academia, 1981);

Oleg Malevich, *Vladislav Vančura* (Leningrad: Chudozhestvennaya literatura, 1973);

Jan Mukařovský, "Vančurovská," *Cestami poetiky a estetiky* (Prague: Československý spisovatel, 1971), pp. 221–276;

Miloš Pohorský, *Portréty a problémy* (Prague: Mladá fronta, 1974);

Jiří Poláček, *Portréty a osudy. Postavy v próze Vladislava Vančury* (Boskovice: Albert, 1994);

F. X. Šalda, *O předpokladech a povaze tvorby* (Prague: Československý spisovatel, 1978);

Šalda, "V. Vančura, Pole orná a valečna," in his *Kritické projevy 13,* edited by Emanuel Macek (Prague: Ceskoslovensky spisovatel, 1963), pp. 181–183;

Šalda, "V. Vančura, Utek do Budina," *Šaldův zápisník,* 5 (1932): 34–37;

Tři studie o Vladislavu Vančurovi (Olomouc: UP, 1970);

Vladislav Vančura mezi dramatem a filmem (Opava: Slezské muzeum, 1973).

Papers:

Vladislav Vančura's literary papers are kept at Památník národního písemnictví (Memorial to Czech Literature) in Prague.

Stanisław Ignacy Witkiewicz
(Witkacy)
(24 February 1885 – 18 September 1939)

Daniel Gerould
City University of New York

BOOKS: *Nowe formy w malarstwie i wynikające stąd nieporozumienia* (Warsaw: Gebethner i Wolff, 1919);

Papierek lakmusowy (Zakopane: "Polonia," 1921);

Tumor Mózgowicz (Kraków: Spółka Wydawnicza "Fala," 1921);

Szkice estetyczne (Kraków: Krakowska Spółka Wydawnicza, 1922);

Teatr. Wstęp do teorii czystej formy w teatrze (Kraków: Krakowska Spółka Wydawnicza, 1923);

Pożegnanie jesieni (Warsaw: F. Hoesick, 1927);

Regulamin firmy portretowej S. I. Witkiewicza (Warsaw: Zakłady Graficzne "Polska Zjednoczona," 1928);

Nienasycenie (Warsaw: Dom Książki Polskiej, 1930); translated by Louis Iribarne as *Insatiability* (Urbana: University of Illinois Press, 1977);

Nikotyna, alkohol, kokaina, peyotl, morfina, eter (Warsaw: Polska Macierz Szkolna, 1932);

Pojęcia i twierdzenia implikowane przez pojęcie istnienia (Warsaw: Kasa Mianowskiego, 1935);

Szewcy (Kraków: Biblioteka Dramatyczna "Nowy Teatr," 1948);

W małym dworku (Kraków: Biblioteka Dramatyczna "Nowy Teatr," 1948).

Editions and Collections: *Dramaty*, 2 volumes, edited by Konstanty Puzyna (Warsaw: Państwowy Instytut Wydawniczy, 1962; revised edition, Warsaw: Państwowy Instytut Wydawniczy, 1972);

Jedyne wyjście, edited by Tomasz Jodełka-Burzecki (Warsaw: Państwowy Instytut Wydawniczy, 1968);

622 upadki Bunga, czyli demoniczna kobieta, edited by Anna Micińska (Warsaw: Państwowy Instytut Wydawniczy, 1972);

Pisma filozoficzne i estetyczne, 4 volumes, edited by Jan Leszczyński and Bohdan Michalski (Warsaw: Państwowe Wydawnictwo Naukowe, 1974–1978);

Stanisław Ignacy Witkiewicz (photograph by J. Kępinska)

Bez kompromisu, edited by Janusz Degler (Warsaw: Państwowy Instytut Wydawniczy, 1976);

Czysta Forma w teatrze, edited by Janusz Degler (Warsaw: Wydawnictwa Artystyczne i Filmowe, 1977);

Niemyte dusze. Studia obyczajowe i społeczne, edited by Micińska (Warsaw: Państwowy Instytut Wydawniczy, 1978);

Wybór dramatów, edited by Jan Błoński (Wrocław: Zakład Narodowy im. Ossolińskich, 1983);

Dzieła wybrane, 5 volumes, edited by Degler, Konstanty Puzyna, and Micińska (Warsaw: Państwowy Instytut Wydawniczy, 1985);

Dzieła wybrane, 23 volumes, edited by Degler, Michalski, Micińska, Konstanty Puzyna, and Lech Sokół (Warsaw: Państwowy Instytut Wydawniczy, 1992–).

Editions in English: *The Madman and the Nun and Other Plays*, edited and translated by Daniel Gerould and C. S. Durer (Seattle: University of Washington Press, 1968);

Tropical Madness: Four Plays, translated by Daniel and Eleanor Gerould (New York: Winter House, 1972);

"Childhood Plays," translated by Daniel Gerould and Jadwiga Kosicka, *yale/theatre*, 5 (1974): 10–58;

The Cuttlefish, or The Hyrcanian World View, translated by Daniel and Eleanor Gerould, in *A Treasury of the Theatre*, edited by John Gassner and Bernard F. Dukore (New York: Crowell, 1976);

The Anonymous Work, translated by Daniel and Eleanor Gerould, in *Twentieth-Century Polish Avant-Garde Drama* (Ithaca, N.Y.: Cornell University Press, 1977);

The Beelzebub Sonata: Plays, Essays, Documents, translated by Daniel Gerould and Kosicka (New York: Performing Arts Journal Publications, 1980);

The Madman and the Nun, The Crazy Locomotive, The Water Hen, edited and translated by Daniel Gerould and Durer (New York: Applause, 1989);

The Witkiewicz Reader, edited, translated, and with an introduction, by Daniel Gerould (Evanston: Northwestern University Press, 1992);

The Mother and Other Unsavory Plays, edited and translated by Daniel Gerould and Durer (New York: Applause, 1993)—comprises *Mother, They*, and *The Shoemakers;*

Country House, edited and translated by Daniel Gerould (Luxembourg: Harwood, 1997).

PLAY PRODUCTIONS: *Tumor Mózgowicz*, Kraków, Teatr Miejski im. J. Słowackiego, 30 June 1921;

Pragmatyści, Warsaw, Teatr Elsynor, 29 December 1921;

Kurka wodna, Kraków, Teatr im. J. Słowackiego, 20 July 1922;

W małym dworku, Toruń, Teatr Miejski, 8 July 1923;

Wariat i zakonnica, czyli nie ma złego, coby na jeszcze gorsze nie wyszło, Toruń, Teatr Miejski, 26 April 1924;

Nowe Wyzwolenie, Zakopane, Towarzystwo Teatralne, 21 March 1925;

Jan Maciej Karol Wścieklica, Warsaw, Teatr im. A. Fredry, 12 April 1925;

Mister Price, czyli bzik tropikalny, Warsaw, Teatr Niezależny, 2 July 1926;

Metafizyka dwugłowego cielęcia, Poznań, Teatr Nowy, 14 April 1928;

Mątwa, czyli Hyrkaniczny światopogląd, Kraków, Teatr "Cricot," 7 December 1933;

Szewcy, Gdańsk, Teatr "Wybrzeże," 12 October 1957 (stopped by the censor after the dress rehearsal);

Oni, Warsaw, Akademicki Teatr Prób "Centon," March 1963;

Matka, Kraków, Teatr Stary, 16 May 1964;

Szalona lokomotywa, Kraków, Studencki Teatr "38," 11 June 1965;

Sonata Belzebuba, czyli prawdziwe zdarzenie w Mordowarze, Białystok, Teatr im. A. Węgierki, 27 January 1966;

Gyubal Wahazar, czyli na przełęczach absurdu, Poznań, Teatr Polski, 10 September 1966;

Karaluchy, Wrocław, Klub "Oławka," November 1966;

Menażeria, czyli wybryk słonia, Wrocław, Klub "Oławka," November 1966;

Księżniczka Magdalena, czyli natrętny książę, Wrocław, Klub "Oławka," November 1966;

Nadobnisie i koczkodany, czyli zielona pigułka, Warsaw, Studencki Teatr Studyjny "IWG," 8 March 1967;

Bezimienne dzieło, Kraków, Teatr im. J. Słowackiego, 21 May 1967;

Odważna księżniczka, Poznań, Teatr Lalki i Aktora "Marcinek," 7 April 1970;

Biedny chłopiec, Poznań, Teatr Lalki i Aktora "Marcinek," 7 April 1970;

Janulka, córka Fizdejki, Wrocław, Teatr Współczesny, 8 September 1974;

Panna Tutli-Putli, Warsaw, Teatr Ateneum, 25 December 1975;

Komedie z życia rodzinnego, Opole, Teatr Lalki i Aktora im. A. Smolki, June 1980;

Niepodległość trójkątów, Katowice, Teatr Śląski im. S. Wyspiańskiego, 28 April 1985;

Maciej Korbowa i Bellatrix, Jelenia Góra, Teatr im. Cypriana Norwida, 6 April 1986.

Stanisław Ignacy Witkiewicz is now accepted as the outstanding Polish dramatist of the interwar

Maria Witkiewicz, the author's mother (photograph by Witkacy)

years and one of the most colorful figures in the European avant-garde. A prolific and multitalented artist, he was also a painter, photographer, philosopher, novelist, aesthetician, and cultural critic who produced a total body of works of disconcerting dimensions. Even before the fall of Communism, Witkacy (his self-created pen name) had become a modern classic, assigned a place in the school curriculum, and the subject of innumerable scholarly books and articles. A huge exhibition of his paintings was held at the National Museum in Warsaw in 1989 and 1990, and a collected edition of his works in twenty-three volumes began to appear in 1992.

Recognition, however, has come slowly, and the story of Witkiewicz's career—both during his lifetime and posthumously—is as full of irony, paradox, and surprise as any of his dramas. For many years a marginal figure ignored, derided, or suppressed by successive Polish cultural establishments, the playwright and his works have always stood in an ambiguous relationship to the styles and fashions of the times. Defying classification, he remains a permanent outsider who cannot be assimilated into any school or movement.

Witkiewicz grew up and reached maturity in a climate of fin de siècle symbolism and modernism. He did his principal work in the 1920s when futurism, Expressionism, Dadaism, Constructivism, and Surrealism were the new trends; he was discovered only in the late 1950s and early 1960s (twenty years after his tragic suicide) when Samuel Beckett, Eugène Ionesco, Max Frisch, and Friedrich Dürrenmatt were the foreign models emulated by writers for the Polish theater, recently liberated from the strictures of Soviet-imposed socialist realism. Previously dismissed by his contemporaries as a madman or practical joker and forgotten during the German occupation and Stalinist era, Witkiewicz made a triumphant posthumous return after the thaw of 1956, becoming an inspiration to a new generation of Polish theater artists (including Józef Szajna and Tadeusz Kantor) and hailed abroad as a brilliant precursor of the theater of the absurd. Often the center of controversy and object of political censorship, Witkiewicz finally achieved success in the sort of totalitarian mass state that he had constantly warned would bring about the end of art and philosophy. In the form of opera, movie, cabaret, jazz, rock, and outdoor spectacle, popular versions of the playwright's works have appealed to ever larger and younger audiences.

In post-Communist Poland, Witkiewicz has been depoliticized and freed from the anti-regime role that his work had automatically acquired after 1956. The overarching theme of both his life and his work now appears to be an ontological quest for identity—personal, artistic, cultural, and national. For Witkiewicz as a philosopher, the central issue is the problem of unity in plurality, including both the existential plight of the individual confronting a world of otherness and the aesthetic dilemma of giving cohesive form to diversity. Witkiewicz's preference for the dramatic mode, in which many voices and masks are assumed by a single author, is an expression of his dialectic between the one and the many.

Witkiewicz's aim was to create a total aesthetic and philosophical system, at the center of which stood the "I," alone in the universe. Unity is imposed by form, the source of aesthetic response, but the creative personality—its richness of experience and imagination—becomes the substance of the work, which is inevitably autobiographical. A portrait of Witkiewicz's life and times is an indispensable introduction to his theory and practice of theater.

Witkiewicz's father, the painter and writer Stanisław Witkiewicz, was one of the creators of Polish cultural life at the end of the nineteenth century. In 1883 he married music teacher Maria Pietrzkiewicz; on 24 February 1885 their only child, Stanisław Ignacy, was born in Warsaw in the Russian sector of partitioned Poland. By 1890 a worsening case of tuberculosis led Witkiewicz senior to move to Zakopane in the Tatras Mountains, then a part of the Austro-Hungarian Empire. The elder Witkiewicz, who popularized Zakopane as a resort for artists and a center of national folk art, held original pedagogic ideas about the free development of creative ability and the nurturing of independent spirits standing above the herd but dedicated to public service. Witkiewicz was educated at home, never attending school and pursuing whatever interested him. By the time he was seven, already immersed in painting and playing the piano, he started writing his own short comedies, such as *Karaluchy* (translated as *Cockroaches*, 1974, printed in 1893 on his own hand press as volume 1 of his comedies), which is about an ominous gray cloud of insects coming from America.

In hundreds of letters full of passionate exhortation, the elder Witkiewicz urged his son to be spiritually free by a perpetual act of Nietzschean self-transcendence. Oppressed by these paternal injunctions to be creative, the adolescent Witkiewicz experienced difficulty in achieving personal definition and treated his own artistic vocation with self-irony.

Young Witkiewicz began to exhibit his Postimpressionistic landscapes as early as 1901. After graduating from secondary school in Lvov by examination in 1903, he studied briefly at the Academy of Fine Arts in Kraków from 1904 to 1905 in defiance of his father's wishes. Under the influence of *Island of the Dead* and other fantastic canvases by Arnold Böcklin, which he saw on visits abroad, Witkiewicz definitively abandoned faithful reproduction of nature in favor of the macabre and grotesque. As the result of a 1907 trip to Paris, where he saw works by Paul Gauguin and Paul Cézanne and discovered the fauves and cubists, the young artist turned to portraits and bizarre charcoal drawings, with titles such as *Książę Ciemności Kusi św. Teresę przy pomocy Kelnera z Budapesztu* (The Prince of Darkness Tempts Saint Theresa with the Aid of a Waiter from Budapest).

At the same time Witkiewicz also began to use the camera to create photographic portraits of himself (and his many playful alter egos or doubles) as well as of his friends and family. These psychic studies reveal the anxiety behind the social mask and highlight the terror of existence caught in the subject's eyes. Among the close friends of his youth,

whom Witkiewicz often drew and photographed, were the anthropologist Bronisław Malinowski and the composer Karol Szymanowski.

In 1908 Witkiewicz met the celebrated modernist actress Irena Solska, with whom he had a stormy love affair lasting four years. With Solska, Witkiewicz discovered "the metaphysical monstrosity of sexuality" and developed a deeply ambivalent attitude toward the histrionic, which he both ridiculed as fraudulent and adopted as an aggressive personal style. In attempting to define his attitude toward the stage and acting, Witkiewicz began to shape a highly personal creative method that combined his own experiences with modernist literary models in the form of grotesque parody and self-conscious reductio ad absurdum. This technique finds its first expression in *622 upadki Bunga, czyli demoniczna kobieta* (The 622 Downfalls of Bungo, or The Demonic Woman, written in 1910–1911 but not published until 1972), an autobiographical roman à clef about his affair with Solska. Daring in its frank treatment of sexuality, *622 upadki Bunga* is a bildungsroman about a would-be young artist's growing alienation from himself and the world. The overly theatrical society of which the hero is a reluctant member turns life into a cabaret where constant metamorphosis produces only pseudochange. Witkiewicz reveals how in periods of cultural crisis the problem of disintegrating identity extends from the personal to the social realm.

At the age of twenty-seven, without a profession and tormented by the enigma of his amorphous self, the young artist felt threatened by incipient madness and underwent a few months of psychoanalysis. Although the therapy proved unsuccessful, Witkiewicz became an admirer of Freud as a theorist of the human psyche.

The suicide of Witkiewicz's fiancée, Jadwiga Janczewska (to whom he had become engaged in 1913) in 1914, for which he held himself responsible, plunged the writer into a state of despair. The circumstances surrounding the suicide remain mysterious, but some imbroglio contrived by Witkiewicz and involving Szymanowski seems likely. In his grief Witkiewicz turned to his friend Malinowski, who invited him to attend the Congress of the British Association for the Advancement of Science in Australia. The journey to the East with Malinowski proved to be Witkiewicz's salvation as both man and artist. The tropics opened his eyes to color, producing a radical transformation in his painting. Discovery of exotic non-Western cultures gave Witkiewicz a new perspective for judging European civilization, and glimpses of rites and ceremonies in

Jadwiga Janczewska, Witkiewicz's fiancée, who killed herself in 1914

Ceylon helped him envisage the modern equivalent of a ritual theater of metaphysical dimensions.

Upon the outbreak of World War I, Witkiewicz volunteered for military service in Russia, where he served as a tsarist officer from 1914 to 1917. He was wounded at the front in 1915 and spent the rest of the war as a convalescent in St. Petersburg. There he witnessed the February Revolution, the overthrow of the Romanov Empire, and the Bolshevik coup d'état "as though from a box in the theater." The experience of revolution as both cultural catastrophe and theatrical spectacle informs much of Witkiewicz's subsequent fiction and drama.

In June of 1918 Witkiewicz returned to Zakopane, where he lived for the rest of his life, occasionally visiting Warsaw and traveling to other cities for sittings with customers. The former tsarist officer brought back with him dozens of canvases he had painted in Russia and the completed manuscript of his first theoretical treatise, *Nowe formy w malarstwie i wynikające stąd nieporozumienia* (New Forms in Painting, 1919), in which he presented his fundamental ideas on the precarious position of art in a mass society.

From 1918 to 1939 Witkiewicz worked in newly independent Poland, earning his living as a portrait painter and writing prolifically in many genres. The first six years were the most productive in his artistic career. In an extraordinary outburst of creative energy, Witkiewicz painted hundreds of compositions and portraits, wrote more than thirty plays (ten of which are lost), and published books and essays on aesthetics and philosophy. For a few years he was associated with the formists, a loose association of artists sharing futurist or expressionist backgrounds, united in their opposition to naturalism and belief in the autonomy of art. Thereafter, Witkiewicz remained an isolated figure, outside the mainstream of Polish culture and in flamboyant opposition to the norms and conventions of his own time.

In the early and mid 1920s Witkiewicz devoted his greatest energies to the theory and practice of theater, feeling that the stage was the chief bastion of artistic conservatism to be overthrown. He had already developed his theory of pure form in the theater that, rejecting referentiality, conceives of drama as pure happening through time. The artistic essence of a play, Witkiewicz argued, does not reside in narrative content or in lifelike characters and actions but rather in the dynamic tensions of its components. Through its formal construction, drama creates the metaphysical feelings of unity in plurality.

To advance his ideas, Witkiewicz wrote theoretical treatises and articles, gave lectures, and engaged in polemics with critics while at the same time fighting to have his plays staged in the face of hostility, ridicule, and indifference. He sought to give modern drama the non-Euclidean coordinates of modern science and to bring the stage into the world of twentieth-century painting. Witkiewicz's attempt to transform the theater focused primarily on the actor, not on stage design, theater architecture, or audience reception. The theory of pure form opened the way for a new sensibility about performing and the performer. Instead of an impersonator pretending to be someone real, faking emotions and futilely trying to compete with nature, the actor-technician could become a true creator, once he was freed of the demands of truth to life and theatrical illusion. For Witkiewicz, theater was a realm of freedom in which the childlike sense of wonder at existence could be reinstated. His early plays are uneven in quality and vary considerably in their degree of departure from the conventions of realism, but all include startling scenic inventions and coups de théâtre.

Written in only ten days in 1918, *Maciej Korbowa i Bellatrix* (Maciej Korbowa and Bellatrix, 1962) is a five-act drama about the violent overthrow of a decadent ancien régime. The play introduces the dramatis personae typical of Witkiewicz's dramas; they are members of a degenerate international band of flamboyant stage characters playing roles from the modernist repertory—crazed artist, demonic woman, cosmopolitan playboy, rapacious tycoon, mad scientist, and ranting tyrant. Pushed to ultimate extremes, these modern *commedia* types grow self-consciously aware of their own theatricality and literary ancestry, upon which they often comment. They speak a bizarre theatrical metalanguage based on verbal games, random borrowings and citations, chance associations, and a variety of incompatible performance styles. There is a postmodern disjunction of action and dialogue. The characters wander off into disquisitions on culture, philosophy, mathematics, and aesthetics; quote the author's own theories of pure form and the death of art; and then suddenly make fervid declarations of love or shoot one another.

In Witkiewicz's first distinctly pure form play, *Pragmatyści* (1920; translated as *The Pragmatists*, 1972), the pseudo-artist Plasfodor and his managerial friend, von Telek, are trapped in a closed world of reciprocal exploitations in the company of Plasfodor's mute mistress and medium, Mammalia (later revealed to be von Telek's sister, whom von Telek seduced when she was eight); his sexually indeterminate maid, Masculette; and a terrifying Chinese mummy from Saigon. In a world of loneliness, boredom, and terror, the only two activities that serve as existential time killers are the orgy (drugs, sex, and endless conversation) and the séance (calling up ghosts). Witkiewicz introduces his most celebrated dramatic device—the rising of the dead. Murdered characters return to life as if nothing had happened—coming back not as otherworldly visions but as perfectly ordinary people resuming their daily lives. Denied the ability to die, Witkiewicz's "pragmatists" are condemned to an eternal repetition of their existence. No longer conclusive but repeatable, death is no more than a sarcastic spasm robbing humankind of any pretensions to greatness or heroism.

During 1920 and 1921, scarcely a year and a half, Witkiewicz wrote fifteen plays, sending copies to professional theaters throughout Poland and dreaming of financial success. In *Mister Price, czyli bzik tropikalny* (1962; translated as *Mister Price, or Trop-*

ical Madness, 1972), the first of several colonial dramas deriving settings and characters from his reading of Joseph Conrad's works, Witkiewicz subverts the conventions of realism by observing them scrupulously, and at the same time he views the greed and lust of the Western imperialists from an ironic distance.

The first of Witkiewicz's plays to be performed, *Tumor Mózgowicz* (1921; translated as *Tumor Brainiowicz*, 1980), provoked scandal and controversy (after being held up for almost a year by the censor). In the words of the author, *Tumor* is "a fantasy on the theme of the revolution in mathematics and physics" and portrays the helplessness of a scientific genius—creator of a new system of transfinite numbers—caught in the grips of an illicit passion for his stepdaughter. The sources of creativity are to be found in eros, the childlike and primitive. Tumor escapes from the children's nursery to the tropical island of Timor but is dragged back to "civilization" by the oppressive forces of the European family and society determined to harness his talent for their imperialist designs.

In the one-act play *Nowe Wyzwolenie* (1922–1923; translated as *The New Deliverance*, 1973), William Shakespeare's *Richard III* occupies a split-stage—half Gothic hall, half bourgeois salon—with an aging demonic woman, Tatiana, engaged in introducing suitors to her young protégée, Amusetta. The sophisticated rites of initiation turn violent when the new favorite, Florestan, is revealed as a guilty fraud, and six thugs with pincers and a blowtorch begin torturing him. Despite his insistence that the meaning of his plays resides solely in their formal structure, Witkiewicz admitted that the catastrophic denouement of this play suggested "the triumph of the organized masses over the remnants of former individualism and self-devouring bourgeois civilization."

An even more prophetic work, *Oni* (1962; translated as *They*, 1968), a play in two and a half acts, dramatizes the tyranny of society over the individual in the form of bizarre cults and conspiracy theories. Having usurped power, a ubiquitous and protean band known as THEY run the secret government within the government and are determined to reform humankind by strict regimentation and the suppression of art.

The more realistic *W małym dworku* (1948; translated as *Country House*, 1997) transposes the theatrical device of the risen dead to the familiar world of the domestic drama of adultery and murder. In this play Witkiewicz specifically parodies a well-known psychological drama by the Polish-Aus-

Scene from a 1974 production of Witkiewicz's Tumor Mózgowicz *at the Jaracz Theatre, Olsztyn, Poland*

trian writer Tadeusz Rittner, but his target is the genre itself. The ghost of the unfaithful wife returns to blur the boundaries of life and death, thereby wreaking havoc on the conventions of the type of realism associated with Konstantin Stanislavsky.

In *Gyubal Wahazar, czyli na przełęczach absurdu* (1962; translated as *Gyubal Wahazar, or Along the Cliffs of the Absurd*, 1972) Witkiewicz creates a sixth-dimensional totalitarian realm where Newtonian physics has been replaced by Einstein's theory of relativity. The absolute dictator Wahazar, who is obsessed with the problem of the one and the many and sees himself as a martyr to his people, is finally assassinated by his own secret police and replaced by a double created through gland transplants and the fission of psychic atoms.

Written in 1921, *Kurka wodna* (1962; translated as *The Water Hen*, 1968), one of Witkiewicz's most

personal plays, is also the most complex realization of his theory of pure form. Through parody the author creates an original dramatic structure out of the skeletal remains of late modernist theater. The antihero Edgar, destined by his father to be an artist, is unable to define himself in relation to a world that has lost all coherence and consistency. The stages of Edgar's life are littered with leftover costumes and ideas, old forms taken out of the theatrical storeroom, scraps of words already spoken, and feelings already felt—all of which reduce him to the role of marionette. Witkiewicz develops the notion of culture as refuse—debris from previous ages, shards and fragments that fail to coalesce. Finally, revolution erupts suddenly as an act of spontaneous combustion, unplanned and unforeseen, revealing the unknown in all its violence and primordial destructiveness. Without a place in the new post-apocalyptic society, the artist, frustrated in his aspirations, kills himself.

In *Mątwa, czyli Hyrkaniczny światopogląd* (1923; translated as *The Cuttlefish, or The Hyrcanian World View,* 1976) Witkiewicz brings together the alienated modern artist Rockoffer, Julius II (a Renaissance pope), and the Nietzschean strongman Hyrcan—each of whom puts forth rival claims for poetry or power. With his invented language and hyperbolic gestures, the dictator Hyrcan exemplifies the performance aspects of totalitarianism, but the artist is the true mythmaker, capable of forging a new reality with words; after killing the posturing histrion, Rockoffer becomes Hyrcan II in order to found a new kingdom built on nonsense.

During his lifetime most of Witkiewicz's dramas were performed, if at all, only two or three times, under special circumstances. A striking exception was *Jan Maciej Karol Wścieklica* (Jan Maciej Karol Hellcat, 1962), which became a genuine hit in 1925 at the Fredro Theatre in Warsaw where it played thirty-four times, then went on tour for another thirty-four performances, and won a prize from the Artists' Union. The play owed its popularity to topical appeal and straightforward dramaturgy; this easily accessible "drama without corpses," as the author subtitled it, in which a country bumpkin rises to be president of the republic, appeared to be a satire on the peasant politician Wincenty Witos, who had recently enjoyed a similar career.

Written in 1923, *Wariat i zakonnica, czyli nie ma złego, coby na jeszcze gorsze nie wyszło* (1925; translated as *Madman and the Nun,* 1968) shows the creative personality as victim of cultural repression in the form of psychiatric confinement. The decadent poet and drug addict Walpurg exemplifies the destiny of exceptional beings who are locked in padded cells and trapped in ever-widening circles of incarceration by body, family, society, state, and cosmos. The poet hangs himself, then comes back to life, leaving his inert corpse in the cell with his former tormentors while he goes free, in defiance of the laws of reality and of theatrical realism.

Subtitled "An Unsavory Play in Two Acts and an Epilogue," *Matka* (1962; translated as *The Mother,* 1968) deals with Leon, a would-be genius at social thought who hopes to combat regimentation and preserve individualism, although he must live off his alcoholic mother, whose constant knitting provides him with financial support. A deformed version of the playwright's relationship to his own mother, *Matka* voraciously devours earlier dramatic structures from Henrik Ibsen to August Strindberg before concluding with a tour-de-force epilogue in

Pure Form. As the consequence of an overdose at a cocaine party, the mother drops dead, and all the characters are suddenly plunged into a black box where Leon confronts a young woman who is his mother twenty-four years earlier, pregnant with her son.

The year 1924 was a turning point for Witkiewicz. He renounced painting as a pure art (formal constructions on plane surfaces) in favor of portraits, done in pastels, a mimetic applied art and commercial activity that the writer treated with self-irony by establishing the S. I. Witkiewicz Portrait Painting Firm, whose "Rules" he published in 1928. The playwright then turned increasingly to the writing of social criticism and fiction, which he hoped would be profitable. Witkiewicz had married Jadwiga Unrug in 1923 and was constantly in need of money to support his wife, who lived apart from him in Warsaw. The more than one thousand letters to his wife from 1923 to 1939 chronicle the writer's day-to-day existence and are testimony to his close and enduring friendship with Jadwiga.

The last surviving play from this most productive period of Witkiewicz's career is *Sonata Belzebuba, czyli prawdziwe zdarzenie w Mordowarze* (1938; translated as *The Beelzebub Sonata,* 1980), a contemporary version of the Faust story that anticipates Thomas Mann's *Dr. Faustus* by some twenty years. Hell has become a Budapest cabaret where the young Hungarian musician Istvan sells his soul to the devil in return for the ability to compose a masterpiece. Creatively exhausted and artistically superfluous once his composition has been written, the lonely musician-hero hangs himself at the end of *The Beelzebub Sonata.*

In 1927 Witkiewicz published his first major novel, *Pożegnanie jesieni* (Farewell to Autumn), which traces the impact of three revolutions, each more drastic than the preceding one, on an alienated group of artists, intellectuals, and pleasure-seekers who travel to India in search of an experience that will give their lives meaning. Athanasius, who returns to a communized Poland, is killed by Russian border guards when he tries to flee into Czechoslovakia. In fiction, as in drama, Witkiewicz reveals himself to be a brilliant analyst of collective states of mind during periods of social instability (when problems of personal identity grow confused with those of class) as well as a sardonic observer of the mechanisms of power and the rise of totalitarian systems.

Nienasycenie (1930; translated as *Insatiability,* 1977) is Witkiewicz's most ambitious and original novel, a vast speculative fantasy in which a bewil-

Scene from a production of Witkiewicz's Sonata Belzebuba *(Beelzebub Sonata) at the Kennedy Theatre, Honolulu, in 1974*

dered young hero's sexual and social initiation and private pursuit of the mystery of existence are interrupted by historical events threatening to the individual—the appearance of the mind-lulling Murti-Bing pill and the arrival of the Chinese Communists, the mobile yellow wall that first lays siege to White Guard Moscow and then threatens Poland and the West. The novel is full of philosophical reflections on the difficulty of conveying what is actually happening, and these epistemological digressions shift emphasis from storytelling to problems of representation: the impossibility of saying anything new, the exhaustion of fictional forms, the inability of language to convey experience, and finally the absence of anything to convey. In *Nienasycenie* the form of the novel starts to break down as the narrator wrestles with the hopeless task of recording the amorphous, hallucinatory experience of life in Poland, a country lacking in coherence and heading toward the void.

To deal with national issues, which had been excluded from his formalist plays, Witkiewicz now cultivated a new type of work, which mixed philoso-

phy, sociology, and psychology with personal confessions and anecdotes, grotesque vignettes, and chatty advice. The first two examples of this form created by Witkiewicz, which moves beyond traditional genres by erasing the boundaries between fiction and life, are the unfinished philosophical novel *Jedyne wyjście* (The Only Way Out, 1968), written between 1931 and 1933, and the drug book *Nikotyna, alkohol, kokaina, peyotl, morfina, eter* (Nicotine, Alcohol, Cocaine, Peyote, Morphine, and Ether, 1932).

Niemyte dusze. Studia obyczajowe i społeczne (Unwashed Souls: Studies of Social Manners and Morals, 1978) is the culmination of the writer's interest in collective psychology and a merciless dissection of the Polish national character. Witkiewicz accuses his fellow countrymen of caring only about appearances, playing stage roles in life, living in a world of illusion, and refusing to be themselves.

Szewcy (1948; translated as *The Shoemakers*, 1968), Witkiewicz's last surviving play, is a sprawling, many-layered work that reflects the author's growing preoccupation with the social and historical issues affecting Poland. Like the unclassifiable prose hybrids from the same period, *Szewcy* is wayward and unruly. A microcosmic vision of the totalitarian ideologies about to overrun Europe, Witkiewicz's grotesque drama, interweaving the philosophical, political, and sexual, lets loose cataclysmic forces on the small stage of the master shoemaker's workshop, where Sajetan and his two apprentices discuss the evils of capitalism while the bourgeois prosecuting attorney Scurvy and the demonic aristocrat Irina carry on a flirtation. After an abortive fascist coup d'état from above and an equally futile socialist rebellion from below, the final revolution, signaling an end to all ideology, is brought about by passionless technocrats who institute a gray reign of uniformity with no place left for individuals or creativity—only mechanized work and trivialized sex.

Witkiewicz devoted the last decade of his life to philosophy, publishing in 1935 his major speculative work, *Pojęcia i twierdzenia implikowane przez pojęcie istnienia* (The Concepts and Principles Implied by the Concept of Existence), a system of biological monadology, attempting to reconcile positivism and metaphysics, on which he had been working since 1917. After first the Germans and then the Soviets invaded Poland, Witkiewicz fled to the East and committed suicide 18 September 1939.

The playwright showed uncanny skill in predicting his own resurrection some twenty years later. On a striking portrait all in red, done in 1931, there is the inscription: "For the posthumous exhibition in 1955." In 1956 Tadeusz Kantor opened his theater Cricot II in Kraków with *Mątwa*, the first postwar production of Witkiewicz's work.

Thirty years later the pariah had become a national treasure. UNESCO declared the year 1985, the one hundredth anniversary of Witkiewicz's birth, the "Year of Witkiewicz," and the Polish People's Republic issued commemorative postage stamps bearing his self-portraits. In 1988 the Polish Ministry of Culture arranged the return of Witkiewicz's "mortal remains" from Ukraine to Zakopane. Party officials from both countries competed in staging solemn ceremonies when the revered author was buried next to his mother. The body, however, proved to be that of an unknown Ukrainian woman. The fraud was exposed almost immediately, and the ensuing scandal led to accusations and recriminations as to who was responsible. The Communist cultural hierarchy, which had suppressed and censored his work, could neither find nor identify his body.

The distinctive qualities of Witkiewicz's work are an acute sense of the grotesque and absurd, a powerful visual imagination that with colors and shapes evokes dream states and drug-induced hallucinations, and a deeply felt philosophy of man's tragic isolation in an alien universe. Once a truly subversive author, whose works are now classics, Witkiewicz remains an elusive but seminal figure in twentieth-century Polish drama.

Letters:

Listy do Bronisława Malinowskiego, edited by Tomasz Jodełka-Burzecki, introduction by Edward C. Martinek (Warsaw: Państwowy Instytut Wydawniczy, 1981).

Bibliographies:

Piotr Grzegorczyk, "Dzieło pisarskie S. I. Witkiewicza 1893–1956," in *Stanisław Ignacy Witkiewicz. Człowiek i twórca,* edited by Tadeusz Kotarbiński and Jerzy E. Płomieński (Warsaw: Państwowy Instytut Wydawniczy, 1957), pp. 351–393;

Lech Sokół, "Stanisław Ignacy Witkiewicz 1945–1969. Przegląd publikacji," *Pamiętnik Teatralny,* no. 3 (1969): 421–425;

Janusz Degler, "Twórczość Stanisława Ignacego Witkiewicza na świecie. Próba bibliografii," *Przegląd Humanistyczny,* 10 (1977): 135–164;

Sokół, "Witkacy w Polsce. Przegląd publikacji 1971–1982," *Pamiętnik Teatralny,* no. 1–4 (1985): 425–481;

Degler, "Witkacy na świecie. Przegląd publikacji 1971–1983," *Pamiętnik Teatralny,* no. 1–4 (1985): 482–543.

References:

Jan Błoński, *Od Stasia do Witkacego* (Kraków: Wydawnictwo Literackie, 1997);

Błoński, *Stanisław Ignacy Witkiewicz jako dramaturg* (Warsaw: Państwowe Wydawnictwo Naukowe, 1973);

Tomasz Bocheński, *Powieści Witkacego. Sztuka i mistyfikacja* (Łódź: Wydawnictwo Uniwersytetu Łódzkiego, 1994);

Cahier Witkiewicz, nos. 1–4 (1976–1982);

Alain van Crugten, *S. I. Witkiewicz: Aux sources d'un théâtre nouveau* (Lausanne: Editions l'Age d'Homme, 1971);

Bożena Danek-Wojnowska, *Stanisław Ignacy Witkiewicz a modernizm: kształtowanie idei katastroficznych* (Wrocław: Zakład Narodowy im Ossolińskich, 1976);

Janusz Degler, *Witkacy w teatrze międzywojennym* (Warsaw: Państwowy Instytut Wydawniczy, 1973);

Degler, ed., *Witkacy: Życie i twórczość* (Wrocław: "Wiedza o Kulturze," 1996);

Dialectics and Humanism. The Polish Philosophical Quarterly, special Witkiewicz issue, 12 (1985);

Ewa Franczak, Stefan Okołowicz, *Przeciw nicości. Fotografie Stanisława Ignacego Witkiewicza* (Kraków: Wydawnictwo Literackie, 1986);

Daniel Gerould, "Stanisław Ignacy Witkiewicz," in *European Writers: The Twentieth Century,* volume 10, edited by Gerould (New York: Scribners, 1990), 1206–1230;

Gerould, *Witkacy: A Study of Stanisław Ignacy Witkiewicz as an Imaginative Writer* (Seattle: University of Washington Press, 1981);

Michał Głowiński and Janusz Sławiński, eds., *Studia o Stanisławie Ignacym Witkiewiczu* (Wrocław: Zakład Narodowy im Ossolińskich, 1972);

Irena Jakimowicz, *Witkacy malarz* (Warsaw: Wydawnictwa Artystyczne i Filmowe, 1985);

Tadeusz Kotarbiński and Jerzy E. Płomieński, eds., *Stanisław Ignacy Witkiewicz. Człowiek i twórca,* (Warsaw: Państwowy Instytut Wydawniczy, 1957);

Bohdan Michalski, *Polemiki filozoficzne Stanisława Ignacego Witkiewicza* (Warsaw: Państwowy Instytut Wydawniczy, 1979);

Anna Micińska, *Witkacy: Life and Work* (Warsaw: Wydawnictwo Interpress, 1991);

Pamiętnik Teatralny, special Witkiewicz issues, 3 (1969); 3–4 (1971); 1–4 (1985);

Piotr Piotrowski, *Metafizyka obrazu* (Poznań: Wydawnictwo Uniwersytetu im. A. Mickiewicza, 1985);

Piotrowski, *Stanisław Ignacy Witkiewicz* (Warsaw: Krajowa Agencja Wydawnicza, 1989);

Polish Review, special Witkiewicz issue, 1–2 (1973);

Przegląd Humanistyczny, special Witkiewicz issue, 10 (1977);

Joanna Siedlecka, *Mahatma Witkac* (Warsaw: Słowo, 1992);

Maciej Soin, *Filozofia Stanisława Ignacego Witkiewicza* (Wrocław: Fundusz Nauki Polskiej, 1995);

Lech Sokół, *Groteska w teatrze Stanisława Ignacego Witkiewicza* (Wrocław: Zakład Narodowy im. Ossolińskich, 1973);

Sokół, *Witkacy i Strindberg,* 2 volumes (Warsaw: Instytut Historii Sztuki, 1990);

Małgorzata Szpakowska, *Światopogląd Stanisława Ignacego Witkiewicza* (Wrocław: Zakład Narodowy im. Ossolińskich, 1976);

Wojciech Sztaba, *Gra ze sztuką: O twórczości Stanisława Ignacego Witkiewicza* (Warsaw: Państwowy Instytut Wydawniczy, 1982);

Sztaba, *Stanisław Ignacy Witkiewicz: zaginione obrazy i rysunki sprzed 1914 roku* (Warsaw: Wydawnictwa Artystyczne i Filmowe, 1985);

Beata Zagodzińska-Wojciechowska and Anna Żakiewicz, eds., *Witkacy; Stanisław Ignacy Witkiewicz in the Museum of Central Pomerania in Słupsk,* translated by Robert L. Kirkland (Warsaw: Wydawnictwa Artystyczne i Filmowe, 1996).

Jiří Wolker

(29 March 1900 – 3 April 1924)

Vladimír Macura

Institute of Czech Literature, Academy of Sciences of the Czech Republic, Prague

BOOKS: *Host do domu* (Plzeň: Karel Beníško, 1921);
Těžká hodina. Verše 1921–1922 (Prague: Václav Petr a
Karel Tvrdý, 1922);
Tři hry (Prague & Nusle: František Svoboda, 1923);
Balady (Prague: Václav Petr, 1925);
Povídky a pohádky Jiřího Wolkra, edited by Max Švabinský (Prague: Václav Petr, 1925);
Svatý Kopeček (Prague: Václav Petr, 1926);
Klytia, 1917 (Prague: Václav Petr, 1928);
Táborový deník šestnáctiletého Jiřího Wolkra, edited by
A. B. Svojsík (Prague: Václav Petr, 1928).

Editions and Collections: *Dílo Jiřího Wolkra*, edited
by A. M. Píša, 2 volumes (Prague: Václav Petr,
1924);
Dílo Jiřího Wolkra, 3 volumes, edited by Miloslav
Novotný (Prague: Václav Petr, 1931–1934);
Spisy Jiřího Wolkra, 4 volumes, edited by Píša, Zina
Trochová, and Julie Štěpánková (Prague:
Státní nakladatelství krásné literatury, hudby a
umění, 1953–1954);
Srdce–štít, edited by Miroslav Florian (Prague: Československý spisovatel, 1964);
Zasvěcování srdce, edited by Vladimír Macura (Prague:
Československý spisovatel, 1984);
Těm, kterým patřím (Prague: Junák-svaz skautů a skautek ČR, 1997).

Editions in English: "The Pillar-Box" and "The
Burial," selected and translated by Paul Selver,
in *An Anthology of Czechoslovak Literature*, edited
by Selver (London: Kegan Paul, Trench, Trübner, 1929), p. 299;
"Dying," translated by Dora Round, in *Heart of
Europe: An Anthology of Creative Writing in
Europe, 1920–1940*, edited by Klaus Mann and
Hermann Kesten (New York: Fischer, 1943),
p. 526;
"Humility," "The Grove," "Love Poem," "Stanzas,"
"The Blind Musicians," and "Ballad from a
Hospital," selected and translated by Ewald
Osers and J. K. Montgomery, in *Modern Czech
Poetry: An Anthology*, edited by Osers and Mont-

Jiří Wolker

gomery (London: Published for Prague Press
by Allen & Unwin, 1945), pp. 40–46;
"Love Poem," translated by Osers and Montgomery,
and "Dying," translated by Round, in *Hundred
Towers: A Czechoslovak Anthology of Creative Writing*,
edited by Franz C. Weiskopf (New York: Fischer,
1945), pp. 71–72;
"The Eyes of the Stoker," translated and edited by
Alfred French, in *A Book of Czech Verse*, edited
by French (London: Macmillan / New York:
St. Martin's Press, 1958), pp. 74–85;
"Whitsun Holidays," "Harvest," and "Autumn,"
translated by Edith Pargeter, in *A Handful of*

Linden Leaves: Anthology of Czech Poetry, edited by Jaroslav Janů (Prague: Artia, 1958), pp. 21, 27, 37;

"The Sea," "Mirogoj," and "Eyes," translated by Pargeter, in *The Linden Tree: An Anthology of Czech and Slovak Literature 1890–1960*, edited by Mojmír Otruba and Zdeněk Pešat (Prague: Artia, 1962), pp. 83–87.

PLAY PRODUCTION: *Nejvyšší oběť*, Prague, Tyl Theater, 11 December 1922.

TRANSLATIONS: *Bratrská poezie*, translated by Wolker and Vojtěch Měrka (Košice: Terezie Štanglerová, 1924);

Dragotin Kette, *Pohádky*, translated by Wolker and Měrka (Košice: Terezie Štanglerová, 1924).

SELECTED PERIODICAL PUBLICATION—
UNCOLLECTED: "Proletářské umění," *Var*, 1, no. 9 (1922): 251–254.

Jiří Wolker belonged to the generation traumatized by World War I but also dazzled by the creation of an independent Czechoslovak state in 1918. The young people of his generation sought a new vision of the world, a new faith, and a new means of expressing their belief in social revolution as the key to the solution of human problems. From the beginning of the 1920s Wolker's work incorporated features of the new literary style: naiveté, primitivism, and harmony among people and objects. Commonplace, everyday life and concrete, simple things became poetic. His death from tuberculosis and meningitis at the age of twenty-four also fixed his image in the public mind. Wolker himself saw his death as part of the all-important task of transforming himself in order to fit the dream of the revolution that he believed to be the only means of saving society and bringing about a new order of creativity.

Jiří Wolker was born on 29 March 1900 in Prostějov. The poet's father, Ferdinand Wolker, was from a family of clothmakers and furriers and was the first to acquire a higher education; he worked in a bank and in 1899 married Zdena Skládalová, the daughter of a wealthy proprietor of a distillery. The family owned an upper-middle-class house with a roof garden in the main square in Prostějov and a luxurious villa, Bellevue, in Svatý Kopeček.

In 1919 Wolker left these secure surroundings to study in Prague. A novice in poetry, he found himself among the left-wing intellectuals of the famous Prague coffeehouse the Union. His simple middle-class ideas were shattered under pressure

from this new environment. He rejected his previous attempts at poetry, which now seemed to him woefully immature. He discovered French unanimism—a literary movement based on the psychological concept for group consciousness—and German expressionism and was encouraged by the first efforts, written in the new style, of his more experienced contemporaries A. M. Píša, Miloš Jirko, František Němec, Zdeněk Kalista, and Josef Suk. Their work rejected the extravagant constructions of symbolism as well as the futurist's obsession with machines. In a letter to a friend, Antonín Dokoupil, in May 1920, Wolker described his feverish search for the new style: "I am growing a new pair of eyes." Soon he began to contemplate the publication of a small book of verse, which confirmed him in his new vision.

Wolker's first published work, *Host do domu* (Welcome, Guest), appeared in 1921. The lyric self is the least of the least, the humblest of the humble, "a child." The concept of the poet as a child was a common theme at the time, but Wolker made it his own. He turned it into a highly personal concept with clear autobiographical elements; but Wolker also declares the general need for a different poetry, simple and unpretentious. The world seen through the eyes of a child is a friendly place. There is intimacy and poetry in ordinary words and everyday objects, as illustrated in "Kamna" (The Stove) and "Poštovní schránka" (translated as "The Pillar-Box," 1929). Wolker links the young speaker's departure for a strange town with a search for his place in the world and a new concept of social and personal relations. These are associated with naive religious symbols (God as an old man visiting people, the Virgin Mary comforting the heartsick boy). Love is a stylized Christian emotion, uncomplicated, touching on the sentimental, and chaste in the extreme. All attempts to enter the real world are directly linked to the poet's all-encompassing love. For Wolker, his collection—consisting of the three sections "Chlapec" (The Boy), "Ukřižované srdce" (The Crucified Heart), and "Host do domu" (Welcome, Guest)—was not a mere exercise in a certain compositional style but a triad, in the Hegelian sense. The boyish vision of the world is the antithesis of the theme of the hero who suffers as he becomes aware of new conflicts. In the end, he has to come to terms with reality, no matter how tragic or contradictory it might be.

Although most of Wolker's readers and some of his reviewers were aware only of the childlike, naive quality of the poems, rebirth is a basic theme in *Host do domu*. Thus, Wolker actually welcomed the criticism that in the future it would be necessary to progress beyond this stage of childlike simplicity. By the time this book was published, Wolker's long poem "Svatý Kopeček" had appeared in the prestigious journal *Červen* (June) in 1921. The young poet clearly regarded this poem as opening up a whole new range of issues. The poem is a lyrical record of a young man's visit to his family's summer residence in Svatý Kopeček; he comes "from distant Prague and homely Prostějov" to the bedside of his sick grandmother. He spends the day talking with her and with friends, thus strengthening his bonds with mankind as a whole. The poem was a direct challenge to Guillaume Apollinaire's "Le Zone," the opening poem of his *Alcools* (1913), which typified modern poetry for Wolker. He adapted many of Apollinaire's concepts in "Svatý Kopeček," but instead of aimless wandering through the world, he offers a concentric movement toward a safe familiar place, the home of his loved ones. Unlike Apollinaire, who saw reality as a constant fluctuation of disparate and chaotic perceptions, Wolker portrays the world as stable, wholly intelligible through the emotions but at the same time governed by reason.

After the publication of *Host do domu* and "Svatý Kopeček" Wolker became the most celebrated poet of his generation. In 1921 he was invited to join the Brno Literární skupina (Literary Group), which chose for its planned journal the name *Host* (The Guest), echoing the title of Wolker's collection. Before the end of the year he had also become a member of the artists' club Devětsil, the name of which may be literally translated as "Nine-Force entity"—signifying the linking of left-wing activists working in nine different artistic disciplines. However, after Literární skupina published its manifesto, which Wolker found utopian, he left the group in September 1922. Soon afterward he also left Devětsil, which had begun turning away from proletarian art to pure, non-ideological poetry. Wolker, disagreeing with the excessive lyricism of the day, began to experiment with drama and prose. His last book to be published during his lifetime was a collection of his prose and one-act plays, *Tři hry* (Three Plays, 1923). In writing "O knihaři a básníkovi" (The Bookbinder and the Poet), "O milionáři, který ukradl slunce" (The Millionaire Who Stole the Sun), "O kominíkovi" (The Chimneysweep), "Pohádka o listonoši" (The Postman's Tale), and "Pohádka o Jonym z cirkusu" (The Tale of Jony from the Circus) Wolker was trying to create a new kind of socialist folktale. His main source of inspiration, however, was the ballad. In a 1 July 1921 letter to his friend and critic Píša he wrote:

I am trying to write narrative verse. It seems to me that that is what is wanted. There is too much lyricism today. There are too many people who do nothing but talk about themselves. I know the poet will always be the strongest element in his own work but I maintain that the poet who can leave his own ego behind and take the narrative of his poem beyond himself proves his strength and courage. Lyricism is a state and narrative writing is action.

Wolker announced his intention of publishing his ballads separately in a book to be titled "Kniha balad" (Ballads), but in the end he included them in the collection *Těžká hodina* (A Difficult Hour, 1922).

In *Těžká hodina* Wolker rejects his original "philosophy of boyhood." The poet contrasts "the heart of a boy," which is "a song beginning," with "a man's heart," which is "hands and calluses," unremitting toil. The boy's new eyes, the recurrent motif in *Host do domu*, are contrasted with eyes disillusioned by suffering and injustice. Wolker centers attention on the downtrodden, the suffering, beggars, prostitutes, servants, and the poor. Increasingly influenced by Marxism and communist ideology, Wolker now classes these people as the "proletariat," the workers, a force capable of shaping the future world as he sees it.

Yet, this highly ideological poetry is at the same time quite personal and surprisingly dynamic. Wolker continued to be obsessed with transformation and rebirth, and this process was not automatic. Everything—love, spring, even life—has to be fought for, chiefly by means of self-restraint. The poems "Pohřeb" (translated as "The Burial," 1929) and "Smrt" (Death), which were inspired by the deaths of Wolker's grandparents, have an important place in this collection. At variance with orthodox communism, they raise the question, on rather intimate terms, of what is a life lived courageously.

In his ballads Wolker merged two disparate Czech ballad traditions, that of Karel Jaromír Erben's classical style and language and that of the social ballads by Jan Neruda and Petr Bezruč. The heroes of Wolker's ballads differ from traditional types. In his "Balada o nenarozeném dítěti" (Ballad of the Unborn Child) the main character is a young lover so poor that she is forced to have an abortion. In "Balada o snu" (The Ballad of the Dream) the hero is a young workman who can rid himself of a recurrent dream of a better world only by realizing that he has to act. By using the ballad form to express the movement from dream to deed, from emotion and vision to toil, from boy to man, and from the notion of harmony to that of revolt,

*Cover for Wolker's 1922 collection of poems, in which he focuses
on the working class and the poor*

Wolker took the ballad beyond its previously
accepted limits.

In April 1923 Wolker became seriously ill, and
X rays revealed that he had tuberculosis. On 19
June, on doctor's orders, Wolker and his mother
went to Tatranská Polianka in the Tatra mountains.
Although suffering from a fever, he kept on writing
and even considered another collection of poems.
He did not give up his theme of struggle; he projected it as a moral imperative into his own fight
against illness:

> Disease forces a man to think only of himself, to
> fear only for himself and to pay attention only to
> himself. This is its greatest anguish and corrupting
> power. The whole universe is narrowed down to his
> feeble body and to what might happen in this poor
> suffering cosmos before misery and pain return! . . .
> If I was ever bothered by suffering or joy (any
> strongly felt joy causes suffering in the end), I
> would try to find release from its torture by transfer-
> ring it from my inner being and placing it outside
> myself so that it could lead its own life without me.

In literary terms, I transformed my subjective torments into poetry.

After seeing a motion picture titled *Tuberculosis*, Wolker began to gather texts for a kind of
"filmed sequence of poems from this terrible environment," as he called it in a letter to Píša on 21
October 1923. At the end of November, having a
premonition that the end was near, he wrote his
own epitaph, which is now inscribed on his grave:

> Zde leží Jiří Wolker, básník, jenž miloval svět
> a pro spravedlnost jeho šel se bít
> Dřív než moh' srdce k boji vytasit
> zemřel, mlád dvacet čtyři let
>
> (This is where Jiří Wolker lies, the poet who loved the
>   world
> and went to fight for its justice.
> Before he could put his heart into action
> he died, twenty four years young.)

In the second half of December, tuberculosis
led to meningitis, and he went into a coma. The
Minister of Education offered to pay for further
treatment, but it was too late. At this critical junc-
ture Wolker's mother decided to make the difficult
journey back to Prostějov, where Wolker died
shortly afterward on 3 April 1924.

His death made the young poet into a cult figure. The extreme political Left took up Wolker's
revolutionary challenge; but the touching, sensitive
simplicity of his work became known to readers
from widely different social backgrounds. Soon
everything he had ever written—juvenilia, diaries,
notes, and rough drafts included—was being published. His collected works came out in edition after
edition, and his poems were included in anthologies and published separately to such an extent that
in 1925 Wolker's contemporaries Artuš Černík,
František Halas, and Bedřich Václavek wrote an article for the journal *Pásmo* (The Zone) titled "Dosti
Wolkera!" (Enough of Wolker!). The authors protested against the appropriation of Wolker by official culture. These avant-garde poets—supporters of
the playful movement of "poetism," which rejected
any connection between lyrical poetry and the portrayal of Social Realism and political programs—dismissed Wolker as "the last great, bad ideological
poet." In the ensuing controversy the Literární
skupina and Julius Fučík, spokesman for the young
Communist intellectuals, supported Wolker. The
arguments continued into the 1930s when an article
written by Bedřich Fučík, Halas, Pavel Levit, and
Vilém Závada and signed "F. Hlz" became the sub-

ject of further controversy. After the Communist coup of 1948 Wolker's works were interpreted as the embodiment of the classic values of socialist poetry and were revered as the pinnacle of Socialist Realism, which finally brought to an end the controversy about Wolker's legacy.

Letters:

Čtyři dopisy Jiřího Wolkra příteli-soudruhu Vladimíru Zelenému (Prague: Václav Petr, 1936);

Listy příteli, edited by A. M. Píša (Prague: Československý spisovatel, 1950);

Korespondence s rodiči, edited by Zdena Wolkerová and Jan Kühndel (Prague: Československý spisovatel, 1952);

Listy dvou básníků, edited by Wolkerová and Kühndel (Prague: Československý spisovatel, 1953);

Do boje, lásko, leť. Dopisy a básně Jiřího Wolkra z roku 1923, edited by Jaromír Dvořák (Prague: Odeon, 1975);

Přátelství a osud. Vzájemná korespondence Jiřího Wolkra a Zdeňka Kalisty, edited by Zdeněk Kalista (Toronto: Sixty-Eight Publishers, 1978);

Dopisy: Korespondence Jiřího Wolkra, edited by Zina Trochová (Prague: Československý spisovatel, 1984).

Bibliographies:

Julie Kuncová, *Jiří Wolker–Bibliografie díla Jiřího Wolkra a literatury o něm* (Prague: Městská knihovna, 1975);

Blažej Belák and others, *Jiří Wolker v slovenskej tlači: Výberová personálna bibliografia* (Martin: Matica slovenská, 1980);

Inna Vasiljevna Toksina, *Irzhi Volker: Bibliograficheskij ukazateľ* (Moscow: Kniga, 1980).

Biographies:

Biografie a vzpomínky: In memoriam Jiřího Wolkera, edited by Konstantin Biebl (Prague: Erna Jánská, 1924);

Jan Kühndel, *Rod Jiřího Wolkera: Genealogická studie* (Prague: Václav Petr, 1934);

Zdena Wolkerová, *Jiří Wolker, jeho dětství, chlapectví a život v rodině* (Prague: Václav Petr, 1934);

Wolkerová, *Jiří Wolker ve vzpomínkách své matky* (Prague: Václav Petr, 1937);

Jan Ryska, *Náš Jiří Wolker* (Prague: Státní nakladatelství dětské knihy, 1956);

Bohuslav Hlinka and Jiří Všetečka, *Den se mi v rukou přelomil: Jiří Wolker neznámý* (Prague: Práce, 1990);

Jiří Wolker ve vzpomínkách současníků: Sborník k 90. výročí narození Jiřího Wolkra, edited by Pavel Marek (Prague: Melantrich, 1990).

References:

Antar (Václav Čedík), *Tak mluvil Wolker: Technika a chemie jeho slov* (Prague: Fischer, 1934);

Milan Blahynka, *Nezval a Wolker* (Ostrava & Brno: Krajské nakladatelství v Ostravě–Krajské nakladatelství v Brně, 1964);

Blahynka, "Nezvalův Wolker a Wolkrův Nezval," *Česká literatura*, 22, no. 5 (1974): 412–416;

Přemysl Blažíček, "Jiří Wolker: Přípravná studie pro 4. díl *Dějin české literatury*," *Česká literatura*, 11, no. 6 (1963): 449–472;

Miloš Dvořák, "Wolkerova balada," *Listy pro umění a kritiku*, 2 (1934): 379–389;

Jiří Fiala, "Báseň Jiřího Wolkra Poštovní schránka," *České jazyk a literatura*, 39, no. 9 (1988/1989): 406–411;

Alfred French, *The Poets of Prague: Czech Poetry Between the Wars* (London: Oxford University Press, 1969), pp. 8–28;

French, "Wolker and Nezval," in *Czechoslovakia Past and Present*, 2 volumes, edited by Miloslav Rechcígl Jr. (The Hague: Czechoslobak Society of Arts and Sciences in America / Mouton, 1968), II: 983–992;

Alena Hájková, "Náboženské prvky v básnické tvorbě Jiřího Wolkra," in *O literatuře* (Prague: Státní pedagogické nakladatelství, 1958), pp. 61–87;

Hájková, "K Wolkrovým baladám," *Česká literatura*, 22, no. 5 (1974): 419–422;

Karel Hausenblas, "O jazyce Wolkrovy poezie," *Studie a práce lingvistické I* (Prague: ČSAV, 1954), pp. 473–493;

Josef Hrabák, "Rým a intonace u Karla Hlaváčka a Jiřího Wolkra," in his *Studie o českém verši* (Prague: Státní pedagogické nakl,1959), pp. 315–325;

Zdeněk Kalista, "Jiří Wolker," *Annali dell' Instituto universitario orientale, sezione Slava*, 18 (1975): 67–108;

Kalista, *Kamarád Wolker* (Prague: Václav Petr, 1933);

Oldřich Králík, "Wolkrovy balady," *Česká literatura*, 18, no. 5–6 (1970): 345–363;

Ladislav Kratochvíl, *Wolker a Nezval: Dvojí sloh generace* (Prague: František Borový, 1936);

Marie Kubínová, *Proměny české poezie dvacátých let* (Prague: Československý spisovatel, 1984);

Vladimír Macura, "Balada Jiřího Wolkra v dobových souvislostech," *Česká literatura*, 32, no. 5 (1984): 431–443;

Pavel Marek, ed., *Na přední stráži: Sborník k 75. výročí narození Jiřího Wolkra* (Brno: Blok, 1975);

Vítězslav Nezval, *Wolker* (Prague: Ústřední studentské knihkupectví a nakladatelství, 1925);

Sergei Vasilyevich Nikolsky, *Dvě epochy české literatury* (Prague: Československý spisovatel, 1986);

Nikolsky, *Myšlenka a obraz ve Wolkrově poezii z let 1920–1921* (Prague: Academia, 1968);

A. C. Nor [Josef Kaván], *Jiří Wolker, básník a člověk* (Prague: Václav Petr, 1934);

Václav Pekárek, *Wolker, Neumann, Hora* (Prague: Československý spisovatel, 1949);

Zdeněk Pešat, "Apollinairovo Pásmo a dvě fáze české polytematické poezie," in *Struktura a smysl literárního díla*, edited by Milan Jankovič (Prague: Československý spisovatel, 1966);

Josef Peterka, "Těžká hodina," in *Rozumět literatuře*, edited by Milan Zeman and others (Prague: Státní pedagogické nakladatelství, 1986), pp. 254–262;

A. M. Píša, *Dvacátá léta* (Prague: Československý spisovatel, 1969);

Píša, "Jiří Wolker," "Lyrik a baladik," and "Vypravěč, dramatik a teoretik," in his *Stopami poezie* (Prague: Československý spisovatel, 1962), pp. 210–250;

Píša, *Soudy, boje a výzvy* (Prague: Tiskové a nakladatelské družstvo československých legionářů, 1922), pp. 264–268;

Píša, Jan Mukařovský, Miloš Tomčík, and Vilém Závada, *Jiří Wolker–příklad naší poezie* (Prague: Československý spisovatel, 1954);

Martin C. Putna, "Wolker–básník náboženský?," *Souvislosti*, 3, no. 1 (1992): 93–100;

F. X. Šalda, "Dvojí pojetí básnické osobnosti Wolkerovy," *Šaldův zápisník*, 1 (1929–1930), pp. 269–328;

Šalda, "Jiří Wolker," "Poezie Jiřího Wolkra," "Radostný fakt," in *O umění* (Prague: Československý spisovatel, 1955), pp. 297–311, 429–430;

Miloš Sedmidubský, "Vytváření idyly v české avantgardě: Jiří Wolker: Svatý Kopeček," *Česká literatura*, 43, no. 2 (1995): 192–214;

Svetlana Sherlaimova, *Irzhi Volker i novye puti cheshskoj poezii XX. veka* (Moscow: Vysshaya shkola, 1965);

Fedor Soldan, *Jiří Wolker* (Prague: Československý spisovatel, 1964);

Jaroslav Tax, "Tvůrčí proměny v uměleckém vývoji Jiřího Wolkera," in *Přednášky z 24. běhu Letní školy slovanských studií v roce 1980* (Prague: Univerzita Karlova, 1983), pp. 61–69;

Tax, "Vztah lyrična a epična v tvůrčím vývoji Jiřího Wolkra," *Přednášky z 28. běhu Letní školy slovanských studií v roce 1984* (1986), pp. 72–100;

Jürgen H. Thumim, *Das Problem von Form und Gattung bei Jiří Wolker* (Hamburg: Universität Hamburg, 1966);

Bedřich Václavek, "Předčasná syntéza," in his *Od umění k tvorbě* (Prague: Odeon, 1928), pp. 113–126;

Štěpán Vlašín, *Jiří Wolker* (Prague: Melantrich, 1974);

František Všetička, "Balada o námořníku" and "Wolkrova dialogizovaná báseň," in his *Stavba básně* (*Acta Universitatis Palackianae Olomucensis. Facultas paedagogica. Monographica XVI*) (Olomouc: Univerzita Palackého, 1994), pp. 85–100;

Wolker dnešku: Z diskuse na vědecké konferenci u příležitosti 80. výročí narození Jiřího Wolkra v roce 1980 v Prostějově (Prostějov: Svaz českých spisovatelů, 1981).

Papers:

Jiří Wolker's papers are in the Literary Archives of Památník národního písemnictví (Memorial to Czech Literature) in Prague, and the Muzeum Prostějovska in Prostějov, Czech Republic.

Books for Further Reading

Aaron, Frieda W. *Bearing the Unbearable: Yiddish and Polish Poetry in the Ghettos and Concentration Camps.* Albany: State University of New York Press, 1990.

Andrups, Janis, and Vitauts Kalve. *Latvian Literature: Essays.* Stockholm: Goppers, 1954.

Anerauds, Janis. *Fifty Encounters: Short Information about Fifty Latvian Soviet Men of Letters.* Riga: Liesma, 1973.

Bălan, Ion Dodu. *A Concise History of Romanian Literature.* Bucharest: Academy of Social and Political Sciences, 1981.

Bantas, Andreí, ed. *Like Diamonds in Coal Asleep: Selections from 20th Century Romanian Poetry.* Bucharest: Minerva, 1985.

Baranczak, Stanisław. *Breathing under Water and Other East European Essays.* Cambridge, Mass.: Harvard University Press, 1990.

Baranczak, and Clare Cavanagh, eds. *Polish Poetry of the Last Two Decades of Communist Rule: Spoiling Cannibals' Fun.* Evanston, Ill.: Northwestern University Press, 1991.

Bart, István, ed. *Present Continuous: Contemporary Hungarian Writing.* Budapest: Corvina, 1985.

Basa, Eniko Molnar, ed. *Hungarian Literature.* New York: Griffon House, 1993.

Baumanis, Arturs, ed. *Latvian Poetry.* Augsburg: A. Baumanis, 1946.

Beissinger, Margaret H. *The Art of the Lautar: The Epic Tradition of Romania.* New York: Garland, 1991.

Beza, Marcu. *Papers on the Rumanian People and Literature.* London: McBride, Nast, 1920.

Bihiku, Koço. *A History of Albanian Literature.* Tirana: "8 Nëntori," 1980.

Bihiku. *An Outline of Albanian Literature.* Tirana: Naim Frasheri State Publishing House, 1964.

Bird, Thomas, ed. *Modern Polish Writing: Essays and Documents.* New York: Queens College Press, 1973.

Birnbaum, Henrik, and Thomas Eekman, eds. *Fiction and Drama in Eastern and Southeastern Europe: Evolution and Experiment in the Postwar Period: Proceedings of the 1978 UCLA Conference.* Columbus, Ohio: Slavica, 1980.

Bisztray, George. *Hungarian-Canadian Literature.* Toronto: University of Toronto Press, 1987.

Bloch, Alfred. *The Real Poland: An Anthology of National Self Perception.* New York: Continuum, 1982.

Bojtăr, Endre. *East European Avant-Garde Literature.* Budapest: Akadémiai Kiadó, 1992.

Brandes, Georg Morris Cohen. *Poland: A Study of the Land, People, and Literature.* London: Heinemann, 1904.

Brogyanyi, Eugene, ed. *DramaContemporary. Hungary: Plays.* New York: P.A.J., 1991.

Călinescu, George. *History of Romanian Literature.* Paris: Nagard, 1988.

Carlton, Charles Merritt. *Romanian Poetry in English Translation: An Annotated Bibliography and Census of 249 Poets in English 1740–1989.* Rochester, N.Y.: University of Rochester Press, 1989.

Carpenter, Bogdana. *Monumenta Polonica: The First Four Centuries of Polish Poetry: A Bilingual Anthology.* Ann Arbor: Michigan Slavic Publications, 1989.

Carpenter. *The Poet Avant-Garde in Poland, 1918–1939.* Seattle: University of Washington Press, 1983.

Catanoy, Nicholas, ed. *Modern Romanian Poetry.* Oakville, Ontario: Mosaic Press, 1977.

Cedrins, Inara, ed. *Contemporary Latvian Poetry.* Iowa City: University of Iowa Press, 1984.

Cejka, Jaroslav. *The New Czech Poetry.* Newcastle upon Tyne: Bloodaxe, 1988.

Chester, Pamela, and Sibelan Forrester, eds. *Engendering Slavic Literatures.* Bloomington: Indiana University Press, 1996.

Chudoba, František. *A Short Survey of Czech Literature.* London: K. Paul, Trench, and Trubner / New York: Dutton, 1924.

Cincura, Andrew, ed. *An Anthology of Slovak Literature.* Riverside, Cal.: University Hardcovers, 1976.

Ciopraga, Constantin. *The Personality of Romanian Literature.* Iaşi, Romania: Junimea, 1981.

Close, Elizabeth. *The Development of Modern Rumanian: Linguistic Theory and Practice Muntenia 1821–1838.* London: Oxford University Press, 1974.

Coleman, Marion Moore. *Our Other World: A Polish Scrapbook.* Cheshire, Conn.: Cherry Hill, 1978.

Coleman. *Polish Literature in English Translation: A Bibliography.* Cheshire, Conn.: Cherry Hill, 1963.

Coleman, ed. *The Polish Land, Ziemia Polska: An Anthology in Prose and Verse.* Trenton, N.J.: White Eagle, 1943.

Coleman and Loretta M. Bielawska, eds. *The Wayside Willow: Prose and Verse.* Trenton, N.J.: White Eagle, 1945.

Collins, R. G. and Kenneth McRobbie, eds. *The Eastern European Imagination in Literature.* Winnipeg: University of Manitoba Press, 1973.

Corbridge-Patkaniowska, Mary. *The Spirit of Polish Literature. Lecture Delivered at the Conference on Poland for Teachers, Held at the University of Liverpool on September 25–26, 1943.* Birkenhead, U.K.: Polish Publications Committee, 1944.

Coulter, Kirkley. *Polish Literature Recently Translated.* Falls Church, Va.: Quarterly Review of Polish Heritage, 1977.

Cummins, Walter, ed. *Shifting Borders: East European Poetries of the Eighties.* Rutherford, N. J.: Fairleigh Dickinson University Press / London & Cranbury, N.J.: Associated University Press, 1993.

Cushing, G. F. *Hungarian Prose and Verse: A Selection with an Introductory Essay.* London: University of London, Athlone, 1956.

Czerniawski, Adam, ed. and trans. *The Burning Forest.* Newcastle upon Tyne, U.K.: Bloodaxe, 1988.

Czerniawski, ed. *The Mature Laurel: Essays on Modern Polish Poetry.* Chester Springs, Pa.: Dufour Editions, 1991.

Czerwinski, Edward Joseph. *Dictionary of Polish Literature.* Westport, Conn.: Greenwood Press, 1994.

Czigány, Lorant. *The Oxford History of Hungarian Literature from the Earliest Times to the Present.* New York: Oxford University Press, 1984.

Czigany, Magda. *Hungarian Literature in English Translation Published in Great Britain, 1830–1968: A Bibliography.* London: Szepsi Csombor Literary Circle, 1969.

Dabrowski, Patrice M. *The Art of Poetic Translation: Russian Variations on Polish Avant-Garde Poetry.* Cambridge, Mass.: Harvard University Press, 1984.

Davie, Donald. *Slavic Excursions: Essays on Russian and Polish Literature.* Chicago: University of Chicago Press, 1990.

Davis, Robert H. *Preliminary List of Polonica in the New York Public Library.* New York: New York Public Library, 1996.

Day, Barbara, ed. *Czech Plays: Modern Czech Drama.* London: Nick Hern Books, 1994.

Degh, Linda. *Folktales of Hungary.* Chicago: University of Chicago Press, 1965.

Deletant, Andrea, and Brenda Walker, trans. *Silent Voices: An Anthology of Romanian Women Poets.* London: Forest Books, 1986.

Deligiorgis, Starvos, trans. *Romanian Poems.* Iowa City: Corycian Press, 1977.

Doležel, Lumbomír. *Narrative Modes in Czech Literature.* Toronto: University of Toronto Press, 1973.

Drăgan, Mihai, comp. *46 Romanian Poets in English.* Iaşi, Romania: "Junimea," 1973.

Duczynska, Ilona, ed. *The Plough and the Pen: Writings from Hungary.* London: P. Owen, 1963.

Durišin, Dionýz. *Sources and Systematics of Comparative Literature.* Bratislava: Univerzita Komenského, 1974.

Dutescu, Dan, ed. and trans. *Romanian Poems: An Anthology of Verse.* Bucharest: Eminescu, 1982.

Dyboski, Roman. *Modern Polish Literature: A Course of Lectures Delivered in the School of Slavonic Studies, King's College, University of London.* London: Oxford University Press, 1924.

Dynowska, Wanda, ed. *The Scarlet Muse: An Anthology of Polish Poems.* Bombay: N. M. Tripathi, 1944.

Eekman, Tomas. *The Realm of Rime: A Study of Rime in the Poetry of the Slavs.* Amsterdam: Adolf M. Hakkert, 1974.

Eile, Stanislaw, and Ursula Phillips, eds. *New Perspectives in Twentieth-Century Polish Literature: Flight from Martyrology.* Basingstoke, U.K.: Macmillan, 1992.

Eimermacher, Karl, Peter Grzybek, and Georg Witte, eds. *Issues in Slavic Literary and Cultural Theory*. Bochum, Germany: Universitätsverlag Dr. N. Brockmeyer, 1989.

Ekmanis, Rolfs. *Latvian Literature under the Soviets, 1940–1975*. Belmont, Mass.: Nordland, 1978.

Elsie, Robert. *Dictionary of Albanian Literature*. Westport, Conn.: Greenwood Press, 1986.

Elsie. *History of Albanian Literature*. Boulder, Colo.: Social Science Monographs, 1995.

Elsie. *Studies in Modern Albanian Literature and Culture*. Boulder, Colo.: East European Monographs / New York: Columbia University Press, 1996.

Eminescu, Mihai. *Works: Hungarian*. Bucharest: Kriterion Konyvkiado, 1989.

Fairleigh, John, ed. *When the Tunnels Meet: Contemporary Romanian Poetry*. Newcastle upon Tyne: Bloodaxe, 1996.

Fenyő, Mario D. *Literature and Political Change: Budapest, 1908–1918*. Philadelphia: American Philosophical Society, 1987.

Fiala, Edward, and Bogumil Pietrasiewicz, eds. *Polish Literature in the Culture of Christian Europe*. Lublin: Catholic University of Lublin, 1983.

Fik, Ignacy. *Selections, 1979*. Warsaw: "Ksiazka I Wiedza," 1979.

Filip, T. M., ed. *A Polish Anthology*. London: Duckworth, 1944.

Folejewski, Zbigniew. *Studies in Modern Slavic Poetry*. Uppsala: Lundequistska Bokhandeln, 1955.

Freeborn, Richard, R. R. Milner-Gulland, and Charles A. Ward. *Russian and Slavic Literature*. Cambridge, Mass.: Slavica, 1976.

French, Alfred. *Anthology of Czech Poetry*. Ann Arbor, Mich.: Czechoslovak Society of Arts and Sciences in America, 1973.

French. *Czech Writers and Politics, 1945–1969*. Boulder, Colo.: East European Monographs/New York: Columbia University Press, 1982.

French, ed. and trans. *A Book of Czech Verse*. London: Macmillan/New York: St. Martin's Press, 1958.

French, ed. *The Poets' Lamp: A Czech Anthology*. Canberra, Australia: Leros Press, 1986.

French. *The Poets of Prague: Czech Poetry Between the Wars*. London & New York: Oxford University Press, 1969.

Frick, David A. *Polish Sacred Philology in the Reformation and the Counter-Reformation: Chapters in the History of the Controversies (1551–1632)*. Berkeley: University of California Press, 1989.

Gardner, Monica Mary. *Poland, A Study In National Idealism*. London: Burns & Oates, 1915.

Garvin, Paul L., ed. *A Prague School Reader on Esthetics, Literary Structure, and Style*. Washington, D.C.: Washington Linguistic Club, 1955

George, Emery, ed. *Contemporary East European Poetry: An Anthology*. New York: Oxford University Press, 1993.

Gergely, Emro Joseph. *Hungarian Drama in New York: American Adaptations, 1908–1940*. Philadelphia: University of Pennsylvania Press, 1947.

Gillon, Adam, and Ludwik Krzyanowski, eds. *Introduction to Modern Polish Literature: An Anthology of Fiction and Poetry*. New York: Twayne, 1964.

Gillon, ed. *Poems of the Ghetto: A Testament of Lost Men*. New York: Twayne, 1969.

Ginsburg, Roderick Aldrich. *The Soul of a Century: Collection of Czech Poetry in English*. Chicago: Czechoslovak National Council of America, 1942.

Goetz-Stankiewicz, Marketa, ed. *Czechoslovakia: Plays*. New York: Performing Arts Journal Publications, 1985.

Goetz-Stankiewicz. *The Silenced Theatre: Czech Playwrights without a Stage*. Toronto: University of Toronto Press, 1979.

Gömöri, György. *Polish and Hungarian Poetry, 1945 to 1956*. Oxford: Clarendon Press, 1966.

Gömöri, and George Szirtes, eds. *The Colonnade of Teeth: Modern Hungarian Poetry*. Chester Springs, Pa.: Dufour Editions, 1996.

Gray, Elizabeth. *The Fiction of Freedom: The Development of the Czechoslovak Literary Reform Movement, 1956–1968*. Clayton, Australia: Monash University Press, 1991.

Grol, Regina, ed. *Ambers Aglow: An Anthology of Polish Women's Poetry (1981–1995)*. Austin, Tex.: Host: 1996.

Grosz, Joseph, and Arthur Boggs, eds. *Hungarian Anthology: A Collection of Poems*. Munich: Griff, 1963.

Harkins, William Edward, and Klement Simonic. *Czech and Slovak Literature*. New York: Columbia University Dept. of Slavic Studies, 1950.

Harkins. *The Russian Folk Epos in Czech Literature*. New York: King's Crown Press, 1951.

Harkins, ed. *Anthology of Czech Literature*. New York: King's Crown Press, 1953.

Harkins, and Paul I. Trenský, eds. *Czech Literature since 1956: A Symposium*. New York: Bohemica, 1980.

Harkins, ed. and trans. *Czech Prose: An Anthology*. Ann Arbor: University of Michigan Press, 1983.

Harris, Ernest Howard. *Estonian Literature In Exile*. London: Boreas, 1949.

Harris. *Literature In Estonia*. London: Boreas, 1943.

Hawkesworth, Celia, ed. *Literature and Politics in Eastern Europe*. New York: St. Martin's Press, 1992.

Hawkesworth, ed. *Writers from Eastern Europe*. London: Book Trust, 1991.

Holton, Milne, and Paul Vangelisti, eds. *The New Polish Poetry: A Bilingual Collection*. Pittsburgh: University of Pittsburgh Press, 1978.

Holton, and Vasa D. Mihailovich. *Serbian Poetry from the Beginnings to the Present*. New Haven: Yale Center for International and Area Studies / Columbus, Ohio: Slavica, 1988.

Hoskins, Geoffrey A. and George F. Cushing, eds. *Perspectives on Literature and Society in Eastern and Western Europe.* Basingstoke: Macmillan in Association with the University of London, 1989.

Hoskins, Janina. *Polish Books in English, 945–1971.* Washington, D.C.: Library of Congress, 1974.

Hribal, C. J., ed. *The Boundaries of Twilight: Czecho-Slovak Writing from the New World.* Minneapolis: New Rivers Press, 1991.

Hruby, Peter. *Daydreams and Nightmares: Czech Communist and Ex-Communist Literature 1917–1987.* Boulder, Colo.: East European Monographs/New York: Columbia University Press, 1990.

Hunt, Rosemary, and Ursula Philips, eds. *Muza Donowa: A Celebration of Donald Pirie's Contribution to Polish Studies.* Cotgrave: Astra, 1995.

Janion, Maria and Nils Ake Nilsson, eds. *Polish-Swedish Literary Contacts: A Symposium in Warsaw September 22–26, 1986.* Stockholm: Kungl. Vitterhets, Historie Och Antikvitets Akademien with Almquist & Wiksell International, 1988.

Jasienczyk-Krajewski, L. R. *Introduction to Polish Literature and Culture.* London: Unicorn, 1989.

Kaari, K. *A Glimpse into Soviet Estonian Literature.* Tallinn: "Eesti Raamat," 1965.

Kabdebó, Thomas, ed. *Hundred Hungarian Poems.* Manchester: Albion Editions, 1976.

Kadic, Ante. *Essays in South Slavic Literature.* New Haven: Yale Center for International and Area Studies / Columbus, Ohio: Slavica, 1988.

Kaleda, Algis. *Echoes of the Years: Contemporary Soviet Lithuanian Literature.* Vilnius: Mokslas, 1988.

Kangro, Bernard. *Estonian Books Published in Exile: A Bibliographical Survey, 1944–1956.* Stockholm: Eesti Rahvusfond, 1957.

Karinthy, Frigyes. *Panorama.* Budapest: Grill Karoly, 1926.

Katzenelenbogen, Uriah. *The Daina: An Anthology of Lithuanian and Latvian Folk-songs.* Chicago: Lithuanian News, 1935.

Kaun, Alexander, and Ernest J. Simmons. *Slavic Studies.* Ithaca, N.Y.: Cornell University Press, 1943.

Kelertas, Violeta, ed. *Come into My Time: Lithuania in Prose Fiction.* Urbana: University of Illinois Press, 1992.

Kerner, Robert Joseph. *Slavic Europe: A Selected Bibliography in the Western European Languages, Comprising History, Languages, and Literatures.* New York: Russell & Russell, 1969.

Kessler, Jascha Frederick. *The Face of Creation: Contemporary Hungarian Poetry.* Minneapolis: Coffee House Press, 1988.

Kirkconnell, Watson. *A Little Treasury of Hungarian Verse.* Washington, D.C.: American Hungarian Federation, 1947.

Kirkconnell. *The Magyar Muse: An Anthology of Hungarian Poetry, 1400–1932.* Winnipeg: Kanakai Magyar Ujsag Press, 1933.

Klaniczay, Tibor. *History of Hungarian Literature.* Budapest: Corvina, 1964.

Klimowicz, Mieczysław, ed. *Sociology of Literature in Poland.* Wrocław: Zaklad Narodowy Ossolinskich, 1978.

Kolumban, Nicholas, ed. *Turmoil In Hungary: An Anthology of Twentieth-Century Hungarian Poetry.* Berkeley, Cal.: Small Press, 1982.

Konnyu, Leslie. *Hungarian Bouquet: Selected Poems.* St. Louis: American Hungarian Review, 1984.

Konnyu. *Modern Magyar Literature: A Literary Survey and Anthology of the XXth Century Hungarian Authors.* Richmond Heights, Mo.: American Hungarian Review, 1964.

Kopta, Flora Pauline Wilson, comp. *Bohemian Legends and Other Poems.* Millwood, N.Y.: Kraus Reprint, 1975.

Kott, Jan, ed. *Four Decades of Polish Essays.* Evanston, Ill.: Northwestern University Press, 1990.

Kovton, George J. *Czech and Slovak Literature in English: A Bibliography.* Washington, D.C.: Library of Congress, 1984.

Kramoris, Ivan Joseph. *An Anthology of Slovak Poetry: A Selection of Lyric and Narrative Poems and Folk Ballads in Slovak and English.* Scranton, Pa.: Obrana Press, 1947.

Kridl, Manfred. *An Anthology of Polish Literature.* New York: Columbia University Press, 1957.

Kridl. *A Survey of Polish Literature and Culture.* New York: Columbia University Press, 1956.

Krżyzanowski, Julian. *A History of Polish Literature.* Warsaw: PWN-Polish Scientific Publishers, 1978.

Krżyzanowski. *Polish Romantic Literature.* Freeport, N.Y.: Books for Libraries, 1968.

Kuniczak, W. S. *The Glass Mountain: Twenty-Six Ancient Polish Folktales and Fables.* New York: Hippocrene, 1992.

Kunz, Egon F. *Hungarian Poetry.* Sydney: Pannoia, 1955.

Landsbergis, Algirdas. *The Green Linden: Selected Lithuanian Folksongs.* New York: Voyages, 1964.

Landsbergis, and Clark Mills, eds. *The Green Oak: Selected Lithuanian Poetry.* New York: Voyages, 1962.

Lankutis, Jonas. *Panorama of Soviet Lithuanian Literature.* Vilinus: Vaga, 1975.

Ledbetter, Eleanor Edwards. *Polish Literature in English Translation.* New York: Wilson, 1932.

Leighton, Lauren. *Studies in Honor of Xenia Gasiorowska.* Columbus, Ohio: Slavica, 1983.

Levine, Madeline G., ed. *Contemporary Polish Poetry, 1925–1975.* Boston: Twayne, 1981.

Lewanski, Richard Casimir. *The Slavic Literatures.* New York: New York Public Library & Ungar, 1967.

Longinovic, Toma. *Borderline Culture: The Politics of Identity in Four Twentieth-Century Slavic Novels.* Fayetteville: University of Arkansas Press, 1993.

Lutzow, Francis. *A History of Bohemian Literature.* Port Washington, N.Y.: Kennikat Press, 1970.

MacGregor-Hastie, Roy, ed. *Anthology of Contemporary Romanian Poetry.* London: Owen, 1969.

Maciuszko, Jerry. *The Polish Short Story in English; A Guide and Critical Bibliography.* Detroit: Wayne State University Press, 1968.

Mägi, Arvo. *Estonian Literature: An Outline.* Stockholm: Baltic Humanitarian Association, 1968.

Makkai, Adam, ed. *In Quest of the 'Miracle Stag': The Poetry of Hungary.* Chicago: University of Illinois Press, 1996.

Mallene, Endel. *Estonian Literature in the Early 1970s: Authors, Books, and Trends of Development,* translated by G. Liiv. Tallinn: "Eesti Raamat," 1978.

Mann, Stuart E. *Albanian Literature: An Outline of Prose, Poetry, and Drama.* London: Quartich, 1955.

Manning, Clarence Augustus. *An Anthology of Czechoslovak Poetry.* New York: Columbia University Press, 1929.

March, Michael, ed. *Description of a Struggle: The Vintage Book of Contemporary Eastern European Writing.* New York: Vintage, 1994.

Martin, Aurel. *Romanian Literature.* New York: Romanian Library, 1972.

Matejka, Ladislav, ed. *Czech Poetry: A Bilingual Anthology.* Ann Arbor: Michigan Slavic Publications, 1979.

Matthews, W. K. *Anthology of Modern Estonian Poetry.* Gainesville: University Press of Florida, 1953.

Mayewski, Pawel, ed. *The Broken Mirror: A Collection of Writings from Contemporary Poland.* New York: Random House, 1958.

Menczer, Béla. *A Commentary on Hungarian Literature.* Castrop-Rauxel: Amerikai Magyar Kiado, 1956.

Michajlow, Adam. *Literary Galicia: From Post War to Post Modern.* Krakow: Oficyna Literacka, 1991.

Mihailovich, Vasa, ed. *Modern Slavic Literatures.* New York: F. Ungar, 1972–1976.

Mihailovich, ed. *White Stones and Fir Trees: An Anthology of Contemporary Slavic Literatures.* Rutherford, N.J.: Fairleigh Dickinson University Press, 1977.

Mikos, Michael J. *Medieval Literature of Poland: An Anthology.* New York: Garland, 1992.

Mikos. *Polish Baroque and Enlightenment Literature: An Anthology.* Columbus, Ohio: Slavica, 1996.

Mikos. *Polish Renaissance Literature: An Anthology.* Columbus, Ohio: Slavica, 1995.

Miłosz, Czesław. *Emperor of the Earth: Modes of Eccentric Vision.* Berkeley: University of California Press, 1977.

Miłosz. *The History of Polish Literature.* New York: Macmillan, 1969.

Miłosz, ed. *Postwar Polish Poetry: An Anthology.* Berkeley: University of California Press, 1983.

Molnar, Ferenc. *The Play's the Thing: A Comedy in Three Acts.* New York: S. French, 1927.

Monumenta, Polonica. *The First Four Centuries of Polish Poetry: A Bilingual Anthology.* Ann Arbor: Michigan Slavic Publications, 1989.

Morson, Bary Saul. *Narrative and Freedom: The Shadows of Time.* New Haven: Yale University Press, 1994.

Nagy, Moses M., ed. *A Journey Into History: Essays on Hungarian Literature*. New York: Peter Lang, 1990.

Nemeskurty, Istvan. *A History of Hungarian Literature*. Budapest: Corvina, 1982.

Nirk, Endel. *Estonian Literature: Historical Survey With Bibliographical Appendix*. Tallinn: Periodika, 1987.

Nosek, Vladimir. *The Spirit of Bohemia: A Survey of Czechoslovak History, Music, and Literature*. London: Allen & Unwin, 1926.

Novák, Arne. *Czech Literature*. Ann Arbor: Michigan Slavic Publications, 1976.

Nyczed, Tadeusz. *Humps and Wings: A Selection of Polish Poetry Since 1968*. San Francisco: Red Hill, 1982.

Opalski, Magdalena. *The Jewish Tavern-Keeper and His Tavern in Nineteenth-Century Polish Literature*. Jerusalem: Zalman Shazar Center for the Furtherance of the Study of Jewish History, 1986.

Opalski. *Poles and Jews: A Failed Brotherhood*. Hanover, N.H.: University Press of New England, 1992.

Oras, Ants. *Estonian Literature In Exile: An Essay*. Lund: Eesti Kirjanike Kooperatiiv, 1967.

Osers, Ewald, and J. K. Montgomery, eds. *Modern Czech Poetry: An Anthology*. London: Allen & Unwin, 1945.

Otruba, Mojmir, and Zdenek Pesat, eds. *The Linden Tree: An Anthology of Czech and Slovak Literature, 1890–1960*. Prague: Artia, 1962.

Pârvu, Sorin. *The Romanian Novel*. Boulder, Col.: East European Monographs/Bucharest: Romanian Cultural Foundation/New York: Columbia University Press, 1992.

Pavlyshyn, Marko, ed. *Glasnost in Context: On the Recurrences of Liberalization in Central and East European Literatures and Cultures*. New York: St. Martin's Press, 1990.

Peterkiewicz, Jerzy, ed. *Polish Prose and Verse: A Selection with an Introductory Essay*. London: University of London, Athlone, 1970.

Peterkiewicz, and Burns Singer, eds. *Five Centuries of Polish Poetry, 1450–1970*. London & New York: Oxford University Press, 1970.

Petro, Peter. *A History of Slovak Literature*. Montreal & Buffalo: McGill-Queens University Press, 1995.

Pienkos, Donals E. *PNA, A Centennial History of the Polish National Alliance of the United States of North America*. New York: Columbia University Press, 1984.

Pipa, Arshi. *Albanian Literature: Social Perspectives*. Munich: R. Trofenik, 1978.

Pipa. *Contemporary Albanian Literature*. Boulder, Colo.: East European Monographs/New York: Columbia University Press, 1991.

Popa, Eli, ed. *Romania Is a Song: Sampler of Verse in Translation*. Cleveland: American, 1966.

Posaga, Wiesied, ed. *The Dedalus Book of Polish Fantasy*. New York: Hippocrene, 1996.

Pranspill, Andres, ed. *Estonian Anthology: Intimate Stories of Life, Love, Labor, and War, of the Estonian People*. Milford, Conn.: Andres Pranspill, 1956.

Pula, James S., M. B. Biskupski, eds. *Selected Essays from the Fiftieth Anniversary International Congress of the Polish Institute of Arts and Sciences of America.* Boulder, Colo.: East European Monographs/New York: Columbia University Press, 1993.

Pynsent, Robert B. *Conceptions of the Enemy: Three Essays on Czech and Slovak Literature.* Cambridge: Cambridge Associates, 1988.

Pynsent. *Questions of Identity: Czech and Slovak Ideas of Nationality and Personality.* Budapest & London: Central European University Press, 1994.

Pynsent, ed. *The Literature of Nationalism: Essays on East European Identity.* New York: St. Martin's Press, 1996.

Pynsent, ed. *Modern Slovak Prose: Fiction Since 1954.* Basingstoke, U.K.: Macmillan/School of Slavonic and East European Studies, 1990.

Pynsent and S. I. Kanikova, eds. *Readers Encyclopedia of Eastern European Literature.* New York: HarperCollins, 1993.

Ray, David. *From the Hungarian Revolution: A Collection of Poems.* Ithaca, N.Y.: Cornell University Press, 1966.

Rechcígl, Miloslav, Jr. ed. *Studies In Czechoslovak History.* Meerut: Sadhna Prakashan, 1976.

Reed-Scott, Jutta. *Survey of Area Studies Collections, Russia and Eastern Europe.* Washington, D.C.: Association of Research Libraries, 1996.

Reich, Emil. *Hungarian Literature, An Historical and Critical Survey.* London: Jarrold & Sons, 1898.

Remenyi, Joseph. *Hungarian Literature.* Washington, D.C.: American Hungarian Federation, 1946.

Remenyi. *Hungarian Writers and Literature: Modern Novelists, Critics, and Poets.* New Brunswick, N.J.: Rutgers University Press, 1964.

Riedl, Frigyes. *A History of Hungarian Literature.* New York: Appleton, 1906.

Rollberg, Peter, ed. *The Modern Encyclopedia of East Slavic, Baltic, and Eurasian Literatures.* Gulf Breeze, Fla.: Academic International Press, 1996.

Rose, William John. *Polish Literature.* Birkenhead, U.K.: Polish Publications, 1944.

Rubulis, Aleksis. *Baltic Literature: A Survey of Finnish, Estonian, Latvian, and Lithuanian Literatures.* Notre Dame, Ind.: University of Notre Dame Press, 1970.

Rubulis, ed. *Latvian Literature.* Toronto: Daugavas Vanags, 1964.

Rudinsky, Norma. *The Context of the Marxist-Leninist View of Slovak Literature.* Pittsburgh: Center for Russian and East European Studies, University of Pittsburgh, 1986.

Rudinsky. *Incipient Feminist: Women Writers In the Slovak National Revival.* Columbus, Ohio: Slavica, 1991.

Rudnyćkyj, J. B., ed. *Readings in Polish Folklore.* Winnipeg: University of Manitoba Press, 1953.

Sandauer, Artur. *Works, 1985.* Warsaw: Czytelnik, 1985.

Schamschula, Walter, ed. *An Anthology of Czech Literature.* New York: Peter Lang, 1990.

Segal, Harold. *Stranger in Our Midst: Images of the Jew in Polish Literature.* Ithaca, N.Y.: Cornell University Press, 1996.

Selver, Paul. *An Anthology of Czechoslovak Literature.* New York: Kraus Reprint, 1969.

Selver. *A Century of Czech and Slovak Poetry.* London: New Europe, 1946.

Shmeruk, Chone. *The Esterke Story in Yiddish and Polish Literature.* Jerusalem: Zalman Shazar Center for the Furtherance of the Study of Jewish History, 1985.

Short, David. *Czechoslovakia.* World Bibliographical Series, volume 68. Oxford & Santa Barbara, Cal.: Clio, 1986.

Short. *Essays In Czech and Slovak Language and Literature.* London: School of Slavonic and East European Studies, University of London, 1996.

Šilbajoris, Rimvydas. *Perfection of Exile: Fourteen Contemporary Lithuanian Writers.* Norman: University of Oklahoma Press, 1970.

Sorkin, Adam J., and Kurt W. Treptow, eds. *An Anthology of Romanian Women Poets.* Boulder, Colo.: East European Monographs/Bucharest: Romanian Cultural Foundation/New York: Columbia University Press, 1994.

Součková, Milada. *A Literature In Crisis: Czech Literature, 1938–1950.* New York: Mid-European Studies Center, 1954.

Spafford, Peter, ed. *Interference: The Story of Czechoslovakia in the Words of Its Writers.* Cheltenham, U.K.: New Clarion Press, 1992.

Speirs, Ruth, trans. *Translations from the Latvian.* Exeter: Exeter University Press, 1968.

Steinberg, Jacob, ed. *Introduction to Rumanian Literature.* New York: Twayne, 1966.

Stoica, Ion, ed. *Young Poets of a New Romania: An Anthology.* London: Forest, 1991.

Striedter, Jurij. *Literary Structure, Evolution, and Value: Russian Formalism and Czech Structuralism Reconsidered.* Cambridge, Mass.: Harvard University Press, 1989.

Sutherland-Smith, James, Stefania Allen, and Viera Sutherland-Smith, trans. *Not Waiting For Miracles: Seventeen Contemporary Slovak Poets,* edited by Peter Milcak and Brano Hochel. Levoca: Modry Peter, 1993.

Szabolcsi, Miklós. *Landmark: Hungarian Writers on Thirty Years of History.* Budapest: Corvina, 1965.

Tabori, Paul, and John Sakeford, trans. *One Sentence on Tyranny: Hungarian Literary Gazette Anthology,* edited by George Horvath. London: Waverly, 1957.

Taborski, Bolesław. *Polish Plays in English Translations: A Bibliography.* New York: Polish Institute of Arts and Sciences in America, 1968.

Talev, Ilya. *Some Problems of the Second South Slavic Influence in Russia.* Munich: Sagner, 1973.

Tappe, Eric Ditmar. *Rumanian Prose and Verse: A Selection with an Introductory Essay.* London: Athlone, 1956.

Terry, Garth M. *East European Languages and Literatures: A Subject and Name Index to Articles in English-Language Journals, 1900–1977.* Oxford & Santa Barbara, Cal.: Clio, 1978.

Terry. *East European Languages and Literatures II: A Subject and Name Index to Articles in Festschriften, Conference Proceedings and Collected Papers in the English Language, 1900–1981.* Nottingham: Astra, 1982.

Terry. *East European Languages and Literatures IV: A Subject and Name Index to Articles in English-Language Journals, Festschriften, Conference Proceedings and Collected Papers, 1985–1987.* Nottingham: Astra, 1988.

Terry. *East European Languages and Literatures V: A Subject and Name Index to Articles in English-Language Journals, Festschriften, Conference Proceedings and Collected Papers, 1988–1990.* Nottingham: Astra, 1991.

Terry. *East European Languages and Literatures VII: A Subject and Name Index to Articles in English-Language Journals, Festschriften, Conference Proceedings and Collected Papers, 1994–1996.* Nottingham: Astra, 1997.

Terry, *A Subject and Name Index to Articles on the Slavonic and East European Languages and Literatures, Music and Theatre, Libraries and the Press, Contained in English-Language Journals, 1920–1975.* Nottingham: University Library, University of Nottingham, 1976.

Tezla, Albert. *Hungarian Authors: A Bibliographical Handbook.* Cambridge, Mass.: Harvard University Press, 1970.

Tezla. *An Introductory Bibliography to the Study of Hungarian Literature.* Cambridge, Mass.: Harvard University Press, 1964.

Tezla, ed. *Ocean at the Window: Hungarian Prose and Poetry Since 1945.* Minneapolis: University of Minnesota Press, 1980.

Theiner, George, ed. *New Writing in Czechoslovakia.* Harmondsworth, U.K. & Baltimore: Penguin, 1969.

Thomas, Alfred. *The Czech Chivalric Romances Vevoda Arnost and Lavryn in Their Literary Context.* Göppingen, Germany: Kummerle, 1989.

Thomas. *The Labyrinth of the Word: Truth and Representation in Czech Literature.* Munich: Oldenbourg, 1995.

Toth, Eva, and the Hungarian Writers' Association, eds. *Ma = Today: An Anthology of Contemporary Hungarian Literature.* Budapest: Corvina, 1987.

Trenský, Paul I. *Czech Drama Since World War II.* White Plains, N.Y.: M. E. Sharpe, 1978.

Tschizewskij, Dmitrij. *Comparative History of Slavic Literatures.* Nashville: Vanderbilt University Press, 1971.

Tschizewskij. *Outline of Comparative Slavic Literatures.* Boston: American Academy of Arts and Sciences, 1952.

Tschizewskij. *On Romanticism in Slavic Literature.* The Hague: Mouton, 1957.

Underwood, Edna Worthley, trans. *The Slav Anthology: Russian, Polish, Bohemian, Serbian, Croatian.* Portland, Me.: Mosher, 1931.

Vaiciulaitis, Antanas. *Outline History of Lithuanian Literature.* Chicago: Lithuanian Cultural Institute, 1942.

Vajda, Miklos, ed. *Modern Hungarian Poetry.* New York: Columbia University Press, 1977.

Varnai, Paul, ed. *Hungarian Short Stories.* Toronto: Exile Editions, 1983.

Veltrusky, F. Jarmila. *A Sacred Farce From Medieval Bohemia–Mastickar*. Ann Arbor: University of Michigan Press, 1985.

Vincenz, Stanisław. *Selections, 1994*. Warsaw: Swiat Literacki, 1994.

Volková, Bronislava. *A Feminist's Semiotic Odyssey through Czech Literature*. Lewiston, Me.: E. Mellen, 1997.

Weiskopf, F. C., ed. *Hundred Towers: A Czechoslavak Anthology of Creative Writing*. New York: Fischer, 1945.

Wellek, René. *Czech Literature at the Crossroads of Europe: A Lecture Delivered at the General Meeting of the Czechoslovak Society of Arts and Sciences at Toronto, Ontario, on September, 7, 1963*. Toronto: Czechoslovak Society of Arts and Sciences, 1963.

Wellek. *Essays On Czech Literature*. The Hague: Mouton, 1963.

Wielewinski, Bernard. *Polish National Catholic Church: Independent Movements, Old Catholic Church and Related Items: An Annotated Bibliography*. Boulder, Colo.: East European Monographs/New York: Columbia University Press, 1990.

Wieniewska, Celina, ed. *Polish Writing Today*. Harmondsworth, U.K. & Baltimore: Penguin, 1967.

Wiles, Timothy. *Poland Between the Wars, 1918–1939*. Bloomington: Indiana University Press, 1989.

World Congress for Soviet and East European Studies. *Aspects of Modern Russian and Czech Literature: Selected Papers of the Third World Congress for Soviet and East European Studies*. Columbus, Ohio: Slavica, 1989.

Yakstis, Frank. *Translations of Lithuanian Poetry*. Ozone Park, N.Y.: Association of Lithuanian Workers, 1968.

Zdanys, Jonas, ed. and trans. *Selected Post-War Lithuanian Poetry*. New York: Manyland Books, 1978.

Contributors

Joachim Baer . . . . *University of North Carolina at Greensboro*

Stanisław Barańczak . . . . *Harvard University*

Péter Bényei . . . . *Institute of Hungarian Philology, Kossuth University*

Andrzej Busza . . . . *University of British Columbia*

John R. Carpenter . . . . *Ann Arbor, Michigan*

István Chován . . . . *University of Debrecen*

Ladislav Čúzy . . . . *Comenius University, Bratislava*

Bogdan Czaykowski . . . . *University of British Columbia*

Ákos Czigány . . . . *Pázmány Péter Catholic University, Budapest–Piliscsaba*

Pál Deréky . . . . *University of Vienna*

Štefan Drug . . . . *Institute for Slovak Literature SAV*

Stanislaw Eile . . . . *University of London*

Ján Gbúr . . . . *University P. J. Šafárika Prešov*

András Gerliczki . . . . *Nyíregyháza Teacher Training College*

Daniel Gerould . . . . *City University of New York*

Elwira M. Grossman . . . . *University of Glasgow*

Gábor Gulyás . . . . *University of Debrecen*

Ondřej Hausenblas . . . . *Charles University, Prague*

Braňo Hochel . . . . *Comenius University*

Jiří Holý . . . . *Charles University, Prague*

Lóránt Kabdebó . . . . *University of Miskolc*

Bożena Karwowska . . . . *University of British Columbia*

Hanna Kirchner . . . . *Institute of Literary Research, Polish Academy of Sciences*

Wladimir Krysinski . . . . *University of Montreal*

Zoltán Kulcsár-Szabó . . . . *Eötvös University, Budapest*

Vladimír Macura . . . . *Institute of Czech Literature, Academy of Sciences of the Czech Republic, Prague*

Jaroslav Med . . . . *Institute of Czech Literature, Academy of Sciences of the Czech Republic, Prague*

Luboš Merhaut . . . . . *Institute of Czech Literature, Academy of Sciences of the Czech Republic, Prague*

Valér Mikula . . . . *Comenius University, Bratislava*

Marcela Mikulová . . . . *Institute for Slovak Literature SAV, Bratislava*

Péter H. Nagy . . . . *Loránd Eötvös University of Budapest*

Šárka Nevidalová . . . . *Ostrava University*

Gábor Palkó . . . . *Eötvös University, Budapest*

Vladimír Papoušek . . . . *South Bohemia University, České Budějovice*

Vladimír Petrík . . . . *Institute for Slovak Literature SAV, Bratislava*

Jiří Poláček . . . . *Masaryk University, Brno*

Bożena Shallcross . . . . *Indiana University*

Wojciech Skalmowski . . . . *University of Louvain*

Richard Svoboda . . *Institute of Czech Literature, Academy of Sciences of the Czech Republic, Brno*

Bònus Tibor . . . . *University of Budapest*

Ferenc Tóth . . . . *Ferenc Kölcsey Pedagogical Institute of the Reformed Church*

Pál S. Varga . . . . *University of Debrecen*

András Veres . . . . *Institute of Literary Studies of MTA, Hungarian Academy of Sciences*

Magdalena J. Zaborowska . . . . *Århus University*

Miroslav Zelinský . . . . *Academy of Sciences of the Czech Republic*

Cumulative Index

Dictionary of Literary Biography, Volumes 1-215
Dictionary of Literary Biography Yearbook, 1980-1998
Dictionary of Literary Biography Documentary Series, Volumes 1-19

Cumulative Index

DLB before number: *Dictionary of Literary Biography,* Volumes 1-215
Y before number: *Dictionary of Literary Biography Yearbook,* 1980-1998
DS before number: *Dictionary of Literary Biography Documentary Series,* Volumes 1-19

G

I

K

L

N

Cumulative Index

ISBN 0-7876-3109-4